COMPETITION POLICY

Theory and Practice

This is the first book to provide a systematic treatment of the economics of anti-trust (or competition) policy. It draws on the literature of industrial organisation and on original analyses to deal with such important issues as cartels, joint-ventures, mergers, vertical contracts, predatory pricing, exclusionary practices and price discrimination, and to formulate policy implications on these issues. The interaction between theory and practice is one of the main features of the book, which contains frequent references to competition policy cases and a few fully developed case studies. The book is written to appeal to practitioners and students, to lawyers and economists. It is not only a textbook in economics for first-year graduate or advanced undergraduate courses, but also a book for all those who wish to understand competition issues in a clear and rigorous way. Exercises and some solved problems are provided. The book is also accessible to readers who are not familiar with modern economics, as the formalisation of the material covered in the main non-technical sections is relegated to separate "technical" sections.

Massimo Motta is Professor of Economics at the European University Institute, Florence, and at the Universitat Pompeu Fabra, Barcelona, from which he is currently on leave. He is a Research Fellow of the Centre for Economic Policy Research, London, and of CESifo, Munich. Professor Motta's main research interests are in industrial organisation and competition policy, but he has also worked extensively on international trade, trade policy and multinational firms. His work has been published in several leading international journals.

Competition Policy

Theory and Practice

MASSIMO MOTTA

European University Institute, Florence
and Universitat Pompeu Fabra, Barcelona

CAMBRIDGE
UNIVERSITY PRESS

PUBLISHED BY THE PRESS SYNDICATE OF THE UNIVERSITY OF CAMBRIDGE
The Pitt Building, Trumpington Street, Cambridge, United Kingdom

CAMBRIDGE UNIVERSITY PRESS
The Edinburgh Building, Cambridge CB2 2RU, UK
40 West 20th Street, New York, NY 10011-4211, USA
477 Williamstown Road, Port Melbourne, VIC 3207, Australia
Ruiz de Alarcón 13, 28014 Madrid, Spain
Dock House, The Waterfront, Cape Town 8001, South Africa

http://www.cambridge.org

First published 2004

Printed in the United States of America

Typeface Minion 10.25/12.75 pt.   *System* LaTeX 2_ε [TB]

A catalogue record for this book is available from the British Library.

Library of Congress Cataloging in Publication Data
Motta, Massimo.
Competition policy : theory and practice / Massimo Motta.
p.   cm.
Includes bibliographical references and index.
ISBN 0-521-81663-7 – ISBN 0-521-01691-6 (pb.)
1. Competition.   2. Competition, International.   3. Competition – Government policy.
4. Antitrust law.   5. Industrial policy.   I. Title.
HD41.M68   2004
338.6′048 – dc21   2003046268

ISBN 0 521 81663 7 hardback
ISBN 0 521 01691 6 paperback

Alle donne della mia vita:
Heike, Enrica, Rina,
ed ai miei bimbi:
Fabio e Alessandro

Contents

Contents

Contents

List of Figures

List of Figures

List of Tables

Preface

Recently, competition policy (or anti-trust policy, as it is more often called in the US) has often made the first pages of newspapers. High-profile cases both in the European Union and in the US have attracted the attention of society at large. Among the possible examples, there are *US v. Microsoft* (see Chapter 7 for a discussion), where the Department of Justice at one point asked for such a drastic measure as the split of the software giant into two separate companies; a few cartel cases with an international dimension (such as those involving the producers of lysine, vitamins, or the famous auction houses Sotheby's and Christie's), that resulted in prison sentences for some of the firms' managers involved; and some EU merger cases, such as *General Electric/Honeywell* (see Chapter 6), which was followed by public opinion on both sides of the Atlantic (and most people were surprised when eventually the European Commission blocked the deal between the two American companies).

What Competition Policy Is and Why We Need It   Rather than starting by defining competition policy in abstract terms, in the book I first provide the reader with an idea of what competition policy is about through a historical approach (see Chapter 1). Only after having briefly described competition laws in the US and in the EU, do I give a formal definition of competition policy (see Chapter 2) as "the set of policies and laws which ensure that competition in the marketplace is not restricted in such a way as to reduce economic welfare".

In this definition two elements should be underlined. The first is that firms might restrict competition in a way which is not necessarily detrimental (for instance, this is the case for most vertical restraints, that is, restrictive clauses between a manufacturer and a retailer, see Chapter 6). The second is that economic welfare, a standard concept for economists (see Chapter 2) is the objective that competition policies should pursue. In this book I assess the anti-competitive potential of business practices, and the desirability of particular competition rules, according to this definition.

Still, a reader might ask why we need competition policy at all. Let me set aside for the moment the case where market failures would require the regulation of the sector (see below), and think instead of an industry where there exist no barriers to entry. One might think that market forces, and in particular the threat of new entrants, will eliminate monopolies (or dominant positions) and reduce prices. Yet, firms might resort to anti-competitive actions that create or strengthen a monopolistic (or dominant) position and, more generally, to actions that increase their profits, but reduce welfare: collusive agreements (see Chapter 4), anti-competitive mergers (see Chapter 5), and exclusionary behaviour (see Chapters 6 and 7) are cases in point. For these reasons, competition laws and competition authorities that enforce these laws are necessary.

Competition Policy and Regulation   In general, competition policy applies to sectors where structural conditions are compatible with a normal functioning of competition (whether the market functions well in practice or not is another matter). Instead, regulation applies to special sectors, whose structure is such that one would not expect competitive forces to operate without problems. Regulation would usually concern markets where fixed costs are so high that no more than one firm would profitably operate (a so-called *natural monopoly*): examples might be electricity (viz., its transmission phase), telecommunications (local loops) and railways (the network). Other industries subject to regulation might be industries that are in a transitory phase, for instance because they used to be legal monopolies (perhaps state-owned), and they were then liberalised. Since it would be unlikely that entrants could compete on an equal footing with an established incumbent, a regulatory body usually supervises the industry to try to ensure a smooth transition toward a regular functioning of competition in the market.[1]

There are several differences between competition policy and regulation (see e.g., Rey, 2000: 44–47). While competition authorities generally limit themselves to checking the lawfulness of firms' activities, industry regulators have more extensive powers (they might impose or control firms' prices, investments, and product choices). While competition authorities usually intervene *ex post* (for instance, checking the legality of a certain business practice after it has already been taken), regulators act *ex ante* (for instance, authorising a certain business practice or not). Regulators' involvement with an industry is long-run and continuous, whereas competition authorities' interventions tend to be occasional.[2] Such differences are also mirrored in the theoretical frameworks adopted to deal with these two issues. While competition policy issues can mostly be analysed with oligopoly theory (that is the main tool used in this book), regulatory issues are more naturally addressed by so-called "principal-agent models", where the principal is the regulatory authority

[1] Other regulatory problems are related to the existence of informational asymmetries between consumers and firms and call for the setting of environmental, health and safety standards.
[2] In some cases, the border between competition policy and regulation is blurred. Merger control, for instance, usually a task carried out by competition authorities, shares several features with regulatory problems. The analysis of the merger is to be done *ex ante* rather than *ex post*, and when conditions are imposed on the merging parties (see Chapter 5), they might involve re-designing the structure of the market (structural remedies), or limit the parties' freedom of choosing contracts or business practices (behavioural remedies), thereby making the competition authorities take actions more typical of a regulator.

and the agent is the regulated firm, with the former having to devise incentives in order for the latter to take the actions that would achieve the principal's objectives.

This book deals only with competition policy, not with regulation.[3]

Objective of This Book, and How to Use It   Previously the domain of lawyers, competition policy today is a field where lawyers and economists work together, and both judges and competition authorities have to master sophisticated economic concepts and theories (and likewise, economists have to understand the legal and institutional framework of anti-trust policy).

The main objective of this book is to provide a guide to all those who have an interest in competition issues, and to offer them the possibility to understand what modern advanced economics teaches us on these issues.

The book deals with both the theory and the practice of competition policy. It draws on the literature of industrial organisation, and on original analyses, to explain the likely effects that firms' practices have on welfare and formulate policy recommendations, which are of practical use for anti-trust authorities.

The interaction between theory and practice is to be regarded as one of the main features of the book, and to this purpose it also contains frequent references to competition policy cases (mostly from the EU and the US), and a few fully developed case studies.

The book is written to appeal to competition policy practitioners as well as students, to lawyers as well as economists. It is also designed to be used as a textbook in economics (in first-year graduate or advanced undergraduate courses) or as a book for those who want to approach competition issues in a clear and rigorous way.

Since the book is meant to be accessible also to readers who are not familiar with modern economics, the formalisation of the material covered in the main non-technical sections is relegated to separate "technical" sections. These sections, which are marked with one or two stars, according to their level of difficulty (*for undergraduates, **for graduates), can be skipped without loss by the readers who are not familiar with modern quantitative economics (or who are not interested in formal models).

Having followed an introductory course in industrial organisation will make reading the technical undergraduate (*) sections of the book easier, but students who have received a basic training in microeconomics should be able to understand them as well. The (*) sections require familiarity with little more than basic calculus, simple game theory (the concepts of Nash equilibrium and sub-game perfect Nash equilibrium) and oligopoly models (e.g., Bertrand competition, Cournot competition).

Nevertheless, to help students and provide them with the necessary background if needed, Chapter 8 offers an introduction to basic monopoly and oligopoly theory

---

[3] For an introduction to regulation with an undergraduate-level treatment, see Viscusi et al. (1995). For an advanced treatment, see Laffont and Tirole (1994).

(as well as to the fundamental concepts of game theory). An instructor who wants to teach a self-contained undergraduate course on the economics of competition policy (or economics of anti-trust policy as it would be called in the US), without requiring any pre-requisite course, might want to devote a few lectures to Chapter 8 before teaching the material contained in the rest of the book.

The book could also be used as a textbook for a course in "applied" industrial organisation at the undergraduate level, as opposed to a traditional course in the theory of industrial organisation. In this case, one could first teach the material contained in Chapter 8 and then select material from the other chapters according to one's priorities.

Each chapter also contains exercises, both at the undergraduate and graduate level, and essays, which instructors might find a useful complement to their teaching. Solutions for the exercises are also provided.

Acknowledgements

My first encounter with anti-trust law dates from 1989–90, when I was at the London School of Economics. John Sutton devoted the classes of his course on Industrial Organisation to the presentation and discussion of anti-trust cases, so I am indebted to him not only for guidance through my first attempts at doing research, but also for introducing me to this fascinating topic. However, I can now confess that I was often very puzzled after class: was that firm really guilty? Was that particular business practice really anti-competitive? And which model was really relevant in that particular case? Some of these questions still accompany me today when I look at anti-trust cases: the interaction between the theory and a complex reality, and the necessity to capture the essential facts of a case and analyse them with the help of models we know, make anti-trust analysis often very difficult.

My curiosity about this topic increased when I met Kai-Uwe Kühn in Barcelona. Given our common interest, we taught a course on competition policy together at Universitat Pompeu Fabra (UPF). I have learned a lot from Kai-Uwe, and discussions with him have shaped my way of thinking about anti-trust issues. The idea of writing a book on competition policy was also conceived together, and for a long time the book was meant to be a common project. Eventually, a continent in between (he moved to Michigan), two small kids each, different research projects, and many other engagements made coordination more difficult and time scarcer, and Kai-Uwe unfortunately did not participate in the project.

Since that first course in 1995, I have taught competition policy to undergraduate and graduate students, to law and economics students, in Barcelona, in Florence, and elsewhere. The questions, comments, and reactions of all these students (many of whom are now colleagues, friends and sometimes co-authors) have constantly pushed me to understand more and to explain better.

As research assistants, some of my students have also helped me in various (but invariably boring) tasks: Elena Argentesi, Inês Cabral, Natalia Fabra, Helder Vasconcelos, as well as Liliane Karlinger and Valanta Milliou (who have been very unlucky to be my research assistants as the deadline for handing in the manuscript was approaching). Thanks for never complaining!

The book has benefited from helpful comments made by a number of people: Mónica Ariño, Joao Azevedo, Jan Boone, Jan Bouckaert, Inês Cabral, Fernando Dominguez, Natalia Fabra, Lapo Filistrucchi, Federico Ghezzi, Mel Marquis, Valanta

Milliou, George Norman, Anne Perrot, Lars Persson, Michele Polo, Francesca Sala, Alexandre de Streel, Paola Valbonesi, Helder Vasconcelos, Filippo Vergara Caffarelli and three anonymous referees.

I also owe special thanks to Pedro Barros, who gave comments on the whole book and who tested it on his students at the Universidade Nova de Lisboa, providing crucial feedback; to Joe Harrington, whose detailed comments have been extremely helpful and pushed me to re-organise the structure of the book and its presentation; and to Patrick Rey, who read and commented on the whole manuscript giving precious advice (over the years, I have learned a lot from Patrick, and not only on economics: how could I live without knowing *Sauternes?*).

I am also extremely grateful to Elena Argentesi, Liliane Karlinger and Laura Ristori, who read several versions of the book, and every time provided me with insightful comments, made corrections, and pointed out omissions; to Christopher Townley, for correcting the whole manuscript and giving me advice on many legal issues; to Marcia Gastaldo, for efficient secretarial support and for managing to assemble the manuscript according to Cambridge University Press instructions, while always smiling; and to Jessica Spataro, for her patience in answering my questions about British English. Thanks also to Scott Parris, who supported this project with contagious enthusiasm, and to Zachary Dorsey and Lee Young for careful handling and editing of the manuscript.

My greatest debt, though, is to Chiara Fumagalli, great friend and co-author, who has helped me throughout this project with encouragement, suggestions, corrections . . . up to the point that I wonder whether I have really ever been her supervisor, or if it has always been the other way around!

Finally, I have a long-term debt to many people, from whom I have learned a lot over the years: my supervisors Claude d'Aspremont and John Sutton; my "old" co-authors Antonio Cabrales, Andrea Fosfuri, Walter Garcia-Fontes, George Norman, Michele Polo, Thomas Rønde and Jacques Thisse; and my colleagues both at UPF and in Florence, in particular Antoni Bosch, Xavier Calsamiglia, Antonio Ciccone, Teresa Garcia-Milà, Giuseppe Bertola and Andrea Ichino.

A large part of this book has been written in three consecutive summers, when we were staying at Otto and Brigitte's: thanks!

Finally, the book could not have been written if Heike had not encouraged me and taken upon herself a lot of tasks that we should have shared. Heike also read and corrected the whole manuscript, but the ultimate proof of love is that she even claims that she liked it!

List of Abbreviations

art.:   article

CFI: Court of First Instance

CS: consumer surplus

DOJ: Department of Justice (in the United States)

EC: European Commission (that is, Commission of the European Communities)

ECJ: European Court of Justice

ET: exclusive territories

EU: European Union

FF: franchise fee

FOCs: first-order conditions

FTC: Federal Trade Commission (in the United States)

HHI: Herfindahl–Hirschman Index

JV: joint-venture

LHS: left-hand side

OFT: Office of Fair Trading (in the United Kingdom)

OJ: Official Journal of the European Communities

para.:   paragraph

PS: producer surplus

R&D: research and development

RHS: right-hand side

RPM: resale price maintenance

s.to: subject to

W: welfare

Competition Policy: History, Objectives, and the Law

1.1 INTRODUCTION

Rather than starting with a long and abstract discussion of what competition policy is, this chapter aims at introducing the reader to competition issues by using a historical approach. Section 1.2 briefly describes the main features that competition policies have exhibited in the past in the US and in Europe. The historical review also shows that in the practice of competition policy a number of public policy considerations and objectives have been (and still are) used. Section 1.3 briefly discusses them, and indicates the possible conflicts between economic and non-economic objectives. Armed with this discussion, at the end of the Section I also provide the definition of competition policy that I use in the book. Section 1.4 describes the main features of competition law in the European Union (EU), to provide the reader with further insight of what competition policy is about.

1.2 BRIEF HISTORY OF COMPETITION POLICY

This section briefly reviews the main historical events in the development of competition (or anti-trust) laws in the US and in the European Union. The purpose here is not to have a complete description of the history of competition laws, but rather to help understand the circumstances in which competition laws were created and enforced, as well as the objectives which they purported to attain.

1.2.1 Anti-Trust Law in the United States

The origins of modern competition policy can be traced back to the end of the 19th century, mainly as a reaction to the formation of trusts in the United States.[1,2]

The Events Leading to the Sherman Act   In the second half of that century, the United States experienced a number of events, which resulted in the transformation

---

[1] "The 'trust' was originally a device by which several corporations engaged in the same general line of business might combine for their mutual advantage, in the direction of eliminating destructive competition, controlling the output of their commodity and regulating and maintaining its price, but at the same time preserving their separate individual existence, and without any consolidation

of manufacturing industries. Perhaps the most important events were the dramatic improvement in transportation and communication. The railways extended rapidly throughout the US territory, as did the telegraph lines and the telephone services. This entailed the formation of a large single market, which in turn gave a powerful incentive to firms to exploit *economies of scale* and *economies of scope*.[3] Along with other technological innovations in several fields (e.g., metallurgy, chemicals, energy), the formation of more advanced capital markets and new managerial methods, this created the possibility for the expansion of the size of the firms.[4] Legal innovations such as the "liberalization of state incorporation laws also contributed [to the creation of larger firms], permitting the acquisition of other firms' stock (e.g., in mergers) and the delegation of stockholders' decision-making power to full time managers" (Scherer, 1980: 492). It is not by chance that the US experienced an impressive merger wave in the 1880s and 1890s.

The last part of the 19th century was characterised by low and unstable prices. This was due in part to macroeconomic factors which gave rise to many recurrent and persistent economic crises (1873–8 and 1883–6) and created instability in several sectors. But most of the price instability was due to the very same factor, which allowed for the creation of larger market opportunities. Indeed, the fall in transportation and communication costs led not only to a large single market for many industries, but also to a rise in competition, since firms now had to compete with more distant rivals, located both in the other American states and abroad (shipping rates fell in this period as well).

Further, the large investments made by firms so as to enjoy scale and scope economies caused lower costs and lower prices. In the words of Chandler (1990: 71), "Increasing output and overcapacity intensified competition and drove down prices. Indeed, the resulting decline of prices in manufactured goods characterised

---

or merger. This device was the erection of a central committee or board, composed, perhaps, of the presidents or general managers of the different corporations, and the transfer to them of a majority of the stock in each of the corporations, to be held in 'trust' for the several stockholders so assigning their holdings. These stockholders received in return 'trust certificates' showing that they were entitled to receive the dividends on their assigned stock, though the voting power of it had passed to the trustees. This last feature enabled the trustees or committee to elect all the directors of all the corporations, and through them the officers, and thereby to exercise an absolutely controlling influence over the policy and operations of each constituent company, to the end and with the purposes above mentioned". (West Group, 1998.)

[2] To write this section, I have consulted a number of sources that describe US anti-trust laws in a historical perspective, among others Amato (1997), Comanor (1990), Fox (2002), Kovacic and Shapiro (2000), Lin et al. (2000), Mueller (1996), Posner (2001: ch. 2), Scherer (1980), and Scherer (1994).

[3] There are economies of scale when unit costs of production fall with the total quantity produced; economies of scope when unit costs fall because two or more goods are produced jointly.

[4] See Chandler (1990), in particular ch. 3, for a rich and fascinating account of the changes taking place in the US economy in the second half of the 19th century.

the economies of the United States and the nations of Western Europe from the mid-1870s to the end of the century".

Also, firms had to make large investments to reorganise their production and distribution activities, to buy new machines or to enter new markets (think for instance of the huge investment railways had to make). In the attempt to operate at full capacity so as to cover the large fixed costs, firms were tempted to decrease prices, giving rise to price wars.

Firms often tried to respond to price wars and market instability by way of price agreements which enabled them to maintain high prices and margins.[5] The organisation of cartels and trusts (railroad and oil companies are the best known examples of these) had exactly this purpose. But the advantages of price stability for the members of cartels and trusts did not come without detriment to other groups in the economy. Final consumers were hurt by higher prices, and so were producers, such as farmers and small industrial firms, which used products of cartelised sectors as an input. Both groups suffered from the low sales prices brought about by the aforementioned crises (the latter also by a less efficient scale of production), and found themselves squeezed in between low sale prices and high input prices (above all, railways and energy). Furthermore, small firms complained of unfair business practices adopted by their large rivals, which allegedly wanted to drive them out of business.

Farmers and small businesses had enough political force and public sympathy to lead to the creation of anti-trust laws in many US states.[6] However, such laws could do very little against agreements, which involved more than one state. But soon there was enough consensus for a federal law and in 1890 the *Sherman Act* was adopted. This is probably the best known example of anti-trust law in the world, although it is not the earliest: Canada, for instance, adopted a similar law in 1889, but enforcement of that law was to be much weaker.

The Sherman Act and Its Early Enforcement For our purposes, the relevant sections of the Sherman Act are Sections 1 and 2. Section 1 prohibits contracts, combinations and conspiracies which restrain trade, and prescribes imprisonment and fines for violators. Section 2 prohibits monopolisation, attempts to monopolise and conspiracies to monopolise "any part of the trade or commerce among the several states, or with foreign nations" (but note that having a monopoly position is not by itself illegal). The Act carries its own criminal penalties, which might include

---

[5] However, price wars might be just one of the phases in the life of a cartel. See Green and Porter (1984) and Porter (1983b). I defer discussion of this issue to Chapter 4.

[6] Note that "small businessmen included not only manufacturers whose small operations gave them a cost disadvantage, but also wholesalers, manufacturers' agents, and other middlemen who were being driven out of business as the volume-producing manufacturers moved forward and the mass retailers moved backwards into wholesaling". (Chandler, 1990: 78–9. See also p. 72.) Consumers' interests are often too fragmented to have an impact on government policies. See also Section 1.3.

imprisonment up to three years (recently jail sentences for anti-trust enforcement have been given more often).[7]

During its first decade of life, enforcement of the Sherman Act was not very strict. It was not until 1897 that a Supreme Court decision on a trust of 18 railways, which fixed the fares for the transport of goods (*Trans-Missouri Freight Association*) clearly established that price agreements were illegal. Indeed, in this decision and in *Addyston Pipe and Steel,* judges refused arguments aimed at justifying price-fixing on the grounds that the rates charged were "reasonable" and that price-fixing was a way to prevent "unhealthy competition". The Supreme Court took the view that, with the Sherman Act, the Congress intended to outlaw all price agreements, and that it was not up to judges to decide which agreements are reasonable and which ones are not.[8] The prohibition of price agreements among competitors is a very strong principle which is still valid, and which has known very few exceptions.[9]

In *Dr. Miles v. Park & Sons* (1911), the Supreme Court applied the Sherman Act's prohibition of price restrictions to vertical relationships as well. The Court established there that a resale price maintenance clause, whereby the manufacturer obliges retailers to sell above a minimum price that it sets, is *per se* illegal.[10] This prohibition has never been reversed since.[11]

This tough stance was then confirmed by the judgments against two of the most important trusts, namely the *Standard Oil Company* (which was split into 34 separate companies in 1911) and *American Tobacco.*

Standard Oil is still one of the most famous cases in the history of anti-trust policy.[12] The trust, a creation of Rockefeller, had engaged in a series of monopolisation practices – such as localised price cuts deemed to be predatory and a number of acquisitions of minor firms – which were judged against Sections 1 and 2 of the Sherman Act. In *American Tobacco,* five tobacco manufacturers had merged into the American Tobacco Company, and engaged in a campaign of purchasing minor

---

[7] Note that EU competition law does not allow imposing criminal penalties in anti-trust violations, although certain EU countries' laws do (for instance, Austria, France, Germany, Ireland, whereas the UK is in the process of introducing them).

[8] See also Posner (2001: 35–6).

[9] However, exceptions to anti-trust rules in the US have been formally granted to many sectors such as insurance, agriculture, fisheries, professional baseball, and labour organisations. There also exists a "state action" doctrine which represents another exception. In particular, horizontal agreements (such as price-fixing), which would otherwise be deemed anti-competitive are allowed insofar as they are promoted by a state regulation. For a discussion see Inman and Rubinfeld (1997).

[10] If a business practice is *per se* illegal, no argument can justify it: it is prohibited without exceptions. Under a *rule of reason* approach, instead, a firm might convince the court that the business practice it adopted does not harm welfare in its particular instance.

[11] Such a *per se* prohibition is not justified on economic grounds: see Chapter 6. Note that only in 1997 did the Supreme Court rule, in *State Oil v. Kahn,* that a firm might impose a *price ceiling* on its dealers.

[12] See Chapter 7 for a brief discussion of the case in the context of the analysis of predatory pricing.

competitors, controlling stock interest in other corporations, and starting price wars to increase its power and drive other manufacturers out of business. The trust was condemned and dismantled.

Another important monopolisation case was *Terminal Railroad* (1912), which prohibited several railways that controlled the terminal facilities of the main bridge in the city of St. Louis to discriminate against competitors, and obliged the former to give access to the latter on reasonable terms.[13]

The Clayton Act and the Federal Trade Commission Act   Note that the Sherman Act covers price fixing and market sharing agreements between independent firms, as well as monopolisation practices by individual companies, but not mergers (which were legal unless formed with the intention to monopolise the market using unfair methods of competition). Therefore, firms wishing to coordinate prices had the option of merging into a single firm and, by so doing, they put themselves beyond the reach of the Sherman Act. The *Clayton Act* of 1914 was therefore introduced to extend anti-trust legislation to cover mergers capable of reducing competition; it was probably the Sherman Act itself that led to a sharp increase in the number of mergers in the US.[14]

> After 1897 began the largest and certainly the most significant merger movement in American history. It came partly because of continuing antitrust legislation and activities by the states, partly because of the increasing difficulty of enforcing contractual agreements by trade associations during the depression of the mid-1890s, and partly because the return of prosperity and the buoyant stock market that accompanied it facilitated the exchange of shares and encouraged bankers and other financers to promote mergers. The merger boom reached its climax between 1899 and 1902, after the Supreme Court had indicated by its rulings in the Trans-Missouri Freight Rate Association case (1897), the Joint Traffic Association case (1889), and the Addyston Pipe and Steel case (1899) that cartels carried on through trade associations were vulnerable under the Sherman Act. (Chandler, 1990: 75, footnote omitted.)[15]

The Clayton Act also explicitly forbids other practices, such as price discrimination, which lessens competition and interlocking directorates among competing firms. The possibility of recovering *treble damages* is also very important: these were introduced by Section 4 of the Clayton Act for private anti-trust suits, and which

---

[13] This case is still mentioned nowadays in discussions related to essential facilites and refusal to supply. See Chapters 6 and 7.

[14] See also Bittlingmayer (1985) for a well documented study.

[15] The extent to which mergers to monopoly were covered by the Sherman Act is unclear. In *US v. Knight* (1895) the Supreme Court did not find against the Sugar Trust, which had gained control of 98% of the US sugar refining capacity through a series of mergers. However, in *Northern Securities v. US* (1904), it blocked the combination of the Northern Pacific and Great Northern railroads which would have monopolised the industry.

gave rise to important transfers of money from offenders to victims of unlawful commercial conduct (the latter can ask a compensation equal to three times the damage they have received, plus attorney's fees).

The *Federal Trade Commission Act* also dates from 1914. It created the FTC, an independent agency that would regulate unfair trade practices, and that shares with the Department of Justice (DOJ), a government agency, the responsibility to enforce anti-trust law in the US at the federal level (at the state level, attorneys general can act on behalf of those injured by anti-trust violations).[16]

The Clayton Act has subsequently been amended. The *Robinson-Patman Act* of 1936 amended its provisions on price discrimination.[17] Later, the Celler-Kefauver Act of 1950 amended the Clayton Act provisions relating to mergers by extending the cross-ownership prohibition among competitors to asset transactions (before, only stock transactions were covered). Another important piece of legislation is the *Hart-Scott-Rodino Act* of 1976 that amends the merger provisions of the Clayton Act by giving the DOJ and the FTC the power to review all mergers of firms above a certain size threshold.

The Inter-War Period   The period between the two World Wars is marked by a less strong enforcement of anti-trust laws. During World War I, it was the coalition between business and politics that governed the economy, rather than market forces, and this model continued to have its advocates even when the war ended. The Great Depression of 1929 reinforced such views and resulted in some price controls and other regulatory initiatives. The Robinson-Patman Act, which aims at avoiding price discrimination that may put small stores out of business to the benefit of large chain-stores, is a product of such an environment.

In the same line is the arguably most noticeable decision of this period, *Appalachian Coals v. US* (1933). This marks one of the very rare exceptions to the *per se* prohibition of price-fixing.[18] This Supreme Court decision can be understood considering only a historical perspective. The Great Depression was having important consequences on many industries, and one such industry which suffered

---

[16] The division of labour between the two agencies is not determined in a precise way. In merger cases, it is typically along sectoral lines that can change over time. However, only the DOJ has enforcement power in criminal cases.

[17] In recent years, provisions against price discriminations have rarely been used.

[18] The *Board of Trade of Chicago* case (1918) might appear an exception to the *per se* prohibition of price-fixing, but it is probably not. The object of the decision was a rule that fixed the price for all the transactions taking place after the normal operating hours at the level set at closing time. The Court decided that the *per se* rule did not apply here because the Chicago Board did not have control over the prices of the transaction and because to judge a restraint one should consider the specificity of the industry, the nature and the effects of the restraint. This seemed to introduce a rule of reason for price-fixing cases, but in *US v. Trenton Potteries* (1927) the Court made it clear that naked agreements to set price among competitors should be under a *per se* prohibition, with a rule of reason assessment being reserved only in exceptional circumstances.

hardship in the crisis was the coal mining industry. Facing a severe reduction in demand, and intending to avoid further losses, 137 producers located in the Appalachian Mountain region formed a company which sought to find the best prices and to allocate outputs among members. The Court found that this agreement was not unlawful since it was to be considered as a reasonable response to protect the market from destructive practices.[19]

This is probably one of the best examples of how competition laws and their enforcement are to be understood in the political, economic, and historic context in which they are made. In *Socony-Vacuum Oil* (1940), when the economic conditions were already very different, the Supreme Court (which in the meantime had changed some of its judges) was to re-establish the principle of the *per se* prohibition of price agreements by declaring unlawful a practice also dating from the time of the Great Depression to counter the price decreases caused by the dumping of gasoline into the market by refiners panic-stricken by the crisis.[20]

Until the Mid-70s: The Activism in Anti-Trust Case Law After *Socony-Vacuum Oil* and until the mid-70s, there was a period of intense anti-trust activity, characterised probably more by the desire to restrain large firms than by the objective of increasing economic efficiency, an attitude which was consistent with the dominant economic thinking of the period.[21]

International Salt (1947) established a *per se* rule prohibiting tie-in sales – situations where a producer sells a given product (or service) only if the customer also purchases another product (or service). In *Schwinn* (1967) the Court ruled against exclusive territorial clauses – clauses that assign a particular distributor to a territory in which other distributors cannot sell the same manufacturer's product.[22]

In *Alcoa* (1945), the Circuit Court of Appeals overruled a lower court judge and found Alcoa guilty of monopolisation in the aluminium ingot market although

---

[19] The anti-competitive effect was also considered to be less strong since there existed many other producers in the industry not taking part in the agreement.

[20] In *Interstate Circuit* (1939), and *American Tobacco* (1946) the Supreme Court took the view that a conspiracy could be found even in the absence of hard evidence: there was no evidence of an explicit agreement or of direct communication among the firms; they simply followed a similar behaviour which had the effect of increasing prices. However, in *Theatre Enterprises v. Paramount* (1954) the Court ruled that conscious parallelism without any additional factor would not be a proof of an unlawful agreement. Chapter 4 discusses at length the issue of the standards of proof in collusion cases. I argue there that hard evidence of communication among firms should be necessary for convicting firms.

[21] See Mueller (1996) and Kovacic and Shapiro (2000) for the relationship between economic doctrines and US anti-trust law over time.

[22] As we shall see in Chapter 6 exclusive territorial protection is generally an efficient practice that encourages retailers to provide services: including it among vertical restraints that were *per se* prohibited is telling of an approach that looked suspiciously at restraints and disregarded efficiency reasons. As for tying (see Chapter 7), it is a practice that might in some circumstances be anti-competitive but often has good efficiency justifications.

there was no intent of monopolisation. The mere fact that Alcoa had monopoly power (as determined by its holding of a 90% share of the market) and that it took actions to increase its business, such as building new capacity, was enough to prove monopolisation (and the intent of it).[23]

Merger decisions of that period also appear to show a similar trend. In *Brown Shoe* (1962), the Supreme Court ruled against a merger that would have given the merging firms a market share of 5%. In *Philadelphia National Bank* (1963), a key issue in the assessment of the merger between two Philadelphia banks was whether the market was to be defined as the Philadelphia metropolitan area or as the New York–Philadelphia region. The Court opted for the narrower market definition and disallowed the merger because it would have created too concentrated a market, and it dismissed the banks' claim that the merger would have allowed them to compete with larger banks by claiming that anti-competitive effects in one market could not be justified by pro-competitive effects in another. In *Procter & Gamble* (1967), the Court ruled in favour of the FTC although the proposed merger was a conglomerate one (it attached great importance to the fact that P&G might have entered the market), and despite the claim of efficiency gains.

From Sylvania Onwards: Chicago School and the Reagan Years   Several authors connected to the University of Chicago heavily criticised the interventionism of the anti-trust authorities and courts, and stressed instead the efficiency rationale behind vertical restraints and mergers.[24] These views started to have an impact on judges and commentators during the 70s.

The joint effect of the Chicago School critique and of the loss of competitiveness of US firms abroad, that directed attention to the efficiency effects of business practices, caused a change in the enforcement attitudes of anti-trust law in the US. The turning-point was certainly *GTE-Sylvania* (1977), in which the Supreme Court decided that non-price vertical restraints should be subject to a rule of reason.

The new trend became a major change during the years of the Reagan administration (1981–8), which introduced a "hands-off" approach, in the conviction that market forces should be left free to select the more efficient firms.[25]

The focus on efficiency also meant that it was more difficult to win a case against a firm, especially in cases involving vertical restraints and monopolisation.[26] As

---

[23] Other monopolisation decisions which have been criticised for not taking into account possible efficiency arguments are *United Shoe* (1953) and *Utah Pie* (1967).

[24] For a view of the so-called Chicago School arguments, see for instance Bork (1978) and Posner (1976).

[25] As a result, important anti-trust investigations carried out by the previous administration, such as the one on IBM, were abandoned. This policy shift was also supported by new theoretical developments such as the "contestable markets theory" (see Chapter 2 for a discussion).

[26] See for instance *Jefferson Parish Hospital* (1984), where the Supreme Court decided that there was no evidence that a tying arrangement (patients of the hospital could get anesthesiologist services only provided by a medical corporation on an exclusive basis) had unreasonably restrained trade.

a consequence, the number of private anti-trust cases filed in US District Courts declined steadily in the 1980s. At the 1977 peak there were 1611 such cases, whereas in 1989 there were only 638.[27]

Recent Events It is more difficult to identify trends when looking at the very recent past. Apart from some very visible events determined by a change in the government,[28] agencies and courts lie somewhere between the interventionism of the 60s and the laisse-faire of the 80s. An important fact is the renewed strength in the fight against cartels, signalled by some prison sentences given in some high-profile international cartel cases, and helped by the introduction of a successful *leniency policy* that grants amnesty to managers that provide proof of the existence of cartels (see Chapter 4 for a detailed discussion).

1.2.2 Competition Laws in the European Union

This section briefly reviews the main historical development of competition laws in the European Union, where there are two different levels of jurisdiction: national and supra-national. The latter is more interesting, as most European countries have not had proper competition laws until very recently, and such national laws are to a large extent reproducing the same features as the laws introduced by the Treaty of Rome and its successive modifications. Therefore, I will devote attention mainly to EU competition policies. However, I find the history of German and British competition laws interesting in several respects, and for this reason I have a cursory look at them.

1.2.2.1 Competition Law in Germany

We have seen that the economic changes in the second half of the 19th century in the US created incentives for the formation of cartels and trusts which were soon to be outlawed by the Sherman Act. In Germany, however, the prevailing view was that cartels were an instrument to control the instability created by cut-throat competition and price warfare.[29] This idea, coupled with the feature that the

---

[27] See Viscusi et al. (1995) and Comanor (1990: 47–8).

[28] The most important and publicised case in recent years was the investigation on the alleged monopolisation of *Microsoft*, started under the Democratic Clinton administration. Under President George W. Bush, the Department of Justice changed attitude completely and looked for a settlement, which was finally approved by a judge in November 2002.

[29] Many of the comments referring here to current German competition law might also apply to other Central European countries such as Austria, Czech Republic, Switzerland, Hungary and Holland. In all of these countries, competition law was inspired by the principle of economic freedom. This might also explain the favourable treatment to cartels accorded in the past by most of the countries mentioned.

freedom of contracting was one of the governing principles of competition laws, implied that in Germany not only price agreements were permitted, but also that they were enforceable in courts. Anti-cartel action was taken only in certain extreme cases, for instance where the cartel could lead to a complete monopoly or to extreme exploitation of consumers (Scherer, 1994: 24). As a result, cartels proliferated in the years around the turn of the century. By 1905 there were 385 cartels involving 12,000 firms, and the number increased steadily. By 1923 there were 1,500 cartels in Germany (Kühn, 1997: 116).

It was only in 1923 that a Cartel Law was introduced, mainly as a reaction to hyper-inflation, as it was feared that price agreements might contribute to the escalation of prices. But even then, the law did not prohibit cartels; it merely required registration with a new agency in charge of ensuring that cartels would not abuse their market power. Not many abuses were pursued and the new law did not have much impact on cartels, whose number continued to rise. New economic conditions soon obviated the desire to limit the power of cartels, and prompted a move in the opposite direction. Indeed, in 1930, under the effect of the Great Depression and the bankruptcy of many firms, participation in cartels was made compulsory for firms operating in vulnerable sectors. Compulsory participation in cartels was made even more extensive under the Nazi regime, with the aim of controlling the national industry and strengthening the sectors involved in the war apparatus, on the grounds that it would be stronger if firms were tightly coordinated.

The idea that allowing firms to cooperate closely or to merge their operations would make them stronger and create some sort of "national champion" which would outperform foreign rivals is a widespread one. After World War II, the Allies wanted to impose anti-trust laws upon both Germany and Japan, not only to promote economic progress but also to break up excessive concentration of economic power, which represented a possible future threat. Accordingly, cartels, syndicates and trusts were forbidden by occupation authorities.[30] But the de-concentration programme of the Allies was soon put to an end, since the US and British governments soon perceived the threat of the Soviet Union and decided that Germany represented a useful force which could help to counter-balance the strength of the Soviet Union. A similar development also occurred in Japan (see Scherer, 1994: 28–32).

Germany passed a strict competition law in 1957, after a long debate.[31] The Federal Cartel Office (Bundeskartellamt) was the main institution called to enforce the rules against price-fixing agreements and other anti-competitive practices. Germany

---

[30] The breaking-up of the German chemical firm IG Farben into BASF, Bayer and Hoechst dates from this period.

[31] See Amato (1997: ch. 3) for a discussion of the ordo-liberal school and its influence on the German competition law.

has had a procedure for merger control since 1973, and this procedure has been enforced relatively strictly, leading not only to a considerable number of merger prohibitions but also to frequent modifications of merger proposals and the abandonment of many others. It has been noted, however, that one of the main principles behind competition policy in Germany is still the protection of economic freedom.[32] Thus, mergers are scrutinised because they could lead to the formation of dominant agents which could then limit the economic freedom of competitors. Provisions against the abuse of a dominant position should be seen in the same perspective.[33]

The strict opposition to practices such as resale price maintenance, which has been *per se* illegal in Germany since 1973,[34] is also consistent with this philosophy, to the extent that the imposition of resale prices by a manufacturer is seen as restraining the liberty of the retailers to set their own price.[35]

1.2.2.2 Competition Law in the United Kingdom

One of the first pieces of legislation introduced in the UK to deal with competition matters was the Profiteering Act 1919, whose main concern was to avoid excessive prices after World War I. Towards the end of World War II, the introduction of new competition rules was discussed, with a different motivation. Indeed, unemployment was a major issue then, and the Monopolies and Restrictive Practices (Inquiry and Control) Act 1948 appears to be motivated by the idea that competition in the marketplace would help attain full employment. Since then, a number of changes have been introduced in the UK, until the Competition Act 1998 brought the UK competition law almost in line with the EU's.

The UK system prior to the recent major changes was principally based upon the Restrictive Trade Practices Act 1956 (RTPA), which was extended among others by the Resale Prices Act 1964 and by the Monopolies and Mergers Act 1965, and amended by a number of other laws. Rather than adopting a system of prohibitions, under the RTPA agreements had to be registered and they could be challenged in

---

[32] See Kühn (1997), also for a discussion of court decisions, which privilege the contractual freedom of agents to the detriment of economic efficiency.

[33] German competition law tends to protect smaller competitors. For instance, the practice of large supermarket chains of selling some products below cost is forbidden because it would damage smaller stores. See the recent decision (11 November 2002) by the German Supreme Court on the Wal-Mart case.

[34] The only sector which is exempted from this prohibition of resale price maintenance is the publishing sector.

[35] According to Kamecke (1998: 147), however, resale price maintenance was prohibited because it was damaging small shop owners. Large chain stores had enough bargaining power to be able to disregard manufacturers' price choices without being challenged, whereas small shops had not. As a result, retail price maintenance had – somewhat paradoxically – the effect of harming small shops.

court if found against the public interest. It is debatable whether or not the Act had a real impact on firms' pricing behaviour.[36]

Several features of the UK competition legislation prior to the 1998 reform are worth mentioning. First of all, its objectives were never clearly specified. Under the wording "public interest" many different considerations can be made. The central role played by the Secretary of State for Industry – who has discretion on whether to accept or reject the Office of Fair Trading recommendations for referrals of merger cases to the Monopolies and Mergers Commission, and discretion on whether to accept the latter body's recommendations – reflects the role that political considerations may have on competition cases.

Second, the UK legislation lacked a system of penalties and tools of enforcement. Until the 1998 Reform, unlike their European counterparts, the UK competition authorities were not entitled to search firms' headquarters and seize documents.[37] This is clearly a serious limitation when it comes to fighting collusive or predatory practices. Further, competition authorities could not impose fines on firms which had been found engaging in practices against the public interest. Penalties could be given only to recidivists: only if a firm had been found guilty by a court of breaching an order of the Secretary of State and was later caught again breaching this court order, could penalties be given, for "contempt of court" (a serious offence). It is not surprising then, that people have been wondering about the effectiveness of the UK competition system in deterring anti-competitive agreements.[38]

The authority of having search power, to impose fines up to 10% of the firms' UK turnover, and the possibility of seeking recovery of damages by third parties through private actions, along with provisions which are clearly derived from the Treaty of the European Community, align the new UK competition policy as designed by the 1998 Act with the EU's.

One of the main differences still existing is that the UK system keeps the possibility of investigating a "monopoly" (defined as a firm having more than 25% market share) or a "complex monopoly" (a group of firms which hold together more than 25% market share) and to make recommendations such as seeking changes in the firms' business practices, imposing price controls and even divestment. This

---

[36] See Utton (2000, pp. 272–5) and Symeonidis (1998).

[37] The Director General of the OFT could ask a company for information, or apply to the courts to have cross-examinations on oath, only if there was suspicion of a restrictive agreement. See Whish (2001).

[38] Other critiques have been made about the quality and variability of the decisions taken. For instance, both Utton (2000) and Symeonidis (1998) mention contradictory judgments (which, incidentally, also have the effect of not giving firms legal certainty about the actions they should take) as well as (early) decisions which are today hard to understand. I found particularly curious two arguments made by the court in two separate cases. The first is that a cartel might benefit consumers because it would save them time wasted in shopping around; the second is that a cartel reduces uncertainty and therefore the return on capital required by firms in the industry, ultimately lowering prices. See Symeonidis (1998: 58 and footnote 3) and Utton (2000: 279).

introduces the possibility of structural interventions, which is more typical of regulatory regimes than competition policy.

1.2.2.3 Competition Law in the European Communities

The starting point of supra-national competition law in Europe was the series of pro-competitive measures adopted by France, Germany, Italy and the Benelux countries in the 1951 Treaty of Paris, which created the European Coal and Steel Community (ECSC). This Treaty prohibits trade barriers as well as discriminatory and other restrictive practices capable of distorting competition among the six countries which were later to become the founding members of the European Economic Community.

There are probably two main reasons behind the introduction of competition policy measures in the Treaty of Paris. The first one is again related to the desire of diminishing the danger of German power by making available to the other European countries such (at the time) essential inputs as coal and steel. The prohibition of discriminatory practices might also be seen as a way to guarantee equal access to these basic resources. The second reason is that the principle of free competition was beginning to be appreciated as the only viable way to attain an efficient functioning of the market, also in view of the success of the US economy which had continuously relied upon anti-trust rules (Goyder, 1993: 19). Free competition was thus preferred to a centralised organisation of markets, even though the High Authority (the body in charge) was authorised to intervene in case serious market imbalances arose.

Some of the key points of current competition law in Europe can be traced back, at least in their basic elements, to the articles dealing with competition issues in the Treaty of Paris. Article 65 of that Treaty prohibits agreements and concerted practices between firms or associations of firms which tend directly or indirectly to prevent, restrict or distort normal competition within the Common Market, and this provision is clearly the model upon which Article 81 of the Treaty of Rome is based.[39] Article 66(7) deals with the abuse of a dominant position by firms which use such a position to pursue objectives which are contrary to the Treaty, and is therefore the close correspondent of Article 82 of the Treaty of Rome.[40]

Article 66 also deals with mergers and concentrations between firms in the coal and steel industry. Consent to such mergers could be given only by the High Authority, which granted approval only where the concentration did not give to the new entity the power to control prices, restrict production and distribution, distort trade among Member States, or create an artificially privileged position in the markets. Attention to prospective mergers in these sectors can be understood by the fear of

---

[39] Previously Article 85. The Treaty of Amsterdam, which entered into force on 1 May 1999, has renumbered the articles of the Treaty of Rome.
[40] Previously Article 86.

concentration of economic power in the hands of a few firms, a fear which had already justified the process of de-cartelisation in Germany. It is noteworthy that the treatment of mergers is not mentioned in the Treaty of Rome. Mergers were not made the explicit object of European competition policy until the adoption of the Merger Regulation in 1989, after a debate which lasted for years, witnessing basic differences in the approach to competition and industrial policy among the different countries. In particular, Germany and the UK wanted mergers to be judged only on the basis of competition issues, whereas France wanted also to consider criteria of industrial policy and social issues. Eventually, the former approach prevailed.[41]

The Treaty of the European Communities deals with competition issues in Articles 81 to 89.[42] However, the logic of free competition is enunciated by Article 3(1)(g), which calls for the institution of "a system ensuring that competition in the internal market is not distorted". Furthermore, one of the major reasons behind the adoption of competition rules under the Treaty of Paris was to avoid discrimination on national grounds. Article 12 confirms that this is also one of the basic principles in the Treaty of the European Communities (the "Treaty"), and it has applications well beyond the rules on competition alone (Goyder, 1993: 26). Therefore one of the main objectives in European competition policy is the elimination in the economic system of any discrimination based on national grounds.[43] This explains in particular the strong position taken by the European Commission – and upheld on several occasions by the European Court of Justice – with respect to price discrimination across countries. Indeed, the Commission has without exception condemned firms which have tried to segment markets across national borders, and practices such as forbidding parallel imports have basically a status of *per se* prohibition within the EU.[44]

It is difficult to see exactly what the objectives of competition policy were for those who drafted the Treaty of Rome. It is probably safe to say that competition was not an end in itself, but was intended as a way to promote economic progress and the welfare of European citizens, the latter being one of the objectives of the EC as stated by Article 2.[45]

---

[41] See Goyder (1998: ch. 18(1)). However, this does not imply that other public policy considerations will never play any role in the EU merger policy. Article 13 of the Merger Regulation states that the EC must assess mergers ". . . within the general framework of the achievement of the fundamental objectives referred to in Article 2 of the Treaty, including that of strengthening the Community's economic and social cohesion".

[42] In the Treaty of Rome the relevant articles were numbered 85 to 94.

[43] This is also clearly stated in recent EC publications, such as European Commission (1996: para 2).

[44] Firms would not be able to charge different prices in different European countries if consumers and retailers made parallel imports, that is, if they engaged in arbitraging by buying cheaply in one country and selling at a higher price in another. See Chapter 7 for a discussion.

[45] That competition policy is a way to achieve the optimal allocation of resources, promote technical progress, and adapt to a changing environment is stated clearly in European Commission (1996: para. 1). The Commission also emphasises that competition helps European firms by pushing them

Today, the main objectives of competition policy as enforced by the EC are most probably economic efficiency and European market integration:

> The first objective of competition policy is the maintenance of competitive markets. Competition policy serves as an instrument to encourage industrial efficiency, the optimal allocation of resources, technical progress and the flexibility to adjust to a changing environment. In order for the Community to be competitive on worldwide markets, it needs a competitive home market. Thus, the Community's competition policy has always taken a very strong line against price-fixing, market sharing cartels, abuses of dominant positions, and anti-competitive mergers. It has also prohibited unjustified state-granted monopoly rights and state aid measures which do not ensure the long-term viability of firms but distort competition by keeping them artificially in business. The second is the single market objective. An internal market is an essential condition for the development of an efficient and competitive industry. . . . The Commission has used its competition policy as an active tool to prevent [erecting private barriers to trade], prohibiting, and fining heavily the parties to, two main types of agreement: distribution and licensing agreements that prevent parallel trade between Member States, and agreements between competitors to keep out of one another's 'territories'. (European Commission, 2000: 6.)

Social reasons are also taken into account in European competition policy. Indeed, the Commission has granted exemptions from competition rules for so-called *crisis cartels* – namely, agreements where firms engage in reciprocal reductions in capacity and output – provided such reductions in over-capacity are permanent, favour specialisation and are implemented in such a way that they minimise the social costs of the unemployment which result from the cutback of production (Goyder, 1993: 162–5). Here it is clear that social and political considerations influence the way in which competition policy is implemented: competition can be sacrificed when the social costs of it might be too high, since many firms might exit an industry under conditions of over-capacity, which would result in considerable job losses. Even if in the long-run a restructuring of the industry would be beneficial, in the short-run there might exist considerable costs that a government might want to avoid for political and social reasons.

A decision which shows that the EC considers arguments other than economic efficiency when deciding on horizontal agreements is *Ford/Volkswagen*, where it exempted a joint-venture for the development and production of a multi-purpose vehicle (that is, a mini-van) between the two major automobile manufacturers. On pure competition grounds, it is very doubtful that this joint-venture should have been cleared (it is likely that the two firms had enough skills and resources to develop

---

to be more competitive and efficient. More generally, Article 3 of the Treaty refers to competition as a way to achieve the objectives stated in Article 2.

and produce this type of vehicle independently). However, the Commission noted that

> the project constitutes the largest ever single foreign investment in Portugal. It is estimated to lead, *inter alia,* to the creation of about 5,000 jobs and indirectly create up to another 10,000 jobs, as well as attracting other investment in the supply industry. It therefore contributes to the promotion of the harmonious development of the Community and the reduction of regional disparities which is one of the basic aims of the Treaty. It also furthers European market integration by linking Portugal more closely to the Community through one of its important industries. (*Ford/Volkswagen:* para. 36.)

The possible consideration of reasons other than efficiency was re-affirmed in *Nestlé-Perrier,* in which the Court of First Instance ruled that, although the Merger Regulation is concerned primarily with questions of competition, this does not preclude the European Commission from taking into account the social effects of a concentration if they affect the level or conditions of employment (European Commission, 1996: 60).

Another element, which affects competition policy in Europe is the importance accorded by the Commission to small and medium-sized enterprises (SMEs).[46] These firms often receive favourable treatment. For instance, the EC looks favourably upon state aid given to SMEs in the form of subsidised loans, R&D support, financial guarantees and other assistance.[47] Further, the European Court of Justice has taken the view that Article 81(1) – which deals with agreements among firms, see Section 1.4 below – is not applicable where the impact of an agreement between firms on intra-community trade or on competition is not appreciable (the so-called *de minimis* doctrine). The European Commission has since set two quantitative criteria specifying when such agreements are deemed of minor importance: (1) a market share criterion and (2) a firm's size criterion.[48]

(1) Two different *aggregate* market share thresholds have been set by the EC: a 10% threshold for an agreement between competitors; and a 15% threshold for an agreement between firms which are not actual or potential competitors in any of the relevant markets affected by the agreement. However, a "black list" exists: if horizontal agreements involve price-fixing, restraints on outputs, market-sharing, or sharing of sources of supply; and if vertical agreements involve resale price maintenance or territorial protection, then Article 81(1) can still be applied.

(2) Even if the above market share thresholds are exceeded, the Commission will not apply Article 81(1) to agreements among SMEs, since they are rarely capable of

---

[46] The EC defines an SME as an enterprise which has a turnover up to 40 million euro, a balance sheet of 27 million euro, and a maximum number of employees of 250. See Commission recommendation of 3 April 1996 published in *OJ L* 107, 30.4.1996, p. 4.

[47] See OJ L 107, 30.4.1996: 4. See also European Commission (1996: para. 201).

[48] See *De Minimis Notice.*

affecting trade and competition within the Common Market, and would not in any case be of sufficient Community interest to justify its intervention. The only exceptions are agreements which might significantly impede competition in a substantial part of the relevant market, or which restrict competition by the cumulative effect of parallel networks of similar agreements between several producers or dealers.

The favourable treatment accorded to small and medium firms finds its rationale in the *de minimis* rule, namely that little harm can be done by firms which are of limited size. Accordingly, it is not efficient for the EC to use resources on agreements which are likely to have little impact on competition and welfare.[49] This has also inspired the recent reform on vertical restraints that allows the EC to focus more on cases that deserve scrutiny (see Section 1.4.1 below).

The European Commission has also looked with favourable eyes at SMEs after the big fall in employment caused in the 70s by the crisis of large firms operating in heavy industries: "the Commission continues to acknowledge the important contribution of SMEs in terms of job creation, innovation and economic development on the one hand and the difficulties SMEs have in raising capital and their insufficient access to information on the other hand".[50]

As the previous quote indicates, a further reason for a more favourable treatment might be to balance disadvantages that SMEs have in the markets because of their smaller dimensions.

1.3 OBJECTIVES OF COMPETITION POLICY AND OTHER PUBLIC POLICIES

The previous short historical review of competition policy illustrates that antitrust and competition laws are often influenced by social and historical factors, and might respond to quite different objectives. In what follows, I first briefly discuss a number of objectives, which have been indicated in different circumstances and in different jurisdictions, as the ones competition policy should pursue. I then deal with some public policy considerations, which have at different times influenced the enforcement of competition policy.

1.3.1 Objectives of Competition Policy

A number of objectives have inspired competition policies. After introducing the concept of economic welfare, I briefly mention some other objectives, and comment upon the possible contradictions between them and the welfare objective.

---

[49] See also Neven, Papandropoulos and Seabright (1998).
[50] EC Competition Policy Newsletter, 2(1), Spring 1996: 34. Similarly, on state aid policy, the EC states: "In general the Commission takes a favourable view of aid to small and medium-sized enterprises, given their structural handicaps as compared with large undertakings and their potential for innovation, job creation and growth" (European Commission, 2000: §245).

1.3.1.1 Welfare (Total Surplus)

Economic *welfare* is the standard concept used in economics to measure how well an industry performs. It is a measure which aggregates the welfare (or surplus) of different groups in the economy (see Chapter 2 for a more detailed discussion). In each given industry, welfare is given by *total surplus,* that is the sum of consumer surplus and producer surplus.[51] The surplus of a given individual consumer is given by the difference between the consumer's valuation for the good considered (or her willingness to pay for it) and the price, which effectively she has to pay for it. *Consumer surplus* (or consumer welfare) is the aggregate measure of the surplus of all consumers. The surplus of an individual producer is the profit it makes by selling the good in question. *Producer surplus* is therefore the sum of all profits made by producers in the industry.

From these definitions it follows that, other things being equal, an increase of the price at which goods are sold reduces consumer surplus and increases producer surplus. It turns out, however, that in general as the price increases, the increase in profits made by the firms does not compensate for the reduction in the consumer surplus (see Chapter 2 for a graphical representation). Hence, welfare is lowest when the market price equals the monopoly price (the highest price firms might want to charge), and highest when it equals marginal costs of production.

It is important to notice that this concept of welfare completely overlooks the issue of income distribution among consumers and producers. This is not because economists think it is an irrelevant issue, but rather because it is a different issue. The welfare measure is a summarising measure of how efficient a given industry is as a whole and does not address the question of how equal or unequal income is distributed, which can be dealt with by other measures. Note also that the rationale for not considering distributional issues is that in principle it is possible to operate redistribution schemes such that consumers and producers are *both* either better off or worse off.[52] Imagine for instance a situation where, as a result of a change in the economy, welfare increases as the net effect of an increase in consumer surplus and a decrease in producer surplus. In theory, it is possible to redistribute gains from consumers to producers in such a way that both groups are at least as well off as they were before the changes took place.[53]

---

[51] More complete measures of welfare might also take into account externalities, taxes paid, subsidies received, government revenues and so on. Some of these items might cancel out. It is also possible to construct measures of welfare which assign different weights to consumer and producer surplus.

[52] The difference between consumers and producers as two completely different groups of citizens should not be overstated. In most countries, consumers are also owners of the firms either directly (as shareholders) or through pension and investment funds.

[53] See Tirole (1988: 7–12) for a discussion of the measures of consumer surplus and welfare. In particular, it should be emphasised that in a partial equilibrium framework (that is, when a sector is considered in isolation from the rest of the economy) such measures are valid as long

Finally, the concept of welfare should not only be interpreted in a static sense but also in its dynamic component. In other words, future welfare matters as well as current welfare. The two things do not necessarily coincide, as we shall discuss in Chapter 2. Imagine the hypothetical case where firms in the industry have already paid their fixed costs and a competition authority is systematically able to impose a price equal to marginal cost. This being the lowest possible price, it would maximise welfare in a static sense. However, one would not have the firms in the industry make any investment in such a situation, as they would anticipate that at a price equal to marginal cost they would not make any profit and hence they would not be able to recover any fixed cost associated with an investment. As a result, in such a hypothetical situation future welfare will be reduced, as new products would not be introduced, innovations would not be made, and the quality levels of goods and services would not be improved. (See Chapter 2 for further discussion of this point.)

1.3.1.2 Consumer Welfare (Consumer Surplus)

Although in most circumstances practices that decrease total welfare also decrease consumer welfare and vice versa (this being the case for cartels, for instance), this is not always necessarily the case. For instance, perfect price discrimination by a monopolist (a situation where each consumer is made to pay exactly its willingness to pay) maximises welfare to the detriment of consumers (see Chapter 7); or, more important since perfect price discrimination belongs to the theoretical realm only, and perhaps is not a very frequent real case, a merger that allows the merging firms to decrease significantly their fixed costs might increase total welfare (due to larger profits) while increasing prices and thus decreasing consumer welfare (see Chapter 5).

Consumer v. Total Welfare Standard in Different Jurisdictions   It is difficult to say whether competition authorities and courts favour in practice a consumer welfare or a total welfare objective. In the EU, Article 81(3) allows any agreement, decision or concerted practice "which contributes to improving the production or distribution of goods or to promoting technical or economic progress, *while allowing consumers a fair share of the resulting benefit*" (emphasis added). Furthermore, Article 2.1 of the Merger Regulation accepts in principle an efficiency defence "provided that it is to consumers' advantage". These provisions might indicate that consumer welfare is among the ultimate objectives of competition law.[54] However, I am not

as consumers are spending on that sector's products just a small fraction of their total incomes. Otherwise, income effects should be taken into account and the consumer surplus measure cannot be relied upon in computing approximations of welfare.

[54] But the Guidelines on Vertical Restraints, at para. 7, state: "The protection of competition is the primary objective of EC competition policy, as this enhances consumer welfare and creates an efficient allocation of resources".

aware of any statement of the ECJ on this point, nor of any (Commission or Court's) decision where reliance on either standard has made a difference in practice.

In the US, both the courts and the anti-trust agencies seem to tend toward a consumer welfare standard too, at least as far as mergers are concerned. Indeed, the last revision of the US merger guidelines states that "the Agency considers whether cognizable efficiencies likely would be sufficient to reverse the merger's potential to harm consumers in the relevant market, e.g., by preventing price increases in that market".

In other jurisdictions, such as in Canada, Australia and New Zealand, competition authorities seem instead to lean towards a total welfare standard (Lyons, 2002: 3).

Consumer v. Total Welfare Standard for Economists   Although I believe that consumer and total welfare standards would not often imply very different decisions by anti-trust agencies and courts, there remains the question of which of the two should be the appropriate objective for competition policy. While economists generally prefer total welfare, arguments have also been raised in favour of a consumer welfare objective.[55]

Consider the following argument (which takes a "political economy" perspective). Very often consumers are not willing (or able) to exert their aggregate power since the effect upon consumers of a given market situation is likely to be dispersed among many of them while it is much less dispersed for producers. Imagine, for instance, that a certain consumer good is usually bought by 100,000 consumers per year, each of which buys only one unit, usually sold at a price of 100 euros. If the two firms producing this good were able to influence the government to enforce a regulation which increases the price by 10% (for instance, through protection from foreign competition, or through authorisation of a collusive agreement), this would bring about huge collective losses for the group of consumers as a whole, but individual losses (10 euros) are probably not large enough for consumers to decide to stand up to defend their position. On the contrary, the two producers would have large individual gains from such a move, and so they would be ready to employ considerable resources to lobby the government into adopting the regulation. The competition authority might then have a role to play if it contributes to balancing the different lobbying powers of the two groups of economic agents in question. Therefore, the argument goes, attaching a heavier weight to consumer surplus than to producer surplus might help redress the balance towards consumers.

Similar arguments in favour of a consumer welfare standard have been made in discussions of merger policy. For instance, Besanko and Spulber (1993) argue

---

[55] A different question, which pertains to politicians rather than economists, is whether – if a total welfare standard is chosen – profits of foreign firms should be included in the measure of producer surplus or not, and in what proportion. The issue is of some importance in European merger policy, since mergers analysed by the EC often involve firms and consumers of different countries.

that merging firms enjoy information advantages (particularly on the efficiency gains associated with the merger) over the competition authority, and that the adoption of a consumer welfare standard (that is, accepting the merger only if it increases consumer welfare, no matter the effects on profits and therefore on total welfare) might counter-balance this asymmetry. Neven and Röller (2000) suggest that competition authority officials might be exposed to the lobbying of firms that can offer them personal reward, and claim that a consumer welfare standard might counter-balance the bias resulting from such lobbying.[56]

Another argument that is sometimes mentioned in favour of the consumer welfare standard is that it might simplify decisions by the anti-trust authorities in merger cases. Suppose for instance that a merger entails some fixed cost savings, but it will likely increase prices. A total welfare standard would entail a difficult exercise of quantification of the changes in consumer surplus and in profits, in order to arrive at a final estimate of the net effects on total welfare. A consumer welfare standard, instead, would not need such an exercise, since it could limit itself to the (relatively) simpler assessment of the effects on prices.

Although these arguments might have some merit, it would not be wise for competition authorities to adopt a consumer welfare objective, for several reasons. First, consumer welfare by definition does not take into account the gains made by the firms. However, in today's advanced economies consumers often own firms (partly or fully), directly or through pension and investment funds. Accordingly, dividends are distributed to a vast number of citizens who would be hurt if profits were reduced. If the adoption of a consumer welfare standard were intended to favour "citizens" as opposed to "firms", it would not be clear that such a goal would be achieved.[57] Second, if one took literally the objective of maximising consumer surplus, this would lead to pricing at marginal costs, with firms exiting the industry in the long-run or having to be subsidised to cover fixed costs, not a reasonable idea, since the market should then be replaced by across-the-board regulation. Third, and of great importance, lower prices and profits would have the effect of depriving firms from the necessary incentives to innovate, invest, and introduce new products.[58] Therefore, at the very least one should consider the objective as that of maximising consumer surplus over time (i.e., in dynamic terms), otherwise by helping consumers today one would hurt consumers tomorrow. But then, it would not be clear to which extent the distinction between consumer and total surplus matters.

---

[56] See Lyons (2002) for a brief discussion on the merits of these papers, as well as for another economic model, which indicates that under certain circumstances a consumer welfare standard might be superior to a total welfare standard when dealing with mergers.

[57] And if one wanted to pursue redistributive goals, for instance favouring labour over capital, it would be more efficient and less distortive to use fiscal policies than anti-trust laws.

[58] See Chapter 2 for a discussion of market power and profits as incentives for firms to invest.

Like most economists, I also prefer the welfare standard. Therefore, in this book the different practices will generally be assessed according to this standard, but their effects on consumer welfare will also be made explicit. In most cases, however, the policy recommendations would not differ if one chose the latter objective over the former.

1.3.1.3 Defence of Smaller Firms

The defence of small firms has often been one of the main reasons behind the adoption of competition laws. The most famous instance is given by anti-trust laws introduced in the US at the end of the 19th century, which were initiated due to the complaints of farmers and small firms against the large trusts, but this motivation probably lies behind the restrictions to discriminatory practices introduced by many pieces of legislation.

The favourable treatment of small firms is not necessarily in contrast with the objective of economic welfare if it is limited to protecting such firms from the abuse of larger enterprises, or giving them a small advantage to balance the financial and economic power of larger rivals.

However, artificially helping small firms to survive when they are not operating at an efficient scale of production is in contrast with economic welfare objectives. Indeed, this would encourage inefficient allocation of resources and would contribute to keep high prices in the economy.

The European Commission seems to have taken the view that small and medium-sized enterprises (SMEs) are more dynamic, more likely to innovate and more likely to create employment than large firms. This would be an additional argument to promote SMEs. However, the empirical evidence is quite ambiguous. It would seem difficult to state that small firms make a larger contribution to growth and innovation than large firms.[59]

As a conclusion, it makes sense that the competition authorities do not use their scarce resources to monitor agreements and mergers which involve smaller firms,[60] but there is little rationale behind a systematic use of competition policy towards helping SMEs.

Smaller firms are often hurt by the lack of proper infrastructure and imperfect markets (larger firms might be able to overcome problems owing to their size, financial means or internal market mechanisms). Such difficulties had better be dealt with by government interventions at the root of the problems, rather than instruments such as competition policy, whose purpose lies elsewhere. There is risk

---

[59] Think, for instance, of the very old issue of whether large firms are more conducive to innovation than the small firms. The vast literature on the subject is far from conclusive.

[60] The practice of granting exemptions to small firms is also useful in that it does not oblige them to spend resources in dealing with administrative matters, such as filling in forms to notify agreements or mergers.

of creating additional distortions in the competition sphere, while giving only a very imperfect answer to the source of the problems.

1.3.1.4 Promoting Market Integration

As we have seen, *promotion of market integration* is one of the key objectives of EU competition policy as stated by the Treaty, enforced by the EC and endorsed by the courts. This is a political objective which is not necessarily consistent with economic welfare. EU competition law *de facto* forbids price discrimination across national borders. There is no economic rationale for such a different treatment.

A priori, it is difficult to say whether price discrimination has a positive or negative impact over welfare, as the following example shows. Imagine that the same good is sold in two countries, say Germany and Portugal. Germans have on average a higher income and willingness to pay for the good than Portuguese. If price discrimination is allowed and it is feasible (arbitrage does not occur, or it occurs only to a limited extent), a monopolist would sell in Germany at a price p_h (where h stands for "high") and in Portugal at a lower price p_l. By making consumers pay according to their different willingness to pay, the firm is able to increase its profit.

Consider now what happens if the monopolist was obliged to set an identical price on the two markets. A possible option is to set an intermediate price p_m (such that $p_l < p_m < p_h$). Hence, Germans would be better off, while Portuguese would be worse off. To judge the overall welfare effect of market integration, three aspects should be accounted for: the consumer surplus of the two groups (Germans would gain, Portuguese would lose) and the profit earned by the monopolist (which is lower when price cannot be segmented). A priori, the welfare effect is therefore ambiguous.[61]

However, there is also another option available to the monopolist. This is to continue to charge the price p_h it was charging in Germany for both markets. It would lose the Portuguese market completely but keep the highest profit in the German market, so that this strategy might well be more profitable than selling at an intermediate price in both markets.

If the second strategy prevails, then the prohibition of price discrimination across countries achieves precisely the opposite effect than intended at first sight: differences in the market conditions between Germany and Portugal end up with being much more pronounced than before.

It is not easy to draw simple and practical policy implications on price discrimination (see Chapter 7). However, as this simple example shows, a *per se* rule, which forbids firms to price discriminate across countries is not justified on economic welfare grounds, and in some circumstances might even work (paradoxically) against the objective of market integration.

---

[61] See Chapter 7 for a simple formal analysis.

1.3.1.5 Economic Freedom

As we have seen, to guarantee economic freedom is probably the main rationale behind competition laws in Germany. The possible contradictions between such an objective and the objective of economic efficiency have been discussed in detail and with reference to specific cases by Kühn (1997). Probably the most obvious source of contrasts arises in vertical restraints, for instance in contracts and clauses imposed by a manufacturer upon the retailers of the good it produces. Although territorial restraints, resale price maintenance and other practices often find strong justification in economic efficiency terms (for instance, by stimulating the efforts of retailers, or by making sure that they would not set prices above those which are optimal for the manufacturer), it is straightforward that they limit the economic freedom of the retailers.[62]

1.3.1.6 Fighting Inflation

Our brief historical excursus has also illustrated how macroeconomic events might affect the implementation of economic policy. Fighting inflation, for instance, has been indicated as one reason for introducing control over cartels in Germany. However, it seems doubtful that competition law might efficiently be used to attain such purposes. If firms are colluding, then breaking a cartel would give a one-time reduction of prices, rather than contributing to a permanent decrease of inflation. Further, in an environment where all prices are continuously increasing, it is likely that firms would react to a common shock on the prices of inputs by simultaneously and independently increasing prices, even in the absence of any collusion.[63,64]

1.3.1.7 Fairness and Equity

Competition laws might also incorporate objectives such as fairness and equity, forcing firms to behave in a certain way both with respect to customers and to rivals.[65]

[62] For the relationship between restrictions on commerce and restrictions on the freedom of contract, see Amato (1997).

[63] Nor would it be reasonable to limit price movements of the firms in a situation where all input prices increase.

[64] However, if price shocks were not perfectly anticipated by the firms, that is, if inflation was highly correlated with price uncertainty, it might be possible that colluding firms (which are able to monitor each other's behaviour and share information) immediately increase prices every time there exists a price increase of inputs, whereas firms which are not colluding are more hesitant to raise prices. I have never seen this argument analysed in formal terms.

[65] Several competition laws refer to terms such as "fairness", "fair", "unfair". Definitions of such concepts are (understandably) rare, and their use is left to the discretion of competition authorities and courts.

As for fairness towards customers, the law might prevent dominant firms from charging excessive prices (as in Article 82 in the EU, see below). From an economic point of view, price controls by authorities are unlikely to be a desirable policy in markets with free entry, apart from exceptional cases. In general, a firm should be free to charge the prices it wants, and if it enjoys market power because of its merits (be they investments in R&D, advertising, or whatever other business strategy) there is little reason to oblige it to give discounts to consumers who are willing to pay a high price for its goods or services.[66] If the market is one where entry is free, and the goods or services under discussion are valuable for consumers, chances are that sooner or later competition from new entrants will appear and prices will move downwards. There are two qualifications to this reasoning, however. The first is that entry in the market in question might not be free. If this is the case, for instance because there exists a legal monopoly, then price intervention would be justified. Usually, such markets should be subject to regulation, but if for some reason sector regulators do not exist or fail to intervene, intervention by competition authorities (if allowed by the institutional setting) might be justified.

The second is that although entry is free on paper, in practice the market does not work well because the monopolist has set up practices which allow it to preserve or reinforce its monopoly position. However, in this case, it would be preferable if anti-trust authorities intervened so as to restore market competition (which is the cause of the problem), rather than to set a ceiling to prices (whose high level is the effect of abusive practices).

This brings us to the next issue, which is fairness and equity in the marketplace. Let us consider first a case where a particular interpretation of the concept of fairness would collide with an economic welfare criterion. Take for instance the politically sensitive issue of small shopkeepers v. large supermarket chains. In many countries, concern is often voiced that the supermarket chains exploit their bigger volumes so as to have bargaining power and buy from manufacturers much more cheaply than small shops. This allows the former to sell at lower final prices than the latter. As a result, small shops have economic difficulties and could be forced to close down. Some people would argue that this is unfair, and that small shops should accordingly be protected.[67] I doubt that this claim is justified from the point of view of fairness. Certainly, such a reasoning would be at odds with basic efficiency principles. Whenever there exist economies of scale in a market, larger firms will have lower costs and will be more competitive. Small firms which fail to reach the minimum efficient scale of production (or distribution) will have to either content themselves

---

[66] See also Chapter 2 on the need to let firms appropriate the fruits of their investments.

[67] An Italian law approved in 2001 (l. 62 of 9-3-2001) prohibited selling books at a discount higher than 10% of the cover price. (The law was later modified, prohibiting discounts higher than 15% and for the period of one year only.) This is an example of a law which distorts competition in the marketplace to protect smaller firms (bookshops in this case) from the competition of more efficient and larger firms (in this case, supermarkets and Internet bookstores).

with lower profits or exit the market. This process of rationalisation whereby only the most efficient firms will stay in the market is beneficial for a community as a whole, as it will bring market prices down to the benefit of consumers. Interfering in this process by limiting the ability of larger firms to charge lower prices would damage welfare.[68]

Note, however, that fairness and efficiency are not always in contradiction. Consider a variation of the previous example, and suppose that in a given market a supermarket chain, which already has a very high share of the market (say, 70%) systematically charges below costs with the aim of forcing all small rivals out of the market (they could not cover their costs at the prices charged by the supermarket). In this case, this practice (which is called *predatory*) is both unfair and welfare detrimental. Indeed, after small shopkeepers have been forced to exit the market, the supermarket chain will start to charge monopoly prices. Therefore, consumers pay low prices during the period in which the supermarket is acting in a predatory way, but they will have to pay much higher prices ever after.[69]

More generally, *ex ante* equity (that is, the fact that firms have the same initial opportunities in the marketplace) is compatible with competition policy, which should guarantee a *level playing field* for all the firms. Instead, *ex post* equity (that is, equal outcomes of market competition) is unfortunately not something, which necessarily coincides with competition policy, since markets work so that firms which invest more, innovate more, or simply are luckier than others will be more successful and reap higher profits.

1.3.2 Other Public Policy Factors Affecting Competition

A number of public policy considerations often affect competition laws and their enforcement. Indeed, the brief historical account above shows that competition authorities and courts often adopt weaker stances on competition issues than economic considerations alone would have suggested, due to social, political or strategic reasons.

1.3.2.1 Social Reasons

Competition rules have sometimes been relaxed to smooth social tensions. US laws were implemented in a more lenient way in the times of the Great Depression, with the view that some price agreement would help firms to avoid bankruptcy, thus

---

[68] If – for whatever reason – it was really felt that small shops have to survive, then rather than using competition policy it would be better to implement this objective through a redistributive policy, for instance by reducing taxes on the personal income of shop-keepers.

[69] Of course, it is not always easy to distinguish predatory behaviour from low prices due to higher efficiency. See Chapter 7 on monopolisation for an analysis of how competition authorities should behave in such cases.

easing social tensions caused by unemployment. If capital markets were imperfect, then a policy trying to reduce bankruptcies might be of help. However, allowing firms to collude to solve the problem is likely to be a remedy worse than the problem itself. This would introduce further distortions into the economy: It would be better to intervene directly with other measures in the banking and financial sphere.

For the same reason, "crisis cartels" are sometimes tolerated by the EC. Although pursuing such objectives might be understandable, it is not clear that the means adopted achieve their purpose. A more favourable treatment for certain firms in bad times might have adverse consequences upon other groups already hit by a recession, like consumers or even other firms using inputs or intermediate goods. As for allowing agreements between firms in a declining sector (often concentrated in a given geographical area), it might have medium- and long-run adverse consequences. Actually, this might allow less efficient firms to stay on to the detriment of more efficient firms which would have survived anyhow. A misallocation of resources might be the result of such a policy.[70]

1.3.2.2 Political Reasons

Political reasons might also justify some competition policy positions. When the Allied Forces decided to break up industrial groups in Germany and Japan, one of the reasons might also have come from the danger of having economic concentration of power being used for political purposes. Indeed, the close connection between political and economic power during the Nazi regime played a role in the attempt of increasing the dispersion of power. More generally, it might be feared that democracy could be put at risk when a few citizens and groups dominate a large share of resources. From a different point of view, calling for a less concentrated distribution of resources can be justified on fairness grounds. Indeed, to reduce inequality in income distribution has also been one of the reasons invoked by the advocates of anti-trust laws in the US, as a reaction to the excessive power accumulated by some large firms and trusts and to the epidemic of bankruptcies of small firms at the end of the 19th century.

1.3.2.3 Environmental Reasons

Environmental reasons might also be taken into account in the enforcement of European competition law, according to Articles 6 and 174 of the Treaty. In a recent decision (*CECED*), for instance, the Commission has approved an agreement

---

[70] However, it is not always the case that market forces left alone would bring about the exit of less efficient firms before the more efficient ones. See e.g., Dierickx et al. (1991). The existence of different financial situations might also explain the permanence in the market of more inefficient firms.

among producers and importers of washing machines which together account for more than 95% of European sales (Martinez Lopez, 2000a). The agreement aims among other things at discontinuing production and imports of the least energy-efficient washing machines, which represent some 10–11% of current EC sales. The agreement removes one of the dimensions along which sellers compete, and as such it might negatively affect competition and increase prices (as a general rule, the most polluting machines are also the least expensive ones). However, the Commission considered that the agreement will benefit society in environmental terms,[71] allowing reduction of energy consumption, and that such an objective would not have been attained without the agreement. This is because consumers do not properly take into account all the externalities involved in their purchase and consumption decisions, and firms would not give up a tool of market competition unless bound by an agreement.[72]

Of course, whenever competition policy is used for other purposes than efficiency, one has to wonder whether this is the optimal solution.[73] In this particular case, the same (or more advanced) objectives might be attained through a number of other public policies, such as the imposition of taxes, which discriminate against more environmental damaging machines or even the imposition of a minimum environmental standard adopted at a European-wide level. However, it might well be that such alternative instruments are politically difficult to attain, and that competition policy might help the environmental objectives. Of course, it is important in these cases to ensure that this use of competition policy does not introduce additional distortions. In this particular case, however, competition among producers did not seem deeply affected, as the agreement did not remove many other competitive instruments at the firms' disposal (prices, technical effectiveness, brand image, advertising and adoption of energy-saving levels above the threshold imposed by the agreement are still available).

1.3.2.4 Strategic Reasons: Industrial and Trade Policies

Supporting *national champions,* or breaking up foreign champions, has also played a role in competition policies. Lax competition policies in some countries can sometimes be explained by the willingness of national governments to allow domestic firms to "go bigger" in the belief that this will help them be more successful vis-à-vis

---

[71] Private energy-saving benefits for consumers should be taken into account by consumers when taking their purchase decisions. It is the environmental externality that the consumers might not take into account.

[72] One could possibly interpret this situation as one where firms play either a coordination game or a prisoner dilemma game. In the absence of the agreement, they would end up selling to a certain part of the market energy-inefficient machines at low prices, whereas the agreement allows them to sell more efficient machines at no less profit.

[73] See also Martinez Lopez (2000b).

foreign rivals. This might for instance explain why France wanted to include social and industrial policy considerations in the Merger Regulation, and *a contrario* inspired the policy of de-cartelisation forced upon Germans after World War II. This means that strategic trade policy considerations might lurk behind competition laws or behind implementation methods.

An example of using competition laws to allow domestic firms to extract rents in foreign markets may be observed in the exception given by US law to *export cartels*.[74] The Webb-Pomerene Act exempts export associations from the anti-trust laws where their sole purpose is to engage in export trade and if their actions (1) do not interfere with or restrain trade in the US; and (2) do not restrain the export trade of domestic competitors.[75] The Export Trading Company Act provides for the issuance of a "certification" of immunity by the Department of Commerce (with the agreement of the DOJ). The certification is issued when the export activity (1) does not result in a substantial reduction of competition in the US or with an export competitor; (2) does not unreasonably affect prices in the US; (3) does not amount to an unfair method of competition against rivals in the export market; and (4) does not engage in the sale or resale of goods in the domestic market.

More generally, competition policy instruments can also be used to achieve *protectionist* goals. A case in point is the use of *anti-dumping laws:* these are laws that in theory aim at preventing foreign firms from selling below their costs (i.e., that they *dump* their goods) in the national market to the detriment of national firms. The existence of such laws is justified on fair trade grounds (if dumping coincides with below cost pricing, it might be indicating predatory behaviour), but that often is used as a way to protect domestic firms from more efficient foreign firms. For instance, anti-dumping laws are often implemented in such a way that it is very easy to prove that there has been dumping by foreign firms, which are being penalised even when they are simply more efficient.[76]

Industrial policy and trade policy considerations have often been an obstacle to the enforcement of competition policy.[77] My view is that competition policy is the best possible industrial policy: it is unlikely that firms in a particular industry are able to grow healthily if sheltered from competition, subsidised, or exempted from anti-cartel laws.[78]

Of course, the clearest case where strategic trade policies are at work is when a country's government subsidises domestic firms. This distorts competition in the

[74] I am grateful to Mel Marquis for the following discussion.

[75] The export association must file reports on its activities with the Federal Trade Commission (FTC). Based on US case law, the association is not permitted to join a foreign cartel, nor may it establish a foreign subsidiary. Finally, it may not join with non-members to restrict competition and price. If the association violates these prohibitions, the FTC refers the matter to the DOJ for prosecution.

[76] On anti-dumping, see Chapter 7. On the possibility that competition policy instruments are used as a protectionist device, see Motta and Onida (1997).

[77] See Gual (1995) on the conflicts among competition, trade and industrial policies in the EU.

[78] See Chapter 2 on the role of competition to promote productive efficiency.

marketplace and has detrimental effects, since it might allow inefficient firms to survive at the expense of more efficient ones. Although in the EU it is the Competition Directorate that is in charge of *state aids,* and such aids do have an effect on competition, I take the view that they pertain more to the domain of trade policy than of that of competition policy. Accordingly, I do not deal with subsidies in this book.

1.3.3 Competition Policy: A Definition

To define *competition policy* (or *anti-trust policy* as it is more often called in the US) is not an easy task. A possible definition might be as follows: "the set of policies and laws which ensure that competition in the marketplace is not restricted in a way that is detrimental to society". This definition admits the possibility that some restrictions might not necessarily be detrimental. For instance, some agreements between a manufacturer and a retailer, which limit competition by other retailers often improve economic welfare (see Chapter 5). But the definition is also empty unless one specifies what "detrimental to society" means. In turn, this calls for a specification of the objectives of competition policy.

In Section 1.3 I have argued that *economic welfare* is the objective competition authorities and courts should pursue. This brings me to define competition policy as "the set of policies and laws which ensure that competition in the marketplace is not restricted in such a way as to reduce economic welfare". In this book I will assess the anti-competitive potential of business practices, and the desirability of competition laws, according to this definition.

This does not imply that objectives or public policy considerations other than economic efficiency are not important, but more simply that if a government wanted to achieve them, it should not use competition policy but resort to policy instruments that distort competition as little as possible. Furthermore, as an economist my role is to stress which measures are aligned with the objective of increasing economic welfare and which are instead in contrast with it. It will be up to others, be they politicians or judges or sociologists, to decide whether to give priority to economic or other considerations when conflicts arise.

1.4 THE MAIN FEATURES OF EUROPEAN COMPETITION LAW

This section gives a short introduction to European competition law, whose main provisions are contained in Articles 81 and 82 of the Treaty of the European Communities and in the Merger Regulation.[79]

---

[79] Articles 83–89 of the Treaty also deal with competition issues, but either contain procedural norms or deal with issues such as public enterprises and state aids, whose detailed analysis goes beyond the scope of this work. For a better understanding of the legal aspects of European competition

Articles 81 and 82 of the Treaty are characterised by "direct applicability": This means that they are part of the law of each Member State and are directly enforceable by national courts. As directly applicable provisions, Articles 81 and 82 are enforced by the European Commission (EC), or more precisely, by the *DG Comp* (the Directorate General for Competition that acts following the directives of the European Commissioner responsible for competition law) at the Community level and by National Competition Authorities at the Member States' level.

At the Community level, the Court of First Instance (CFI) has, since 1989, jurisdiction in all actions brought against the decisions of the EC by any natural or legal person in competition law matters.[80] The European Court of Justice decides on appeal actions brought against the judgments of the CFI.

At the national level, national courts decide according to the different systems provided by each Member State against the decisions of National Competition Authorities.

1.4.1 Article 81: Horizontal and Vertical Agreements

Article 81(1) prohibits

> all agreements between undertakings, decisions by associations of undertakings and concerted practices which may affect trade between Member States and which have as their object or effect the prevention, restriction or distortion of competition within the common market, and in particular those which: (a) directly or indirectly fix purchase or selling prices or any other trading conditions; (b) limit or control production, markets, technical development, or investment; (c) share markets or sources of supply; (d) apply dissimilar conditions to equivalent transactions with other trading parties, thereby placing them at competitive disadvantage; (e) make the conclusion of contracts subject to acceptance by the other parties of supplementary obligations which, by their nature or according to commercial usage, have no connection with the subject of such contracts.

Article 81(2) declares that "any agreements or decisions prohibited pursuant to this Article shall be automatically void".

Article 81(3) states that such prohibition does not apply to any agreement, decision or concerted practice,

> which contributes to improving the production or distribution of goods or to promoting technical or economic progress, while allowing consumers a fair share of the resulting benefit, and which does not: (a) impose on the undertakings

---

law, see e.g., Bellamy and Child (2001), Goyder (1998), Korah (1994a), Ritter et al. (2000) or Whish (2001).

[80] Actions brought by Member States against other Member States or community institutions and actions brought by any community institution against any other community institution are, however, heard only by the European Court of Justice.

concerned restrictions which are not indispensable to the attainment of these objectives; (b) afford such undertakings the possibility of eliminating competition in respect of a substantial part of the products in question.

Whereas a full discussion and interpretation of this article is not possible here, a few remarks are needed. First, Article 81 deals with both horizontal and vertical agreements. This is a source of potential problems, as economics shows that one should generally expect these agreements to have quite different competitive effects. Horizontal agreements, that is agreements among competitors, usually restrict competition and thus reduce welfare (see Chapter 4) and should therefore be prohibited apart from very specific cases (such as, for instance, co-operative agreements in R&D). By contrast, vertical agreements, that is agreements between firms operating at different stages of the production processes (for instance, between a manufacturer and a retailer) are often efficiency enhancing and pose problems to competition, if any, only when they are undertaken by firms which enjoy considerable market power (see Chapter 6). To treat agreements which have such a different nature and such different expected competitive effects with the same legal provision is therefore unlikely to be efficient.

Recently, the EC perceived this problem and adopted an approach on vertical restraints which is more in line with economic thinking. Regulation 2790/1999 introduces a block exemption from Article 81(1) on vertical restraints, subject to (i) a market share criterion and (ii) a "black list" of clauses, which are not exempted.[81] (i) The block exemption is limited to vertical agreements in which the market share of the supplier is below 30% (in case of agreements containing an exclusive supply obligation, it is the buyer's market share which may not exceed 30% in order for the block exemption to hold).[82] (ii) However, there are some types of restraints which are considered so harmful by the Commission that the block exemption does not apply to them even if the market share threshold of 30% is not attained.[83] These so-called "hard-core" practices mainly relate to resale price maintenance (clauses which fix, directly or indirectly, resale prices) and (some types of) territorial restrictions which might lead to market partitioning by territory or by customer,[84] and are justified

---

[81] Adopted on 22 December 1999 and published in *OJ L* 336, 29.12.1999, this regulation replaces three expired block exemptions regulations, on exclusive distribution, exclusive purchasing and franchise agreements. For a better understanding of this regulation, see also the Commission Notice *Guidelines on Vertical Restraints*.

[82] See Article 4(b) of the *Vertical Block Exemption*.

[83] However, the *de minimis* rule (discussed above in Section 1.3) may still apply.

[84] However, this does not mean that exclusive territory agreements are illegal: a supplier is allowed "to restrict *active* sales by its direct buyers to a territory or a customer group which has been allocated exclusively to another buyer or which the supplier has reserved to itself". (See Guidelines, §50.) A supplier is not normally allowed to restrict passive sales, i.e., sales to satisfy unsolicited requests from individual customers, but can prevent its distributors from actively approaching customers located in territories assigned to other distributors.

more by the desire to promote identical prices and sales conditions in the EU than by an economic rationale.

Second, note that agreements need not be written or be formal agreements for them to be prohibited, as the reference in Article 81 to the term of *concerted practices* makes clear. However, the term itself leaves space for interpretation. Today pure market "parallel behaviour" without any attempt from the firms involved to communicate with each other or establish practices which help sustain collusion would probably not be judged by the Court of First Instance and the European Court of Justice as a concerted practice within the meaning of Article 81 (see Chapter 4 for a discussion).

Third, for different reasons such sectors as agriculture, defence, and (road, rail, inland waterways, air and maritime) transports have been granted block exemptions from Article 81(1). In other words, agreements between firms in such sectors are not subject to the same prohibition.

Fourth, Article 81(3) clearly states that even agreements among competitors do not fall under a *per se* rule of prohibition. Some horizontal agreements have been covered by so-called "block exemptions". The EC has adopted over the years a number of regulations which specify the conditions under which specialisation, research and development, or technology transfer agreements are not subject to the prohibition of Article 81(1). The block exemptions have been extremely useful in saving time in dealing with agreements that the EC thought would pose few competition problems. Otherwise, firms could still apply for an individual exemption from Article 81(1). In such cases, until 2002 they had to notify the EC of their agreement, which could (implicitly or explicitly) clear them if the conditions indicated by Article 81(3) were met.[85]

The recent reform of Regulation 17 of 1962 (due to come into effect 1 May 2004) has modified the implementation of Article 81, and introduced a "directly applicable exception system".[86] There have been two main changes. First, the authorisation arrangement system and the notifications which are its corollary would be abolished, passing to a system of *ex post* control. Second, the EC has given up some of its "monopoly power" over Article 81(3): national authorities and judges could also give exemptions.[87] This new system will – in the intention of the EC that proposed it – lead to a more efficient application of Article 81, allowing it to focus on the most important agreements rather than having to review hundreds of minor ones. Nevertheless, due to the decentralisation of competition policy, the system might

---

[85] The Commission did not have enough resources and personnel to review each notification in depth. More than 90% of cases were closed informally by so-called "comfort letters", which probably did not have binding legal value. See European Commission (2000: §25).

[86] *Regulation implementing Articles 81 and 82 of the Treaty* of 26 November 2002.

[87] For an economic analysis of these changes, see Bergès, Loss, Malavolti and Vergé (2002), who focus on the implications of *ex post* rather than *ex ante* control regime, and Barros (2001), who focuses on the decentralisation aspects.

lead to heterogeneous enforcement, with some national agencies and courts being more lax than others.

1.4.2 Article 82: Abuse of a Dominant Position

Article 82 states:

> Any abuse by one or more undertakings of a dominant position within the common market or in a substantial part of it shall be prohibited as incompatible with the common market in so far as it may affect trade between Member States. Such abuse may, in particular, consist in: (a) directly or indirectly imposing unfair purchase or selling prices or other unfair trading conditions; (b) limiting production, markets or technical development to the prejudice of consumers; (c) applying dissimilar conditions to equivalent transactions with other trading parties, thereby placing them at competitive disadvantage; (d) making the conclusion of contracts subject to acceptance by other parties of supplementary obligations which, by their nature or according to commercial usage, have no connection with the subject of such contracts.

The list of possible abuses is not exhaustive and it is included just to give possible examples. In general, Article 82 is related to exploitative behaviour (excessive pricing) and such exclusionary practices as predatory pricing, exclusive dealing, refusal to supply, and tying (see Chapter 7).

It is important to stress that for an abuse of a dominant position to exist, *first* it must be established that a *dominant position* exists, *then* that this dominant firm has engaged into an *abusive behaviour*. I look at these two elements in turn.

Dominance In one of the first Article 82 (then Article 86) cases, *Hoffmann-La Roche*, the European Court of Justice gave the definition of market dominance which is still used nowadays:

> The dominant position ... relates to a position of economic strength enjoyed by an undertaking, which enables it to prevent effective competition being maintained on the relevant market by affording it the power to behave to an appreciable extent independently of its competitors, its customers and ultimately of the consumers. Such a position does not preclude some competition, which it does where there is a monopoly or quasi-monopoly, but enables the undertaking, which profits by it, if not to determine, at least to have an appreciable influence on the conditions under which that competition will develop, and in any case to act largely in disregard of it so long as such conduct does not operate to its detriment.

It is difficult to translate into economic terms the precise meaning of the legal expression "the power to behave to an appreciable extent independently of its competitors, its customers and ultimately of the consumers".[88] For sure, dominance relates to a situation where a firm enjoys a very high degree of market power, but the jurisprudence has made it clear that a firm with 40% of the relevant market – far from being a monopolist – might well be a dominant one.[89] In practical terms, the analysis of dominance by the Commission and the courts coincides with the economic analysis of market power. A firm will be judged dominant when it has a high degree of market power, and the process of finding dominance involves the study of those factors that are relevant for the determination of market power (see Chapter 3).

Abuse of Dominance   As for the concept of abuse of a dominant position, *Hoffmann-La Roche* defined it as follows:

> [a behaviour] which, through recourse to methods different from those which condition normal competition in products or services on the basis of the trans-actions of commercial operators, has the effect of hindering the maintenance of the degree of competition still existing in the market or the growth of that competition.

Abusive behaviour consists mainly of exclusionary practices. A possible exception is price discrimination across member states, which occupies a special place in view of the economic integration objective of the European Union.[90]

Another possible exception is an "exploitative abuse", which consists of charging excessive prices to buyers (or extorting too low prices from suppliers). This is an area where European competition law differs from US law, which does not pro-vide the competition agencies with the power to intervene in case of "too high" prices.[91]

One important point to emphasise is that European law does not punish the creation of a dominant position, just its abuse. In other words, if a firm builds market power – however strong – through innovation, investment, marketing activities, this is perfectly legal. It is only the abuse, not the creation, of a dominant position which

---

[88] In modern industrial economics terms, one could perhaps say that behaving independently of competitors might be formalised as a situation where the (dominant) firm maximises its profits taking into account the best replies of its competitors (which simply best respond).

[89] The threshold of 40% comes from one of the early cases of abuse of dominance, *United Brands*, and it is still considered as a relevant threshold for the purpose of the determination of dominance, although the market share possessed by a firm is neither a necessary nor a sufficient condition to prove its dominance.

[90] Note that predatory price discrimination would be an exclusionary practice.

[91] See Section 1.3.1.7 above and especially Chapter 2 for why price controls are not a good idea. For cases where the EC and the courts have applied Article 82 for excessive pricing, see Ritter et al. (2000: 357–60). The most famous case is *United Brands*, where the ECJ found that the EC had not proved the allegation of excessive pricing.

is forbidden. This makes sense from the point of view of economic efficiency. One does not want to punish firms just because they are better, more successful, or even luckier, than others, as this would reduce incentives for firms.

However, in the practice of European law, a dominant firm might not be entitled to engage in the same practices as non-dominant firms. Aggressive competitive practices might be allowed to competitors, but not to a dominant firm, which has a "special responsibility".

As we shall see in Chapter 7, proving that a firm has engaged in exclusionary practices is not an easy task. This is an area of competition law where it is difficult to adopt simple rules and where each case is often a special one. Not surprisingly, Article 82 cases are much rarer than Article 81 cases, and often controversial.

1.4.3 Mergers

Both horizontal and vertical mergers are regulated by the Merger Regulation 4064/89 and successive modifications. This regulation, which as seen above has been adopted after many discussions and a long time after the Treaty of Rome, consists of an authorisation procedure with strict time deadlines. Each project of *concentration* (the law uses this term to encompass both mergers and takeovers and refers to all situations where the operation allows a firm to take *de facto* control of the operations of another firm) should be reported to the Merger Task Force (MTF), a special unit of the Competition Directorate of the European Commission, within seven days of the agreement or the announcement of the public bid. The MTF has then one month to carry out a first round of investigation.[92] At the end of it, it might decide either to allow the merger or that such a merger "raises doubts as to its compatibility with the Common Market". In the latter case, the MTF has four additional months at its disposal to decide on the concentration proposal, during which it will engage in deeper investigation of the possible effects of the merger. In the end, there are mainly three possible outcomes to this process. The merger might be allowed, prohibited, or allowed subject to certain conditions, or *remedies* (see Chapter 5 on the distinction between behavioural and structural remedies).

The fact that the EC decides on mergers within strict time deadlines is a notable feature of the Merger Regulation, and one which should be praised. Indeed, firms and the markets need to know as quickly as possible if a merger can be carried out or not. The uncertainty related to long regulatory processes is always very costly but it is especially so for mergers, where firms need to deeply restructure and reorganise their production, distribution, research and marketing activities. It is crucial that this uncertainty is over as quickly as possible. The preventive authorisation system

---

[92] Under special circumstances, for example the submission of a remedy, the one-month limit can be extended.

also responds to an efficiency criterion. It would simply be wasteful to let firms carry out the merger first and then rule that they should return to the original situation.[93] Forced spin-offs would be extremely inefficient. It is precisely for this reason that the European legislators decided to introduce the Merger Regulation. In *Continental Can* and *Philip Morris*, the European Court of Justice had ruled that Article 81 and 82 might have been used *ex post* to deal with merger operations. It is to avoid this danger that the Merger Regulation was introduced in 1989.[94]

The Merger Regulation does not deal with all merger proposals in the EU, of course. Rather, it provides a good example of the *subsidiarity principle* whereby decisions should be taken at a decentralised level (i.e., by the national authorities) unless there are good reasons to take them at a centralised one (i.e., by the supra-national administration body which is the EC). The EC has jurisdiction on a merger if certain thresholds are met (see Article 1). Such thresholds ensure that the mergers reviewed by the EC are mergers among large firms which have an important presence in several EU countries.[95] Mergers between "small" firms, and mergers which mainly interest a single country, will be dealt with by national authorities and not by the Commission. Note that this regulatory rule is to the advantage of the firms, since it spares them from asking for an authorisation in each of the countries in which they operate, a process which might involve a considerable waste of time and legal expenses (this is known as the *one-stop shop* principle of regulation).

The substantive aspects of the merger regulation and merger practice will be discussed in Chapter 5. For the time being, however, note that Article 2(3) of the Merger Regulation states that

> A concentration which creates or strengthens a dominant position as a result of which effective competition would be significantly impeded in the Common Market or in a substantial part of it shall be declared incompatible with the Common Market.

In other words, only mergers which create or reinforce a dominant position will be prohibited. This is a crucial feature of the Merger Regulation, and to anticipate the discussion in Chapter 5, it is a feature at odds with economic principles, since there may well be mergers which do not create a dominant position but still decrease

---

[93] Article 7(1) of the Merger Regulation states that no merger may be put into effect before being declared compatible with the Common Market. However, in some special circumstances firms might want to take the risk of a merger being undone. Article 7(4) allows for derogation from the suspensory provisions of Article 7(1) if certain conditions apply.

[94] On the events preceding the Merger Regulation, see Goyder (1998: 379–85).

[95] Notice that merger projects by firms, which are non-Europeans also fall within the scope of the Merger Regulation, as long as the thresholds above are met, that is, as long as a merger has effects in the EU. Two well-known merger operations among non-EU firms that were blocked by the EC are *Gencor/Lohnro* and *General Electric/Honeywell.*

welfare (in markets with few firms, a merger might result in considerable price increases and diminished competition even if it does not establish or reinforce a dominant position).

1.5 EXERCISES

Exercise 1.1   Describe the concepts of consumer surplus (or consumer welfare) and total surplus (or total welfare). What are the arguments in favour and against using consumer surplus rather than total surplus as the objective of competition policy?

Exercise 1.2   In which competition law jurisdictions that you know can competition authorities intervene in case of excessive pricing by a firm? Briefly discuss whether such intervention should be welcomed.

Exercise 1.3   To what extent might trade policy and competition policy be in conflict with each other?

Exercise 1.4   Large firms sometimes have advantages over small ones, for instance because of economies of scope, stronger bargaining power with suppliers that allow them to buy inputs at lower prices, better financial resources and access to credit. As a consequence of these advantages, large and small firms are not on equal competitive grounds. Should competition policy intervene, and if so in what way, so as to balance these asymmetries?

Exercise 1.5   What other policies might be pursued by competition policies? What are some advantages and disadvantages of distorting competition to achieve these ends?

2

Market Power and Welfare: Introduction

2.1 OVERVIEW OF THE CHAPTER

The basis of competition policy is the idea that monopolies are "bad". Indeed, Section 2.2 shows that a monopoly causes a static inefficiency: for given technologies, monopoly pricing results in a welfare loss. Further, there generally is an inverse relationship between market power (the ability of firms to set prices above marginal costs), of which monopoly power is the most extreme form, and (static) welfare.

Sections 2.3 and 2.4 show that by looking only at allocative inefficiency one might actually underestimate the welfare loss from market power. A monopoly (more generally, high market power) might also result in productive and dynamic inefficiencies. Not only does a monopolist charge too high a price, but it might also have too high costs and innovate too little, since – sheltered from competition – it is not pushed to adopt the most efficient technologies and to invest much in R&D.

One might be tempted to conclude that if having one firm (or very few firms) leads to welfare losses, then competition policy should try to increase the number of firms, which operate in the industry (for instance subsidising and protecting less successful firms). Section 2.3 shows that such a conclusion would not be correct, because keeping less efficient firms artificially alive would distort the allocation of resources and reduce economies of scale, thus reducing welfare. In short: (1) *competition policy is not concerned with maximising the number of firms*, and (2) *competition policy is concerned with defending market competition in order to increase welfare, not defending competitors.*

Although there is an inverse relationship between market power and welfare under static analysis, it is not clear that the same unambiguous relationship exists when productive and dynamic inefficiencies are considered. In any event, Section 2.4 argues that market power is certainly not *per se* bad. Indeed, the prospect of enjoying some market power (and profits) is the main incentive for firms to invest and innovate. If firms were not able to appropriate the results of their investments – whether they be advertising outlays, capacity, R&D expenditures or other – they would not invest at all, with the result that consumers would not benefit from lower costs, higher quality goods, new product varieties and so on.

Section 2.5 shows that there often exists a trade-off between *ex post* and *ex ante* considerations. If *ex post* (i.e., for given qualities, technologies, varieties) one would be tempted to eliminate market power so as to reduce prices and increase allocative efficiency, *ex ante* such a policy would be detrimental, because it would eliminate the incentives for firms to improve their quality offerings and their technologies. Public policies should guarantee firms some market power, that is appropriability of their R&D and investments, and competition policy should not aim at "destroying" monopolies, or more generally firms' market power, as long as they are established on the basis of legitimate business practices. A firm which enjoys a monopoly after having successfully invested in, innovated, and introduced new products, is a firm which receives a reward for its activities. The expectation that – if doing well – a firm will receive profits is the incentive which pushes such a firm to do well. Any attempt to eliminate market power after a firm has successfully attained it gives the wrong incentive signals to this and all other firms. Competition policy is therefore not concerned with monopolies *per se,* but rather only with monopolies which distort the competitive process.

The previous arguments suggest that competition policy should not be too interventionist. Some theories go further, and suggest that there exist market mechanisms, which prevent a monopolist from exercising market power, thereby reducing further the scope for competition policy. Section 2.6 discusses these views, and in particular the argument that free entry acts as a restraint to the market power of a monopolist. Although it is true that potential entrants can play a role in disciplining incumbents, monopolists often continue unperturbed to charge high prices even when entry is possible, for a number of reasons, such as the existence of sunk costs, consumer switching costs, and network effects, as well as business practices carried out by incumbents to exclude potential entrants (such practices will be analysed in Chapter 7).

Section 2.7 ends the chapter with some policy conclusions.

2.2 ALLOCATIVE EFFICIENCY

Section 2.2.1 defines market power. Section 2.2.2 shows that market power brings about a welfare loss due to prices being too high: This welfare loss is labelled "allocative inefficiency", and is highest when market power coincides with monopoly power. Section 2.2.3 suggests that the welfare loss might be larger when firms engage in unproductive activities in order to grab market power. Other reasons why the welfare loss from market power might be even higher are analysed in Sections 2.3 and 2.4.

2.2.1 Market Power: A Definition

Market power is a crucial concept in the economics of competition law. It refers to the ability of a firm to raise price above some competitive level – the benchmark price – in a profitable way. Since the lowest possible price a firm can profitably charge is the price which equals the marginal cost of production,[1] market power is usually defined as the difference between the prices charged by a firm and its marginal costs of production.[2]

Since market power refers to the ability of firms to charge prices above marginal costs, we expect firms to have some degree of market power in the real world (not least because if they had zero profits they could not cover their fixed costs), with an unchallenged monopolist enjoying the highest possible market power. The issue of how to measure market power in practice is put off to the next chapter, but note that in many circumstances competition policy will be concerned only with those firms which have "large enough" market power, where "large enough" will be arbitrary to some extent, and might be different according to the particular competition problems being scrutinised.[3]

The concept of "market dominance" which is used in European competition law (see Chapter 1) does not have a clear equivalent in economic terms,[4] but can be interpreted as a situation where a firm has a large degree of market power, which allows it to charge prices which are "close enough" to those that a monopolist would charge.

2.2.2 The Allocative Inefficiency of a Monopoly

Let us now analyse why market power reduces static welfare. I focus here on allocative efficiency, and assume that technologies (costs) are given, and that the most efficient technology available is used (these assumptions are relaxed in later sections). In what follows, a simple graphical analysis illustrates the main argument: when prices are above marginal costs, this entails higher producer surplus but not enough higher to compensate for the lower consumer surplus caused by higher prices.

---

[1] In a model where firms sell perfectly identical products, have zero fixed costs, and choose prices (the so-called *Bertrand* model), price is equal to marginal cost at the equilibrium. (See Chapter 8 for a brief description.) The same outcome also arises under perfect competition.

[2] An alternative definition would be to define market power not by how far the prices are with respect to marginal costs, but by how close they are to monopoly prices. Conceptually, these definitions are very similar. Operationally, one is not easier to estimate than the other: the former requires an estimation of marginal costs, the latter of the industry's monopoly prices. Since the former definition is more widely used, I shall adopt it.

[3] For instance, competition laws might fix some minimum market power thresholds below which some rules do not apply, under the presumption that firms with little market power can do little damage. Different thresholds might also be adopted for different practices, such as various types of vertical restraints, which have different potential of harming competition. The market power thresholds used in merger analysis or in cases of abuse of dominant position also need not be the same.

[4] See Section 1.4.2 for a discussion.

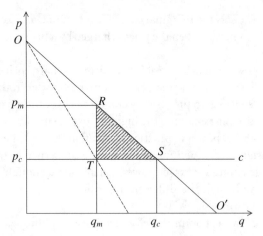

Figure 2.1. Welfare loss from monopoly.

A Simple Graphical Analysis   Assume for simplicity that there exists a linear market demand, described by the line OO' in Figure 2.1, and a constant returns to scale technology, represented by the line of constant marginal costs $p_c c$. In the most competitive case, our benchmark case,[5] the price is $p_c = c$ and the quantity sold to consumers is equal to q_c. Consider then the extreme case where market power is maximum: the industry is monopolised by a single firm, which charges the monopoly price p_m.[6,7] The equilibrium output would be given by q_m.

Recall that welfare is defined as the sum of consumer surplus and producer surplus. Under the most competitive equilibrium, welfare is given by the triangle $O p_c S$, which also corresponds to the consumer surplus (firms do not have any surplus, since profits are equal to zero).[8] Under *monopoly*, welfare is given by the area described by the points $O p_c T R$, which is itself the sum of producer surplus

[5] The most competitive case corresponds to the Bertrand (or perfectly competitive) equilibrium.

[6] The monopoly price is determined as the price at which marginal revenue (the dotted line in the figure) equals marginal cost. To understand this basic equilibrium condition between marginal revenue (MR) and marginal cost (MC), consider the case where, at a certain number of units sold, the monopolist finds that MR > MC. Then it means that by selling an extra unit of output it would obtain a higher profit, since this extra unit would give a higher revenue than cost. Therefore, MR > MC cannot be an equilibrium. By increasing output, the monopolist would go down the curve MR, getting closer to the equilibrium. By the same reasoning, MR < MC would imply that the last unit sold by the monopolist costs more than it brings revenue to it. Therefore, MR < MC cannot be an equilibrium. The monopolist would rather reduce the number of units sold, and by reducing output, MR will increase by getting closer to the equilibrium.

[7] Note that the same price p_m might be set if there were full collusion among several identical firms operating under constant marginal costs.

[8] Consumer surplus is the area that lies between the segment OS in the demand line (which describes the willingness to pay of people who buy the good) and the line $p_c c$ (which describes the price they pay).

$p_m p_c TR$ and of consumer surplus $Op_m R$. The net efficiency loss caused by the monopoly is given by the difference between the areas $Op_c S$ and $Op_c TR$, namely by the area of the triangle RTS, which is the deadweight loss, D, for the economy.[9]

Note also that, relative to monopoly, competition increases net welfare but does not bring about a *Pareto improvement* (i.e., not everybody is better off), since the producer surplus shrinks with respect to the monopoly case. This might be trivial, but it illustrates the main interests behind the different situations. An industry's producers will try to lobby in favour of more protection and less competitive pressure, while consumers and users of the industry products will have an interest in backing proposals of more competition.[10]

The Determinants of the Deadweight Loss   A welfare loss occurs not just for the monopoly price but for any price above marginal costs. To see this with the help of the figure above, just redo the same analysis as above by comparing the welfare level attained when $p = c$ with that attained under any arbitrary price $p > c$.

One can also check that the higher the price p the larger the welfare loss caused by market power (the triangle, which represents the loss, gets bigger as p gets close to p_m), suggesting that welfare decreases with market power.

Furthermore, the graphical example also suggests that the deadweight loss caused by monopoly power also depends on the elasticity of market demand. If demand were perfectly elastic (OO' horizontal in the figure), then the monopolist would not be able to set any price above marginal cost (consumers would not buy the good if there was an even slight increase in price). Hence, the deadweight loss would be nil in this case. As market demand elasticity decreases, the ability of the monopolist to charge higher prices rises and the deadweight loss increases.[11]

---

[9] The monopolist is not able to appropriate all the consumer surplus, which is lost by consumers whose willingness to pay is higher than marginal costs. However, if the monopolist was able to set a different price for each consumer (i.e., if it were able to do perfect price discrimination), then its profit would be equal to the whole area of the triangle $Op_c S$. Perfect price discrimination is unlikely to happen, since it requires that the monopolist knows perfectly the willingness to pay of each consumer. See also Chapter 7.

[10] As discussed in Chapter 1, because of the fragmentation of their interests, in practice consumers do not often lobby for more competition, whereas firms are strong advocates for less competition.

[11] Let me make two technical notes that can be skipped by readers who are not interested in such details. (1) If demand is perfectly inelastic, the deadweight loss will disappear. Consider the case where consumers are willing to pay up to a price V for a unit of the good: the monopolist will set precisely that price V and – as with perfect price discrimination – appropriate all the surplus of consumers. As a result, market power is the highest but there is no deadweight loss. (2) Tirole (1988: 68 and 88) shows that the *absolute* welfare loss DWL does not necessarily decrease with the elasticity of demand. For example, with a constant elasticity demand function $p = q^{-\varepsilon}$, there exists a non-monotonic relationship between welfare loss from monopoly and elasticity. However, with this demand function the size of the market increases with ε. Tirole shows that the *relative* welfare loss, namely DWL/W (where W is welfare) is indeed decreasing with ε.

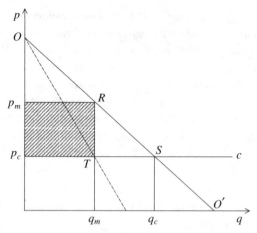

Figure 2.2. Possible additional loss from rent-seeking activities.

Finally, the absolute value of the deadweight loss depends on the size of the market. The intercept of demand (the point O) in the figure can be seen as the size of the market. If demand OO' shifted in a parallel way towards the origin, that is if it kept the same slope but had a lower intercept, then the deadweight loss associated with monopoly power would be smaller in absolute terms.

2.2.3 Rent-Seeking Activities

The allocative inefficiency identified above might understate the actual negative effect of monopoly. It has been suggested that – when monopolies are allowed – firms might try to use their political influence and lobbying power to keep or increase their monopoly power. In this process, they would use resources which could instead be put in more productive use. Hence, rent-seeking activities enlarge the expected welfare loss from monopoly.

Posner (1975) argues that the social cost of a monopoly should include an area which might be as large as the overall monopoly profit a firm obtains (that is the area of the rectangle $p_m p_c T R$ in Figure 2.2). This is because firms would waste resources in activities which do not have any social value in the attempt to maintain or acquire monopoly power. A monopoly, whether private or caused by public regulation, creates rents. Agents would compete to appropriate these rents by bribing officials, by forming lobbying groups, or by resorting to other such activities.[12] Because of competition among such agents, the amount of their expenditure in rent-seeking activities would equal the amount of expected profit from monopoly, which leads to

---

[12] The argument is familiar to those who have studied the political economy of protection. See for instance Krueger (1974).

a complete dissipation of the rents. (See Exercise 2.1 for a formalisation.) Posner's argument (1975: 257) crucially hinges on three assumptions: (1) there exists perfect competition among agents who engage in rent-seeking activities. (2) The rent-seeking "technology" is characterised by constant returns to scale. (3) The costs incurred in obtaining a monopoly do not have any socially valuable by-product. Under these assumptions, it is easy to see that the welfare loss of monopoly should include all the profit as well.

The assumptions made by Posner are questionable.[13] In particular, it might well be that some agents are better than others and very "efficient" in their rent-seeking operations, which means that the dissipated rent, if it exists, does not necessarily coincide with the monopoly profits. Further, the assumption that rent-seeking activities never create socially valuable results is questionable. Advertising outlays, for instance, indicated by Posner as rent-seeking activities, might increase information available to consumers as well as their "perceived" value of the good.[14]

The result that competition in rent-seeking activities among agents might lead to a complete dissipation of rents, which would then be completely wasted for welfare purposes, is certainly a very extreme and provocative one. Nevertheless, the argument itself makes sense. In their effort to get hold of rents, firms might well use resources which could be put to more productive use elsewhere. Rent-seeking activities may certainly generate inefficient distortions. The actual amount of these distortions is an empirical issue whose treatment is beyond the scope of this work.

2.3 PRODUCTIVE EFFICIENCY

We have seen that for given production costs a monopolist (more generally, a firm enjoying large market power) charges too high a price, leading to a welfare loss called allocative inefficiency. However, there might be an additional welfare loss, called productive inefficiency, if a firm operating under monopoly has a higher cost than if it were operating in more competitive environments.

From an empirical point of view, the evidence is mixed, but points to significant productive efficiency losses, which might even be larger than the more usual allocative inefficiency ones.[15]

This section first shows the possible additional welfare losses which arise if a monopolist chooses inefficient technologies, and then analyses why a monopolist might indeed end up with such inefficient technologies, discussing briefly both the theoretical and the empirical literature on these issues.

[13] See Fisher (1985) for a critique of Posner's arguments.

[14] More generally, expenses to increase the probability of obtaining rents will go to agents active elsewhere in the economy. A partial equilibrium framework is not appropriate any longer to compute welfare.

[15] See Scherer and Ross (1990: 668–72). The first work that tried to estimate welfare losses from monopoly (in the US) was Harberger (1954).

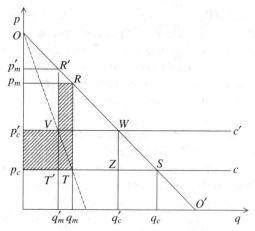

Figure 2.3. Additional loss from productive inefficiency.

2.3.1 Additional Welfare Loss from Productive Inefficiency

Let us consider how a productive inefficiency increases the welfare loss due to monopoly power.[16]

Suppose that while firms operating in a more competitive industry have marginal cost c, a monopolist would operate at a higher cost, say $c' > c$. This will imply that the welfare loss is bigger than the area RTS identified in Figure 2.1. Figure 2.3 illustrates this idea. If the monopoly operates at the higher cost c', then welfare under monopoly is given by the area $OR'Vp_c'$. At the competitive equilibrium, firms would instead operate at a cost c, and welfare is (as in Figure 2.1) given by the area OSp_c. Therefore, the welfare loss from monopoly is given by the sum of areas $R'T'S$ and $p_c'VT'p_c$. This is clearly a bigger area than the deadweight loss triangle RTS which considered only allocative inefficiency: the shaded areas in Figure 2.3 represent the additional welfare loss due to productive inefficiency.

2.3.2 Why Is a Monopolist Less Efficient?

The argument is still incomplete. I have argued so far that *if* a monopolist adopts a less efficient technology than firms operating under competition, then the monopoly entails an additional productive efficiency loss. However, I have not yet explained why one should expect a monopolist to be less efficient. Somehow, it does seem reasonable to claim that a firm that does not face any competitive pressure will not make much effort to use the best available technologies, to improve its products

---

[16] See Section 8.2.1 for a simple example that shows that the more inefficient a monopolist the higher the price it will charge.

and to innovate, but one should look more carefully at the theoretical and empirical arguments that support this claim.

There are two main arguments which suggest that a monopoly is likely to involve productive inefficiency. First, managers of a monopolistic firm have less incentive to make effort. Second – a Darwinian selection argument – when competition exists, more efficient firms will survive and thrive, whereas less efficient firms will shut down. If a monopoly exists, the market will not operate any selection and an inefficient firm is as likely to survive as an efficient one. I analyse each argument in turn.

2.3.2.1 Monopoly and Managerial Slack

The idea that competitive pressure leads a firm to look for the most efficient way to organise its production and reduce its cost is a very old one, which dates at least from Adam Smith and has also been discussed by John Hicks. Leibenstein (1966) introduced the concept of "X-inefficiency" to restate the idea that monopoly power – and the "quiet life" which comes with it – brings about managerial inefficiency.

Although it meets the consensus of economists, the idea that a firm might end up operating with inefficient techniques when more efficient ones are available is not self-evident and deserves explanation. To understand why this might happen, one has to consider that in reality firms are complex organisations, and that decisions regarding the adoption of technologies – and more generally decisions affecting the overall level of efficiency of the firm – are taken by managers who might have objectives other than maximisation of profits. Consider a firm in which there exists a separation between ownership (shareholders) and control (managers). Shareholders care about profits, but managers care about their individual utility, determined by wage, career prospects, as well as the level of effort and time they have to put into the job. The manager might also care about profits (typically, the shareholders will write a contract where his remuneration increases with the firm's profits), but in general he will care about other things, too. As a result, when he takes decisions about technologies (or he has to take actions, which affect the firm's costs) he might not have the right incentives to adopt the most efficient ones (that is, those which maximise profits).

To understand why a firm might choose inefficient technologies one has therefore to resort to so-called *principal-agent models,* that is models where a principal (say, the owner of the firm) wants to induce an agent (the manager of the firm) to take the actions that maximise her (the principal's) payoff. Within these models, one can study how market structure would affect (via the decisions of the owner) the actions of the manager, and hence the cost of the firm.

Principal-agent models do not unambiguously show that competition reduces managerial slack.[17] A tentative conclusion from this literature is that increasing

---

[17] For instance, in Hart (1983), competition increases managers' efforts, but Scharfstein (1988) shows that the result depends on a strong assumption on the managers' preferences, i.e., that they are infinitely risk-averse. If the manager's marginal utility from income is strictly positive,

competitive pressure in a market where there is a monopolist will lead it to be more efficient, but increasing pressure in a market where there is already a great deal of competition might reduce efficiency. (See Section 2.3.2.2 for a brief account of a model where this relationship emerges.)

Finally, note that managerial slack is an argument, which applies not only to productive inefficiency, but also to dynamic inefficiency (quiet life does not push the managers to innovate either).

2.3.2.2 Empirical Evidence on Individual Firms' Productivity

The managerial slack hypothesis is difficult to test empirically, but there exists some evidence that *individual firms' productivity* is higher in more competitive markets.

Nickell (1996) analyses panel data of around 700 UK manufacturing firms over the period 1972–86. He finds that the larger the market share, a possible proxy for market power, the lower the firm's productivity *levels*.[18] Furthermore, he finds that the stronger the competition (measured either by increased number of rival firms or by lower levels of rents), the higher the total factor productivity *growth*.[19]

Nickell, Nicolitsas and Dryden (1997), based on data and analysis similar to that of Nickell (1996), confirm that product market competition improves firms' productivity performance, but also indicate that the role of competition in disciplining managers and improving company performance is lower when firms are already subject to financial pressure or external shareholder control.[20]

Overall, even though the empirical evidence collected so far is far from conclusive, it does seem that competition affects productivity, and therefore environments where firms enjoy monopoly power would be characterised by lower productive efficiency.[21]

Competition and Efficiency: Schmidt's Model* In Schmidt's (1997) model, a firm might go bankrupt, and a manager would incur a loss when his firm closes down (a reasonable assumption). A firm's owner has to devise a contract to induce

competition would *reduce* managerial effort. Other models dealing with the effect of competition upon managers' effort include Hermalin (1992), Horn, Lang and Lundgren (1994) and Martin (1993).

[18] For a discussion of the possible problems associated with the use of market shares as market power indicator, see Nickell (1996: 733–7).

[19] Hay and Liu (1997) also look at the components of firms' efficiency in nineteen UK sectors and find some evidence that competition does play some role in determining efficiency and market shares of firms.

[20] On the relationship between product market competition, corporate finance and managerial effort (and innovation), see Aghion, Dewatripont and Rey (1998, 1999).

[21] There is also some evidence that trade liberalisation (or trade openness) – an indicator of the degree of competition firms in a country face – results in higher efficiency levels. See Tybout (2000) for a survey.

more effort by her manager: since effort (which is not observable by the owner) is costly for the manager, the owner might have to pay some rents to the manager in order to increase his effort. Note that the manager's effort makes the firm more efficient. Therefore, it not only increases the expected firm's profit but also reduces the probability that the firm will face bankruptcy (a more efficient firm will be more sheltered from negative shocks).[22]

Market competition reduces the firm's profit, and this has two different effects on managerial effort. The first effect, labelled "threat of liquidation effect" is unambiguously positive. When competition rises, the threat of going bankrupt becomes more important (profits are lower), and this pushes the manager to exert higher effort in order to avoid the loss from liquidation. The second effect, though, has an ambiguous sign. When competition rises, profit decreases, and as a consequence the value of inducing a given cost reduction *might* also decrease. If it does decrease, then the owner will not want to pay a rent to the manager in order to induce higher effort and thus obtain a cost reduction. Competition might then reduce effort if this adverse effect on the profitability of a cost reduction is sufficiently strong.[23]

Schmidt identifies sufficient conditions to guarantee that competition increases managerial effort, but these conditions are not mild enough to expect that this is the only realistic outcome. In an extension, he studies the impact of competition upon managers' effort in a Bertrand competition example. Competition is measured here by the number of firms that operate in the market, and effort increases the probability of obtaining an innovation which makes the firm a monopolist (if more than one firm obtains the innovation, they will each receive zero profit). He finds that the highest level of effort is given by the duopoly case,[24] therefore finding a non-monotonic relationship between competition and effort (and innovation), which is reminiscent of some empirical studies.[25]

---

[22] The assumption that the manager is wealth constrained excludes the possibility of attaining the first-best simply by selling the firm to the manager, who would then choose effort in order to maximise profit.

[23] Another way of describing these two effects is as follows. The first effect is a Darwinian one: more competition pushes the manager to do better to fight for survival. The second effect is a Schumpeterian one: more competition diminishes expected future profits and therefore reduces the owner's incentives to induce more effort from the manager.

[24] In the working paper version of the model, Schmidt also analysed the Cournot competition case, finding the same non-monotonic relationship, but with a maximal effort for number of firms in the market higher than two. (In this result, it is not the actual number of firms under which effort is the highest, but the existence of a non-monotonic function competition/effort, to which I want to draw attention).

[25] For instance, Caves and Barton (1990) look at US data and find that efficiency is the highest for intermediate levels of concentration (as measured by the 5-firm concentration ratio). Green and Mayes (1991) find a similar result on UK data. See also the discussion in Section 2.4 below.

2.3.2.3 A Darwinian Mechanism: Competition Selects Efficient Firms

In an industry where there exist more efficient and less efficient firms, competition will force the inefficient firms to exit; thus welfare improves because output will be produced at a lower cost. A related argument is that when competition exists a lot of different projects, products and technologies are possible. The market will then allow only the best among them to survive and thrive whereas the others will disappear. Obviously, under monopoly this sort of Darwinian process will not occur.[26] The example in technical Section 2.3.5.1, although extremely simple and unable to reproduce the richness of the "Darwinian" argument, shows that market competition might drive the less efficient firm out of the industry, and that this would be beneficial.

From an empirical point of view, the selection argument predicts that competition will increase *industry productivity* through a process of entry into and exit from the industry. Olley and Pakes (1996) have carried out one of the most careful studies of the reasons behind changes in productivity in a given industry, and give strong support to the selection effect of competition. They analysed the impact of technological change and de-regulation in the industry for telecommunications equipment in the US in the period 1963–87. This is a period in which the industry was deeply de-regulated. For a large part of the twentieth century, AT&T was given exclusive monopoly in the provision of telecommunications equipment, so that its manufacturing subsidiary, Western Electric, dominated the industry for a long time. Competition in the industry rose gradually, thanks to an anti-trust decision in 1968, a regulatory decision in 1975 which allowed the connection of private equipment to the network, and the 1982 Consent Decree which led to the divestiture of AT&T. The creation of seven regional Bell operating companies, free to buy their equipment from any supplier, and which could not produce equipment themselves, effectively completed this de-regulation process. As a result, there was considerable entry (and exit) in the sector between 1967 and 1987, due to both domestic and foreign producers.[27] Olley and Pakes first used sophisticated econometric techniques to estimate the parameters of a production function for the industry, and then used these estimates to understand the role of technological change and de-regulation in explaining the changes in the distribution of plant-level performance between 1974 and 1987.

They found that it is the larger share in output of the more productive firms, which explains the rise in productivity in the industry: "the productivity growth that followed regulatory change seemed to result from the downsizing (frequently the shutdown) of (often older) unproductive plants, and the disproportionate growth of productive establishments (often new entrants)".[28]

---

[26] See Jovanovic (1982) for a formalisation of market selection.

[27] See Olley and Pakes (1996: 1266–70) for a description of the industry and a statistical account of entry and exit in the period.

[28] Olley and Pakes (1996: 1266).

The role played by exit and entry in increasing productivity is confirmed also by recent studies on both US and UK data.[29] Disney, Haskel and Heden (2000) also find that the exit and entry of *plants* is important in explaining productivity increases. The group of single-establishment firms experienced no productivity growth at the firm level: the productivity growth of this group came entirely from entry and exit. Likewise, when looking at the group of multi-establishment firms, they find that most of the productivity growth of these firms is due to closing down of the less efficient plants and the opening of new and more efficient plants. In their paper, Disney et al. (2000) also carry out a detailed analysis of the impact of competition upon productivity and confirm that an increase in market power (measured by either market shares or rents) reduces both the level and the growth of productivity.[30]

Overall, it seems that empirical studies confirm the important role played by competition in selecting the most efficient firms and thus raising productive efficiency. This has also an additional implication for competition policy: if less efficient firms were protected or subsidised, this would prevent market competition from selecting the best firms, which will actually result in higher prices and lower welfare.

2.3.3 Number of Firms and Welfare

Since market power decreases with the number of firms in the industry, one might be tempted to conclude that the larger the number of firms the higher the welfare. This is not the case, however, when firms have to incur (recurrent or set-up) fixed costs. Indeed, the presence of fixed costs – which gives rise to scale economies – implies the existence of a trade-off. On the one hand, a higher number of firms entails more competition in the market and lower prices, which undoubtedly increases consumer surplus (and allocative efficiency). On the other hand, it also entails a duplication of fixed costs, which represents a loss in terms of (static) productive efficiency. The net effect on welfare is *a priori* ambiguous, as technical Section 2.3.5.2 shows.

This trade-off between allocative and productive efficiency (a larger number of firms increases competition and drives prices downward but at the same time involves a loss in economies of scale) implies that a policy aimed at maximising the number of firms in any given industry would be unsound. If an authority tried not

---

[29] For the US, see Foster, Haltiwanger and Krizan (1998). In an earlier work, Baily, Hulten and Campbell (1992) had found that more than entry and exit, productivity growth was mainly due to increasing output shares in high-productivity plants and decreasing output shares in low-productivity ones. For the UK, see Barnes and Haskel (2000). Sorting (or "external") effects, i.e., productivity increases due to entry or growth of more efficient plants and exit of less efficient plants are found to account for roughly 30–60% of productivity increases, according to different data and studies. The remaining is accounted for by "internal growth", i.e., improved productivity at the plant level.

[30] They also argue that there is a potential selection bias in analyses as in Nickell (1996) which look at productivity growth in a sample of *surviving* firms (see Disney et al., 2000: 22). Correcting for this bias reduces but does not eliminate the impact of competition over productivity.

just to guarantee that entry is possible in an industry and that all firms compete on equal grounds, but also tried to use subsidies or other industrial policy instruments to actively promote entry in an industry or to artificially prevent firms from exiting, this would conflict with an economic welfare criterion.[31]

These considerations should act as a warning that competition policy should be about *defending competition* and not about *defending competitors,* which are less efficient. In particular, we have seen in Chapter 1 that in many cases antitrust laws have tried to defend small firms as such (that is, in the absence of an abuse by large firms, and just because the latter enjoy a more efficient scale of production). This might be a legitimate political or social objective, but it is not justifiable from an economic welfare perspective: "Twisting" the market so as to have more firms than market forces left alone would support may decrease welfare.

2.3.4 Conclusions

This section has considered two arguments suggesting that market power decreases productive efficiency. The first is that competition (which lowers market power) pushes managers to make effort and be more productive; the second is that competition selects the more efficient firms, which results in lower market prices. Both theory and evidence seem to give some support to these arguments although with some qualification. One should expect that introducing more competition in a monopolistic industry is welfare improving, but it is possible, in principle, that increasing competition in an industry where a lot of competition already exists *might* not increase welfare further.

In a similar vein, it is not necessarily true that the larger the number of firms in an industry the higher the welfare, because of the inefficient duplication of fixed costs.[32]

2.3.5 Competition and Productive Efficiency*

In this technical section, I present two simple models. The first illustrates how competition might select the most efficient firms; the second analyses the relationship between number of firms and welfare.

---

[31] This conclusion is reinforced when firms are not symmetric (as in Section 2.3.5.1). When there exist firms producing at higher costs, their exit from the industry might carry additional efficiency gains.

[32] Similar studies could be carried out by keeping fixed the number of firms and looking at the effect of tougher product market competition on welfare in a situation where entry is free, a situation analysed by d'Aspremont and Motta (2000). Since firms have to cover fixed set-up costs of entry, and anticipate lower profits when market competition is tougher, there exists a positive relationship between the toughness of competition and industrial concentration. As a result, markets where competition is the toughest might not be associated with the highest welfare since fewer firms will co-exist at the equilibrium. Yet, a situation where cartels are allowed (that is, a monopolistic outcome) is the worst in terms of welfare. Exercise 2.4 develops this result in a simple example.

2.3.5.1 Competition and Selection of Firms: An Example*

To illustrate the possible beneficial effect of competition in selecting the most efficient firms, consider the following example. Assume a homogenous good industry where firms compete in quantities. Firms have different efficiency levels (different technologies): out of a population of n firms, there are nk firms with a high marginal cost technology c_h and $n(1 - k)$ more efficient firms whose technology allows them to produce at a marginal cost c_l. Assume that demand is given by $p = 1 - Q$, where Q is the aggregate output. $Q = \sum_{i \in L} q_i + \sum_{j \in H} q_j$, where we have denoted with L and H respectively the set of low-cost and high-cost firms. The profit functions are given by $\pi_j = (p(Q) - c_h)q_j$ for any $j \in H$, and by $\pi_i = (p(Q) - c_l)q_i$ for any $i \in L$. One can then write the FOCs $\partial \pi_j / \partial q_j = 0$ and $\partial \pi_i / \partial q_i = 0$:

$$-q_j + 1 - \sum_{i \in L} q_i - \sum_{j \in H} q_j - c_h = 0, \tag{2.1}$$

$$-q_i + 1 - \sum_{i \in L} q_i - \sum_{j \in H} q_j - c_l = 0. \tag{2.2}$$

Focusing on the symmetric solution (symmetric in the sense that firms of a given type produces the same output at equilibrium), the FOCs can be simplified as follows:

$$q_h = \frac{1 - c_h - (1 - k)nq_l}{1 + kn}; \qquad q_l = \frac{1 - c_l - knq_h}{1 + (1 - k)n}, \tag{2.3}$$

where q_h and q_l denote the output of a high-cost and a low-cost firm respectively. The equilibrium solution can then easily be found:

$$q_h^* = \frac{1 - c_h - n(1 - k)(c_h - c_l)}{1 + n}; \qquad q_l^* = \frac{1 - c_l + nk(c_h - c_l)}{1 + n}. \tag{2.4}$$

The equilibrium price is given by

$$p^* = \frac{1 + nkc_h + n(1 - k)c_l}{1 + n}. \tag{2.5}$$

Note that the high-cost firms can produce a non-negative output if and only if $c_h \leq [1 + n(1 - k)c_l] / [1 + n(1 - k)]$. This condition becomes the more stringent the larger the n. In other words, if we proxy the degree of competition in the industry with the number of firms which operate in such an industry, then the stronger the competition and the more likely that the inefficient firms will exit at equilibrium.[33]

Suppose therefore that competition brings the more inefficient firms to exit the market. I now show that, despite the decrease in the number of sellers, price in

---

[33] Another way to express the idea that competition increases efficiency could be to proxy fiercer competition not by the larger number of firms, but by a switch from Cournot to Bertrand: the high-cost firms would immediately exit the market.

the industry will decrease. In other words, exit is beneficial because it allows a reallocation of output from inefficient to efficient firms.

To see this, compute the equilibrium if the inefficient high-cost firms exit. There will be only the $(1 - k)n$ firms with identical low-cost technology. The equilibrium per firm quantity and price will be

$$q_l^{**} = \frac{1 - c_l}{1 + (1 - k)n}; \qquad p^{**} = \frac{1 + n(1 - k)c_l}{1 + n(1 - k)}. \tag{2.6}$$

One can easily check that $p^* > p^{**}$ if $c_h > [1 + n(1 - k)c_l] / [1 + n(1 - k)]$. But the last inequality is precisely the same condition under which the high cost firms exit the industry. Therefore, the exit of the inefficient firms improves welfare through a reduction in the market prices.[34]

2.3.5.2 Too Many Firms in the Industry*

Consider a homogenous good industry with n firms, which are perfectly symmetric. The firms simultaneously decide on the quantity to bring to the market, and have a production cost $C = cq + F$, where c is the marginal cost and F a fixed cost. Market demand is characterised by $p = 1 - Q$, p being the market price and Q the aggregate output.

Each firm i will choose q_i to maximise its profits:

$$\Pi_i = \left(1 - q_i - \sum_{j \neq i} q_j\right) q_i - cq_i. \tag{2.7}$$

The first-order condition is given by

$$q_i = \left(1 - c - \sum_{j \neq i} q_j\right) / 2. \tag{2.8}$$

By imposing symmetry, so that $q_i = q_j = q^c$, we obtain the equilibrium solution (it is straightforward to check that second-order conditions are satisfied):

$$q^c = \frac{1 - c}{n + 1}. \tag{2.9}$$

By substitution, one can also obtain the equilibrium price as a function of the number of firms operating in the industry: $p^c = (1 + nc)/(n + 1)$. Note that when the number of firms n increases, the market price decreases and the aggregate

---

[34] See Vickers (1995) for a more general treatment of the homogenous good model with Cournot competition and asymmetries. In particular, it is not always true that exit brings about a welfare rise, although this occurs under fairly mild assumptions in the case where consumer and producer surplus have the same weight in the welfare function. (Vickers' paper also considers the case where consumer surplus has a larger weight than profits.)

output $Q^c = nq^c$ increases, so that the consumer surplus unambiguously rises with n. Indeed, $\partial CS/\partial n > 0$, since

$$CS = (1 - p^c)Q^c/2 = \frac{n^2(1 - c)^2}{2(n + 1)^2}. \tag{2.10}$$

However, a larger number of firms brings about an inefficient multiplication of fixed costs. This can be easily seen by noticing that the individual firm's profit is

$$\pi^c = \frac{(1 - c)^2}{(n + 1)^2} - F. \tag{2.11}$$

As a result, the producer surplus in the industry is

$$PS = \frac{n(1 - c)^2}{(n + 1)^2} - nF, \tag{2.12}$$

which is decreasing with n. In particular, note that as n increases and eventually tends to infinity total welfare becomes negative and then tends to $-\infty$.

Therefore, a policy which aims at maximising the number of firms in the industry would be in contrast with an objective of economic efficiency.[35]

2.4 DYNAMIC EFFICIENCY

So far I have considered static, rather than dynamic, properties of market power: Section 2.2 showed that a monopoly involves an allocative inefficiency, since a firm (for any given technology) charges too high a price; Section 2.3 showed that monopoly involves a productive inefficiency, since a monopolist might not adopt the most efficient technology *available*. This section considers dynamic efficiency, which refers to the extent to which a firm introduces *new* products or processes of production. In other words, whereas Section 2.3 studied whether competition pushes firms to operate at or closer to the current efficient frontier of production, this section considers whether competition pushes them to move the efficient frontier of production faster or further forward.

Section 2.4.1 shows that a monopolist might indeed have lower incentives to innovate, thus adding dynamic inefficiency to the list of welfare losses created by a monopoly. However, a monotonic relationship might not exist between market power and innovation. Section 2.4.2 shows that firms are unlikely to make any investment unless they can expect to appropriate them. This implies that the expectation of market power has an important role as it gives firms incentives for R&D, a theme which will be further analysed in Section 2.5.

---

[35] Exercise 2.8 analyses the equilibrium of this game when entry is endogenous.

2.4.1 The Lower Incentives to Monopolist Innovation

In what follows, I use a simple example to show that a monopolist might be dynamically inefficient because it has little incentive to adopt new technologies. Suppose that a monopolist has the possibility to adopt a process innovation, which allows it to produce at the lower marginal cost c_l rather than at the current cost c_h by paying a fixed cost F. Call Π_l and Π_h respectively the profit made under the (low-cost) new and the (high-cost) old technology. To decide whether to make this innovation or not the monopolist will have to compare the *additional* profit $\Pi_l - \Pi_h$ it will make with the fixed outlays F it has to spend. The new technology is adopted only if $\Pi_l - \Pi_h > F$.

Consider now the same decision about whether to adopt the new technology or not for a firm which operates in a competitive environment. With the current technology entailing marginal cost c_h that all firms have, firms charge $p = c_h$ and make zero profit: $\Pi'_h = 0$. Suppose now that one of them has the chance to adopt the new technology, which allows it to operate at cost c_l, whereas all other firms will still be operating with the old technology.[36] By adopting the new technology, the firm will have the possibility to make a profit Π_l.[37] Hence, this firm operating under competition will innovate if $\Pi_l > F$, whereas the monopolistic firm will innovate only if $\Pi_l - \Pi_h > F$, a much stricter condition. Therefore, the monopolist would have lower incentives to innovate given that it would consider the "additional" profit brought by the new technology, while a competitive firm would consider the whole profit brought by it.[38]

This simple example illustrates the idea that monopolistic firms often have lower incentives to innovate than firms which face rivals.[39,40] The analysis of the formal models in Sections 2.4.3.1 and 2.4.3.2 confirms that a monopoly is dynamically inefficient, in that it has less incentive to innovate and invest. In a nutshell, the intuition behind this result is as follows. Competition pushes firms to invest, in order to improve their competitive position relative to their rivals. The absence of

---

[36] This is the case, for instance, when the innovation is perfectly protected by a patent.

[37] For simplicity, I assume here that a firm operating under Bertrand (or perfect) competition makes the same profit Π_l as the monopolist by adopting the same low-cost technology. This need not be the case. Technically, I assume that the innovation is "drastic". The technical Section 2.4.3.1 shows that the same qualitative results are obtained if one assumes that the innovation is "non-drastic".

[38] The property that a monopolist gains less from an innovation than a competitive firm is also known as Arrow's *replacement effect*.

[39] Another reason why monopolists might innovate less comes from the managerial slack argument analysed above: quiet life does not put enough pressure on a monopolist to do better.

[40] Aghion, Dewatripont and Rey (1999) analyse a growth model where entrepreneurs do not aim at maximising profits, but are "conservative": they want to avoid the private cost of adopting new technologies and they will adopt them in so far as they will allow the firm to avoid bankruptcy. The paper shows that in this setting competition disciplines the entrepreneurs and increases adoption of new technologies and growth.

competition (whether because there is only one firm, or because there are several firms but they collude) reduces this incentive to innovate, and this in turn means that a monopolist will be less efficient (less innovative) than firms which operate under competition.

This example cannot be generalised to conclude that the more competition exists in a market the more likely that firms will innovate. There is an old debate in the economic literature on the link between monopoly power and innovations. This debate goes as far back as Schumpeter (1912) who suggested that monopoly power encourages research and development efforts.

Both theoretical and empirical research on the link between market structure and innovation is not conclusive, even though a "middle ground" environment, where there exists some competition but also high enough market power coming from the innovative activities, might be the most conducive to R&D output.[41] This is precisely the result which emerges from the model analysed in the technical Section 2.4.3.2. In a context where the R&D choices of firms are studied, and the number of firms in the industry is taken as a measure of the degree of competition in the industry, increasing competition when there is already much of it is not necessarily good for welfare. Indeed, firms' incentives to innovate are determined not only by the existence of competition but also by the possibility of appropriating the results of their investment. If competition is too strong, appropriability is reduced, and so is the incentive to invest and innovate.

The result is that some intermediate levels of competition might be optimal for innovations and productive efficiency, a result which is found also in a completely different theoretical framework (based on endogenous growth models) and is confirmed in empirical studies that do find an inverted U relationship between competition and innovation.[42]

Note, however, that it would be extremely difficult to use this result for practical policy purposes, for instance to choose the "right" level of competition. Different assumptions on parameters and on the game being played by the firms would give different results as to which ones should be the optimal levels of competition in the marketplace. Hence, intervening on given industries by reducing the level of competition (whatever the mechanism to obtain it) in order to get closer to some theoretically optimal level of competition would not be justified by any robust theory. The only sound and robust conclusion we can derive from analyses like the one above is that a monopoly (or a cartel) is worse than competitive market structures, because it fails to stimulate dynamic efficiency.[43] Accordingly, steps should be taken to restore competition in markets where there is none.

---

[41] See Scherer and Ross (1990: ch. 17) for a review.

[42] Aghion et al. (2002) present a growth model that suggests such a relationship and conduct an empirical test (on UK panel data) of this prediction.

[43] Exactly the same interpretation should be applied to the result obtained by d'Aspremont and Motta (2000) and illustrated in Exercise 2.4.

2.4.2 Incentives to Invest in R&D

Competition stimulates innovations, but so does the expectation of being able to appropriate investment in R&D through market profits. To show the importance of market power as an incentive to innovate, reconsider the simple example of Section 2.4.1, but assume that when there is competition no firm can appropriate the innovation: if one firm adopts the technology all other firms are able to produce at the same cost as well, perhaps because there is no patent protecting the innovating firm, or perhaps because of policies which oblige firms to give away their technology to rivals (*compulsory licensing*). In this case, no firm has an incentive to innovate: diffusion of the technology prevents an innovator from benefiting from it, since after an innovation all firms would charge $p = c_l$ and make zero profit: $\Pi'_h = 0$. The fixed cost F of the innovation could never be recovered, and no innovation will arise under competition.

This simple example is admittedly extreme (see Section 2.4.3.3 below for a slightly more general setting), but its purpose is to draw the reader's attention to the fact that market power (or the expectation to exercise it) has an important role in maintaining the firms' incentives to innovate, invest, introduce new goods, and improve product quality. Eliminating market power cannot be an objective that any public policy should pursue, as I will argue in Section 2.5.

2.4.3 Models of Competition and Innovation*

This technical section provides a formalisation of some of the arguments made above.

2.4.3.1 Monopoly Gives Fewer Incentives to Innovate: An Example*

Here I present a simple example with deterministic R&D which illustrates the lower incentives to innovate in a monopoly than in a duopoly.

Monopoly   Consider first a monopolist operating at a cost c^h and facing a linear demand $Q = 1 - p$. It can adopt a technology which gives lower marginal cost $c^l = c^h - x$ (with $x \in [0, c^h]$) if it pays a fixed cost F. The monopolist first decides whether to innovate or not, and then decides how much to sell in the market.

The monopolist's profit is given by $\Pi = (p - c^i)(1 - p)$, with $i = l, h$ depending on whether it has low or high cost (that is, if it has innovated or not). From the FOCs $\partial \Pi / \partial p = 0$, it is straightforward that the optimal price is given by $p = (1 + c^i)/2$.

Therefore, if it does not innovate, the monopolist will charge $p = (1 + c^h)/2$ and earn $\Pi = (1 - c^h)^2/4$. If it does innovate, it will charge $p_I = (1 + c^h - x)/2$ and earn the gross profit $\Pi_I = (1 - c^h + x)^2/4$, but will have to pay the cost F.

Hence, the monopolist will innovate if

$$\Delta \equiv \Pi_I - \Pi = \frac{x}{4}\left(x + 2(1 - c^h)\right) \geq F. \qquad (2.13)$$

Duopoly Consider now the duopoly case. The two firms (which sell a homogenous good) face the same market demand $Q = 1 - p$ as above. The firm which charges the lowest price p will face all demand, and the one with the highest price will get no demand. If both firms charge the same price, they will share equally demand.

They play the following game. In the first stage, they simultaneously have to decide whether they want to pay the fixed cost F to adopt the technology which gives lower marginal cost $c^h - x$, or keep the current technology giving marginal cost of production c^h. In the second stage, they simultaneously choose prices. I look for the sub-game perfect Nash equilibrium in pure strategies of this game.

Price Stage of the Game If both firms choose to innovate in the first period, in the second period they will both have the same cost $c^h - x$. This is the standard Bertrand game (see Section 8.3), and the only solution is that both firms will charge at marginal cost ($p = c^h - x$) and get zero gross profit. If none innovate in the first period, firms will again charge at marginal cost at equilibrium (this time, however, $p = c^h$) and get zero profit.

If only one innovates in the first period, at the price sub-game we have two possible situations: either the innovating firm sets the monopoly price (if this is lower than the marginal cost of the non-innovating firm); or it sets a price slightly below the marginal cost of the non-innovating firm (if the monopoly price is higher than the rival's cost).[44] The first case refers to a "drastic" innovation, the second to a "non-drastic" innovation. I assume that the innovation is non-drastic, that is the marginal cost reduction is small enough: $x \leq 1 - c^h$. (Exercise 2.5 examines the "drastic" innovation case.)

Then the innovating firm will charge a price slightly lower than the rival, $c^h - \varepsilon$, and make gross profit $\Pi_{nd} = x(1 - c^h)$.

Innovation Stage of the Game At the first stage of the game firms correctly anticipate the profit they make in the following stage. Firms' payoffs are as follows. If both firms innovate, they will both get $-F$. If none innovate, they will both get 0. If only one firm innovates, the innovating firm will get $\Pi_{nd} - F$ and the other firm 0.

This game has the following solutions: If $\Pi_{nd} \geq F$ the only equilibrium is one where one firm innovates and the other does not. If $\Pi_{nd} < F$, then no firm will innovate at the equilibrium.

Comparison between Monopoly and Duopoly Either market structure does not affect the adoption of innovation (innovations occur under both market structures,

---

[44] Other equilibria in pure strategies are eliminated because they involve weakly-dominated strategies (see Section 8.3 for a discussion).

or do not occur under either), or an equilibrium with innovation occurs under duopoly but not under monopoly. Indeed, it can be easily seen that $\Pi_{nd} \geq \Delta$ for $x \leq 2(1 - c^h)$, which is in the domain we are considering. Therefore, for values of fixed cost of innovation such that $\Pi_{nd} \geq F > x \left(x + 2 \left(1 - c^h\right)\right) / 4$, there will be an innovation under duopoly but not under monopoly. For values of fixed cost such that $F \leq x \left(x + 2 \left(1 - c^h\right)\right) / 4$, an innovation will occur in both market structures. For $F > \Pi_{nd}$, no innovation will be adopted under either market structure.

This analysis confirms that a monopolist's incentive to innovate might indeed be lower than the incentive of firms which face competitors.

2.4.3.2 R&D and Competition**

I present now another simple model, where firms first invest in R&D and then compete in quantities, to show that the degree of market competition has an effect on dynamic efficiency. More particularly, a monopolistic market structure is going to lead to lower R&D investments (and therefore higher production costs) than a market structure where several firms co-exist and behave non-cooperatively.

Consider the demand function for a homogenous good $p = a - Q$, with Q being the sum of individual output. Firm i ($i = 1, \ldots, n$) is characterised by marginal costs $c_i = C - x_i$, where x_i is the R&D investment made by firm i. The cost of R&D is given by the function $g x_i^2 / 2$, where $g > 0$ is a parameter expressing the efficiency of R&D production.[45]

The game is a simple two-stage game. Firms simultaneously invest in R&D at the first stage; they then simultaneously choose quantities in the second stage. As usual, I look for the sub-game perfect Nash equilibrium of the game.

At the *last stage* of the game, it is easily checked that the (Cournot) equilibrium output is given by

$$q_i^c = \frac{a - c_i + \sum_{j \neq i}(c_j - c_i)}{1 + n}, \tag{2.14}$$

and the profit will be given by $\Pi_i = (q_i^c)^2$. (See Section 8.3 for an introduction to the Cournot model.)

At the *first stage* of the game, each firm will have the following profit function:

$$\pi_i = \left(\frac{a - (C - x_i) + \sum_{j \neq i}(x_i - x_j)}{1 + n}\right)^2 - \frac{g}{2} x_i^2. \tag{2.15}$$

---

[45] I therefore look at process innovations, and assume that R&D is a deterministic, rather than stochastic. This simplifies the model without depriving it of interesting insights.

By taking the first derivative we obtain the FOC for the ith firm:[46]

$$\frac{\partial \pi_i}{\partial x_i} = \frac{2n\left(a - C + x_i + \sum_{j \neq i}(x_i - x_j)\right)}{(1 + n)^2} - g x_i = 0. \qquad (2.16)$$

Notice that by taking all the rival firms' R&D levels x_j ($j \neq i$) as given and equal to $\bar{x}$ ($x_j = x_k = \bar{x}$, for $j, k \neq i, k \neq j$), the marginal effect of R&D on firm i's profit can be written as

$$\frac{\partial \pi_i}{\partial x_i} = \frac{2n(a - C + x_i)}{(1 + n)^2} + \frac{2n(n - 1)(x_i - \bar{x})}{(1 + n)^2} - g x_i = 0. \qquad (2.17)$$

This is helpful because it reveals that there are three different effects that govern the optimal R&D levels. The first one is what we could label *appropriability effect*: the larger demand (or net demand, $a - C$) the stronger the incentive to do R&D. This term decreases with n, and it is highest when $n = 1$, that is, when there is a monopoly. The second term is a *competition effect*. When there is a monopoly ($n = 1$), this term disappears completely, while it is strictly positive when there is competition: it therefore captures the incentive to innovate determined by the existence of competition. Notice that the competition effect increases with n, but at a slower pace as n rises: $2n(n - 1)/(1 + n)^2$ is concave in n, and reaches an asymptote when $n \to \infty$. The third term captures instead the marginal cost of R&D, and the efficiency parameter g is the only parameter affecting it. It is the interplay between these effects which will determine the R&D levels chosen at equilibrium by firms and how the number of firms affects the equilibrium solutions.

If we focus on the symmetric equilibrium $x_i = \bar{x} = x$, we obtain the equilibrium R&D level for each firm:

$$x^c = \frac{2n(a - C)}{g(1 + n)^2 - 2n}. \qquad (2.18)$$

From this solution, one can then obtain by substitution the equilibrium levels of quantity, price and profit (omitted for shortness). The total level of R&D in the industry will be given by $R^c = nx^c = 2n^2(a - C)/\left[g(1 + n)^2 - 2n\right]$. Note that

$$\frac{\partial R^c}{\partial n} = \frac{2n(a - C)(g(1 + n) - n)}{\left[g(1 + n)^2 - 2n\right]^2} > 0. \qquad (2.19)$$

The last expression tells us that the more firms in the industry (that is, the more competition in the marketplace) the larger the amount of R&D carried out. However, this does not necessarily mean that welfare increases as n increases. It might be that

---

[46] The second-order condition requires $g > 2n^2/(1 + n)^2$. The stability condition requires instead $\left[\partial^2 \pi_i/\partial x_i dx_{-i}\right]/\left[\partial^2 \pi_i/\partial x_i^2\right] = 2n(n - 1)/\left[g(1 + n)^2 - 2n^2\right] < 1$. This is satisfied for $g > 2n(2n - 1)/(1 + n)^2$. The latter is clearly a more stringent condition. Note that an increase in n tightens this condition. However, a sufficient condition for stability to be met is that $g > 4$.

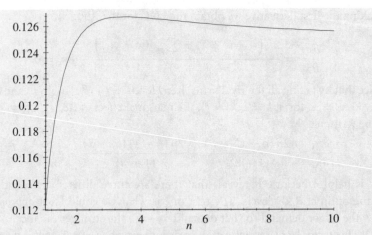

Figure 2.4. Welfare W^c as a function of the number of firms n ($a = 1; c = .5; g = 4$).

there exists too much R&D with respect to what is optimal for society (that is, that too many resources are devoted to R&D).

To this purpose, let us first compute welfare under competition. As is standard, we take welfare as $W = CS + PS$. In our case

$$CS^c = \frac{(a - p^c)nq^c}{2} = \frac{[(a - C)ng(1 + n)]^2}{2[g(1 + n)^2 - 2n]},$$ (2.20)

and total profits are

$$PS^c = n\pi^c = n\frac{(a - C)^2 g\left(g(1 + n)^2 - 2n^2\right)}{[g(1 + n)^2 - 2n]^2}.$$ (2.21)

Therefore, welfare will be given by

$$W^c = \frac{(a - C)^2 ng\left((2 + n)g(1 + n)^2 - 4n^2\right)}{2[g(1 + n)^2 - 2n]^2},$$ (2.22)

which is a non-monotonic function in n.

As shown in Figure 2.4, the welfare function $W^c(n)$ increases up to a certain value $n_m(g)$ and then decreases, with a horizontal asymptote at $W = (a - C)^2/2$. In other words, an increase in competition (in the sense of an increase in the number of firms in the market) from low initial levels (when appropriability is high) raises welfare; but when competition is large enough, a further increase in it would decrease welfare, since an increase in the number of firms n does not add much to R&D levels (and hence quantities sold in the market) but it decreases profits.[47] Note that when

---

[47] Boone (2000) finds that increasing competition (as proxied by a switch from Cournot to Bertrand) when firms are asymmetric may lead to lower R&D investments. In industries where the technological gap is larger, the laggard's gain from catching up with the leader may fall with more competition. A similar result is also found in Aghion et al. (2002).

n increases there will be a larger number of firms, which have to pay R&D costs, and this duplication of costs determines a productive inefficiency.[48]

2.4.3.3 Appropriability and R&D*

Assume a homogenous good duopoly where firms have initial marginal cost levels c. Market demand is $q = a - p$; the cost function is $C_i = (c - x_i - lx_j)q_i - x_i^2$, where x_i is the R&D investments made by firm i ($i, j = 1, 2; i \neq j$). Here R&D takes the form of a process innovation (it reduces production cost) and for simplicity it is deterministic. Also assume that there exist R&D spillovers (or externalities): a fraction $l \in [0, 1]$ of the R&D carried out by a firm i will benefit its rival j (and vice versa). This is a crude but simplifying way to formalise the idea that innovations can be (partly or completely) copied, imitated or reverse-engineered by rival firms.[49] The game is as follows. First, firms have to simultaneously decide their R&D investment levels x_i; then, they compete on prices. The objective here is to compare equilibrium outcomes with and without patents.

Duopoly under Price Competition Note that one can immediately rule out equilibria where both firms innovate, since at least one firm would not be able to recover the fixed cost of R&D expenditures. At the equilibrium of the whole game, only one firm innovates. In general, there are two possible cases to consider. (1) The innovation is drastic. In this case, the monopolistic price of the innovating firm is lower than the cost of the non-innovating firm. For this to happen, the following condition must hold: $(a + c - x)/2 < c - lx$, or $x \geq (a - c)/(1 - 2l)$. (2) The innovation is non-drastic. In this case, $x < (a - c)/(1 - 2l)$. I focus here on non-drastic innovations (it can be shown that at the equilibrium of this specific model the optimal level of the innovation corresponds to a non-drastic one).

Let us now look at the R&D stage and find the optimal value of x. The profit function of the innovating firm will be given by $\pi_{nd} = x(1 - l)(a - c + lx) - x^2$. Note that $x(1 - l)$ is the profit margin of the innovating firm: the higher the spillover l, the lower its market power.

From solving $\partial \pi_{nd}/\partial x = 0$ it follows that the function π_{nd} has a maximum at $x^*(l) = (1 - l)(a - c)/[2 - 2l(1 - l)]$, which is the equilibrium level of R&D. Note that the higher the spillover l the lower the R&D made at equilibrium.

Patent (No Spillovers) Imagine now that a patent is awarded to the firm which makes an innovation. As before, we know that the two firms would compete à la Bertrand: at the equilibrium in pure strategies only one of them will do a positive amount of R&D. The treatment is the same as in the previous case, but for the particular value where $l = 0$, i.e., no spillovers could arise (the patent is protecting the innovating firm from spillovers).

---

[48] See also Section 2.3.5.2 for another example of this duplication effect.
[49] Assume for simplicity that imitation and reverse engineering are costless.

The optimal level of R&D under patents will therefore be $x^p = x^*(l = 0) = (a - c)/2$. Clearly, $x^p > x^*(l)$ for all $l > 0$: there is always more R&D under patents.

Conclusions In this simple model, a patent improves welfare. Because of spillovers, R&D is a public good. Since firms are not able to appropriate their R&D efforts, they will invest less in R&D than what would be optimal for society. The patent removes the negative externality given by the spillovers and restores the incentive to do R&D.

It should be noted, however, that this model is rather extreme in that it suggests that patents might be optimal whatever the level of spillovers. This needs not be the case under more general models. Here there are homogenous goods and price competition, so competition is very fierce and has a very strong impact on the returns of R&D. If we assumed weaker competition (for instance, by allowing for some product differentiation) then we might find that patents increase R&D levels when spillovers are large enough.[50]

A final qualification is as follows. This simple model does not capture another important feature of patents, that is the fact that a firm is granted a patent only if it discloses completely the technology to other firms. The purpose of this rule is that all rival firms are able (at least in principle) to share perfectly the technology with the innovating firm and use it as soon as the period of patent protection expires.

2.5 PUBLIC POLICIES AND INCENTIVES TO INNOVATE

From the previous sections it emerges that market power reduces allocative efficiency, but also that a clear-cut relationship between market power on one side and productive and dynamic efficiency on the other side is more difficult to establish. Therefore, there would be no justification for the elimination of market power as an objective of competition policy.

More importantly, the very existence of some market power helps competition. It is precisely the prospect of enjoying some market power (i.e., of making profit) that pushes firms to use more efficient technologies, improve their product quality, or introduce new product varieties. If anti-trust agencies tried to eliminate or reduce market power whenever it appeared, this would have the detrimental effect of eliminating firms' incentives to innovate.

This section stresses the importance of the incentives to innovate (and more generally, to invest), and argues that public policies should maintain such incentives.

---

[50] Under Cournot competition and homogenous goods, market competition is "too weak" and as a result spillovers do little to dissipate the incentive to innovate (at least at the symmetric equilibrium). As a result, a patent might not be better than allowing spillovers.

2.5.1 *Ex Ante* v. *Ex Post:* Property Rights Protection

The trade-off between *ex ante* efficiency (one wants to preserve the firms' incentives to innovate) and *ex post* efficiency (once firms have innovated it would be better if all the firms in the economy had access to the innovation) is at the core of public policies towards investments and innovations. A government faces a time-consistency problem here. Before firms decide whether to invest in R&D, the government will always want to promise firms that they can fully benefit from their R&D results (to make them invest as much as possible), but once such R&D results are obtained, it will be tempted to renege on this promise; by cancelling exclusivity rights on innovations, the government would allow for the innovation to be used by a maximal number of firms (including those that did not contribute to the R&D efforts), so that as many consumers as possible can immediately enjoy the benefits of the new technology. But firms would anticipate that the government has such an incentive to renege on the promise, and as a consequence, firms would not innovate at all, resulting in the worst possible solution for welfare. The government is therefore hurt by the possibility to renege on the promise, that is by its lack of commitment. It would be better off by tying its hands and committing to keep its promise. This way, firms would be ensured that they will be able to enjoy the rewards from their R&D.

Patent laws (and other intellectual property rights) are a way for governments to commit not to expropriate an innovating firm *ex post*. A firm knows that for a certain period of time it will be able to exploit fully its R&D results.

The trade-off between the necessity of granting firms the appropriability of their innovations and the desire that the benefit of such innovations spread to other firms and to consumers has given rise to a vast literature on the optimal design of patents.[51] This literature aims at identifying the optimal breadth and length of patents. In theoretical terms, the problem is the following. One does not want to give too broad a protection to an innovation, otherwise rival firms would be discouraged to introduce innovations, which are only vaguely related to the patented innovation. On the other hand, the protection cannot be too narrow, otherwise a rival firm might make any small and artificial incremental innovation and get away with the infringement of the patent. The same is true for the length of the patent. A too long period of protection makes it impossible for rival firms to challenge the incumbent innovator with new discoveries; but too short a period of protection would not give enough appropriability for innovators. In practical terms, though, it is difficult to go beyond the recognition of such a trade-off and it is very hard to identify a breadth and length of protection which is not arbitrary.

Besides patent laws, there are other laws which help a government solve the commitment problems in a relative straightforward way. Copyright and trademark

---

[51] See Tirole (1988: ch. 11) for references.

laws ensure that a successful product or brand can be used by another firm only under an agreement with the firm which owns the rights. Trade secret laws aim – among other things – at making sure that employees who have been informed of business secrets in a firm cannot bring them to a rival firm which hires them. Non-competition clauses also help firms keep their know-how intact, as they limit the freedom of workers to move to rival firms.[52]

More generally the issue involves not only intellectual property rights but property rights *tout court*. Imagine that a firm invests in a certain plant or in a certain physical asset that later turns out to be a crucial competitive advantage for all other firms in the industry. A competition agency might then be tempted to give access to such a crucial asset to all firms: again, if this were possible, firms would not make much effort to invest in the first place. Property laws solve this commitment problem by ensuring that expropriation will not occur.

A similar problem occurs with respect to pricing. Suppose that a firm has introduced a new product or created such a strong brand image of a given product that consumers would love to buy it even at extremely high prices. A government might then be tempted to intervene and impose price ceilings to increase surplus. It is therefore important to have a clear legal framework which guarantees firms against such a possibility. We elaborate on the last two points in the following sections.

2.5.2 Essential Facilities

Any input which is deemed necessary for all industry participants to operate in a given industry and which is not easily duplicated might be seen as an *essential facility* (see also Chapter 6). There are many examples that might satisfy this very loose definition of essential inputs. In the airline industry, slots in an airport; for maritime transportations, a port's installations; in fixed telephony, the local loop, which links each home's telephone with the network; for electrical power generation, the transmission and distribution network of electricity; for the production of pharmaceuticals, a certain chemical component; and so on.

These are theoretical examples, in the sense that understanding whether a given input truly is an essential facility is a complex issue. How indispensable is a certain input? Very often, an input gives its owner a competitive advantage over rivals which have inferior inputs. Obviously, one cannot call "essential" an input which just gives a minor competitive advantage to a firm. On the other hand, there might be alternative inputs that are such poor substitutes that they would not allow rivals to compete at all. It might therefore not be easy to establish where a certain input begins to be so superior as to be judged "necessary".

---

[52] See Motta and Rønde (2002) for a formalisation of such clauses.

How easy is it to duplicate an input? Clearly, if reproducing the input were easy, cheap and practical, then it would be difficult to say that it is an essential input. But how costly and difficult should reproduction be in order to conclude that the input is essential?

Imagine for instance that a shipping company X integrates backwards and builds new port installations in a certain town A, located in the "home" country. Given the location, using this port's infrastructure gives firm X a great advantage in serving the maritime route from the home country to a certain other foreign country. Company Y now requests use of the port and firm X denies it (*refusal to supply*). Then, firm Y complains with the competition authorities that it should also have access (possibly even at a price, provided it be fair) to town A's port installations.

Competition authorities in different countries have often been too ready to accept allegations like that made by firm Y, and too easily embraced the so-called *essential facilities doctrine,* thereby deciding that the owner of the input had engaged in an illegal practice and was obliged to make the facility available to competitors.[53]

But there are a number of considerations which should be properly analysed before granting rivals access to a facility owned by a firm. In the port example, for instance, it should be seen to which extent transport from ports other than port A is really such a poor substitute for the maritime route to the foreign country. Are all the other ports really so far away? Are their facilities so inferior? Second, supposing that there are no other existing ports which might provide a substitute route for transport to the foreign country, is it feasible for company Y to reproduce a similar investment and build (or improve) port facilities in another nearby town, say B? Notice that here it would not be enough to answer that it would be too expensive. It should be argued that there are no other towns in the area which are served by train and/or highways so that shipping would be impossible; or that the government would not authorise the building of other ports in a close area because of environmental or other reasons, and so forth. Third, it should also be checked that by letting rivals access the infrastructure the owner of the facility would not find it more costly to produce. If, for instance, there is no spare capacity, then it would be more difficult to argue for access.

If all the previous tests were favourable to the firm requesting use of the input, the possibility of using access pricing to cope with this issue could be considered. However, there is another argument which suggests caution before granting access to rivals too generously. In our example, the new port installation has been the

---

[53] In a stream of cases related to the transport sector, the EC has been too ready to find "essential" facilities and abuses of dominant positions on the side of the firms that owned such facilities. Most of these cases were related to port infrastructures: *B&I Line/Sealink* and *Sea Containers/Stena* (both concerning the port of Holyhead in Wales), *Port of Rødby,* and *Irish Continental Group/Morlaix* (port of Roscoff in Brittany). However, the subsequent decision by the ECJ in the *Bronner* case has set a higher standard for the application of the essential facilities doctrine, putting a brake on the interventionist approach of the Commission.

result of a deliberate (and presumably costly) investment by a firm. Obliging it to share its facilities with rivals would be an infringement of its property rights. More importantly, it would have the effect of discouraging similar investments elsewhere, as the prospect of being expropriated of their investments discourages firms from introducing new inputs and facilities in the first place.

The last observation is crucial. There is an important difference between firms which have invested and firms which have obtained the right of using a certain facility without having borne the risk of its creation or having paid for it. In the above example, one should not consider in the same way the case where firm X has built itself (bearing the risk and cost of the investment) the port installations and the case where the investment has been made by the state and the firm has received the monopoly rights to use them.

Take for instance the case – common in Europe – where the "flag carriers" had received from their government, at the time where they were the national monopolists, the right of using most of the landing and take-off slots at domestic airports. Availability of slots in a given airport is an essential input for many routes (alternative, less crowded, airports might be too far away for most consumers, for instance), and once de-regulation occurs and entry in the sector is "free", it would be hard to argue that the slots should be kept by the former monopolist. In this case, even if the monopolist holds a contract, which gives it exclusive rights for the slots, competition would require letting competitors have access to some of them: there is no issue of protecting the firm's investments here.

Similarly, in some instances firms might obtain intellectual property rights protection over an input without having made any innovation which is worth being protected. In my view, this has been the case in two important EU cases, *Magill* and *IMS*. In *Magill*, a small company (Magill) was accused of infringing upon the copyright of three TV chains because it had offered a weekly TV guide that included the programmes of all the three broadcasters. Before Magill, the only products available were each broadcaster's weekly TV guide (that did not include the other TV's programmes), or the listing of all programmes by newspapers, but only for the current day (such information was freely supplied to newspapers by the TV chains). It is doubtful that the weekly listing of programmes by each broadcaster is an innovation which deserves copyright protection (especially if considered that broadcasters spread the relevant information).

In *IMS*, a German firm (IMS) collected data about pharmaceutical product sales in Germany. To do so, it had divided the country into zones, thus creating a reference map that firms in the industry had helped to draw and were using. When a new competitor tried to offer the same service, it had to organise sales data according to the same map (firms refused alternative ways of organising the data because they were accustomed to the old system), over which IMS claimed copyright. In this case as well, it is difficult to see the map as an innovation worthy of protection.

2.5.3 Price Controls and Structural Remedies

While regulation generally provides regulatory authorities with some sort of control over the prices charged by the firms in the sector, this is not the case for competition policy authorities, whose intervention in the marketplace is assumed to be occasional. Use of price controls and price caps in general is in contrast with competition policy. However, many competition laws, such as for instance Article 82 of the EU Treaty, allow authorities to intervene if prices set by a dominant firm are "too high" (see Section 1.4). These are very dangerous provisions, for at least two reasons. First, deciding if a price is too high or not involves a high degree of arbitrariness. Second, and more important, even if it was established that a firm is charging too high a price (whatever this means), why should it be punished for it? Imagine that the firm is a monopolist and is charging the monopoly price (which is the highest profitable price a firm would set). Such a dominant position in the market might come from different sources.

First, it might come from past illegal behaviour, such as predation. If it did, then the competition authority should open a proceeding directly for the infringement of some competition laws, rather than for high prices.

Second, it might be due to present legal barriers to entry. In this case the sector should be subject to regulation, since market forces are not free to operate. If legal barriers to entry have already been removed, though, an industry regulator should operate for a transition period, because free entry does not by itself and immediately eliminate the power of the incumbent (see Section 2.6 below). If for some reason there are no sector regulators and the competition authorities are competent, then it makes sense that they intervene, either by imposing lower prices or, in exceptional circumstances, by the use of structural remedies, that is measures that modify the property rights of a firm, for instance by imposing the disposal of certain assets (patents, brands, plants) or – even more dramatically – by breaking a firm into several units. This measure should be taken only in really extraordinary cases, and should be adopted only if all other measures have failed, for example, if it is clear that incumbents will never be challenged by entrants, and if the dominant position has been acquired not on the merits but because of a legal monopoly.[54]

Third, the firm might have acquired its market power through investments, innovations, and advertising (and maybe even a good share of business luck). If this is the case, then there is no reason to punish it for it. The firm has the right to set high prices since these are the reward for its investments. Intervening by imposing lower prices would be tantamount to depriving it of its risky investments, and discourage it and other firms from investing in the future.

---

[54] The only case of break-up in the recent anti-trust history is that of the Bell Telephone System, which was divided into regional companies (the so-called Baby Bells). This had indeed been the legal monopolist in the US telecom industry for a long time.

In such a case, the competition authority should just be vigilant, and intervene only if the dominant firm engages in exclusionary practices aimed at preserving its market position. If predation does not occur (and that would be the case in most situations) then either the firm keeps on investing to keep its position, or other firms will sooner or later challenge it and prices will decrease over time.

For the same reasons, targeting firms because they are "too profitable" is wrong. High prices and high profits might be an indication that it is worth looking at the industry (for instance, there might be collusion, or some other infringement of competition law), but certainly by themselves they cannot justify intervention by competition authorities.

2.5.4 Internal v. External Growth

The view proposed above is one where firms should enjoy market power if it is the result of their investment. Market power, and profit, are the legitimate reward for the fact that a given firm has been more successful than others (whatever the reason, provided not illegal). Call this situation where a firm acquires market power and grows on the merits "internal growth". Contrast it now with a situation – call it "external growth" – where a firm grows and acquires market power not because of its investments but simply because it takes over other firms (or merges with them). In this case, market power is not the legitimate reward of some risky activities of the firm, but it is the product of the direct elimination of competitors via compensation (that is, at the price of the takeover). Conceptually, this is quite a different thing, and competition authorities should take care to prevent this. Chapter 5 will show that a merger between small firms is unlikely to create anti-competitive problems, whereas a merger between firms holding large market shares should be allowed only if it creates substantial, verifiable, merger-specific efficiency gains. That is, if there are strong reasons to believe that by combining the two firms together the result is a much more efficient firm, able to produce at lower cost and sell at lower prices.

2.6 MONOPOLY: WILL THE MARKET FIX IT ALL?

It has been suggested that market mechanisms prevent even a monopolist from exercising market power. One such argument says that a durable good monopolist is unable to keep prices high because consumers anticipate that it will reduce prices in the future. Another says that if there is free entry, this will prevent the monopolist from setting high prices, as they would trigger entry. Taken at face value, these arguments – derived from the *Coase conjecture* and the *contestable markets theory* – would imply that one should not worry about market power, at least when durable good sellers are involved and when there exists free entry. In this section, I present and discuss both arguments, to conclude that – although they offer interesting and valuable insights – the extreme versions of such theories are unlikely to hold. I will also mention a number of reasons why market forces alone are unlikely to reduce market power in a number of cases (if sunk costs are important, if consumers have switching costs, if there are network externalities, and if a monopolist can engage in anti-competitive practices). Unfortunately, even when entry is in principle free, reasons to worry about monopolies still exist.

2.6.1 Durable Good Monopolist

Coase (1972) suggested that the producer of a durable good might price at marginal cost even if it is a monopolist.[55] To gain some insight for this result, suppose that a producer is facing two groups of potential clients who have a different valuation for the durable good it sells. Presumably, the producer will first try to charge a high price and sell to consumers who have a high valuation for the good. In the period after these consumers have bought the good (being a durable good they will not buy again), it would then decrease the price to be able to sell to the low-valuation consumers as well. However, it is reasonable to expect that the high-valuation consumers understand that the producer will decrease the price in the future. Unless they incur a high cost from delaying the purchase by one period, they will abstain from buying until the price for the good has decreased. As a result, the monopolist will not be able to sell at a high price in the first period.

Suppose now that there are not only two groups of consumers but an extremely large number of them, and that they have valuations for the same durable good that are between the marginal cost and the monopoly price. (Suppose too that each period is very short, so that price adjustments occur continuously.) The monopolist would then have an incentive in each period to reduce the price to sell to those who have not previously bought. Since each consumer will expect that the monopolist will eventually reduce the price to marginal cost to sell to the lowest valuation group of consumers, each consumer will postpone buying until price is equal to marginal cost. We might therefore arrive at the paradoxical result (conjectured by Coase) that the monopolist will lose all its possible market power because consumers anticipate that it will reduce prices down to marginal cost in the future.

The Coase conjecture has been formally proved, but it relies on such "heroic" assumptions that it should not be taken literally.[56] However, the insight behind the result is valid, important, and applies to several situations (see for instance Chapter 6, where this principle is applied to understand the logic and effects of vertical restraints). The crucial issue is that the monopolist is hurt by its *flexibility* to change

---

[55] Durable goods are goods that last for a certain period of time such as cars, computers, photocopiers, dishwashers and so on.

[56] Notably, the assumptions are that both monopolist and consumers live forever, that the good also has infinite durability, that consumers have unit demand, and that the period between successive price adjustments tends to zero. See Tirole (1988: ch. 1.5) for references, a formalisation and discussion.

prices in future periods. If it could commit not to reduce prices in a credible way, then it would be better off. Suppose for instance that it could publicly announce that it charges the monopoly price for its durable good and that it will not change the price as long as the good is sold. Suppose also that the monopolist writes a contract (a so-called *most-favoured nation* clause) specifying that if it ever did decrease the price all consumers who have paid a higher price are entitled to the reimbursement of the difference between the original price they paid and the lower price. Then, this contract (enforceable in law courts) would allow it to credibly commit to monopoly pricing and the monopolist would be able to restore all its market power.

Note, however, that the pure announcement of intending not to reduce the price, without any explicit and enforceable commitment, would not be enough to solve its problem. After the first group of consumers have bought the good, the monopolist would have an incentive to renege on the promise and would find it profitable to decrease price.[57]

In conclusion, price flexibility might indeed hurt a seller of durable goods, as well as of other goods which have similar characteristics. But what the example above tells us is that the monopolist might also find a way to solve the commitment problem.

Some Instruments Solve (or Alleviate) the Commitment Problem   As seen above, one possible way for the monopolist to evade the Coase problem is to resort to contractual clauses (such as most-favoured nation clauses) that make its commitment not to lower prices credible.[58]

Another possibility is that, instead of selling the durable good, the producer might rent it (or lease it) to customers. In this way, it commits itself not to decrease price in the future, since a decrease would hurt it by reducing the value of a good it owns. (Exercise 2.14 formalises this idea and shows that for a durable good monopolist leasing gives higher profit than selling.) One should be aware, though, that leasing is not always feasible or without problems, due for instance to moral hazard problems (consumers who do not own the good might not take care of it and damage it) and the associated monitoring costs.

Yet another possibility is that if there is not one, but a stream of products that the monopolist will bring to the market, it might be able to alleviate the commitment

---

[57] The problem of inter-temporal credibility and commitment is one which can be found in several circumstances and across fields. Consider for instance a government that wants to stimulate foreign direct investment into the country. It would have an incentive to promise an exemption from corporate taxes. But once firms have established themselves in the country, the government might be tempted to make foreign affiliates pay high taxes. Similar issues might apply to monetary and macroeconomic policies as well.

[58] Of course, the clauses themselves must be credible. If for instance the price is not publicly observable (when the good sold is an intermediate good and the buyers are firms this is generally the case) then a most-favoured nation clause might be of little use, since a buyer would not easily know prices charged to other buyers later. In such a case, the monopolist will have to find another solution to the commitment problem.

problem through establishing a reputation of not flooding the market of a good after the introductory periods.

Conclusions   Although theoretically a durable good monopolist might be unable to charge prices above marginal costs, in practice it is unlikely that its market power will disappear because of the commitment problem. If consumers incur costs when delaying their purchases, potential buyers increase over time, or menu costs reduce the monopolist's flexibility in changing prices over time, the monopolist will be able to set prices close to the monopoly level. Above all, a durable good monopolist will have several instruments available, such as leasing, reputation, or various contractual clauses, to solve (or alleviate) the commitment problem and exercise all its market power.

2.6.2 Contestable Markets

It is sometimes argued that monopoly power is likely to be a temporary situation, since the existence of profits would attract the entry of new firms and erode market power. Even if at a given point in time the static deadweight loss was large, from a dynamic point of view the overall expected loss from monopoly power would be much smaller, because of new entrants.[59] If this was the case, there would be little scope for competition policy, since market forces would re-establish a more favourable social outcome without the need of any anti-trust actions.

It is therefore important to analyse whether free entry is likely to decrease market concentration, or in any case to decrease the welfare loss which is due to monopoly power. A useful starting point to discuss this issue is the so-called "contestable markets theory", proposed by Baumol, Panzar and Willig (1982).

A simple illustration of the argument proposed by these authors might go as follows. Consider an industry which produces a homogenous good by means of a technology which is equally accessible by both an incumbent monopolist and a potential entrant. In particular, to produce the good a firm incurs a fixed cost F plus a variable cost cq. Assume also that the market is large enough for the monopolist to earn enough profits to recover the fixed cost F.

One then obtains the surprising result that the incumbent firm will not charge the monopoly price, but the price which is just enough to cover its average cost ($p_a = c + F/q$). The proof of this result is straightforward and can be obtained by *a contrario* reasoning, as follows. First, if the monopolist charged a price above average cost, it would obtain positive profits; attracted by these profits a new firm would enter, charge a price slightly lower than the price set by the incumbent, steal all the market from the latter, and earn positive profits. Hence, price above average cost cannot be an equilibrium.

---

[59] See for instance Schmalensee (1982) and Ordover (1990).

Second, at an equilibrium the incumbent cannot set a price below average costs, because it would not be able to cover its fixed costs and would accumulate losses.

Therefore, price equal to average cost must be the only possible equilibrium outcome under free entry.

The result that a monopolist would not charge a price exceeding average cost is striking. If this outcome were robust and based on reasonable assumptions, its implications for competition policy would be extremely strong. Since it is the very presence of potential entrants in the industry which disciplines the monopolist, any market where entry is not forbidden would attain the socially efficient output (at least when government subsidies are not admitted). Also, since the monopolist would continue to be the only firm operating in the sector, duplication of fixed costs is avoided, and technological efficiency is attained. Indeed, at the equilibrium one would not observe any entry in the market, because no firms would start operating in the industry when the monopolist makes zero profit. Therefore, even the finding that in a given market there exists a persistent monopolist and no entrants over the years would be perfectly compatible with a socially efficient situation. Anti-trust authorities would have no reason to intervene in such a world.

Unfortunately, there are two problems in the reasoning above. The first problem comes with the assumption that the monopolist is not able to change its price when it faces new competition. The argument above hinges crucially on the hypothesis that the incumbent sticks to the pre-entry price for at least some time after observing actual entry by another firm. In other words, there would be a higher flexibility in an entry decision by a potential producer than in the price decision of the incumbent. This is unrealistic. The degree of commitment of a firm to its pricing decision is generally low and one would not expect a firm to have such rigid prices that it cannot revise them downwards while it observes a new firm first preparing entry, and then actually entering, its market. In turn, the potential entrant knows very well that the incumbent is able to modify its price and it would rationally expect the price after entry to be lower than that before entry. If there is no room for two firms at more competitive prices, no entry will occur in the industry.

The second problem lies in the nature of the fixed costs F. The theory describes a situation where the potential entrant observes the existence of profit in a given industry, quickly converts part of its existing capacity (or establishes a new plant) to produce the good demanded in that market and sells it. It earns positive profits for some time and then, when the monopolist finally reacts and lowers its price to match the entrant's, would exit the industry and reconvert its capacity to the old production without additional cost (or sell the plant to somebody else, at the same value as the purchase value).

This story depends on the assumption that the entrant does not incur any *sunk* cost to start production in the new sector. A sunk cost is a cost, which is not recoverable. Generally, setting up new capacity or a new plant involves some degree of fixed sunk costs. To establish new production requires some dedicated, specific investments which cannot be easily recovered, at least not totally, after ceasing production. As an example, an economist who decides to work in industrial organisation has to make an initial investment and devote part of her time to get familiar with the work done in that area. When "recycling" herself into another field (say, macroeconomics), a part of her investment will be lost, since the other field will use different methods. Likewise, to start production in whatever sector involves some fixed set-up costs which are not perfectly recoverable at the moment of leaving the industry. The theory of contestable markets requires that there are zero sunk costs. If the entrant had to commit resources in order to produce in the industry, then the "hit-and-run" strategy that this theory proposes would not be possible any longer.

Although its extreme result (that a monopolist would charge at average cost) is unwarranted in most cases, the contestable market theory has had the merit of underlining the role played by potential entry in constraining the market power of incumbents. It is now commonly accepted that a firm is unlikely to exercise such market power if it faces potential rivals that could rapidly and cheaply enter the industry. In many markets, firms have to bear large fixed sunk costs and their investment projects are long and risky. But when this is not the case, one should expect potential entrants to significantly limit prices of established firms. This important insight is crucial for merger policy, as discussed in Chapter 5.

2.6.3 Monopoly and Free Entry

The contestable markets theory invites us to think more seriously about the relationship between monopoly (more generally, market power) and entry. Recent oligopoly models show that free entry is not enough to guarantee that market power in the industry decreases. In this section, I first show that a highly concentrated industry structure can arise under free entry even when firms are *ex ante* identical; then, that there are a number of reasons why it might be difficult for entrants to challenge incumbent firms, even if there are no legal barriers to entry. Of course, monopolists might also resort to exclusionary practices to hinder entry.

Monopolies Might Exist under Free Entry   Consider a situation where many firms might decide to enter an industry. They are all endowed with the same technology and knowledge, they have to incur the same fixed sunk costs if they enter, and they decide simultaneously. They all know that if only one firm enters the market, it will get a large profit, which outweighs the fixed costs. But they also know that, if more than one firm enters, competition will be so fierce (this is a crucial assumption) that even duopoly profits will not be enough to cover fixed costs. Then, as technical Section 2.6.3.1 shows, a monopoly will arise at equilibrium. The expectation of intense product market competition will prevent more than one firm from operating in the industry.[60]

Persistence of Concentration when (Endogenous) Sunk Costs Exist   The previous result is certainly an extreme one. However, a more general and robust result exists. It is called "finiteness property", and states that in markets where consumers value quality of the products, industrial concentration will not fall below a certain threshold even if market size grow arbitrarily large. Intuitively, this is because as demand increases, firms' expenditures in R&D or advertising (which are endogenous sunk costs) escalate to raise the quality of their products. In turn, only a limited number of firms can profitably sustain these large endogenous sunk costs. This property is briefly discussed in technical Section 2.6.3.1.

2.6.3.1 Concentration under Free Entry*

A Simple Example   Consider a homogenous product which can be produced by two different firms which are perfectly identical (they possess the same technology and are equally efficient) and analyse the following game. In the first stage of the game the two firms have to decide whether to enter the industry or not. If they do, they have to incur a fixed set-up cost f, which is necessary to start production. Once made the investment, the cost f is sunk and cannot be recovered if the firm exits the industry. In the second stage of the game the firms choose prices, that is, they play a "Bertrand" game. The timing of such a game reflects the idea that the entry decision is a long-run decision whereas price decisions are short-run ones. The equilibrium concept for such a multi-stage game is the standard sub-game perfect Nash equilibrium and is found by first looking at the equilibrium of the last stage and then moving backwards (see Chapter 8). I focus on pure strategies.

To find the solution start from the price sub-game. Here there are three possible cases. First, both firms have entered in the previous stage. Because of price competition, they will earn zero gross profits. Second, only one firm has entered. Hence this firm earns the monopoly profit Π_M (which we assume to be larger than the fixed cost f) and the other firm zero profit. Third, no firm has entered the industry. Profits are zero for both. Once the solutions for the last stage of the game are found we can then pass to the first stage.

The payoff matrix at the first stage of the game is summarised in Table 2.1. Note that when both firms enter they incur a loss due to the fixed set-up cost. There exist two equilibria in pure strategies of the game. One (E, NE) where firm 1 enters and firm 2 does not, and the other (NE, E) where firm 2 enters while firm 1 does not. Consider first the pair (E, NE). For this to be an equilibrium, each firm must not have an incentive to deviate from it for the given strategy of the other player. If firm 1

---

[60] The milder product market competition the higher the number of firms that will enter at equilibrium. See d'Aspremont and Motta (2000) and Sutton (1991).

Table 2.1. The Entry Game

1 \ 2	E	NE
E	$-f, -f$	$\Pi_M - f, 0$
NE	$0, \Pi_M - f$	$0, 0$

deviates from the strategy "enter" given that firm 2 does not enter, it would attain a payoff $0 < \Pi_M - f$. The deviation is clearly unprofitable. The other possible deviation is that firm 2 chooses the strategy "enter" given firm 1's decision to enter. In this case, however, firm 2 would receive a payment $-f < 0$. It would be worse off with respect to the zero profit associated with the decision of not entering. This deviation is not profitable either. Therefore, the pair (E, NE) is an equilibrium. Since the game is perfectly symmetric, one finds that the pair (NE, E) is also an equilibrium.

No matter which firm ends up being the only producer, a monopolistic structure arises in the market. Despite free entry, the market outcome is a monopoly, and the monopolist does earn supra-competitive profits. This simple example shows that the anticipation of market competition might lead one firm not to enter the market even when entry is not restricted. The same argument is developed in what follows, in the context of a more sophisticated setting.

Finiteness Property in Vertical Differentiation Models* One of the most important recent contributions in oligopoly models is the work of Shaked and Sutton (1982, 1983, 1987). They analyse a *vertical product differentiation* model, that is a model where consumers agree on the ranking they give to products of different qualities. Whereas everybody agrees on the quality of the goods, differences in incomes exist which do not necessarily allow each consumer to buy the best products. Shaked and Sutton (1982, 1983) analyse a game where firms choose whether to enter the industry or not at the first stage, choose quality of the good at the second stage, and choose price at the third stage. They show that the number of firms which can co-exist in an industry described by the aforementioned characteristics is bounded above even when the size of the market tends to infinity. In the limit, if the distribution of incomes is narrow enough, only one firm will operate in the industry despite free entry and a number of potential firms. Also, the monopolist will earn supra-normal profits. This result is in sharp contrast with the standard homogenous good with Cournot competition and the *horizontal product differentiation* models (that is, models where consumers differ in their preferences over distinct varieties of the same product), where an increase in market size allows more firms to cover their fixed costs, leading to a more fragmented market structure.

The intuition for the finiteness property result, given in very loose terms, is as follows. Imagine that a new firm considers entry in an industry monopolised by a firm producing a good of quality u_1. If the new entrant chooses a quality $u_2 < u_1$, then it will have to offer the good at a lower price as well, since consumers have a preference for quality. However, competition would bring down the price of the high-quality good, making it more attractive to all the consumers. In the extreme case where people have similar enough incomes (or, equivalently, tastes for quality), all of them would continue to buy the top-quality good, despite the appearance of a new quality. Note also that given price competition in the market, firms would never choose a similar quality to the existing one, since this would increase competition in the marketplace. Producing identical qualities would make the goods homogenous, and the game at the last stage would be like the Bertrand one, with zero profit at equilibrium.

The new entrant might be able instead to enter with a higher quality than u_1, but in this case it would be the incumbent firm which would have to leave the market. From the point of view of the final result on welfare, it would not make any difference which firm stays in the market at equilibrium. However, it is unlikely that the entrant would be able to replace an incumbent, since the latter has a strategic first-mover advantage.[61]

The finiteness property result rests on many assumptions, of which the strongest may be the following: the costs of producing a higher quality fall on fixed costs such as R&D investments and advertising, rather than on variable costs such as better raw materials and more expensive high-skilled labour. If this assumption is relaxed, then the top-quality firm will have higher variable production costs than a low-quality firm, and this restricts its possibility to decrease prices. Under fixed costs of quality and identical marginal costs, a high-quality firm has a better ability to set prices which are as low as those set by a low-quality firm and steal the market share of the latter (recall that at identical prices everybody would buy the high-quality product). But under variable costs of quality, the top firm has higher marginal costs as well, and this reduces its ability to compete on prices. Therefore, the finiteness property does not hold when variable costs of quality are relatively more important than fixed costs of quality, as shown in Shaked and Sutton (1987).

Shaked and Sutton (1987) and Sutton (1991) reformulate the finiteness property result in a weaker but more robust version, in the sense that it holds across a number of specifications, and in particular when firms produce goods which are not only qualitatively different, but are also horizontally differentiated. According to this version, as the size of the market increases, a very large number of firms may survive in the industry, but there always exists at least one firm whose market share is significantly bounded away from zero (whereas in the homogenous good case, when the number of firms tends to infinity, their market share tends to zero).

---

[61] See Motta, Thisse and Cabrales (1997) for an analysis of a quality race between firms which start from different levels of quality. This paper shows that persistence of leadership is the likeliest outcome in this type of games.

Sutton (1991) puts the model to a test, and gathers impressive econometric, as well as case-study, evidence in favour of this result. In particular, the key role played by advertising expenditures (which allow the firms to increase the perceived quality of the product for the consumers) emerges clearly. In most of the sectors analysed (food and beverage industry), firms have been able to conquer large market shares by escalating advertising expenditures. When market size increases, advertising outlays of the firms tend to increase as well, since there exists an incentive to increase quality (the marginal cost of quality-enhancing spending is unchanged, but the marginal benefit is higher because of the larger market size). This increases the fixed sunk costs of the investments needed, and tends to limit the number of firms in the market. More precisely, new entrants might still enter the industry and manage to operate profitably, but they would have to rely on a low-price, low-quality strategy, which does not jeopardise the market positions of the incumbents.[62]

2.6.3.2 Switching Costs

Another situation where market power does not necessarily decrease under free entry arises when there exist consumer switching costs.[63] There are many reasons why consumers might prefer to stick to products already bought in the past, other things being equal. Switching to a new product (or a new supplier) might entail transaction costs (when one closes an account in a bank and opens another in a new bank, for instance) and learning costs (the cost of passing to a new software application, after having learned how to operate with a different one, for instance). Some of these switching costs might also be artificial or contractual, that is created on purpose by the firms in order to make it more difficult for consumers to pass to new products. Think of "frequent-flyer" programmes, for instance, that make travellers keener on continuing to use the services of the same airline: if after having accumulated miles with an airline, they switched to another, they would not reach the number of miles necessary to have a free flight. Another example of artificial switching cost is fees charged by banks to close an account.

In all these cases, the existence of switching costs effectively differentiates goods which would otherwise be perceived as perfectly identical. One might be perfectly indifferent, *before* opening a bank account, between two banks that charge similar rates and give similar services. However, *after* having opened an account at a particular bank, the existence of switching costs would make it worth changing banks only if the alternative bank will give much better rates or services. Products that are *ex ante* identical after a purchase become *ex post* differentiated.

---

[62] It should be emphasised that advertising expenditures are not an exogenous sunk cost but rather an endogenous variable for the firm. If they were exogenous sunk costs, namely exogenous barriers to entry, then market size increases would allow a larger number of firms in the industry and a more fragmented market structure. However, this occurrence is rejected by the data.

[63] For models with switching costs, see Klemperer (e.g., 1987a and 1987b). For surveys on this topic, see Klemperer (1995) and Padilla (1991).

When such switching costs exist, and one can realistically think that this is the case for many industries, new entrants generally have a harder time in getting market shares from the incumbents. Firms which have already developed a large base of customers will have a large advantage, since very important price cuts should be offered by new firms to attract committed customers. Again, free entry does not guarantee that market power will decrease.[64]

Switching costs might also allow incumbent firms to choose pre-entry prices and quantities so as to strategically deter entry in later periods. For instance, a firm that is a monopolist today might under-price in order to build a large customer base and make it more difficult for a potential entrant to enter the market tomorrow.[65]

The Competitiveness of Switching Cost Markets   Switching costs are not necessarily always as anti-competitive as they might appear at first sight. Suppose for instance that there are two firms which are both new entrants in an industry where consumers will have some kind of switching costs. In each period, the firms must simultaneously decide the prices to be charged in the market. Then the degree of competitiveness in each period will be very different. In the second period, each firm will have some captive customers: the consumers who have already bought from the firm in the first period will tend to buy from the same firm in the second period too (they are locked-in, at least partially). Therefore, we should expect their lower elasticity of demand with respect to price to be reflected in higher prices charged by the firms in the second period. Notice that the larger the first-period market share of a firm the larger the profit it will make in the second period.

In the first period, however, we should expect stronger competition than in a situation without switching costs. Since the first-period market share (or customer base) has a positive impact on the second-period profit, each firm will price more aggressively in the first period. Overall, therefore, it is not possible to conclude whether switching costs will result in higher or lower total welfare. In two-period models, the net effect on competitiveness due to switching costs is therefore ambiguous.

However, the presumption that switching costs decrease competition is reinforced by the analysis of models where firms interact not for only two but for many periods. Beggs and Klemperer (1992) examine a market where, in each period, firms must set prices, some new consumers arrive, some old consumers leave the market. They show – under relatively general assumptions – that in such a situation

---

[64] However, switching costs might sometimes make the incumbent firm less keen on fighting entry and more tempted instead to set high prices to exploit its customer base. In other words, prices might be higher relative to a situation where there are no switching costs, and this in turn makes entry more likely other things being equal.

[65] In some circumstances, for instance when tomorrow's demand is much larger than today's, a firm might instead want to overprice today, thereby committing to more aggressive behaviour tomorrow. See Klemperer (1987c) for an analysis of entry deterrence behaviour.

switching costs relax competition, that is, prices are higher than in markets without switching costs. Intuitively, there are two different effects at work when firms set prices in any current period. On the one hand, they would like to charge higher prices to exploit the current customer base. On the other hand, they would like to set lower prices to expand the future customer base (in order to be able to exploit it later). For several reasons one should expect the former effect to dominate. First, because today is more important than tomorrow, it is better to have higher profits today than tomorrow. Second, lower prices today are relatively ineffective in attracting consumers, since consumers would correctly anticipate that they will face higher prices tomorrow. Hence, it is unlikely that today's prices will be much lower to attract future customers.[66]

Conclusions Although an unqualified proposition is not possible, especially in the light of the various strategic effects that they bring into play, switching costs are generally detrimental to welfare, among other things because they make entry more difficult and markets less competitive. After a long and detailed review of switching costs and their effects, Klemperer (1995) arrives at the conclusion that

> public policy should discourage activities that increase consumer switching costs (such as airlines' frequent-flyer programmes), and encourage activities that reduce them (such as standardization that enhances compatibility and reduces learning costs of switching, and quality regulation and information sources that reduce consumer uncertainty about untested brands). (Klemperer, 1995: 536.)

It would be difficult to argue that competition authorities should systematically forbid firms from introducing contracts and practices which involve switching costs, among other reasons because some of these practices might have motivations other than the desire to reduce market competition. However, authorities should check that firm-created switching costs are not preventing competition in markets. When deregulating a previously monopolised sector, for instance, authorities should make sure that consumers are not locked-in by artificial switching costs (as when switching telephone providers would imply changing one's telephone number). When analysing mergers, authorities should use their bargaining power to reduce switching costs which are artificial and not motivated by any possible transaction cost savings.[67]

---

[66] Additionally, one should expect that in most situations prices will be "strategic complements" across periods. If a firm charges a higher price today, its rival will have a larger customer base today. Therefore, it will be more likely to charge higher prices tomorrow, since it will want to exploit its larger customer base. In turn, higher rival prices will make one firm's profit larger.

[67] In mergers of airlines, for instance, the European Commission is right in asking the merging companies to make smaller rival airlines also benefit from their frequent-flyer programmes. See for instance the *Lufthansa/SAS* decision.

2.6.3.3 Network Effects

Other industries where a monopoly might persist despite the absence of barriers to entry are those characterised by network effects. In such industries, consumers derive utility from the number of other consumers who choose the same product. If most consumers have already bought a given product, it will be difficult for new firms to attract demand.

Network effects are mainly of two types.[68] The first type is given by *physical,* or communications, networks. In this case, a consumer's utility in the consumption of a good increases *directly* with the number of other people consuming the same good. The prototypical example for such a network is telephones. One would not do much with a telephone if there were no other people with telephones with whom one could communicate. The larger the number of people in a given telephone network the more useful the telephone service. Fixed telephones, mobile telephones, fax, telefax, telex, and e-mail services clearly belong to the same category.[69] The second type is given by *virtual,* or hardware–software, networks. In this case, a consumer utility increases *indirectly* with the number of other consumers buying the same good because of its effects on the availability of a complementary product. Think for instance of a credit card network. As a card-holder, my utility is not directly affected by the number of other consumers using the same type of credit card. However, the larger the number of holders of the same credit card the more likely that shop-keepers will accept it. Similarly, a consumer's utility from a given computer hardware (or any type of durable good, be it a car, a washing machine, or a VCR) increases with the number of other buyers of the same computer (or durable good), since this will increase the likelihood that computer software for it will be developed (or spare parts, post-sales services, or video cassettes will be available).

In all these situations, consumers have to face coordination problems, since their choices are based on what other people will also do. In some cases, this might not be a problem. For instance, nobody will wonder today whether there will be enough people with whom to communicate by fixed-line phones or e-mail. But in other cases, when completely new networks/products are introduced, expectations about what other people will do are relevant. The development of a new generation of mobile phones might be hindered by doubts about how many other consumers will adopt them (and how quickly). Likewise, when a new firm launches a network with a different standard than the one currently used, a potential buyer has to guess the likelihood that this network will be successful, in order to avoid being locked in with a product

---

[68] The first articles on network effects were Katz and Shapiro (1985) and Farrell and Saloner (1985). For a survey, see for instance Katz and Shapiro (1994), and for a simple introduction to these topics, Shy (2001).

[69] But communication might not be necessary for a direct increase in utility. Think for instance of some fashion products, where the perceived value of wearing a certain type (or brand) of shoes or jacket or watch often depends on many other people also having the same product.

that gives her little possibility of communication (communications networks) or little software/services/complementary goods (hardware–software networks).

Therefore, expectations play a crucial role in network industries. Suppose for instance that a new type of mobile phone service were introduced by an entrant firm, whose standard is incompatible with existing mobile phones. Each prospective customer has to take a purchase decision on the basis of her expectations of other prospective customers. If all consumers have reasons to believe that millions of other people will rush to buy the new type of phones, all will buy. If none think that anybody would buy it, none will. Notice that here expectations will be self-fulfilling: in the first case, the service will be successfully established; in the second, it will not.[70]

These features of network effects explain why a potential entrant might find it very difficult to challenge an incumbent in these industries. It is not enough to have a better product, or to provide it at a lower price, since a crucial component of the utility of people is given by the number of (current and future) users of it. If the new product is not compatible with the established one, the firm has to convince prospective buyers that enough other buyers will buy it. The larger the number of consumers already locked in with the current standard the more difficult will be its task. The stronger the reputation of the new entrant and the more resources it commits to the new product the higher the chances that it will succeed. A number of strategies might be used to such purposes, from introductory price offers (or even giving away the product for free), to convincing firms selling complementary services (or spare parts, or software applications) to develop them.

However, incumbents can also adopt a number of strategies which might delay or completely deter new entrants. First of all, incumbents will want to make sure that the new products cannot be compatible with theirs (on compatibility and interoperability, see also Chapter 7). As long as a standard is proprietary, this strategy will be legal. However, the incumbent might also engage in anti-competitive practices. For instance, faced with an entrant which offers a product with new features, an incumbent might want to announce that soon it will introduce an upgrade of its product that incorporates these new features even if this is not true.[71] Likewise, it might advertise that the entrant is making very slow progress in building a customer base (or equivalently, that the incumbent's market share is high and growing). Such

---

[70] Satellite-based mobile phones failed to attract enough consumers, and the firm providing its services went bankrupt. GSM services in the US have developed very slowly (relative to Europe), among other reasons because of uncertainty on the winning standard. DIVX, a technology offering similar services as DVD, but based on a different standard, also failed in attracting enough customers and disappeared from the market. On the last case, see Dranove and Gandal (2000) for a description on how the uncertainty of consumers about the dominant standard can affect the evolution of the market.

[71] Product pre-announcements can strongly affect consumers' expectations, but it might be difficult to check to what extent they are false, since they refer after all to intentions and plans.

announcements will likely have an impact on the expectation of consumers about the viability of the entrant, and should therefore be carefully monitored by the anti-trust authorities, and promptly punished if false.[72]

Given that entry might be difficult under incompatible standards, another route that anti-trust authorities might pursue to avoid such problems is to force compatibility in the industry. For instance, they might impose on an incumbent full inter-operability with an entrant's products. However, this solution reminds us of the discussion on patents and essential facilities (see above). *Ex post* (that is, after a given standard is dominant), the imposition of inter-operability sounds beneficial because it allows more competition. However, *ex ante* (that is, before a given product appears on the market) it has an adverse effect on innovations, since it discourages firms from introducing new products and to fight for them to become the standard in the industry. Therefore, such measures do not appear convincing in general.[73]

A full analysis of the welfare effect of industries with network effects is beyond the scope of this section. Nevertheless, it is important to deal – albeit briefly – with the idea that such industries are particularly prone to dominance, and are therefore naturally associated with the existence of monopolies. The basic concept here is that of *market tipping*, which refers to the fact that when there are competing systems, once a system manages to gain a certain advantage in consumer preferences, then it might become more and more popular (think of the role of expectations discussed above: once consumers see that a product gains a large enough market share, then it is expected to become the industry's standard), and its rivals might fade out.

Market tipping is certainly an important phenomenon in network industries, but some qualifications should be made before jumping to general conclusions. First, there are many situations in which different standards might co-exist in a given industry. For examples of incompatible systems, think of different credit card and ATM networks,[74] or different brands of video games. In many cases, consumers do value variety and differentiated systems will survive in the same industry. Second, the existence of tipping and of the large profit that can be reaped once their own product is established as the industry's standard, will prompt firms to compete fiercely to win the "standards war". Intense promotional activities of various types, as well as aggressive pricing in the introductory periods, might characterise the initial stages of a given product life, as a firm attempts to increase market shares

---

[72] For a discussion of anti-competitive practices in network industries, see also Rubinfeld (1998).

[73] For a more thorough discussion of public policies about compatibility, and their possible effects on innovations, see Farrell and Katz (1998). An issue they also discuss is that interfaces that do not involve many innovation efforts should not receive protection. For instance, imposing *number portability* to telephone companies rightly ensures that the interface "telephone number" is not protected (assigning telephone numbers to consumers is certainly not worth protection).

[74] In some countries, there exist different networks of Automatic Teller Machines.

so as to gain the edge it needs to make the market tip.[75] As a result, it might well be that the large profit made by a firm after its product has become the dominant standard might just cover the cost incurred during the standards war.[76] Third, the existence of only one network in the market might even benefit consumers, to the extent that they will be able to enjoy more communication possibilities or more complementary services, whereas under competing networks they will not be able to.

Likewise, the difficulties faced by entrants in markets which exhibit important network effects should not be generalised to imply that all these markets will naturally show "excess inertia" (or persistence of dominance). As Katz and Shapiro (1994: 108) note, examples of entrants which manage to establish a product incompatible with previous standards abound in the real world. Further, from the welfare point of view, it is not even clear that entry – if it occurs – would always be beneficial. Suppose for instance that – due to consumers' expectations, perhaps helped by the reputation of the entrant – a new standard which does not offer advantages over the previous one affirms itself in the industry. This will lead to "stranding" of the buyers who have locked themselves into the old technology: their purchases will rapidly become obsolete, and duplication of purchases will have to follow.

2.6.3.4 A Model of (Physical) Networks*

In this section, I present a simple model of physical (communications) networks proposed by Fumagalli, Karlinger and Motta (2003), to illustrate the coordination problems that arise for consumers when network externalities exist, and show that this might result in the entrant staying out of the industry even when it is a more efficient producer.[77]

Following Katz and Shapiro (1985), assume that consumers value a network good i as follows:

$$U_i = r + v_i(n) - p_i, \tag{2.23}$$

where r is the intrinsic value of the good in the absence of network effects, $v_i(n)$ is the valuation for the good (n consumers join network i), and p_i is the price a

---

[75] Rey, Seabright and Tirole (2001) stress a "topsy-turvy" principle of competition. The higher the profits to be made in a market the stronger the competition to obtain them. This should hold in industries with network effects, switching cost, lock-in effects, economies of scale, and generally all situations where the "winner takes all".

[76] This reminds us of the analysis of the competitiveness of markets with consumer switching costs. Indeed, switching costs and network industries share a number of similar features, as stressed in Farrell and Klemperer (2001).

[77] Fumagalli et al. (2003) develop the model to analyse how the incumbent and the entrant might resort to different strategic variables so as to make consumers coordinate on (respectively) an exclusionary or an entry equilibrium.

consumer has to pay to join network i. For simplicity, assume that $r = 0$, so that the network good has value only for its "network" component.

Assume that $v_i(n)$ is non-decreasing and concave, but that after a certain number of consumers z the network exhausts its positive externalities. In other words, $v_i(z) = v_i(z+j)$ for all $j > 0$. (The reason behind this assumption will be explained shortly.) Assume also that $v_i(1) = 0$: there is no value from buying a network product of which one is the only consumer.

In the market for this network good, there is an incumbent, I, and a potential entrant, E. The entrant is more efficient and can produce at a cost $c_E < c_I$. The two networks are homogenous in the sense that if they are of the same size, they create the same externality for their consumers: $v_I(\cdot) = v_E(\cdot) = v(\cdot)$. Assume also that the entrant has an arbitrarily small fixed cost of entry, ε, to underline that entry barriers come only from network effects.[78]

There are two groups of consumers, each of size z. The first group of ("old") consumers have already bought the incumbent's product in the past, and enjoy a utility $v(z)$. The second group of ("new") consumers is on the market now.

Note that the assumption that the incumbent has already served z consumers in the past has a two-fold role. First, it implies that new consumers, should they join the incumbent's network, do not have any externality on the z old consumers; second, it implies that the asymmetry between the incumbent and the entrant is maximal, since the incumbent has already reached the highest possible externality level.

The game is as follows.

1. E decides whether to enter or not.
2. Active firms set prices simultaneously. Assume for the time being that prices must be the same for all customers.
3. Buyers decide which network to join, and pay either p_I or p_E.

Two Types of Equilibrium   There exist two very different types of equilibrium in this game. The first type is an "entry" equilibrium, where the entrant enters and all new consumers join its network. The second type is an inefficient "persistence of monopoly" equilibrium, where consumers fail to coordinate on the outcome that would be more efficient. Let me characterise and prove the existence of each equilibrium as follows.

Entry Equilibrium   Consider the following entry equilibrium:[79] E enters, I sets a price c_I and E a price a shade below c_I, and all z new consumers join the entrant's network.

---

[78] Note that here networks are incompatible: there exist network externalities only among consumers who buy from the same network. See Chapter 7 for a model where inter-operability (or compatibility) is an endogenous choice of firms.

[79] There might also exist other equilibria of the same type.

To see why this is an equilibrium, consider consumers first. At this equilibrium, they have a surplus $v(z) - c_I$. If one of them deviated and bought I's product, when all others are joining E's network, it would get a utility $v(z) - c_I$. Therefore, it has no incentive to deviate.

Firms have no incentives to deviate, either. Firm I would have no incentive to decrease its price given that, should it get consumers, it would experience losses. Firm E would not have an incentive to increase its price because otherwise customers would switch to the incumbent.

Persistence of Monopoly (or Mis-coordination) Equilibrium   An equilibrium with mis-coordination is as follows: E does not enter, I sets a price $p_I = v(z)$, thereby extracting all surplus from consumers, and all z new consumers join I's network.

To see why this is an equilibrium of the game, consider the case where the entrant has entered and has offered a price which might be as low as c_E. It is easy to see that everybody buying from the incumbent is still a Nash equilibrium at the consumers' stage of the game. At the proposed equilibrium, all consumers buy the incumbent's product, and have surplus 0. However, if any of them deviated and bought from E, given that all others buy from I, it would receive utility $v(1) - c_E = -c_E$. Therefore, it would worsen its position.

As for the firms, at this equilibrium I has no incentive to change its price (it is earning monopoly profits), and E has no incentive to deviate, as by entering it would not be able to recover its fixed cost, however small.

This is clearly a mis-coordination equilibrium, in the sense that consumers are unable to coordinate on the outcome that is more convenient for them. Were they able to coordinate and decide together, the only equilibrium of the game would be the one where entry occurs. (I shall come back to mis-coordination problems in Chapter 3, when discussing buyers' power, and in Chapter 6, when discussing exclusive dealing as an entry deterrence device.) On the other hand, the incumbent might also resort to strategies that allow it to exclude entry, as I now show.

Price Discrimination to Exclude Entry in a Network Industry   Assume now that the incumbent can price discriminate among new consumers, and that its costs are not too high, that is, $2c_I < v(2) + c_E$. For simplicity, set $z = 2$, and call the new consumers 1 and 2. I now show that even if the entrant entered and offered its network product at a price c_E, it would not get any demand if the incumbent is able to price discriminate.[80] Therefore, the only equilibrium of the game is the one with persistence of monopoly.

If the entrant sets a price c_E, and the incumbent sets prices p_1 and p_2, consumers' payoffs will be as in Table 2.2. An entry equilibrium, which corresponds to the pair (buy E, buy E), does not exist any longer. If both consumers bought from the entrant,

---

[80] The incumbent would be able to deter entry also if consumers bought sequentially. See also Chapter 6 for an exclusive dealing model, which exhibits very similar features.

Table 2.2. Consumers 1 and 2's Payoffs under
Price Discrimination

1 \ 2	buy I	buy E
buy I	$v(2) - p_1, v(2) - p_2$	$v(2) - p_1, -c_E$
buy E	$-c_E, v(2) - p_2$	$v(2) - c_E, v(2) - c_E$

the incumbent might deviate and offer a price $p_1 < c_E$ to one buyer, say consumer 1, and a price $p_2 = v(2)$ to the other consumer. Consumer 1 would decide to buy from I, whatever the other consumer does. If consumer 2 bought from E, consumer 1 would get surplus $v(2) - p_1$ buying from I, and $v(2) - c_E$ buying from E. Since $p_1 < c_E$, the former is higher. If consumer 2 bought from I, consumer 1 would get surplus $v(2) - p_1$ buying from I, and $-c_E$ buying from E. Also in this case he is better off buying from I. Given that consumer 1 would buy from I, consumer 2 could not do better than buying from I ($v(2) - p_2 = 0 > -c_E$). Thus, the incumbent's deviation would be followed by both consumers buying from it.

But is it profitable for the incumbent to deviate and deter entry? Clearly, it would not be profitable if it had to offer a price below cost to each buyer. However, under price discrimination, it can offer a price below cost to only one buyer, while setting the monopoly price to the other. If total revenues are higher than total costs ($v(2) + p_1 \geq 2c_I$) the deviation would be profitable. Since by assumption $v(2) + c_E > 2c_I$, if both buyers decide to buy from E, the incumbent would have an incentive to deviate and an entry equilibrium could not exist.

Instead, equilibria with persistence of monopoly still exist. The argument is the same as before. For instance, if the incumbent sets prices $p_1 = p_2 = v(2)$, both consumers buying from it form a Nash equilibrium. Since $0 > -c_E$, no consumer has incentive to deviate.

2.6.3.5 Exclusionary Practices

As we have seen, free entry does not guarantee that an industry structure will become less concentrated over time. In markets characterised by endogenous sunk costs, consumer switching costs or network effects, for instance, entrants will often find it difficult to challenge successfully incumbents, even if the latter do not behave strategically.

When incumbents behave strategically, things turn even more difficult for entrants. A monopolist (or more generally a firm with large market power) might engage in many different practices aimed at deterring entrants. Investing in extra capacity, setting prices below cost, flooding a market with many different product specifications, foreclosing access of rivals to crucial inputs, bundling, price discriminating, and tying are all possible examples of strategies that can prevent entry. The analysis of exclusionary practices is delayed until Chapter 7, but it is worth recalling here that competition authorities should be vigilant and promptly intervene whenever monopolists impede entry through practices whose profitability derives only from their ability to keep entrants off the market. This is an important issue, as well as a difficult one, since in most cases it is hard to tell genuine competitive strategies from predatory ones.

2.7 SUMMARY AND POLICY CONCLUSIONS

This chapter has illustrated the relationship between market power and welfare. The analysis of allocative efficiency has shown that market power brings about a welfare loss, due to higher prices than in a competitive situation. Productive and dynamic inefficiencies (higher production costs and lower innovation rates) might also be associated with market power. This explains why competition policy should be concerned with market power.

However, I have also argued that the elimination of market power – even if it were practicable – is not one of the objectives competition policy agencies should pursue. Indeed, the prospect of having some market power (i.e., some profit) represents a most powerful incentive for firms to innovate and invest. Competition laws and their enforcement should therefore ensure that firms will be able to enjoy the rewards for their investments. I have therefore argued that any expropriation of firms' assets (whether material or immaterial) should be avoided. As a consequence, resorting to the doctrine of essential facilities (granting access of crucial assets to competitors), to price controls, or even more drastic structural remedies must be carried out only in truly exceptional circumstances.

I have also tackled other misconceptions of competition policy. In particular, I have underlined that defending competition is not tantamount to defending competitors. Indeed, competition often leads inefficient firms to exit, and this is beneficial from a welfare point of view. Protecting inefficient firms so as to prolong their life artificially in an industry would be detrimental from a welfare perspective.

Finally, market forces alone will not "fix it all": for several reasons, very often incumbent firms are able to keep and reinforce their market power. Competition policy must be vigilant, and guarantee an environment where potential and actual competitors are able to challenge firms enjoying a position of large market power.

2.8 EXERCISES

Exercise 2.1 *An example of rent-seeking.[81] Consider a market where a total profit Π can be earned by the firm which obtains the monopoly right to sell in that market. Suppose that there exist n identical firms, which participate in the competition to

[81] I am grateful to Joe Harrington for suggesting this formalisation.

obtain this monopoly right. Each firm i has to simultaneously decide the amount x_i it wants to spend, knowing that the probability to win the race is given by $x_i / \sum_{j=1}^{n} x_j$. (a) Find the symmetric equilibrium level of expenditure of each firm, and the expected equilibrium profit of each firm. (b) Show that as n tends to infinity, the total expenditures made by the firms equal the total monopoly profit.

Exercise 2.2 By making use of graphs, identify the welfare loss occurring in a market where the price is higher than the marginal cost of production, and then discuss how this loss could be higher due to possible rent-seeking activities and productive inefficiency.

Exercise 2.3 Explain why there is a possible tension between allocative efficiency on the one hand and productive and dynamic efficiency on the other hand.

Exercise 2.4 *Inspired by d'Aspremont and Motta (1990). Consider a homogenous good industry with two potential firms. Market demand is given by $Q = S(1 - p)$, where S is market size and Q is industry output. Firms have zero constant marginal costs but incur a fixed cost $k \in (0, S/9)$ if they are active. The game they play is as follows. First, they decide whether to enter or not. Then, they compete in the product market. Consider three different cases of product competition: (i) firms non-co-operatively choose quantities (Cournot); (ii) firms non-co-operatively choose prices (Bertrand); (iii) a cartel is allowed: firms set quantities (or prices, it is equivalent) so as to jointly maximise their profits (monopoly). Focus on pure strategies and find (sub-game perfect Nash) equilibrium quantities, prices, profits, consumer surplus and welfare for each of the three cases above. Show that for low enough fixed costs Cournot competition gives rise to higher welfare than Bertrand competition, and that monopoly always gives the lowest welfare level at equilibrium.

Exercise 2.5 *Consider the same example as in Section 2.4.3.1, but assume that there is a drastic innovation, that is the reduction in marginal cost is large enough: $x > 1 - c^h$. Compare the equilibrium under duopoly with the one obtained above under monopoly.

Exercise 2.6 **Consider a variant of the model dealt with in Section 2.4.3.1 where the amount of innovation is continuous and endogenously determined rather than exogenously given. The cost of innovation is not constant, but is a quadratic function of the amount of innovation made. More explicitly, a firm faces an investment cost $C(x_i) = x_i^2$. By investing x_i^2 in innovation (such an investment still occurs in the first stage and it is therefore sunk in the second stage), a firm will have marginal cost $c^h - x_i$ in the following price sub-game. Apart from this variant, consider the same set of assumptions as above. (1) Find the optimal amount of investment x_m for a monopolist. (2) Find the equilibrium amount of investment in the duopoly. Does it correspond to a drastic or non-drastic innovation? Is the equilibrium investment bigger or smaller than x_m?

Exercise 2.7 Why should one expect an inverted U relationship between competition and innovation?

Exercise 2.8 **Consider a homogenous good industry with perfectly symmetric firms. The firms play the following game. In the first stage, they simultaneously decide whether they enter the industry or not. In the second, they simultaneously decide on the quantity to bring to the market. If they enter, they have to incur a fixed set-up cost F. Production occurs at a constant marginal cost c. Market demand is characterised by $p = 1 - Q$, p being the market price and Q the aggregate output. (a) Find the number of firms n that would enter at the sub-game perfect Nash equilibrium. (For simplicity, consider n as continuous in the whole exercise.) (b) Consider now the following game. In the first stage, a social planner decides the number of firms (and pays the fixed costs of firms). The social planner maximises welfare, as given by the sum of consumer surplus and producer surplus minus the entry costs it has to pay. In the second stage, the same quantity competition game as above is played. Find the optimal number of firms chosen by the social planner and compare it with the number of firms that would enter at the sub-game perfect Nash equilibrium.

Exercise 2.9 **Consider the model analysed in Section 2.4.3.2. Assume that a social planner maximises total welfare taking the number of firms n as given. First the social planner has to choose R&D levels, and then output. Find the (symmetric) optimal levels of R&D and output, and compare them with the equilibrium levels obtained in the model of Section 2.4.3.2.

Exercise 2.10 *Consider the same model as in Section 2.4.3.2 but assume that the n firms jointly determine their output levels: in the first stage of the game, each firm independently sets its R&D level; in the second stage, the firms act as a cartel, that is they choose their output levels so as to maximise joint profits. Find the equilibrium levels of R&D and output and compare them with those obtained in the model of Section 2.4.3.2.

Exercise 2.11 Industrial organisation models suggest that – left alone – market forces will result in any given industry in equilibrium levels of quality, variety, innovation, or number of competitors that are different from the optimal levels for society (that is, from the levels of quality, variety, innovation or number of firms that would maximise economic welfare). This is because firms take their decisions on the basis of their profits, not taking into account the externality that such decisions exercise over competitors, or over consumers. What are the possible practical implications of this result? Can competition authorities try to move each industry towards the optimal outcome?

Exercise 2.12 In a country, the fixed telephone market has just been deregulated and new entrants are allowed to challenge the incumbent monopolist telecom operator. Soon, the entrants discover that it is very difficult to persuade customers to switch operators, because they do not want to change their telephone number, over which the incumbent claims intellectual property rights. Should the Court decide in favour of the incumbent (in which case, customers who patronise the new operators should change telephone number) or the entrants?

Exercise 2.13   *(Loosely inspired by the Bronner case)* The leading national newspaper in the country has established a system of home delivery services that allows it to distribute copies of the newspaper in the early morning all over the country. A regional newspaper has decided to sell over the whole national territory, and accordingly increases coverage of news from local to national. However, it discovers that the lack of a home delivery distribution makes it difficult to increase national sales, and that building such a distribution system is too expensive and risky. It asks the leading newspaper to grant it access to its home delivery distribution system against a fair compensation, but the latter refuses. Should the Court decide in favour of the national newspaper or the local one?

Exercise 2.14   **Leasing v. selling (From Tirole, 1988, Section 1.5.2.1) Consider a two-period game where a monopolistic firm wants to sell its durable good. The durable good will last only two periods, and after that it will become obsolete. There is no depreciation of the good between the two periods. The discount factor δ is identical for all consumers and the firm. Demand for the utilisation of the good will be given by $p = 1 - Q$ (Q being aggregate quantity). Production is assumed to be costless. A resale market exists: consumers who buy the good in one period might want to re-sell (or lease) it in the second period.

1. Consider first the case where the firm sells in each period. Find the equilibrium prices charged by the monopolist in each period, and show that they decline over time. Find the total equilibrium profit.

2. Consider then the case where the monopolist leases (rents) the good in each period, and find equilibrium prices and profits. Are they higher or lower than the profit made under sales?

Exercise 2.15   Vertical product differentiation models suggest that high concentration might arise in markets characterised by endogenous sunk costs such as, for instance, advertising outlays. In such markets, firms investing heavily in advertising typically have larger market shares, charge higher prices and get higher profits than their rivals. Their leadership also tends to persist over time. What policy implications should we derive from such models?

Exercise 2.16   ** *(From Klemperer, 1988: Welfare effects of entry)* Consider the following two-stage game between an incumbent firm and a potential entrant. In the first stage, the entrant decides whether to enter or not. Entry is costless. In the second stage, existing firms in the market (simultaneously) choose the quantity to be sold. Firms have the same constant unit cost c. Consumers who buy the entrant's product will have to incur a switching cost s. (For simplicity, assume that there is no switching cost when buying from the incumbent.) Assume that there is linear demand $p = \alpha - \beta q$ (in other words, this is the qth consumer reservation price net of switching costs).

1. Find the equilibrium output and prices for the game according to the different levels of switching costs s.

2. Is it possible that entry diminishes welfare?

3. Consider the case where the switching cost is zero. Would welfare be higher or lower than under positive switching costs?

Exercise 2.17 ** (*Examples 0 and 1 in Klemperer, 1995.*) Consider the following two-stage game. Assume that there are N consumers who are distributed along a line $[0, 1]$ which measures their (linear) cost of learning how to use a (homogenous) product. Firms A and B sell the same product but are located at 0 and 1 respectively, and have the same unit cost $c = 0$ in each period. Therefore, a consumer located at point y has a learning cost ty of using firm A's product and $t(1 - y)$ of using B's product ($t > 0$). Consumers do not have any physical transport cost. At period 1, consumer utility is given by $U = r - p_i - t \, |l_i - y|$, for $i = A, B$, where l_i stands for the location of firm i. Assume also that goods cannot be stored and consumers have the same discount factor $\delta = 1$. At period 2, each consumer has a reservation price R to buy the good. Goods are perceived as perfectly homogenous, but there are switching costs: if one changes provider, one has to pay a cost s, which for simplicity is assumed to be independent of the distance which separates the consumer from the firm. Firms set simultaneously prices in each period. Assume also $R > c$; $s \geq R - c$; $r - 2t > c$.

1. Find the equilibrium prices of each period of the game.

2. Find the equilibrium price for the game where the first period is like the above, but in the second period there are no switching costs at all. Show that under switching costs prices are higher in the second period but lower in the first period.

Exercise 2.18 *Monopoly threatened by entry. (From Tirole, 1988: Section 10.1.4) Consider the case of two firms in an output market. There is also a third firm which cannot produce in this output market but has generated an innovation which can lower the unit production cost from $\bar{c}$ to $\underline{c} < \bar{c}$ (process innovation). This third firm puts this innovation up for bidding between the two producing firms and the innovation is protected by a patent of unlimited duration. Before the bidding process takes place, firm 1 is a monopolist and produces at unit cost $\bar{c}$. Firm 1's profit at this status quo market structure is denoted by $\Pi^m (\bar{c})$. Firm 2 is a potential entrant whose unit cost is infinite. Let $\Pi^d (\bar{c}, \underline{c})$ and $\Pi^d (\underline{c}, \bar{c})$ denote the profits for the monopolist and the entrant, respectively, if the entrant alone adopts the new technology with marginal cost $\underline{c}$ and, consequently, the monopolist's marginal cost is still $\bar{c}$.

1. Find the value of the innovation (i.e., the difference between the profits a firm earns if it is the one that wins the bidding competition for the innovation and the profits it earns in case it does not win the bidding competition) for the monopolist (V^1) and for the entrant (V^2).

2. Show that $\Pi^m\left(\underline{c}\right) \geq \Pi^d\left(\bar{c}, \underline{c}\right) + \Pi^d\left(\underline{c}, \bar{c}\right)$ is a sufficient condition for $V^1 \geq V^2$.

3. Consider the case in which the innovation is drastic, $p^m\left(\underline{c}\right) < \bar{c}$. If this is the case, what is the value of the innovation for firms 1 and 2?

2.8.1 Solutions to Exercises

Exercise 2.1   The expected profit of a firm i is given by $\pi_i = \left(x_i / \sum_{j=1}^{n} x_j\right) \Pi - x_i$. The FOCs are therefore given by the system of equations $\partial \pi_i / \partial x_i = \left(\sum_{k \neq i}^{n} x_k\right) \Pi / \left(\sum_{j=1}^{n} x_j\right)^2 - 1 = 0$. (a) At the symmetric equilibrium $\forall i \in \{1, \ldots, n\}$, $x_i = x$, each firm spends $x^* = (n-1)\Pi / \left(n^2\right)$. By substitution, one can find that the expected equilibrium profit is $\pi^* = \Pi / \left(n^2\right)$. (The second-order conditions for a maximum are satisfied.) (b) Total expenditure nx^* to obtain the monopoly rent Π is given by $(n-1)\Pi / (n)$, which tends to Π as $n \to \infty$.

Exercise 2.4   (i) (Cournot) To analyse the case of quantity competition, first find the inverse demand function, which is $p = 1 - Q/S$. A firm i chooses q_i to maximise $\pi_i = [1 - (q_i + q_j)/S]q_i - k$. The FOCs are $\partial \pi_i / \partial q_i = 1 - 2q_i/S - q_j/S = 0$. At the symmetric equilibrium $q_i = q_j = q$ the solution will be given by $q^C = S/3$. Equilibrium prices and individual profits will be $p^C = 1/3$ and $\pi^C = S/9 - k > 0$. It is easy to find consumer surplus and total welfare as $CS^C = 2S/9$ and $W^C = 4S/9 - 2k$.

(ii) (Bertrand) Given that products are homogenous, competition would bring about zero (short-run) profits, which would not allow both firms to cover fixed costs. Therefore at the (long-run) equilibrium in pure strategies only one firm will be active in this market. This firm will choose Q so as to maximise $\pi = Q(1 - Q/S) - k$. From $\partial \pi / \partial Q = 0$ it follows that equilibrium output, price and profits will be $Q^B = S/2$, $p^B = 1/2$ and $\pi^B = S/4 - k > 0$. Consumer surplus and total welfare are $CS^B = S/8$ and $W^B = 3S/8 - k$.

(iii) (Monopoly or cartel) Firms will set outputs q_1 and q_2 so as to maximise the joint profits $\pi_1 + \pi_2 = [1 - (q_1 + q_2)/S](q_1 + q_2) - 2k$. Clearly, this gives rise to the same solution as in the Bertrand case but with a duplication in the fixed costs. Consumer surplus and total welfare are $CS^M = S/8$ and $W^M = 3S/8 - 2k$.

The welfare comparisons are straightforward. If $k \in (0, 5S/72]$, then $W^C \geq W^B$. If $k \in (5S/72, S/9)$, then $W^C < W^B$. It is enough to inspect W^C, W^B, W^M to see that W^M is always the lowest.

Exercise 2.5   Assume $x > 1 - c^h$. Then at the last (price) stage of the game, the innovating firm will be better off by charging the monopoly price $(1 + c^h - x)/2 < c^h$. It will earn gross profit $\Pi_d = (1 - c^h + x)^2/4$.

At the first stage of the game firms correctly anticipate the profit they would make in the following stage. Firms' payoffs are as follows. If both firms innovate, they will both get $-F$. If none innovate, they will both get 0. If only one firm innovates, the innovating firm will get $\Pi_d - F$ and the other firm 0. This game has the following solutions: if $\Pi_d > F$ the only Nash equilibrium is one where one firm innovates and the other does not. If $\Pi_d \leq F$, then no firm will innovate at the equilibrium.

Comparison between monopoly and duopoly

Either market structure makes no difference (innovations occur under both market structures, or do not occur under either), or an equilibrium with innovation occurs under duopoly but not under monopoly. To see why, consider that $\Pi_d > \Delta$ as $(1 - c^h + x)^2/4 > (1 - c^h + x)^2/4 - (1 - c^h)^2/4$. Therefore, for values of fixed cost of innovation such that $\Pi_d > F > x \left(x + 2 \left(1 - c^h \right) \right)/4$, there will be an innovation under duopoly but not under monopoly. For values of fixed cost such that $F \leq x \left(x + 2 \left(1 - c^h \right) \right)/4$, an innovation will occur in both market structures. Finally, for $F \geq \Pi_d$, no innovation will be adopted, independently of market structure.

Exercise 2.6   (1) The monopolist will earn profit $\Pi_m(x) = (1 - c^h + x)^2/4$ in the last stage. Therefore, its optimal investment will be determined by finding the value x_m which maximises $\pi_m(x) = (1 - c^h + x)^2/4 - x^2$. It is easy to check that $x_m = (1 - c^h)/3$.

(2) In the case of duopoly the analysis is similar to the one carried out for exogenous levels of R&D. In particular, there will be only one equilibrium where one firm innovates and the other does not. However, here we also have to determine whether the optimal investment corresponds to a drastic or non-drastic innovation. Therefore, we have to compute the profit made for the optimal drastic innovation and compare it with the profit made for the optimal non-drastic innovation. For a drastic innovation, the domain is $x \in \left[1 - c^h, c^h \right]$. The problem is then the same as the monopolist's. The profit function reaches a maximum at $x = (1 - c^h)/3$ and then decreases. However, the maximum is not in the domain, and therefore the maximum under a drastic innovation is attained at $x = (1 - c^h)$. In the case of a non-drastic innovation, the optimal amount of R&D x_{nd} is given by the maximisation of the profit function $\Pi_{nd} = x(1 - c^h) - x^2$. Therefore $x_{nd} = (1 - c^h)/2$. It is easy to check that a non-drastic innovation gives a higher profit to the innovating

firm, and that the equilibrium level of R&D under duopoly is larger than under monopoly.

Exercise 2.8   (a) Since the equilibrium has to be found by backward induction, first solve the last stage of the game, where firms choose quantities given the number of firms that have entered the market in the previous stage. This problem has already been solved in Section 2.3.5.2.

Since n is a real number, the equilibrium number of firms in the industry will be given by the solution of $\pi^c(n) = 0$, which is given by $n^c = (1 - c)/\sqrt{F} - 1$.[82]

(b) The social planner will choose n to maximise total welfare $W = CS + PS = n(1 - c)^2(n + 2)/[2(n + 1)^2] - nF$, leading to $n^* = \sqrt[3]{(1 - c)^2/F} - 1$.[83]

By comparing the optimal number of firms n^* with the number of firms entering at the free entry equilibrium, n^c, it is clear that there exists excess of entry in the industry.[84]

Exercise 2.9   Welfare can be written as $W(q(x), x) = (a - p)nq/2 + n(pq - (C - x)q - (g/2)x^2)$. Given x, the efficient output will be found by taking $\partial W/\partial q = 0$. It can be seen that this gives the per-firm output $q^{sP}(x) = (a - C + x)/n$. Note that at the first-best firms make zero gross profit, since they set prices equal to marginal cost ($p = C - x$). The social planner must cover firms' R&D fixed outlays by using subsidies.

It is now possible to replace this in the previous expression so as to obtain $W(x)$. By solving the FOCs one gets the individual firm's efficient R&D level as $x^{sP} = (a - C)/(gn - 1)$, which is the socially optimum level of R&D in the industry.

We can now compare the optimal R&D levels with those which arise from competition. It can be checked that the inequality $x^{sP} < x^c$ is satisfied for $n^2 - 2n - 1 > 0$. Hence, when the number of firms is small ($n = 1$ or $n = 2$), then the market produces too little R&D. When the number of firms is larger ($n = 3, 4, \ldots$), then there is too much R&D as compared to the social optimum.

Exercise 2.10   Let us start from the last stage of the game. The case of a cartel among the n firms is equivalent to the case of a monopoly, as the n firms behave as if they were a single firm. In this case, the total quantity sold in the industry is $Q = (a - C + x)/2$ and the joint profit is $\Pi = (a - C + x)^2/4 - gx^2/2$.

---

[82] If n were to be treated as a discrete number, the equilibrium number of firms in the industry would be given by the value of n which solves $\pi^c(n) \geq 0$ and $\pi^c(n + 1) < 0$. This would make calculations slightly less simple but would not change the qualitative results.

[83] The formulation proposed here is inspired by Tirole (1988: 466, Exercise 24). He also points out that at the first-best the social planner makes only one firm produce and sell at $p = c$.

[84] The result that free entry gives rise to a number of firms which is larger than the socially optimum number is not robust. In general, the market equilibrium under free entry might involve either too many or too few firms. See also Tirole (1988: ch. 7).

The first-order condition is given by $(\partial \pi_i / \partial x_i)|_{x_i = x} = (a - C + x)/2 - gx = 0$, which corresponds, for $n = 1$, to the expression we obtained in the case of competition in Section 2.4.3.2 (note that the competition effect term is absent here). Solving the FOCs will give the per-firm individual R&D level $x^m = (a - C)/(n(2g - 1))$.

The total R&D carried out in the industry will be $R^m = (a - C)/(2g - 1)$. This coincides with $R^c(n = 1)$. Since R^c is increasing with n, it follows that there will always be more R&D under competition than under a cartel. It can also be checked that under a cartel there is always less R&D than at the efficient (social planner) level.

One could also compare welfare levels. Welfare under a monopoly (or cartel) coincides with the expression $W^c(n = 1)$: $W^m = (a - C)^2 g(3g - 1)/(2[2g - 1]^2)$.

I showed in Section 2.4.3.2 that the lowest level attained by welfare under competition corresponds to the limit case where $n \to \infty$, where W^c tends to $(a - C)^2/2$. It can be shown that for $g > 4$ (which satisfies both second order and stability conditions) W^m is always lower than W^c.

Exercise 2.14

1. If the monopolist decides to sell, the quantity sold during period 1 is re-offered in period 2 (remember a resale market exists). Hence, a monopolist who has produced q_1 in period 1 will sell in period 2 the quantity which maximises its profit, $\max_{q_2} q_2 (1 - q_1 - q_2)$. Notice that the price of the good at period 2, p_2, is the one for which the total quantity produced in *both* periods ($q_1 + q_2$) is equal to the quantity demanded, $p_2 = 1 - q_1 - q_2$. Simple algebra shows that $q_2 = (1 - q_1)/2$, $p_2 = (1 - q_1)/2$ and $\Pi_2 = (1 - q_1)^2/4$. Now, at stage 1, the price consumers will be willing to pay for the good will obviously depend on their expectations of p_2. Assume that $E(p_2) = p_2$. Hence, consumer willingness to pay is given by $p_1 = (1 - q_1) + \delta p_2$, the current value of the good plus what resale would give in discounted terms. But, since $p_2 = (1 - q_1)/2$, by substitution one has that $p_1 = (1 - q_1)(1 + \frac{\delta}{2})$. Notice that $p_1 > p_2$. When the monopolist sells in each period, prices fall over time. The monopolist then chooses q_1 so as to maximize its present value of (selling) profits Π_s, that is $\max_{q_1} [q_1 (1 - q_1)(1 + \delta/2) + \delta(1 - q_1)^2/4]$. Some algebra shows that $q_1 = 2/(4 + \delta)$, $p_1 = (2 + \delta)^2/2(4 + \delta)$ and $\Pi_s = (2 + \delta)^2/4(4 + \delta)$.

2. If, instead, the monopolist decides to lease, then at each period of time t, $t = 1, 2$, it sets a price such that $\max_{p_t} p_t(1 - p_t)$. This implies that $p_1 = p_2 = 1/2$. Then, it produces $q_1 = 1/2$ and $q_2 = 0$, since it was assumed that there is no depreciation. The present value of its (leasing) profits is given by $\Pi_l = 1/4 + \delta(1/4) = (1 + \delta)/4$. As can be easily checked, $\Pi_l > \Pi_s$, the monopolist prefers leasing.

Exercise 2.16

1. At the second stage of the game, if there is entry then the incumbent's (I) and the entrant's (E) prices will respectively be $p_I = \alpha - \beta(q_I + q_E)$ and $p_E = p_I - s$. Note that here we are using the simplifying assumption that no switching costs of buying from the incumbent exist.[85] If there is no entry, the monopolist will set $q_M = (\alpha - c)/2\beta$ and $p_M = (\alpha + c)/2$. The associated welfare will be $W_M = 3(\alpha - c)^2/8\beta$. If there is entry, then $q_I = (\alpha - c + s)/3\beta$, $q_E = (\alpha - c - 2s)/3\beta$ and $p_I = (\alpha + 2c + s)/3$, $p_E = (\alpha + 2c - 2s)/3$. Associated welfare will be $W_E = (8(\alpha - c)^2 + 11s^2 - 8s(\alpha - c))/18\beta$. At the first stage of the game, entry will be chosen only if $s \leq (\alpha - c)/2$.[86] Indeed, for entry to be profitable it must be that $p_E = ((\alpha + 2c - 2s)/3) \geq c$. This condition can be simplified to $s \leq (\alpha - c)/2$. Therefore, if switching costs are large enough, there will be no entry.

2. It is easy to see that $W_E > W_M$ if $s < 5(\alpha - c)/22$. Therefore, for $s \in [0, 5(\alpha - c)/22]$ entry occurs and it is beneficial, whereas for $s \in (5(\alpha - c)/22, (\alpha - c)/2)$ entry occurs but it is detrimental to welfare. This result is due to the fact that entry has two effects: a positive effect, since it decreases prices and increases allocative efficiency; and a negative effect, since consumers who choose the entrant will have to pay a switching cost they would not incur if they bought from the incumbent.

3. If there are no switching costs, then entry will always occur in this model with no fixed cost. The equilibrium output and prices are given by $q_i = q_e = (\alpha - c)/3\beta$, and $p_i = p_e = (\alpha + 2c)/3$. Welfare is given by $W_e = (8(\alpha - c)^2)/18\beta$. This is always higher than welfare under entry and switching cost.

Exercise 2.17

1. Let us look at the last stage of the game and solve backwards. At period 2, a consumer who has previously bought from a firm i can be induced to buy from firm j only if $p_j + s < p_i$. For this to be profitable, a necessary condition is $p_j > c$, or $p_j + s > c + s$. Therefore, it must be $c + s < p_j + s < p_i < R$ (the last inequality to ensure that the market exists). Hence, it must be $c + s < R$, which is ruled out by assumption. It follows that undercutting to increase market share relative to period 1 is not feasible, and each firm will then set the monopoly price, that is the maximum price that consumers are willing

---

[85] Otherwise, we should consider a slightly more complex two-period game where only people who have bought from the incumbent will pay no switching cost, whereas people who have never previously bought the good will have to pay the switching cost if they buy from either the incumbent or the entrant. But a two-period game would open the possibility for the incumbent to choose output in period one in a strategic way. See Klemperer (1987c) for an analysis of such a game.

[86] Notice that $q_E \geq 0$ if and only if $s \leq (\alpha - c)/2$.

to pay. In sum, at period 2, $p_A^2 = p_B^2 = R$ and period 2 profits are given by $\Pi_A^2 = q_A^1 N(R - c)$ and $\Pi_B^2 = q_B^1 N(R - c)$, where q_i^1 is the quantity sold by firm i in period 1.

What happens in period 1? First of all, notice that in period 2 at equilibrium the consumer will always pay up to her reservation price, R. Therefore, second period considerations do not affect at all consumers' decisions in period 1. A consumer y will prefer to buy from firm A than B if the former gives her higher utility: $r - p_A^1 - ty \geq r - p_B^1 - t(1 - y)$, which can be rewritten as $y \leq 1/2 + (p_B^1 - p_A^1)/(2t)$. All consumers whose learning costs are included in $[0, y]$ will buy from A, the remainder will buy from B: $q_A^1 = 1/2 + (p_B^1 - p_A^1)/(2t)$; and $q_B^1 = 1/2 + (p_A^1 - p_B^1)/(2t)$. Therefore, total profits after discounting the second-period profit are $\Pi_A^2 = [1/2 + (p_B^1 - p_A^1)/(2t)] [N(p_A^1 - c) + N(R - c)]$; and $\Pi_B^2 = [1/2 + (p_A^1 - p_B^1)/(2t)] [N(p_B^1 - c) + N(R - c)]$. First-order conditions are $\partial \Pi_i^2/\partial p_i^1 = N[1/2 + (p_j^1 - p_i^1)/(2t) - (p_j^1 + R - 2c)/(2t)] = 0$ (for $i, j = 1, 2$ and $i \neq j$). Focusing on the symmetric equilibrium we obtain $p_A^1 = p_B^1 = t - R + 2c$.

2. If there are no switching costs in the second period, the two firms are selling products that are regarded as perfectly homogenous by all consumers. At period 2, therefore, the only possible equilibrium is the usual Bertrand solution, where each firm charges marginal cost: $p_A^2 = p_B^2 = c$. At period 1, consumers's choices will not depend on the second period since they will buy the good at marginal cost anyhow. We therefore have the standard Hotelling-like game being played in the first period. Each firm's profit will be $\Pi_i^2 = [1/2 + (p_j^1 - p_i^1)/(2t)] N(p_i^1 - c)$. First-order conditions are $\partial \Pi_i^2/\partial p_i^1 = N[1/2 + (p_j^1 - p_i^1)/(2t) - (p_j^1 - c)/(2t)] = 0$. At symmetry, we shall have $p_A^1 = p_B^1 = t + c$. Therefore, in a market with switching costs there will be lower first-period prices and higher second-period prices than in a market without switching costs.

Exercise 2.18

1. For each firm, the value of the innovation is given by the difference between the profits the firm expects to earn if it wins the bidding competition for the innovation and the profits it expects to earn in case it does not adopt the innovation and the competitor does. Hence, $V^1 = \Pi^m(\underline{c}) - \Pi^d(\bar{c}, \underline{c})$ and $V^2 = \Pi^d(\underline{c}, \bar{c})$.

2. Notice that $V^1 - V^2 = \Pi^m(\underline{c}) - (\Pi^d(\bar{c}, \underline{c}) + \Pi^d(\underline{c}, \bar{c}))$. Hence, if $\Pi^m(\underline{c}) \geq \Pi^d(\bar{c}, \underline{c}) + \Pi^d(\underline{c}, \bar{c})$, then one has that $V^1 \geq V^2$. This property is called the *efficiency effect*, and is crucial in many models which study whether there is persistence of monopolies: when the industry profits are higher

under monopoly than under duopoly, one should expect monopolies to persist.

3. If the innovation is drastic and the entrant wins the bidding competition for the innovation, then it completely eliminates the monopolist from the market. Therefore, $\Pi^d\left(\bar{c}, \underline{c}\right) = 0$ and $\Pi^d\left(\underline{c}, \bar{c}\right) = \Pi^m\left(\underline{c}\right)$. This in turn implies that $V^1 = V^2 = \Pi^m\left(\underline{c}\right)$.

3

Market Definition and the Assessment of Market Power

3.1 INTRODUCTION

As we have seen, the concept of market power is central to competition policy. So far, we have dealt with this concept from a theoretical point of view. This chapter introduces the reader to the issue of how market power should be assessed in practice. Many competition law investigations will start with such an assessment.[1]

Ideally, one would like to estimate directly the extent to which a firm has (or increases its) market power. In merger cases, for instance, one might want to understand whether the merging firms will be able to profitably raise prices above the current level. Some modern econometric techniques (briefly analysed in the technical Section 3.3.2) allow us to do precisely that.

However, in many circumstances these econometric exercises are not feasible for lack of reliable data, and even when they are feasible, it might be a good idea to complement their results with the more traditional approach that evaluates the market power of firms by analysing the market in which they operate. In turn, this requires defining the "relevant market", that is the set of products and geographical areas to which the products of the merging firms belong. It is such a set of products (and areas) that might create competitive constraints to the firms under analysis.

In this perspective, the definition of the market (both from its product and geographical points of view) is a preliminary step towards the assessment of market power.

In this chapter, I first discuss how to define a market (Section 3.2) and then how to assess market power (Section 3.3) so as to mimic the sequence that cases often follow in many anti-trust jurisdictions. Nevertheless, it should be stressed first that market definition is not of interest by itself, but only as a preliminary step towards the objective of assessing market power.

---

[1] In merger cases and in monopolisation (or abuse of dominant position) cases, it is critical to determine the market power enjoyed by the firm(s) under investigation. But an assessment of market power is necessary also for tying and private price-fixing cases in the US (see Landes and Posner, 1981: 937–8).

3.2 MARKET DEFINITION

Since market definition is instrumental only to the assessment of market power, the relevant market should not be a set of products, which "resemble" each other on the basis of some characteristics, but rather the set of products (and geographical areas) that exercise some competitive constraint on each other. Suppose for instance that the anti-trust problem one faces is the likely effect of a merger between two sellers of bananas. The final objective being to which extent those sellers' market power is enhanced by the merger, the market definition investigation should reflect that objective. Accordingly, whether bananas are to be in a separate market, or not, should not depend on some particular characteristics they may or may not share with other fruits (for instance, they are "exotic" fruits, so that they might be put in the same market as pineapples, mangos and papayas), but rather on whether there exist other fruits that are substitutable enough to bananas so as to limit the possibility to raise the price of bananas.

The test that satisfies this requirement, and that should guide the analysis of market definition in both the product and the geographic dimension, is the so-called SSNIP (or hypothetical monopolist) test. For simplicity, I discuss this test and its practical implications first with reference to product market definition and then to geographic market definition.

3.2.1 Product Market Definition

3.2.1.1 The SSNIP (or Hypothetical Monopolist) Test

Let me continue with the previous example and suppose that we are interested in the impact of a merger between two sellers of bananas, and first focus on product market definition.[2] To find the relevant market, the US Department of Justice has introduced a test that is currently being used by anti-trust authorities worldwide.[3] The test is called SSNIP (Small but Significant Non-transitory Increase in Prices), and works as follows.

Suppose that there exists a hypothetical monopolist that is the only seller of bananas. Would this hypothetical monopolist find it profitable to increase the price of bananas above the *current* level in a non-transitory way, say by 5–10%?[4]

Imagine that the answer to this question is yes, that such a price rise would be profitable. This will mean that bananas do not face significant competitive

---

[2] In non-merger cases, the SSNIP test presents some difficulties (related to the so-called "cellophane fallacy" problem), as I discuss in Section 3.2.1.2 below.

[3] See US *Horizontal Merger Guidelines*, revised in 1992; *Commission Notice on the definition of the relevant market* and OFT *Market Definition Guidelines*.

[4] The US Department of Justice refers to a 5% increase in prices. The EC and the UK guidelines refer to a 5–10% increase.

constraints from other products, that is there are no other products that substitute enough for bananas for the hypothetical monopolist to lose much demand when it raises the prices of bananas. Accordingly, bananas should be considered as a separate market, and the test has already given its response.

Suppose now instead that the hypothetical monopolist would not find it profitable to increase prices by that amount, for instance because after the price rise a significant part of demand is redirected from bananas to kiwi fruits and to a lesser extent to pineapples and other fruits. Then this will imply that bananas should not be considered as a separate market on their own, as there exist other products that exercise a competitive constraint on sellers of bananas. The test should then continue, to consider a wider market, for instance bananas and kiwi fruits together. Would a hypothetical monopolist that is the only seller of bananas and kiwi fruits find it profitable to increase the price of these fruits above their current level by 5–10%? Again, if the price rise is profitable, the relevant market for our investigation will be found. Otherwise, the test should continue to include those products/fruits that exercise a constraint on bananas and kiwi fruits, and so on until a separate market has been found.

Demand and Supply Substitutability   When looking for the products that exercise a competitive constraint upon the group of products we are analysing, it is natural to think first of products that are perceived by consumers as substitutes. This is substitutability on the side of demand. But there might also be substitutability on the side of supply, when producers that are currently supplying a different product possess those skills and assets that make it possible to switch production in a short period of time (say, up to six months or one year) if a price rise occurs. In this case, the competitive constraint would not come from the fact that a considerable part of demand would be addressed to competing products when the price rises, but rather that the price rise attracts producers that are currently selling some other products.

Suppose for instance that we are considering a merger between the only two providers of bus services between city A and city B. This is a commuter route and the train is not a good substitute because it takes too long and there is no direct service between the two cities. Accordingly, demand substitutability alone would call for a definition of bus services between A and B as the relevant market. However, there are other bus companies active in both cities A and B. Although they are operating other routes, say to cities C and D, to the extent that it is not difficult to obtain a license to operate the A to B service and there is some spare capacity on the other routes, these bus companies will exercise a competitive constraint and prevent a price rise on the A–B route from being profitable. Accordingly, the market can be defined more widely (say, bus services in cities A, B, C and D) than it would be by taking into account demand substitutability alone.

In *Torras/Sarrio*, the EC found that under demand substitutability alone separate markets should have been defined, each corresponding to a different degree of quality paper (for instance, art books need high-quality paper, and low-coating paper would not be a good substitute for art publishers). However, paper manufacturers can easily and immediately change the degree of coating in the production, to make paper of a higher or lower quality, so that a wider product market was defined taking into consideration supply substitutability.

Supply Substitutability v. Entry That Constrains Market Power   Note that there are several conditions that should be fulfilled for supply substitutability to widen the relevant market. In particular, switching production must be easy, rapid and feasible. The producer of another good must already have the skills and assets required to produce the product under consideration, it should not incur considerable sunk costs, and any barriers to entry must be surmountable in a rapid and relatively cheap way. For instance, markets for civil air transport services in the EU are usually defined route by route,[5] say Brussels – Milan, Brussels – Munich, and so on. Supply substitutability cannot be invoked to widen the market in such cases, because most airports are congested and obtaining landing and take-off slots is a lengthy and sometimes impossible process. Likewise, the market for cola drinks cannot be widened by using supply substitutability arguments: although the technology of producing a cola is simple and some firms operating in other markets (say, producers of mineral water and those of other carbonated drinks) might have the necessary technology (bottling plants and distribution networks), important advertising campaigns are crucial to determine success in the cola market, and these entail huge sunk costs that make entry difficult and risky. In the *Nestlé/Perrier* case, for instance, the EC found that producers of soft drinks could have in principle started to produce and sell purified tap water immediately. However, for such a product to compete with spring mineral waters, producers should have incurred huge advertising outlays, so that supply substitutability could not be invoked to include soft drinks in the same market as mineral waters.[6]

As argued in Section 3.3, entry into an industry is also considered in the stage of the investigation which deals with the assessment of market power. (If entry is likely and relatively easy – even if not as timely as under supply substitutability – then it will constrain the market power of the firms in the market.) One can then wonder why it is necessary to consider supply substitutability at the market definition stage as well. The answer is that there is no reason to delay the moment at which substitutes on the supply side are considered. Immediate consideration of the existing competitive constraints will save time and help the investigation. Drawing the borders of the market in a narrower way than supply considerations would

---

[5] See for instance *Lufthansa/SAS*.

[6] In fact, the investigation indicated that purified tap water would not constrain the market power of mineral water producers even on a longer time horizon.

authorise might force an anti-trust agency to spend time and energy in justifying why a firm with a considerable market share does not actually have considerable market power. In contrast, if immediate consideration of supply substitutability arguments leads to a correct wider market, and accordingly a low market share, there will be an immediate presumption of absence of market power.[7]

3.2.1.2 A Problem in Non-Merger Cases: The "Cellophane Fallacy"

The use of the SSNIP test presents some difficulties when it is to be used in non-merger investigations. Consider for instance Article 82 under EU competition law, where a firm is investigated for alleged abuse of dominant position. In this case, a preliminary step in the investigation is to establish whether such a firm is dominant at all, that is if it has sufficient market power. But in such a case, the appropriate market definition test should not ask whether a hypothetical monopolist can increase prices in a small but significant way relative to *current* prices, but rather relative to *competitive* prices. Applying the SSNIP test to a current prices benchmark might lead to a too-wide definition of the market precisely *because* the firm under investigation has a dominant position. Suppose for instance that the firm is the only seller in the correctly defined product market. Being a monopolist, it might have set its prices at such a high level that a further increase above the current prices would not be profitable. Therefore, the SSNIP test might lead to a too-wide market definition, which in turn might lead to a calculation of small market shares, and to a finding of no dominance, for the firm under investigation.

This argument is known as the "cellophane fallacy", from the widely discussed *du Pont* case. The US Supreme Court maintained that the existence of high cross elasticity of demand between cellophane (sold by du Pont) and other flexible wrapping materials (such as paper bags) called for a wide definition of the market to include all possible wrapping materials. This decision was later criticised on the grounds that the presence of such a high elasticity of substitution was by itself an indication of the high market power enjoyed by du Pont. During the trial there was evidence that the firm was setting the price of cellophane so high that consumers of the product would have considered replacing it with inferior substitutes.

The cellophane fallacy argument calls for some caution in applying the SSNIP test in non-merger cases. Evidence that, say, a 5% price rise would lead to more than a 10–15% decrease in demand (which presumably implies non-profitability of the increase) should not be taken as decisive proof that the market delineation should be wider.

---

[7] Not considering supply substitution might distort an investigation. The finding of, say, an 80% market share would usually be associated with a presumption of dominance that would be hard to break at the market power stage of the investigation.

3.2.1.3 Implementing the SSNIP Test

The SSNIP test provides a very useful approach to market definition, but we should still discuss how to make it operational. Indeed, the very reliance on a hypothetical (monopoly) situation means that there exist no data that would allow for a literal application of the test. In what follows, I briefly discuss the tools that can be used to implement the test. The most important thing to recall throughout is that all the data and information available should be interpreted in the light of the test above.

Own-Price Elasticity   One of the most useful pieces of information towards the definition of a product market is the own-price elasticity of demand, which is defined as the percentage change in the quantity demanded that follows a one-percent increase in the price of a product.[8] Suppose for instance that we are still interested in the merger between two sellers of bananas and we want to define the relevant market. Knowing that the own-price elasticity is, say, 0.2, one can infer that a 10% increase in the price of bananas will lead to a 2% decrease in the demand for bananas. (Note that I refer to prices and quantities of all bananas, and not just to those of the two firms whose merger is investigated.) Since only a very small number of consumers will turn to other fruits (or stop buying altogether) the price rise is likely to be profitable.[9] Hence, with these (imaginary) data it would be appropriate to define the relevant market as the market for bananas.

The simple statistical observation that over a certain period a 10% increase in banana prices has been associated with a 2% decrease in the number of bananas sold does not get us very far: a number of other variables will probably play a role in the demand for bananas, such as the prices and availability of other fruit, the general price level, disposable income and so on. Imagine for instance that in the period considered the price of bananas rose by 10% but the prices of oranges, apples, pineapples and kiwi fruits all rose by a different extent. Then the observation that demand for bananas has decreased by 2% is of no help, as many other variables affecting the demand for bananas have also changed.

---

[8] Own-price elasticity ε is therefore defined as: $\varepsilon = -(dQ/Q)/(dP/P)$, where Q and P are quantities and prices of the product. In discrete terms, it will be $\varepsilon = -(\Delta Q/Q)/(\Delta P/P)$, where the operator Δ expresses the difference between the level of a variable after and before the change. Since demanded quantities usually decrease in response to a price rise, the fraction is multiplied by (-1) so as to define elasticity as a positive number.

[9] Call $R_0 = P_0 Q_0$ the revenue before the change, and $R_1 = P_1 Q_1$ the revenue after the change. One can then write $\Delta R = R_1 - R_0 = P_1 Q_1 - P_0 Q_0$. Dividing by R_0 both sides and re-arranging, one obtains $\Delta R/R_0 = (P_1/P_0)(\Delta Q/Q_0) + \Delta P/P_0$, which can be further simplified to become: $\Delta R/R_0 = (1 + \Delta P/P_0)(\Delta Q/Q_0) + \Delta P/P_0$. In the example, $\Delta P/P_0 = .1$ (that is, 10%), and $\Delta Q/Q_0 = -.02$ (that is, 2%). Therefore, we shall have $\Delta R/R_0 = .078$. In other words, revenue following a price rise will increase by 7.8%. Of course, to determine profitability one will have in general to consider also the reduction in total costs that follows a reduction in output. In this example, any decrease in costs would further increase profitability.

To take into account the different variables that are likely to have an impact on the demand for bananas, one should formulate and estimate an econometric model. It is from such a model, and to the extent that it gives results that are statistically significant, that one should obtain estimates of elasticities that can be safely used for anti-trust analysis. (The discussion of how to build an econometric model, evaluate the goodness of fit of the model and the significance of the estimates obtained is well beyond the scope of this book.)

As final (and perhaps very obvious) remarks, note that elasticity estimates should be obtained from representative data, and that the time span one looks at matters: consumers might take time to adjust their behaviour to a price change, and the demand reduction after a price rise is not likely to be immediate. (The appropriate time span will probably change from market to market.)

Cross-Price Elasticities   If obtained from a properly specified econometric model, cross-price elasticities might also help to understand the competitive constraints exercised by other products on the product (or group of products) under examination for market definition purposes. The cross-price elasticity between products A and B is defined as the percentage change in the demand for product B when there is a one-percent increase in the price of product A.[10]

When own-price elasticity for the product considered, say product A, is high enough to lead us to believe that a hypothetical monopolist would not profitably raise prices of A in a small but significant way, it becomes important to identify which products exercise a constraint on A. Cross-price elasticities might help us to rank the closest substitute (which, together with A, will become the object of the next step of the hypothetical monopolist test).

When estimates of cross-price elasticities, say between bananas and any other fruit, are low, they indicate that such products are not perceived by consumers as substitutes for bananas, and suggest a separate market for bananas.

Price Correlation Tests   To help define a relevant market, one can also use *price correlation* tests, which look at how price series of different products evolve over time. Stigler and Sherwin (1985: 555), the most authoritative proponents of this test, justify its use by resorting to the classical Marshallian definition of a market area: "A market for a good is the area within which the price of a good tends to uniformity, allowance being made for transportation costs".

The idea is therefore that if two products (but the same would hold for two geographical areas) belong to the same market, their prices will tend to move in the same way over time. Suppose for instance that a shock increases the price of product A. If product B is in the same market (that is, it is a good enough substitute

---

[10] Cross-price elasticity ε_{AB} between products A and B is therefore: $\varepsilon_{AB} = (dQ_B/Q_B)/(dP_A/P_A)$, or, in discrete terms, $\varepsilon_{AB} = (\Delta Q_B/Q_B)/(\Delta P_A/P_A)$.

of product A), then its demand will increase, leading also to an increase in its price.[11]

Stigler and Sherwin propose a number of possible correlation tests (correlation of prices, logarithms of prices, and first differences of logarithms of prices) based on this idea. In all cases, the higher the correlation the more likely two goods are within the same market area (or two regions in the same geographic market).

Some remarks should be made here. The first one is about how to choose the frequency of data. Should one take daily, monthly, or annual data when analysing price correlation? The results are likely to be affected by this choice, since price adjustments might take time. As for estimates of demand elasticity, the appropriate frequency will probably be different according to the nature of the product, and although common sense might be a good guide, it will be appropriate to repeat the test with different time spans to check the robustness of the results.

Second, other difficulties may arise from the fact that price series might diverge over time because the quality mix of different product specifications changes, or because the transportation and transaction costs vary.

Finally, a serious difficulty with price correlation tests is that common factors might induce a similar movement in prices of products that are in different markets. Imagine for instance that there exist variations in cost or demand conditions which depend on a common cause (for instance, inflation, an increase in property prices or in a common input). If this is the case, then we would observe price correlations even between products which are clearly not in the same industry. This is the problem of *spurious correlation*, which has called for more sophisticated tests relying on econometric techniques based on Granger causality tests and co-integration tests. Such techniques might be used to correct the results obtained from the impact of common shocks.[12]

Even without resorting to more sophisticated econometric techniques (the simplicity of the price correlation test being the main reason why one wants to perform such a test), one can derive useful information from price correlation tests. In particular, the presence of common shocks is likely to bias correlation tests in the sense of including two products in the same market when they should not. Accordingly, this test provides a useful screening device in indicating products that are *not* part of the same market, rather than products that are in the same market. For instance, a *correlation coefficient* between the price series of products A and B that is estimated

---

[11] A similar mechanism might be identified on the supply side too. If there exists supply substitutability between A and B, a shock that increases the price of A will lead some producers of B to switch and sell A, thereby causing a decrease in the supply of B and an increase in its price, whereas the price of A would move downwards after the supply adjustment. In the end, relative prices must be aligned again.

[12] See for instance Slade (1986) for the use of Granger-causality in price correlations tests. Werden and Froeb (1993) provide a detailed critique of price tests used for delineation of market areas. See also Sherwin (1993) for a reply to such arguments.

to be below a certain threshold (which may be, for instance, 0.8) will give us a strong presumption that these two products are not in the same market.[13]

In *Nestlé/Perrier*, the EC found that the correlation coefficients between prices of mineral water and prices of soft drinks were either very low or negative: in the five years before the investigation started, mineral water prices tended to increase whereas soft drink prices tended to decrease. This led the EC to (correctly) conclude that soft drinks did not exercise a competitive constraint on mineral waters. Similarly, in *Du Pont/ICI*, low correlation over time between the average prices of nylon fibres and polypropylene fibres suggested that these two products were not in the same market.

One must be more cautious in drawing conclusions when two products exhibit a very high correlation in prices, and analyse other tests before concluding that they are in the same market.

Price Differences   The theoretical basis for the price correlation test is the idea that two products in the same market will tend to have the same price. One might then be tempted not only to look at whether price *changes* of two products are similar over time, but also at whether price *levels* of the two products are similar. In the past, for instance, the EC has used the existence of large differences in prices between two products as an indicator that they were not in the same market. In *Aérospatiale-Alenia/de Havilland*, jet aircraft and turbo-propeller aircraft were put in different markets because the prices of the former were on average twice as much as the prices of the latter. In *Du Pont/ICI*, the fact that nylon fibres and polypropylene fibres exhibited large price differences was taken as an indication that they belonged to different markets. In *Nestlé/Perrier*, large price differences between mineral waters and soft drinks also contributed to defining the relevant market as mineral waters alone.

However, using price differences as a criterion to define the relevant market is unsound. Recall that ultimately what we are interested in is the extent to which a product exerts a competitive constraint on the other (as expressed by the hypothetical monopolist test), but price differences do not give us any information on this point. It might well be, for instance, that the price of product *A* is twice as much as the price of *B*, but that it would not be profitable to raise the price of *A* even by a small amount since most of those buying it would switch to *B*. Markets that exhibit quality differentials are likely to be a case in point. Organic bananas might command a large price premium over bananas grown in plantations that use pesticides, a fact reflected in a higher price of the former over time. However, a further increase in the prices of organic bananas (say, because of a merger) is not profitable if there is

---

[13] The correlation coefficient between the price series of A and B will be given by $\rho = \sigma_{AB}/(\sigma_A \sigma_B)$, where σ_A, σ_B are the standard deviations of the price series of A and B respectively, and σ_{AB} is the covariance between them.

a sizeable proportion of consumers less keen on organic food who will then switch to non-organic bananas.

Hence, products at the bottom of the quality scale might well constrain the pricing behaviour of those at the top of the scale.[14] Price differences are not a good indicator for the purposes of the market delineation.

Characteristics and Usage of Products and Consumer Preferences   Physical characteristics of products and their use might give some indication as to the possible degree of substitutability between products, but only insofar as this information is used in the framework of the hypothetical monopolist test. The fact that both mineral waters and soft drinks are consumed with the purpose of quenching one's thirst does not necessarily imply that these products should be included in the same relevant market. Conversely, the fact that two products obviously differ does not mean that they cannot be included in the same market: trains and buses are indeed different products, but to the extent that they provide a similar service in transporting people from city A to city B they might well be included in the same market.

Consumer surveys and market research studies might also contribute to understanding consumers' preferences and their perceived degree of substitution between different products.

Temporal Markets, Seasonal Markets, Multiple Markets   In the spirit of defining markets according to the competitive constraints that products exercise on each other, notice that relevant markets might be defined in a way that might not appear *a priori* obvious. For instance, in most cities (including my home town, Milan, and my adoptive town, Barcelona) restaurants and bars might be part of the same market at lunch time, when most people look for a quick and light meal during the short office break; but at dinner time, when people go to restaurants to spend their evening in a nice environment and pleasant company, it is unlikely that good sandwiches sold by a bar would provide a good substitute for a good restaurant meal.[15]

Bananas are by and large available throughout the year, whereas oranges are mainly available in winter months, and much rarer in other seasons. Accordingly, bananas might belong to the same market as oranges in winter months but be in a separate market for the rest of the year.

Another consequence of the conceptual framework provided by the hypothetical monopolist test is that one can arrive at different definitions of markets according

---

[14] The UK *Market Definition Guidelines* are explicit about this point: "Although [a product] is of a lower quality, customers might still switch to this product if the price of the more expensive product rose and if they no longer felt that the higher quality justified the price differential".

[15] In Barcelona, it would not be uncommon to have lunch for 5–10 euro and dinner for three times as much in the same restaurant and for comparable meals.

to the starting point of the investigation. Consider the different ways of getting from city A to city B, and vice versa. One might expect some degree of substitutability between airplanes and trains, and between trains and buses, but air ticket prices are unlikely to be constrained by the existence of bus services. Suppose that we now look at a merger between an airline and a train company that both operate services between these two cities. Given the limited substitutability between air and bus travels, it is likely that air and train services will be found to be the relevant market.

Consider instead an investigation prompted by a proposed merger between a train and a bus company operating the same route as above. In this case, and for similar reasons, we might end up with a market definition that includes trains and buses, but not airplanes. Therefore, the same product (trains, in this example) might be placed in different markets, according to the nature of the investigation (that is, if the test starts from airplanes, or from buses).

After-Markets (or Secondary Markets) One important question that often arises is how to define markets when there exist primary and secondary products (also called *after-markets*), such as cars (primary product) and spare parts (secondary product), or washing machines (primary product) and technical assistance (secondary product). Often, a certain type of secondary product is designed for and can fit only a certain brand of the primary product. For instance, a certain brand of cars requires special headlights that do not fit any other brand. If the car-maker also produces headlights, defining the relevant product market as headlights for a particular brand of cars might result in a dominant position of the car-maker in the secondary market, even if the car-maker has a weak position in the primary market.

The framework offered by the SSNIP test turns out to be helpful in addressing this problem. The relevant question is whether a hypothetical monopolist (to continue the example) selling spare parts for a certain car brand would be able to profitably increase prices in a significant way. Note that if existing consumers have already bought that certain car brand they cannot turn to other spare parts (we are supposing they are incompatible). However, consumers who are considering whether to buy that particular brand of car might turn to other car-makers instead, to the extent that they base their purchase decision on the overall estimated life-time cost of the car, which includes the price of the car and the expected cost of replacing spare parts (and getting after-sales services, and so on). If the spare parts at hand are sufficiently important for the overall expected cost of the product, and there are a sufficient number of buyers who will take it into account, the hypothetical monopolist will not find it useful to raise prices in a small but significant manner, and the market should be defined as the market for cars and spare parts together.

In practice, the answer to the question of whether secondary products should be defined as a separate market will depend on the following variables. First, whether the price of the secondary product at issue is a considerable proportion or not of the price of the primary product: ash-trays will more likely to be put into a separate market than car engines. Second, not only the price of the spare part but also the probability of replacement matters: prices being equal, a spare part which is commonly known as very likely to break down will be less likely to be put into a separate market than a spare part whose failure probability is widely expected to be very low (the latter would not be considered by consumers when buying the car). Third, some buyers are more sophisticated than others. When the buyers are final consumers, they might be less informed about the probability that spare parts or after-sales services are needed and they might be less aware of those secondary products' prices. Conversely, when the primary product is an input which is bought by a firm, we should expect the buyer to be better informed about the expected cost (both the probability that they are needed and their costs) of secondary products. In the latter case, the market definition will *ceteris paribus* be wider than in the former.

The most famous case about after-markets is *Kodak,* where that company's practice of tying the sales of spare parts for its photocopiers with assistance services was being considered. In this case, the US Supreme Court defined the market (in a majority decision) in a narrow way, as the secondary market for spare parts and services of Kodak photocopiers. Using this definition, Kodak was found to have almost 100% of the market for spare parts of Kodak photocopiers and 80–90% of the market for services and assistance of Kodak photocopiers. This led in turn to the finding that it had market power, despite the fact that Kodak had market shares which ranged from 2% to 23% in the primary markets. This judgment has been widely debated because it is far from clear that Kodak could really exercise market power in the secondary markets, given the strong inter-brand competition in the primary markets. It is also unclear whether this decision has had a permanent impact on the way secondary markets are defined. According to Peritz (1999), lower courts in the US have continued to define markets in a wider way, making it less easy to find market power by firms that face considerable inter-brand competition in the primary products.

In *Hugin v. Commission,* the market was defined as the UK market for spare parts of the cash registers manufactured by Hugin, a Swedish company that was found dominant although it had only 13% of the UK market for cash registers.[16]

In another European case, Kyocera, a producer of printers for computers, had been accused of having abused a dominant position in the market for secondary products of its printers. However, the EC rejected the complaint since it found that consumers took into account the prices of the secondary products (that accounted

---

[16] The *Hugin* case is probably more famous because Hugin's refusal to supply spare parts to Lipton was found to have no effect on the trade between Member States, and Article 82 of the Treaty did not apply.

for an important part of the cost of the life-time purchase of a printer) when buying the primary product, and that there was significant competition in the market for printers.[17]

Consistency of Market Definitions over Time   A final observation pertains to the consistency that anti-trust agencies show with respect to market definitions over time. It might happen that the same firms, or similar products, are investigated on different occasions. In such cases, it would be of course recommendable that agencies would adopt the same market definitions for the same type of problem (we have just seen that if the anti-trust problem is different, a different market definition is fully justified). However, consumer preferences and technological conditions change over time, and consistency in such cases might be at the cost of making serious mistakes.[18]

For instance, advances in transportation technologies, in greenhouse cultivation, and in storing and refrigerating techniques imply that not only bananas, but also many other fresh fruits can nowadays be consumed all year round by European consumers. However correct the ECJ decision was of placing bananas in a separate market forty years ago, it would be much less likely today to find that other fruits do not exercise competitive constraints on bananas.[19]

3.2.2 Geographic Market Definition

Most of the considerations I have made above with respect to the definition of product markets hold good when considering how to define geographic markets. In particular, the SSNIP test is still the conceptual framework to be used and it is in its light that data and information must be interpreted.

Suppose for instance that a merger between mineral water producers in Italy is being considered. The SSNIP test then takes the following form: would a hypothetical monopoly seller of all Italian mineral waters find it profitable to increase the price of mineral water by 5–10%? If the answer is affirmative, then the geographic market will be defined as Italy. If not, for instance because one expects imports from France to render such a price rise unprofitable, as a considerable part of consumers

---

[17] *Pelikan/Kyocera*, in European Commission (1996: 140).

[18] More generally, an anti-trust authority should not feel constrained by a bad decision taken in the past. Such an issue has arisen in the past in merger investigations of the Merger Task Force of the EC. The MTF has to publish decisions under very tight constraints, and it might come up with incorrect market definitions for a merger analysed superficially because it obviously creates no competition problems. It would be wrong to ask it to adopt the same market definition when analysing subsequent mergers if it turned out to be incorrect after a closer investigation.

[19] Likewise, the existence of high-speed trains, which make use of a new tilting technology to work on the existing tracks might impose a competitive constraint on airlines for routes between cities located within a range of 300–600 kilometers. Such a constraint was much weaker only ten years ago.

demand French mineral water, then the test should be repeated on a hypothetical monopolist of Italian and French mineral waters, and so on.

When implementing the test in order to define a geographic market, in addition to estimates of elasticities and correlation tests, information related to imports and transportation costs might also be used, as indicated below.

3.2.2.1 The Role of Imports (Shipment Tests)

Elzinga and Hogarty (1973) propose to use shipment data to identify geographic market areas. The test has two components, the first to establish whether there is "*little in from outside*" (that is, imports account for a small part of local consumption) and the second that there is "*little out from inside*" (exports account for a small part of local production). The idea behind the test is that a given geographical area is defined as a relevant geographical market if both tests are satisfied, that is there is little movement of the product to and from other geographical areas.

The test might provide useful information, but it is likely to be biased and its results should accordingly be interpreted with care. Suppose for instance that a considerable proportion of trade was observed between one region and another. This would be a clear indication that the regions' producers are exercising a competitive constraint on each other. Accordingly, the two regions should not be defined as separate markets, and the test should be carried out again on further regions.

Suppose instead that the test is satisfied, in the sense that few shipments occur between region A and region B. This is not necessarily an indication that the two regions are not in the same market. If prices are the same, and there are some (even very small) transportation costs, one would not observe any delivery from one region to the other, even though they produce exactly the same good and are neighbouring. Yet, producers in one region strongly constrain those in the other. If A's producers tried to increase prices by even a small amount, A's consumers would switch to B's producers: such a price rise would not be profitable. Hence, the shipment test is biased, and its results should accordingly be discounted.

3.2.2.2 Transportation Costs

One useful piece of information that can supplement other tests is given by the importance of transportation costs relative to the prices of a given product. Even if no shipments had occurred in the past between one region and another, the fact that transport costs are low relative to prices would imply that such shipments are possible and that a competitive constraint will prevent that prices in a region are increased.

In some situations, these considerations will make the geographic extent of the market very small. Consider for instance a merger between food retailers in a given city. It would make little sense to define the market beyond the city borders, as transportation costs (which in this case include time spent by consumers travelling to a shop) would prevent most citizens from going to neighboring cities to do their shopping.

At the other side of the spectrum, there are markets which are correctly defined as global. A case in point is markets for aircraft, where transportation costs are irrelevant relative to their prices.[20]

3.2.2.3 Other Characteristics

In some cases, especially when the question is whether to define a market at a national or supranational level, consumer preferences might be an important variable. For a number of products, preferences follow national borders. This implies that separate markets should be defined. Different national tastes might be reflected in different perceived qualities, and in turn different market prices across countries. Yet, as we have seen above when discussing price differences, this does not necessarily mean that imports do not exercise a competitive constraint: a further increase in prices in a country's products might trigger a substantial diversion of demand towards foreign products. In some cases, however, taste differences might be so strong that it would make little sense to define markets across countries: Italians would not buy pasta unless made of durum wheat, whereas French and Germans would buy it in any case.

An example of markets that are (at the moment) unlikely to be defined at the supranational level are media (publishing and broadcasting) markets. A merger between two French newspapers will probably result in a geographic market definition not wider than France, in part due to language, in part because it is unlikely that French citizens are interested in the Swiss and Belgian news covered by newspapers in Geneva or in Brussels. For language reasons, a merger between two German television broadcasting companies will lead at most to a geographic market comprehending also Austrian and Swiss–German television stations.[21]

3.3 THE ASSESSMENT OF MARKET POWER

Market power is defined as the ability of a firm to raise prices above its marginal cost.[22] However, firms lack market power only in the abstract and unrealistic world of perfect competition or in the Bertrand model with homogeneous goods and perfectly symmetric firms (see Chapter 8). In real-world industries, where there

---

[20] World markets have been found by the EC in *Aérospatiale-Alenia/de Havilland, Boeing/McDonnell Douglas*, and *General Electric/Honeywell*.

[21] Examples of media markets where language has determined a less-than-European wide geographic market are *Kirch/Richemont/Telepiù, CLT/Disney/SuperRTL* and *Nordic Satellite Distribution*.

[22] Sometimes, it is defined as the ability to set prices above the *competitive* price level. But the competitive price is nothing else than the price that a firm would charge under perfect competition, that is, its marginal cost.

exist fixed costs and products are unlikely to be perceived as perfect substitutes by all consumers, we should expect every firm to have *some degree* of market power.

This calls for two issues to be addressed. First, which measure of market power should be used, and second, which threshold of market power should be taken to indicate that a firm has enough market power for it to call for the attention of competition authorities. The second question calls largely for an arbitrary answer, and it is solved in different ways by the different anti-trust legislations, or even within the same legal framework (see below for the different threshold values of market share used by the EC and the ECJ in their decisions). Let us dwell upon the first question before coming back to the second issue.

A (theoretical) measure of market power is given by the *Lerner index*, defined as the firm's mark-up (that is, the difference between the price p_i and the marginal cost C_i') over price ratio: $L_i = (p_i - C_i')/p_i$. The index increases with the mark-up charged by the firm, which should be the most desirable feature of any index of market power.

One might be tempted to apply the Lerner index directly to real-world cases. However, its direct application would create problems of a different nature.[23] Firstly, estimating the marginal cost of a firm is not an easy task. Marginal cost is mainly a theoretical concept. Determining the impact of a marginal change in the quantity produced by a firm on the total cost of production is often beyond practical feasibility even with the best knowledge of the technological conditions under which a firm operates. Indeed, there might be large differences in the estimates of marginal costs even within the management of the same firm. Competition agencies with an imperfect knowledge of the sector, the technology, and the firm itself would certainly have a much more difficult task.[24]

Secondly, high costs can be inherent to monopoly power. As seen in Chapter 2, one should expect a monopolistic firm to be characterised by productive inefficiency. Paradoxically, by applying the Lerner index one might find that a firm is not dominant because it has (relatively) high costs (and relatively low margins), whereas such high costs are the result of its monopoly power.[25, 26]

Given the difficulties entailed by the direct application of the Lerner index, an alternative approach might be based on the fact that the Lerner index of a

---

[23] See also Landes and Posner (1981) and Neven et al. (1993, ch. 2) among the many contributions that start from the Lerner index in their discussion on how to evaluate market power.

[24] Note that a firm would not have an incentive to reveal its true costs to the anti-trust agencies. Rather, it might try to artificially inflate its costs through the manipulation of its accounting books.

[25] See for instance Neven and Röller (1996), who find that airlines less exposed to competition share rents with workers, thereby increasing costs.

[26] Of course, low prices might also be the *result* of monopoly power: In predatory pricing cases (see Chapter 7), a price very close (or inferior) to marginal costs should obviously not be taken as a proof that a firm has no market power.

monopolistic firm corresponds to the inverse of the elasticity of demand faced by it: $L_i = 1/\varepsilon_i$ (see Chapter 8.2, as well as 3.3.1.6). Indeed, the direct estimate of the elasticity of the (residual) demand faced by a firm is at the core of one of the modern econometric techniques of assessment of market power, as I discuss in Section 3.3.2.1 below.

However, the estimate of the residual demand elasticity faced by a firm, as well as the use of other econometric techniques aiming at estimating (or forecasting) directly from market data the market power enjoyed by a firm or a group of firms, is not always possible (for lack of data) and, when possible, is not necessarily without problems, as discussed in Section 3.3.2 below. These econometric techniques certainly represent a very promising tool for anti-trust analysis, but as reliable data do not always exist and such techniques are not completely standard, a more traditional approach might be used for the assessment of market power.

The traditional approach assesses market power in an indirect way. It attributes a key role to the market share held by the firm(s) under investigation, but market share is only one of the variables that one must look at in order to determine market power. Other variables are the relative position of competitors, the existence of potential entrants, and the countervailing power of buyers.

In what follows, I discuss how these different variables contribute to the assessment of market power.

3.3.1 Traditional Approach: (Indirect) Assessment of Market Power

3.3.1.1 The Central Role of Market Shares

The typical procedure followed by anti-trust authorities all over the world is to first define the relevant market and then assess market power in that market. In this second step, the analysis rotates around the measurement of market shares held by the firm (or firms).

Giving an important role to market shares in a market power analysis makes sense. After all, one would expect (other things being equal) a monopolistic firm, that is one that has 100% of the market, to have the highest possible market power. Conversely, one would expect a firm holding a tiny share of the market to be unable to exercise much market power; a restraint on the ability of setting high prices will come from competitors, and a firm's low market share will indicate that this firm has strong competitors.

However, a firm's high market share is not sufficient to conclude that it is dominant. As we shall discuss below, such a firm would not be able to increase prices substantially if entry in the industry was very easy, or if there was a strong buyer ready to use its countervailing power and switch to competing suppliers (or to integrate vertically). None the less, it is reasonable to start from a measurement of market share as a first step of the analysis of market power of a firm, and the simple technical Section 3.3.1.6 below confirms the positive relationship between market share and market power.

3.3.1.2 Which Thresholds for Market Shares?

The centrality of market shares in market power assessments suggests that they might be used as a screening device. For instance, if the market share of a firm being investigated were below a certain threshold (say, 40%) there might be a presumption that the firm does not hold enough market power to be considered dominant, and the case might be dismissed (or the burden of proving that there is dominance should fall entirely on the anti-trust authority). If it were above another threshold (say, 50%) there might be a presumption that the firm is dominant, and the burden of proving that dominance does not exist should fall on the defendant; and for intermediate market shares a more open investigation might take place.

This approach would be helpful to increase legal certainty and reduce the cost of the investigations. Of course, using such thresholds aims at distributing the burden of proof, and should not hide that many other elements (see below) must be assessed before reaching a final conclusion about the market power of a firm.

Some anti-trust authorities are explicit in the way they would use market share thresholds as a screening device. The "Assessment of Market Power" Guidelines (point 2.11) released by the UK Office of Fair Trading indicate two thresholds that appear very sensible: below 40% it is unlikely that a firm is considered dominant; above 50% dominance can be presumed.

Neither the EC nor the European Court of Justice are equally explicit, but in practice their approach is probably not so different. Since the earliest cases, the ECJ has indicated that a number of factors must be considered in assessing dominance, but has attributed an important role to market shares:

> The existence of a dominant position may derive from several factors which taken separately are not necessarily determinative but among these factors a highly important one is the existence of very large market shares.[27]

In *United Brands*, the defendant was found to be dominant with market shares around 40–45% (but again, this was only one of the elements considered by the ECJ), and somehow this range is still considered to cover the benchmark levels for the presumption of dominance. In *Akzo v. Commission* the ECJ stated that a market share persistently above 50% is an indication that the firm is dominant in the absence of evidence to the contrary.

It is not clear below which threshold the ECJ would consider a firm *not* to be dominant. The European Commission would probably set that threshold at 25%, given that Article 15 of the Merger Regulation states that a concentration is presumed

---

[27] *Hoffman/La Roche:* 520. A similar statement is also made in *United Brands.*

not to impede competition if the merging firms' combined market share does not exceed 25%.

US courts seem to indicate higher thresholds for finding dominance. In *Alcoa*, Judge Learned Hand wrote that a market share of 33% is certainly not sufficient to establish dominance, and in *Jefferson Parish Hospital* a 30% market share has been deemed far too low for dominance. In *Times-Picayune*, a firm with a 40% market share was not found to be dominant.

3.3.1.3 Measuring Market Shares and Assessing Relative Strengths

Once a market has been defined, market shares of all the relevant firms in the market can be calculated. This will give a first picture of the relative competitive positions of the firms in that market.

If the relevant market in the investigation at hand coincides with the market that firms and business magazines usually make reference to, there might be several sources that one can use to derive market shares. A more unusual market definition might imply a divergence between desired data and firm or industry data, but even so, sales data are usually readily available.

In some cases, market shares both in number of *units* and in *values* might be available. The latter generally have more economic meaning, although the former might contain some additional information about the relative market positions.[28]

In certain industries where production is limited by a crucial input, existing *reserves* might be more informative than market shares. For instance, if one looks at a mineral industry, it would be meaningless for competition analysis purposes to report that a certain firm has (or had) a 20% market share, if its reserves will be completely exhausted within little time: the future market share of that firm is going to be nil, and it will not exercise any competitive constraint on its rivals.[29]

Similar considerations might apply when one of the market participants is very unlikely to be a relevant market player in the near future, because of an older or less efficient technology or other reasons. In this case, considering the current (or past) market share would over-estimate the competitive constraints that this firm exercises on its competitors. It might then be appropriate to exclude its current sales from the calculations of market shares.[30]

The degree of *excess capacity* held by rival firms also gives important information. If the existing capacity of these firms is just enough to satisfy their current demand,

---

[28] For instance, in *Nestlé/Perrier*, the EC calculated market shares in the French mineral water industry both in volumes and values. The three major firms held higher shares when total values were considered, indicating that consumers were willing to pay higher prices for a bottle of their water than for that of competitors.

[29] See for instance *Gencor/Lohnro*.

[30] In *Boeing/McDonnell Douglas*, it was debated to which extent McDonnell Douglas (that in the long-run would be unlikely to survive) obliged Boeing and Airbus – the two main players in the market for aircraft – to set lower prices.

their supply elasticity (that is, their ability to react to an increase in prices and serve new customers) is very low. If, on the other hand, they have a considerable excess of capacity, then it is reasonable to expect that the market power of the firm being investigated is reduced. Because of this observation, the share of the capacity of each firm over total industry capacity might be relevant information.[31]

For the cases where supply substitution has been taken into account, and hence the relevant market includes firms that are not currently selling the market products, an estimate of capacity might again be used as a proxy for sales, and market shares should be estimated accordingly.

Some markets are characterised by large and infrequent orders made by a small number of buyers. In these markets, there might be a large variance in market shares if they are calculated over a small time period, as one order alone might represent a considerable proportion of the period's sales. As a consequence, market shares should be calculated over a relative long period, say three to five years (depending on the frequency of the orders).[32]

Furthermore, it is not only the existence of a certain pattern, but its *persistence* over time that might give a strong indication of an industry situation. If a firm's market share was consistently above say 50% over a time horizon of five to ten years, that might be a further indication (other things being equal) of its likely dominance. Conversely, a distribution of market shares among the main players that varies considerably over a relatively short time period might be suggestive of a more competitive situation where no single player is dominant.[33]

As a final remark, note that the aggregate level of market power (that is, the extent to which firms in the industry can on average raise prices above their marginal costs) increases with the degree of concentration, other things being equal (see also technical Section 3.3.1.6). This observation is not relevant for the assessment of individual market power, but it is very important when mergers are analysed (see Chapter 5). Indeed, measures of industrial concentration are often used as a first device to screen mergers that might have some anti-competitive effects.

3.3.1.4 Ease and Likelihood of Entry

If a firm tried to increase its prices, its existing competitors might react by increasing their capacity. To the extent that its competitors will respond aggressively, the market power of a firm is limited.

---

[31] In *Nestlé/Perrier*, distribution of capacities was again an important consideration.

[32] Examples of industries that fit this description of large and infrequent orders are aircraft and trains, as in *Aérospatiale-Alenia/de Havilland, Boeing/McDonnell Douglas, General Electric/Honewell* and *ABB/Daimler-Benz*.

[33] In *Airtours*, the market shares held by the leading firms had changed considerably in the few years prior to the Commission investigation of the proposed merger between Airtours and First Choice. See Section 5.6.1.1 for a discussion of the case.

Aside from existing competitors, potential entrants might also constrain the ability of a firm (or a group of firms) to raise prices. Indeed, the most important insight of contestable markets theory (see Chapter 2) is that if entry is easy, rapid and costless, a firm would not be able to charge a high margin because large profits would attract competitors into the industry.

The criticisms addressed to this theory have stressed the key role played by fixed sunk costs as an obstacle to entry. The higher sunk costs the less likely that entry will occur, which in turn makes it less likely that new firms will discipline the incumbents. Note that fixed sunk costs can be either exogenous or endogenous, or both.[34] Exogenous sunk costs refer to the investment a firm has to incur in order to endow itself with the plants and machines (or more generally, technology) it needs for producing and distributing the good. By and large, such an investment is not a choice variable for the firms operating in the industry. Endogenous sunk costs refer to R&D and advertising outlays that firms make in order to increase the perceived quality of their products, and they are indeed a choice variable for the firm. As discussed in Chapter 2, endogenous sunk cost industries are typically characterised by a lower bound to concentration and it is unlikely that entry will discipline the market power of the incumbents in such industries.

When analysing market power in an industry, it is crucial to understand the likelihood of entry, and care should be devoted to a number of details. For instance, the existence of switching costs, lock-in effects and network externalities (see again Chapter 2) might represent an obstacle to entry, as consumers do not have the right incentive to turn to new suppliers, even when they are more efficient and/or offer superior products.

Care should also be devoted to the history of the industry, in particular previous episodes of entry and the incumbent's reactions. Suppose for instance that the market leader has consistently priced aggressively whenever new competitors have entered the industry. Then it will have built a reputation of being a tough player, and potential entrants will take this into account at the moment they decide on entry: the expectation that the incumbent will set low prices after their entry might discourage them from entering in the first place (see Chapter 7 for a discussion of predatory behaviour by an incumbent dominant firm).

3.3.1.5 Buyers' Power

The ability of a firm to charge high prices also depends on the degree of concentration of the buyers. A firm is clearly more free to exert market power if it faces a large number of dispersed consumers or buyers than if it faces one or a few strong buyers.[35] A strong buyer can make use of its bargaining power to stimulate

---

[34] See Sutton (1991, 1998).

[35] Galbraith (1952) is probably the first author who has argued that countervailing power of buyers can considerably restrain the market power of sellers.

competition among sellers, either by threatening to switch orders from one seller to another, or by threatening to start upstream production itself.[36]

Because of coordination problems, entry into the sellers' industry by new firms can also be easier when buyers are concentrated. Imagine for instance a situation where there is an incumbent monopolist, and where potential entrants would have to make a considerable sunk investment to operate in this market. If buyers are dispersed, and potential entrants have similar cost levels, orders are likely to be distributed across sellers. Winning orders from a few buyers might not be enough to justify this investment, and as a result no new firm might enter the industry, even though each potential entrant is more efficient than the monopolist. Because buyers are not coordinating their decision of which seller to select, they might end up having the monopolist as the only seller in the industry, and hence face much higher bills than if entry had occurred. When instead there is just a single buyer (or all the buyers coordinate), then it will order from one of the entrants, thereby making entry into the industry possible.[37]

Several empirical works have tried to test the countervailing power hypothesis, and there appears to be some evidence that buyer concentration does negatively affect the market power of the sellers.[38]

The role of buyer power in constraining sellers is typically well taken into account by anti-trust agencies. In European merger cases, for instance, it has led the EC to clear mergers that would otherwise have been blocked.

In *Enso/Stora*, the merging firms produced Liquid Packaging Board (LPB), used for the packaging of milk and fruit juice. The merger was expected to give them a market share between 50 and 70%. Other industry characteristics, such as high barriers to entry, also suggested an anti-competitive impact. Yet, the merger was approved on the grounds that buyer power in this industry was so large (Tetrapak alone buys 60–80% of total sales) that the merging firms would have been unlikely to exercise market power. The EC argued that the main buyer, Tetrapak, "would have the option of developing new capacity with other existing or new suppliers, should the parties attempt to exercise market power" (*Enso/Stora*: para. 91).

A similar argument was used by the EC in the *ABB/Daimler-Benz* case, which was cleared (subject to conditions) mainly on the grounds that Deutsche Bahn (the German railways operator), the only buyer for mainline trains, would have exerted

---

[36] See Scherer and Ross (1990: ch. 14) for a discussion and a number of examples. An interesting case is in particular when a buyer produces itself a part of the inputs it needs (*tapered integration*). This makes a potential switch from suppliers to internal production more credible and has the additional advantage of giving the buyer information about the cost of production in the upstream industry, information which can be very useful in price negotiations.

[37] For a formal presentation of this argument, see Fumagalli and Motta (2000).

[38] See Scherer and Ross (1990: 533–5) for a review of this literature, initiated by Lustgarten (1975). Among more recent works, Schumacher (1991) also supports the countervailing power hypothesis in a study based on US manufacturing industries, whereas Connor, Rogers and Bhagavan (1996) find no evidence of countervailing power in the US food manufacturing industries.

competitive pressure on the producers of trains and railways materials (see Chapter 5 for a detailed discussion).

Finally, an interesting issue is to what extent final consumers benefit from buyer power. Von Ungern-Sternberg (1996) and Dobson and Waterson (1997) find that lower prices obtained by buyers are passed on to consumers only if there exists enough competition among the buyers themselves.

3.3.1.6 Market Power, Market Shares and Concentration*

Suppose we are interested in studying the market power of a firm i in a certain (well-defined) market. Assume also that firms compete in quantities, produce a homogenous good (there is only one market price, p), and have a constant marginal cost c_i. Firm i's profits can be written as

$$\pi_i = p(Q)q_i - c_i q_i, \tag{3.1}$$

where $Q = q_i + \sum_{j \neq i} q_j$ is the total industry output and q_i and q_j denote respectively the output of firm i and that of any of its rival firms j. Maximisation of its profits given the output of its rivals will lead to the following FOC:

$$\frac{d\pi_i}{dq_i} = p(Q) + \frac{dp}{dq_i}q_i - c_i = 0. \tag{3.2}$$

The equilibrium price p^* in this market will be defined by the solution of all the FOCs. At such a price, the FOC for firm i can be re-written as

$$p^*(Q) - c_i = -\frac{dp}{dQ}\frac{dQ}{dq_i}q_i, \tag{3.3}$$

Dividing both sides of this expression by p^*, multiplying and dividing by Q the RHS, and noting that in a Nash equilibrium in quantities rivals' quantities are given (so that production of one additional unit by a firm corresponds to production of an additional unit for the industry as a whole: $dQ/dq_i = 1$), we have

$$\frac{p^* - c_i}{p^*} = -\frac{dp}{dQ}\frac{Q}{p^*}\frac{q_i}{Q}, \tag{3.4}$$

which one can finally re-write as

$$L_i = \frac{m_i}{\varepsilon}, \tag{3.5}$$

where L_i is firm i's Lerner index of market power, m_i is firm i's market share, and $\varepsilon = -(dQ/Q)/(dp/p)$ is the elasticity of *market* demand with respect to price. Note that for the monopoly case one finds the well-known relationship $L_i = 1/\varepsilon$.

Building on this result, one can also find an aggregate index of market power for an industry as a whole. Denoting with $L = \sum_i m_i L_i$ such an index, and using (3.5) one obtains

$$L = \sum_i \frac{m_i^2}{\varepsilon} = \frac{HHI}{\varepsilon}, \tag{3.6}$$

where $HHI = \sum_i m_i^2$ is the Herfindahl–Hirschman Index of concentration. This establishes that there is a direct relationship between the degree of industrial concentration and the average degree of market power, a result that has been used to justify the prominent role assigned by the US DOJ to the HHI as a screening device in merger analysis.[39]

Other works have shown that the individual Lerner index depends on the firm's market share as well as the market demand elasticity and the elasticity of the supply of the rivals.[40] This stresses that firm i's market power is constrained by the extent to which rival firms are able to respond to an increase in firm i's prices by increasing their output.

3.3.2 Econometric Techniques: (Direct) Assessment of Market Power*

The purpose of this section is to give an overview of two recent quantitative techniques that are used to assess market power and estimate the likely effects of a merger. Section 3.3.2.1 briefly describes the method based on the estimation of residual demand elasticities, and Section 3.3.2.2 deals with logit demand models that can be used both to estimate market power and to simulate effects of mergers.

One reason for the popularity of these two techniques is that they both allow us to reduce dimensionality problems when dealing with differentiated product industries (logit models and residual demand elasticities methods therefore provide two alternative answers to the same problem). Suppose for instance that one wanted to estimate market power in a market characterised by n differentiated products. A natural approach would be to specify a system of n demand equations, where the demand for each product is expressed as a function of the prices of all products in the market. Even with linear or log–linear demands, estimating such a system would imply estimating more than n^2 parameters, since each of the n demand equations will contain the prices of all n products, plus all other relevant explanatory variables. It is clear that as n becomes large, the dimensionality problem becomes very important (even when imposing restrictions, such as symmetry, on the model). Residual demand analysis and logit models offer two ways to deal with this dimensionality problem.

A complete analysis of these and other techniques is beyond the scope of this book, but the following notes, however incomplete and short, should give an idea of

---

[39] See Dansby and Willig (1979) and, more recently, the discussion in Rey (2000: 32–4). See also Chapter 5 on the role of the HHI in US merger investigations.

[40] See for instance Encaoua and Jacquemin (1980), Landes and Posner (1981) and Neven et al. (1993: 20–8).

the help modern econometric and computing tools might give in concrete anti-trust cases.

3.3.2.1 Elasticity of Residual Demand*

A very useful quantitative technique for evaluating market power and assessing the effects of mergers is due to Baker and Bresnahan (1985, 1988), and is based on the direct estimation of residual demand elasticities. Here I briefly recall the main features of this technique.

I have already mentioned the dimensionality problem when dealing with differentiated products. An additional problem arises because a price increase by firm A would generally not leave the price set by the other firms unchanged (as it was implicit in technical Section 3.3.1.6): for a correct assessment of the market power enjoyed by a firm, one should also estimate to what extent a price increase by such a firm would be followed by each of the rivals. This would add complexity to the task of assessing market power.

The estimation of the residual demand function is a technique which considerably simplifies this task, and reduces the need for data. To assess the market power of firm A, this technique involves the estimation of just one coefficient. This is the elasticity of its *residual demand function,* that is the demand function faced by firm A once the reaction of all the other firms is taken into account. Instead of asking by what percentage a price rise of firm A would increase demand of firm B, C, and so on, this technique just asks by what percentage a price rise of firm A would decrease its own residual demand, that is the demand that is left after all the other firms have satisfied theirs. A low estimate of the residual demand elasticity would then suggest high market power of firm A, as a considerable proportion of consumers would continue to buy from firm A rather than switching to other firms (or ceasing to buy the product). Vice versa, a high estimate would suggest low market power.

Regressing the residual demand function of a firm alone would result in an estimator which is not *consistent,* as equilibrium price (and quantity) are jointly determined by both the demand and the supply schedules of a firm. Therefore, the estimation of the residual demand elasticity is usually accompanied by the use of the *instrumental variable* method (for which firm-specific cost data of the firm whose market power we would like to assess are needed), to solve the simultaneous relation problem and obtain consistent estimators.

Note that the estimation of the residual demand elasticity cannot tell us whether market power is low because of competition from firm B, or C, or other, since the rival firms are considered as a collective, and their specific role in constraining the market power of firm A cannot be singled out. However, the advantage of this method is that it allows us to save on the data required to perform an econometric assessment of the market power of a firm. Since it is very often the case that data at the disaggregated level are scarce or difficult to obtain, this is an important step for the feasibility of the application of quantitative methods to the analysis of market power.

The application of this method to the analysis of mergers is straightforward. Imagine that one is interested in knowing the likely market power enjoyed by a firm which results from the merger of, say, firms A and B. One could use the technique briefly described above with a minor modification, that is by computing two (*partial*) residual demand elasticities for each of the two firms.[41] For instance, for firm A, the first is its own elasticity, ϵ_{AA}^{pr}, which estimates the percentage decrease in the residual demand of firm A following a one percent increase in A's price; the second is the cross-elasticity ϵ_{AB}^{pr}, which estimates the percentage increase in the residual demand of firm A following a one percent increase in the price of firm B. This helps to understand how these two firms restrain each other in the market. By subtracting the two elasticity estimates thus obtained, one obtains the value $(\epsilon_{AA}^{pr} - \epsilon_{AB}^{pr})$ which is an assessment of the market power enjoyed by the merging firm. This difference expresses the idea that when the insiders coordinate their actions and increase their prices simultaneously, firm A will lose all the consumers going to all the other firms *minus* the consumers who would have gone to firm B if the merger had not occurred (and firm B had therefore priced its product independently of firm A).

This way, with relatively small data requirements, it is possible to obtain an estimate of the likely effects of a merger. This technique is increasingly being used by economic experts and in court proceedings, and although it is unlikely that merger appraisal will be based uniquely on it, it certainly complements other information collected and the analysis of the market where the merger takes place. Residual demand estimation can also be used to define the relevant market in merger cases, as explained in Scheffman and Spiller (1987).[42]

Estimation of the Residual Demand Elasticity**   Consider an industry with n single product firms. First we want to derive the residual demand faced by one such firm, and see how it can be used to estimate its market power. Then we extend this approach to estimate the market power created by a merger.[43]

Direct demand faced by a firm $i = 1, \ldots, n$ can be written as

$$q_i = D_i\left(p_i, \mathbf{p}_{-i}, \mathbf{y}\right), \tag{3.7}$$

where bold-faced letters indicate vectors and $-i$ refers to all other firms but i. The vector $\mathbf{y}$ denotes a vector (of size S) of exogenous variables which affect demand.

---

[41] When estimating the residual demand of firm A one takes into account how an increase in the price of A redirects customers to all rivals, without separating the effect of competition from B or any other $(n - 2)$ firms. With the concept of partial residual demand function, instead, the merging partner's reaction (B's reaction) is separated from that of the other firms.

[42] See Froeb and Werden (1991) for a critical assessment.

[43] The use of residual demand elasticities as a method to measure market power of one or more firms is due to Baker and Bresnahan (1985, 1988).

For each of the firms, the first-order conditions of profit maximisation define the best-reply functions

$$p_i = R_i \left(\mathbf{p}_{-i}, \mathbf{y}, \mathbf{w}, c_i \right), \qquad (3.8)$$

where $\mathbf{w}$ denotes the vector of size L which contains the industry-specific cost variables, and c_i denotes the firm-specific cost of firm i. From the previous expression one can obtain the vector of the best-reply functions of all firms but i as

$$\mathbf{p}_{-i} = R_{-i} \left(p_i, \mathbf{y}, \mathbf{w}, \mathbf{c}_{-i} \right), \qquad (3.9)$$

where $\mathbf{c}_{-i}$ denotes the vector of all the firm-specific cost variables apart from those specific to firm i. By substituting back into the direct demand, we obtain the residual demand function of a firm i, $q_i^r = D_i(p_i, \mathbf{p}_{-i}(p_i, \mathbf{y}, \mathbf{w}, \mathbf{c}_{-i}), \mathbf{y})$or, more simply[44]

$$q_i^r = D_i^r \left(p_i, \mathbf{w}, \mathbf{c}_{-i}, \mathbf{y} \right). \qquad (3.10)$$

The equation to be estimated would then take the form

$$\ln q_i^r = \alpha_i + \beta_i \ln p_i + \sum_{s=1}^{S} \gamma_{is} y_s + \sum_{l=1}^{L} \mu_{il} w_l + \sum_{k \neq i} \delta_{ik} c_k + v_i, \qquad (3.11)$$

where α_i is a constant; β_i gives the estimate of the (opposite of) residual demand elasticity (because $d \ln q_i^r / d \ln p_i = -(dq_i^r/q_i^r)/(dp_i/p_i) = \epsilon_{ii}^r$);[45] the coefficients $\gamma_{is}, \mu_{il}, \delta_{ik}$, are the parameters of demand, industry-wide costs and cost other than firm i; and v_i is the error term.

However, regressing (3.11) alone would not give a consistent estimator, as there is a problem of simultaneity between p_i and q_i which are jointly determined in the supply – demand system (they are both endogenous variables, and p_i appears at the right-hand side of equation (3.11)).

Typically, this problem is solved by estimating equation (3.11) by using the instrumental variable method. In this case, the method implies using c_i as an instrument for the price p_i, since c_i (the firm-specific cost of firm i) is correlated with p_i, is not correlated with the residuals, and is not an explanatory variable in (3.11).

By doing so, we obtain an estimate of the residual demand elasticity of firm i, which in turn, is an estimate of its market power: the lower the estimated value of ϵ_{ii}^r, the higher the market power of the firm.

Note that the only firm-level data needed for this method are those on the price, quantity and firm-specific cost of the firm whose market power we are interested in.[46]

---

[44] Note that this way of proceeding amounts to assuming that the firm whose residual demand function we build behaves as a Stackelberg leader.

[45] Note that $\epsilon_{ii}^r = \epsilon_{ii} - \sum_{j \neq i}^{n} \epsilon_{ij} \eta_{ij}$, where $\epsilon_{ii} = -(\partial q_i/q_i)/(\partial p_i/p_i)$ is the own price elasticity of the (standard) demand function, $\epsilon_{ij} = (\partial q_i/q_i)/(\partial p_j/p_j)$ is the cross-price elasticity between firm i and firm j and $\eta_{ij} = (\partial p_j/p_j)/(\partial p_i/p_i)$ is the elasticity of best reply functions, and measures by how much a rival j increases its price following a price increase by firm i.

[46] Possibly complemented by data which can summarise $\mathbf{c}_{-i}$.

Residual Demand Elasticity in Merger Analysis   The same method can be applied to the analysis of mergers to estimate the joint market power possessed by two merging firms. Suppose for instance that we are interested in the likely impact of a merger between the first two firms, call them 1 and 2, in our industry of n firms. By proceeding in a similar way as above, one obtains the (partial) residual demand functions for firms 1, 2 as

$$q_i^{pr} = D_i^{pr}\left(p_1, p_2, \mathbf{w}, \mathbf{c}_{-1\&2}, \mathbf{y}\right), \qquad i = 1, 2, \tag{3.12}$$

which in logarithm becomes

$$\ln q_i = \alpha_i + \beta_{ii} \ln p_i + \beta_{ij} \ln p_j$$

$$+ \sum_{s=1}^{S} \gamma_{is} y_s + \sum_{l=1}^{L} \mu_{il} w_l + \sum_{k=3}^{n} \delta_{ik} c_k + v_i, \qquad (i, j = 1, 2; i \neq j) \tag{3.13}$$

By using the firm-specific cost variables c_1 and c_2 as instruments for p_1 and p_2, and jointly regressing the two partial residual demand curves (3.13), the coefficients β_{ii}, β_{ij} give an estimate of the partial residual demand elasticities $\epsilon_{ii}^{pr} = -(dq_i^{pr}/q_i^{pr})/(dp_i/p_i)$ and $\epsilon_{ij}^{pr} = (dq_i^{pr}/q_i^{pr})/(dp_j/p_j)$.[47]

These coefficients provide an estimate not only of the market power of each of the two firms, but also of how much the market power of, say, firm 1, is constrained by firm 2 (and vice versa). Note that the value $\left(\beta_{ii} - \beta_{ij}\right)$ gives an estimate of the market power that the merging firms will enjoy in the market, as the difference between these two coefficients tells us by how much the demand faced by firm 1 decreases if both p_1 and p_2 increase by the same percentage after the merger. The lower the estimated value of this difference, the higher the market power that the merging firms are likely to enjoy, and hence the more adverse effects of the merger (other things being equal, of course).

3.3.2.2 Logit Models**

In this section, I briefly introduce the main features of a technique which is based on a *multinomial logit demand*, itself derived from a discrete choice model of consumers' behaviour.[48] Logit models, due to McFadden (1973), allow one to sharply reduce the dimensionality problems when dealing with differentiated products. They have become very popular in recent years, and have been used to estimate market power of firms and to test whether there is collusion in an industry. They also provide the

---

[47] Baker and Bresnahan (1985) estimate the partial residual demands jointly for the two firms by the method of three-stage least squares, to increase the power of the estimators. See Baker and Bresnahan (1985: 436–7).

[48] I draw here mainly on Werden and Froeb (1994) and Werden, Froeb and Tardiff (1996). See also Anderson, De Palma and Thisse (1992).

basis for simulations that aim at predicting the likely effects of mergers, that is the extent to which market power will be exercised by merging firms.[49]

The Logit Demand Model Suppose there exist n products that are mutually exclusive alternatives for consumers and that exhaust the set C of possible choices. Assume that consumer i has the following utility from consuming product j:[50]

$$U_{ij} = \alpha_j - \beta p_j + e_{ij}, \tag{3.14}$$

where the explanatory variable, the price, is alternative-specific (that is, it refers to the products) and it has the same coefficient for all alternatives ($\beta_j = \beta_k = \beta$ for all j and k),[51] α_j is a product-specific constant, and where the random component e_{ij} can be either unobservable product characteristics or (equally unobservable) subjective preferences of individual i.

Maximisation of the individual utility gives the probability that j will be chosen for the population of all consumers:

$$\pi_j = \Pr(U_j > U_k), \qquad \text{for all} \quad k \in C, \quad k \neq j, \tag{3.15}$$

which can be re-written as

$$\pi_j = \Pr[(e_{ik} - e_{ij}) < (\alpha_j - \beta p_j) - (\alpha_k - \beta p_k)], \qquad \text{for all} \quad k \in C \quad k \neq j. \tag{3.16}$$

Note that each $(e_{ik} - e_{ij})$ is a random variable. By specifying the distribution of all residuals, one can obtain the joint cumulative distribution of the multivariate random variable (of $n - 1$ dimensions), which expresses π_j, the probability of choice of product j, as a function of product characteristics and parameters. More specifically, it is possible to prove that if all residuals are independently and identically distributed according to the *extreme value distribution*, one obtains that π_j takes a logistic distribution function (Anderson et al., 1992: 39–40):

$$\pi_j = \frac{\exp(\alpha_j - \beta p_j)}{\sum_{k \in C} \exp(\alpha_k - \beta p_k)}. \tag{3.17}$$

Estimation of Logit Models The parameters that one would like to estimate in the logit model are those pertaining to the utility functions, that is the α_js and β. Now that we know the probability π_j, and given the availability of data on individual choices and on prices, the Maximum Likelihood method can be used

---

[49] Willig (1991) is perhaps the first author who has suggested the use of the logit model for merger analysis.

[50] For simplicity, I assume from the outset that the utility function takes a linear form and that the price is the only relevant product characteristic.

[51] This model is known as a *conditional logit* model.

to estimate the α_js and β.[52] To solve the problem of indeterminacy inherent to the logit model, one of the α_j must be set equal to an arbitrary value, and the nth product is taken as an outside good, whose price is assumed to be zero. Call *inside goods* all goods but the nth.

There is one difficulty with this method. The probability of choosing a certain product depends not only on the utility of that product, but also – as we have seen from equation (3.15) – on the utility of the other products that have not been chosen. This requires us first to identify the set of the possible choices available and second to find data on the characteristics of all the choices that have not been made, which might well be very difficult and costly.

Alternative ways of proceeding are to use *choice-based sampling*, that is to use data only on individuals who make certain choices; or data on the ranking of choices that particular individuals would make.[53]

Estimation of logit models with data on individuals and the choices they make will present *endogeneity* problems when observed choice characteristics co-vary with unobserved choice characteristics. This is the case, for instance, when the unobserved quality of a product increases the price of that product (the ML estimate might suggest that consumers will want to buy a product with higher prices, whereas it is the unobserved quality variable which drives them). The use of instrumental variables estimation can help solve this problem.[54]

The own-price (here expressed as a positive number) and cross-price elasticities of demand are given by

$$\varepsilon_{jj} = \beta p_j (1 - \pi_j); \qquad (3.18)$$

$$\varepsilon_{jk} = \beta p_k \pi_k. \qquad (3.19)$$

The estimates of the α_js and the β obtained above are therefore used to compute all the relevant elasticities of the model (since from those estimates one can obtain all probabilities π_j, as in Equation (3.17)).

Independence of Irrelevant Alternatives and Nested Logit Models   A crucial property of the logit model is the so-called property of *Independence of Irrelevant Alternatives* (IIA), according to which the odds ratio of any two choices is independent of other available choices. In other words, the choice of a consumer between buying product A or product B must be independent of whether any product C is also available or not. An implication of the IIA property is that the cross-price

---

[52] McFadden (1973) studied ML estimation and its properties. He showed that ML estimators are asymptotically efficient under general conditions.

[53] See Werden et al. (1996: 90–2) for a discussion of this point.

[54] See Berry, Levinsohn and Pakes (1995); and Hausman, Leonard and Zona (1994), who use the price in other cities to instrument for the price of any given city.

elasticity between a given product j and any product $k \neq j$ is always the same (Anderson et al., 1992: 44). Clearly, this property is based on assumptions about the pattern of substitutability that might be too strong. Consider for instance the choice of an individual who is indifferent between buying a general newspaper, call it *Corriere*, and a sports newspapers, call it *Gazzetta dello Sport*. If these two are the only newspapers available, then the probabilities of buying one or the other will be equal: $\Pr(Corriere) = \Pr(Gazzetta) = 1/2$.

But suppose now that the same consumer is given another choice, which is another sports newspaper, *Tuttosport*, very similar to *Gazzetta*. Now this consumer should be indifferent between buying the general newspaper and one of the two sports newspapers and, conditional on buying a sports newspaper, indifferent between *Gazzetta* and *Tuttosport*. Therefore, the probability of choosing each newspaper will be $\Pr(Corriere) = 1/2$ and $\Pr(Gazzetta) = \Pr(Tuttosport) = 1/4$. In this example, the IIA property does not hold, because the odds ratio of any two choices is not independent of the presence or the absence of other possible choices. Indeed, the ratio between the probabilities of buying *Corriere* and *Gazzetta* is 1 if *Tuttosport* is not an available choice for the consumer, but 2 if *Tuttosport* is available.

To see whether the substitutability among the products in the industry is compatible with the IIA property or not, econometric tests can be employed. The idea behind such tests is as follows. Suppose that in the market being analysed there exist subsets of products that might be closer substitutes for each other, for instance, in newspaper markets one can suspect that general newspapers are close substitutes among each other and poorer substitutes of sports newspapers, and that sports newspapers are close substitutes among each other but poorer substitutes of general ones. One could first run estimates of a model where observations on the choice of all newspapers are included in the sample, and then run estimates with only a subset of observations (for instance, dropping the observations related to *Tuttosport* in the above example). If the two estimates obtained are close enough to each other, then the pattern of substitution implied by the data is compatible with the IIA property; otherwise, it is not. (Whether the coefficients are close enough or not should be assessed with a formal test, such as the Hausman test, that provides a formal test of the null hypothesis that the coefficients obtained from the two estimations are "identical".)

If the econometric tests indicate that the IIA is not consistent with the data, one could adopt a so-called *nested logit* model, where choices of different orders are assumed. With a single nest, for instance, the set C of all possible choices is divided into two subsets: one, that groups all products included in the nest, and the other that includes all the remaining products. (For instance, in the example above one could put all the sports newspapers in a nest.) There exist then expressions that give the unconditional choice probabilities for products that belong to the set and for the remaining ones and, starting from these probabilities, one can proceed towards an estimate of the model.

Nested logit models become more complex as one adds more nests into the analysis. An alternative approach, when the pattern of substitutability among products is unlikely to be reflected in a simple nested model, is to use *random-coefficients logit* models. Such models assume that consumer preferences are heterogenous, and estimate the unknown parameters of the distribution of consumers' heterogeneity. Some of the most interesting contributions in the econometric estimates of market power and collusion make use of this technique.[55]

Simulating Effects of a Merger with Logit Models   So far, I have presented the logit model as a model used to estimate with a maximum likelihood approach the elasticities of demand of certain products. The logit model, however, intended as a model of consumer choice, can also be used to simulate the effects of a merger. This different approach is not aimed at providing econometric estimates, but rather at predicting the after-merger prices from some available data.

The methodology that follows is taken from Werden and Froeb (1994) and Werden et al. (1996), who re-parameterise the model by using as primitives an aggregate demand elasticity (see below) and market shares.

Consider a version of the logit model where the nth product is the outside good whose price is set equal to zero. Werden and Froeb (1994) define an *aggregate elasticity price of demand for the inside goods* as

$$\varepsilon \equiv [\partial \pi_I(\lambda \mathbf{p})/\partial \lambda]\,[\overline{p}/\pi_I(\mathbf{p})] = \beta \overline{p} \pi_n, \qquad (3.20)$$

where $\mathbf{p}$ is the vector of the prices of all inside goods, $\overline{p}$ is some benchmark weighted average price, $\pi_I \equiv 1 - \pi_n(\mathbf{p})$ is the sum of the choice probabilities of the inside goods, and λ is a scalar. This industry elasticity measures the increase in the demand of the set of all inside goods when all inside prices are increased by a factor λ. Werden and Froeb (1994) and Werden et al. (1996) take it as a primitive of the model. The other primitive of their model is given by individual *market shares*, that is the choice probabilities for the inside goods conditional on an inside good being chosen. They are given by

$$s_j = \frac{\pi_j}{1 - \varepsilon/(\beta \overline{p})}. \qquad (3.21)$$

By replacing $\pi_j = s_j\,(1 - \varepsilon/(\beta \overline{p}))$ in equations (3.18) and (3.19) and rearranging, one obtains the individual own-price and cross-price elasticities (which are going

---

[55] The main references are Berry (1994), Berry, Levinsohn and Pakes (1995) and Nevo (2001). Nevo (2000) offers a discussion of the recent advances in such models.

to be used below to derive the price–cost margins) as

$$\varepsilon_{jj} = \frac{p_j}{p} \left[\beta \overline{p}(1 - s_j) + \varepsilon s_j \right];$$ (3.22)

$$\varepsilon_{jk} = \frac{p_k s_k}{p} \left[\beta \overline{p} - \varepsilon \right].$$ (3.23)

Given prices and market shares, β and ε (which are industry, and not individual firm's, variables that might be available from previous studies, might be estimated, or are guessed at) the own- and cross-price elasticities of demand can be recovered.

The choice probabilities of an inside product j and of the outside good are given by expression (3.17), and the logarithm of their ratio will be

$$\ln \left(\frac{\pi_j}{\pi_n} \right) = \ln \left(\frac{e^{\alpha_j - \beta p_j}}{e^{\alpha_n}} \right),$$ (3.24)

where $p_n = 0$ has been used. By simplifying and rearranging this becomes

$$\alpha_j = \alpha_n + \beta p_j + \ln \pi_j - \ln \pi_n, \qquad j = 1, 2, \ldots, n-1.$$ (3.25)

From (3.20) we know that $\pi_n = \varepsilon/(\beta \overline{p})$, and we also know that $\pi_j = s_j (1 - \varepsilon/(\beta \overline{p}))$, where $\overline{p}$ is the share-weighted average pre-merger price. Substituting them into the previous expression (3.25) gives

$$\alpha_j = \alpha_n + \beta p_j + \ln s_j + \ln \left(\frac{\beta \overline{p}}{\varepsilon} - 1 \right), \qquad j = 1, 2, \ldots, n-1.$$ (3.26)

This equation says that the α_j's can all be found analytically, given that the variables at the RHS are known (and α_n is set equal to an arbitrary constant): β and ε are known; and prices and market shares are data that are assumed to be available.

To complete the model, assume that (1) each firm before the merger produces only one differentiated product; (2) each firm has no fixed costs and a constant marginal cost c_j; (3) firms compete in prices; (4) all other product characteristics are fixed (that is, the merger could neither lead to entry nor product re-positioning by the existing firms).

Under such assumptions, we know that the FOCs for profit maximisation can be re-written as: $(p_j - c_j)/p_j = 1/\varepsilon_{jj}$ (this is nothing else than the Lerner index). By using expression (3.22) we can then obtain each firm's margin as

$$p_j - c_j = \frac{\overline{p}}{\beta \overline{p}(1 - s_j) + \varepsilon s_j}, \qquad j = 1, 2, \ldots, n-1,$$ (3.27)

which implies that a firm's margin increases with its market share (s_j) and decreases with the substitutability among the inside products (β), and decreases with the substitutability between inside and outside goods (ε). Equation (3.27) allows us to find analytically the marginal costs of each firm, since it expresses c_j as a function of p_j, $\overline{p}$, β, s_j, and ε, which are all given.

The next step is to see what happens under a merger. Without loss of generality, suppose that firms 1 and 2 merge, and call m the resulting firm. The FOCs of price maximisation for firm m imply that

$$p_1 - c_1 = p_2 - c_2 = \frac{\overline{p}}{\beta \overline{p}(1 - s_m) + \varepsilon s_m}, \qquad (3.28)$$

where s_m is the pre-merger market share and $\overline{p}$ is the share-weighted average price before the merger. Since all parameters are known (marginal costs have been derived by using the FOCs and actual pre-merger prices, as explained above), replacing them in equations (3.28) gives the predicted post-merger prices. From these, one could also predict the effect of the merger on consumer surplus and total welfare.[56]

3.4 EXERCISES

Exercise 3.1   Briefly describe the hypothetical monopolist test and explain the rationale for using it as a market definition test. Then apply the test to define markets for goods you are familiar with. For instance, (a) is there a separate market for pizzerias in your town? Or should pizzerias be included in a wider market including also fast-foods and restaurants? (b) Is there a separate market for the bus service (or train, or airplane services) between your home town and your university town (or any two towns you know)? Or is there a wide market including all types of transportation between such two towns? (c) Is there a separate relevant market for anti-trust textbooks?

Exercise 3.2   The extent to which a firm can exercise market power is limited by the existence of potential entrants, or more generally by firms that can start supplying a competing product once attracted by higher prices in the market. Should these considerations be taken into account when defining the relevant market or when assessing market power?

Exercise 3.3   A well-known premium brand of tennis shoes and a cheap minor brand of tennis shoes are considering a merger, and you have to determine the relevant market. One piece of information you have is the wholesale prices set by the producers for the last five years, and this shows that the premium brand's price is consistently twice as much as the minor brand's price. Will you conclude that the two products should be put in the same, or in separate markets?

---

[56] See Werden and Froeb (1994) and Werden et al. (1996) for a complete discussion, that includes an overview of the implications of the logit demand model, reports the expressions that can be used to compute consumer surplus and welfare, and presents some applications.

Exercise 3.4 What considerations should be taken into account when defining product markets and assessing market power in after-markets or secondary markets (that is, the markets for spare parts or services for a particular brand of a product)?

Exercise 3.5 What is the rationale for using market shares as a screening device in the assessment of market power stage of investigations? What other variables would you like to know before concluding whether a firm with a given market share is dominant?

Exercise 3.6 *Briefly explain the rationale for using the residual demand elasticity analysis and the logit model for investigations on market power in differentiated products industries.

Exercise 3.7 **(*Buyer power coordination – from Fumagalli and Motta (2000)*) An incumbent firm, I, has already sunk its market-specific cost, and a potential entrant, E, still has to incur this fixed sunk cost, F. If it enters, it would produce the same homogenous good as the incumbent. The potential entrant is more efficient, with a unit variable cost c_E strictly lower than the cost of the incumbent, c_I. Buyers have unit demands for the good and their maximum willingness to pay (valuation for the good) is V. At $t = 0$, N buyers call a procurement auction for the good. At $t = 1$, the incumbent and the potential entrant simultaneously make their (public) bids to all the buyers. At $t = 2$, each buyer observes the bids and (independently of the others) decides whether to accept the incumbent's or the entrant's offer. At $t = 3$ the incumbent fulfils all the orders it has received; the entrant observes the number of buyers who addressed it, and decides whether to actually enter the industry or not. In the former case, it immediately makes the necessary investment and fulfils the orders. In the latter case, it stays out and has payoff 0. At $t = 4$, the buyers whose orders have not been fulfilled by firm E can turn to the incumbent. We assume that (A1) $F > V - c_E$, i.e., a single buyer is never enough to trigger entry, and (A2) $F < N(c_I - c_E)$, i.e., entry is viable if the entrant charges some price $p \geq c_I$ and is addressed by all buyers. Show that there exists an equilibrium where the potential entrant does not enter the industry and indicate under which condition this occurs.

3.4.1 Solutions to Exercises

Exercise 3.7 We will solve the game by backward induction.

$t = 4$: If E did not enter, I will offer the good at $p_I = V$ to the buyers who addressed E in $t = 2$ but were not served by E.

$t = 3$: E receives a number S_E of orders. Given the price he quoted in $t = 1$, he will enter if $S_E(p_E - c_E) \geq F$.

$t = 2$: Buyers observe the bids p_I and p_E. Case 1: $p_I < p_E \leq V$ (we will ignore cases where either of the two firms quotes a price above V). All N buyers will address I. Case 2: $c_I \leq p_E \leq p_I \leq V$ (we will ignore cases where either of the two firms quotes a price below c_I). Then, buyers know that E will only enter if $S_E \geq F/(p_E - c_E) = S_E^*(p_E)$. By (A1), we know that a single buyer will never be enough to trigger entry, i.e. $S_E^*(p_E) > 1$ for all $p_E \in [c_I, V]$. At this stage, the buyers' choice game has only two equilibria: $S_E = N$, $S_I = 0$ (all buyers patronise the entrant, who will enter since by (A2) entry is worthwhile, and supply the good at a lower price than I); and $S_I = N$, $S_E = 0$ (the "mis-coordination" equilibrium, where all buyers address the incumbent; note that a single buyer has no incentive to deviate, as he alone would not be able to trigger E's entry, so he would have to turn to I in $t = 4$ and buy the good at price V instead.)

$t = 1$: equilibrium 1: $S_E = N$, $S_I = 0$ will only be sustained by the price pair $p_E^* = p_I^* = c_I$ (quasi Bertrand with unequal marginal cost). Equilibria 2 (mis-coordination equilibria): $S_I = N$, $S_E = 0$ will be sustained by $p_I^* = V$ and any $p_E^* \leq p_I^*$ (I will anticipate buyers' mis-coordination and therefore charge the maximum price they are willing to pay, i.e., V).

4

Collusion and Horizontal Agreements

4.1 INTRODUCTION

Collusive agreements can take different forms: firms might agree on sales prices, allocate quotas among themselves, divide markets so that some firms decide not to be present in certain markets in exchange for being the sole seller in others, or coordinate their behaviour along some other dimensions. Institutional arrangements to sustain collusion might range from a very well organised cartel-like structure where a central office (secret, if anti-trust laws exist) takes the main decisions, to situations where firms merely find some form of communication to sustain the agreement. Further, a collusive outcome might be sustained even in a situation where firms never meet to discuss prices or never exchange sensitive information (but I shall argue that in such a case, labelled "tacit collusion", the law should not intervene.)

Collusive practices allow firms to exert market power they would not otherwise have, and artificially restrict competition and increase prices, thereby reducing welfare.[1] Accordingly, they are prohibited by any anti-trust law, and a large part of the anti-trust authorities' efforts is devoted to fighting such practices. However, while any serious anti-trust authority would certainly attack a cartel or an explicit agreement among competitors to set prices, or share markets, there might be divergences as to the standard of proof required in less blatant infringements of the law, and as to the treatment of cases where firms manage to keep prices high without overtly colluding.

The main purpose of this chapter is to identify the main mechanisms behind collusion, to study the factors which facilitate it, and to explain which behaviour should be treated as an infringement of the law and which one should not. I shall also analyse what actions anti-trust authorities should take in order to deter and break collusion.

The chapter is structured in the following way: Section 4.1.1 briefly sketches the main features of collusion from an economic point of view. Section 4.2 investigates the industry features, contractual characteristics, and other factors that make collusion more likely to occur. These two sections are theoretical in nature, and draw on the existing and well-developed industrial organisation literature on collusion.

---

[1] See Chapter 2 on the relationship between market power and welfare.

Section 4.3 is also theoretical, but it deals with technical issues and is intended for advanced readers only. Section 4.4 instead deals with the "practice" of collusion: I will indicate what should be the legal standards for finding firms guilty of collusion, and what actions to take to deter and break collusion. Section 4.5 is devoted to the discussion of agreements among competing firms, which do not concern the fixing of prices, outputs or markets. This is the case, for instance, when firms create a joint-venture or collaborate in research and development activities. Finally, Section 4.6 studies the *Wood pulp* case, which gives the opportunity to discuss further the issue of the standard of proof in collusion cases.

4.1.1 What is Collusion?

... First, a Warning   In this section, I briefly characterise the concept of collusion from the point of view of industrial economics. Note that here I will not use the term "collusion" as a synonym for "collusive agreement that should be outlawed". Indeed, one of the main themes of this chapter is that whereas in economic theory collusion is defined as a market outcome (i.e., "high prices", in a sense to be specified further below), anti-trust authorities and judges should consider as illegal only practices where firms *explicitly* coordinate their actions to achieve a collusive outcome.

The reader should then be aware that in Sections 4.1.1 and 4.2 I will use the term "collusion" in a way that adheres to economic theory but might be slightly misleading, as it comprehends both explicit and tacit collusion, whereas the law should punish only explicit agreements (as Section 4.4 will argue).[2]

Defining Collusion in Economic Theory   In economics, collusion is a situation where firms' prices are higher than some competitive benchmark.[3] A slightly different definition would label collusion as a situation where firms set prices which are close enough to monopoly prices.[4] In any case, in economics collusion coincides with an outcome (high-enough price), and not with the specific form through which that outcome is attained. Indeed, as I explain below, collusion can occur both when firms act through an organised cartel (explicit collusion), or when they act in a purely non-co-operative way (tacit collusion).

---

[2] I will argue that anti-trust authorities should also deal with tacit collusion, but in a preventive way, that is trying to eliminate business practices that might facilitate collusion and through merger control.

[3] In technical terms, the benchmark is usually the equilibrium price of a game where firms meet only once in the marketplace (a situation where collusion would not arise). For instance, in a homogenous goods game where firms choose prices, a collusive outcome would exist whenever prices are higher than the one-shot Bertrand equilibrium price; where firms choose quantities, whenever they are lower than the one-shot Cournot equilibrium quantities.

[4] See Kühn (2001). Monopoly, or joint-maximisation prices, are the prices which would be set if all the firms in the industry were affiliates of the same company, or managed by the same manager.

What Are the Main Ingredients of Collusion?   It is not easy for firms to achieve a collusive outcome, even if they are free to agree on the prices they set. In particular, every firm would have the temptation to unilaterally deviate from a collusive action, as by doing so it would increase its profit.

Consider for instance an imaginary industry consisting of two fruit sellers in a street market. Imagine they both sell pears of identical quality, and that they each pay $1 per kilo to their suppliers. Imagine also that each seller thinks that $2 per kilo is the monopoly price, and believes the other thinks in the same way. When a seller arrives at his stall, he has to decide the sales price. Suppose that he thinks the rival is setting a price of $2. If he charges $2 for his pears, he will get roughly half of the buyers, as people who want to buy pears are indifferent between buying from him or from the other vendor. But he will have a strong temptation to *deviate*, that is to charge a lower price than his rival: if he sets a price of, say, $1.9, consumers will all buy from him (why pay more for an identical product?). As a result, he will still enjoy a high unit margin but he will sell more units: in short, he will make more profits than if he sold at the "collusive" price of $2.[5]

The acknowledgement that any collusive situation naturally brings with it the temptation to *deviate* from it and therefore to break collusion leads us to the identification of the two elements which must exist for collusion to arise. First, its participants must be able to *detect* in a timely way that a deviation (a firm setting a lower price or producing a higher output than the collusive levels agreed upon) has occurred.[6] Second, identifying the deviation is not enough: there must also be a *punishment*, which might take the form of rivals producing much higher quantities (or selling at much lower prices) in the periods after the deviation, thus depressing the profit of the deviator.[7]

Only if a firm knows both that a deviation will be identified quickly and that it will be punished (i.e., it will have to forego enough profits because of the market reaction of the cartel members) might it refrain from deviating, so that the collusive outcome will arise.[8]

---

[5] Of course, for this simple example to hold it is necessary that at the collusive price of $2 the seller does not manage to sell all the pears he comes to the market with. Otherwise, he would not have an incentive to cut his price in order to increase sales.

[6] Detection of a deviation is not always easy: in many markets, firms' prices and outputs are not directly observable. Stigler (1964) was probably the first to underline this problem, and its consequences upon the likelihood of collusion.

[7] Note that a punishment should be thought of as a more aggressive market behaviour, and not as a direct monetary (or physical!) punishment. Note also that generally a punishment also hits the punishing firms, and not just the deviating firm, precisely because it has to rely on market mechanisms (a low price affects all the firms' profits). It is therefore crucial that firms are willing to take part in the punishment.

[8] In turn, this implies that collusion can be sustained only if firms meet repeatedly in the marketplace. Otherwise, a punishment cannot take place. In technical terms, collusion will never arise in a one-shot game. This is why collusion should be modelled through dynamic (repeated) games.

To continue our example, after having seen why a fruit seller has a temptation to cut prices below the collusive level of $2, let us see under which conditions he will deviate. If the street market is small enough, and if the sellers post the prices of the fruit they sell, detection of the price cut will be immediate. After the price cut has been identified, one can bet that a seller who has so far sold at the price of $2 will immediately retaliate, and likely will start to sell at a price lower than $1.9 per kilo. The result will be a price war which will reduce the profit of both. A seller contemplating a deviation will certainly expect that the rival will retaliate. As a result, the prospect of selling for much of the day at very low prices will deter him from deviating in the first place. In other words, the awareness that a deviation will be easily detected and that a market punishment will ensue will make each seller refrain from deviating and convince him to stick to the collusive price instead.

To summarise, for collusion to occur, firstly, there must be the possibility to *detect* deviations from a collusive action in a timely way. Secondly, there must be a credible *punishment* which follows a deviation.

It is important to stress that in the example, the two fruit vendors do not talk to each other, neither directly nor through intermediaries: collusive prices will arise through purely non-co-operative behaviour of the sellers. In other words, if detection of deviations is rapid, and if (market) punishments of deviations are likely and credible, then *tacit collusion* can arise: firms do not necessarily have to talk to each other, let alone agree on complicated schemes, for a collusive outcome to be sustainable. All that is needed is the awareness that a deviation will be identified, and that a "punishment" will follow.

Which Collusive Price?   A difficulty in the example above is that it is not clear how the "collusive price" is chosen. Imagine that, for some reason, each seller thinks that the other would set a price of $1.5, rather than a price of $2. Then, again a collusive situation might occur in equilibrium, but this time with sellers setting a price lower than the monopoly price. In other words, the collusive mechanism I have described works for many different prices and results in firms getting quite different levels of profits.[9]

This result raises the important issue of *coordination*. Firms that are tacitly colluding might arrive at the fully collusive price, but this is just one of the many possible equilibrium outcomes (one of these also being the competitive outcome, i.e., the one-shot game equilibrium price). So, is there an outcome that is more likely than the other? And, since firms have an interest in coordinating on an outcome with the highest possible prices, how can they achieve that outcome?

[9] The 'folk theorem' (Friedman, 1971) says that in games with infinite horizon if the discount factor is large enough, firms can have any profit between zero and the fully collusive profit at the "collusive" equilibrium. See Section 4.2.5.3 for a simple formal argument.

Coordination: The Difference between Tacit and Overt Collusion Under *tacit collusion*, it is difficult for the firms to solve the coordination problem. If firms cannot communicate with each other, they can make mistakes, and select a price (or a quantity) which is not jointly optimal for the firms, and might be difficult to change. Using the market to signal intentions to coordinate on a different price might be very costly. If a firm believes the "right" price for the industry is higher and increases its own price to signal it, it will lose market share in the adjustment period. If a firm decreases its own price to try to coordinate on a lower equilibrium price, this move might be understood as a deviation and trigger a costly price war. Therefore, experimenting with price changes to coordinate on another collusive equilibrium might be too costly.

Under *explicit collusion*, instead, firms can talk to each other and coordinate on their jointly preferred equilibrium without having to experiment with the market, which is costly. Furthermore, if there are some shocks which modify market conditions, communication will allow the firms to change to a new collusive price without the risk of triggering a period of punishment.

Suppose for instance that, in the example above, one seller knows that demand for pears has decreased, so that he thinks the optimal price is now lower, say $1.8. Absent communication with the other vendor, our seller faces a problem: If he reduces the price to $1.8, as new market conditions suggest, collusion might break. Indeed, the rival vendor might have a different perception of market demand, and/or misinterpret the new low price as a "deviation", and start a price war as a punishment. However, if he sticks instead to the usual price of $2, he will make lower profits, because demand is lower.

Explicit collusion avoids this problem: our vendor could simply tell his rival that he thinks it would be better to decrease the price, and communication will allow them to decide on a new price that suits them both, without risking any price war or a lengthy adjustment period.

Market allocation (or market-sharing) schemes, according to which a firm sells in a certain region (or serves customers of a certain type), whereas the rivals sell in other regions (or serve customers of a different type) – whether achieved by explicit collusion or historical accidents – have the advantage of allowing for prices to adjust to new demand or cost conditions without triggering possible price wars. A market allocation scheme avoids the possibility that, if a shock reduces production costs or market demand, a price reduction might trigger a price war. As long as each firm does not serve segments of demand (explicitly or tacitly) allocated to rivals, prices can change without the collusive outcome being disrupted. This probably explains why such collusive schemes are often used.[10]

I revisit the question of communication and coordination among firms in Section 4.2.2.2, and consider why competition policy should focus on explicit collusive

[10] I am grateful to Joe Harrington for stressing this point.

practices (that is, when some communication and coordination exists) in Section 4.4. Before doing that, however, it is appropriate to study collusion more deeply, and in particular to study the factors which facilitate collusion. This is done in the following Section 4.2.

4.2 FACTORS THAT FACILITATE COLLUSION

The analysis of collusion in modern industrial economics is based on the so-called *incentive constraint* for collusion: each firm compares the immediate gain it makes from a deviation with the profit it gives up in the future, when rivals react. Only if the former is lower than the latter will the firm choose the collusive strategy. In general, collusion is more likely to arise the lower the profit that a firm would obtain from deviating, the lower the expected profits it would make once the punishment starts, and the more weight firms attach to the future (i.e., when the "loss from deviation" occurs). (See Section 4.2.5.1 for a formal analysis.)

In this section, I briefly review the factors that are more often mentioned as those which foster collusive outcomes, and explain under which circumstances one should expect them to have that role. The discussion (see Section 4.2.5 for the formal analysis) is based on the framework delineated above (that is, the condition that says that a firm is better off colluding than deviating): if a given factor relaxes the incentive constraints of the firms, then it facilitates collusion; if it makes it more binding, it hinders it; if the effect is ambiguous, then the factor does not have a clear impact on collusion.

There are two main practical reasons behind the exercise conducted in this section. First, it is important to identify the factors that facilitate collusion so that anti-trust authorities can intervene so as to eliminate them whenever possible. Second, in some cases, especially in merger analysis, one has to evaluate whether a particular industry is prone to a collusive outcome or not. Studying the industry and assessing whether there are factors likely to lead to collusion become crucial.

Somehow arbitrarily, and mainly for the ease of presentation, I divide the study of facilitating factors into different categories.

4.2.1 Structural Factors

Concentration　　Other things being equal, collusion is the more likely the smaller the number of firms in the industry. The comparison between gains and losses from deviations illustrates why this is the case. Imagine that there are many firms of identical size and of large capacity, which co-exist in the industry. In a collusive situation, each of them will set a high price and get a (small) share of the total profits. However, if one of them deviates and sets a price lower than the rivals, it might get all the market for itself. Even if the punishment was harsh, so that a very small stream of expected profits would follow after a deviation, the gains from deviating would be so extraordinarily large in the deviation period that they would outweigh the collusive profits foregone during the punishment period. Compare this situation with the extreme one where there are only two firms in the industry. At a collusive equilibrium, each would get half the market, so that the gains from deviating are smaller relative to the lower profits due to the punishment which follows.

If firms are symmetric, a lower number of firms is equivalent to a higher degree of concentration, which is therefore associated – *ceteris paribus* – with more likely (tacit or explicit) collusion.

However, we shall see below that the more firms are asymmetric (in capacities, market shares, costs, or product range) the less likely collusion will be. This qualifies the finding that concentration facilitates collusion, in the following sense. If a measure of concentration rises with the asymmetric distribution of assets among the firms – as is the case with the Herfindahl–Hirschman Index (see Chapter 3) – then one should expect an ambiguous relationship between concentration and collusion: such a measure confounds two factors – higher average market share and asymmetry – that affect collusion in opposite ways. If instead the measure of concentration used does not vary with asymmetry – as for the concentration ratios, C_k, that sum the market shares of the k largest firms in the industry – then an increase in measured concentration should correspond to higher likelihood of collusion.

Finally, note that concentration also helps firms' coordination on a collusive outcome, not only its enforcement: the lower the number of players in the industry the easier for them to coordinate their behaviour.

Entry The easier entry into an industry (the lower entry barriers) the more difficult to sustain collusive prices. When prices and profits are high, new firms will be attracted into the industry, and this tends to disrupt the collusive outcome, by two possible mechanisms. Suppose first that the entrant does not want to pursue a collusive strategy and behaves aggressively.[11] This will subtract market shares to the incumbent firms that will have to decrease prices to keep their customers, thereby breaking the collusive equilibrium. Anticipating that entry might occur, the incumbents will be forced to keep prices low.

Suppose instead that both the entrant and the incumbent firms follow an accommodating strategy, with the entrant taking part in the (explicit or tacit) collusive behaviour. Since the larger the number of firms the less likely that collusion can be sustained, entry might break the collusive outcome. All the more so since if a new firm does enter and takes its share of the industry collusive profits, more entrants will be induced to follow the same strategy, and sooner or later collusion will be unsustainable.

---

[11] Such a firm might be a so-called "maverick". A maverick might also be a firm that is substantially different from the rivals (for instance because it has a smaller discount factor, a different utilisation of capacity or a smaller portfolio of brands). See the discussion on symmetry and collusion.

Overall, therefore, one should expect that the lower entry barriers (as determined by fixed entry costs that new firms would have to sink into the industry) the more difficult it will be to sustain collusion. Nevertheless, the existence of potential entrants might not always necessarily break collusion. Suppose for instance that an entrant expects the incumbent firms to react very aggressively to entry.[12] If the threat of such a strong reaction by the incumbents is credible, the entrants might decide not to enter in the first place.[13]

Cross-Ownership and Other Links among Competitors   If a firm has participation in a competitor, even without controlling it,[14] the scope for collusion will be enhanced. First and more obvious, if a representative of a firm is sitting in the board of directors of a rival firm, it will be easier to coordinate pricing and marketing policies. It might also be easier to exchange information on the marketing and pricing policies, which makes it easy to monitor a rival's behaviour and – as I discuss below – is an important facilitating factor for collusion. Second, even if a firm did not have any say in the business policies of the other, but just owned a share of it without representation on the board, the incentives to compete in the marketplace might be reduced. This is because the profits of the rival firm would affect the firm's own financial performance, composed of market profits and financial returns: an aggressive market strategy (like a deviation from a collusive price) would be less profitable than if there was no stake in the rival firm, because it would decrease the returns on financial investments.[15]

Overall, it would therefore seem wise not to allow a firm to have minority (*a fortiori*, controlling) shareholding in a competitor.[16]

[12] There is no reason to believe, *a priori*, that incumbents would always accommodate, or always fight, entry. In a nice empirical study, Scott Morton (1997) analyses the British shipping cartels at the turn of the last century and finds that some entrants were accepted and joined the cartel, whereas others (the weaker entrants) were fought.

[13] Gilbert and Vives (1986) analyse the case where joint predation occurs without the need for predators to coordinate. In Harrington (1989b), entry triggers the same (strongest possible) punishment as a deviation from collusive actions by the incumbents, hence reacting strongly to entry without more coordination than needed to devise the punishment strategies. But if incumbents did coordinate, then they would breach both Articles 81 and 82 in the EU, and Sections 1 and 2 of the Sherman Act in the US. The EC's *CEWAL* decision provides an interesting recent case study where incumbents (members of a maritime shipping conference) put in place a sophisticated mechanism to fight entry.

[14] If there is control, then this will be a merger (see Chapter 5). A minority shareholding is not subject to EU merger control.

[15] See Exercise 4.2 to formalise this idea. Similar considerations might also apply to cases where competing firms have common interests – such as joint-ventures – in certain markets or products. See also Martin (1995).

[16] Ritter et al. (2000: 553–4) say that it is not clear whether minority shareholdings are compatible with Article 81 of the Treaty, although "the acquisition of 10% or less in a *competitor* which is not associated with a representation in the board or veto rights may be considered as a *purely passive* shareholding for investment purposes".

Regularity and Frequency of Orders   *Regular orders* facilitate collusion. Indeed, an unusually large order would give a very strong temptation to deviate: by deviating, a firm would make unusually large profits, and the perspective of losing collusive profits obtained under the typically small expected demand is not enough to deter the deviation. The high *frequency of orders* also helps collusion because it allows for a timely punishment. If orders arrive only with large time intervals between them, one has a higher incentive to deviate because the punishment will be started only much later in the future, and will accordingly be discounted.

Buyer Power   The ability to sustain collusive prices in a given industry also depends on the degree of concentration of the buyers. A strong buyer can make use of its bargaining power to stimulate competition among the sellers, either by threatening to redirect orders from a current seller to others or to potential entrants (whose entry prospects would be rosier if guaranteed demand by a large buyer), or by threatening to start upstream production itself.

By concentrating its orders, a powerful buyer can also manage to break collusion. Rather than keeping a steady flow of small orders, by grouping them into large and less frequent orders a large buyer can induce suppliers to deviate from the collusive strategy (Snyder, 1996).

Finally, strong buyers might design procurement auctions so as to minimise the risk of collusive behaviour among suppliers (see Section 4.4.2 for a discussion of auction design).

Demand Elasticity   Although the elasticity of market demand is a factor that is sometimes mentioned as facilitating collusion, it is not clear why it should affect the *likelihood* of collusion. If demand is very elastic, then a given price cut will determine a large increase in the quantity demanded, but this is true both for the price cut in a deviation and for the price cut in the punishment period. In other words, elasticity of demand will in general affect both sides of the incentive constraint for collusion, and its net effect on sustainability of collusion is ambiguous.

However, demand elasticity will affect the *level* of the maximum collusive price (the lower the elasticity of demand the higher the monopoly price), which implies that there will be less reason to worry about possible collusion if demand elasticity is high.

Evolution of Demand   The impact of demand evolution over time upon collusion depends on the nature of demand shocks.[17] Suppose that current demand conveys no information about future demand – that is, demand shocks are independently and identically distributed, as in Rotemberg and Saloner (1986). Then, it is as if a large order suddenly arrived, and the analysis would be as above: firms would break

---

[17] It also depends on whether demand movements are *ex post* observable or not, as discussed in Section 4.2.2.1 below.

collusion to capture the profit of unusually large demand.[18] (Conversely, collusion will be more likely if a negative shock occurs.)

Suppose instead that demand movements are correlated over time, so that today's large order signals that demand will increase steadily. In this case, collusion is more likely: why should a firm give up the prospect of large future collusive profits for a small gain today, when the market is still small? (Conversely, collusion will be less likely when firms face a future of declining market demand.)[19]

Demand stability might help sustain collusion, to the extent that it increases the degree of observability in the market (see also Section 4.2.2.1). In a market characterised by frequent demand shocks or large uncertainty it might be difficult to understand whether poor sales are due to demand variability or to price undercutting of rivals. Accordingly, collusion might be more difficult to sustain. By contrast, in a mature stable market it would be easier to spot deviations and punish them, rendering collusion easier.

Product Homogeneity   Practitioners, anti-trust authorities and judges often maintain that it is easier to reach collusion with homogenous than differentiated products.[20] Theory is less clear about this point. Suppose that products are differentiated. In this case, it is harder to punish a deviant firm, since even a considerable reduction in prices by rivals would leave the deviant firm with a positive demand. This effect tends to discourage collusion, as only the fear of punishment makes firms refrain from deviating. However, for precisely the same reasons, under differentiated products a deviation is also less profitable: a deviant firm cannot expect to gain very large market shares from rivals unless it makes a very considerable cut in price, an effect that tends to facilitate collusion. Therefore, product homogeneity does not unambiguously raise the scope for collusion.[21] *A priori*, then, it is not clear – other things being equal – that collusion should be more likely in products like cement and gasoline than, say, cigarettes, colas or mineral waters, which are all consumer goods characterised by a high degree of consumer loyalty.[22]

---

[18] A market characterised by frequent and drastic innovations will also be less prone to collusion, as less weight is attached to the future (as incumbents anticipate that they might not be competitive in the near future) and the incentive to deviate is therefore higher. See Rey (2002).

[19] There are a number of papers that have formally studied the problem of sustainability of collusion over the business cycle. The intuitive results reported here coincide with the results of Haltiwanger and Harrington (1991), who find that collusion is more likely to break when demand is declining. But Fabra (2001b) extends their analysis by also considering possible capacity constraints, and she shows that Haltiwanger and Harrington's results hold only when aggregate industry capacity is large enough, whereas when it is small enough, collusion is less likely to be sustained when demand increases.

[20] For instance, product homogeneity is one of the recurrent features in European merger cases suspected to give rise to collusion.

[21] See, for instance, Ross (1992) for a formal analysis.

[22] The large advertising expenditures sustained in these markets explain why these products are perceived by consumers as very differentiated from each other. See Sutton (1991).

However, homogeneity might help collusion if firms sold not a single well-defined product but very many different product variants, so it would be more difficult for them to attain a collusive outcome. This makes sense, insofar as it reduces the visibility of deviations, and would thus diminish the possibility to resort to quick punishments.[23]

Symmetry Competition authorities and courts also regard symmetry among firms as a factor which facilitates collusion. Symmetry can concern different dimensions (such as market shares, number of varieties in the product portfolio, costs and technological knowledge, capacities), whose importance will clearly differ across industries. Many informal arguments support the idea that symmetry helps collusion: for instance, it is intuitive that people who are in a similar position would find it easier to arrive at an agreement which suits all of them. Recently, there have been some formal contributions to the literature which give further support to this idea.[24]

Compte, Jenny and Rey (2002) analyse a model where firms produce homogenous goods and have identical costs but differ in their capacities. In their model, the largest firm has the highest incentive to deviate from collusion (a firm whose capacity is filled when the price is at the collusive level does not have any incentive to cut the price) and the smaller firms have difficulties to punish (since they are capacity constrained, they cannot credibly threaten to punish a deviant firm). A more equal distribution of capacities would help collusion. If firms' positions were more similar, their incentives to deviate and to punish would be more aligned and collusion could be more easily sustained.

In Kühn and Motta (1999), there are multi-product firms that sell a different number of product varieties. The larger the firm (the higher the number of product varieties it sells) the stronger its interest in keeping prices high. Similarly to a firm having a large share of the market, for which a marginal reduction in the price would hurt all the infra-marginal units, here a price reduction in one variety would negatively affect all other varieties (the larger the firm the stronger pricing externalities). Instead, a small firm (that sells only one or few varieties) has a stronger incentive to deviate and free ride on high prices, as by decreasing prices it would capture demand from all rivals' products. Therefore, in this model the large firm finds it more difficult to punish and the small firms have the larger temptation to deviate from the collusive price.

Note that the mechanisms at work are quite different in Compte, Jenny and Rey (2002) and in Kühn and Motta (1999), but the results are the same: a more equal

---

[23] An alternative explanation of why product homogeneity might help collusion has been offered by Raith (1996a). He argues that different products might be subject to different demand shocks. If product homogeneity means that there is correlation in the demand shocks, then this might help collusion.

[24] There also exists some evidence from empirical analysis: See Barla (2000) on firm-size inequality and collusion in the airline industry.

distribution of assets relaxes the incentive constraints of both the small and the large firm and would help collusion.[25]

Multi-Market Contacts   For a long time, it has been argued that multi-market contacts – defined as the same firms meeting in more than one market – would help collusion. Indeed, there also exists some empirical evidence that this is the case. Evans and Kessides (1994) find that airline fares are significantly higher in routes where there exist carriers that have contacts on several routes; Parker and Röller (1997) find that prices tend to be higher in US mobile telephone markets characterised by multi-market contacts.

The suggested explanation used to be that when firms co-exist in several markets, then it is more costly for them to deviate from a collusive outcome, since they would be punished in all the markets at the same time. But this intuitive argument is incomplete and therefore faulty. Indeed, if a firm is present in many markets, it can also deviate in *all of them* at the same time, and this increases its incentive to deviate. *A priori*, the very fact that the same firms co-exist in several markets rather than in just one might not be sufficient to explain why the latter should help collusion. Indeed, Bernheim and Whinston (1990) show that when firms and markets are perfectly symmetric, multi-market contacts do not change the incentives for collusion. It is only when there are asymmetries that multi-market contacts might help.

The intuition behind the result that multi-market contacts might help collusion is not straightforward, but an example might help. Suppose that there exist two markets that are asymmetric in the following sense. In market A there are only two firms, call them 1 and 2, that have a similar share of that market. In market B, there are n firms, two of them being 1 and 2 (our multi-market firms), which equally share the market. Suppose that if the two markets were taken in isolation (that is, if in market B the n firms were only single-market firms), then collusion would arise in market A but not in market B (we know that collusion is harder to sustain where there are more firms). This is equivalent to saying that, at the prevailing discount factor, the incentive constraints (ICs) of the multi-market firms in market A are lax, whereas the ICs in market B (taken in isolation) are not satisfied. But the ICs of the multi-market firms are given by the pooling of the two ICs, one for each market. To understand why multi-market contacts help sustain collusion, consider two points. First, if the other $n - 2$ firms in market B had a larger share of the market, then their incentive to deviate would be reduced. (Recall that the larger the firm the lower its incentive to reduce its price.) Second, for each multi-market firm, the pooled IC will still hold if

---

[25] Vasconcelos (2001b) confirms these results within a very elegant model where he analyses optimal punishment schemes. He has a homogenous good model where firms differ in their capacities, but contrary to Compte et al. (2002) higher capacity implies lower cost. In his paper, large firms have higher incentives to deviate along the punishment path and small firms along the collusive path. Again, symmetry would help collusion. Harrington (1989a) analyses collusion when firms have different discount factors. He shows that when firms are asymmetric they manage to reach a collusive outcome by redistributing market shares.

the firm sold a bit less in market B. Indeed, accepting a lower market share in market B would increase the incentive to deviate in market B, but this can be outweighed by the fact that the incentive to deviate in market A is low. By pooling the ICs, the slackness of the IC in market A can be used to enforce collusion on the other market.

To further clarify the concept, consider the following example. Suppose that in market A a firm has 70% of the market and the other has 30%, whereas exactly the opposite situation occurs in market B. Apart from one firm selling more in one market (and vice versa), the firms have similar characteristics, and the markets present similar features and sizes. Also suppose that, if the two markets were taken in isolation, collusion would not be sustainable (the asymmetry in market shares being too strong). But now the same two firms operate in the same two markets: when they analyse whether they prefer to collude or to deviate, they will look at both markets together. This implies that they will have a single IC where the gains and losses from deviations are pooled across both markets. Effectively, under pooling it is as if there were now two symmetric firms in one large market, each firm holding a 50% share of it. Multi-market contacts here smooth the market asymmetries and by making the ICs of the firms more symmetric they help collusion.[26]

Inventories and Excess Capacities   Generally speaking, the role played by the presence of large levels of inventories and large excess capacity is ambiguous. Suppose for instance that all firms in an industry are endowed with excess capacity with respect to the expected levels of demand. Then this affects both sides of the incentive constraints in a similar way, rendering ambiguous the final effect on the condition for collusion. On the one hand, large excess capacity implies that there is a stronger incentive to deviate (a price reduction would help fill capacity). On the other hand, if rivals are also endowed with large capacities, the punishment is more likely to be strong.[27]

Since both theory and empirical evidence on this point are ambiguous,[28] it is unclear whether excess capacity helps collusion.

---

[26] Another reason why multi-market contacts might help collusion is that they tend to increase the frequency of the firms' contacts.

[27] Of course, this would be different if excess capacities (or large inventories) were unequally distributed. In this case, the arguments made above about asymmetry would apply: the more unequal the distribution of capacities, the less likely that collusion can be sustained.

[28] The first to model the relationship between capacity and collusion were Brock and Scheinkman (1985). Benoit and Krishna (1987) find that excess capacity is needed to sustain collusive outcomes, and Davidson and Deneckere (1990) that the greater the degree of excess capacity (which is determined endogenously in their game, and depends on the cost of capital) the more collusive the prices that can be sustained at equilibrium. These two papers suggest that the punishment effect of excess capacity (the fact that it allows for punishment to occur) is stronger than the cheating effect (the fact that excess capacity makes it more tempting to deviate). However, in a different setting, Compte et al. (2002: 10) find that – for symmetric firms – the higher industry capacity the less likely that collusion can be sustained. Some empirical papers on this point are mentioned in Davidson and Deneckere (1990: 525–6).

4.2.2 Price Transparency and Exchange of Information

In this section, I first emphasise the role of observability of prices and quantities in sustaining collusion (Section 4.2.2.1). This leads to the discussion of one practice, which helps firms improve observability of their actions, namely agreements to exchange past and current individual data. I also discuss (Section 4.2.2.2) the role of communication among firms. This also helps collusion as it might help firms coordinate on a particular outcome.

4.2.2.1 Observability of Firms' Actions Facilitates Enforcement

Identifying Deviations to Sustain Collusion: Theoretical Considerations   Detection of deviations is a crucial ingredient for collusion, and Stigler (1964) argued that collusive agreements would break down because of *secret* price cuts. In fact, Green and Porter (1984) show that if actual prices (or price discounts) are not observable, collusion would be more difficult to sustain, but it could still arise at equilibrium. Their important contribution can be summarised in the following way. Imagine an industry where sellers cannot observe the prices charged by rivals and where market demand levels are also unobservable. Then, a seller would not know if a lower than expected number of customers served is due to a negative shock in demand or to a price cut by a rival, which has stolen some (or all) of his business. Green and Porter show that if the discount factor is high enough, there exists a set of collusive strategies that represent an equilibrium. The strategies are such that each firm sets a collusive price (which might be the price that maximises joint profits) as long as every firm faces a high level of demand. When a firm faces low (or zero) demand, then the punishment is triggered and each firm sets the one-shot equilibrium price for a finite number of periods. After this finite punishment phase, all firms revert to the collusive price.

Therefore, the model implies that collusion can be sustained at equilibrium, but unlike the standard model with perfect observability, collusive prices and profits will never be observed forever, even if no firm deviates. Indeed, the punishment is triggered whenever a low level of demand is observed, and will last for a certain number of periods, after which firms revert to the collusive prices.[29] The model has therefore an important implication. The observation of some periods with low prices is not sufficient to exclude that the industry is at a collusive equilibrium. Rather, price wars simply are the indispensable element of a collusive strategy when rivals' prices and market demand realisations are unobservable.[30]

---

[29] Playing price equal to marginal cost forever, that is an infinite punishment, would clearly be suboptimal here: since the punishment is triggered even if nobody has actually deviated, it would not make sense to condemn the industry to zero profit forever whenever a low level of demand is observed.

[30] On the other hand, as I discuss below, the alternance of high and low price levels is no proof either of a collusive outcome, since an industry at a non-collusive equilibrium might have lower prices under negative demand (or common input) shocks or increased capacities.

Since observability of prices and quantities helps firms to reach the most collusive outcomes (under perfect observability, price wars that are costly for the firms would not occur), competition policy should pay special attention to practices that help firms monitor each other's behaviour. One example of such a practice is given by information exchange agreements; that is discussed next. In Section 4.2.3, I also address other pricing practices that increase observability of firms' actions, such as resale price maintenance and best price clauses.

Exchange of Information on Past or Current Prices and Quantities   It is often the case that via trade associations or in other ways, firms in a given industry exchange data on prices, quantities, or other variables such as capacities, customer demand, cost and so on. In the light of the discussion above, it becomes important to identify the collusive potential of such communications among firms.[31]

First, we have seen above that exchange of information on past prices and quantities (or of verifiable information on prices and quantities set in the current period) of each individual firm facilitates collusion, as it allows to identify deviators and better target market punishments, which then become more effective and less costly for the punishing firms.

In the absence of disaggregate information on past prices and quantities, availability of more precise estimates of aggregate (market) demand would also help, as it allows firms to see whether a decrease in individual demand is due to cheating of rivals or to a negative shock in market demand. In turn, this implies that there would be no need for punishment phases which are triggered not by deviations but by a general decrease of market demand.[32]

Exchange of information about past (and current) prices and quantities helps firms sustain collusion, but it is possible that there might also be efficiency effects behind exchange of such data. For instance, better information about demand might allow firms to increase production in markets, times, and areas where demand is higher. The literature on information exchange has ambiguous findings.[33] Theoretically, it is possible in certain circumstances that exchanging information helps

---

[31] On collusion and exchange of information between competitors, see Kühn (2001).

[32] Porter (1983a) shows that exchange of private information about market demand reduces demand uncertainty and allows more collusive outcomes to be sustained. In a similar vein, Kandori (1992) shows that as demand uncertainty decreases, firms can attain higher collusive outcomes (and punishment phases become more severe), and Kandori and Matsushima (1998) also find that communicating information about past realisations helps collusion. Technically, the last paper differs from Green and Porter (1984), Porter (1983a) and Kandori (1992) in that it assumes that firms receive private rather than public signals, so that each firm might have a different belief of what has happened in the industry. (Has there been a demand shock, or has somebody deviated?). Other papers that deal with collusion under imperfect monitoring and private signals are Compte (1998) and Athey and Bagwell (2001).

[33] The incentives for firms to exchange private information, and more importantly the welfare effects of such exchange are not robust, as they crucially depend on whether the firms compete on prices or quantities, or whether the uncertainty concerns costs or demand. See Kühn and Vives (1995) or Raith (1996b) for surveys.

welfare. However, it is unlikely that firms need to exchange individual and disaggregate data in order to achieve whatever efficiency there might be. Kühn (2001) also argues that information about the industry might help firms devise incentive schemes for their personnel, based on relative productivity, but again, for such schemes to work firms do not need detailed data at a disaggregate level.[34]

Kühn (2001) convincingly concludes that while both types of information exchange help firms to collude, the observation of past and present quantities and prices of firms is a more effective collusive device than the exchange of private information about market demand. Further, if efficiency gains of information exchange exist, they would be reaped already with the exchange of aggregate data. This should lead competition policy to a more severe treatment of agreements concerning exchange of information about individual prices and quantities (especially the more disaggregate and the more recent). Indeed, his conclusion that communication between firms about such individual firm data should be forbidden is compelling.

4.2.2.2 Coordination and the Role of Communication

Coordinating on a Particular Collusive Outcome: Introduction   When firms repeatedly meet in the marketplace, if the discount factor is large enough, any price between marginal cost and fully collusive price might be sustained. This raises the issue of which price is likely to arise as the market outcome. Habit, history, or particular events might provide firms with a *focal point* on which to coordinate.

Consider for instance a situation where two firms are told by a regulator that their prices cannot be higher than a certain level, say 100. In this case, this price will provide a clear benchmark (the focal point) for the firms, and one can bet that 100 will be the price that they will set.[35]

History might also provide hints. Many European markets have been protected from foreign competition for a long time, resulting in several national monopolies in many industries. Once tariff and non-tariff barriers started to fall, this created a potentially pan-European market. However, a situation where each firm stays in its own market without entering foreign ones would provide a good collusive equilibrium, which is just the continuation of something which has happened for a long time. Starting to export instead might be considered a deviation and might trigger retaliation in the home market, with rivals exporting in turn. Therefore, the

---

[34] Some exceptions about detailed data might occur in particular sectors. In banking and insurance, for instance, markets are characterised by asymmetric information. If firms had information about clients' solvency history, this would be efficiency enhancing as it would lessen adverse selection problems and foster competition by helping customers to switch firms. See Padilla and Pagano (1997). Note, however, that although disaggregate, this is not information about prices set or quantities produced by firms.

[35] Schelling (1960) was the first to introduce the notion of focal points (or conventions) and show how they can help people to coordinate.

status quo might be a focal point, and only when demand and technology conditions substantially change might firms be tempted to break the current situation.

Whatever the reason, if firms have coordinated in the past on a certain collusive price or divided markets in a certain way, it might be too risky for them to experiment so as to change it. Firms might simply update such a price more or less mechanically with inflation or when raw materials commonly used in the industry become more expensive.

If firms were colluding explicitly they would simply communicate with each other and they could achieve higher collusive prices (provided that firms are symmetric enough, they would have similar preferences over prices) and/or more efficient market sharing rules.[36] But even if they did not overtly collude, they could still try to overcome coordination problems by transmitting information to each other, as I discuss in what follows.

Exchange of Information on Future Prices and Quantities   Announcement of future prices (or production plans) might help collusion, in that it might allow firms to better coordinate on a particular equilibrium among all the possible ones.[37] Farrell (1987) was the first to show the role of non-binding and non-verifiable communication (known as "cheap talk") in achieving coordination among players in games with multiple equilibria.[38] Since then, both theory and experimental evidence seem to indicate that announcements about price intentions might help firms to coordinate, although not under all circumstances.[39]

However, not all announcements about future actions should be treated in the same way. One should distinguish two different situations, according to whether the announcements are (1) *"private" announcements* directed only to competitors (these include communication in auctions) or (2) *"public" announcements* with commitment value to consumers.

"Private" Announcements   In the first case, announcements are directed only to competitors. To help fix ideas, think of a firm sending a fax to rivals where it is

---

[36] But explicit agreements might theoretically render collusion more difficult when it allows firms to renegotiate the punishment following a deviation, thereby undermining the collusive mechanism. See the technical Section 4.3.2.

[37] Unilateral announcements help players to select a jointly optimal price, on which it would otherwise be difficult to coordinate if a focal price (that is, an obvious price to be chosen) does not exist.

[38] Farrell (1987) analysed a game with different features from supergames. He looked at a "battle of the sexes" situation, where there are two asymmetric equilibria, as in an industry where at equilibrium only one of two firms could profitably enter, whereas if both entered they would suffer losses.

[39] See Farrell and Rabin (1996) for a non-technical discussion of the possible role of cheap talk in different games, and of the conditions under which one should expect it to affect equilibrium outcomes or equilibrium selection. A number of experiments have been performed on this issue, see for instance Cooper et al. (1992). See Kühn (2001) for other references on experiments on the collusive effects of information.

stated that from next month it intends to set a certain price. As Kühn (2001) remarks, it is hard to imagine any efficiency reason behind such announcements. Most likely, they just help rivals to coordinate on a particular collusive price, and therefore help them collude by avoiding costly periods of price wars and price instability.

Advance notice of intended price changes, as long as it does not fully commit the firm to the price announced, might also be a tool to avoid costly experimentation with the market.[40] A firm might announce a price increase effective, say, in 60 days, but then revert to the current price if the other firms did not follow suit with similar announcements of price changes.[41] This way, firms might arrive at a commonly agreed price without incurring the risk of losing market shares or triggering price wars during the period of adjustment to the new prices.

Particularly instructive in this respect is the *Airline Tariff Publishers* (ATP) case in the US.[42] ATP is a company owned by the major US airlines whose main purpose is to disseminate price information to airlines and to operators such as travel agents, using computer reservation systems. Such information is fed to the ATP by each company, and it contains several elements, such as the fare and the route to which the fare is applied, the possible restrictions to this fare (for instance, which type of consumer can buy it, if advance payment is required, if a minimum number of days of stay are required and so on), *first and last ticket dates* (which indicate the period during which the fare can be sold), and *first and last travel dates* (which indicate when the travel for which the fare applies should take place).

The DOJ alleged that airlines used this information to coordinate price increases without any explicit collusion taking place. For instance, airline A could announce today a price increase on the route from city 1 to city 2 and put a first ticket date in thirty days' time, so that nobody could actually sell a ticket for that route at the new fare. Since this information was public to all other airlines, airline A could then wait and see the reaction to this price announcement. If its competitor on the same route, say airline B, matched the price increase, then it would be left unchanged and later become effective. But if airline B did not match the price increase, then airline A could still revise the fare. The process could then continue, with airlines adjusting their fares until a convergence is reached, but without consumers ever having the possibility to buy tickets at the announced future fares.[43]

An Example of Private Announcements: Communication in Auctions   An interesting example of how firms manage to achieve collusive outcomes through communication is given by their bidding behaviour in *simultaneous ascending auctions*. These are first-price auctions where several objects are for sale at the same

[40] However, advance notice of *effective* price changes could be in the interest of consumers, who might want to know in advance the prices they will have to pay, and so reduce uncertainty.

[41] See Hay (1999) for the *Ethyl* case, where this was one of the allegedly anti-competitive practices used by the firms.

[42] See Borenstein (1999) for a detailed account of this intriguing case.

[43] The case ended by a settlement, with the firms involved agreeing to discontinue these practices.

time,[44] and the auction ends only when no new higher offer is made on any of the objects. These auctions have good efficiency properties (the value of one object might depend on which other objects are also obtained; information about the value of an object is increased by observing the bids made by rivals), but they are not immune to collusion, as players might use their bids to signal a way to share the objects.[45] For instance, if the government was auctioning off an asset in Milan (whose area code is 02) and other assets elsewhere, I might indicate my interest in the Milan asset by submitting one or more bids for, say, 1,002 euro each. Other bidders will then understand that I am proposing to share objects in such a way that I obtain that particular asset.

A number of such signalling examples are described in Cramton and Schwartz (2001), who discuss collusion in the FCC auctions in the US, where licenses in different markets were simultaneously for sale. For instance, after a number of rounds where it had not bidden for Amarillo, Texas, the firm Mercury PCS made the highest bid for that market, bumping a rival firm, High Plains Wireless, from it. High Plains had been an aggressive bidder in another market, Lubbock, Texas, and Mercury's bid was intended as a signal to its rival that if it had not stopped bidding for Lubbock, it would have retaliated by increasing the price in Amarillo. To make sure that the signal was clear, Mercury's bid for Lubbock had "013", the code number of Amarillo, as its last three digits, and its bid for Amarillo ended with "264", the code number of Lubbock.[46]

Another case is given by a 1999 auction of ten identical blocks of spectrum in Germany.[47] This was again a simultaneous ascending auction, with the rule that any new bid had to be at least *10% higher* than the previous one. Mannesmann and T-Mobil, the strongest incumbent firms, were the only serious players. In the first round, Mannesmann bid 18.18 million DM per megahertz on blocks 1–5 and 20 million DM on blocks 6–10, and T-Mobil had even lower bids. By making different bids for otherwise identical objects, Mannesmann was signalling the intention to share the market. Further, by choosing 18.18 and 20 it was signalling the fact that it would have been happy with its rival increasing its bid on blocks 1–5 by 10% (the minimum admissible bid increase), so that both would have ended up with five blocks each paid at 20 million DM. Sure enough, T-Mobil's managers got the message (as they admitted in public declarations, see Klemperer (2002: 170)), and

[44] The most standard auction is the first-price auction on a single object. Think for instance of the way works of art are often sold: people in a room make higher and higher bids for a particular object, until a bid will no further be matched by anybody.

[45] See Klemperer (2002) and Cramton and Schwartz (2001) for a more detailed analysis.

[46] See Cramton and Schwartz (2001: 8–9). Such examples of communication of intentions are not restricted to auctions. In the *ATP* case discussed in the text above, airlines included "footnote designators" attached to a particular announced fare so as to indicate their intentions to punish a competing airline on a particular route: See Borenstein (1999: 314–6) for details.

[47] See Klemperer (2002).

in the second round they bid 20 million DM on blocks 1–5, after which the auction ended.

These examples clearly show that communication among players helps them reach collusive outcomes in auctions. Therefore, public statements about bidding intentions should not be allowed,[48] and measures might be taken to avoid signalling through bids: "For example, bidders can be forced to bid 'round' numbers, the exact increments can be pre-specified, and bids can be made anonymous" (Klemperer, 2002: 179).

"Public" Announcements   In the second case, price announcements are public, and therefore seen by rival firms as well as consumers. Think for instance of a firm advertising the prices of its products in newspapers. On the one hand, it might be argued that transparency of prices still helps collusion, for the reasons indicated above. On the other hand, market transparency is good for consumers, as it allows them to "shop around" for the best offer. The latter positive effect is generally considered stronger than the collusive effects of the announcements. Both theoretical arguments and empirical evidence suggest that price advertising in this sense is generally beneficial and brings prices down.[49] Therefore, when prices are "transparent" for both consumers and firms, this should not be considered as an anti-competitive practice.

In some cases, however, prices are made public mainly to increase transparency among rival firms, rather than to the benefit of customers. The *Ethyl* case provides an interesting example.[50] In that case, the four producers of anti-knock gasoline additives allegedly used facilitating practices to decrease competition. One such practice was that firms issued press notices on price increases (the other practices were advance notice of price changes, uniform delivered pricing, and most-favoured nation clauses). In that industry, there were few large buyers and prices were set by negotiation, and it seems reasonable to think that the press notice did not have the purpose of informing buyers, but of letting rivals know intentions about price changes.[51]

To conclude, whereas announcements directed only to rivals should be forbidden, announcements about current and future prices which carry commitment value *vis-à-vis* consumers should be regarded as welfare enhancing.

4.2.3 Pricing Rules and Contracts

Most-Favoured Nation and Meeting-Competition Clauses   Some clauses in long-term contracts between a seller and a buyer might condition the price paid by

---

[48] Klemperer (2002) reports episodes where bidders disclosed their objectives to the press, thereby affecting the behaviour of rivals in a straightforward way.

[49] For a survey of both the theoretical and the empirical literature on price advertising, see Fumagalli and Motta (2001).

[50] See Hay (1999).

[51] Note, however, that the FTC was overturned by an appeal court, that found there was insufficient evidence to prove the existence of a cartel.

the buyer either to the price offered by the seller itself to its other buyers, or to the price offered by other sellers to the same buyer. I look at these two types of clauses in turn, and argue that the latter is more likely to have anti-competitive effects.[52]

A *most-favoured nation* (or most-favoured customer) clause (MFN) engages a seller to apply to a buyer the same conditions offered (by the same seller) to other buyers. The clause can be of two types. A *retroactive MFN* states that the buyer will be offered a price reduction if future buyers will get a lower price for the same good (the reduction being equal to the difference between present and future price); a *contemporaneous MFN* engages a seller to offer a buyer the same price as its other buyers (usually in the same area), and effectively amounts to an engagement not to price discriminate.

These clauses are often said to be anti-competitive, because they make it more costly for firms to give price discounts: a firm that wants to attract new customers must also reduce its price and margins on existing customers. However, it is not clear that a MFN clause would facilitate (tacit or overt) collusion.[53] On the one hand, the clause makes it harder to deviate from a collusive outcome (the additional profit to be gained is smaller because a price reduction would apply to existing customers); on the other hand, it also makes it more costly to carry out a punishment, for precisely the same reason (the punishment cannot be selective and target only rivals' customers).

Meeting-competition clauses are different. They state that if the buyer receives a better price offer from *another* seller, the current seller will match that price.[54] In this case, the potential for collusion is higher, and twofold. First, the clause works as a device to exchange information: whenever a buyer is offered a better price, it will have an incentive to report that information to the current seller. This will make firms immediately aware of a deviation from a collusive outcome in the industry, and we know that timely detection of deviations is a crucial element for collusion. Second, the clause reduces the incentives to deviate in the first place: if rivals can retain their current customers due to a meeting-competition clause, the price decrease can only attract new buyers, but cannot steal existing buyers from other firms.

Both MFN and meeting-competition clauses might have efficiency explanations.[55] First, if buyers are risk-averse, these clauses might have some insurance properties: for a retroactive MFN from the possibility that only future buyers will benefit from future shocks; for a contemporaneous MFN from the possibility that

---

[52] Salop (1986) was among the first to point out the possible anti-competitive effects of these clauses.

[53] There is little literature that shows that if a MFN clause is adopted, firms might enjoy higher prices and profits than without it. See for instance Cooper (1986), Holt and Scheffman (1987) and Schnitzer (1994). But these are all models where firms play a finite horizon game, and collusion as we have defined it would not arise. In other words, I know of no model where MFN is found to increase sustainability of collusion in an infinite horizon game.

[54] A *meet-or-release* clause gives the seller the possibility to match the price or free the customer from the contract.

[55] See Salop (1986: 283–4) and especially Crocker and Lyon (1994).

rival buyers will get the same input at lower prices; for a meeting-competition clause from the possibility that a price reduction will be offered by other sellers (although, as pointed out above, the very existence of the clause might push other sellers to not offer lower prices!). Second, if gathering information about prices is a costly process, these clauses might speed up purchase since they insure the early buyer that it is not missing better deals. Third, they introduce some price flexibility in long-term contracts, by ensuring that shocks that affect outside options are internalised in the contracts.

There is certainly need for more research on the possible anti-competitive effects of the MFN and meeting-competition clauses. Overall, however, the pro-collusive impact of meeting-competition clauses seems so strong that anti-trust agencies should probably put them under a *per se* prohibition rule.

Resale Price Maintenance   Resale (or retail) price maintenance (RPM) is a verti-cal agreement whereby a manufacturer imposes upon its retailer(s) the price at which the good should be sold in the final market. As I will show in Chapter 6, there are a number of reasons why RPM can be efficient, and therefore pro-competitive. However, RPM might also facilitate collusion among manufacturers. The intuition is clearly conveyed in the following quote:

> With a competitive retail market and stable retail cost conditions, manufacturers could assume agreed-upon retail prices by fixing their wholesale prices appro-priately. In reality, however, variation over time in the costs of retailing would lead to fluctuating retail prices. If wholesale prices are not easily observed by each cartel member, cartel stability would suffer because members would have diffi-culty distinguishing changes in retail prices that were caused by cost changes from cheating on the cartel. RPM can enhance cartel stability by eliminating the retail price variation.[56]

This story has been recently formalised by Jullien and Rey (2001). In their paper, manufacturers can sell only through local retailers, and there exist local shocks on retail cost or demand. Only the retailer will observe the local shock on the demand for the product it sells, or on its distribution cost. If the retailer were free to choose the price of the final good, the price would be more flexible and would reflect the shock. RPM would therefore be less efficient because it would not allow for adjustment to local conditions. However, RPM implies that prices would be uniformly set by the manufacturers, and therefore allows them to better identify deviations from a collusive action, as the quote above suggested. Jullien and Rey show that whenever the manufacturers find it optimal to adopt RPM, collusion can be sustained and the result will be welfare detrimental.

---

[56] Mathewson and Winter (1998: 65).

Other Pricing Practices that Increase Observability When producers are located in different geographic areas and serve consumers that are also spread out over the territory, it might be difficult for firms to compare prices and to detect price changes, since prices vary with transportation costs. The practice of setting *uniform delivered prices* would then facilitate price observability among rivals. A firm would set the same price inclusive of transportation cost throughout its territory, and independent of the customers' locations. Somebody located next to a firm's plant would pay exactly the same as somebody located hundreds of kilometres away.

A similar effect is achieved by *basing point pricing*, a system whereby each producer sets the final price as the mill price at the common basing point (which might be the seat of plants of one or more firms or it might be completely arbitrary) plus transport cost from that point to the final destination. Again, this allows to increase transparency on the producers' side, in that it allows firms to better compare prices.[57]

4.2.4 Analysis of Collusion: Conclusions

The above analysis has identified the main factors which affect the likelihood of collusion. For the purpose of competition policy, this should be useful in two respects. First, it indicates which factors an anti-trust authority should pay attention to in order to prevent (explicit or tacit) collusion. I shall rely on this analysis in Section 4.4, where I focus on the legal treatment of collusion. Second, in a merger case which raises doubts of coordinated effects (joint dominance), it is important to correctly assess the role played by each variable in determining the likelihood of future collusion in the industry. The analysis will often be very complex. Apart from the cases where all factors point in the same direction, in general one should expect that the analysis of these factors will leave some room for discretion, as it is difficult to understand how such factors interact and whether collusion is likely to arise from the merger or not.[58]

4.2.5 Factors That Facilitate Collusion*

In this section, I first formalise the basic model of collusion based on the so-called incentive constraints, then I analyse the factors that facilitate collusion, relying on the standard industrial organisation textbook model.[59]

---

[57] While delivered pricing and basing point pricing have been claimed to facilitate collusion for a long time, I am not aware of any model that shows rigorously their pro-collusive effect in a supergame context. However, see Thisse and Vives (1992: 257–8) for some considerations on this issue.

[58] See also the section on joint dominance of Chapter 5.

[59] See Tirole (1988: ch. 6).

4.2.5.1 Conditions for Collusion to Arise*

Consider an industry where n firms play an infinite horizon game.[60] Call π_i^c and V_i^c respectively the current profits and the present discounted value of profits that firm i receives if it chooses a certain collusive action, given that all firms also collude. Call π_i^d the current profit of firm i if it deviates when all other firms take the collusive action, and V_i^p the present discounted value of firm i's profits in the punishment phase, that is in all periods that follow the deviation period. Denote with $\delta \in (0, 1)$ the discount factor, assumed identical for all firms in the industry. Note that the discount factor can be expressed as $\delta = 1/(1 + r)$, where r is the interest rate between two periods of time, and therefore the value in today's terms of 1 euro that one receives in the following period. Therefore, $\delta \to 0$ corresponds to the case where $r \to \infty$: one euro earned in the future is not worth anything in today's terms (people are infinitely impatient, and do not attach any value to the future); at the other extreme, $\delta \to 1$ corresponds to the case where $r = 0$: one euro earned in any future period has the same value as 1 euro earned today (people are infinitely patient, and they attach equal value to the future as to the present).

Collusion can arise only if each firm will prefer to play the collusive action rather than deviate from it (and be punished). Therefore, the following *Incentive Constraints* (ICs) must hold, one for each firm in the agreement:

$$\pi_i^c + \delta V_i^c \geq \pi_i^d + \delta V_i^p \qquad i = 1, \dots, n. \tag{4.1}$$

Clearly, the lower the deviation profit one makes relative to the collusive profit, and the lower the profit in the punishment phase, the more likely that collusion will be sustained. (The harsher the punishment the stronger the deterrent to cheating on the collusive agreement.) The n incentive constraints can also be written as

$$\pi_i^d - \pi_i^c \leq \delta(V_i^c - V_i^p) \qquad i = 1, \dots, n, \tag{4.2}$$

which states that the gains from deviating obtained today must be lower than the losses from deviating from the collusive strategy, incurred from tomorrow onwards. Again, this condition must be satisfied for all firms, otherwise one or more deviations will occur and collusion cannot be sustained.

Finally, another way to express the same incentive constraint is

$$\delta \geq \frac{\pi_i^d - \pi_i^c}{V_i^c - V_i^p} \equiv \bar{\delta}_i \qquad i = 1, \dots, n. \tag{4.3}$$

This is the form in which the condition for sustainability of collusion is most often

---

[60] If firms played a repeated game with a finite (and certain) horizon, the collusive outcome would never be attained at equilibrium. At the last stage of the game, all firms would play the Nash equilibrium action, since it is as if they played a one shot game. By backward induction, the Nash equilibrium would be played in each period. See Chapter 8.

expressed. Collusion arises at equilibrium only if the discount factor is large enough, that is, if it is larger than a certain "critical discount factor", $\bar{\delta}$. Only if firms are patient enough will the collusive agreement be sustained. This is very intuitive: if the discount factor is very low, firms do not give importance to what will happen in the future, and they will prefer to cheat so as to reap all the benefit they can today. Hence, collusion will not arise.

Note that the conditions identified above hold for both tacit and explicit collusion.

4.2.5.2 The Basic Model to Analyse Facilitating Factors*

Consider an industry where n identical firms play a repeated game with infinite horizon (or, with an uncertain final date, which is equivalent). They produce the same homogenous good at the same unit cost c. In each period t of the game, firms set prices simultaneously and non-cooperatively.[61] They all have the same discount factor δ. (If one prefers to consider the game as one where the market exists in the following period with a probability $\phi \in (0, 1)$, take the discount factor to be equal for all firms and label it d. By setting $\delta = d\phi$, the analysis is equivalent.) Assume also that there are no capacity constraints, and that each firm wants to maximise its present discounted value of profit.

Finally, specify firm i's demand in the following way (which is the usual one for a Bertrand game with homogenous products). If all the firms charge the same price $p_i = p_j = p$, then they share demand equally, so that $D_i = D(p)/n$ and $\pi_i = \pi(p)/n$, where π_i denotes firm i's profit and $\pi(p)$ is the aggregate profit when all firms charge price p. If firm i sets a price $p_i < p_j$, for any $j \neq i$, then $D_i = D(p_i)$ and $\pi_i = \pi(p_i)$. Finally, if there exists a k such that firm i sets a price $p_i > p_k$, then $D_i = 0$ and $\pi_i = 0$.

Consider the following *trigger strategies*. At the initial period $t = 0$, each firm sets the collusive price p_m (that is, the price that maximises joint profits).[62] At time t, it sets the price p_m if all firms have set p_m in every period before t. Otherwise, each firm sets $p = c$ forever. In words, each firm behaves in a collusive way as long as all others do, but if one of them deviates from the collusive action, then the punishment is triggered and they all revert to the one-shot Bertrand equilibrium for the rest of the game.[63]

Collusion arises at equilibrium if no firm has an incentive to deviate from the behaviour indicated by the trigger strategies. Since all firms are identical, we need

---

[61] Exercises 4.11 and 4.12 analyse the case of quantity competition.

[62] As I shall discuss below, this is not the only price that can be sustained as an equilibrium of the game under the same conditions on the discount factor.

[63] This is the harshest punishment: after a deviation occurs, all firms earn zero profit forever. No credible punishment can be harsher than that. Therefore, with homogenous products and price decisions, no other set of strategies can improve the chances of collusion upon these trigger strategies.

to consider the incentive constraint for only one firm:

$$\frac{\pi(p_m)}{n}(1 + \delta + \delta^2 + \delta^3 + \cdots) \geq \pi(p_m). \qquad (4.4)$$

The LHS gives the total payoff a firm receives if it colludes (i.e., if it follows the trigger strategy when all other firms do). In each period, and for all periods, the firm receives its share $1/n$ of the aggregate monopoly profit. Profits earned at a time t are discounted by a factor δ^t. The RHS gives the profit under the optimal deviation. If a firm decides to "cheat" when all others collude, the best payoff is obtained by slightly undercutting p_m. By setting $p_m - \varepsilon$, all consumers will buy from the deviating firm, which will thus earn a profit $\pi(p_m - \varepsilon)$. For ε small enough, the firm will therefore get a profit that is very close to $\pi(p_m)$ in the period it deviates. In the following period, however, the punishment occurs as all firms will revert to the Nash equilibrium forever. Therefore, the deviating firm (like all others) will make zero profit in all periods of the game.

Note that $\sum_{t=0}^{\infty}\delta^t = 1/(1-\delta)$. Hence, after simple algebra, the incentive constraint above becomes

$$\delta \geq 1 - \frac{1}{n}. \qquad (4.5)$$

For $n = 2$ we have the standard textbook (duopoly) case: collusion is sustainable as long as $\delta \geq 1/2$; for $n \to \infty$, collusion is impossible, as a discount factor higher than one would be necessary for the incentive constraint to hold, whereas $\delta \in (0, 1)$.

Concentration   From the inequality above it is easy to see that the larger the number of firms n the tighter the incentive constraint, that is the less likely that collusion will be sustained at equilibrium. In a model where firms are symmetric, this is tantamount to saying that an increase in concentration ($1/n$ being an index of concentration) makes collusion more likely.[64]

Regular Orders Facilitate Collusion   To see how regular orders facilitate collusion, it is convenient to show how a *large* order would break collusion. Suppose that we have the same game as above but that at $t = 0$ market demand and market profit are respectively $kD(p)$ and $k\pi(p)$, with $k > 1$. In the following periods, $t = 1, 2, \ldots$, demand and profit are back to the usual levels $D(p)$ and $\pi(p)$. This is equivalent to saying that there is an unusually large order in one period. The incentive constraint would then become

$$\frac{\pi(p_m)}{n}(k + \delta + \delta^2 + \delta^3 + \cdots) \geq k\pi(p_m). \qquad (4.6)$$

---

[64] But recall that asymmetries – that might increase concentration measures – hinder collusion: see Section 4.2.1.

This can be rewritten $\delta \geq (n-1)k/[1+(n-1)k]$. The IC is the more binding as k is larger, as k increases the RHS more than the LHS. In the limit, if $k \to \infty$, there would be no value of the discount factor that can satisfy the condition for collusion.

Exercise 4.1 shows that high frequency of market contacts also helps collusion.

Demand Elasticity   Since demand elasticity enters the IC for collusion only through the expression of profits, $\pi(p_m)$, and these cancel out, this variable does not seem to have any obvious impact on the likelihood of collusion.[65]

Collusion and the Evolution of Demand   One of the first papers to analyse the effects of the evolution of demand on the likelihood for collusion is Rotemberg and Saloner (1986). In their model, demand can be either in a low (d_L) or in a high (d_H) demand state, and each state occurs with a probability $1/2$. The crucial assumption in their model is that shocks are independently and identically distributed: there is no correlation between today's and tomorrow's state of demand. Rotemberg and Saloner show that collusion is less likely to hold in the states of high demand: firms' temptation to deviate is higher then. Full collusion, defined as firms setting the monopoly price in both states of demand, can be achieved only for very high discount factors. For intermediate discount factors a less than fully collusive outcome can be achieved: firms set the monopoly price in low state of demand, and lower prices in the high state of demand.[66]

To understand the mechanism behind Rotemberg and Saloner's paper, note that in their model the occurrence of a high state of demand is equivalent to a situation where there is an unexpectedly large order today, but tomorrow the market goes down to the usual demand levels. The expected level of demand in their paper is $(d_L + d_H)/2$, so if there is a high demand shock a firm faces a demand higher than the expected: $d_H > (d_L + d_H)/2$. Everything is the same as in the previous section when the usual level of demand is D, and there is an unexpected large order such that demand in the current period is $kD > D$.

The introduction of a positive correlation among the demand shocks changes the scenario completely. If the boom is likely to continue in the future, then the incentives to deviate are reduced: the punishment reduces profit in periods of high demand. If instead a decline in demand is expected to be persistent, then collusion is less likely to be sustainable, as one would prefer to deviate now that demand is

---

[65] To see it better, write the collusive profit as $(p_m - c)D(p_m)$. The IC becomes: $(p_m - c)D(p_m)(1 + \delta + \delta^2 + \cdots)/n \geq (p_m - c)D(p_m)$, which simplifies to become the usual condition $\delta \geq 1 - 1/n$, where the demand function does not figure.

[66] In this sense, there are "price wars during booms". However, note that the actual (lower than monopoly) price set in the high state of demand might be higher than the monopoly price set in the lower state of demand. The term price war just means that firms are not able to set the fully collusive price in the high demand state.

high, since the cost of the punishment is lower tomorrow when demand is lower. The following example shows these effects.

At time $t = 0$, demand and profit are given by $D(p)$ and $\pi(p)$. At time t, they are given respectively by $\theta^t D(p)$ and $\theta^t \pi(p)$, with $\theta > 0$. The incentive constraint can then be rewritten as

$$\frac{\pi(p_m)}{n}(1 + \delta\theta + \delta^2\theta^2 + \delta^3\theta^3 + \cdots) \geq \pi(p_m), \tag{4.7}$$

or $\delta \geq (1/\theta)(1 - 1/n)$. We now have to distinguish two cases.

(1) (Continuous) demand growth. If $\theta > 1$, it is easy to see that collusion is easier (the IC is relaxed): the expected rise in future demand increases the future cost of a deviation.

(2) (Continuous) demand decline. If $\theta < 1$, collusion is less likely to be sustained (the IC is tightened): the temptation to deviate is stronger because the future cost of deviating, that is the punishment, is lower.

In the real world demand is likely to fluctuate in cycles, with periods of growth followed by periods of decline. However, Harrington and Haltiwanger's (1991) results on collusion over the cycle are consistent with the picture given by this simpler model: collusion is more likely to break when demand is falling.[67]

Symmetry Helps Collusion   Consider a market A where two firms 1 and 2 operate. Firm 1 has market share λ and firm 2 has market share $1 - \lambda$.[68] Assume $\lambda > 1/2$: firm 1 is "large" and firm 2 is "small". The firms have the same technology, summarised by a constant marginal cost c and the same discount factor δ. The firms play the price game for an infinite number of times. Denote the fully collusive price by p_m, and consider simple trigger strategies with Nash reversal forever. The incentive constraint for firm $i = 1, 2$ is given by

$$\frac{s_i(p_m - c)\,Q(p_m)}{1 - \delta} - (p_m - c)\,Q(p_m) \geq 0, \tag{4.8}$$

where $s_1 = \lambda$, and $s_2 = 1 - \lambda$ are respectively firm 1 and 2's market shares. The IC of the two firms in market A are therefore given by $IC_1^A : \lambda/(1 - \delta) - 1 \geq 0$, and $IC_2^A : (1 - \lambda)/(1 - \delta) - 1 \geq 0$. The former can be simplified as $\delta \geq 1 - \lambda$ and the latter as $\delta \geq \lambda$. Clearly, the binding constraint for collusion in market A is $\delta \geq \lambda$, that of the small firm. The intuition is simple: along the collusive path, the large firm has a larger share of the market, while by deviating each firm obtains (for

---

[67] But see Fabra (2001b) for the case of capacity constraints.

[68] The assumption that market shares are exogenously given is simplistic: typically, market shares should be determined endogenously. However, one could interpret this example as the reduced form of a richer game where firms differ in some assets – capacities as in Compte et al. (2002) and Vasconcelos (2001b), or number of brands as in Kühn and Motta (1999) – and market shares will mirror the distribution of those assets.

one period) all the market for itself. Clearly, the incentive to deviate is higher for the small firm, which can capture a higher additional share by decreasing prices. Collusion is limited by the extent to which the market shares are asymmetric. In the symmetric case, where firms have the same market share, we fall back onto the standard condition for collusion $\delta \geq 1/2$. The higher the asymmetry the more stringent the IC of the smallest firm.

Multi-Market Contacts   Consider now another market B with identical features as market A above, but where the same two firms have reversed market positions. Firm 1 has a market share λ (respectively $1 - \lambda$) in market A (resp. B) and firm 2 has a market share $1 - \lambda$ (resp. λ) in market A (resp. B), with $\lambda > 1/2$, so that firm 1 is large in market A but small in market B, and vice versa for firm 2.

Consider the ICs for collusion, first for each market in isolation and then for both markets together. We shall see that multi-market contacts help facilitate collusion in this example.

The IC for firm $i = 1, 2$ in market $j = A, B$ *considered in isolation* is

$$\frac{s_i^j (p_m - c) \, Q(p_m)}{1 - \delta} - (p_m - c) \, Q(p_m) \geq 0, \tag{4.9}$$

where s_i^j is the market share held by firm $i = 1, 2$ in market $j = A, B$. We have seen that the ICs in market A are given by $IC_1^A : \delta \geq 1 - \lambda$, and $IC_2^A : \delta \geq \lambda$. In market B the two ICs are $IC_1^B : (1 - \lambda)/(1 - \delta) - 1 \geq 0$ and $IC_2^B : \lambda/(1 - \delta) - 1 \geq 0$, that reduce to $\delta \geq \lambda$ and $\delta \geq 1 - \lambda$. Firm 1 is the small firm in market B so its IC, $\delta \geq \lambda$, is the binding one.

We can now conclude that by looking at the two markets *in isolation* (or, equivalently, by assuming that firms 1 and 2 operating in the two markets are different) collusion will arise in each market if $\delta \geq \lambda$, where $\lambda > 1/2$.

So far, we have assumed that each firm makes its decision about collusion in each market separately. However, this is not correct: Each firm $i = 1, 2$ is selling in two markets, and it will therefore take into account both markets when making its decisions (recall that if a firm deviates it will deviate in both markets, since after a deviation collusion would be broken in both markets), so its IC is

$$\frac{s_i^A (p_m - c) \, Q(p_m)}{1 - \delta} + \frac{s_i^B (p_m - c) \, Q(p_m)}{1 - \delta} - 2 (p_m - c) \, Q(p_m) \geq 0, \tag{4.10}$$

Both incentive constraints simplify to $\lambda + 1 - \lambda \geq 2(1 - \delta)$, whence $\delta \geq 1/2$. In the case where firms 1 and 2 were operating in only one market, collusion would arise if $\delta \geq \lambda$. Multi-market contacts help collusion, since the critical discount factor is lower: $1/2 < \lambda$.

These results follow from the fact that under multi-market contacts firms pool their incentive constraints and can use slackness of the constraint in one market to enforce more collusion in the other.[69] More intuitively, in the example presented here multi-market contacts restore symmetry in markets which are asymmetric. Under multi-market contacts, collusion arises if $\delta \geq 1/2$, which is precisely the same condition faced by symmetric firms in a given market (when looked at in isolation).[70]

4.2.5.3 A Problem with Supergames: Multiple Equilibria*

One problem with games where firms play over an infinite horizon is that they admit a continuum of equilibrium solutions. Consider for instance precisely the same basic model as the one analysed in the previous Section 4.2.5 but assume that firms have the following trigger strategies. Each firm sets a price $p \in [c, p_m]$, where c is the marginal cost and p_m the joint profit maximisation price, at $t = 0$. It sets p at period t if all firms have set p in every period before t; otherwise, it sets $p = c$ forever. These strategies, which differ from those studied in the previous section only in that those restricted the collusive price to be $p = p_m$, represent an equilibrium of the game if the following IC holds:

$$\frac{\pi(p)}{n}(1 + \delta + \delta^2 + \delta^3 + \cdots) \geq \pi(p). \tag{4.11}$$

It is straightforward to rewrite the IC and check that it amounts to $\delta \geq 1 - 1/n$. Therefore, the same value of the discount factor allows for a continuum of equilibrium solutions to hold: any price between the Bertrand price and the monopoly price can be sustained at equilibrium![71]

This result is not entirely satisfactory, since a number of outcomes are possible, and *a priori* it cannot be said which ones are more likely than others. More work is needed to understand if some particular equilibria are more likely to be selected. In turn, this calls for more theoretical analysis on the refinements of the equilibrium in supergames, but also for experimental evidence which helps understand how agents in the real world are coordinating on certain equilibria rather than others. See also Section 4.2.2.1 for a discussion on the practical implications of this multiplicity of equilibria.

---

[69] Of course, the example given here is extreme and very simplified for illustrative purposes.

[70] Spagnolo (1999) assumes that firms have a strictly concave objective function (for instance, instead of maximising the sum of profits $\pi_A + \pi_B$, they would maximise $\ln(1 + \pi_A + \pi_B)$) and finds that multi-market contacts facilitate collusion also under market symmetry.

[71] The result that the critical discount factor is independent of the collusive price is an artefact of the Bertrand model. In general, one should expect that the lower the collusive price the easier to sustain collusion (that is, the lower the critical discount factor). This is shown in Exercise 4.11.

4.3 ADVANCED MATERIAL**

4.3.1 Credibility of Punishment and Optimal Penal Codes**

I have so far not discussed the credibility of punishments once a deviation takes place, but this is a key issue for both tacit and explicit collusion. If firms were not willing to carry out the punishment, that is entering a phase of low prices, once a deviation is actually observed, then the threat of the punishment would not exist, and collusion could not be sustained. Formally, this implies that for collusion to be sustained other incentive constraints (one for each firm) should hold, that is that a firm prefers to engage in the punishment action (i.e., retaliate) rather than to deviate from it (i.e., not retaliate).

There are (at least) two different technical solutions for the credibility of the punishment. In "trigger strategies" models, after a deviation from the collusive action is observed the punishment consists in all firms reverting to the one-shot Nash equilibrium forever. Clearly, participating in the punishment is rational here: given that all other firms play the Nash equilibrium actions, a firm has no incentive to deviate from its own Nash equilibrium action. Accordingly, I have so far not explicitly introduced incentive constraints along the punishment path because they are always satisfied.

In another class of models, due to Abreu (1986, 1988) and Abreu, Pearce and Stacchetti (1986), firms carry out optimal penal codes that involve *stick and carrot* strategies. Abreu notes that playing Nash equilibrium forever is not necessarily the optimal punishment, whenever V_i^p is positive. If a harsher punishment can be imposed, this will improve the likelihood of collusion.[72]

Abreu's proposed punishment involves a very strong punishment (the *stick*) immediately after a deviation, resulting in firms making negative profits during the punishment period. To make participation in such a strong market punishment credible, the penal code also establishes that firms will immediately revert to the collusive actions if they do take part in the punishment (the *carrot*), whereas the punishment would continue unless all firms take part in it. If the present discounted value of profit after a deviation is zero ($V_i^p = 0$), the sustainability of collusion will be maximal, since a harsher punishment cannot be built (a firm would never be willing to take part in a punishment which leaves it with a negative present discounted value of profits, because it would be better off producing zero forever). The following section illustrates a simple model with symmetric two-phase punishments, and shows how they can improve upon Nash reversal trigger strategies.

---

[72] Note that playing the Bertrand equilibrium forever is the optimal penal code when firms choose prices and they have homogenous products, since it gives firms zero payoff along the punishment path, $V^p = 0$.

An Example of Optimal Punishments   Consider $n \geq 2$ firms producing homogenous goods and choosing *quantities* in each period for an infinite number of periods. Demand in the industry is given by $p = \max\{0, 1 - Q\}$, Q being the sum of individual outputs. All firms in the industry are identical: they have the same constant marginal costs $c < 1$, and the same discount factor δ.

Nash Reversal Trigger Strategies   Let me first give the conditions for collusion under trigger strategies with Nash reversal. Exercise 4.12 shows that in this industry individual outputs and profits under collusion are given by $q^m = (1 - c)/(2n)$ and $\pi^m = (1 - c)^2/(4n)$; the optimal outputs and profits a firm can make by deviating under collusion are given by $q^d = (n + 1)(1 - c)/(4n)$ and $\pi^d = (1 - c)^2 (n + 1)^2/(16n^2)$; finally, the Cournot quantities and profits are given by $q^{cn} = (1 - c)/(n + 1)$ and $\pi^{cn} = (1 - c)^2/(n + 1)^2$.

The ICs for collusion are given by $\pi^m/(1 - \delta) \geq \pi^d + \delta \pi^{cn}/(1 - \delta)$, which after substitution and rearranging becomes

$$\delta \geq \frac{(1 + n)^2}{1 + 6n + n^2} \equiv \delta^{cn}. \tag{4.12}$$

Optimal Punishment Strategies[73]   Under the above trigger strategies with Nash reversal forever, firms make positive profits along the punishment path: $V^p = \delta \pi^{cn}/(1 - \delta) > 0$. Abreu (1986) stresses that by strengthening the punishment, that is reducing the present discounted value of the profits made after the deviation, call it V^p, collusion might be achieved under milder conditions on the discount factor. He focuses on *stick and carrot* (or two-phase) strategies, and shows conditions under which there exists a symmetric optimal punishment where each firm produces the same quantity q^p and earns negative profit π^p for the period immediately after the deviation, to then revert to the collusive quantity in the following period: $V^p(q^p) = \pi^p(q^p) + \delta \pi^m/(1 - \delta)$. The punishment is optimal in the sense that the quantity q^p is chosen in such a way that $V^p = 0$, which is the worst possible punishment that firms can resort to.

Of course, the punishment must be credible, that is firms should not have an incentive to deviate from the punishment path. Denoting with $\pi^{dp}(q^p)$ the profit made by deviating from the punishment path (that is, the one-shot game best response when all other firms set quantity q^p), it must be $V^p(q^p) \geq \pi^{dp}(q^p) + \delta V^p(q^p)$, or $\pi^p(q^p) + \delta \pi^m/(1 - \delta) \geq \pi^{dp}(q^p) + \delta(\pi^p(q^p) + \delta \pi^m/(1 - \delta))$. (Note that after a deviation the punishment would be restarted.)[74]

---

[73] There are two differences between my treatment here and Abreu (1986), who also analyses the Cournot model. First, he focuses only on the conditions under which the optimal punishment is sustained (but V^p is not necessarily the best firms can do, as shown below). Second, he does not restrict attention to the highest collusive payoff π^m as I do. As a result, he finds optimal symmetric punishments but for varying levels of collusion.

[74] Note also that the punishments are "history-independent": the punishment scheme is the same when a firm deviates from the collusive path and when it deviates from the punishment path.

The conditions for collusion are then determined jointly by a pair of ICs (since the firms are symmetric and we focus on symmetric optimal punishments, the two ICs are identical for all the firms), which slightly rearranged are

$$\delta \geq \frac{\pi^d - \pi^m}{\pi^m - \pi^P(q^P)} \equiv \delta^c(q^P) \qquad \text{(IC collusion)} \qquad (4.13)$$

$$\delta \geq \frac{\pi^{dp}(q^P) - \pi^P(q^P)}{\pi^m - \pi^P(q^P)} \equiv \delta^P(q^P) \qquad \text{(IC punishment)}. \qquad (4.14)$$

First of all, note that the two ICs depend on the harshness of the punishments. The harsher the punishment (the higher the output q^P and the lower $\pi^P(q^P)$ after the deviation) the more likely that the IC for collusion is satisfied: $\partial \delta^c(q^P)/\partial q^P < 0$. However, a harsher punishment also tightens the IC along the punishment path: *ceteris paribus,* the punishment is sustainable only for a higher discount factor. Indeed, the higher the output q^P the lower $\pi^P(q^P)$; further, one can check that the higher q^P the lower $\pi^{dp}(q^P)$ (we are dealing with strategic substitutes: the higher the aggregate output produced by the $(n-1)$ rivals, the lower the quantity the nth firm wants to produce as its best response): $\partial \delta^P(q^P)/\partial q^P > 0$.

More specifically, in the linear demand Cournot example, we have

$$\pi^P(q^P) = \begin{cases} (1 - nq^P - c)q^P, & \text{for } \dfrac{1-c}{n+1} < q^P < \dfrac{1}{n} \\[2ex] -cq^P, & \text{for } q^P \geq \dfrac{1}{n}. \end{cases} \qquad (4.15)$$

Note first that I focus on $q^P > (1-c)/(n+1)$, which is the Cournot–Nash output; second, that the punishment profit function changes when $q \geq 1/n$, because the market price becomes zero (I assume p is non-negative).

$$\pi^{dp}(q^P) = \begin{cases} (1 - (n-1)q^P - c)^2/4, & \text{for } \dfrac{1-c}{n+1} < q^P < \dfrac{1-c}{n-1} \\[2ex] 0, & \text{for } q^P \geq \dfrac{1-c}{n-1}. \end{cases} \qquad (4.16)$$

Note that $\pi^{dp} = 0$ if a firm cannot make positive profits even if it reduces its output unilaterally given that all the other firms set output q^P. In the present setting, this translates into the condition $p = 1 - (n-1)q^P \leq c$, or $q^P \geq (1-c)/(n-1)$. (Only in this case is the punishment optimal, in the sense that $V^P = 0$. To see this, note that the harshest punishment is credible only if $0 = V^P \geq \pi^{dp} + \delta V^P$, which implies $\pi^{dp} = 0$.)

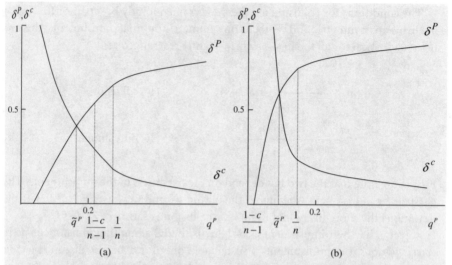

Figure 4.1. Incentive constraints along collusive and punishment paths.

Accordingly, one can now substitute and write the ICs as functions of q^P:

$$\delta^c(q^P) = \begin{cases} \dfrac{(1-c)^2(n-1)^2}{4n(1-c-2nq^P)}, & \text{for } \dfrac{1-c}{n+1} < q^P < \dfrac{1}{n} \\[3ex] \dfrac{(1-c)^2(n-1)^2}{4n(1-2c+c^2+4ncq^P)}, & \text{for } q^P \geq \dfrac{1}{n}, \end{cases} \tag{4.17}$$

and

$$\delta^P(q^P) = \begin{cases} \dfrac{n(1-c-q-nq^P)^2}{(1-c-2nq^P)}, & \text{for } \dfrac{1-c}{n+1} < q^P < \dfrac{1-c}{n-1} \\[3ex] \dfrac{4nq^P(-1+c+nq^P)}{4n(1-c+2nq^P)}, & \text{for } \dfrac{1-c}{n-1} \leq q^P < \dfrac{1}{n} \\[3ex] \dfrac{4ncq^P}{1-2c+c^2+4ncq^P}, & \text{for } q^P \geq \dfrac{1}{n}. \end{cases} \tag{4.18}$$

Figure 4.1 illustrates the problem: by making a stronger punishment (that is, by increasing q^P), one relaxes the IC on the collusive path, but tightens the IC on the punishment path. The point of intersection between the two ICs determines the output level $\tilde{q}^P$, which most relaxes the conditions for both collusive and punishment path to be sustainable (that is, the lowest possible δ).

It turns out that there are two possible points of intersection of these two curves. In Figure 4.1(a) the output level $\tilde{q}^P$ that makes collusion more likely is lower than

$(1 - c)/(n - 1)$, that is, $V^p = 0$ cannot be enforced. In Figure 4.1(b), instead, $\widetilde{q}^p$ is such that $V^p = 0$.[75]

Note that only in the second case $\widetilde{q}^p$ is such that $V^p = 0$. In other words, the best possible strategies (in the sense that they allow firms to enforce collusion for the largest possible range of discount factors) are not necessarily those which require the strongest possible punishment $V^p = 0$. The harsher the punishment, the higher the discount factor needed for making the return to collusion desirable enough to participate in the punishment itself. Imposing $V^p = 0$ might make the IC along the punishment path even tighter than the IC along the collusive path. This is precisely what happens when a small number of firms operate in the industry, as in Figure 4.1(a): setting a punishment $q^p \geq (1 - c)/(n - 1)$ (which implies $V^p = 0$) requires too high a discount factor for the punishment to be enforced. Hence, it is better to resort to a milder punishment under which $V^p > 0$.

One can then check that the lowest possible critical discount factor $\underline{\delta}$ for which the highest level of collusion can be sustained is given by

$$\underline{\delta} = \begin{cases} \dfrac{(n + 1)^2}{16n}, & \text{for } n < 3 + 2\sqrt{2} \\[3mm] \dfrac{(n - 1)^2}{(n + 1)^2}, & \text{for } n \geq 3 + 2\sqrt{2}. \end{cases} \tag{4.19}$$

Figure 4.2 (which makes sense for $n \geq 2$) illustrates the critical discount factor $\underline{\delta}$ obtained under these carrot and stick strategies, and compares it with the critical discount factor δ^{cn} obtained under Nash reversal strategies.

4.3.2 Cartels and Renegotiation**

As we have said, a collusive outcome can be reached without actual meetings ever taking place. But suppose now that we consider explicit agreements (rather than tacit collusion), with firms meeting to coordinate on prices and punishment strategies. McCutcheon (1997) shows that the possibility that firms meet again and renegotiate the agreement might actually break the cartel, a result which has probably limited practical applications but is nevertheless very interesting and deserves attention.

Consider again our simple model of collusion with two homogenous product firms choosing *prices* in every period and reverting to the one-shot Nash equilibrium after a deviation. This model calls for both firms to have zero profit forever along the punishment path. Indeed, if they cannot meet and renegotiate their behaviour (or if for some reason renegotiation costs were prohibitively high), neither firm would

---

[75] Figure 4.1 is drawn for $c = 1/2$ and (a) $n = 4$; (b) $n = 8$. Formally, in Figure 4.1(a) $\widetilde{q}^p = (3n - 1)(1 - c)/[2n(n + 1)] \equiv \widetilde{q}_1^p$. In Figure 4.1(b), $\widetilde{q}^p = (1 + \sqrt{n})^2(1 - c)/[4n\sqrt{n}] \equiv \widetilde{q}_2^p$. It turns out that $\widetilde{q}_1^p < (1 - c)/(n - 1)$ for $n < 3 + 2\sqrt{2} \simeq 5.8$, whereas $\widetilde{q}_2^p > (1 - c)/(n - 1)$ for $n > 3 + 2\sqrt{2}$. Recall that n is the number of firms, a discrete variable, which is treated as continuous in the text just for simplicity.

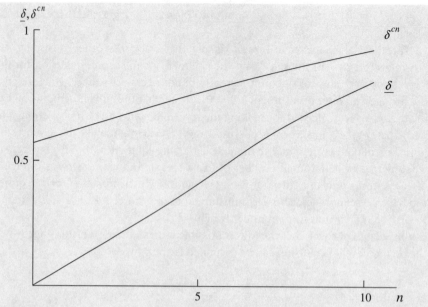

Figure 4.2. Conditions for collusion: Nash reversal (δ^{cn}) v. two-phase ($\underline{\delta}$) punishment strategies.

have an incentive to deviate from the punishment path: given that the rival charges at marginal cost, a firm cannot obtain higher profits by adopting a different price.

But consider now the possibility that the two firms could meet again (and assume that it is costless for them to do so, for the time being) and renegotiate their strategies. After a deviation has taken place, they would have an incentive to agree not to punish each other and restart colluding instead. Indeed, it is in their mutual interest to try to avoid a situation where they would both make zero profits forever. In other words, the enforcement of such a punishment would not be renegotiation-proof. This has a strong implication for the existence of collusion: since firms anticipate that the punishment would be renegotiated and therefore would not take place, there is nothing that will prevent them from cheating in the first place. Only if firms could commit not to meet again or they found it very costly to meet would they be able to sustain collusion at equilibrium.[76]

This conclusion still holds if one considers a different set of strategies than simple grim strategies, for instance one where asymmetric punishments exist and where the punishment lasts for a finite number of periods.[77] It makes sense to consider asymmetric treatment of players because one way to reduce the incentive to renegotiate is to give different payoffs to the firms along the punishment path: this way, one

---

[76] Note again that this argument does not apply to tacit collusion, where no meeting ever takes place.
[77] Only equilibria that use finite punishments are renegotiation-proof.

might want to renegotiate while the other does not. In particular, the non-deviant must get at least as much as it would obtain by accepting to renegotiate. Therefore, in this game, in order not to be induced to forgive the deviant, it should get at least $\pi(p^m)/2$.

Consider therefore a set of strategies which, for T periods after a deviation, calls for the non-deviant and the deviant firm to charge respectively prices p^p and $p > p^p$, where p^p is chosen so that the non-deviant gets at least $\pi(p^m)/2$.[78] After T periods, firms would revert to monopoly pricing.[79] Of course, T should be chosen appropriately, so as to give a low enough payoff along the punishment path that a firm is not tempted to deviate. In other words, T should satisfy the incentive constraint along the collusive path:

$$\frac{\pi(p^m)}{2(1-\delta)} \geq \pi(p^m) + \frac{\delta^{T+1}\pi(p^m)}{2(1-\delta)}, \tag{4.20}$$

which could be rewritten $\delta(2 - \delta^T) \geq 1$.

However, for collusion to hold the deviant must be induced to punish itself. The incentive constraint along the punishment path described by the strategies above would be

$$\frac{\delta^T \pi(p^m)}{2(1-\delta)} \geq \frac{\pi(p^m)}{2} + \frac{\delta^{T+1}\pi(p^m)}{2(1-\delta)}. \tag{4.21}$$

The LHS denotes the payoff the deviant would get if it accepts to get zero payoff for T periods. The RHS denotes the payoff it would get if it deviated and charged a price slightly lower than p^p, thereby getting all the demand and a profit slightly lower than $\pi(p^m)/2$ in the deviation (from the punishment path) period, but then the punishment would be restarted the next period.[80]

We can readily check that the previous condition can be rewritten as $\delta^T \geq 1$, which is false. Therefore, an alternative set of collusive strategies, which call for asymmetric payoffs during the punishment, cannot be sustained at equilibrium.

[78] The non-deviant firm might also be rewarded and get a profit as high as the monopoly profit along the punishment path.

[79] Note that this would not be an optimal punishment strategy, since it would leave the deviant with a strictly positive payoff along the punishment path, unlike the grim strategy. However, an optimal punishment strategy that gives a zero present discounted value of profits to the deviant along the punishment path would not eliminate the incentives of the non-deviant to renegotiate. Consider for instance a strategy which calls for the deviant firm to make negative profits for one or more periods. This requires the deviant to supply all demand below marginal cost for one or more periods. But then the non-deviant firm would not be able to make positive profits during the punishment period (either it also supplies below cost or it does not sell anything). Hence, it would have an incentive to renegotiate and restart a collusive phase.

[80] I am assuming that the non-deviant firm gets $\pi(p^m)/2$ along the punishment path. It could get any profit up to $\pi(p^m)$ (in which case the deviation from the punishment path would give a profit $\pi(p^m)$ too) without changing the conclusion that collusion cannot be sustained.

Hence, we are left with the conclusion that a collusive outcome cannot be sustained at equilibrium when renegotiation is allowed.[81]

Costly Renegotiation McCutcheon (1997) uses this framework to argue that intermediate fines might even be counterproductive and promote collusion. Suppose that every meeting entails a probability θ of being found out, leading the firm to receive a fine F. The expected cost of a meeting, whether the first one or a renegotiation one, is therefore θF. The benefit of the initial meeting is given by the difference between the stream of collusive profits and the one-shot equilibrium payoff (equalling zero): $\pi(p^m)/(2(1-\delta))$. This meeting would therefore take place if $\theta F < \pi(p^m)/(2(1-\delta))$.

Consider now the incentive to have another meeting after a deviation took place. Under grim strategies that involve zero profit forever, the expected gain from renegotiation would again be $\pi(p^m)/(2(1-\delta))$. Therefore, a renegotiation meeting would take place again if $\theta F < \pi(p^m)/(2(1-\delta))$. Hence, collusion could never be sustained, since renegotiation would always take place. It makes sense, therefore, to focus on strategies that reduce the benefit from renegotiation after a deviation, that is, strategies that reduce the cost of the punishment. A strategy which calls for a punishment to take place during the minimum possible number of periods T, rather than forever, fulfils this task. This number T is the one that satisfies the incentive constraint along the collusive path (4.20), $\delta(2 - \delta^T) \geq 1$, with equality.

Accordingly, the cost of the punishment or, which is equivalent, the benefit from renegotiating amounts to forgoing the collusive profits $\pi(p^m)/2$ for T periods is:

$$\sum_{t=0}^{T-1} \delta^t \frac{\pi(p^m)}{2} = \frac{\pi(p^m)}{2}\left(\frac{1-\delta^T}{1-\delta}\right). \tag{4.22}$$

Therefore, a renegotiation meeting would take place after the punishment if $\theta F < \pi(p^m)(1-\delta^T)/(2(1-\delta))$. Otherwise, renegotiation has no bite: firms would prefer to go through the punishment and collusion will arise.

We can then summarise the analysis as follows, according to the expected cost of a meeting, θF.

1. $\theta F \geq \pi(p^m)/(2(1-\delta))$. In this case, each meeting is very costly because it would involve a high expected fine: firms would never start to collude in the first place: no collusion arises at equilibrium.
2. $\pi(p^m)/(2(1-\delta)) > \theta F \geq \pi(p^m)(1-\delta^T)/(2(1-\delta))$. The fines and the probability of being found out are small enough for the initial meeting to take place, but high enough for a subsequent renegotiation meeting not to take

---

[81] Note that the same result holds for any possible collusive price (just replace p^m with any $p > c$ in the discussion above to verify it). Given that firms are organised in a cartel, however, it makes sense to focus on the joint profit maximising price p^m.

place. This leads to the worst outcome, where collusion arises at equilibrium since the punishment will not be renegotiated.

3. $\pi(p^m)(1 - \delta^T)/(2(1 - \delta)) > \theta F$. Here the expected cost of a meeting is so small that renegotiation will take place, bringing the initial agreement to collapse: No collusion can be sustained at equilibrium.

Discussion McCutcheon's analysis is interesting because it underlines the importance of bargaining and negotiation among potential colluders.[82]

This work emphasises the negative (from the point of view of prospective cartel members) aspects that renegotiation of a collusive agreement might have. Yet, in different contexts, such further meetings might have a different role. For instance, after some shocks occur, meetings might be indispensable for collusion to continue without having the industry entering costly punishment phases.

We know little about the actual working of cartels, but Genesove and Mullin (2001), one of the few rich descriptions we have of collusion (they analyse the Sugar Institute, an industry association that fixed rules conducive to a collusion outcome among sugar refiners), indicate that renegotiation meetings were important to face new unforeseeable circumstances, which intervened in the sector, and that punishments did not occur nearly as frequently as theory would suggest, despite actual deviations taking place, perhaps due to such meetings, which did not lead to the collapse of the collusive agreement. It seems an area where further research is needed.

4.3.3 The Green–Porter (1984) Model**

Consider an industry with n identical firms selling a homogenous good and simultaneously playing the Bertrand game for an infinite number of times.[83] Demand realisations are stochastic and independently and identically distributed. In each period, demand is either in a low state ($D = 0$) with probability α, or in a high state ($D > 0$) with probability $1 - \alpha$, and firms do not know the state of demand at the moment they set their prices, nor can they know it afterwards. Each firm does not observe the prices set by rivals either. Hence, a firm facing zero demand does not know if this is due to some rivals having undercut its price, or rather to a low demand state. (Keep the usual assumptions of the Bertrand game: if demand is positive, then all demand is shared among the firms setting the lowest price, whereas firms with higher prices receive zero demand.)

[82] I do not find the policy implications of this model very relevant. Note also that the model applies only to cartels, where there are explicit meetings, and not to tacit collusion, where no meetings take place. Some of the assumptions she makes are questionable too: the initial meeting – which has to define all the collusive strategies – might well be more costly than the following ones.

[83] In their paper, Green and Porter (1984) assumed firms to choose quantities. I follow here Tirole's (1988) version of the model, that is much simpler but equally insightful.

Clearly, reverting to Nash equilibrium (with zero profit) forever after observing zero demand cannot be an optimal strategy any longer, as a punishment might be triggered even if no firm has actually deviated from the collusive path. Consider the following collusive strategy instead. Each firm sets the collusive price p^m at the outset of the game and continues with it as long as all firms have positive demand. When at least one firm observes zero demand,[84] the industry enters a punishment phase, which lasts for T periods and during which each firm sets price equal to marginal cost. After the punishment phase ends, all firms revert to collusive behaviour.

As usual, to see whether these strategies represent an equilibrium, one has to derive the IC by comparing the profit from collusive strategies and from deviating from them (given that all other firms follow these strategies). To do so, it is convenient to define the following two variables, V^+ and V^-, which represent respectively the present discounted value of a firm's profit in a period which belongs to the collusive phase and in a period where a punishment phase has just started.

$$V^+ = (1 - \alpha) \left(\frac{\pi(p^m)}{n} + \delta V^+ \right) + \alpha \delta V^-, \qquad (4.23)$$

where the first term is the payoff when all firms collude and demand is positive (which occurs with probability $1 - \alpha$), with the result that the following period is a collusive phase again; and the second term is the payoff if a negative demand shock occurs (it does so with probability α), thereby triggering a punishment phase. Next, write V^- as

$$V^- = \delta^T V^+; \qquad (4.24)$$

note that firms do not get any profit during all the T periods a punishment phase lasts. The two equations above form a system in the two unknowns V^+ and V^-, whose solution is given by

$$V^+ = \frac{(1 - \alpha)\frac{\pi(p^m)}{n}}{1 - (1 - \alpha)\delta - \alpha\delta^{T+1}}, \qquad V^- = \frac{\delta^T(1 - \alpha)\frac{\pi(p^m)}{n}}{1 - (1 - \alpha)\delta - \alpha\delta^{T+1}}. \qquad (4.25)$$

We now need to write the incentive constraint of a firm. If it abides to the collusive strategy, a firm gets V^+, whereas by (optimally) deviating it gets $V^d = (1 - \alpha)\left(\pi(p^m) + \delta V^-\right) + \alpha\delta V^- = (1 - \alpha)\pi(p^m) + \delta V^-$. Indeed, if after having slightly undercut the other firms a high-demand state occurs (which happens with probability $1 - \alpha$), the deviating firm gets all the industry profit by itself in the current period, but it then triggers a punishment phase, which means that the present discounted value of all its profit at the beginning of the next period is V^-. If however

---

[84] Note that the event "at least one firm has zero demand" is common knowledge in this model. A firm can always infer if all firms have positive demand or not. If it receives positive demand and it did not undercut, it knows that all others have positive demand too. If it receives negative demand or if it has undercut, it knows that at least one firm has zero demand.

a low-demand state arises (which occurs with probability α), then the deviating firm (like all other firms) will get zero in the current period, followed in the next period by V^- as the total value of all the future profit.

One can now write the IC as $V^+ \geq (1 - \alpha)\pi(p^m) + \delta V^-$. After substitution, and some simple algebra, the IC becomes

$$[\delta n(1 - \alpha) - (n - 1)] + [\delta^{T+1}(\alpha n - 1)] \geq 0. \tag{4.26}$$

The first term is non-negative if $\alpha \leq (1 - n + n\delta)/(n\delta) \equiv \alpha_1$; the second term is non-negative if $\alpha \geq 1/n \equiv \alpha_2$. Since $\alpha_1 < \alpha_2$, there are three possible cases. If $\alpha \leq \alpha_1$, (4.26) may hold; if $\alpha_1 < \alpha \leq \alpha_2$, both terms are negative and it will not hold; finally, if $\alpha > \alpha_2$, (4.26) does not hold because the second term (which is positive) is lower in absolute value than the first term (which is negative).

Therefore, the two *necessary* conditions for the IC to hold are as follows. First, $\alpha < 1/n$: if there is a high probability to be in a low-demand state, collusion cannot be sustained. Intuitively, this is because there is a high probability that demand will be zero anyhow, so the loss from deviating is low, which tightens the IC. Second, $\delta \geq (n - 1)/(n(1 - \alpha))$, which corresponds to $\alpha \leq \alpha_1$.[85] Note also that, even if these necessary conditions are satisfied, if $T = 0$ the IC will never be satisfied,[86] whereas if $T \to \infty$ (which makes the second term equal zero) it will always be satisfied if $\delta \geq (n - 1)/(n(1 - \alpha))$ holds.

For further use, (4.26) can be re-written as

$$\delta^T \leq \frac{\delta n(1 - \alpha) - (n - 1)}{\delta(1 - \alpha n)}. \tag{4.27}$$

The IC implicitly defines the values of the punishment length T for which collusion can be sustained. To find the optimal punishment length (which corresponds to the highest sustainable collusive outcome), note from (4.25) that V^+ decreases with T, so firms would like to have the lowest possible punishment phase. Formally, the optimal T can be found by solving the problem $\max_T V^+$, subject to (4.27). The solution is given by the IC holding with equality. To find the optimal T explicitly, take the logarithm of both sides of expression (4.27), and readjust. It then becomes

$$T^* = (\ln \delta)^{-1} \ln \frac{\delta n(1 - \alpha) - (n - 1)}{\delta(1 - \alpha n)}. \tag{4.28}$$

One can check that $\partial T^*/\partial \alpha > 0$: the higher the probability to be in a low-demand state the longer the punishment phase will have to be.

[85] Note that for $\alpha = 0$, this condition is $\delta \geq 1 - (1/n)$, the usual condition for collusion in the demand certainty case.

[86] If $T = 0$, expression (4.26) simplifies to $\delta > 1$, which is false. The punishment phase cannot be of negligible duration.

4.3.4 Symmetry and Collusion**

In this section, I extend the treatment of the relationship between symmetry and collusion that has also been considered in Sections 4.3.4 and 4.2.5.

Consider a differentiated product industry where firms do not necessarily produce the same number of products. A "large" firm is one which sells a large number of products, while a "small" firm is one which sells a more limited range of products. Assume the following demand function:

$$q_i = \frac{1}{n} \left[v - p_i (1+\gamma) + \frac{\gamma}{n} \sum_{j=1}^{n} p_j \right],$$ (4.29)

where q_i and p_i are the quantity and the price of the ith product, v is a positive parameter, n is the number of products in the industry, and $\gamma \in [0, \infty)$ represents the degree of substitutability between the n products. (See Section 8.4.2 for a brief description of the utility function on which this demand function is based, and of its properties.)

Each firm sells a number k of products, with $k \in [\kappa, K]$, and $\kappa \geq 1$, $K < n$. Assume for simplicity that there exist no economies of scope or multi-product economies, so that the marginal production costs are constant (set them equal to c) and identical for each product, independently of the number of varieties produced by each firm.

Firms meet in the marketplace an infinite number of times, and choose market prices at each period. All firms have the same discount factor, $\sigma \leq 1$. Denote the (per product) jointly maximising profit as π_M,[87] the profit a firm obtains if it deviates as $\pi_D(k)$, and the profit in a punishment phase as $\pi_P(k)$, k being the number of products sold by this firm.[88] Each firm prefers to play the collusive strategy at time t rather than deviate if the following holds:

$$\pi_M \left(\sum_{t=0}^{\infty} \sigma^t \right) \geq \pi_D(k) + \sigma \pi_P(k) \left(\sum_{t=0}^{\infty} \sigma^t \right).$$ (4.30)

The condition is the more likely satisfied the higher the collusive profit π_M earned by a firm with k products if it does not deviate from the tacitly collusive behaviour, the lower the profit $\pi_D(k)$ it makes if it does deviate, and the lower the profit $\pi_P(k)$ earned during the punishment phase (that is, the stronger the punishment).

---

[87] Under a collusive agreement that involves all the firms, each product is sold at the same price $p_M = (v + c)/2$ and gives the same profit $\pi_M = (v - c)^2 /(4n)$, which is independent of the number of product varieties produced by each firm.

[88] To be precise, prices and profits during a deviation or a punishment phase depend not only on the number of products k a firm sells, but also on the distribution of products of all other firms. To make the notation lighter, I omit the rivals' number of products from the argument of the price and profit functions of each firm, and write only the number k of products it sells.

Consider "grim" strategies: after a deviation occurs, all the firms set the Bertrand price forever, that is they will always charge the price, which represents the one-shot equilibrium action.[89] Therefore, $\pi_P(k) = \pi_b(k)$. Since $\sum_{t=0}^{\infty} \sigma^t = 1/(1-\sigma)$, the condition for which a firm with k products prefers not to deviate is

$$\sigma \geq \sigma_k' \equiv \frac{\pi_D(k) - \pi_M}{\pi_D(k) - \pi_b(k)}, \tag{4.31}$$

where σ_k' is the "critical" discount factor. For the jointly maximising outcome to arise (that is for complete collusion to exist) we must have that $\sigma \geq \text{Max}(\sigma_\kappa', \ldots, \sigma_K')$. I shall prove that the firm which has the strongest incentive to deviate is the smallest one in the industry, so that for complete collusion to be sustained the condition $\sigma \geq (\sigma_\kappa')$ must be satisfied, where κ refers to the firm having the smallest number of products in the industry.

To obtain this result proceed as follows. When a firm decides whether to stick to the collusive prices or not, it compares the stream of monopoly profit $(\pi_M/(1-\sigma))$ with the stream of profit it would make by deviating $(\pi_D + \sigma\pi_P/(1-\sigma))$. While the per-product monopoly profit is the same independent of the size of the firm, I shall show sufficient conditions for both deviation and punishment profits to decrease with the number of products sold by a firm (thus implying that the smaller the firm the more likely it will deviate).

The intuition behind this result is as follows. A large firm has a number of varieties: when choosing prices, it takes into account the externality that it imposes on all the varieties it produces (a lower price reduces demand on all the other products), and this restrains its interest in reducing prices. A firm which has a lower number of varieties will also benefit from higher prices set by the larger firms, so that (deviation and punishment) profits decrease with the size of the firms.

We start from the profits in the punishment phase. The following lemma tells us that the smallest firm in the industry makes the highest per-product profit in the industry, and the largest firm the lowest per-product profit.[90]

Lemma 4.1   *At the non-cooperative equilibrium of the one-shot price-competition game the profits earned by each product variety can be ranked as follows:*

$$\pi_b(\kappa) > \cdots > \pi_b(k) > \cdots > \pi_b(K), \qquad \text{with} \qquad K > \cdots > k > \cdots > \kappa.$$

Proof   The proof consists of two steps. The first shows that the larger the number of products sold by a firm the higher the price it sets at equilibrium. The second, a consequence of the previous result, proves that the larger the firm the lower the per-product profit it gets. See Section 4.3.4.2 for detailed proofs. ■

---

[89] These are not necessarily the optimal punishment strategies. Kühn and Motta (1999) extend the model analysed here by considering general demand functions and using two-phase punishment strategies.

[90] This result is identical to the one obtained in Deneckere and Davidson (1985), who use a very similar demand function. The proof is also similar to theirs.

We now have to rank the profits made by deviating firms. There exist two possible types of deviation by a firm. The first consists of setting a price $p_D < p_M$ such that all other firms in the industry can still sell a (lower but) positive output. The second involves setting a price $\tilde{p} < p_D$ resulting in none of the other firms being able to sell and the deviating firm being a monopolist in the deviating period.[91] In both cases it will be the smallest firm which obtains the highest deviation profit.

Consider first the case where a deviation is such that all the products sell a non-negative quantity. The following holds:

Lemma 4.2 *The per-product deviation profits when a deviation involves $q_i \geq 0$, for all $i = 1, \ldots, n$ can be ranked as follows:*

$$\pi_D(\kappa) > \cdots > \pi_D(k) > \cdots > \pi_D(K), \qquad with \qquad K > \cdots > k > \cdots > \kappa.$$

Proof　I omit the proof of this lemma, since it involves exactly the same steps as the proof of Lemma 4.1. ∎

For the case where the deviation leaves all the market to the deviating firm, the following lemma holds.

Lemma 4.3 *The per-product deviation profits when a deviation by a k-products firm i involves $q_i > 0$, and $q_j = 0$, where $j = k+1, \ldots, n$, $j \neq i$, can be ranked as follows:*

$$\tilde{\pi}(\kappa) > \cdots > \tilde{\pi}(k) > \cdots > \tilde{\pi}(K), \qquad with \qquad K > \cdots > k > \cdots > \kappa.$$

Proof　See Section 4.3.4.2. ∎

These two lemmata are not enough to rank deviation profits of firms according to their size. We should check in which interval of values of γ the actual profit obtained by a deviating firm corresponds to π_D or to $\tilde{\pi}$, and then establish a ranking in that interval. In other words, for any given γ we are not sure whether two firms with, say, size l and m, would both choose a deviation leaving them with profit π_D or $\tilde{\pi}$. The previous lemmata indicate how to rank deviation profits of the same type, but do not tell us, for instance, how $\pi_D(l)$ would compare with $\tilde{\pi}(m)$. The next proposition does precisely this.

Proposition 4.1 *Write $\tilde{\gamma}_{\min} = \min\{\tilde{\gamma}_\kappa, \ldots, \tilde{\gamma}_K\}$ and $\gamma'_{\max} = \max\{\gamma'_\kappa, \ldots, \gamma'_K\}$. If $\gamma \in [0, \tilde{\gamma}_{\min})$ and if $\gamma \in [\gamma'_{\max}, \infty)$, then it is always the smallest firm (that is, the firm with the lowest number of products, κ), which has the highest incentive to deviate, and the fully collusive outcome in the industry can be sustained only if the discount rate*

[91] Since all the non-deviating firms charge the same monopoly price, intermediate situations where some firms continue to sell but others do not sell after a deviation do not occur. This is because the quantity sold by a non-deviating firm is not a function of the own number of varieties, but only a function of the number of varieties sold by the deviating firm.

$\sigma \geq \sigma_\kappa$, where

$$\sigma_\kappa = \sigma_\kappa' = [\pi_D(\kappa) - \pi_M] / [\pi_D(\kappa) - \pi_b(\kappa)] \text{ for } \gamma \in (0, \tilde{\gamma}_{\min}),$$

and

$$\sigma_\kappa = \tilde{\sigma}_\kappa' = [\tilde{\pi}(\kappa) - \pi_M] / [\tilde{\pi}(\kappa) - \pi_b(\kappa)] \text{ for } \gamma \in [\gamma_{\max}', \infty).$$

Proof   See Section 4.3.4.2. ∎

4.3.4.1 Discussion and Implications**

This proposition gives a sufficient condition for the critical discount rate to coincide with the one which avoids the deviation of the smallest firm. To extend the proof to intervals where the substitution parameter takes intermediate values is difficult, since in such intervals the smallest firm will have the highest profit under the punishment phase but not under the deviation, and it is impossible to give the general conditions on γ, n, k for which the same ranking of profits holds.

Nevertheless, this model suggests that a collusive agreement depends mainly on the incentive constraint of the smallest firms in the industry to be satisfied. The implication of this analysis is that symmetry among the firms does help collusion. An industry where the existing number of product varieties is distributed evenly will reach the fully collusive outcome more easily than one where product varieties are distributed unevenly between small and large firms.[92]

The previous analysis suggests that asymmetries between large and small firms represent an obstacle for industry-wide collusion. It is therefore natural to wonder whether large firms could try to reach a collusive outcome without involving small firms. Unfortunately, the analysis of partial collusion raises several difficulties, as one should model a situation where a group of firms collude whereas others simply best respond. Solving such a model analytically is not easy, and further work is needed on this issue.[93]

4.3.4.2 Proofs**

This section contains the proofs of the propositions stated above.

Proof of Lemma 4.1   First, the following remark will turn out to be useful:

Remark 4.1   *At the non-co-operative equilibrium of the one-shot price-competition game the prices at which each product variety is sold can be ranked as follows:*

$$p_b(\kappa) < \cdots < p_b(k) < \cdots < p_b(K), \qquad \text{with} \qquad K > \cdots > k > \cdots > \kappa.$$

---

[92] As repeatedly mentioned, the result that symmetry facilitates collusion – although not the result that it is the smaller firms that have the highest incentive to deviate – can also be found in Compte, Jenny and Rey (2002) and Vasconcelos (2001b).

[93] Vasconcelos (2001b) uses simulations to obtain further insights on partial collusion.

This remark tells us that the smallest firm in the industry charges the lowest per-product prices in the industry, and the largest firm the highest per-product prices.

Proof   We can prove this remark by contradiction. Suppose that $p_b(m) \equiv p_m < p_k \equiv p_b(k)$ when $m > k$. The profit function of the firm having the first m products is given by

$$\pi(m) = m\left[\left(\frac{p_m - c}{n}\right)\left(v - p_m\left(1 + \gamma - \frac{\gamma m}{n}\right) + \frac{\gamma}{n}\sum_{i=m+1}^{n} p_i\right)\right], \quad (4.32)$$

where we have made use of the fact that all the m products sold by the firm have the same price p_m. The first-order condition of the maximisation problem of this multi-product firm is given by

$$\frac{\partial \pi(m)}{\partial p_m} = v - p_m\left(1 + \gamma - \frac{\gamma m}{n}\right) + \frac{\gamma}{n}\sum_{i=m+1}^{n} p_i - (p_m - c)\left(1 + \gamma - \frac{\gamma m}{n}\right) = 0,$$

$$(4.33)$$

which can be re-written as $q_m = (p_m - c)(1 + \gamma - \gamma m/n)$, where q_m is the quantity sold by the firm for each of its m products. By analogy, the maximisation of its profit requires the following condition for a firm with k products: $q_k = (p_k - c)(1 + \gamma - \gamma k/n)$.

Since by assumption $p_m < p_k$ and $m > k$, it must follow that $q_m < q_k$. But from the demand function, it must hold that $q_m = v - p_m(1 + \gamma) + (\gamma/n)\sum_{j=1}^{n} p_j$ and that $q_k = v - p_k(1 + \gamma) + (\gamma/n)\sum_{j=1}^{n} p_j$.

By subtracting the latter from the former we obtain $q_m - q_k = (p_k - p_m)(1 + \gamma)$. Since $p_m < p_k$ by assumption, it must be that $q_m > q_k$, but this contradicts what we have found above. This completes the proof of the remark on the ranking of prices. ∎

Let us now turn to the proof of lemma 4.1. We have to show that $\pi_m < \pi_k$ if $k < m$. Write the per-product profit π_m that the large firm with m products obtains at equilibrium as $\pi_m = \pi_m(p_m, \ldots, p_m, p_k, \ldots, p_k, p_{m+k+1}, \ldots, p_n)$, where the first m prices p_m are those charged by the m products of the large firm, and the prices p_k (from $m + 1$ to $m + k$) are those charged for the k products of the smaller firm.

Consider now what happens if the k products from $m + 1$ to $m + k$ had the higher price p_m instead of p_k. Since we are considering products which are demand substitutes, it must be that π_m would increase. Therefore, it must be that

$$\pi_m = \pi_m(p_m, \ldots, p_m, p_k, \ldots, p_k, p_{m+k+1}, \ldots, p_n) < \pi'_m$$

$$= \pi_m(p_m, \ldots, p_m, p_m, \ldots, p_m, p_{m+k+1}, \ldots, p_n). \quad (4.34)$$

Since firms are symmetric except for the number of products produced, the per-product profit earned by the large firm when both the small and the large firm charge prices p_m on all their product varieties must coincide with the per-period profit earned by the small firm when both firms charge prices p_m:

$$\pi'_m = \pi_m(p_m, \ldots, p_m, p_m, \ldots, p_m, p_{m+k+1}, \ldots, p_n)$$

$$= \pi'_k = \pi_k(p_m, \ldots, p_m, p_m, \ldots, p_m, p_{m+k+1}, \ldots, p_n). \quad (4.35)$$

The previous expression π'_k gives the per-product profit earned by each of the k products of the small firm when it sells all its products at the same price p_m charged by the large firm. But at the non-co-operative equilibrium the best response of the small firm when the large firm sells its products at p_m requires charging the price $p_k < p_m$. Therefore, it must be that

$$\pi'_k = \pi_k(p_m, \ldots, p_m, p_m, \ldots, p_m, p_{m+k+1}, \ldots, p_n) < \pi_k$$

$$= \pi_k(p_m, \ldots, p_m, p_k, \ldots, p_k, p_{m+k+1}, \ldots, p_n). \quad (4.36)$$

This shows that at the non-co-operative equilibrium $\pi_m < \pi_k$ if $k < m$. ∎

Proof of Lemma 4.3 For the quantities sold by the non-deviating firms to be positive when a firm with k products deviates by undercutting its prices to $\tilde{p}$, we must have

$$q_j = \left(\frac{1}{n}\right)\left(v - p_M(1+\gamma) + \frac{\gamma(n-k)p_M}{n} + \frac{\gamma k\tilde{p}}{n}\right) \geq 0, \quad (4.37)$$

where $p_M = (v+c)/2$.[94] After some algebra, it can be checked that a deviating firm obtains all the market if

$$\tilde{p}(k) = \frac{(\gamma k - n)v + (\gamma k + n)c}{2\gamma k}. \quad (4.38)$$

Note that a large firm with many product varieties will find it easier to undercut a rival, since the RHS of the expression above increases with k. In other words, a large firm does not need to cut its prices as much as a small firm should do in order to be able to exclude the rivals from the market during a deviation period. (However, we shall see that the large firm has also less incentive to undercut.) A necessary condition for such a deviation to be profitable is $\tilde{p}(k) > 0$. Therefore, it must be that $\gamma > n(v-c)/[k(v+c)] \equiv \widehat{\gamma}(k)$.

Suppose now that such a deviation is profitable for a firm with k products and one with $r < k$ products. A firm with k products obtains from the deviation a per-product profit $\tilde{\pi}(k) = \tilde{\pi}(\tilde{p}(k), \ldots, \tilde{p}(k))$, corresponding to the situation where it sells k products all selling at the same price $\tilde{p}(k)$. By eliminating some products and keeping the price unchanged, the per-product profit will increase: $\tilde{\pi}(k) < \tilde{\pi}'(k) =$

[94] Whether another firm is able to sell or not after a firm deviates by setting a price $\tilde{p}$, depends on the number of varieties k of the deviating firm.

$\tilde{\pi}'(\bar{p}(k), \dots, \bar{p}(k))$, where the price vector is now composed of $r < k$ identical elements $\bar{p}(k)$.

Finally, we have $\tilde{\pi}'(k) = \tilde{\pi}'(\bar{p}(k), \dots, \bar{p}(k)) < \tilde{\pi}(\bar{p}(r), \dots, \bar{p}(r)) \equiv \tilde{\pi}(r)$, where the latter inequality comes simply from the fact that the optimal deviation price for a firm with r products is $\bar{p}(r)$ and not $\bar{p}(k)$. Hence, we have shown that $\tilde{\pi}(k) < \tilde{\pi}(r)$ for $k > r$. ∎

Proof of Proposition 4.1   The first step is to compute $\pi_D(k)$ explicitly. This can be done as follows. By replacing q_j in the first-order condition above and solving with respect to the price, one obtains the optimal deviation price when all the firms have a positive output. This is given by

$$p_D(k) = \frac{(2n + \gamma n - \gamma k)v + c(3\gamma n - 3\gamma k + 2n)}{4(n + \gamma n - \gamma k)}. \tag{4.39}$$

By substitution one can find the optimal deviation profit:

$$\pi_D(k) = \frac{(2n + \gamma n - \gamma k)^2 (v - c)^2}{16n^2 (n + \gamma n - \gamma k)}. \tag{4.40}$$

It is easy to check that $\partial \pi_D(k)/\partial k < 0$, which confirms that the higher the number of product varieties of a firm, the lower the deviation profits it can make. However, we also have to check if the deviation price $p_D(k)$ is consistent with all the firms selling a positive output. This is satisfied as long as $p_D(k) > \bar{p}$. By substituting and solving with respect to γ, this condition can be expressed as

$$\gamma < \gamma'(k) = \frac{n}{k}\left(1 + \frac{\sqrt{n^2 - k^2}}{n - k}\right). \tag{4.41}$$

Therefore, the function $\pi_D(k)$ has values in $\gamma \in (0, \gamma'(k))$, and it is increasing in its domain.

The next step is to study the function $\tilde{\pi}(k)$. If the deviating firm charges the highest possible price $\bar{p}$ which guarantees it will be the only firm selling in the market, its profit is

$$\tilde{\pi}(k) = \frac{(\gamma^2 k^2 - n^2)(v - c)^2}{4\gamma^2 k^3}, \tag{4.42}$$

which is an increasing and concave function in its domain $\gamma \in (\widehat{\gamma}(k), \infty)$.

Since $\widehat{\gamma}(k) < \gamma'(k)$, we have that in the interval $(\widehat{\gamma}(k), \gamma'(k))$ both types of deviation give positive profits to the deviating firm. We should then try to see which type of deviation is optimal in this interval. The following can be shown:

Remark 4.2   There exists a value $\tilde{\gamma}(k) \in (\widehat{\gamma}(k), \gamma'(k))$, which is obtained as the solution of the equality $\pi_D(k) = \tilde{\pi}(k)$, such that for $\gamma < \tilde{\gamma}(k)$ the optimal deviation profit is $\pi_D(k)$.

Proof   Unfortunately, to find the explicit form of $\bar{\gamma}(k)$ turns out to be a difficult task. To prove this remark we proceed in two steps. First we prove that if $\bar{\gamma}(k)$ exists it must be $\bar{\gamma}(k) > \widehat{\gamma}(k)$. We know that in the point $\gamma = \widehat{\gamma}(k)$ we have $\tilde{p}(k) = 0$. Therefore, $\tilde{\pi}(k) = 0$, whereas $\pi_D(k \mid \gamma = \widehat{\gamma}(k)) > 0$. Therefore, by continuity there must exist an interval $(\widehat{\gamma}(k), \gamma)$ for which $\pi_D(k) > \tilde{\pi}(k)$.

Next step is to prove that $\bar{\gamma}(k) < \gamma'(k)$. When $\gamma = \gamma'(k)$, we have:

$$\tilde{\pi}(k \mid \gamma = \gamma'(k)) - \pi_D(k \mid \gamma = \gamma'(k))$$

$$= \frac{(v - c)^2 (n - k)^2 \left(n^2 + n\sqrt{n^2 - k^2} - k^2\right)}{4nk \left(n + \sqrt{n^2 - k^2}\right) \left(n + \sqrt{n^2 - k^2} - k\right)^2} > 0. \qquad (4.43)$$

Since both functions are continuous and increasing in $(\widehat{\gamma}(k), \gamma'(k))$ from $\pi_D(k) > \tilde{\pi}(k)$ in $\gamma = \widehat{\gamma}(k)$ and $\pi_D(k) < \tilde{\pi}(k)$ in $\gamma = \gamma'(k)$, it follows that there exists only one point $\gamma = \bar{\gamma}(k)$, where $\pi_D(k) = \tilde{\pi}(k)$. This completes the proof of the remark.

We can now establish the proposition. If $\gamma \in (0, \bar{\gamma}_{\min}]$ then all the firms have deviating profits $\pi_D(k)$. In this interval, the incentive constraint of each firm will be given by $\pi_M \geq (1 - \sigma)\pi_D(k) + \sigma\pi_b(k)$. But π_M and σ are identical for all firms, while both the deviation profit $\pi_D(k)$ and the punishment profit $\pi_b(k)$ are the higher the lower the number of products of a firm. Therefore, the constraint is the most binding for the smallest firm in the industry, the one with κ products. Full collusion is sustainable only if $\sigma \geq \sigma'_k = [\pi_D(\kappa) - \pi_M] / [\pi_D(\kappa) - \pi_b(\kappa)]$. ∎

If $\gamma \in [\gamma'_{\max}, \infty)$, then all the firms have deviating profits $\tilde{\pi}(k)$. The incentive constraint is given by $\pi_M \geq (1 - \sigma)\tilde{\pi}(k) + \sigma\pi_b(k)$. In this case as well, both the deviation profit $\tilde{\pi}(k)$ and the profit in the punishment phase $\pi_b(k)$ are the highest for the smallest firm, and collusion can be sustained only if $\sigma \geq \tilde{\sigma}'_k = [\tilde{\pi}(\kappa) - \pi_M] / [\tilde{\pi}(\kappa) - \pi_b(\kappa)]$. ∎

4.4 PRACTICE: WHAT SHOULD BE LEGAL AND WHAT ILLEGAL?

In this section, I first deal with the standards of proof for collusion (Section 4.4.1), then with the possible measures to deter collusion (Section 4.4.2), and finally with those that might break ongoing collusive practices (Section 4.4.3).

4.4.1 Standards of Proof: Market Data v. Hard Evidence

Although industrial economics has been successful in identifying the mechanisms through which collusion acts and the factors that facilitate it, its practical implications for legal purposes are less straightforward and require some discussion. Consider for instance a literal use of the economic definition of collusion. Since a collusive outcome is defined as a situation where prices are "high enough", one could think that to verify the existence of collusion in the legal sense (that is, of anti-competitive behaviour), one has to analyse price data in a given industry, and infer if they are above some threshold levels above which they should be considered collusive.

However, it would be very difficult in practice to look at market outcomes to decide whether there has been an infringement of anti-trust law, for several reasons.[95] First of all, in many circumstances price data might not be available, and when they are they might refer to list prices rather than effective prices (in many industries, actual prices are negotiated between buyers and sellers and in others they might differ from list prices because of discounts, which might also differ across customers).

Second, even if reliable data existed, there would probably be disagreement about the monopoly price in an industry. Sellers might have very different views of what that price would be, and an outside observer could have yet different perceptions. It is also well known that estimates of costs differ widely, sometimes even within the management of the same firm.

Third, suppose that there is agreement on what the monopoly price in the industry would be: how close to the theoretical monopoly price should sales prices be for them to be judged "too high" and therefore collusive?

Fourth, the very principle that firms could be convicted solely on the grounds that they charge "too high" prices is a dangerous one, and it might open the way for anti-trust interventions whenever firms are successful enough to find consumers willing to pay high prices for their products. As I have repeatedly argued in Chapter 2, it is not market power by itself that anti-trust intervention should punish.

Rather than looking at the *level* of prices in the industry, one might then be tempted to infer the existence of collusion (as an infringement of the law) by analysing the *evolution* of industry prices over time. For instance, courts and anti-trust authorities have sometimes been tempted to infer the existence of collusive (illegal) behaviour from the fact that sellers charge similar prices over time, the so-called "price parallelism" (or "conscious parallelism").[96] But to observe that prices move in a similar way is not enough to establish that firms are guilty of collusion. Common exogenous shocks such as the increase in input prices of all the suppliers, or an increase in inflation, or an increase in property prices would probably lead all the sellers to increase prices proportionally, without implying that they are colluding.

Further, we have already noticed that a collusive outcome might arise without firms agreeing or communicating to coordinate their behaviour. Suppose for instance that – even without common shocks on demand or input prices – one day a seller increases prices by 10%, and that the next day a rival follows suit. Is this price

---

[95] Of course, looking at market outcomes is important to the extent that it helps identify those sectors where there might be collusion, and that therefore should be subject to a more thorough investigation.

[96] See Scherer and Ross (1990: 339–46) for a discussion of the conscious parallelism doctrine and its evolution in the US.

parallelism enough evidence to convict firms? Surely not. It is of course possible that the two firms have talked to each other and previously agreed on changing prices. But it is also possible that they have taken their decisions without communication. The first firm might have simply raised prices in the expectation that the rival would follow its price rise, and the rival might have simply decided to follow, either happy to raise prices or in the expectation that a failure to do so would trigger a price war that would reduce profits. In the absence of hard evidence, a court would have to prove infringement of the law by second-guessing the firms' intentions and their motivations.

An example where history provides a focal point for tacit collusion is given by the *Soda-Ash* case. Soda-ash is a commodity used as a raw material in the production of glass. ICI, a British company, and Solvay, a Belgian company, are the main producers in the industry. The two firms had a long history of explicit market-sharing agreements (at times when cartels were not illegal), started in the 1870s and renewed immediately after the Second World War with a so-called 'Page 1000' agreement, which divided Europe (and some overseas markets) into spheres of influence: for instance, ICI was to sell in the United Kingdom and Solvay in Continental Europe.

The agreement (which the defendants indicated as being out of date since 1962) was terminated as of 31 December 1972, when the UK entered the European Community (so as to comply with the anti-trust rules of the Treaty), but as the EC said in its decision:

> The alleged desuetude of the 'Page 1000' arrangement did not however manifest itself in any significant change in the commercial policy of Solvay or ICI in the soda-ash sector, either in 1962 or at any later stage. Neither ever competed with the other in their respective home markets in the Community. Similarly in overseas export markets each continued to respect the other's sphere of influence. (*Soda-Ash*: 27.)

What is noticeable is that each firm admitted that it had no intention of invading the other's home market, but simply because it feared retaliation if it had done so (*Soda-Ash*: 43–44). They therefore justified a collusive outcome as the result of independent decisions that made sense from a business viewpoint. In this case, continuing to share markets was an easy way to reach tacit collusion.

The other interesting point here is whether tacit collusion is an infringement of Article 81 (ex-85). In this case, the Commission decided that it was, and that the term "concerted practice" mentioned in Article 81 among the prohibited practices also covered tacit collusion:

> The Commission fully accepts that there is no direct evidence of an express agreement between Solvay and ICI to continue to respect the 'Page 1000' cartel in practice. However, there is no need for an express agreement in order for article 85 to apply. A tacit agreement would also fall under Community competition law. (*Soda-Ash*: 55.)

Note, however, that in some cases price parallelism can be credibly explained only by coordination among firms, even if there is no proof of the latter. For instance, in *Dyestuffs*, price rises were so simultaneous that it is impossible that they had not been previously agreed upon:

> In Italy, apart from Ciba who had already ordered its Italian subsidiary to increase prices, all other producers, with the exception of ACNA, sent by telex or fax – from their headquarters, seated in places very distant from each other – instructions to their respective agents in the afternoon of 9 January: Sandoz at 17.05, Hoechst at 17.09, Bayer at 17.38, Francolor at 17.57, BASF at 18.55, Geigy at 19.45 and ICI at an undetermined time, since instructions were given by phone. (*Dyestuffs:* 2. My translation.)

The "parallelism plus" rule, which consists of finding illegal behaviour whenever price parallelism is accompanied by a facilitating factor (such as for instance resale price maintenance, best price clauses, or exchange of information) is not more convincing either, unless it can be proved that firms have coordinated in order to introduce or keep the facilitating practice at stake. In other words, if there is no proof that they have agreed on a particular practice, the very fact that they have followed that practice should not be proof of collusion. For instance, in the *Wood pulp* decision, the EC saw a facilitating practice in the fact that producers of pulp for paper production announced their price changes with the same advance. Together with parallel price movements, this was seen as evidence of collusion. However, the ECJ found that the wood pulp sellers introduced this practice at the request of their customers, the paper producers, who wanted to have more price transparency as well as to be informed in time about input price changes, so as to take the appropriate steps to face them. Accordingly, the ECJ quashed the EC decision (see Section 4.6).[97]

The presence of periods of price wars is no proof of collusion either. We have seen that under imperfect price observability (and demand uncertainty), full collusion cannot be sustained and price wars are an integral part of collusion. However, observing that there are episodes in an industry where prices fall considerably might be consistent with either Green and Porter's type of collusion or with some other events, such as new capacity appearing in the market, occasional competitors that are temporarily in the market (e.g., imports), a reduction in demand and so on. Certainly, repeated episodes of this type would raise suspicion and deserve a careful scrutiny of the industry, but they should not be seen as the ultimate proof that collusion exists. Again, it is possible that firms trigger price wars so as to sustain a Green and Porter's type of collusion, but in the absence of communication among them, I do not see why they should be convicted. Firms would probably argue that lower prices in some particular periods were due to particular capacity or demand

---

[97] Similarly, in the *Ethyl* case in the US, a Court of Appeal ruled that the pricing practices adopted by Ethyl had been introduced when it was still a monopolist, and that other firms had later independently adopted them. See Scherer and Ross (1990: 345).

conditions, or that they simply behaved so as to match prices set by one of them, or again that prices fell but not to the competitive (or sub-competitive) levels predicted by theory, and it would be very difficult for a court to rule out such arguments, unless there existed evidence of communication among firms to coordinate their behaviour.

The use of econometric techniques, however sophisticated, does not change the nature of the arguments above. It is instructive to look at the estimates carried out on the railroad cartel in the US, which pre-dated the Sherman Act (and for which therefore public data exist). This cartel was studied first by Porter (1983b), whose econometric analysis found that the data were not inconsistent with the firms in the industry behaving à la Cournot (and therefore not colluding). However, Ellison (1994) studied the same data but used a slightly different econometric specification, and he found that firms' behaviour was close to full collusion.[98]

The lesson from these papers is that even if one thought that collusion might be proved on the basis of market outcomes alone, and if good and reliable data existed, econometric techniques might not always provide unambiguous answers as to the existence of collusive prices in a given industry. Perhaps in the future there will be more consensus on how to design and assess econometric exercises of this type, but for the time being econometrics is more likely to give complementary evidence, rather than conclusive proof, of collusion.

For all these reasons, inferring *illegal* collusive behaviour – i.e., inferring conspiracy in the US or infringement of Article 81 in the EU – from market data (that is, looking only at the outcomes) would not be desirable, and the legal approach which requests some hard evidence as proof of collusion is sensible practice. Firms should be convicted for anti-competitive behaviour only insofar as there is proof that they have communicated with each other to sustain collusion. Such communication can be of various kinds. First of all, and most obvious, minutes of meetings, e-mail messages, memos and other written (or recorded) evidence concerning agreements on prices and quantities are still the most likely proof of collusion. But firms might also sustain collusion without openly discussing prices or quantities, but coordinating so as to establish the environment that facilitates collusion. For instance, they might decide to exchange detailed price and quantity information via their trade association, or they might set up a forum where they can announce future prices to each other (as in the *Airline Tariff Publishing* case), or agree on a resale price maintenance scheme or other practices that makes their prices more uniform or transparent.[99] In all such cases, if there is evidence that firms have not acted unilaterally, firms should be found guilty of collusion.[100]

---

[98] In the same vein, and using the same data on the railroad cartel, Porter (1985) and Vasconcelos (2001a) find a different impact of entry upon collusion.

[99] See the *Sugar Institute* case, described in Genesove and Mullin (2001).

[100] If they have acted unilaterally, or on the basis of habit, but the investigation determines that the practices in place favour collusion but do not entail any efficiency gain, the court should not fine them but impose a cessation of such practices.

This approach has the advantage that it is based on observable elements verifiable in court: if there is any evidence of communication or coordination (on prices, quantities, or on facilitating practices in the sense described above) among the firms, then courts and competition authorities should fine them for anti-competitive (collusive) behaviour. Otherwise, they should not.

Too Lenient with the Firms?   It might seem that this approach is particularly generous with firms. After all, I have explained above that they might be able to sustain high prices even without communicating with each other. Therefore, why should they take actions that could leave hard evidence? And if they do not need to communicate, is there any hope to punish (and deter) supra-competitive pricing?

Two considerations can be made. First, it is true that tacit collusion *might* be sustained by firms. However, we have also seen that there are very good reasons why firms would like to communicate and/or to coordinate their actions. They might want to avoid unnecessary and costly experiments with the market and choose instead the best (for the firms) prices, or they might want to create facilitating practices and more generally an environment which improves observability of firms' actions so as to favour collusion. This will lead firms to try to communicate among themselves so as to coordinate their actions, thereby leaving traces of hard evidence behind them. Firms have known for a long time that they will be found guilty if there is any written proof of their coordination, and yet anti-trust authorities keep on uncovering such hard evidence in cartel cases.[101]

Second, there is no alternative to such an approach. Any other rule – such as for instance inference from market data – which is not based on observables could not be easily enforced in courts. It would also be detrimental to legal certainty, as firms would not know whether their pricing policies might be accepted or fined. At the same time, competition authorities would have to decide on a case-by-case basis, rather than follow a clear rule.

Still, it might appear that this approach does not do enough to deter and punish collusion. What else can be done, then? There are two types of competition policy interventions which might help deter tacit or explicit collusion or break explicit collusion (i.e., cartels). I divide them into *ex ante* and *ex post* measures.

4.4.2 *Ex Ante* Competition Policies against Collusion

Collusive agreements are possibly the most serious infringement of competition law in any jurisdiction, and they are accordingly heavily fined. Firms might be subject to different penalties if they are found guilty of collusion. First, they will generally

---

[101] Noteworthy are a stream of high profile international cartels prosecuted by both US and EU authorities in the late 1990s, among which *Citric Acid, Lysine, Vitamins* and *Graphite Electrodes*.

pay a fine (which usually is a transfer to the country's general budget). Second, they might have to pay damages to private parties (in the US, treble damages). Third, the firms' managers might be given prison sentences. Recently, in the UK and in the EU there have been discussions about making collusion a criminal offence. If this were the case, executives found guilty of collusive agreements could be imprisoned, as in the US. Arguably, this provides a stronger deterrent of collusion as risk-averse managers would find it very dangerous to collude.

However, what matters for deterrence purposes is not the size of the fine if found guilty of collusion, but the expected fine, namely the amount of the fine multiplied by the probability of being caught and found guilty. In turn, this raises the issue, so far little studied, of how anti-trust authorities should design their policies and organise their investigations so as to efficiently deter collusion.[102]

Apart from making firms face tougher penalties, I argue in what follows that other *ex ante* measures might have an important role in deterring collusion.

Black List of Facilitating Practices   Since collusion is facilitated by certain practices, competition authorities should identify business practices that should be forbidden and others which might be tolerated apart from specific cases. Some practices should therefore be on a black list and be *per se* prohibited, and others should be under a rule of reason. In terms of European competition law, for instance, the EC might issue guidelines indicating black-list practices that would represent an infringement of Article 81(1) – but firms might ask for an individual exemption under Article 81(3) provided that they prove that they achieve efficiency gains.

Such practices should include announcements about future price and quantity conduct; exchange of disaggregate information about individual prices and outputs; any *co-ordination* among firms aimed at harmonising business practices that increase price observability among sellers (without increasing transparency for buyers), such as resale price maintenance, basing point pricing, and best price clauses. Minority shareholdings among competitors also appear as a pro-collusive practice that should be authorised only if efficiency effects can be shown.

Auction Design to Avoid Bid-Rigging   In Section 4.2.2.1, I have discussed the possibility of collusion in auctions, and more particularly in simultaneous ascending auctions. One problem there was that players might use their bids to signal their collusive intentions. Since it is difficult to intervene *ex post* to contest the legality of certain bids, Klemperer (2001) suggests to intervene *ex ante* by choosing an auction design that can minimise such problems. This suggestion is in the same

---

[102] For instance, it might make sense to tolerate prices that are perceived to be above some competitive benchmark by not much, but intervene as soon as prices are above a certain threshold, as argued in Besanko and Spulber (1989). See also Section 4.4.3 below on how anti-trust authorities might optimally use their limited resources. The issue of how colluding firms change their conduct in the presence of an anti-trust authority is also analysed in LaCasse (1995).

spirit as what I propose here: it is better to try to create an environment that discourages collusion in the first place than trying to prove unlawful behaviour afterwards. A clear advantage of auction markets is that the environment can be affected directly, since the rules of the game are specified at the beginning by the auctioneer.

In simultaneous ascending auctions signalling can be avoided by authorising round number and/or anonymous bidding only, and objects can be aggregated into larger lots so as to make it harder for players to divide them, and/or a final round with sealed bid offers among the two remaining players can be introduced.[103]

More generally, collusion in auctions can be made more difficult by appropriate auction design. Consider for instance the school milk cartels in Florida and Texas studied by Pesendorfer (2000, especially p. 389). The market was characterised by many small contracts (on average, 239 per year in Florida, and 136 in the Dallas–Forth Worth area), which allowed the cartels to better divide the spoils. The boards of education in every school district awarded contracts independently of each other, and at different dates. They also publicly announced bids and identities of all bidders. This made it possible for the bidding firms not only to spot immediately deviations from a collusive agreement but also to punish a deviation in the following auctions. A different procurement strategy might have helped. For instance, the school districts might have coordinated and acted as a single buyer (recall that large orders break collusion), or they could have fixed the auctions for the same day, or again they could have not revealed information about bids and bidders.

Merger Analysis   Another *ex ante* instrument to prevent collusion from arising is given by merger control. Indeed, we know that a reduction in the number of firms in the industry or a more symmetric distribution of their assets would favour collusion. Therefore, by increasing concentration, and to the extent that they increase symmetry, mergers might create favourable conditions for collusion to be sustained in a given industry. It is crucial, therefore, that competition authorities should be vigilant on mergers (see Chapter 5).

4.4.3 *Ex Post* Competition Policies against Collusion

Surprise Inspections ("Dawn Raids")   Next to *ex ante* measures aimed at preventing collusion, competition authorities should also intervene to try to break existing cartels. From the discussion above, which attributes great importance to

---

[103] This is the so-called Anglo-Dutch auction. See Klemperer (2002) for details and discussion. The UK generation market is also a case where auction design matters. Before the 2001 reform, there was a (sealed-bid) *uniform price* auction, where generators submit a bid that states the different quantities they are ready to supply and at which price. All generators will then be paid the highest accepted bid. Fabra (2001a) formally shows that this type of auction has a higher collusive potential than a *pay-as-bid* auction, where the generator will be paid at its own bid. See her paper for a discussion.

the discovery of hard evidence as a proof of collusion, it is obvious that one such measure is dawn raids. Police searches in the headquarters of firms suspected of collusive conduct (or trade associations, or even executives' homes) often result in crucial evidence being uncovered. Accordingly, competition authorities should be given extensive search powers so that they can, in collaboration with police forces, seize documents which might help prove collusive agreements. But competition authorities might also resort to more clever ways to break collusion, and provide incentives for firms to withdraw from collusive agreements and reveal hard information needed as proofs in courts. It is to such measures that I turn next.

Leniency Programmes   In recent years, competition authorities have devoted a lot of attention to more sophisticated fine schemes. Such schemes are called "leniency programmes" and grant total or partial immunity from fines to firms that collaborate with the authorities. They work on the principle that people who break the law might report their crimes or illegal activities if given proper incentives.[104] In competition law, the Anti-trust Division of the Department of Justice (DOJ) in the US has been the first to introduce such a law, in 1978, granting immunity from criminal sanctions if certain conditions occurred.[105] In August 1993, this scheme – that had not been particularly successful – was thoroughly redesigned by the DOJ, and it now works as follows.

There is *automatic leniency* for firms that report evidence of a cartel *before* an investigation has begun, provided that the firm is the first to come forward; it terminates participation in the illegal activity; it fully and continuously collaborates with the DOJ; it makes restitution to injured parties; it did not coerce another party in the activity; nor was it its leader or originator. *Discretionary leniency* exists for firms that report evidence *after* an investigation has started, provided that the DOJ does not yet have evidence against the company that is likely to result in a sustainable conviction (plus similar accessory conditions as above).

The 1993 reform has improved the leniency programme in two major ways. First, it has extended the possibility of leniency to firms that cooperate *after* an investigation is already under way (that is precisely what theory would suggest, see below). Second, it is now *clear and certain* since – at least for the case where co-operation unveils a cartel before an investigation started – amnesty is automatic rather than discretionary.[106] The changes have been extremely fruitful: while under

---

[104] Similar schemes are routinely used in several fields other than anti-trust, such as fiscal law and environmental law. In Italy, the so-called "turncoat laws" ("*leggi sui pentiti*") have been successfully used to fight organised crime such as the mafia and terrorist organisations such as the Red Brigades. Of course, there are ethical issues involved because punishment is abandoned in exchange for deterrence of further crimes: criminals might be set free (and sometimes even rewarded) in exchange for information that allows to imprison other criminals.

[105] Recall that in the US, unlike Europe, managers risk prison sentences up to three years and criminal fines if their firms are found guilty of price-fixing.

[106] An additional novelty is that all officers, directors and employees who cooperate are protected from criminal prosecution.

the old policy on average only one corporation per year applied for amnesty, under the revised policy applications for amnesty have come in at the rate of approximately two per month (Spratling, 1998: 2).

The EU introduced a leniency policy in 1996.[107] It established that a fine might have been very substantially (75–100%) reduced if a company informed the European Commission before an investigation started; and substantially (50–75%) reduced if co-operation started after an investigation had started, but before the EC had obtained sufficient grounds for initiating the procedure; in both cases, the company had to be the first to report, terminate all cartel activities and must not have been the instigator of the cartel. The fine might have been significantly (10–50%) reduced if the company cooperated with the EC in the investigations (for instance by not challenging the EC findings and allegations) without the previous conditions for more generous reduction of fines being met.

However, this policy did not give the results the EC hoped for, mainly for two reasons.[108] First, leniency was given in a discretionary way by the EC (rather than being automatic as in the US), and firms did not know what fines they would get until the final decision was adopted. This clearly reduced the benefit from disclosing evidence. Second, firms did not receive immunity if an investigation had already begun.

In February 2002, the EC adopted a new leniency policy.[109] It improves on the first point since it introduces transparency and certainty: complete immunity from fines is given to the firm first reporting a cartel and, after providing evidence, the firm will receive (conditional) immunity in writing from the EC. Further, the new rules specify that any firm can apply for immunity as long as it had not coerced other firms to participate in the cartel (the previous condition, requiring a firm not to be an "instigator" of the cartel, left room for interpretation).

It also improves on the second point, since immunity is given to a firm that provides evidence that enables the EC to establish an infringement even when the EC is already in possession of enough information to launch an inspection (but not to establish an infringement).[110]

The use of leniency programmes in anti-trust enforcement has been studied first by Motta and Polo (1999, 2003).[111] They show that such programmes might have an important role in the prosecution of cartels provided that firms can apply for

---

[107] *Commission Notice on the non-imposition or reduction of fines in cartel cases.*

[108] Although a reduction of fines was given in several cases, full immunity was granted only three times under the old leniency policy: to Rhône-Poulenc (in two vitamins cartels), Interbrew (Luxembourg brewers cartel) and Sappi (carbonless paper cartel). All three decisions were taken in November and December 2001, when the change in policy was already under way. See European Commission Press Release IP/02/247 of 13 February 2002.

[109] New *Commission Notice on immunity from fines and reduction of fines in cartel cases.*

[110] A reduction of fines is granted to firms that do not fulfil the previous conditions, but provide evidence that has *significant value added* for the investigation.

[111] See also Spagnolo (2000) and Rey (2000).

leniency *after* an investigation has started. When a firm decides whether to join a cartel, it takes into account the risk of being caught. In other words, its decision of colluding or not weighs the benefit of collusive profits against the expected cost of it, namely the probability μ of being caught times the fine F it expects to pay in such a case. If, after having decided to take part in a cartel, a firm receives the opportunity to report itself (that is if a leniency programme becomes available), but the expected cost μF of it does not change, then there is no reason why the firm should report the cartel. If the benefit of collusion was already higher than its expected cost, and nothing changes in the information available to the firm, then the firm will continue to collude even if a lower fine is available in case of reporting.[112]

But consider now a leniency programme that is open to firms even after an investigation has already begun. Decompose the probability μ of being caught as the probability α that the cartel is investigated times the probability p that the competition authority gathers enough hard evidence for the investigated cartel to be proved guilty. (Therefore, $\mu = \alpha p$.) In this case, a decision to start a cartel is taken when the expected cost of being caught is $\alpha p F$, but *after* an investigation of the industry has started (if any), the expected cost is $p F$, which is higher than $\alpha p F$ (since $\alpha < 1$): The trade-off is changed, as the expected cost of continuing to collude has become higher, whereas the collusive profit is the same. If given the possibility to apply for leniency, the firm might well decide to give up its participation in the cartel.

Leniency also helps in that it saves resources of the authority: building up a convincing enough case to be defendable in courts is very costly, but the cost of this prosecution stage can be avoided or greatly reduced by leniency, since the firms would bring themselves enough evidence to the authority.

Leniency Programmes** This section presents a simple model, by Motta and Polo (1999), to study whether the effects of reduced fines for firms co-operating with the anti-trust authority (AA from now on) can be useful.

The timing of the (infinite horizon) game is as follows:

At time $t = 0$, the AA can commit to a leniency programme (LP) which allows for reduced fines $0 \leq R \leq F$ for firms which reveal information useful to prove collusion,[113] F being fixed by law as the maximum fine that firms can receive if found guilty of collusion.[114] This policy is observed by all firms, which

---

[112] Only if new managers with a different perception of the risk of being caught have meanwhile taken over the firm, would the leniency programme have some effect.

[113] I assume that information given by a single firm is enough to prove that all the firms which have taken part in the collusion are guilty. This might be the case when each firm has access to the minutes of the meetings, or has other written evidence of communication that the firms have used to coordinate on the collusive outcome.

[114] It is always optimal for the AA to set the fine for non-co-operating firms at the maximum level.

also know the probability α that the AA will open an investigation and the probability p that it will be able to prove colluding firms guilty.[115] Note that the reduced fine R will be granted to any firm co-operating even *after* the investigation is opened.[116]

At time $t = 1$, n identical firms decide whether to collude or deviate and realise the per-period associated payoffs, respectively Π_M and Π_D (with $\Pi_N < \Pi_M < \Pi_D$). Consider grim strategies: a deviation triggers the punishment by the other firms, which will play the one-shot non-co-operative equilibrium action forever afterwards, giving a payoff Π_N to each firm.

Assume that the existence of a collusive outcome in the industry is perfectly observed by the AA, but this is not enough for collusion to be proved in courts. To build a case against the firms, the AA needs to find some "hard" proof of co-ordination.[117] Perfect observability of collusive prices also implies that the AA will never investigate firms, which do not collude at equilibrium.

At time $t = 2$, the AA opens an investigation with probability $\alpha \in [0, 1]$. If the inquiry is not opened, each firm realises the profit Π_M. If it is opened, firms simultaneously decide whether or not to reveal information to the AA; if at least one firm reveals, the AA is able to prove them all guilty. A firm which co-operates with the AA pays $R \leq F$ whereas one that does not pays the full fine F. If no firm reveals information, the AA is able to prove them guilty with probability $p \in [0, 1]$. If the AA has not been able to prove the firms guilty of collusion at the end of this inquiry, the firms will never be investigated again in the future. If proved guilty, they will behave non-co-operatively forever in the future. After the investigation has ended, payoffs are realised. Figure 4.3 illustrates the game at period $t = 2$.

For any $t > 2$, if up to the previous period the AA has not started an investigation, with probability α it opens an inquiry in t, firms decide whether to reveal, and so on. We restrict attention to the case where $\delta \geq (\Pi_D - \Pi_M)/(\Pi_D - \Pi_N)$: in the absence of anti-trust policy, collusion would arise at equilibrium.

---

[115] The former refers to the preliminary activities (general monitoring) necessary to open an investigation such as collecting information about the firms in the industry, interviewing firms, suppliers and customers, collecting data from the different sources; the latter (prosecution) involves collecting more focused information on the case, ordering surprise "raids" in the firms' headquarters, processing the information collected and preparing the case against the firms according to the existing laws. Here α and p are exogenously given for simplicity. See Motta and Polo (1999) where they are determined by the AA.

[116] Spagnolo (2000) shows that it might be optimal not only to give fine discounts to collaborating firms, but also to reward them ($R < 0$). However, giving extra benefit to firms reporting evidence of a cartel is unlikely to be used in practice because of moral issues. Further, it might give firms incentives to fabricate evidence in order to get an extra benefit. The authorities might then have to invest resources to check the claims of the reporting firms, thereby losing much of the appeal of the leniency programme itself.

[117] Since there exists a continuum of possible equilibria, firms need some coordination to select the fully collusive outcome giving them the per-period profit Π_M.

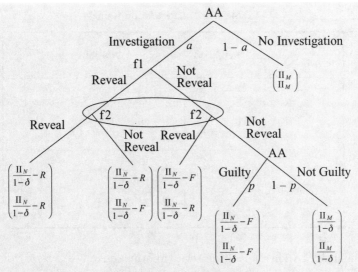

Figure 4.3. Game tree, at $t = 2$.

Solution To look for the sub-game perfect equilibria of the game, consider first the "revelation game" which is played once an investigation is opened by the AA (see Table 4.1). If a firm reveals, it gets a payoff of $\frac{\Pi_N}{1-\delta} - R$ independently of the action chosen by the other firms. If a firm does not reveal any information but at least one other firm does, then the former firm receives a payoff of $\frac{\Pi_N}{1-\delta} - F$. Finally, if no firm reveals any information, each firm receives an expected payoff

$$p\left(\frac{\Pi_N}{1-\delta} - F\right) + (1-p)\frac{\Pi_M}{1-\delta}. \qquad (4.44)$$

It is easy to show that the n-tuple (*reveal*, ..., *reveal*), which we denote as $(R, \ldots, R)$, in which all firms choose to co-operate with the AA obtaining a reduction in fines, is always a Nash equilibrium. Instead, the n-tuple (*no reveal*, ..., *no reveal*), or $(NR, \ldots, NR)$, is an equilibrium: (1) if $pF < R$, always; (2) if $pF \geq R$ if the following condition holds:

$$p \leq \frac{\Pi_M - \Pi_N + R(1-\delta)}{\Pi_M - \Pi_N + F(1-\delta)} = \bar{p}(\delta, R, F). \qquad (4.45)$$

Note that when the $(NR, \ldots, NR)$ equilibrium exists, it would also be the one selected by standard criteria of equilibrium selection such as Pareto-dominance or

Table 4.1. The Revelation Game

firm 2 / firm 1	Reveal	Not Reveal
Reveal	$\dfrac{\Pi_N}{1-\delta} - R,$ $\dfrac{\Pi_N}{1-\delta} - R$	$\dfrac{\Pi_N}{1-\delta} - R,$ $\dfrac{\Pi_N}{1-\delta} - F$
Not Reveal	$\dfrac{\Pi_N}{1-\delta} - F,$ $\dfrac{\Pi_N}{1-\delta} - R$	$p\left(\dfrac{\Pi_N}{1-\delta} - F\right) + (1-p)\dfrac{\Pi_M}{1-\delta},$ $p\left(\dfrac{\Pi_N}{1-\delta} - F\right) + (1-p)\dfrac{\Pi_M}{1-\delta}$

risk dominance.[118] Therefore, firms reveal information only if $p > \bar{p}$. Note that (a) when no leniency programme exists $R = F$ and $\bar{p} = 1$: firms will never collaborate with the AA even after an investigation has started; (b) to induce revelation the best the AA can do is to set $R = 0$.

As for the decisions taken by the firms at $t = 1$, we have to find the discounted sum of profits if a firm decides to collude and compare it with the discounted sum of profits if it decides to deviate from the collusive strategy. This comparison must be done for both cases, when firms will decide to reveal once investigated, and when they will prefer not to co-operate with the AA.

(1) *Collude and reveal: $p > \bar{p}$.* In this case firms reveal if an investigation is opened by the AA. Define Π_R as the expected profit immediately before an investigation is opened. It is easy to see that

$$\Pi_R = \alpha\left(\frac{\Pi_N}{1-\delta} - R\right) + (1-\alpha)(\Pi_M + \delta\Pi_R), \qquad (4.46)$$

which can be rewritten as

$$\Pi_R = \frac{(1-\alpha)\Pi_M + \alpha\left(\frac{\Pi_N}{1-\delta} - R\right)}{1 - \delta(1-\alpha)}. \qquad (4.47)$$

If a firm decides to set the collusive price, then its expected discounted payoff will be

$$V_{CR} = \Pi_M + \delta\Pi_R = \frac{\Pi_M + \delta\alpha\left(\frac{\Pi_N}{1-\delta} - R\right)}{1 - \delta(1-\alpha)}. \qquad (4.48)$$

[118] It is also reasonable to believe that if firms are able to coordinate on the collusive outcome, they will also be able to coordinate not to reveal when this is an equilibrium, which gives them a Pareto superior payoff.

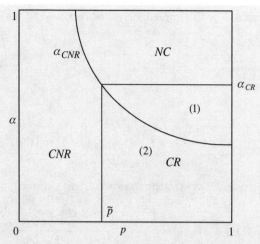

Figure 4.4. Equilibrium solutions for given policy parameters.

If instead a firm decides to deviate from the collusive strategy, then its payoff is given by

$$V_D = \Pi_D + \frac{\delta \Pi_N}{1 - \delta}. \qquad (4.49)$$

Collusion can arise if $V_{CR} \geq V_D$, that is if the following condition is satisfied:

$$\alpha \leq \frac{\Pi_M - \Pi_D + \delta(\Pi_D - \Pi_N)}{\delta(\Pi_D - \Pi_N + R)} = \alpha_{CR}(\delta, R). \qquad (4.50)$$

Figure 4.4 illustrates α_{CR} in the plane (p, α), for given values of δ and R: this locus does not depend on p since in the region considered here firms cooperate with the AA once an investigation is opened.

Below the line, firms prefer to collude even though they anticipate that, if an investigation is opened, collusion would collapse because firms would reveal information to the AA. Above the line, firms, anticipating revelation, prefer to deviate, and the collusive outcome never occurs.

Note also that the less generous the leniency programme (the higher the reduced fine R) the lower α_{CR}: if firms expect that in case an investigation is opened they can reveal and get away with a small fine, they will have an extra incentive to choose the collusive strategy. In other words, a generous leniency policy might stimulate *ex ante* collusion. (I shall come back to this issue below.)

(2) *Collude and not reveal: $p \leq \tilde{p}$.* In this case, firms anticipate that even if an investigation is started, no firm will reveal any information. Only by beginning an investigation and then proving the firms guilty can the AA break the cartel.

Write the expected profit immediately before knowing if an investigation is opened as

$$\Pi_{NR} = \alpha \left[p \left(\frac{\Pi_N}{1-\delta} - F \right) + (1-p) \left(\frac{\Pi_M}{1-\delta} \right) \right] + (1-\alpha)(\Pi_M + \delta \Pi_{NR}),$$

$$(4.51)$$

whence

$$\Pi_{NR} = \frac{\alpha \left[p \left(\frac{\Pi_N}{1-\delta} - F \right) + (1-p) \left(\frac{\Pi_M}{1-\delta} \right) \right] + (1-\alpha)\Pi_M}{1 - \delta(1-\alpha)}. \qquad (4.52)$$

If a firm follows the collusive strategy its expected discounted payoff is given by

$$V_{CNR} = \Pi_M + \delta \Pi_{NR} = \frac{\Pi_M \left(1 + \frac{\delta \alpha (1-p)}{1-\delta} \right) + \delta \alpha p \left(\frac{\Pi_N}{1-\delta} - F \right)}{1 - \delta(1-\alpha)}. \qquad (4.53)$$

As before, a firm which deviates obtains a payoff $V_D = \Pi_D + \frac{\delta \Pi_N}{1-\delta}$. Some simple but boring algebra shows that the inequality $V_{CNR} \geq V_D$ is satisfied for

$$\alpha \leq \frac{(1-\delta)[\Pi_M - \Pi_D + \delta(\Pi_D - \Pi_N)]}{\delta[pF(1-\delta) + p(\Pi_M - \Pi_N) + \Pi_D(1-\delta) - \Pi_M + \delta \Pi_N]}$$

$$= \alpha_{CNR}(\delta, p, F), \qquad (4.54)$$

when $p[F(1-\delta) + \Pi_M - \Pi_N] > \Pi_M - \Pi_D + \delta(\Pi_D - \Pi_N)$, and always satisfied otherwise. Figure 4.4 illustrates the curve, which decreases with p: other things being equal, an increase in the probability of being found guilty will make collusion less likely (and at low enough p, collusion is always preferred). Of course, when F rises, given p, collusion will be less profitable.

Figure 4.4 illustrates the equilibrium solutions of the game. Note that if no LP is introduced ($R = F$) firms have no reason to reveal information to the authority once an investigation is opened, and the equilibrium outcomes would be defined uniquely by the line α_{CNR}. Below the line, firms would collude (CNR); above it, they would not (NC), because any proposed agreement would break down immediately.

Reduced fines ($R < F$) modify the situation, when $p < \bar{p}$ firms do not reveal if monitored, and the analysis above still applies: the line α_{CNR} distinguishes the equilibrium where firms collude and not reveal from that where no collusion occurs. When $p \geq \bar{p}$ firms anticipate that they reveal information if monitored: above α_{CR} they prefer not to collude, and below α_{CR} they initially collude and then reveal if monitored.

To understand the role of leniency on the sustainability of collusion, consider what happens when, starting with a situation in which no LP is used, we introduce reduced fines. This has two effects which are shown in Figure 4.4. On the one hand, the LP might have an adverse, pro-collusive effect. By reducing the expected value of the fine to be paid if an investigation is opened, the LP might give an incentive to collusion. This occurs in the area (1) included between the curve α_{CNR} and the line α_{CR}. In this region, no collusion can be sustained in the industry if full fines are given, but under a LP firms would engage in collusion and, if monitored, they would reveal and pay the reduced fine $R < F$.

On the other hand, there exists an area (2) where collusion will break down (because the firms reveal information) if the AA starts monitoring the industry, whereas in the absence of a LP collusion could stop only after a successful complete investigation. This is the area between the curve α_{CNR} and the line $\bar{p}$.[119]

Implementing the Optimal Policy A leniency programme is therefore not unambiguously optimal, as it might introduce a trade-off between lower *ex ante* deterrence and *ex post* desistence of cartels. Motta and Polo (1999, 2003) formally analyse the optimal anti-trust policy, and show that leniency should be used when the AA has limited resources. A full analysis requires maximising the objective function of the AA, which is welfare, subject to its budget constraint. However, even without a full analysis, note that the AA will rank the regions as follows: NC > CR > CNR. Cartels entail an allocative efficiency loss, and so the AA wishes to deter or break them. In the first case (NC), cartels are deterred; in the second (CR), cartels are broken as soon as an investigation is started, because firms reveal information to the AA; in the third, they are broken only if an investigation is started and prosecution is successful.

Intuitively, if the AA had a high budget, it could set high values of (p, α) and would be able to achieve full deterrence by using the full fine F, while introducing a leniency programme might result in lower deterrence (i.e., ending up in region (1)). Instead, if the AA had lower budget, full deterrence can never be achieved and it becomes better to implement the outcome where firms collude and reveal (CR) by granting maximum discounts ($R = 0$) rather than having full collusion (CNR).

Fine Reductions Only before the Inquiry Is Opened An alternative leniency policy where firms can apply for fine discounts only *before* an inquiry is opened would correspond to the same game as above, with the difference that at the beginning of time $t = 2$, firms simultaneously choose whether to reveal the cartel to the AA, or not; if no firm reveals, the AA opens an investigation with probability α, proving them guilty with probability p, and after the investigation is resolved, payoffs are realised.

Under this alternative regime the leniency programme is completely ineffective. An equilibrium in which firms choose to collude and reveal does not exist. By colluding when expecting the cartel to be broken by information given to the AA, a firm would get $V_c = \Pi_M + \delta(\Pi_N/(1 - \delta) - R)$. By deviating, it would get $V_d = \Pi_D + \delta\Pi_N/(1 - \delta)$. Since $\Pi_D > \Pi_M$ and $R \geq 0$, it follows that $V_c < V_d$.

---

[119] If the Leniency Programme was unanticipated, firms would decide whether to collude or not on the basis of an expected fine $R = F$ and therefore would not co-operate unless $\alpha < \alpha_{CNR}$. When unexpectedly the leniency program is introduced, collusion would break down in all the area (2), without any adverse effect arising.

In the case where firms were entitled to fine discounts *after* the opening of an investigation, the expected profit from collusion decreases when the event "opening of an investigation" occurs, leading firms to reveal. In the case we are considering here, instead, nothing new happens between the moment firms decide on collusion and the moment they are asked to cooperate with the authorities to break down the cartel. If leniency programmes are to be effective in breaking down cartels, they should be extended to benefit firms which reveal information after the industry is put under monitoring.

4.5 JOINT-VENTURES AND OTHER HORIZONTAL AGREEMENTS

In this section, I analyse horizontal agreements other than collusive ones. Section 4.5.1 deals with joint-ventures in general; Section 4.5.2 looks at research joint-ventures; Section 4.5.3 at other forms of co-operation involving technology and innovations.

4.5.1 Joint-Ventures

There are a number of horizontal agreements that go under the name of *joint-ventures* (JVs). These are agreements between competitors that create a new entity that carries out some activities instead of the partners. An example of JVs are *research joint-ventures:* in that case, two or more partners cease doing independent research and development (perhaps in a particular field only) to do it together, within the new entity jointly set up. There are many other possible activities that could make the object of a joint-venture. *Production* JVs and *marketing and sales* JVs are other examples. In the former, two (or more) partners delegate production to a common entity; in the latter, they continue to manufacture independently, but market jointly.

Given their nature, joint-ventures are a hybrid entity that can lie somehow inbetween cartels and mergers. Consider for instance a sales JV between two competitors, whose only purpose is to set prices or quantities in the final market without any additional activity. This is nothing other than a cartel between the two competitors (and should accordingly fall under Article 81 of the Treaty in the EU and under Section 1 of the Sherman Act in the US). At the other extreme, consider two competitors that give all their research, production and sales assets in a certain sector to a newly created firm whose ownership they share. Since the partners cease any independent business in the sector, the JV is akin to a merger, and should be treated accordingly by the law.[120]

[120] *A priori* it is difficult to say whether a joint-venture should be considered as a horizontal agreement or as a merger by the law. In the EU, the distinction was not very clear, and I have probably not been the only one to struggle to understand the difference between co-operative and concentrative JVs (the former used to fall under Article 81, the latter under the Merger Regulation). After the

Apart from the extreme cases where the JV is nothing other than a cartel (this happens when partners simply agree on some decisions rather than carrying out some activities together),[121] the economic analysis of the effects of a joint-venture is not very different from that of mergers (see Chapter 5). In both cases, there might be a trade-off between market power and efficiency. For instance, an operation whereby two competitors decide to delegate their marketing and sales activities to a jointly-owned entity might have anti-competitive effects because the joint-venture would have larger market power than if the partners operated independently. However, it might also entail pro-competitive effects if the coordination of activities through the joint-venture allows them to rationalise their distribution and marketing efforts. The net impact of the operation can be assessed only after having analysed the industry (to see whether there is indeed scope for exercising market power) and the likely efficiency gains of the joint-venture. As for mergers, a good screening device is to look at the initial market power of the partners: if they have only small market shares, there would be little point in a detailed analysis of the operation, and the joint-venture should be cleared.

Additional care should however be devoted to ancillary restraints. Unlike pure mergers, where the partners disappear and their assets are entirely transmitted to the merged entity, in a joint-venture partners might continue activity in the sector. Therefore, their decisions – and welfare as a consequence – might be affected by restraints to their behaviour. Anti-trust authorities should avoid restraints unnecessary for the operations of the JV, such as output and price restrictions in markets unaffected by the JV.[122]

4.5.2 Research Joint-Ventures

Collaborative agreements between firms on research and development (R&D) activities deserve special treatment due to the particular nature of R&D (more generally, of knowledge), which is often characterised by *spillovers* and *non-rivalry*.

Spillovers are a distinctive feature of R&D because technology and know-how often flow from one firm to another, for instance through imitation (and reverse-engineering) and workers' mobility. This reduces the extent to which firms can *appropriate* the results of their R&D efforts, which in turn reduces their incentive to invest in R&D. True, there exist various forms of protection of intellectual property rights (patents, copyrights, trade secret laws) but often they are imperfect.

R&D is also non-rival in the sense that it can be used by other parties without its value being diminished. Knowledge might be costly to create the first time, but once

---

amendment (Regulation 1310/97) of the Merger Regulation, *full-function* JVs are treated as mergers, whereas JVs that perform only a few specific functions are evaluated under Article 81. See Ritter et al. (2000: ch. 6, E).

[121] See Correia (1998: 738–9) and Werden (1998: 714).

[122] See also Werden (1998: 723–5).

it exists, its diffusion does not modify its nature. In this sense, *ex post* one would like R&D to spread as much as possible in society.

Further, it is undesirable for firms to repeat large investments to get knowledge which already exists: diffusion would avoid duplications of costs.

As a result of these two features, the market alone is unlikely to give rise to socially optimal levels of research. Research joint-ventures might help to cope with these problems and create appropriate levels of R&D. If firms collaborate in research, they will share the cost of R&D, thereby increasing their incentives to invest; they will also have immediate access to R&D output, thereby increasing diffusion; finally, they can coordinate their effort, thereby avoiding duplication of investments.

This simple reasoning provides the rationale for *research joint-ventures,* even when they involve competing firms. However, allowing competitors to carry out R&D together might also have costs. For instance, the main motive behind doing R&D might be the hope to get a lead over rivals: if all the main firms in the industry take part in a co-operative venture, the incentive to carry out R&D might dramatically fall; if the joint-venture does not only concern the research stage but also the production and marketing stages, co-operation might extend to the product market and result in collusive behaviour. Therefore, while there are good reasons to allow for research joint-ventures among competitors, such horizontal agreements should be limited in scope.

Technical Section 4.5.4 provides a very simple analysis of the welfare effects of research joint-ventures. This is an issue which has attracted a lot of attention in the last fifteen years. Overall, this line of research shows that allowing competitors to carry out joint research projects might be a sensible policy, but with two caveats. First, such a policy is beneficial only insofar as there exist high enough spillovers. Indeed, if spillovers are high, firms are unable to appropriate their R&D effort, and co-operation increases R&D. Unfortunately, the need for clear rules and for avoiding arbitrariness, on the one hand, and the difficulty of measuring spillovers on the other, make it impossible to limit the policy to particular sectors or technologies where more spillovers are likely to arise. However, a R&D project is composed of many stages, from basic research to applied research, to development, production and marketing. Externalities being higher at the earlier stages of this path, it makes sense to exclude marketing operations from R&D co-operative agreements among competitors. In other words, one should make sure that co-operation does not extend too far into the product market. One way to do this is to require that the R&D results are used independently by collaborating firms.

This leads us to the second point, which is that the authorities should make sure that the R&D co-operation does not "spill over" to the product market competition stage. It is conceivable that firms that start to work very closely on R&D projects might start to extend the coordination of their behaviour onto other spheres of the life of the firms (see Martin, 1985). Anti-competitive effects of a research joint-venture are less likely if the collaborating firms have limited market power. Therefore, a market share criterion might be used as a proxy to screen potentially harmful ventures from others, the former having to be cleared only after a thorough investigation.

Furthermore, competition authorities should scrutinise *ancillary restraints* to the agreement for possible anti-competitive clauses. This might be the case, for instance, if the agreement setting up the research joint-venture divides (geographical or product) markets among the participating firms, thus relaxing competition artificially; or if it calls for the payment of per-unit royalties to the joint-venture: this would increase the unit costs of output, and would have the effect of increasing prices (see also below, Section 4.5.3.1).[123] If payments are due to old patents owned by the firms, or by the joint-venture, fixed rather than per-unit of output payments would avoid distortion of competition.

4.5.2.1 Treatment of Research Joint-Ventures in US and EU Law

In the US and in the EU, research joint-ventures have been seen with favour since the early 1980s. Due also to political and industrial policy reasons (it was felt at the time that the success of domestic firms in international markets crucially depended on their advances in technology, and that more incentives to innovate should be given to domestic firms), a more lenient anti-trust approach was followed for firms collaborating in R&D.

In the US, the National Co-operative Research Act of 1984 established that joint-ventures in R&D should be subject to a *rule of reason* rather than being *per se* illegal, and that – with proper notification to the anti-trust agencies – they should be subject to single rather than treble damages in case a court would find the partners guilty of anti-trust infringement.

In the EU, the *R&D Block Exemption* issued in 2000 exempts from Article 81 of the Treaty certain forms of co-operative agreements in R&D, subject to certain conditions. In particular, partners should normally be free to use the results of R&D independently in production and distribution (to avoid restrictions of competition), and when they are competing firms their combined market share should not exceed 25%.[124] Note, however, that where the joint-venture does not qualify for the *R&D Block Exemption*, it is still possible for the parties to apply for an individual exemption to Article 81.

---

[123] A similar effect would result from a rule which establishes that the cost of financing the joint-venture falls on partners according to their *ex post* output (that is, the output they sell and which incorporates the results of the joint venture). Instead, financing the joint-venture on the basis of the *ex ante* market shares would not distort the incentives to compete *ex post*.

[124] This may rise to 30% under certain conditions, see Articles 4 and 6.

4.5.3 Other Forms of Co-Operation Regarding Technology

There are a number of other agreements that competing firms might have to share R&D results, or to fix technological standards. Like research joint-ventures, they can have beneficial welfare effects, although some caution is needed to prevent ancillary clauses that might end up distorting competition. In what follows, I briefly discuss them.

4.5.3.1 Cross-Licensing and Patent Pooling

Cross-licensing occurs when two firms reciprocally allow each other to use technology protected by patents. In principle, it is possible that such an agreement might be used to restrict competition in the marketplace. This is the case, for instance, when the technologies at stake are substitutable, and the cross-licensing agreements contain per-unit royalties that reduce the incentive to market aggressively (for a technical argument see Exercise 4.2).[125]

However, it often happens that firms have essential (or "blocking") patents that are needed for further technological progress or for final production. Suppose that two firms could introduce a new process (or manufacture a new good) that requires use of complementary technologies protected by two patents, each owned by one of the two firms. In this situation, cross-licensing might allow technological advance (or production).

Furthermore, if the patents are complementary, it would be better for each firm to own both patents. Recall that when two firms produce complementary goods each of them fails to internalise the externality that it imposes on the other, resulting in too-high prices at equilibrium relative to a firm which has both (we shall see in Chapter 6 an application of this principle in the case of vertically related products, where vertical integration would get rid of double marginalisation). For complementary technologies, the same principle would hold, and cross-licensing would reduce prices (see also Exercise 4.19).

Note also that the best situation for competition would arise when cross-licences are royalty-free, or when they specify fixed payments rather than unit royalties, as the latter would amount to higher variable costs and reduce output.

Similar reasoning applies to a *patent pool*, which might be a firm or other organisation that holds the patent rights of two or more firms and licenses them to third parties as a package. Again, if the patents are essential inputs in the technological process, their availability as a package is highly desirable, and as they are complementary, having them pooled would keep royalties lower.[126]

---

[125] See Eswaran (1994) for a repeated game in which cross-licensing facilitates collusion.

[126] Of course, not all patent pools necessarily package only complementary patents. In the *Summit/VISX* case, the two leaders in laser eye surgery formed a patent pool and the FTC challenged the agreement because it involved competing, rather than complementary, patents (see Shapiro, 2000).

Patent pools might have the additional positive feature of decreasing transaction costs, as one firm would be spared multiple time-consuming bilateral negotiations and could instead deal with only one party, namely, the patent pool (see Merges, 2001).

4.5.3.2 Co-Operative Standard-Setting

There are many examples (compact discs, television, encrypting of digital music, digital TV, Web protocols, videocassettes) where firms that compete in the development of a new technology decide to set common standards. The question is whether such co-operation in fixing standards is welfare improving or rather anti-competitive. It turns out to be a difficult question, which has no *a priori* answer. Following Shapiro (2001), I briefly summarise the main arguments for and against co-operative standard-setting. An understanding of network externalities and of their effects is crucial here (see also Chapters 2 and 7).

The main benefit of common standards is that consumers will belong to the same single network. Therefore, they will be able to communicate directly with each other in physical networks (for instance, each consumer can exchange files with all computer users who have the same operating system), and they will enjoy a larger variety in indirect networks (for instance, software programmers will face a larger market and will develop a larger number of applications). It is not a small advantage. Think for instance of the inconveniences if you could call only half of the population because the other half uses a different telephone standard!

An additional benefit is that consumers do not risk being stranded with a product that uses a standard that turns out to be abandoned later. A standards war can create a lot of uncertainty as to which standard will win, resulting in consumers delaying their purchase for fear of being stuck with the wrong product,[127] and the market not taking off when it could.

A common standard also implies fiercer competition, since consumers will face greater choice within the same standard (although smaller choice across standards, see below). Instead, if standards were different, consumers would tend to be locked-in with a given product standard, and competition would be reduced.

However, setting a common standard means that there is no competition for the dominant standard. This might have several implications. First of all, it is not clear that the industry will pick the best standard, or the one that would prevail if there were market competition for the dominant standard. A standard might be chosen on criteria that follow more the different bargaining powers of the firms involved than other, more worthy, considerations (government organisations might also be

---

[127] See Dranove and Gandal (2000) for an interesting account of the standard war between DVD and DVXX.

involved in the standard setting process, which might add bureaucracy but could also help find a good compromise). In other words, it is possible that competition for the standard would help select the standard which is more appreciated by the market, whereas under a co-operative standard this selection process would not occur. Second, precisely because network externalities are important, in absence of a co-operative standard the market will usually end up with one standard, with incompatible products disappearing altogether. After an initial phase where different standards co-exist, one will usually prevail. Anticipating the fact that eventually the market will *tip* towards one standard or the other, firms engage in intensive competition in these initial phases. Consumers will benefit from this competition, even though they will pay higher prices after the standards war has settled and one firm will prevail. This mechanism is very similar to the one which occurs under switching costs: *ex ante* competition is very intense to acquire a large customer base, but *ex post* competition is relaxed once consumers are locked-in with a particular product (see also Chapter 2).

Therefore, co-operative standard-setting implies a clear trade-off between *ex ante* and *ex post* competition: it eliminates the former but it intensifies the latter. It is very difficult to conclude *a priori* whether the net effect is positive or not. Shapiro (2001) emphasises that the case for co-operative standard setting is very strong if a standards war is likely to delay (or fail altogether) the market because consumers fear being stranded with a product that has the losing standard.[128]

Co-operative standard-setting also helps when the product being developed needs complementary technologies owned by different firms. In this case, it would allow to pool mutually blocking patents together, with the same benefits as described in the previous section.

Overall, it makes sense to allow co-operative standard-setting, but with some caution. In particular, ancillary agreements should be carefully scrutinised. For instance, side clauses which call for per-unit of output royalty cross payments should be avoided because they tend to relax competition in the product market.

4.5.4 Co-Operative R&D*

Consider a simple model by d'Aspremont and Jacquemin (1988), which analyses the effects of co-operative agreements in R&D.

The demand function for the homogeneous good produced by the two firms is $p = a - Q$, with $Q = q_1 + q_2$, the sum of individual outputs. Firm i ($i = 1, 2$) is characterised by marginal costs $c_i = C - x_i - lx_j$, where x_i is the R&D investment made by firm i, and $l \in [0, 1]$ is a parameter that indicates the spillover from the R&D investment x_j made by the rival firm. The cost of R&D is given by the function

---

[128] However, it is also true that some negotiations for setting the standard co-operatively might be very slow. A case in point is the standard for High-Definition Television, which took ten years to be set, considerably delaying the take-off of the market for digital TV.

$gx_i^2/2$, where $g > 4/3$ is a parameter expressing the efficiency of R&D production.[129] (See Chapter 2 for very similar models of innovation.)

Consider two cases. In the first, firms compete both in R&D and in quantities. In the second, they co-operate in their R&D investment decisions, but then compete in the marketplace, that is they choose quantities non-co-operatively.

Competition in Both Stages   In the first case, firms simultaneously invest in R&D at the first stage; they then simultaneously choose quantities in the second stage.

At the last stage of the game, each firm i chooses q_i to maximise its profit function $\pi_i = (a - q_i - q_j - c_i(x_i, x_j))q_i - gx_i^2/2$, given (x_i, x_j). It is easily checked that the (Cournot) equilibrium output is given by

$$q_i^c = \frac{a - 2c_i(x_i, x_j) + c_j(x_i, x_j)}{3} = \frac{a - C + x_i(2 - l) + x_j(2l - 1)}{3}. \quad (4.55)$$

After substitution, one can check that profits are given by

$$\pi_i(x_i, x_j) = \left(\frac{a - C + x_i(2 - l) + x_j(2l - 1)}{3}\right)^2 - \frac{g}{2}x_i^2. \quad (4.56)$$

At the first stage of the game, each firm will choose x_i to maximise $\pi_i(x_i, x_j)$. By taking the first derivatives $\partial\pi_i/\partial x_i = 0$ and solving the system of FOCs,[130] and focusing on the symmetric equilibrium $x_i = x_j = x^c$, we obtain the equilibrium R&D level for each firm:

$$x^c = \frac{2(a - C)(2 - l)}{9g - 4 - 2l + 2l^2}. \quad (4.57)$$

From this solution, one can then obtain by substitution the equilibrium levels of quantity and profit:

$$q^c = \frac{3(a - C)g}{9g - 4 - 2l + 2l^2}; \quad \pi^c = \frac{(a - C)^2 \left(9g - 8 + 8l - 2l^2\right)}{(9g - 4 - 2l + 2l^2)^2}. \quad (4.58)$$

Consumer surplus is given by

$$CS^c = \frac{(a - p^c)Q^c}{2} = \frac{18(a - C)^2 g^2}{(9g - 4 - 2l + 2l^2)^2}. \quad (4.59)$$

---

[129] The restriction $g > 4/3$ derives from the stability conditions of the game, which are stricter than the second-order conditions (that also require g to be large enough). See next footnote.

[130] The second-order condition requires $g > 2(2 - l)^2/9$. The stability conditions for the R&D stage require $(\partial^2\pi_i/\partial x_i dx_{-i})/(\partial^2\pi_i/\partial x_i^2) = \left|[-2(2 - l)(2l - 1)]/[2(2 - l)^2 - 9g]\right| < 1$. These are satisfied for $g > 2(2 - l)(1 - l)/3$. A sufficient condition for stability to be met is that $g > 4/3$, which also satisfies the second-order condition.

Finally, welfare is

$$W^c = 2\pi^c + CS^c = \frac{4(a-C)^2\left(9g-4-4l+l^2\right)}{(9g-4-2l+2l^2)^2}. \tag{4.60}$$

Co-Operation in R&D   I will now consider the case where firms compete in quantities in the product market, but co-operate in their R&D investment decisions.[131] Since firms take non-co-operative decisions in the product market place, the last stage is the same as before.

At the first stage of the game, however, firms will choose x_1, x_2 to maximise their joint profit $\pi^J(x_i, x_j) = \sum_{i\neq j}\pi_i(x_i, x_j)$:

$$\pi^{JV}(x_i, x_j) = \sum_{i\neq j}^{2}\left[\left(\frac{a-C+x_i(2-l)+x_j(2l-1)}{3}\right)^2 - \frac{g}{2}x_i^2\right]. \tag{4.61}$$

Focusing on the symmetric equilibrium, we find

$$x^{JV} = \frac{2(a-C)(1+l)}{9g-2(1+l)^2}. \tag{4.62}$$

By substitution the equilibrium levels of a firm's quantity and profits are

$$q^{JV} = \frac{3(a-C)g}{9g-2(1+l)^2}, \qquad \pi^{JV} = \frac{(a-C)^2g}{9g-2(1+l)^2}. \tag{4.63}$$

We can now compute consumer surplus as

$$CS^{JV} = \frac{(a-p^{JV})Q^{JV}}{2} = \frac{18(a-C)^2g^2}{(9g-2-4l-2l^2)^2}, \tag{4.64}$$

and welfare as

$$W^{JV} = 2\pi^{JV} + CS^{JV} = \frac{4(a-C)^2\left(9g-1-2l-l^2\right)}{(9g-2-4l-2l^2)^2}. \tag{4.65}$$

The Effect of a Joint-Venture in R&D   It is now possible to compare the results under the two regimes, and check that $l \geq 1/2$ guarantees that R&D investments, outputs and welfare are higher under the regime of co-operative R&D than under the regime of competition in both stages. Indeed, $x^c > x^{JV}$ amounts to the inequality

$$\frac{18g(a-C)(1-2l)}{(9g-2-4l-2l^2)(9g-4-2l+2l^2)} > 0, \tag{4.66}$$

---

[131] I assume here that firms continue to have the same degree of spillovers even when they co-operate. Perhaps it would be natural to suppose that when they co-operate they also share completely their R&D results, leading to $l = 1$; see Motta (1996) for such a formalisation. In this case, the private and social benefits from R&D co-operation would be stronger.

which holds for $l < 1/2$; $q^c > q^{JV}$ can be re-written as

$$\frac{6g(a - C)(1 - l - 2l^2)}{(9g - 2 - 4l - 2l^2)(9g - 4 - 2l + 2l^2)} > 0, \tag{4.67}$$

which also holds for $l < 1/2$. Finally, $W^c > W^{JV}$ can be re-written as

$$\frac{36g^2(a - C)^2(1 - 2l)\left(9g - 4 + l\left(36g - 12 - 12l - 4l^2\right)\right)}{(9g - 2 - 4l - 2l^2)^2(9g - 4 - 2l + 2l^2)^2} > 0; \tag{4.68}$$

Since the last term in the numerator of the LHS is always positive (given that $l \leq 1$ and that $g > 4/3$), again the inequality holds for $l < 1/2$. In other words, a research joint-venture raises welfare if spillovers are large enough ($l \geq 1/2$).

When spillovers are large enough, non-co-operating firms anticipate that they would not be able to appropriate the result of their R&D investments, and reduce their investments accordingly. Under R&D co-operation, they internalise the effect of the spillover and this results in higher R&D expenditures.

One can check that profits are always higher under the co-operative R&D regime, which means that there would be no need for subsidies (or other financial incentives) for firms to coordinate their R&D levels: they have private incentives to do so.

Extensions and Discussion   This simple model has given rise to a vast literature dealing with the effects of R&D co-operation. A number of extensions have been considered, such as price competition, generalising cost, demand functions, the number of firms, and so on.[132] However the main qualitative results of the analysis do not change across all these specifications.

Leahy and Neary (1997) analyse R&D co-operation in a general model, and compare it with alternative R&D policies to increase R&D investments, such as R&D and output subsidies. They conclude that the former policy is better than the latter, but they also warn that the welfare improvement to be obtained through R&D co-operative agreements is unlikely to be of a high order of magnitude. They also stress that R&D co-operation is privately profitable, so there is no need for further government incentives beyond allowing competing firms to engage in co-operative projects.

4.6 A CASE OF PARALLEL BEHAVIOUR: *WOOD PULP*

In 1984, the European Commission adopted a decision (*Wood pulp*) that found that forty wood pulp producers (six from Canada, ten from the US, eleven from Finland, ten from Sweden, one each from Norway, Portugal and Spain) and three of their trade associations (KEA from the US, Finncell from Finland and Svenska Cellulosa

---

[132] I confess I have contributed to raise the number of papers on this topic well above the social optimum: Motta (1992) looks at the effects of R&D joint-ventures upon entry and Motta (1996) considers them in an international economics context.

from Sweden) had infringed Article 81 (then Art. 85) of the Treaty by concerting on prices. Several of the firms involved appealed the decision, and in 1993 the European Court of Justice issued a judgment (*Ahlström and Others v. Commission*) that annulled most of the EC decision, partly on procedural grounds (which will not be discussed here) and partly on substantive issues. In what follows, I briefly describe the case and I argue that the ECJ was right in finding that the EC had not established a convincing case for collusion.

A Brief Description of the Industry   The product market concerned in the case is *bleached sulphate pulp*, obtained from the chemical processing of cellulose (which consists of plant fibres) and used in the production of high-quality paper.[133] The properties of this product vary according to the type of wood used (softwood or hardwood, wood pulp produced in northern latitudes or in southern latitudes).

Because of their different properties, paper manufacturers usually mix different types of wood pulp to obtain paper of a certain grade. Within any product category, pulp is interchangeable to a considerable extent, but once a given mixture has been determined, there might be large *switching costs* for a paper manufacturer, since adjustments should be made to its equipment and there may be time-consuming and costly trials before arriving at the optimal result. These characteristics (combination of different wood pulps and switching costs) have led buyers of wood pulp to purchase from different producers and to have long-term relationships with them.

The wood pulp price is important for paper manufacturers, as it accounts for 50–75% of the cost of paper. This pushes manufacturers to diversify their sources of supply to avoid becoming over-dependent on one producer.

In the years considered in the decision, there were more than fifty producers selling wood pulp in Europe. The forty firms involved in the decision accounted for roughly 60% of overall European sales. The industry is characterised by vertical integration, with most wood pulp producers being also paper manufacturers, but even vertically integrated firms sold and bought wood pulp in the market.

Some producers were selling through agents, which often were common to more wood pulp producers.

As said above, pulp producers were generally linked to their buyers by long-term contracts of up to five years. "Under such contracts, the producer guaranteed his customers the possibility of purchasing each quarter a minimum quantity of pulp at a price, which was not to exceed the price announced by him at the beginning of the quarter. The customer was free to purchase more or less than the quantity reserved for him and could negotiate reductions in the announced price" (*Ahlström and Others v. Commission*, para. 13).

---

[133] There also exist other chemical pulps, or mechanical pulps, but they are of inferior quality. Note that in a collusion case the definition of the relevant market is not particularly important, since an assessment of the market power of the firms involved is not necessary.

Important for the case at hand, a consolidated trading practice in this market is a system of quarterly announcements of prices. Some weeks or days before the beginning of each quarter, producers communicate to their customers and agents the prices for that quarter (although, as just said, rebates might be negotiated).

Also important, manufacturers generally quoted their prices in US dollars.

The Commission Decision   In 1977, the EC opened a proceeding against fifty-seven producers and associations alleged to have participated in price-fixing. On 19 December 1984, forty-three producers and associations were found to have infringed the EU competition rules. More specifically: (1) all the US producers members of KEA (that is, all US firms but one) were found to have concerted on prices and exchanged individualised price data. (2) Finncell and Svenska, which embraced the Finnish and Swedish producers, one Canadian firm, and the Norwegian, Portuguese and Spanish firms, were found guilty for having exchanged individualised data on prices of hardwood pulp from 1973 to 1977, within the framework of Fides, the (Swiss-based) research and information centre of the European pulp and paper industry. (3) All the producers involved were found to have concerted on (announced or actual) prices of wood pulp for the whole or parts of the period from 1975 to 1981.[134]

As I discuss shortly, the first two accusations were supported by hard evidence. The third one is much broader, both because it involves all the firms and because it relates to a different period (which goes beyond the starting date of the EC investigation), but is not substantiated by hard evidence. Rather, it is based on the parallel conduct of the producers. This third point is the most interesting, and will be discussed at length after a brief discussion of the first two points.

(1) Concertation within KEA   Except one, all the US wood pulp producers involved used to belong to the Pulp, Paper and Paperboard Export Association of the United States, formerly known as Kraft Export Association (KEA), an abbreviation still used at the time of the Decision. KEA was an *export cartel* registered in 1952 under the Webb-Pomerene Act (see Chapter 1). Its members met to unanimously fix export prices of wood pulp. They were then free to deviate from those prices, but they were required to give advance notification to KEA, which may then convene a meeting to discuss appropriate action. As such, there is little doubt that the members of KEA had engaged in concerted practices forbidden by EU competition law.

---

[134] The decision (confusingly) distinguishes between concertation in announced prices and concertation in transaction prices. This distinction which is not well explained by the EC is not very relevant for the following discussion. However, it is interesting to the extent that it reveals at the outset that announced and actual prices did not necessarily coincide. As a separate remark, note that the Canadian and Swedish producers were also found guilty for having used clauses prohibiting export or resale of wood pulp to their European customers, a point I do not discuss here.

(2) **Concertation within Fides**   Within Fides, and apparently at the initiative of the Finnish and Swedish producers, some wood pulp producers (mentioned above) exchanged data concerning individual prices and capacities, agreed on a selling price, and committed to justify divergences between the commonly agreed prices and the prices they effectively charged. Proof of these practices was provided by hard evidence, consisting of various documents, telex messages, minutes of some meetings, internal letters and notes relating to meetings or their outcomes (*Wood pulp*: paragraphs 44–60). Some of these documents are interesting because they hint at the sort of problems arising in a collusive agreement.[135]

Borregaard, the Norwegian producer, stated in a letter to its London subsidiary:

> Officially we keep the KEA price of US $405, but here are possibilities of going below this price, although we are somewhat afraid of doing too much of this in the UK market which is a key market and very important to everybody ... There is a lot of sympathy and understanding among our colleagues and competitors at present because the French group and Borregaard are the worst hit from the bad hardwood pulp market. We believe they would oversee the fact that we in some cases give a better price or a longer credit[136] (*Wood pulp*: para. 49).

The minutes of the management board meeting (14 April 1977) of GEC, relating to a trip to Sweden and Finland of Mr Jooris, GEC's sales manager at the time, state: "Supported by data, Mr. Jooris persuaded them that it was not GEC that was charging the lowest prices, especially in Italy. He will go again to Helsinki on the 11th of May, to study the possibility to raise prices in the second semester ... The Scandinavians have abandoned their threat to redirect to France important amounts of wood pulp"[137] (*Wood pulp*: para. 53).

The minutes of a meeting of the Bristol Club (also called "mini-Fides", because it grouped a subset of the producers belonging to Fides) state:

> Price increases for export of pulp are perhaps premature for the third quarter. Everybody is, however, keen on reaching higher levels as soon as possible. Criticism is still heard from Scandinavians as to Continental hardwood pulp prices. Through curtailments and sacrifices the Scandinavians are contributing to a stabilisation that can fail completely if discipline is not shown by the Continental producers. In case the second quarter has not yet been price-fixed, wholly or partly, the low

---

[135] This topic is studied in Genesove and Mullin (2001), who analyse in depth the working of the Sugar Institute, the trade association of US sugar refiners. The Sugar Institute did not fix prices, but imposed business practices that help sustain collusion, and provided its members with a forum where they could analyse suspected deviations and possible punishments.

[136] This sentence shows that the firm expected a retaliation not to take place as long as the deviation was not too considerable. Also, it shows that some price undercutting was tolerated if special circumstances (such as local shocks which hit differently producers) occurred.

[137] This sentence shows the role of meetings to justify a firm's actions, so as to avoid possible retaliations. See also Genesove and Mullin (2001) for an account of a similar role in the Sugar Institute meetings.

price sellers should try to increase their levels. Everybody seems to be aware of the necessity of increasing prices as soon as possible but maybe the third quarter is still premature. Cirnelima from Riocel has admitted that in the Federal Republic of Germany their prices are US $335 to 340. However, no lower prices have been given Jacobson ... Mueller: Difference of US $25 has not caused problems, but now the difference is US $80 to 100, which is intolerable. If this gets on, the birch kraft cannot hold its position. He as well as Nykopp stated that US $390 is holding! ... Nykopp: The Finns will respect the Spanish dominance in Spain if ENCE really increase their prices in other countries. If Finncell learns about prices below US $360 also in the future, they will reconsider their policy as to sales in Spain![138] (*Wood pulp:* para. 60.)

(3) Parallel Behaviour   If it was uncontroversial that firms belonging to KEA and Fides explicitly colluded, the Commission went beyond that, and found an infringement of Article 81 due to parallel behaviour, which concerned also firms not involved in KEA and Fides, and which allegedly continued until 1981. Such parallel behaviour consisted of (i) the system of quarterly price announcements; (ii) the simultaneity or quasi-simultaneity of the announcements; (iii) the fact that announced prices were identical. As the ECJ rightly argues, absent documents, which *directly* establish the existence of collusion between the producers concerned, the problem is then to understand whether the three elements (i), (ii), and (iii) are proof of collusion ("constitute a firm, precise and consistent body of evidence of prior concertation") or can instead be explained by normal competitive behaviour:

> In determining the probative value of those different factors, it must be noted that *parallel conduct cannot be regarded as furnishing proof of concertation unless concertation constitutes the only plausible explanation for such conduct.* It is necessary to bear in mind that, although article 85 of the Treaty prohibits any form of collusion which distorts competition, *it does not deprive economic operators of the right to adapt themselves intelligently to the existing and anticipated conduct of their competitors.* (*Ahlström and Others v. Commission,* para. 71; emphasis added; note that art. 85 is now art. 81.)

To establish whether parallel conduct was in this case proof of collusion, the ECJ commissioned two experts' reports, whose conclusions were devastating for the Commission, in that they indicated that parallelism could well have been the result of the normal oligopolistic interdependence among competitors. In what follows, the reasoning of the ECJ, which completely relies on the experts, is described.

(i) The system of price announcements   The Commission believed that the system of quarterly price announcements and the fact that all firms quoted prices in the same currency were practices expressly adopted by the wood pulp producers so as to increase the transparency of the market, thus rendering collusion easier.

---

[138] Clearly, the meetings allow the firms to coordinate on new prices, as well as make sure that price cutters know of the risks of retaliation. See also Section 4.2.2.

The experts found that it was the purchasers who, after World War II, demanded the introduction of that system of announcements, in order to estimate their costs (recall that wood pulp accounts for 50–75% of the costs of a paper manufacturer) and to fix the prices of their (downstream) products. The quarterly periodicity appeared to be a compromise between the buyers, who would have liked price stability over a longer period, and the sellers, who did not want to commit to the same price for too long (recall that under the long-term contracts used in the industry, the prices were renegotiable downwards, but not upwards).

Further, they found that the US dollar was first introduced by the North American producers during the 1960s (before the period of the alleged concerted practices), and subsequently adopted by other producers; they also found that this development was welcomed by the buyers.[139]

(ii) The near-simultaneity of the announcements According to the EC, the close succession of price announcements could be explained only by a concerted practice:

> There is no valid explanation of how such information spreads so rapidly (i.e., within a matter of days, in some instances, on the same days) between such a large number of firms, especially since information normally passes from one producer to another in a multi-stage process: from the producer to his agent or subsidiary, from the agent or subsidiary to the customer, from the customer to the agent or subsidiary of another producer who is ultimately informed and then makes his own announcement. (*Wood pulp:* para. 89.)

However, the simultaneity or near-simultaneity of the announcements had another, innocent, plausible explanation according to the experts' reports. Several market features, some already mentioned above, explain why information could spread very rapidly: each buyer is in contact with several producers (because of the mixture of wood pulp used and because of diversification in the sources of supply), and would have an incentive to reveal prices set by other suppliers – at least when they are cut; most wood pulp producers are also paper manufacturers, and purchase some of their input from upstream rivals, thus being immediately informed of upstream prices; the existence of common agents that work for several wood pulp producers. All these elements, combined with the use of telephone and telex, imply that "notwithstanding the number of stages involved – producer, agent, buyer, agent, producer – information on the level of the announced prices spreads within a matter of days, if not within a matter of hours on the pulp market" (*Ahlström and Others v. Commission,* para. 88).

---

[139] The reason reported in the judgment (para. 79) is that purchasers "regarded it as a means of ensuring that they did not pay a higher price than their competitors". This seems a rather unusual explanation, also in the light of the fact that these were ceiling prices subject to negotiation. Another reason might be that a common currency allowed buyers to better compare prices offered by the different suppliers.

Furthermore, the fact that information spreads so rapidly was stressed in the Commission Decision as well. Paragraph 19 recites: "Telex dated 19 November 1975 from Continental Cellulose to its principal Stora Kopparbergs: "We just learned that SCA have decided to offer henceforth their pulps in Belgium in US dollars at the following levels: . . . As your agents, and in order to help the stability of the market – which needs it because of the very low and bad paper prices – we beg to recommend to follow such levels. Please instruct". SCA (Svenska Cellulosa AB) announced its prices on 19 November 1975".[140]

(iii) Parallelism of announced prices   The third element in the EC's construction consists of the fact that the prices announced by the wood pulp producers involved were the same (or very similar) although they had different production costs, different rates of capacity utilisation, and different costs of transportation to a given market; they were at an artificially high level, especially in 1976, 1977 and 1981; in 1977 and 1982 the fall in prices was particularly abrupt.

The pattern and evolution of price levels described in this case might be consistent with the Commission's hypothesis that there existed collusion, the low prices in 1977 and in 1982 corresponding to a punishment phase. However, as the experts and the ECJ noted, it is also consistent with an alternative explanation, that is competitive behaviour in an oligopolistic industry.

First, let us deal with the evolution of (average) prices, that is, the fact that they were high in some years and low in others. The experts' findings suggest that this might well be explained by the evolution of demand and by other factors. In modern terms, this means that it was consistent with non-collusive (say, Cournot) behaviour in presence of demand or supply shocks.

In 1974, demand for wood pulp was very strong, and led to an increase in prices. In 1975 and 1976, prices were stable although demand was low. However, several factors might explain the fact that price did not fall despite the decline in capacity utilisation rates and the increase in inventory levels. First, a high rate of inflation implies that real prices had actually fallen; second, the Swedish government introduced a storage subsidy scheme that granted Swedish producers a tax rebate on stock building that was related to the value of inventories; third, Canadian and US producers were operating close to capacity because the US market was buoyant at that time; fourth, in 1976 world demand for paper had started to recover, resulting in optimistic forecasts for the demand of wood pulp.

The analysis of the market can equally explain the 1977 price fall without resorting to a collusive hypothesis. The Swedish government had ended its storage subsidy scheme, and the expected increase in wood pulp demand had never materialised. A fall in prices was therefore the result of excess supply (inventories had increased over the two previous years).

---

[140] Svenska Cellulosa AB is a producer. It should not be confused with the Swedish Pulp and Paper Association, which bears the same name.

In 1978, demand recovered and then exceeded supply. With producers having no spare capacity, prices started to rise and stayed high until the end of 1981, when the world demand for paper fell and excess capacity was growing accordingly. As a result, prices rapidly fell as well (unlike 1976–7; this time inflation was not high, and there was no incentive programme to artificially increase supply).

Second, it still remains to be explained why prices over the economic cycle were the same (or similar) across producers. Here there are two possible theoretical explanations, which are compatible with the firms behaving independently. The first theory is the tacit collusion hypothesis that has been at the heart of this chapter (which, as I have repeatedly argued, deserves a different legal treatment than explicit collusion). Given the existing price (for instance the high price established after the strong demand in 1974), and given that that is one of the several possible (tacitly collusive) equilibrium prices, no firm light-heartedly wants to decrease prices when (as in 1975) demand starts to fall, fearing that this would trigger a reaction from rivals that would accelerate the price fall. Also, consider that the transparency of the market implies that a price cut is immediately spotted by rivals, so the incentive to decrease prices to gain market shares is very small. It is only when excess capacity becomes untenable that prices will fall. In this tacit collusion hypothesis prices are close to each other because the lack of coordination implies that there is no possibility to coordinate on a collusive equilibrium, which is more efficient for the producers. The second theory is the one favoured by the experts of the Court, and corresponds to the *kinked demand curve* hypothesis.[141] According to this theory, there is a lot of price rigidity in markets because a firm expects that if it increases prices the rivals will not follow and therefore it will lose market shares, and that if it decreases prices the rivals will immediately follow and therefore it will not benefit from the price cut (an analysis of the market shows that the paper manufacturers' demand for wood pulp is inelastic to price; hence, no market expansion would follow from a generalised price reduction of wood pulp). Therefore, the same price would continue to hold unless major shocks intervened (as in the previous case, the theory does not explain why a certain price has formed in the market, but at that given price there would be not much room for firms to move from it because of the existing expectations).

The Court's Conclusions, and a Discussion   In the light of the economic analysis of the market briefly described above, the ECJ arrived at the conclusion, from which it is hard to dissent, that "concertation is not the only plausible explanation for the parallel conduct" (*Ahlström and Others v. Commission*, para. 126).

At this point, one can ask the broader question of whether one can ever find an infringement of anti-trust laws by simply looking at parallel conduct. The answer is

---

[141] This is an old theory in industrial organisation that has been formalised by Maskin and Tirole (1988) in a model where firms take alternating moves and that makes use of a Markov-perfect equilibrium concept.

that this is possible, but the standard of proof is (rightly) high, as one should prove that communication and/or coordination of some kind among the firms must be the only plausible explanation for parallelism. In *Dyestuffs* (see Section 4.1), firms were found sending similar price instructions to their agents and subsidiaries basically at the same hour and day. The probability that this could happen without firms having previously talked to each other was nil: concertation was in that case the only plausible explanation for parallel conduct.

Finally, a question of some interest in *Wood pulp*, especially for those who are interested in market outcomes (and think that it is not intent or communication that matters, but rather whether prices are above some competitive level), is whether market prices were collusive or not? The published documents do not offer much data that can help answer this question, but some considerations might none the less be made. On the one hand, the market was very transparent from the point of view of the firms: there is little doubt that if a firm made a generalised deviation from a collusive price, the deviation will be immediately detected by rivals (via the connections between wood pulp producers, agents and buyers described above). We also know that at least some of them, for at least some time, had coordinated on prices and had exchanged information on prices and capacity utilisation. On the other hand, it is far from clear that in this industry the collusive outcome can be easily reached. Firms can coordinate on list prices, but the effective transaction prices are determined by the bargaining between a buyer (some of them were buying large quantities, although the published documents do not offer precise information) and a seller. Apparently, secret price cuts were widespread in the industry, and announced and effective prices did not generally coincide (although the actual divergence is somehow disputed in the proceedings), which results in the market shares of producers varying during the period at issue (*Ahlström and Others v. Commission*, para. 119). Finally, and no less important, the firms involved in the investigation accounted only for 60% of the market. It seems hard to believe that they could sustain a collusive outcome with outsiders supplying a 40% share of the total consumption of wood pulp.

4.7 EXERCISES

Exercise 4.1   *(From Tirole (1988).)* Consider n firms producing homogenous goods and choosing prices in each period for an infinite number of periods. Suppose that the market meets every two periods, rather than every period. Write the incentive constraint for collusion under trigger strategies and show that collusion is less likely to hold than when the market meets every period.

Exercise 4.2   *Consider two firms producing homogenous goods and choosing prices in each period for an infinite number of periods. Each of the two firms owns a share σ of its rival. This share is small enough for each firm to keep full control of its own activities and decisions: the rival is a minority shareholder, who is not represented in the board and receives just a share σ of the firm's profits. Is the likelihood of collusion affected by this cross-ownership?

Exercise 4.3   There are only three sellers in a given industry. One day, one of the firms sends the following fax to its two competitors: "In the interest of fair competition, and for the sake of market transparency, we hereby inform you that the Board of our company has decided that from the next quarter our sales prices will be increased by 10%". Do you think that the competition authority should allow or forbid sending such faxes? Why?

Exercise 4.4   In a given sector there are n firms that sell directly to consumers. They sell a homogenous good which is subject to very frequent shocks, giving rise to high price instability. Every week, these firms communicate the price at which they will sell the product in the following week to the central office of their trade association. The trade association then publishes the (following week's) prices of all the firms in national newspapers. The national anti-trust authority argues that this practice allows firms to exchange information thereby increasing the likelihood of collusion. Do you agree?

Exercise 4.5   *Consider a homogenous good industry where n firms produce at zero cost and play the Bertrand game an infinite number of periods. When firms choose the same price, they earn a per-period profit $\Pi(p) = p\alpha D(p)/n$. When a firm i charges a price p_i lower than the price of all the other firms, it earns a profit $\Pi(p_i) = p_i\alpha D(p_i)$, and all other firms obtain zero profits. The parameter α represents the state of demand. Imagine that in the current period demand is characterised by $\alpha = 1$, but starting from the following period demand will be characterised by $\alpha = \theta$ in each of the following periods. All the players know exactly the evolution of the demand state at the beginning of the game. Firms have the same common discount factor, δ. (a) Assume $\theta > 1$ and consider the following trigger strategies. Each firm plays the monopoly price p_m in the first period of the game and continues to charge such a price until a profit equal to zero is observed. When this occurs, each firm charges price equal to zero forever. Under which conditions does this n-tuple of strategies represent an equilibrium? In particular, show how θ and n affect such a condition, and give an economic intuition for this result. (b) Can other prices be sustained at equilibrium under strategies similar to the ones above? Under which condition? (c) Assume now $\theta < 1$, and find the conditions under which the n-tuple of strategies delineated above represent an equilibrium.

Exercise 4.6   In a country there are three large automotive firms, which have together 100% of the market (the existence of a prohibitive tariff excludes imports). During the last weeks, these firms have been engaged in a promotional campaign in the major newspapers of the country. In these announcements, separately made by each of the firms, a firm announces a price for each of the models produced and says it will sell at such a price to any buyer who produces the newspaper cutting containing the announcement. The anti-trust agency has opened an investigation, suspecting a collusive agreement. The announcements are very similar, since they use similar wording and even prices appear to be very close to each other for comparable models. Give your opinion on the basis of what has been reported here about whether or not collusive agreement exists.

Exercise 4.7 *Consider a sector Y where two firms sell a homogenous good at a marginal cost c. They have the same discount factor δ. The firms play the Bertrand game for an infinite number of times. That is, in each period they have to choose the price at which they sell. They face a market demand $D(p)$. When they charge the same price, one firm sells a market share λ (with $1/2 < \lambda < 1$) and the other a market share $1 - \lambda$. (It does not matter why one firm has a higher market share than the other.) The two firms have the following trigger strategy. In the first period they set a price $\bar{p}$, where $\bar{p} > c$. In the following periods, they choose the same price $\bar{p}$ if both firms have chosen $\bar{p}$ in all previous periods. Otherwise, they choose the one-shot Bertrand equilibrium price forever. (a) Find the condition under which these trigger strategies represent an equilibrium. (b) Practitioners often argue that symmetry among firms facilitates collusion. Does this simple model support their claim? (c) Under which condition can the trigger strategies above sustain a fully collusive equilibrium where the firms charge the joint-profit maximising price p_m in each period?

Exercise 4.8 The time-series of price data of a given industry reveals that prices are not stable over time. During the last ten years, one can observe periods in which prices are high and periods where prices are low (about 30% less than the high price level). (a) Can one infer from the existence of periods with low prices that there is no collusion in this industry? Why? (b) Can one infer from the existence of periods with low prices that there is collusion in this industry? Why?

Exercise 4.9 Can you explain why and under what circumstances resale price maintenance can facilitate collusion?

Exercise 4.10 *In a small town, Fiesole, there is a street market twice a week, all year round and every year (so we can approximate the game being played with an infinite horizon game). In a market day, n vendors sell their perfectly homogenous apples (they produce them at a marginal cost c and without fixed costs). When they arrive at the market in the morning, they each have to simultaneously hand in to the market authorities a sealed envelope which contains the price at which they will sell their apples during the day. Once the envelopes are opened, the prices are public, but they cannot be changed for the whole day. (Assume also that they are not capacity constrained: each of them brings to the market enough apples to satisfy all the demand at any price above marginal cost.) In another small town far away, Schriesheim, a very similar situation and game occur, with just two small differences: the street market takes place once a week only, and there are only two vendors that sell their (homogenous) apples (they also have marginal cost c and no fixed cost). Would you expect that a collusive equilibrium (with trigger strategies) would be more likely to arise in Fiesole or in Schriesheim? Show your point formally.

Exercise 4.11   *Consider two firms producing homogenous goods and choosing quantities in each period for an infinite number of periods. Demand in the industry is given by $p = 1 - Q$, Q being the sum of individual outputs. Firms are identical: they have zero constant marginal costs, and the same discount factor δ. Consider the following trigger strategies. Each firm sets the output $q \in [1/4, 1/3]$ at the beginning of the game, and continues to do so unless a deviation occurs. After a deviation, each firm sets the quantity q^{cn}, which is the Nash equilibrium of the one-shot game. (a) Find the condition for collusion to arise in this industry. (b) Show that the lower q (i.e., the more collusive the output choice) the less likely that the collusive trigger strategies above are sustained at equilibrium.

Exercise 4.12   *Consider n firms producing homogenous goods and choosing quantities in each period for an infinite number of periods. Demand in the industry is given by $p = 1 - Q$, Q being the sum of individual outputs. All firms in the industry are identical: they have the same constant marginal costs $c < 1$, and the same discount factor δ. Consider the following trigger strategies. Each firm sets the output q^m that maximises joint profits at the beginning of the game, and continues to do so unless one or more firms deviate. After a deviation, each firm sets the quantity q^{cn}, which is the Nash equilibrium of the one-shot game. (a) Find the condition for collusion to arise in this industry. (b) Indicate how the number of firms in the industry affects the possibility of reaching the tacit collusive outcome, and discuss. (c)** Do you know any other punishment strategy under which firms can sustain the collusive outcome under weaker conditions?

Exercise 4.13   **Consider two perfectly symmetric firms that sell a differentiated good and consider collusion. The fully collusive price in the market is given by p_m, and gives firms a profit π_m each. Firms also have the same discount factor δ. They play the Bertrand game an infinite number of periods. There also exists an antitrust authority, which investigates the industry in every period. If firms collude, the authority will find them guilty with a probability p and will accordingly give them a fine $F > \delta\pi_n$. If they are found colluding, also assume that the authority will prevent them from colluding in the future: they will forever earn market profit $\pi_n > 0$ each, where the index n stands for Nash. If firms do not collude, they cannot be fined. (a) Focus on simple trigger strategies with Nash reversal forever. Write the incentive constraints for collusion to be sustained at equilibrium, and discuss the effects that p and F have upon collusion. (b) Consider a value of the discount factor high enough for collusion to be sustainable. Are prices other than p_m sustainable at equilibrium of this infinite horizon game? (c) Do you know of any other strategies that could allow firms to sustain collusion under a slacker condition?

Exercise 4.14   Very often, in cartel investigations, lawyers, judges and economic experts state that collusion is more difficult in periods of declining demand than in periods of boom. Can you briefly mention theoretical arguments which support this view?

Exercise 4.15   If one discovers that two or more firms change prices by the same proportion within a few days of each other, then is this proof that these firms have a collusive agreement? Discuss.

Exercise 4.16   *Consider a sector where n firms play a non-co-operative game that will continue in each of the following periods with a probability α. (That is, in any period T, the game can either continue with probability α, or stop forever with a probability $1 - \alpha$.) In each period where the game takes place, a firm has to choose a certain action. If all firms choose the "collusive" action, they will all share the market and gain a profit Π_m/n each. If one firm deviates from the collusive action, this firm will earn $\Pi_d > \Pi_m/n$. Firms have the following strategies. In the first period of the game, they take the collusive action. In any of the following periods where the game takes place, they choose the collusive action if all firms have obtained profits Π_m/n in any of the previous periods. Otherwise, they choose a punishment action, which results in all firms making profits Π_c for all future periods of the game. (a) Show that if the discount factor δ (which is equal for all firms) and the probability α are high enough, these strategies form an equilibrium of the game. (b) Show that collusion is the more likely to happen the stronger the punishment, the lower deviation profits, and the smaller the number of firms. (c) Is the collusive equilibrium the unique equilibrium of this game?

Exercise 4.17   *Consider the model of Section 4.5.4, where two firms face a demand $p = a - Q$ and have costs $A_i = (C - x_i - lx_j)q_i + (g/2)x_i^2$, where $0 \le l \le 1$ is a spillover parameter and $g > 4/3$ is an investment efficiency parameter. They sequentially choose first R&D levels x_i and then output levels q_i. (a) Suppose that firms could co-operate at both the R&D and the output stage of the game. Find the equilibrium R&D investments and outputs. (b) Suppose now that firms behave non-co-operatively in both stages. Find the equilibrium R&D and outputs. (c) Compare the equilibrium outcomes under the two regimes. [A possible variant of this exercise is to find R&D and outputs when firms behave co-operatively at the R&D stage, and then compare the results with those of full co-operation.]

Exercise 4.18   *(*Anti-competitive cross-licensing*) Consider two firms that play the following game. In the first stage, they jointly decide whether they want to cross-license their technologies. The technologies are assumed to be perfect substitutes and are used to produce the same homogenous good. At this stage, if cross-licensing is agreed upon, they also jointly decide the same per-unit of output royalty c_L for the cross-licence. In the following stage, they compete in quantities. Assume for simplicity that the only unit cost, if any, is given by c_L. Assume linear demand $p = 1 - Q$, where Q is total output. Show whether at equilibrium they will decide to cross-license and at which royalty level.

Exercise 4.19 *(Pooling of complementary patents)* To produce a certain (homogenous) final good, n manufacturers need two complementary technologies, whose patents are owned by two firms A and B, who separately license the technologies at a unit royalty fee w_i ($i = A, B$). The game is as follows. In the first stage, the patent-holders independently and simultaneously decide the royalty level. In the second stage, the manufacturers compete à la Bertrand, and incur unit costs $c + w_A + w_B$. They face market demand $q = 1 - p$ (as usual, if several firms all charge the same lowest price, demand is equally shared among them; zero demand goes to firms having higher prices). (a) Find the equilibrium values of royalties and final prices. (b) Consider an alternative situation where the two patent-holders assign the right of exploitation of their patents to a patent pool. It is now the pool which sets the value of both royalties. Find equilibrium values of royalties and final prices under the patent pool and compare them with the previous case. (c) Show that forming the patent pool is both profitable for the patent-holders and good for consumers.

Exercise 4.20 *Suppose there are two separate geographic markets, a and b, and two firms, 1 and 2, located respectively in a and in b. Unit transportation costs (production costs are zero) from one market to the other are given by $t < 1/2$. Firms produce a homogenous good whose demand in country $k = a, b$ is $p_k = 1 - 2Q_k/s$.[142] We assume that each firm $i = 1, 2$ simultaneously chooses quantities q_{ia} and q_{ib} to be sold in both markets in each period of an infinite horizon game with common discount factor δ. Consider the following trigger strategies, which define a collusive market allocation scheme. At the beginning of the game, each firm sells only in its own market ($q_{2a} = q_{1b} = 0$). If a deviation occurs (that is, if a firm starts to export), then both firms revert to the Nash equilibrium forever (at the Nash equilibrium, both firms export). Find the conditions for collusion and show how they vary with t.

4.7.1 Solution to Exercises

Exercise 4.1 The IC becomes $\pi(p_m)(1 + \delta^2 + \delta^4 + \cdots)/n \geq \pi(p_m)$. Write $\delta^2 = d$. Then the IC can be written $d \geq 1 - (1/n)$, whence $\delta \geq \sqrt{1 - (1/n)}$. Since $\sqrt{x} >$

x when $x < 1$, the incentive constraint is less likely to be satisfied than under the standard case.

Exercise 4.2 Yes, cross-ownership makes collusion more likely. To see why, consider that firm i's profit will be given by $\pi_i(1 - \sigma) + \sigma\pi_j$, and that if firm i deviates, in the deviation period $\pi_j = 0$. The incentive constraint for collusion can then be written as $\pi(p^m)/(2(1 - \delta)) \geq \pi(p^m)(1 - \sigma)$, which simplifies to $\delta \geq 1 - 1/[2(1 - \sigma)]$.

If there were no cross-ownership, $\sigma = 0$, and the condition would be less likely to hold.

Exercise 4.5 Let us denote the collusive price by $p^c \in (c, p_m]$. At time $t = 0$, $\alpha = 1$, whereas at time $t \in \{1, 2, \ldots\}$, $\alpha = \theta$. The incentive constraint then becomes $\pi(p^c)(1 + \delta\theta + \delta^2\theta + \delta^3\theta + \cdots)/n \geq \pi(p^c)$, or, equivalently, $\delta \geq (n - 1)/(n - 1 + \theta) \equiv \tilde{\delta}(n, \theta)$.

(a) When firms play the monopoly price along the collusive path, $p^c = p_m$ and the condition for the n-tuple of firms' strategies to be an equilibrium is given by the incentive constraint just derived, which is the same for all firms. Now, some simple algebra shows that $\partial\tilde{\delta}(n, \theta)/\partial\theta = -(n - 1)/(n - 1 + \theta)^2 < 0$, whereas $\partial\tilde{\delta}(n, \theta)/\partial n = \theta/(n - 1 + \theta)^2 > 0$.

The higher the value of θ, the higher the one-time change in demand will be. Hence, the higher is θ, the higher the present value of the stream of profits received from $t = 1$ onwards. The opportunity cost of deviation increases with θ. Hence, the higher θ is, the less likely it is that firms will disrupt the collusive agreement today (at $t = 0$). On the other hand, when n increases, the tighter the incentive constraint becomes, that is, the less likely it is that collusion will be sustained at equilibrium. The intuition that underlies this result is the standard one: the higher the number of firms in a collusive agreement, the more difficult it becomes to reach and sustain collusion.

(b) Notice that the incentive constraint derived above is valid for all $p^c \in (c, p_m]$. Hence, under strategies similar to the ones above, a collusive price $p^c \in (c, p_m]$ can be sustained at equilibrium if $\delta \geq (n - 1)/(n - 1 + \theta) \equiv \tilde{\delta}(n, \theta)$.

(c) The condition is the same as in (b), and it implies that an anticipated drop in demand would lead to a more stringent condition for collusion.

Exercise 4.7 Let us denote by s_i the market share of firm i, $i = 1, 2$. Assume, without loss of generality, that $s_1 = \lambda$ and $s_2 = 1 - \lambda$.

(a) The incentive constraint for firm i, $i = 1, 2$, is given by $s_i(\bar{p} - c) D(\bar{p})/(1 - \delta) - (\bar{p} - c) D(\bar{p}) \geq 0$, or, equivalently, $\delta \geq 1 - s_i$.

Hence, the described trigger strategies represent an equilibrium if and only if $\delta \geq \max\{\lambda, 1 - \lambda\}$. But, since $1/2 < \lambda < 1$, the previous condition reduces to $\delta \geq \lambda$.

(b) Yes. Notice that in a symmetric industry structure $s_1 = s_2 = 1/2$. Therefore, the incentive constraint (which is now common for both firms) reduces to $\delta \geq$

226 Collusion and Horizontal Agreements

1/2, which is the condition for the standard textbook symmetric duopoly case. Since by assumption λ is greater than 1/2, the condition $\delta \geq \lambda$ is more stringent than $\delta \geq 1/2$. Collusion is less likely to be sustained in an asymmetric market structure.

(c) If $\bar{p} = p_m$, then the incentive constraint for firm i, $i = 1, 2$, is $s_i (p_m - c) D(p_m)/(1 - \delta) - (p_m - c) D(p_m) \geq 0$. It is straightforward to show that it amounts to $\delta \geq \max \{\lambda, 1 - \lambda\}$, the same condition we have derived in (a). Thus, the same interval of values for the discount factor δ allows for a continuum of equilibrium solutions to hold.

Exercise 4.10 Assume that one unit of time is half a week. In Fiesole, the market runs twice a week and there are n vendors. Therefore, the incentive constraint of a representative vendor in Fiesole is given by $\pi^f (p^c) / [n(1 - \delta)] \geq \pi^f (p^c)$, where $\pi^f (p^c)$ denotes the aggregate profit in the Fiesole market when all vendors set a (collusive) price $p^c > c$.

This condition in turn implies that the critical discount factor in Fiesole is given by $\delta \geq (1 - 1/n) \equiv \widetilde{\delta}_f$.

As far as Schriesheim is concerned, there the market runs only once a week and only two vendors exist. The incentive constraint faced by a vendor in this other small town is given by $\pi^s (p^c) (1 + \delta^2 + \delta^4 + \cdots)/2 \geq \pi^s (p^c)$, where $\pi^s (p^c)$ denotes the aggregate profit in Schriesheim when both vendors fix the same collusive price $p^c > c$.

Collusion will therefore arise at equilibrium under trigger strategies if $1/(1 - \delta^2) \geq 2$, which in turn implies that $\delta \geq 1/\sqrt{2} \equiv \widetilde{\delta}_s$.

Notice that in Fiesole, as compared to Schriesheim, we have more firms, which tends to hurt collusion, on the one hand, and a higher frequency of orders (market interactions), which tends to facilitate collusion, on the other. So, in order for collusion to be less likely in Fiesole than in Schriesheim, the first effect must more than compensate the second. In formal terms, $\widetilde{\delta}_f > \widetilde{\delta}_s$ if $(1 - 1/n) - 1/\sqrt{2} > 0$, which holds if $n \in \{4, 5, 6, \ldots\}$.

Exercise 4.11 (a) First of all, it is useful to find the Cournot equilibrium of the game, which is given by $q^{cn} = 1/3$ and $\pi^{cn} = 1/9$ (see Chapter 8). By following the trigger strategies and setting output q between the joint profit maximisation output $q^m = 1/4$ and the Cournot output $q^{cn} = 1/3$, a firm has profits $\pi = (1 - 2q)q$. When the rival sets q, the optimal deviation can be found by choosing $q^d = \arg\max_{\widetilde{q}} \pi^d = (1 - \widetilde{q} - q)\widetilde{q}$. By setting $\partial \pi^d/\partial \widetilde{q} = 0$, one can find that $q^d = (1 - q)/2$, and $\pi^d = (1 - q)^2/4$.

The IC can be written as $\delta \geq (\pi^d - \pi)/(\pi^d - \pi^{cn})$, and by substitution this becomes $\delta \geq 9(1 - 3q)^2/(9q^2 - 18q + 5) \equiv \bar{\delta}$, which is the condition for collusion to be sustainable.

(b) To see how the critical discount factor varies with the degree of collusion, just compute $\partial\bar{\delta}/\partial q = -108/(5 - 3q)^2 < 0$. As q increases in the interval $[1/4, 1/3]$, the critical discount factor $\bar{\delta}$ decreases: the lower the degree of collusion the more easily sustainable.

Exercise 4.12 (a) First find the quantities that maximise joint profits $\Pi = (1 - Q - c)Q$. It is easily checked that $Q = (1 - c)/2$.

Therefore, at the symmetric equilibrium individual quantities are $q^m = (1 - c)/(2n)$ and individual profits under the collusive strategy are $\pi^m = (1 - c)^2/(4n)$.

As for the deviation profits, the optimal deviation by a firm is given by $q^d(q^m) = arg\,max_q(1 - (n - 1)q^m - q - c)q$. It can be checked that $q^d(q^m) = (n + 1)(1 - c)/(4n)$, and that the profits obtained by deviating from the collusive output are $\pi^d = (1 - c)^2(n + 1)^2/(16n^2)$.

Finally, it is standard to check that the Cournot quantities and profits are given by $q^{cn} = (1 - c)/(n + 1)$ and $\pi^{cn} = (1 - c)^2/(n + 1)^2$.

The IC for collusion is given by $\pi^m/(1 - \delta) \geq \pi^d + \delta\pi^{cn}/(1 - \delta)$, which after substitution and rearranging becomes $\delta \geq (1 + n)^2/(1 + 6n + n^2) \equiv \delta^{cn}$.

Hence, under punishment strategies that involve a reversion to Cournot equilibrium forever after a deviation takes place, tacit collusion arises if and only if firms are sufficiently patient.

(b) By carrying out a simple exercise of comparative statics using the critical threshold for the discount factor, one concludes that $\partial\delta^{cn}/\partial n = 4\left(n^2 - 1\right)/\left(1 + 6n + n^2\right)^2 > 0$.

Hence, other things being equal, as the number of firms in the agreement increases, the more difficult it is to reach and sustain tacit collusion (the tighter the firms' incentive constraint becomes). Since firms are assumed to be symmetric, an increase in the number of firms is equivalent to a lower degree of concentration. Therefore, lower levels of concentration are associated – *ceteris paribus* – with less likely collusion.

(c) Yes. In order to determine the highest level of profits that a fixed number of firms can sustain as a sub-game perfect equilibrium, Abreu (1986) studied punishments more severe than reversion to Cournot forever after a deviation takes place. By being able to credibly threaten with a harsher retribution for defection, an oligopoly is able to sustain a collusive outcome for a *wider range of discount factors*. For the case of symmetric punishments, Abreu found that an optimal punishment strategy takes a very simple form. In the first period after deviation, each individual firm produces a high level of output so that all firms get negative profits. In order to induce firms to go along with the punishment first phase, the oligopoly agrees to produce the most collusive sustainable output in the ensuing periods, provided that no firm has deviated from the punishment first phase (period). Otherwise, the punishment is restarted.

Exercise 4.13 (a) If the AA investigates the sector in every period, the present discounted value of collusion is given by $V^c = p(\pi_m - F + \delta\pi_n/(1 - \delta)) +$

$(1 - p)(\pi_m + \delta V^c)$, and the incentive constraint each firm faces is given by $[p(\pi_m - F + \delta\pi_n/(1-\delta)) + (1-p)\pi_m]/[1 - \delta(1-p)] \geq \pi_d + \delta\pi_n/(1-\delta)$, where π_d denotes the one-shot deviation profit. Notice that the previous condition can be re-written as follows: $[\pi_m - p(F - \delta\pi_n) - \delta\pi_n]/[1 - \delta(1-p)] \geq \pi_d$.

Hence, collusion is self-enforcing if the long-run expected losses due to the punishment are no smaller than the one-shot expected net gains from deviation. The higher p and F the less likely for collusion to be sustained at equilibrium, other things being equal.

(b) The described game, being a supergame, admits a continuum of solutions. If we consider exactly the same model but assume that firms, along the collusive equilibrium, set the price $\bar{p} \in (c, p_m)$, which gives firms a profit $\bar{\pi}$, then it is straightforward to show that firms' incentive constraint would be similar to the one derived in (a), the only difference being that π_m would be substituted by $\bar{\pi}$.

(c) Yes, two-phase punishment strategies would increase the interval of discount factors under which collusion might be sustained.

Exercise 4.16 (a) In order for collusion to be self-enforcing, the following incentive constraint should be satisfied: $\delta\alpha(\pi_m/n - \pi_c)/(1 - \delta\alpha) \geq \pi_d - \pi_m/n$.

Since the LHS of the previous condition increases with δ and α, one concludes that if the discount factor and the probability of continuation are high enough, then these strategies form an equilibrium of the game.

(b) It is straightforward to see that the incentive constraint derived in (a) is relaxed when the punishment becomes stronger (i.e., π_c decreases), the deviation profits π_d decrease and the number of firms n decrease.

(c) No. Another feasible equilibrium of this game is the one in which firms play the Nash equilibrium of the stage game at each period of the repeated game.

Exercise 4.17 (a) The joint profit of the two firms are $\pi^M = \sum_{i=1}^{2}[(a - q_i - q_j - C + x_i + lx_j)q_i - gx_i^2/2]$ and the problem of the firm is to choose q_i, q_j, which maximise it. Solving the FOCs $\partial\pi^M/\partial q_i = 0$ and focusing on the symmetric solution gives $q = ((a - C) + (1 + l)x)/4$. At the first stage of the game, the joint profit becomes $\pi^M = ((a - C) + (1 + l)x)^2/4 - gx^2$. Maximisation requires $\partial\pi^M/\partial x = 0$, which is solved by $x^M = (a - C)(1 + l)/[4g - (1 + l)^2]$, and after replacement this gives the equilibrium output: $q^M = (a - C)g/[4g - (1 + l)^2]$.

(b) This is done in the text.

(c) Comparison of the equilibrium levels reveals that $x^M > x^C$ for $l > 7/17$, whereas $q^M > q^C$ for $3g + 1 - 4l - 5l^2 > 0$. Again, l must be high enough for monopoly to give rise to a superior outcome: if $l < (-2 + \sqrt{29})/5 \simeq .677$, then $q^M < q^C$ whatever g. But for higher levels of the spillover parameter, there exist combinations of g and l for which full co-operation is better. Intuitively, there is a trade-off under full co-operation, between higher R&D due to internalisation of the spillover, which restores R&D incentives, and lack of competition in the product market which reduces equilibrium outputs. The former effect is stronger when spillovers are very high.

[The variant of the exercise involves finding equilibrium R&D levels and outputs under R&D co-operation, which is done in the text, and then comparing them to those obtained in the full co-operation regime. It is easy to check that $x^M > x^{JV}$ for all l, whereas q^M is always strictly lower than q^{JV} ($q^M < q^{JV}$ amounts to $g > (1 + l)^2/3$, which is always true since $g > 4/3$ and $l \leq 1$).]

Exercise 4.18   At the last stage of the game, the Cournot equilibrium is found by solving each firm' problem $\max_{q_i} \pi_i = (1 - q_i - q_j - c_L)q_i + c_L q_j$. Note that each firm has to pay the other a unit royalty on the own output, which implies that the royalties appear both as a cost and as a revenue in the profit function. From the FOCs one obtains the equilibrium output at the symmetric equilibrium as $q^*(c_L) = (1 - c_L)/3$. The associated per-firm profits are $\pi^*(c_L) = (1 + 2c_L)(1 - c_L)/9$.

At the first stage, firms jointly decide on the cross-licensing agreement and on the level of c_L. Note that the function π^* reaches its maximum in $c_L = 1/4$. The firms will therefore have an incentive to cross-license and will optimally choose $c_L = 1/4$. Their outputs and profits will be equal to $q^*(1/4) = 1/4$ and $\pi^*(1/4) = 1/8$. These values correspond to the joint profit maximisation solutions. In other words, by cross-licensing the firms manage to reach the monopoly solution, improving upon the Cournot solution obtained when $c_L = 0$: $q^*(0) = 1/3$ and $\pi^*(0) = 1/9$.

Exercise 4.19   (a) In the last stage, given that manufacturers compete in prices, the Bertrand equilibrium applies: the market price will be $p = c + w_A + w_B$, and final demand $q = 1 - (c + w_A + w_B)$.

In the first stage, each patent-holder decides the royalty fee so as to $\max_{w_i} \pi_i = w_i(1 - c - w_i - w_j)$. From $\partial \pi_i / \partial w_i = 0$, it follows that the symmetric equilibrium is $w^* = (1 - c)/3$, and the final price (by substitution) is $p^* = (2 + c)/3$. Patent-holders' profits are $\pi^* = (1 - c)^2/9$.

(b) Under the patent pool, there is joint-profit maximisation of the patent-holders. The pool's problem is therefore $\max_{w_i, w_j} \pi_P = w_i(1 - c - w_i - w_j) + w_j(1 - c - w_i - w_j)$. Solving the FOCs gives the symmetric solution $w^P = (1 - c)/4$. By substitution prices and (per-firm) profits are obtained as $p^P = (1 + c)/2$ and $\pi^P = (1 - c)^2/8$.

(c) It is straightforward to see that the patent pool Pareto dominates the situation where the two patents are licensed independently. Final prices (as well as royalties) are lower (therefore, consumers are better off) and patent-holders' profits are higher. (Manufacturers in this example always get zero profits.)

Exercise 4.20   Let us first derive the market allocation scheme solution when each firm sells only in its own market. In this case, profits are given by $\pi = (1 - 2q/s)q$. From $\partial \pi / \partial q = 0$ it follows that $q_{1a} = q_{2b} = s/4$, and $q_{1b} = q_{2a} = 0$, $\pi_1^m = \pi_2^m = s/8$.

Punishment. If firms were playing the one-shot Nash game in quantities, they would sell in both markets. Their profits would be $\pi_1 = p_a(q_{1a}, q_{2a})q_{1a} + (p_b(q_{1b}, q_{2b}) - t)q_{1b}$ and $\pi_2 = p_b(q_{1b}, q_{2b})q_{2b} + (p_a(q_{1a}, q_{2a}) - t)q_{2a}$, where $p_k = 1 - 2(q_{1k} + q_{2k})/s$, for $k = a, b$. Firm i's programme is $\max_{q_{ia}, q_{ib}} \pi_i$. Therefore, finding the equilibrium solutions involves solving the system of four equations $\partial \pi_i/\partial q_{ia} = 0$, $\partial \pi_i/\partial q_{ib} = 0$, for $i = 1, 2$.

It is easy to check that the solution is given by the four prices: $q_{1a} = q_{2b} = s(1 + t)/6$, $q_{2a} = q_{1b} = s(1 - 2t)/6$, and that firms' profits are given by $\pi_1^e = \pi_2^e = s\left[(1 + t)^2 + (1 - 2t)^2\right]/18$.

Deviation. The optimal deviation of, say, firm 1 consists of setting its monopoly quantity in the home market a, but choosing the (positive) output q_{1b}^d that maximises its export profits π_{1b} given that the rival sets $q_{2b} = s/4$. In other words, q_{1b}^d is the quantity q that maximises $\pi_{1b} = (1 - t - 2(q + s/4)/s)q$. From $\partial \pi_{1b}/\partial q = 0$ it can be found that $q_{1b}^d = s(1 - 2t)/8$, and that $\pi_1^d = s/8 + s(1 - 2t)^2/32$ (the first component of the profit being the home monopolistic profit).

The incentive constraint for collusion is given by the standard condition $\pi_i^m/(1 - \delta) \geq \pi_i^d + \delta \pi_i^e/(1 - \delta)$, from which the critical discount factor is derived as $\delta^e = \left(\pi_i^d - \pi_i^m\right)/\left(\pi_i^d - \pi_i^e\right)$. After substitution, it can be checked that $\delta^e = 9(1 - 2t)/(13 + 22t)$, so that collusion can be achieved only if $\delta \geq \delta^e$.

Note that $\partial \delta^e/\partial t < 0$, so that as transportation costs increase, collusion becomes easier to sustain. This is because the higher the transportation cost the smaller the market share that can be obtained through a deviation. In the limit case where $t = 1/2$, the transport cost becomes prohibitively high, so that no exports would occur at the one-shot equilibrium: a firm would not have any temptation to deviate from the (monopolistic) autarky equilibrium.

5

Horizontal Mergers

5.1 INTRODUCTION

Nowadays most countries have laws or regulations which call for anti-trust author-ities to scrutinise mergers.[1] For instance, since 1989 the European Union has had a Merger Regulation, which establishes a system of preventive control on mergers (see also Chapter 1). The Merger Regulation entered into force in September 1990, and between that time and the end of the year 2000 some 1,500 mergers have been noti-fied to and reviewed by the European Commission (EC).[2] Figure 5.1 illustrates the evolution in the number of final decisions taken by the EC.[3] Note that the growth in the workload of the EC has been impressive, rising from 63 notifications in 1991 (the first full year of implementation of the Merger Regulation) to 292 notifications in 1999.

The objective of this chapter is to analyse the welfare effects of *horizontal* mergers – that is mergers between competitors – and identify the main circumstances under which such mergers should or should not be allowed.[4]

There are two main cases which should be considered when studying the effects of mergers. First (Section 5.2), the case where the merger might allow the merged firm to *unilaterally* exercise market power and raise prices. Second (Section 5.3), the case where a merger might favour collusion in the industry. Here, the merging firm would not be able to unilaterally raise prices in a significant way, but the merger could generate new industry conditions which enhance the scope for collusion. Prices could then increase as firms are more likely to attain a (tacitly or explicitly) collusive outcome.

---

[1] Throughout this chapter I will use the term "merger" as a synonym for the more general term used in European law, "concentration". When analysing the economic effects of a concentration, the distinction between a hostile takeover and a commonly agreed merger is largely irrelevant, so I will not deal with takeovers separately.

[2] Own calculation, based on the data contained in the Annual Reports of Competition Policy of DG Competition. Only thirteen mergers have been blocked over this period.

[3] The number of notifications follows a similar pattern. Note that decisions on mergers in the coal and steel sectors were taken not under the Merger Regulation but under the EC Steel and Coal Treaty before that treaty expired.

[4] *Vertical* mergers, that is mergers between firms operating at successive stages of the production process, are discussed in Chapter 6.

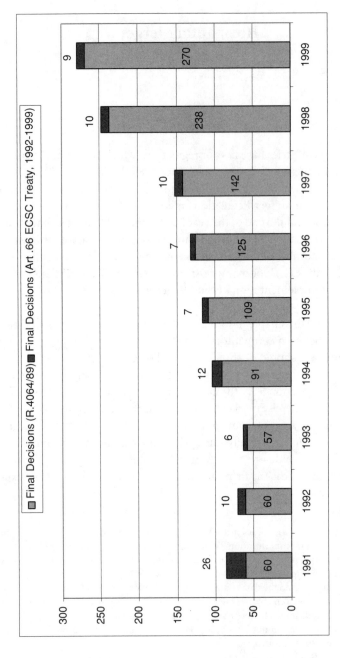

Source: Report on Competition Policy, European Commission, DG IV (various years)

Figure 5.1. Number of final decisions on mergers taken by the European Commission.

The distinction between unilateral and pro-collusive effects mirrors that used in the US merger policy (where the latter are called *coordinated effects*). There, a merger is evaluated according to a "substantial lessening of competition" test: what matters is whether the merger will lessen competition and raise prices. In the EU, where a "dominance" test exists, the concept of joint dominance corresponds to pro-collusive effects, but that of single-firm dominance does not correspond to unilateral effects under the current Merger Regulation. See Section 5.6.

Section 5.4 offers an advanced formalisation of merger effects that readers un-interested in technical details can skip without loss. Section 5.5 deals with *merger remedies,* that is with the conditions that an anti-trust authority might require in or-der to correct for the possible anti-competitive effects of a merger. Section 5.6 briefly discusses EU merger policy and some of its recent developments. Section 7 analyses two case studies.

5.2 UNILATERAL EFFECTS

This section focuses on the *unilateral effects* of a merger.[5] It first shows that a merger is likely to increase the market power of the merging firms and decrease both consumer surplus and total welfare (Section 5.2.1). It then emphasises (Section 5.2.3) that if the merger increases efficiency in the merging firms, the net effect on welfare of the merger is ambiguous, as the rise in market power can be outweighed by the price decrease possibly brought about by efficiency gains. Section 5.2.4 offers a technical treatment of these issues.

5.2.1 Absent Efficiencies, a Merger Increases Market Power

To understand why a merger might allow a firm to unilaterally increase market power, consider a simple example. Imagine that in a given town there are a few independent grocery stores. Competition constrains the market power of each store: if one of them tries to increase prices in a significant way, many among its current consumers would start to shop at one of the other stores. Anticipating this, the store considering the price increase will refrain from doing so. Its market power, that is its ability to charge consumers a high price, is therefore limited by the presence of the rival stores.

Such market power, however, will increase if two or more stores merged to give rise to a chain of grocery stores. A contemporaneous increase by the merged stores in the price of each product sold might now be profitable, because the number of rival stores is reduced. Consumers might have to travel greater distances to find a store with lower prices, and many of them will shop at their usual store despite higher prices.

---

[5] In technical terms, we are comparing the one-shot non-co-operative equilibrium in the industry before and after the merger.

In general, therefore, the merger increases (by some degree) market power of the merging firms, which in turn will increase prices (see Section 5.2.4.1 for a formal treatment).

To be more precise, there exists a small difference in the predictions about the price effects of mergers made by different models in the industrial economics literature. In particular, models, which assume that firms' decision variable is price, predict that the prices charged both by the merging firms and by the outsiders would rise; conversely, models which assume that firms' decision variable is quantity predict that the merging firms would reduce their outputs (that is, they would raise their price), whereas the outsiders would *increase* their outputs (they would reduce their price).[6] This difference is not important, however, as both models predict that the overall effect of the merger (in the absence of efficiency gains) is to reduce consumer surplus.[7]

The effect of a merger on the rival firms' profits is of some interest. What is perhaps surprising to some readers is that, absent efficiency gains, the merger will benefit the outsiders. This is because the insiders, by increasing prices and/or reducing output, benefit the rivals.[8] Indeed, the rivals might gain more than the insiders from the merger.[9]

In sum, because they increase market power, mergers which do not entail efficiency gains hurt consumers and society at large.[10] As we shall see in Section 5.2.3, the presence of efficiency gains can change this result, and makes a merger beneficial from the point of view of consumer and total welfare. Before showing that, however, let me briefly discuss the variables which affect the extent to which a merger will raise market power.

5.2.2 Variables Which Affect Unilateral Market Power

The previous section has explained why a merger – absent efficiency gains – will tend to increase market power. However, several variables affect the extent to which

---

[6] For papers where firms choose quantities (technically, firms' decisions are *strategic substitutes*) see for instance Salant, Switzer and Reynolds (1983), and Farrell and Shapiro (1990). For a paper where firms choose prices (i.e., decisions are *strategic complements*), see Deneckere and Davidson (1985). See also technical Section 5.2.4.1.

[7] Section 5.4 provides a proof of this result for the case of price competition. See for instance Farrell and Shapiro (1990) for the case of quantity competition. Even in the models where firms set quantities, the increase in quantities sold by the outsiders is outweighed by the decrease in the quantities sold by the insiders.

[8] A merger might therefore be seen as a sort of "public good" (the public good being high prices) provided by the insiders, while the outsiders might "free-ride" on the provision of the public good.

[9] In models where firms choose quantities, and there are no efficiency effects, the insiders might *lose* from the merger; the profits of the merged firms can be lower than the sum of the profits they make when they are independent. See Section 5.2.4.1 for a discussion.

[10] A possible exception to this result might arise when two small firms merge. In that case (briefly discussed in the next section), total welfare (but not consumer welfare) might increase even absent efficiency gains. However, as we shall see below, anti-trust authorities will typically not scrutinise mergers between firms which have low market shares.

the merged firms will be able to exercise more market power. If, because of certain industry characteristics, the actual impact of the merger is expected to be small or nil, then there will be no need for intervention.[11] Since these characteristics have been analysed in depth when dealing with the assessment of market power in Chapter 3, their treatment here will be kept brief.

Concentration   Other things being equal, the larger the number of independent firms operating after the merger the less likely it is to be detrimental to consumers (see 5.2.4.1). The intuition for this result is straightforward, as the ability of merging firms to exert market power clearly depends on the number of rivals. In the case of a merger to monopoly, for instance, the new firm will not face any restraint from competitors in its pricing decisions. At the other extreme, in an industry which is extremely fragmented and in which each firm has only tiny market shares, the impact of a merger on the market price will be irrelevant.

This gives us a rationale for using a concentration index, such as the Herfindahl-Hirschman Index (HHI),[12] as a first screening device for the unilateral effects of mergers: *ceteris paribus,* we should worry more about a merger in an industry which is highly concentrated than about one which occurs in a fragmented industry.

For the same reasons, and whatever the existing *level* of concentration, we should pay more attention to a merger which *increases* in a sensitive way industry concentration than to one which increases it only marginally. This gives us a rationale for using a proxy for the likely change in concentration (such as ΔHHI, that is, the difference between post- and pre-merger concentration) as an additional screening device.

According to the US Merger Guidelines, US competition agencies should rely on these two indices to screen mergers and decide which ones are likely to raise adverse competitive consequences.[13] If the post-merger HHI is lower than 1,000 (low concentration), the merger will be approved.[14] If the post-merger HHI is between 1,000 and 1,800 (moderate concentration), the merger is approved as long as it does not result in an increase in concentration of more than 100 points. If the post-merger HHI is more than 1,800 (high concentration) the merger is not challenged only if

---

[11] Even very small efficiency gains can outweigh the possible negative effect of market power when the latter is very small.

[12] The HHI is a standard index of concentration and it is the most often used in anti-trust analysis. It is given by the sum of the squares of market shares of the firms in the industry. It can vary between 0, when the market is entirely fragmented (each firm has a market share close to 0) and 10,000, when there is only one firm in the industry which has 100% of the market. The index takes values between 0 and 1 if fractions instead of percentage values are used.

[13] See US Merger Guidelines (sect. 1.5). In practice, however, the US agencies do not apply these thresholds strictly.

[14] The (expected) post-merger HHI is computed by assuming that each firm keeps the same market share after the merger, and that the merging firms will simply have the sum of their pre-merger shares.

it increases concentration by less than 50 points. In all other cases, a merger raises "significant competitive concerns" and is likely to be investigated.

Market Shares and Capacities   Another simple but useful indicator of the likely market power created by the merger is given by market shares. Farrell and Shapiro (1990), for instance, show that the lower the market share of the merging companies the less detrimental the effect on market prices. Furthermore, a merger between small firms might increase welfare even in the absence of efficiency gains.[15] In a model based on Perry and Porter (1985), McAfee and Williams (1992) find that mergers, which result in a new largest firm, and mergers, which increase the size of the largest firm always reduce welfare. These findings justify using market shares of the merging firms as another possible screening device in merger control. If the merger involves firms with low market shares then it is unlikely that considerable adverse effects would arise.

The analysis of productive capacities is also very important. The ability to raise prices by any given firm is limited by the existence of rivals to which consumers can switch. It is therefore crucial that such rivals be effectively competitive, and be able to satisfy the possible additional demand addressed to them. Therefore, other things being equal, the larger the unused capacity of rivals the less likely it is that the merging firms will exercise much market power.[16]

Entry   The firms' ability to raise prices after a merger is also limited by the existence of potential entrants.[17] Firms which would find it unprofitable to enter the industry at pre-merger prices might decide to enter if the merger brings about higher prices or lower quantities.[18] By anticipating this effect, post-merger prices might not rise at all; or, if they do, the price increase would be transitory. The extent to which potential entrants restrain the market power of actual industry participants crucially depends

---

[15] In technical terms, this is because under Cournot competition (strategic substitutes) the outsiders react to the lower quantity of the insiders by increasing their own output. When the insiders are small firms, their output reduction might be of a lower order of magnitude than the output expansion of the large outsider firms. This effect would not appear in a model like the one used in the technical Section 5.2.4.1, where firms' actions are strategic complements (as the price increase of the insiders is followed by a price increase of the outsiders). However, under both types of models, the existence of asymmetries opens the possibility that a merger might improve welfare in very particular circumstances. For instance, if the outsider firms are more efficient than the insiders, the merger would reallocate production to outsiders, which has a welfare improving effect.

[16] Similar considerations apply to the availability of raw materials, reserves, or other indispensable inputs.

[17] The contestable markets theory (see Chapter 2) has the merit of having emphasised the role of potential entrants in restraining the market power of the incumbents.

[18] Entry might also take the form of imports from abroad. If after a merger prices rise, foreign firms' competitiveness will increase. As a result, imports might discipline the market in the same way as local entrants.

on fixed sunk costs. The larger (and the more sunk, i.e., committed to the industry and not recoverable) the costs that an entrant has to incur, the higher the scope for a price increase.[19]

The evaluation of the likelihood of entry involves some difficulties. Anti-trust authorities have to judge whether there are firms which consider entry, how likely they are to enter, what are the possible barriers they face[20] and how long it might take for entry to be accomplished (the longer it takes the higher the damage to consumers and social welfare). This is recognised by both the EC and the US Department of Justice (see for instance US Merger Guidelines, Section 3).

Demand Variables   Of course, not only supply variables but also demand variables must be taken into account to understand to what extent the merging firms enjoy market power. For instance, in industries characterised by very high switching costs, consumers would not easily change their providers, who will then enjoy market power. More generally, the lower the elasticity of market demand the higher the scope for raising prices.

Buyer Power   As discussed in Chapter 3, the merging firms' ability to charge high prices also depends on the degree of concentration of the buyers. Strong buyers can constrain upstream market power by threatening to withdraw orders from one seller to give them to another or by threatening to start upstream production itself. An example of a merger where the consideration of buyer power had a strong influence on the decision to authorise it is provided in Section 5.7.3, which discusses the *ABB/Daimler-Benz* decision.

Failing Firm Defence   To decide on the desirability of a merger it is important to understand what is likely to happen after it takes place (for instance, do entry, or buyer power, or demand factors constrain the ability of the merging firms to increase prices?), but it is also relevant to assess what would happen were the merger not to take place. Suppose for instance that the merger involves a *failing firm*, that is a firm that would, in the absence of a merger, not have been able to survive in the industry. In that case, the *ex post* merger situation should be compared not with the *ex ante* merger situation, but with the situation occurring after the failing firm would have exited the industry.

---

[19] See Werden and Froeb (1998) for a study that casts some doubts over the possibility that entry would reduce or eliminate the anti-competitive effects of mergers.

[20] Barriers to entry can be technological (know-how to be learned, but also patents which protect the existing firms), administrative (e.g., when government licences or permits are needed to operate), linked to the financial market (firms might have problems in obtaining financing for the new venture), and so on. Switching costs of various nature, or network effects (see Chapter 2) might also be an obstacle to new entrants.

The failing firm defence is clearly stated in the US Merger Guidelines, Section 5.1, where an otherwise anti-competitive merger is accepted if: 1) the failing firm would be unable to meet its financial obligations in the near future; 2) it would not be able to reorganise successfully under Chapter 11 of the Bankruptcy Act; 3) there are no suitable alternative buyers that would keep the failing firm's tangible and intangible assets in the relevant market while having lower anti-competitive effects than the proposed merger; and 4) in the absence of the merger, the failing firm's assets would have exited the relevant market.

The first two conditions require that the failing firm must not only have short-run problems, but be unlikely to be viable in the medium-long term. The other conditions require that the proposed merger is the only (or the best) way to keep the assets of the firms in productive use.[21]

I will turn now to the case where the merger does involve efficiency gains.

5.2.3 Efficiency Gains

In the absence of efficiency gains, a merger should be expected to lower both consumer surplus and total welfare. However, it is well established in the economic literature that efficiency gains might offset the enhanced market power of merging firms and result in higher welfare.[22] This is because the merger might cause the insiders to be more efficient and save on their unit costs. If these savings are large enough, they will outweigh the increase in market power and result in lower prices, to the benefit of consumers.

To better illustrate the opposite forces at work, consider again the example made above, where two or more stores in the same town merge. The merger allows them to exercise more market power. In the absence of efficiency gains, this means that the new chain store would find it profitable to charge higher prices. But consider now the case where the merger allows the partner stores to rationalise their activities, better organise their transportation network, and so forth. In this case, the merger allows the chain store operations to be run more efficiently than before, so that savings in unit costs will occur.

The new merged firm might of course still increase its prices (its sales decreasing but its mark-up increasing both because of the price rise and because of the lower costs). This strategy would be profitable because we have seen it was so even in the absence of any cost saving. However, it is not necessarily optimal (that is, *the*

---

[21] The failing firm defence has been rarely used both in the US and in the EU, where the EC adopted it in the *Kali&Salz/MdK/Treuhand* decision, albeit with some modifications with respect to the US requirements (see para. 71). The ECJ accepted the EC's arguments in *France v. Commission* (see para. 111 and following).

[22] See Section 5.2.4.1 for a simple formalisation, and 5.4.3 for a more general one. The first to point out that efficiency gains might offset enhanced market power was Williamson (1968). See also Farrell and Shapiro (1990) for an elegant and rich analysis of the role of efficiency gains.

most profitable strategy) any longer. Indeed, because of efficiency gains, another profitable strategy might now be to reduce prices and attract new customers. For instance, in the case where prices and unit costs decreased proportionally, the unit mark-up would be exactly the same as before the merger, but total profits would be higher as lower prices increase demand of the chain store.

In general, therefore, with efficiency gains the merging firms have two possible ways to increase their profits: to increase prices (reduce sales) or to decrease prices (increase output). Which of these two ways is the most profitable cannot be said *a priori*, but the higher the efficiency gains the more likely it is that the second effect will dominate. If efficiency gains are large enough then the insiders to the merger will decrease sales prices and both consumer and total welfare will increase (see Section 5.4.3 for a proof).

The Effect of Efficiency Gains on Outsiders' Profits   It should be noted that the impact of a merger on the distribution of firms' profits might be very different when there are efficiency gains. Indeed, unlike the case where there are no efficiency gains, outsiders will lose from the merger, and thus oppose it, when the merger allows insiders to cut their costs: intuitively, this is because the merger changes the competitive positions of the firms in the industry to the detriment of the outsiders.

The analysis of merger effects reveals therefore that rival firms' profits will decrease when the merger will have a positive effect on welfare, namely when there exist sufficiently large efficiency gains. This idea has led Eckbo (1983) to look at the impact of the merger announcement on the stock market prices of the outsider firms in order to have an indication of the significance of efficiency gains. If the competitors' share prices decrease, then this means that market analysts and observers anticipate the existence of merger efficiencies. In turn, this should imply that the merger will increase consumer and total surplus. If instead the competitors' share prices increase, one should expect efficiency gains to be minimal or absent, and as a consequence the merger to be welfare detrimental.[23]

Yet this method is not without difficulties. First, it assumes that the stock market correctly anticipates the effects of the merger, which implies, among other things, that it is also able to assess claims of efficiency gains made by the merging parties (which often overstate the profitability of the merger, as discussed in Section 5.2.4 below). Second, the formal announcement of the merger might be followed by a period of speculation about the possibility that the merger will occur, so one should check and correct for this possibility. Third, exogenous shocks related to the sector profitability or the economy as a whole might have an impact on firms' stock prices.[24] Fourth, the response of the stock market to the announcement of

---

[23] For a recent evaluation of European merger policy using this test, see Neven and Röller (2002).

[24] Also events or public declarations related to the merger might affect the stock prices. Consider for instance the case where the managers of the merging firms state in public that after the merger

the merger might also be affected by the expectations of the anti-trust authorities' decisions. Suppose for instance that there is a correct expectation that the merger involves efficiency gains, but there is also anticipation that anti-trust authorities will not clear the merger (for instance, because they do not properly take efficiency gains into account, which might have been the case so far in the EU). Then, rivals' share prices would not decrease, and might even increase in the expectation of the regulatory costs incurred by the merging parties.

The result that welfare increases and outsiders' profits decrease when efficiency gains are large should also have another important implication on the reliance anti-trust authorities place on the information they receive from interested parties. Clearly, claims from rival firms that the merger will be anti-competitive should be received with great scepticism from the authorities: The fact that rivals complain about the merger probably signals that there might be significant efficiency gains. If anything, then, their complaint might be taken as a first indication that the merger will improve welfare![25] In sum, while buyers and final consumers should have an incentive to complain when the merger is likely to increase prices (and therefore reduce welfare), the opposite will often be true for rivals. Anti-trust authorities should accordingly scrutinise their complaints with extra care.

The Nature of Efficiency Gains and Their Assessment   So far, I have been rather vague about the sources of possible efficiency gains. There are several reasons why firms which combine their assets might decrease their costs. The most obvious are the existence of economies of scale and economies of scope. Due to a merger, firms might be able to reorganise their production so as to improve the division of labour and attain economies of scale; or they might benefit from lower costs due to joint production. Other possible gains might come from synergies in research and development, rationalisation of distribution and marketing activities and cost savings in administration. Another possible efficiency argument is that takeovers might improve efficiency via the substitution of less able managers with more successful ones. However, empirical studies do not give strong support to this "managerial discipline" theory.[26]

they will behave more aggressively and be able to increase their share of the market. Even if the merger did not really entail efficiency gains, this statement may affect the market's expectations, and competitors' share prices might well decrease in anticipation of tougher market competition. Similar considerations appear to have distorted this test when it was carried out in the *Volvo/Scania* merger.

[25] Of course, this is not necessarily always the case. Suppose that there is a vertical merger that is likely to lead to foreclosure of rival firms. In this case, the latter will complain, but the merger might also reduce consumer surplus and welfare. In Chapter 6, however, I will argue that foreclosure is a relatively rare event and that a number of conditions must be fulfilled in order for a vertical merger to be detrimental.

[26] McGuckin and Nguyen (1995) find mixed results in their analysis of an unbalanced panel of some 28,000 plants for the period 1977–87. On the one hand, a change in ownership is generally

From the theoretical point of view, one would like to draw a distinction between cost savings that will directly affect variable production costs and cost savings that mainly affect fixed costs. The former type of efficiency gains are likely to have a direct impact on prices, while the latter type would affect fixed (i.e., independent of the volume of production) costs and thus would not modify the price decisions of the firms (which depend only on variable costs). Efficiency gains in fixed costs might still lead to a positive welfare effect, but this would come only from an increase in profits due to lower duplication of fixed costs, since consumer surplus would not change. If competition agencies attach a higher weight to consumer welfare, or competition laws require that some of the firms' gains should be passed on to consumers, then efficiency gains which are mainly due to savings in fixed costs should be looked at less favourably.

The US Merger Guidelines come to a similar conclusion, although for different reasons, that is, because efficiencies derived from technical rationalisation are easier to demonstrate than efficiencies obtained through the reduction of administrative costs, personnel savings and other fixed outlays.[27]

Next, efficiency arguments should be accepted only as long as costs savings achieved by the merger could not be achieved otherwise. If, for instance, the firms claimed that the merger would create efficiency gains because it would reduce personnel costs, one should wonder if these savings could not be achieved without a merger. Where efficiency gains could be achieved without a merger they should not be accepted as an efficiency defence of the merger, as they could be obtained without a reduction in the number of independent competitors.

Farrell and Shapiro (2001) thoroughly discuss how to assess efficiency gains in horizontal mergers, building on the results of the model they studied in Farrell and Shapiro (1990). They argue that it is *synergies* – defined as efficiencies obtained through the "intimate integration of the parties' unique, hard-to-trade assets" – that competition authorities should particularly welcome, while "no-synergy" efficiencies such as mere reorganisation of output among the facilities of the merging firms should be looked at with scepticism. This is because the latter are less likely to outweigh the negative effect of increased market power,[28] and can often be obtained without resorting to a merger. Indeed, they stress the importance of understanding

associated with the transfer of plants which have an above average productivity. On the other hand, after a change in ownership the plants which have been transferred do show higher productivity than before. Matsusaka (1993) studies stock market response to acquisition announcements. He finds that the market responds positively to bidders who retain the management of target companies and negatively to bidders who replaced their management, thus suggesting that the market does not like takeovers, which aim at disciplining the management of the target companies.

[27] US Merger Guidelines, Section 4.
[28] Note, however, that Farrell and Shapiro (2001) base their discussion mainly on the assumption that consumer surplus, rather than total surplus, is the objective of competition policy. This implies that firms' profits are not taken into account.

how likely it is that efficiencies would be attained in the absence of the merger, that is through internal growth, and argue that only synergies that cannot be achieved unilaterally should be considered.[29] Furthermore, if "no-synergy" efficiency gains are likely to be of considerable magnitude, then a firm will have a stronger incentive to pursue them unilaterally, which in turn implies that they are less likely to be merger-specific.

Asymmetric Information   A crucial issue in the discussion of efficiency gains is the assessment of the likelihood of the gains from a merger. There is in general asymmetric information between a competition authority and the merging parties: the latter are clearly more informed about the structure of production and the functioning of the market than the former. When efficiency gains are a crucial determinant in the decision on the prohibition or acceptance of the merger, it is clear that the merging firms have an incentive to overstate efficiency claims.[30] On the other hand, and for opposite reasons, the rival firms which fear that the merger could jeopardise their competitive positions have an incentive to understate the efficiency gains of a merger. Agencies will therefore want to rely on independent studies to try to evaluate efficiency considerations.[31]

Balancing Efficiency and Market Power Considerations   Finally, even if it appeared that there exist efficiency gains (and that they are merger-specific),[32] one has to evaluate if they are sufficiently large to lead to a positive effect on consumer and total surplus. In practice, to compute the likely net result of the market power and efficiency effects is a very difficult operation, but certainly the stronger the likelihood that the merger allows the parties to exercise higher market power, the larger should be the efficiency gains required to authorise the merger.

---

[29] They also warn about the danger of falling into two extreme and opposed positions. The first one, that there always exist contracts that would allow a firm to replicate cost savings obtained through a merger (that is, no efficiency would be truly merger-specific). The other, that if it were possible to attain an efficiency gain without the merger, the firm would already have done it.

[30] Merging partners often have a genuine tendency to overstate the benefits from combining their activities and assets. Even strictly internal and confidential documents often report too optimistic an assessment of the merger's efficiency gains.

[31] Neven, Nuttall and Seabright (1993) suggest that the EC should create a unit of auditors within the Merger Task Force, specialising in assessing the likelihood of efficiency gains.

[32] The hypothesis that mergers occur because they bring efficiency gains, and thus by their own nature are beneficial, is not confirmed by evidence. Note for instance the result of the empirical analysis on the US airline industry carried out by Kim and Singal (1993). They analyse data from the period 1985–8, a period where the anti-trust agency, in line with the philosophy of the Republican administration, did not contest mergers. The authors find that prices increased on the routes served by the merging firms relative to a control group of routes which have not been affected by the merger. Therefore, if mergers did result in more efficient operations, efficiency gains were not enough to outweigh the exercise of increased market power, the final effect having been an increase in prices.

This concludes the analysis of the unilateral effects of mergers. The next technical section formalises some of the arguments so far presented. Readers who are not interested in the technical treatment should go directly to Section 5.3.

5.2.4 Modelling Unilateral Effects of Mergers*

Modelling mergers and their effects is difficult. The basic feature of mergers is that they create a new firm which combines the assets of the merging parties, so one needs some type of *asset-based model* if one wants to capture the essence of mergers. There are two relatively simple asset-based models: models of product differentiation, where the assets at hand are the product varieties sold by the firms (I follow this approach), and models where firms produce a homogenous good but differ in their production capacity, capacity being the asset they own (see e.g., Perry and Porter, 1985).

For this reason, the simplest oligopoly models, where firms sell homogenous goods, have constant returns to scale, and are able to supply all of the demand they face (think for instance of the standard Cournot model), fail to capture the basic nature of mergers: in such models, a merger between two firms simply amounts to one firm disappearing from the market.

A further weakness of the standard Cournot model derives from the fact that a merger among symmetric firms is not profitable unless it involves 80% or more of the firms in the industry, a result due to Salant, Switzer and Reynolds (1983), which Exercise 5.2 invites you to reproduce. (See also Section 5.2.4.1 below for a discussion.) Clearly, it is not without problems to study the effects of mergers by relying on a model where the merger itself is unprofitable, since the model would not be able to explain why the merger is done in the first place.[33,34]

---

[33] Nevertheless, Farrell and Shapiro (1990) manage to provide several insights into the welfare effects of mergers by using a Cournot competition model (with asymmetric firms). Their approach is to focus on the external effects of the merger, that is its impact on consumer surplus and outsiders' profits, rather than the insiders' profits.

[34] Interestingly, though, empirical evidence is not conclusive about whether the merger is (statistically) profitable for insiders: see, among others, Mueller (1985), Ravenscraft and Scherer (1987), Caves (1989), Frank, Harris and Titman (1991). Several explanations have been suggested as to why mergers *might* be on average unprofitable. Roll (1986) suggests that managers of bidding firms overestimate their ability to run other companies and this makes them overpay for their targets. Morck, Schleifer and Vishny (1990) suggest that merger unprofitability is due to a divergence between shareholders' and managers' objective functions: while the former care about profits, the latter are interested in the size, growth or risk-diversification of the company they run. According to Faulí-Oller and Motta (1996) unprofitable mergers might occur not because managers are irrational or they pursue objectives other than profit maximisation, but because owners (rationally) give them contracts which include incentives to increase the firm's size, to make them more aggressive in the marketplace. These contracts might have the side-effect of inducing managers to take rival firms over even when it is not profitable for the owners. Fridolfsson and Stennek (2002)

To be precise, merger profitability can be restored in the Cournot model if one assumes that the merger entails sufficiently large efficiency gains (as shown in Exercise 5.3). However, I believe it is instructive to study the (unilateral) effects of mergers in the absence (Section 5.2.4.1) and with (Section 5.2.4.1) efficiency gains. Accordingly, in this section I use a model where firms have different products and a merger creates a new firm endowed with a larger product portfolio. To keep the model as simple as possible, in this section I analyse the case where only three products exist. The model is generalised to n products in the advanced technical Section 5.4.

5.2.4.1 Unilateral Effects of Mergers, Absent Efficiency Gains*

Using a product differentiation model, this section shows that mergers which do not entail efficiency gains enhance market power and decrease welfare. The case of efficiency gains will be formally studied in Section 5.4.3. Furthermore, I consider here the case of the unilateral effects of a merger, that is, I exclude the possibility that firms could collude before or after the merger.

To keep things as simple as possible, assume that there exist three single product firms (see Section 5.4 for a more general treatment). Firms' marginal production costs are identical and equal to $c \geq 0$. Consumers have the following utility function:

$$U = v \sum_{i=1}^{3} q_i - \frac{3}{2(1+\gamma)} \left[\sum_{i=1}^{3} q_i^2 + \frac{\gamma}{3} \left(\sum_{i=1}^{3} q_i \right)^2 \right] + y, \qquad (5.1)$$

which – after solving for the consumer problem – gives the direct demand functions (see Chapter 8 for details):

$$q_i = \frac{1}{3} \left[v - p_i (1+\gamma) + \frac{\gamma}{3} \sum_{j=1}^{n} p_j \right], \qquad (5.2)$$

where $\gamma \in [0, \infty)$ is the parameter of product substitutability, and $v > c$. Note that in this model firms' products are given exogenously, and that a merger affects neither product choice nor the degree of product substitutability, which is assumed to be symmetric among all products.[35]

Pre-Merger	Before the merger takes place, we have three identical single-product firms with a profit function $\pi_i = (p_i - c)q_i$, where q_i is given by the demand function above ($i = 1, 2, 3$).

---

argue that a merger might be unprofitable, but still gives the merging parties higher profits than if they did not merge.

[35] See Levy and Reitzes (1992) for a model of localised competition. In their model, products are located along a circle line (therefore, two adjacent products are closer substitutes than distant ones), and only a merger which involves neighbouring products would raise prices.

The FOCs $\partial \pi_i / \partial p_i = 0$ are

$$p_i = \frac{3v + (3 + 2\gamma)c + \gamma p_j + \gamma p_k}{2(3 + 2\gamma)}, \qquad i, j, k = 1, 2, 3; \ i \neq j \neq k. \quad (5.3)$$

By solving the system of FOCs and imposing symmetry on prices one obtains

$$p_b = \frac{3v + c(3 + 2\gamma)}{2(3 + \gamma)}, \quad (5.4)$$

where the index "b" stands for "before the merger". Outputs and profits at equilibrium are

$$q_b = \frac{(v - c)(3 + 2\gamma)}{6(3 + \gamma)}, \qquad \pi_b = \frac{(v - c)^2 (3 + 2\gamma)}{4(3 + \gamma)^2}. \quad (5.5)$$

Note that as substitutability among the products increases (higher γ), equilibrium prices and profits decrease. Finally, we can derive consumer surplus as $CS = U(q_b) - 3 p_b q_b$ by substitution of the equilibrium values, and welfare as the sum of consumer and producer surplus:

$$CS_b = \frac{(v - c)^2 (3 + 2\gamma)^2}{8(3 + \gamma)^2}; \qquad W_b = \frac{(v - c)^2 (27 + 24\gamma + 4\gamma^2)}{8(3 + \gamma)^2}. \quad (5.6)$$

A Merger between Two Firms Suppose a merger takes place between firms 1 and 2. In the industry there is now firm I, selling two products and firm O, selling one product (respectively the insider and outsider parties to the merger), with profits

$$\pi_I = \sum_{i=1}^{2} \frac{(p_i - c)}{3} \left(v - p_i(1 + \gamma) + \frac{\gamma}{3}(p_1 + p_2 + p_3) \right), \quad (5.7)$$

$$\pi_O = \frac{(p_3 - c)}{3} \left(v - p_3(1 + \gamma) + \frac{\gamma}{3}(p_1 + p_2 + p_3) \right). \quad (5.8)$$

By taking the first derivatives $\partial \pi_I / \partial p_i = 0$ (with $i = 1, 2$) and $\partial \pi_O / \partial p_3 = 0$, one obtains the FOCs as

$$\begin{cases} 3v + c(3 + \gamma) - 2(3 + 2\gamma)p_i - 2\gamma p_j + \gamma p_3 = 0, & i, j = 1, 2; i \neq j. \\ 3v + c(3 + 2\gamma) - 2(3 + 2\gamma)p_3 + \gamma(p_1 + p_2) = 0 \end{cases}$$
$$(5.9)$$

We can then find the post-merger equilibrium prices p_I, p_O as

$$p_I = \frac{c(2 + \gamma)(3 + 2\gamma) + v(6 + 5\gamma)}{2(\gamma^2 + 6\gamma + 6)}; \qquad p_O = \frac{c(3 + \gamma)(1 + \gamma) + v(3 + 2\gamma)}{(\gamma^2 + 6\gamma + 6)}. \quad (5.10)$$

After substitution, one obtains the quantities and per-variety profits of the merged firm and the outsiders as

$$q_I = \frac{(3+\gamma)(6+5\gamma)(v-c)}{18\,(6+6\gamma+\gamma^2)^2}; \qquad q_O = \frac{(3+2\gamma)^2\,(v-c)}{9\,(6+6\gamma+\gamma^2)}. \qquad (5.11)$$

$$\pi_I = \frac{(3+\gamma)\,(6+5\gamma)^2(v-c)^2}{36\,(\gamma^2+6\gamma+6)^2}, \qquad \pi_O = \frac{(3+2\gamma)^3(v-c)^2}{9\,(\gamma^2+6\gamma+6)^2}. \qquad (5.12)$$

The Effect on Prices   It is now easy to see that *the merger increases prices,* and therefore *decreases consumer surplus.* To do that, note that the inequality $p_I > p_b$ can be rewritten as

$$(3+2\gamma)\,\gamma\,(v-c)\,/\,\big[2(3+\gamma)\,(6+6\gamma+\gamma^2)\big] > 0.$$

To illustrate this result, it is helpful to write the best reply functions of the firms before and after the merger. Consider for instance product 1 and product 3. In the space (p_1, p_3), and for given p_2, before the merger the best replies of the insider firm 1 and the outsider firm 3 are obtained from FOCs (5.3):

$$R_I : p_1 = \frac{3v + (3+2\gamma)c + \gamma p_2 + \gamma p_3}{2(3+2\gamma)};$$

$$R_O : p_1 = \frac{-3v - (3+2\gamma)c - \gamma p_2 + 2(3+2\gamma)p_3}{\gamma}. \qquad (5.13)$$

After the merger, the best replies are derived from FOCs (5.9) as

$$R'_I : p_1 = \frac{3v + (3+\gamma)c + 2\gamma p_2 + \gamma p_3}{2(3+2\gamma)};$$

$$R_O : p_1 = \frac{-3v - (3+2\gamma)c - \gamma p_2 + 2(3+2\gamma)p_3}{\gamma}. \qquad (5.14)$$

As Figure 5.2 illustrates, the merger determines a shift upwards of the best reply function of the insider product, which in turn will cause the equilibrium prices after the merger to increase.[36] Note that the price increase of the insider product is larger than that of the outsider product, which implies a reallocation of output in favour of the outsider.

Another intuitive way to understand this result is as follows. When firms behave non-co-operatively in the marketplace, each of them imposes a negative externality on all the others by choosing a price which is too low with respect to the price which would be optimal for the maximisation of joint profits. If two firms merge, they will take into account the negative externality which they impose on each other, and raise their price. The other firms will react by increasing their price (recall that in

---

[36] Note that at equilibrium it must be that $p_2 > c$. Hence, the intercept of R'_I is higher than that of R_I.

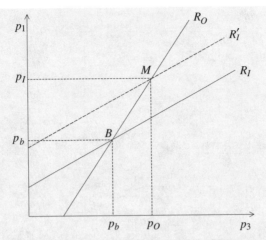

Figure 5.2. Effects of a merger absent efficiency gains: Strategic complements.

this model the actions are strategic complements) but not as much as the merging firm.

The Effect on Insiders' Profits   The next result is that *the merger benefits the merging firms*. To see that, one has to compare the per-product profits before and after the merger. The inequality $\pi_I > \pi_b$ can be rewritten as

$$\gamma^2(27 + 63\gamma + 42\gamma^2 + 7\gamma^3)(v - c)^2 / \left[36\left(\gamma^2 + 6\gamma + 6\right)^2 (3 + \gamma)^2\right] > 0.$$

The result that the merger *always* benefits the merging partners is not robust, as it critically depends on the assumption that firms compete on price. It is useful to review briefly the literature on merger profitability.

Salant, Switzer and Reynolds (1983) analyse a homogenous good model and assume (i) quantity competition and (ii) no efficiency gains from the merger. They find that a merger between two firms is always detrimental to the partners unless it gives them a monopoly (that is, unless $n = 2$).[37] The intuition behind this result is that the merging partners internalise the negative pecuniary externality given by the too-low prices in the industry, and reduce their outputs (which would tend to increase prices). The firms' actions being strategic substitutes (as is the case with quantity competition and linear demand functions), the outsiders to the merger will respond by increasing rather than decreasing their outputs, which allows them to gain market share but moderates the increase in the price. As a result, insiders

---

[37] See Exercise 5.2. More generally, a merger involving two or more firms is not profitable unless they account for more than 80% of the total number of firms.

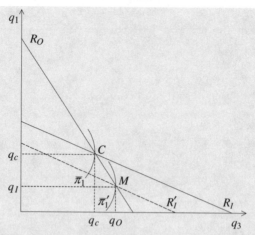

Figure 5.3. Effects of a merger absent efficiency gains: Strategic substitutes.

lose market share and profits, as the lower quantity produced is not compensated for by the price rise in the industry.

Figure 5.3 shows these arguments graphically. The merger shifts the best reply function R_I of the insiders downwards to R_I'. As a result a new equilibrium will be at point M, characterised by higher production of the outsiders and lower production of the insiders. Profits for the insiders decrease, as the iso-profit curve π_I' lies above π_I. (See also Exercise 5.7.)

This article opened a debate on the profitability of mergers, and subsequent research has shown that by relaxing assumptions (i) and (ii) above, profitability of the merger would be restored. As for (i), Davidson and Deneckere (1985) show that when actions are strategic complements, the price increase of the merger firms is followed by a price increase by the outsiders (see again Figure 5.2 above). Their case corresponds to the analysis being carried out here.

As for point (ii), Perry and Porter (1985) show that even under the assumption of homogenous goods and quantity competition, if there exist enough efficiency gains the merger will be profitable.[38]

The Effect on Outsiders' Profits   Next, one can check that *the merger increases the outsiders' profits*. We can do that by comparing the per-product profits before and after the merger. The inequality $\pi_O > \pi_b$ can be rewritten as

$$\gamma^2(36 + 36\gamma + 7\gamma^2)(3 + 2\gamma)(v - c)^2 / \left[36\left(\gamma^2 + 6\gamma + 6\right)^2 (3 + \gamma)^2\right] > 0.$$

---

[38] They do so in a model where the merger amounts to the partners joining their respective capital assets, which in turn gives them the benefit of economies of scale.

This result does not depend on whether firms compete on prices or quantities, and hinges on the free-riding effect enjoyed by the outsiders: when the merging firms increase their prices (or reduce their output), they reduce a negative externality for all the industry. The outsiders will therefore benefit from the merger. However, notice that we are assuming here that the merger does not create cost savings for the insiders. When it does, outsiders might be worse off from the merger.

The Effect on Total Welfare   The final result I want to show is that in this model the merger decreases total welfare. So far, we have seen that the merger decreases consumer surplus (as it increases prices without changing the number of products on offer) and increases producer surplus (as it increases both insider and outsider firms' profits). We now have to look at the net effect of these two opposing forces (which unfortunately involves some simple but tedious algebra). Consumer surplus can be derived as $CS = U(q_O, q_I) - 2p_I q_I - p_O q_O$ and welfare by summing it to the producer surplus (itself the sum of the two firms' profits):

$$CS_m = \frac{(v - c)^2 \left(9 + 9\gamma + 2\gamma^2\right)\left(18 + 26\gamma + 9\gamma^2\right)}{36\left(\gamma^2 + 6\gamma + 6\right)^2};$$

$$W_m = \frac{(v - c)^2 \left(486 + 1044\gamma + 765\gamma^2 + 215\gamma^3 + 18\gamma^4\right)}{36\left(\gamma^2 + 6\gamma + 6\right)^2}. \qquad (5.15)$$

To show that the net effect of the merger on welfare is negative one has therefore to check that $W_b > W_m$. This inequality amounts to the following:

$$W_b - W_m = \frac{(v - c)^2 \left(648 + 1242\gamma + 738\gamma^2 + 129\gamma^3 + 2\gamma^4\right)}{72\left(\gamma^2 + 6\gamma + 6\right)^2(3 + \gamma)^2} > 0. \qquad (5.16)$$

Efficiency Gains   To gain some insights into how the analysis changes when efficiency gains exist, continue the example above with three firms, but with the *ad hoc* assumption that when two firms merge they will generate cost savings that allow them to produce each variety at a marginal cost ec, with $e \leq 1$. The parameter e represents then an inverse measure of the efficiency gain from the merger. I assume here that the cost advantage acquired by the merged firm is not large enough to force the outsider to exit the market (this possibility is considered within the general model, in Section 5.4.4).

The profit functions of the merged firms and of the outsider are given by $\pi_I = \sum_{i=1}^{2}(p_i - ec)q_i$ and $\pi_O = (p_3 - c)q_3$, where q_1, q_2, q_3 are defined by the demand functions (5.2). By taking the FOCs $\partial\pi_I/\partial p_1 = 0$, $\partial\pi_I/\partial p_2 = 0$, $\partial\pi_O/\partial p_3 = 0$, and rearranging, one can derive the best reply functions for one of

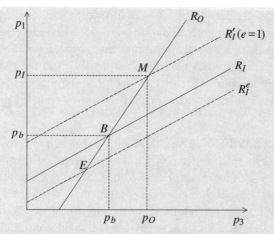

Figure 5.4. Effects of a merger with efficiency gains.

the products of the merged firm and for the outsider, as follows:

$$R_I^e : p_1 = \frac{3v + (3 + \gamma)ce + 2\gamma p_2 + \gamma p_3}{2(3 + 2\gamma)};$$

$$R_O : p_1 = \frac{-3v - (3 + 2\gamma)c - \gamma p_2 + 2(3 + 2\gamma)p_3}{\gamma}. \qquad (5.17)$$

As Figure 5.4 shows, the existence of efficiency gains affects the position of the best reply functions of the insider products: the lower e the lower R_I^e. In particular, if e is small enough the new best reply function R_I^e will be below (rather than above) the pre-merger function R_I, determining a price reduction (rather than a price rise) at the new merger equilibrium. Hence, when there are large enough efficiency gains consumer surplus will increase with the merger.

Further, note that when the new equilibrium prices are lower (as in point E), the outsider will be hurt by the merger: both firms set lower prices than at the pre-merger situation, and the outsider has the same production cost as before (while the merged firm has lower costs). Hence, the merger will decrease its profits.

A formal proof that when efficiency gains are large enough the merger increases consumer surplus and welfare is given in Section 5.4 for the general case of n firms.

5.3 PRO-COLLUSIVE EFFECTS

I have considered so far just one of the possible mechanisms through which a merger can negatively affect welfare, namely the case of unilateral market power. A second important mechanism is given by pro-collusive (or coordinated) effects, where the merger does not pose a threat of market power by a single firm, but generates more favourable conditions for collusion in the industry. In other words, before a merger firms might not be able to reach a collusive outcome, whereas the merger might create the structural conditions for the firms to (tacitly or explicitly) attain a collusive outcome. The concept of *joint dominance* in the EU refers to this situation.

There are two main reasons why a merger might favour the creation of collusive outcomes. Firstly, a merger by definition reduces the number of independent firms. Since it is possible to show that the lower the number of market participants, the higher the scope for collusion in the industry, the merger makes it more likely that firms will charge higher prices. Secondly, a merger *might* give rise to a more symmetric distribution of assets. When this is the case, we know from Chapter 4 that a collusive equilibrium will also be more likely.

The extent to which collusion (that is, joint dominance) might occur after the merger depends on a number of factors. Since Chapter 4 has dwelt at length upon the factors that facilitate collusion, the next section looks only very briefly – as a reminder – at them.

5.3.1 Factors which Affect Collusion (Reminder)

The more an industry is already characterised by the co-existence of factors which favour a collusive outcome, the more risky to allow a merger, as it would further increase the likelihood of collusion. Such factors include (see Chapter 4) the importance of entry barriers, the presence of structural links such as cross-ownership, the existence of information exchange among firms, the presence of multi-market contacts, the regularity and frequency of market interactions, the absence of countervailing power, and the existence of clauses such as best-price clauses and retail price maintenance.

The analysis of joint dominance will therefore have to take into account all such factors. Clearly, it is very difficult *a priori* to predict whether a merger might lead to a collusive outcome or not. In principle, the more an industry contains elements, which are likely to favour collusion the stricter the competition agencies should be towards the merger. However, the analysis will typically be very complex. Apart from a few rare cases where all factors point in the same direction (see the *Nestlé/Perrier* case, analysed in Section 5.7.2), in general there will be much room for discretion, as it is difficult to understand how such factors interact and whether collusion is likely to arise from the merger or not. Economic analysis indicates the factors that affect collusion, but it is silent (and it could not be otherwise) on what is the net effect upon the likelihood of collusion whenever an industry presents some circumstances which favour and others which discourage collusion.[39] There simply exists no rule on how to weigh these different factors, and the final judgement on whether a merger will be likely to result in collusion will depend on which factors are more important in the case at hand.

---

[39] A similar point is also made by Bishop (1999).

5.3.2 Efficiency Gains and Pro-Collusive Effects

The effect of efficiency gains in joint dominance analysis is slightly less clear-cut than in single-firm dominance. In general, an improvement of the efficiency of operations should be looked at very positively as it should decrease prices, other things being equal. This is more so when the merger results in a firm which has lower costs, or a larger capacity, than the rivals, as these elements might disrupt collusion since they create a stronger incentive to deviate. It might be conceivable, however, that the merger and its efficiency gains create symmetric conditions in the industry. Think for instance of a situation where the second and the third largest firm merge and reach the same product range and technological level as the industry's leader. It is possible that this might favour collusion by creating a more symmetric environment. However, it is unlikely that this effect might outweigh the potential welfare benefits of the efficiency gains. In particular, if such a merger is not allowed, there is the risk that the gap with respect to the leading (more competitive) firm would widen and in the long run this could result in single-firm dominance.

5.4 A MORE GENERAL MODEL**

In this section, I present a more general, n-products version of the model analysed in the previous sections. I will briefly analyse the effects of a merger along the same lines as above, with the additional treatment of the case where the merger might lead to the exit of outsiders.

5.4.1 The Model

I assume the following utility function:

$$U = v \sum_{i=1}^{n} q_i - \frac{n}{2(1+\gamma)} \left[\sum_{i=1}^{n} q_i^2 + \frac{\gamma}{n} \left(\sum_{i=1}^{n} q_i \right)^2 \right] + y, \qquad (5.18)$$

where y is an outside good, q_i is the quantity of the ith product, v is a positive parameter, n is the number of products in the industry, $\gamma \in [0, \infty)$ represents the degree of substitutability between the n products. This utility function being quasi-linear, the consumers' decisions on the outside good y do not affect their decisions taken with respect to the differentiated good, which we can analyse in a partial equilibrium framework.

From the maximisation of the utility function subject to the income constraint, one can derive the inverse demand functions as

$$p_i = v - \frac{1}{1+\gamma} \left(nq_i + \gamma \sum_{j=1}^{n} q_j \right). \qquad (5.19)$$

By inverting this system we can find the following direct demand functions (see

Section 8.6 for the derivation):

$$q_i = \frac{1}{n}\left[v - p_i(1+\gamma) + \frac{\gamma}{n}\sum_{j=1}^{n} p_j\right]. \tag{5.20}$$

Among the properties of this demand function, notice that the aggregate demand $Q = \sum_{i=1}^{n} q_i$ does not depend on the degree of substitution among the products, as $Q = \sum_{i=1}^{n} q_i = v - \frac{1}{n}\sum_{i=1}^{n} p_i$. Note also that in the case of symmetry ($p_i = p_j = p$) aggregate demand does not change with the number of products n existing in the industry, as $Q = \sum_{i=1}^{n} q_i = v - p$. Assume also, unless stated otherwise, that all the firms have identical cost functions $C(q_i) = cq_i$, with $c < v$.

5.4.2 Unilateral Effects without Efficiency Gains

In this section, I show that mergers which do not entail efficiency gains enhance market power and decrease welfare. I consider here the case of unilateral effects of a merger. Therefore, I assume that a collusive outcome cannot be reached, both before and after the merger.

5.4.2.1 Merger Effects, and Market Power

Consider first the case where there exists a multi-product firm, I, which sells the first m products in the industry, whereas the remaining $(n - m)$ products are sold by single-product firms. A merger between the "large" multi-product firm and a "small" single-product firm can then be studied by looking at the effect of an increase by one unit (from m to $m + 1$) in the number of products belonging to the large firm, all remaining firms still selling one product only.

To find the industry equilibrium write the profit functions of the multi-product firm and of each of the outsiders as follows:

$$\pi_I = \sum_{i=1}^{m} \frac{(p_i - c)}{n}\left(v - p_i(1+\gamma) + \frac{\gamma}{n}\left(\sum_{j=1}^{m} p_j + \sum_{k=m+1}^{n} p_k\right)\right), \tag{5.21}$$

$$\pi_k = \frac{(p_k - c)}{n}\left(v - p_k(1+\gamma) + \frac{\gamma}{n}\left(\sum_{l=1}^{m} p_l + p_k + \sum_{j=m+1, j\neq k}^{n} p_j\right)\right),$$

$$k = m+1, \ldots, n \tag{5.22}$$

By taking the first derivatives $\partial\pi_I/\partial p_i = 0$ and $\partial\pi_k/\partial p_k = 0$, imposing symmetry on the prices of the multi-product firm ($p_i = p_I$ for $i = 1, \ldots, m$), and of the outsiders ($p_k = p_o$ for $k = m+1, \ldots, n$), the first-order conditions are

$$
\begin{cases}
v + c\left(1 + \gamma - \dfrac{m\gamma}{n}\right) + \dfrac{\gamma(n-m)p_o}{n} - 2p_I\left(1 + \gamma - \dfrac{m\gamma}{n}\right) = 0 \\[4mm]
v + c\left(1 + \gamma - \dfrac{\gamma}{n}\right) + \dfrac{m\gamma p_I}{n} - p_o\left(2(1+\gamma) - \dfrac{\gamma(n-m+1)}{n}\right) = 0.
\end{cases}
\tag{5.23}
$$

By solving the system one obtains the equilibrium prices as

$$
p_I(m_j) =
$$

$$
\frac{c\left(n\gamma\left(4n - 2m - 1\right) + 2n^2 + \gamma^2\left(2n^2 - nm - 2n - m^2 + 2m\right)\right) + nv\left(2n + \gamma\left(2n - 1\right)\right)}{\gamma^2\left(2n^2 - nm - 2n - m^2 + 2m\right) + 2\gamma n\left(3n - m - 1\right) + 4n^2},
\tag{5.24}
$$

$$
p_o(m_j) =
$$

$$
\frac{c\left(n\gamma\left(4n - m - 2\right) + 2n^2 + \gamma^2\left(2n^2 - nm - 2n - m^2 + 2m\right)\right) + nv\left(2n + \gamma\left(2n - m\right)\right)}{\gamma^2\left(2n^2 - nm - 2n - m^2 + 2m\right) + 2\gamma n\left(3n - m - 1\right) + 4n^2}.
\tag{5.25}
$$

One can check that $\partial p_I/\partial m > 0$ and $\partial p_o/\partial m > 0$, implying that the larger the multi-product firm (the higher m for any given number of products n sold in the industry) the higher the equilibrium prices of both insiders and outsiders after the merger. Conversely, $\partial p_I/\partial n < 0$ and $\partial p_o/\partial n < 0$: a merger which involves a certain number of firms m will result in higher equilibrium prices the lower the number of firms in the industry, that is, the more concentrated the industry.

5.4.2.2 The Welfare Effects of a Merger

To show more formally the effects of a merger, let us focus upon the case where there exist n single-product firms and a merger between two of such firms occurs. Therefore, we have to compare the equilibrium solution for the pre-merger case $m = 1$ with that of the post-merger case $m = 2$.

By replacing $m = 1$ in the expression (5.24), we obtain the pre-merger equilibrium price $p_b = p_I(1) = p_o(1)$:

$$
p_b = \frac{\left(v + c\left(1 + \gamma - \frac{\gamma}{n}\right)\right)}{2 + \gamma - \frac{\gamma}{n}},
\tag{5.26}
$$

The quantity sold by each firm at equilibrium is given by

$$
q_b = \frac{(v - c)(n + n\gamma - \gamma)}{n(2n + n\gamma - \gamma)},
\tag{5.27}
$$

and the per-firm profit is

$$\pi_b = \frac{(v-c)^2 \, (n+n\gamma-\gamma)}{(2n+n\gamma-\gamma)^2}. \tag{5.28}$$

A merger creates a firm with two products. We can find the post-merger equilibrium values $p_I(2)$, $p_o(2)$ (we shall denote them for simplicity p_I, p_o) by replacing $m = 2$ in the expressions (5.24) and (5.25):

$$p_I = \frac{c\left(2n\,(n-2)\,\gamma^2 + n\,(3n-5)\,\gamma + 2n^2\right) + nv\,(2n + (2n-1)\gamma)}{2n\,((n-2)\gamma^2 + 3(n-1)\gamma + 2n)}, \tag{5.29}$$

$$p_o = \frac{c\,(n+(n-2)\gamma)\,(n+n\gamma) + nv\,(n+(n-1)\gamma)}{n\,((n-2)\gamma^2 + 3(n-1)\gamma + 2n)}. \tag{5.30}$$

After substituting, one obtains the quantities and per-product profits of the merged firm and the outsiders as

$$q_I = \frac{\left(2n^2 + n(4n-5)\gamma + (2n^2 - 5n + 2)\gamma^2\right)(v-c)}{2n^2 \, (2n + 3(n-1)\gamma + (n-2)\gamma^2)^2}; \tag{5.31}$$

$$q_o = \frac{(n+(n-1)\gamma)^2 (v-c)}{2n^2 \, (2n + 3(n-1)\gamma + (n-2)\gamma^2)}. \tag{5.32}$$

$$\pi_I =$$
$$(n+(n-2)\gamma)\left(\frac{c\left(n\,(n-2-3(n-1))\,\gamma - 2n^2\right) + nv\,(2n+(2n-1)\gamma)}{2n\,((n-2)\gamma^2 + 3(n-1)\gamma + 2n)}\right)^2, \tag{5.33}$$

$$\pi_o = (n+(n-1)\gamma)\left(\frac{-c\left(n\,(n-1)\,\gamma + n^2\right) + nv\,(n+(n-1)\gamma)}{2n\,((n-2)\gamma^2 + 3(n-1)\gamma + 2n)}\right)^2. \tag{5.34}$$

Lemma 5.1 *The merger increases prices and decreases consumer surplus.*

Proof The first part of the lemma has been shown above: the merger increases m from 1 to 2, and both insiders' and outsiders' prices increase with m. Since all the products are sold before and after the merger, consumers are worse off with the merger, because it raises prices of all the products. ∎

When two firms merge, they take into account the negative pecuniary externality they impose on each other, and raise their price. The other firms will react by increasing their price (in this model the products are strategic complements) but not as much as the merging firm.[40]

Lemma 5.2   *The merger benefits the merging firms.*

Proof   First, notice that $p_b < p_I$ and $p_b < p_o$. This follows from the result that $\partial p_I / \partial m > 0$ and $\partial p_o / \partial m > 0$, and recalling that $p_I = p_I(2) > p_b = p_I(1)$ and that $p_o = p_o(2) > p_b = p_o(1)$.

Denote the per-product profit earned by the merging firm as $\pi_I = \pi_I(p_I, p_o)$, where p_I denotes the vector of the own (two) product prices and p_o the vector of the other $(n-2)$ prices charged by the outsiders. Since goods are demand substitutes, it must be that $\pi_I(p_b, p_b) < \pi_I(p_b, p_o)$. In other words, the equilibrium profits obtained by the merging firms before the merger must be lower than the profit they would get if the rival firms charged a price $p_o > p_b$. However, we also know that the best response of the merging firms to the price p_o chosen by the outsiders is $p_I > p_b$. Therefore, it must be: $\pi_I(p_b, p_o) < \pi_I(p_I, p_o)$. So $\pi_I(p_b, p_b) < \pi_I(p_I, p_o)$. ∎

Lemma 5.3   *The merger increases outsiders' profits.*

Proof   We know that $p_b < p_I$ and $p_b < p_o$. Using the same notation as in the previous lemma, and given that the goods are demand substitutes, we have that for each of the outsiders $\pi_o(p_b, p_b) < \pi_o(p_I, p_b)$. Further, we know that the best response of each outsider to the price p_o chosen by the merging firm is $p_o > p_b$. Therefore, it must be $\pi_o(p_I, p_b) < \pi_o(p_I, p_o)$. This allows us to conclude that $\pi_o(p_b, p_b) < \pi_o(p_I, p_o)$. ∎

This result does not depend on whether firms compete on prices or quantities, and hinges on the free-riding effect enjoyed by the outsiders: when the merging firms increase their prices (or reduce their output), they reduce a negative externality which affects all the industry. The outsiders will therefore benefit from the merger.

We can now state the following:

Lemma 5.4   *The merger increases producer surplus.*

Proof   It follows trivially from the fact that the merger increases both the profits of the merging firms and of the outsiders, as established by the previous lemmata. ∎

Lemma 5.5   *The merger reduces net welfare.*

Proof   See Section 5.4.5. ∎

---

[40] In Section 4.3.4, I showed that when firms have the same technology, the larger the firm the higher the price it would charge: $p_m > p_k$ for $m > k$, m and k being the number of products sold by respectively a large and a small firm. See also Deneckere and Davidson (1985).

5.4.3 Efficiency Gains from Mergers

In this section, I illustrate the role of efficiency gains in merger analysis. The pre-merger case has already been analysed in the previous section, for the case where $m = 1$: equilibrium prices, quantities and profits are given by expressions (5.26), (5.27) and (5.28) above.

A merger between two firms creates a larger firm which will own and sell two product varieties.[41] Assume that by combining their assets, the merging firms might gain in efficiency with respect to the single-product firms, and be able to operate at a unit cost ec, with $e \leq 1$. The lower the parameter e, the higher the efficiency gains entailed by the merger. In other words, the proportion of costs saved by the merger is $100(1 - e)\%$. I shall show, among other things, that the higher the efficiency gains it creates, the more likely a merger is to be welfare improving.

To find the industry equilibrium after a merger between the first two firms $(I = 1, 2)$, write the (per-variety) profit functions of the merging firms (insiders) and of each of the outsiders as follows:

$$\pi_I = \frac{(p_I - ec)}{n}\left(v - p_I(1 + \gamma) + \frac{\gamma}{n}\left(2p_I + \sum_{i=3}^{n} p_i\right)\right), \quad I = 1, 2 \qquad (5.35)$$

$$\pi_j = \frac{(p_j - c)}{n}\left(v - p_j(1 + \gamma) + \frac{\gamma}{n}\left(2p_I + p_j + \sum_{i=3, i \neq j}^{n} p_i\right)\right), \quad j = 3, \ldots, n, \qquad (5.36)$$

where I have used symmetry on the merging firms' prices: $p_1 = p_2 = p_I$. Once imposing symmetry on the outsiders, so that $p_i = p_j = p_o$, the first-order conditions are given by

$$\begin{cases} v + ec\left(1 + \gamma - \frac{2\gamma}{n}\right) + \frac{\gamma(n-2)p_o}{n} - 2p_I\left(1 + \gamma - \frac{2\gamma}{n}\right) = 0 \\ v + c\left(1 + \gamma - \frac{\gamma}{n}\right) + \frac{2\gamma p_I}{n} - p_o\left(2\left(1 + \gamma - \frac{\gamma}{n}\right) - \frac{\gamma(n-3)}{n}\right) = 0. \end{cases} \qquad (5.37)$$

By solving the system above in p_o and p_I, one obtains the equilibrium prices after

---

[41] The analysis could be extended to consider mergers between m firms, but we would lose in simplicity and not gain any further insights by doing so.

the merger as

$$
p_I = \frac{c\left((n-2)(en+n+e-1)\gamma^2 + n(3en-3e-2)\gamma + 2en^2\right) + nv(2n+(2n-1)\gamma)}{2n((n-2)\gamma^2 + 3(n-1)\gamma + 2n)},
$$

(5.38)

$$
p_o = \frac{c(n+(n-2)\gamma)(n+(n-1+e)\gamma) + nv(n+(n-1)\gamma)}{n((n-2)\gamma^2 + 3(n-1)\gamma + 2n)}.
$$

(5.39)

After substituting, one obtains the per-product profit of the merged firm and the outsiders as

$$
\pi_I = (n+(n-2)\gamma)
$$

$$
\times \left(\frac{c\left((1-e)(2-3n+n^2)\gamma^2 + n(n-2-3e(n-1))\gamma - 2en^2\right) + nv(2n+(2n-1)\gamma)}{2n((n-2)\gamma^2 + 3(n-1)\gamma + 2n)}\right)^2,
$$

(5.40)

$$
\pi_o = (n+(n-1)\gamma)\left(\frac{-c\left((1-e)(n-2)\gamma^2 + n(n-e)\gamma + n^2\right) + nv(n+(n-1)\gamma)}{2n((n-2)\gamma^2 + 3(n-1)\gamma + 2n)}\right)^2.
$$

(5.41)

I now find the effects of the merger on consumer surplus, firms' profits and net welfare, using as the benchmark the equilibrium solutions in the industry before the merger, and under the assumption that the merger does not reduce the number of products, which are sold in the market (Section 5.4.4 relaxes this assumption).

The Merger Effect on Consumer Surplus   The following lemma gives a necessary and sufficient condition for the merger to result in lower prices and thus benefit consumers.

Lemma 5.6   *The merger is beneficial to consumers if and only if it involves enough efficiency gains, i.e., if and only if*

$$
e \le \bar{e} \equiv \frac{c\left((n^2-3n+2)\gamma^2 + n(3n-4)\gamma + 2n^2\right) - nv\gamma}{c(n+(n-2)\gamma)(2n+(n-1)\gamma)}.
$$

(5.42)

Proof   Since we are considering the case where all the products are sold before and after the merger, a sufficient condition for consumers to be better off with the merger is that prices of all the products are lower after the merger. However, it turns out that the condition for which $p_o \le p_b$ coincides with the condition for which $p_I \le p_b$, both of them requiring that $e \le \bar{e}$. This implies that the condition is both necessary and sufficient. It is easy to check it is the case by doing some simple but tedious algebra. Write $\Delta p_o(e) = p_o(e) - p_b$. The inequality $\Delta p_o(e) \le 0$ is satisfied only by $e \leq \bar{e}$. Likewise, one can check that $\Delta p_I(e) = p_I(e) - p_b \leq 0$ is also solved only by $e \leq \bar{e}$. ∎

The lemma above can be read as follows. First, consumers will benefit from the merger only if it decreases prices. Second, prices decrease only if there are enough efficiency gains.

Note also that $\bar{e} < 1$ can be rewritten as $-n\gamma(v-c) < 0$. This implies that a merger which does not entail any efficiency gain (that is, a merger such that $e = 1$) will always increase prices and thus will never improve consumer surplus.

The reader can check that $\partial \bar{e}/\partial n > 0$. The higher the number of firms the smaller the efficiency gains that are required to raise consumer surplus: since the critical value $\bar{e}$ increases, it is easier that the condition $e \leq \bar{e}$ be satisfied. When a large number of firms operate in the industry, the extent to which prices increase after the merger between two of them is much reduced. Each firm internalises the externality on the price of the partner, but with a large number of outsiders the effect of the merger on prices becomes marginal, and a small efficiency gain can outweigh this negative effect. At the other extreme, when there are only two firms in the industry the merger will create a monopoly and thus result in the maximal increase in market power: only extremely high efficiency gains might in principle outweigh the negative welfare effect due to higher prices. This strengthens the rationale for challenging mergers which occur in a more concentrated industry (see Section 5.2.2).

The Impact of the Merger on Producer Surplus   Let us now turn to the effect of the merger on the firms' profits, keeping our assumption that the merger does not force output of the outsiders to zero. The first step is to study the impact of the merger on the insiders' profits. In the price-competition setting we are analysing, the firms which undertake the merger always gain from it, independently of the efficiency gains, as the following remark states.

Remark 5.1   *The merger benefits the merging firms.*

Proof   Recall that even without efficiency gains, a merger is profitable for the merging firms (see Lemma 5.2). This implies that $\Delta_{Ib}(e) \equiv 2(\pi_I(e) - \pi_b) > 0$, for $e = 1$. Next, it can be checked that the function $\Delta_{Ib}(e)$ is convex:

$$\frac{\partial^2 \Delta_{Ib}}{\partial e^2} = \frac{c^2(n+(n-2)\gamma)\left(3n(n-1)\gamma + 2n^2 + (n^2-3n+2)\gamma\right)^2}{n^4\left((n-2)\gamma^2 + 3(n-1)\gamma + 2n\right)^2} > 0,$$

(5.43)

To make sure that Δ_{Ib} is always positive, we just need to check that the first derivative does not change sign in its domain. Since $\partial \Delta_{Ib}/\partial e$ is negative when evaluated at $e = \bar{e} < 0$, this amounts to checking that $\partial \Delta_{Ib}/\partial e < 0$ at $e = 1$. Some algebra shows that

$$\frac{\partial \Delta_{Ib}}{\partial e}(e=1)$$

$$= -\frac{c(v-c)(n+\gamma(n-2))\left(2n^2+3n(n-1)\gamma+(n^2-3n+2)\gamma^2\right)\left(2n^2+n(2n-1)\gamma\right)}{n^4\left((n-2)\gamma^2+3(n-1)\gamma+2n\right)^2} < 0.$$

$$(5.44)$$

The lower e (the stronger efficiency gains), the more profitable the merger. This completes the proof that the merging firms always gain from the merger. ∎

The next step is to show that the merger always benefits the outsiders unless there are high enough efficiency gains for the merging firms.

Remark 5.2   *The merger increases outsiders' profits if efficiency gains are small enough, i.e., if $e > \bar{e}$.*

Proof   We know from the previous section that if there are no efficiency gains, the outsiders gain from the merger: $\pi_o(p_b, p_b) < \pi_o(p_I, p_o)$, for $e = 1$. The next step is to define the function $\Delta_{bo}(e) \equiv (n-2)(\pi_b - \pi_o(e))$, whose sign will tell us whether outsiders gain from the merger. First, note that $\Delta_{bo}(\bar{e}) = 0$. When $e = \bar{e}$, we have $p_o = p_I = p_b$. Therefore, it must be also that $q_o = q_I = q_b$. This implies that $\pi_o = (p_o - c)q_o = (p_b - c)q_b = \pi_b$, since the merger does not affect production costs of the outsiders. Finally, it is easy to see that while π_b is not a function of e, the function $\pi_o(e)$ increases with e. Hence, $\Delta_{bo}(e)$ is decreasing in its domain. Therefore, $\pi_b \leq \pi_o(e)$ for $e \geq \bar{e}$. ∎

The following proposition establishes that even though the outsiders might lose from the merger (if there exist important efficient gains for the merging partners), the industry profits increase with the merger.

Lemma 5.7   *The merger always increases producer surplus.*

Proof   See Section 5.4.5. ∎

The Net Welfare Effect of Mergers   We can now look at the overall effect of the merger upon welfare, and establish the following sufficient condition:

Lemma 5.8   *The merger improves net welfare if it involves enough efficiency gains, i.e., if*

$$e \leq \bar{e} \equiv \frac{c\left((n^2-3n+2)\gamma^2+n(3n-4)\gamma+2n^2\right)-nv\gamma}{c(n+(n-2)\gamma)(2n+(n-1)\gamma)}.$$

Proof   A sufficient (but not necessary) condition for welfare to increase with the merger is that both consumer surplus and producer surplus increase. The two lemmata above have showed that for $e \leq \bar{e}$ consumers gain and aggregate profits also rise. Therefore, welfare increases in this interval. ∎

This concludes our technical treatment of efficiency gains, made under the assumption that all outsiders continue to operate in the industry after the merger takes place. The following section considers the possibility that after the merger some outsiders are driven out of the market.

5.4.4 Efficiency Offence: When the Merger Leads to the Exit of the Outsiders

It is conceivable that the merger, by making the merging partners more efficient with respect to the outsiders, might allow the former to push some of the latter firms out of the market. I now analyse this possibility and its implications.

In order for the outsiders not to sell anything after the merger, it must be that $q_o \leq 0$. The quantity sold by the outsiders can be derived from equations (5.38) and (5.39). The merger leads to the merging firms to be the only seller if

$$e \leq e_{ex} = \frac{c\left(n^2(1+\gamma) + (n-2)\gamma^2\right) - n(n + (n-1)\gamma)\,v}{c\gamma\,(n + (n-2)\gamma)}. \tag{5.45}$$

Note that e_{ex} is negative when n is large enough and when γ is small enough, implying that if the industry is not very concentrated and products are imperfect substitutes the merger will never result in outsiders exiting the industry, even in case of important efficiency gains for the insiders. It is also straightforward to see that $\partial e_{ex}/\partial n < 0$, and that $\partial e_{ex}/\partial \gamma > 0$. In the extreme case where the goods are perfectly homogenous, a marginal cost improvement is enough to force the other firms out of the industry ($\lim_{\gamma \to \infty} e_{ex} = 1$).

When the merged firm is the only one left in the market, it will charge the monopoly price $p_m = (ec + v)/2$ for each variety. It is easy to check that the welfare level attained in this situation is given by

$$W_M = \frac{3(v - ec)^2}{8}. \tag{5.46}$$

The merger is beneficial to society as a whole if $W_M > W_b$, where the latter indicates the welfare level before the merger and is given by $W_b = \left(\gamma^2(n-1)^2 + 4\gamma n(n-1) + 3n^2\right)(v-c)^2 / \left[2\left(2n + (n-1)\gamma\right)^2\right]$. It can be shown that $W_M \geq W_b$ if[42]

$$e \leq e_w = \frac{v}{c} - \frac{2\sqrt{3n^2 + 4n(n-1)\gamma + (n-1)^2\gamma^2}}{\sqrt{3}c\,(n + (n-1)\gamma)}. \tag{5.47}$$

It can be checked that $\partial e_w/\partial \gamma < 0$ and $\partial e_w/\partial n < 0$. This means that the more substitutable the products and the larger the number of firms, the more unlikely that a merger which gives rise to a (two-product) monopoly would be welfare improving. The reason behind this result is that a higher number of firms or less differentiated

---

[42] The second root of the associated equation is higher than one, and therefore it should be discarded.

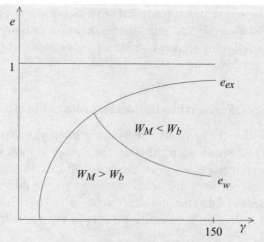

Figure 5.5. Levels of efficiency gains and exclusion of competitors.

goods make the before-the-merger welfare level higher, due to stronger competition in the market.

Figure 5.5 helps explain the effects of a merger which gives rise to a monopoly of the merging firms (i.e., where $e < e_{ex}$). There exist two different possibilities:

- $e_w < e < e_{ex}$. In this case, the efficiency gain is enough for the merging firms to be the only seller, but its monopoly power goes to the detriment of consumers and total welfare.
- $e < e_w < e_{ex}$. In this case, the merger creates such an efficient firm that the lack of competition in the market is more than outweighed by the efficiency gains. Total welfare rises as a result.

In other words, even if the merger gave rise to a monopoly, it would not be possible to conclude that this necessarily leads to a welfare loss, since the very same efficiency gains which oblige the rival firms to exit the market might benefit consumers.

To better interpret the results obtained, consider that the example I have set up here is somehow extreme, for at least three important reasons. First, it does not consider capacity constraints, since I have implicitly assumed that the two merging firms are able to supply all the market demand which would have been supplied by n firms before the merger. This is a very strong assumption, which makes it possible for a single firm to cover all the market.

Second, in this model if one outsider goes out of the market, all the outsiders also cease production. As a result, strong enough efficiency gains lead to monopoly for the merging firm, which in turn creates strong monopoly power and worsens welfare. In a more sophisticated model, one would like to assume a range of production costs for the outsiders, with some of them being forced out of the market by the merger's efficiency gains, and some others not. The welfare impact of the merger would then be less adverse. In fact, it might lead to a more efficient outcome, made possible by the shut down of the less efficient competitors.

Third, this is a static model, where outsiders cannot react to a firm's merger. But if a merger leads to such high efficiency gains, it should be expected that the rivals would merge too. This would call for a more complete model where the number of mergers should be determined endogenously, something beyond the scope of the present work.[43]

To summarise, the possibility that a merger which entails efficiency gains might decrease welfare by forcing out most or all of the competitors seems unlikely, as this result can be obtained only under very strong assumptions.

5.4.5 Proofs

Proof of Lemma 5.5   Welfare is defined as the sum of consumer surplus and producer surplus. In the case of the merger, welfare is given by

$$
\begin{aligned}
W_m &= U(q_I, q_o) - 2p_I q_I - (n-2)p_o q_o + 2(p_I - c)q_I + (n-2)(p_o - c)q_o \\
&= v\left(2q_I + (n-2)q_o\right) - \frac{n}{2(1+\gamma)} \\
&\quad \times \left(2q_I^2 + (n-2)q_o^2 + \frac{\gamma}{n}\left(2q_I + (n-2)q_o\right)^2\right) - 2cq_I - (n-2)cq_o.
\end{aligned}
\tag{5.48}
$$

By replacing equilibrium quantities in the above expression we obtain

$$
W_m =
$$

$$
\frac{\left(2\gamma^4(n-2)^2 n^2 + 6n^4 + 4\gamma n^4(5n^2 - 5n - 1) + 3n\gamma^2(8n^3 - 16n^2 + 4n + 1) + \gamma^3(12n^4 - 36n^3 + 24n^2 - n + 2)\right)(v - c)^2}{4n^2\left(2n + 3(n-1)\gamma + (n-2)\gamma^2\right)^2}.
\tag{5.49}
$$

Welfare before the merger is instead given by

$$
W_b = vnq_b - \frac{n^2 q_b^2}{2} - ncq_b.
\tag{5.50}
$$

By replacing quantities, we obtain

$$
W_b = \frac{\left(\gamma^2(n-1)^2 + 4\gamma n(n-1) + 3n^2\right)(v - c)^2}{2\left(2n + (n-1)\gamma\right)^2}.
\tag{5.51}
$$

---

[43] Motta and Vasconcelos (2003) analyse efficiency gains in a homogenous goods model where firms might differ in capacity. They study a dynamic game where mergers are decided sequentially, and must be authorised by an anti-trust authority. In their model, efficiency gains prompt outsiders to merge as well, and the ultimate structure of the market is more concentrated but is also associated with a higher welfare level. In other words, taking account of outsiders' reactions eliminates the rationale for an efficiency offence argument.

The difference in welfare $\Delta W = W_m - W_b$ is given by

$$\Delta W =$$

$$- \frac{\gamma \, (v-c)^2 \, \left(\gamma^4(n-2)(n-1)^2 + 16n^4 + 4\gamma n^3(10n-7) + 4\gamma^2 n^2(8n^2 - 11n + 2) + \gamma^3 n(8n^3 - 15n^2 + 5) \right)}{4n^2 \, (2n + (n-1)\gamma)^2 \, \left(2n + 3(n-1)\gamma + (n-2)\gamma^2 \right)^2} < 0.$$

$$(5.52)$$

It is straightforward to see that the difference is negative, given that the numerator is always positive for $n \geq 2$. This proves that (when there are no efficiency gains) the merger always reduces welfare. ∎

Proof of Lemma 5.7   We know that total industry profits increase when $e \in [\bar{e}, 1]$, as in this interval both insiders and outsiders gain from the merger. Therefore, we only need to show that aggregate profits rise in the interval $e \in [0, \bar{e})$.

Denote the producer surplus after the merger as $PS' = 2\pi_I + (n-2)\pi_o$, and producer surplus before the merger as $PS_b = n\pi_b$. For producer surplus to increase with the merger, we must therefore have $PS' > PS_b$, or equivalently: $\Delta_{Ib}(e) \equiv 2\,(\pi_I(e) - \pi_b) > \Delta_{bo}(e) \equiv (n-2)\,(\pi_b - \pi_o(e))$. To prove that this is the case in the interval $e \leq \bar{e}$, we move in three steps.

1. $\Delta_{Ib}(\bar{e}) > \Delta_{bo}(\bar{e})$.

2. $\dfrac{\partial \Delta_{Ib}}{\partial e}(\bar{e}) < \dfrac{\partial \Delta_{bo}}{\partial e}(\bar{e}) < 0$.

3. $\dfrac{\partial^2 \Delta_{Ib}}{\partial e^2} > 0 > \dfrac{\partial \Delta_{bo}^2}{\partial e^2}$.

Taken together, these three conditions ensure that $\Delta_{Ib}(e) > \Delta_{bo}(e)$, for $e \leq \bar{e}$, as shown in Figure 5.6.

Let us start with 1. To show that $\Delta_{Ib}(\bar{e}) > \Delta_{bo}(\bar{e})$, recall that $\Delta_{Ib}(e) > 0$ in all its domain, and that when $e = \bar{e}$, we have $\pi_o = \pi_b$. Hence, $\Delta_{Ib}(\bar{e}) = 2\,(\pi_I(\bar{e}) - \pi_b) > 0 = \Delta_{bo}(\bar{e}) = (n-2)\,(\pi_b - \pi_o(\bar{e}))$.

As for point (2), we have to compute the derivatives and take their value in $e = \bar{e}$. After some algebra, one finds that

$$\frac{\partial \Delta_{Ib}}{\partial e}(\bar{e}) = - \frac{2c\,(v-c)\,(n+(n-1)\gamma)\,\left(3n(n-1)\gamma + 2n^2 + (n^2 - 3n + 2)\gamma \right)}{n^2\,(2n+(n-1)\gamma)\,((n-2)\gamma^2 + 3(n-1)\gamma + 2n)} < 0,$$

$$(5.53)$$

$$\frac{\partial \Delta_{bo}}{\partial e}(\bar{e}) = - \frac{2c\,(v-c)\,\gamma\,(n-2)\,(n+(n-2)\gamma)\,(n+(n-1)\gamma)}{n^2\,(2n+(n-1)\gamma)\,((n-2)\gamma^2 + 3(n-1)\gamma + 2n)} < 0, \quad (5.54)$$

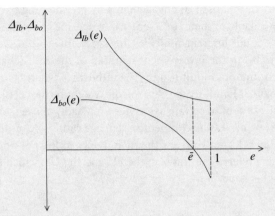

Figure 5.6. Study of functions used in Lemma 5.7.

The inequality $\partial \Delta_{Ib}(\bar{e})/\partial e < \partial \Delta_{bo}(\bar{e})/\partial e$ can be re-written as

$$-\frac{2c\,(v-c)\left(2n^3 + n^2(4n-3)\gamma + (n^2-3n+2)\gamma^3 + n(2n^2-2n-1)\gamma^2\right)}{n^2\,(2n+(n-1)\gamma)\,((n-2)\gamma^2 + 3(n-1)\gamma + 2n)} < 0,$$

(5.55)

which proves point 2.

We are now left with point (3), which just consists of computing the second derivatives and showing that $\Delta_{Ib}(e)$ is convex whereas $\Delta_{bo}(e)$ is concave. It can be checked that

$$\frac{\partial^2 \Delta_{bo}}{\partial e^2} = -\frac{2c^2\,(n-2)\,(n+(n-2)\gamma)^2\,(n+(n-1)\gamma)}{n^4\,((n-2)\gamma^2 + 3(n-1)\gamma + 2n)^2} < 0.$$

(5.56)

This completes the proof. ∎

5.5 MERGER REMEDIES

An anti-trust authority (AA) might approve a merger only if certain "remedies" were adopted by the merging firms.[44] This is not an uncommon event: for instance, a considerable proportion of the mergers reviewed by the EC are approved after remedies have been offered by the merging parties.[45]

Merger remedies fall into two categories. (i) *Structural remedies* modify the allocation of property rights: they include divestiture of an entire ongoing business, or partial divestiture. (ii) *Behavioural remedies* set constraints on the merged firms'

[44] This section follows closely Motta, Polo and Vasconcelos (2002).
[45] 40 out of 345 in the year 2000, according to the EC Report on Competition Policy (2001).

property rights: they consist of engagements by the merging parties not to abuse certain assets available to them, or to enter into specific contractual arrangements.

Of course, not all different remedies are applicable to the same merger. They typically differ also in the involvement required of the AA. Behavioural remedies usually entail continuous monitoring by the authorities, whereas structural remedies do not. On the other hand, structural remedies might be more risky, as they are not reversible: if divestment of certain assets has been badly chosen, or these assets end up with the wrong buyer, the competitive damage cannot be undone.

In what follows, I briefly review the main issues in the policy on merger remedies, occasionally referring to cases in the EU and the US, which have very similar approaches to this issue.[46]

5.5.1 Divestitures

When two firms merge, there might be substantial overlaps in particular geographic areas and/or lines of business. Whereas the merger does not create problems overall, an AA should also avoid anti-competitive effects in those particular markets, and selected divestment of assets might be the natural remedy to solve the problem.

Divested assets can either be bought by a new firm or be acquired by an existing competitor. In both events, the AA should ensure that the acquirer of the assets will be an active competitor in the market. To this end, the acquirer should have the possibility to purchase "all the elements of the business that are necessary for the business to act as a viable competitor in the market: tangible (such as R&D, production, distribution, sales and marketing activities) and intangible (such as intellectual property rights and goodwill) assets, personnel, supply and sales agreements (with appropriate guarantees about the transferability of these), customer lists, third party service agreements, technical assistance (scope, duration, cost, quality), and so forth". (*Commission Notice on Remedies*, para. 46)

In some cases, due to the existence of economies of scope or network effects, to have an effective competitor in the affected markets might also require the merging parties to divest assets which do not raise competition concerns.[47]

When the acquirer of divested assets is a firm that is already active in the market, the divestiture might be limited to particular assets that would be integrated into the business of the acquirer. However, this "mix-and-match" approach may create

---

[46] For the EU, see *Commission Notice on Remedies*. Parker and Balto (2000) nicely review the evolution in the US policy and the recent changes after the FTC Divestiture Report (Federal Trade Commission, 1999). The FTC experience has considerably influenced the EC policy.

[47] The FTC often asks for divestiture of a greater set of assets than those that participate in the overlapping market if ancillary assets are required to replicate economies of scale or economies of scope without which competition could not be restored. See Parker and Balto (2000). The same practice has been followed by the EC, among other cases, in *Unilever/Bestfoods* and *Total Fina/Elf Aquitaine*.

additional risks as to the viability and efficiency of the resulting business: the FTC divestiture study reveals that the likelihood of successful entry was much higher when an entire ongoing business was divested, whereas entry was significantly more problematic in the case of divestiture of selected assets (Parker and Balto, 2000).[48]

5.5.1.1 Problems with Divestitures

Structural remedies are often the best corrective measure for potentially anticompetitive mergers, but they might not be without problems (Parker and Balto, 2000).

First of all, the merging parties have all the incentive to make sure that the purchaser of the divested assets will *not* be a competitive firm. The seller might therefore try to decrease their value (by transferring valuable personnel, disposing of certain brands, patents and activities, or not maintaining properly the production plants or the shop premises), and would use very different criteria than the AA to select the buyer. This implies that the AA should ensure that the seller does not engage in activities that could reduce the value of the assets or hinder the sales, and should keep control of the identity of the buyer.[49]

Second, the FTC *ex post* study of merger remedies emphasises the significant *informational asymmetries* between the seller and the buyer. When the latter is not already operating in the industry, it often does not know what are the crucial assets to be an effective competitor in the industry, and it might end up with a package of assets that falls short of what is needed to be successful.[50]

Third, whenever some relationships were needed between the seller and the buyer of the divested assets (for instance, if the buyer needs supply of certain inputs or technical assistance) the remedy is unlikely to restore competition. In the FTC study, in thirteen out of the nineteen cases reviewed where there existed such a relationship, either the buyer did not manage to operate effectively, or there was collusion between the two firms (Parker and Balto, 2000).

Fourth, it is obvious that the merging parties have all the incentives to select a buyer that does not jeopardise their market position, but – perhaps less obvious – it

---

[48] In *MCI WorldCom/Sprint*, the EC found that this merger, involving the world's leading provider of Internet connectivity (MCI WorldCom) and one of its main competitors, Sprint, would have resulted in the creation of a dominant position in the market for top-level universal Internet connectivity. The parties proposed to divest Sprint's Internet business, but the EC did not accept this remedy, since it argued that Sprint's internet business was completely intertwined with the rest of Sprint's telecom business, and the divested business would never have constituted a strong and viable competitor of the merged entity.

[49] The figures of the "hold-separate trustee" and of the "divestiture trustee" replace the EC in these tasks.

[50] The problem is made more serious by the fact that the seller has all the incentive to design a package that does not include the right (from the point of view of the competitor) assets, and that a competition authority is not an industry regulator and has thus limited expertise in any given sector.

is far from clear that a buyer that intends to be a fierce competitor will end up with the divested assets. Suppose that there are two potential buyers, identical in other respects but who differ in their market attitude. One plans to use a soft pricing policy, or (tacitly or overtly) collude with the seller. The other plans an aggressive price strategy. It is likely that the expected profit of the former is higher than that of the latter, and it will accordingly be willing to pay more to obtain the assets. An auction will therefore not guarantee the best possible outcome from welfare's point of view.

Fifth, the use of structural remedies might increase the risk of collusion in the industry if the divested assets increase *symmetry* between the buyer and the merging partners and if they create *multi-market contacts* between them (see Chapter 4 on why symmetry and multi-market contacts increase collusive outcomes).

This points to a tension between two problems. On the one hand, AAs should guarantee the reinforcement or the creation of a viable firm to avoid problems of unilateral effects (single-firm dominance by the merging firms). On the other hand, they should also avoid pro-collusive effects after the merger (joint dominance). This implies that the evaluation of merger remedies should follow the same twofold test used in merger analysis, that is the evaluation of unilateral effects and pro-collusive effects. Remedies should be accepted, and the merger proposal cleared, only if both tests are satisfied.

5.5.2 Behavioural Remedies

Behavioural remedies consist mainly of commitments aimed at guaranteeing that competitors enjoy a level playing field in the purchase or use of some key assets, inputs or technologies that are owned by the merging parties.

Such commitments might be purely behavioural, as in *Vivendi/Canal+/Seagram*, regarding the European pay-TV market. Seagram has control over content through its subsidiary Universal, one of the six major Hollywood studios. Canal+ is the largest pay-TV operator and also the first acquirer of premium films for pay-TV from the US major studios and in particular Universal. The EC worried that up-stream content providers could deny or limit the access to premium films to some downstream active users or potential entrants. The parties proposed a mechanism that would not discriminate against rivals. The EC, however, showed scepticism towards this "essentially behavioural" remedy and considered it unsatisfactory. The concentration was afterwards cleared subject to the parties' commitment not to grant Canal+ "first-window" rights covering more than 50% of Universal production and co-production.

Non-structural remedies may also be of a contractual type, and therefore "quasi-structural". For instance, the merging parties might be obliged to license a given technology to a rival. Or, in case the merging parties' key assets are not owned but were secured by exclusive long-run contracts, the remedy might involve giving up or shortening part or the totality of such contracts. This specific type of commitment was used both in *Astra/Zeneca* and in *Lufthansa/SAS*.[51]

In *Astra/Zeneca*, the EC investigations showed that, in the market for plain betablockers in Sweden and Norway, Zeneca is Astra's main competitor. In particular, Zeneca has been very actively promoting its plain betablockers (Tenormin) as a competitive alternative to Astra's largest selling betablocker in those countries. Therefore, a merger between the two companies would eliminate competition between these two products. This concern was addressed by the parties' undertaking to "grant a viable independent third party exclusive distribution rights for Tenormin in Sweden and Norway for a period of at least 10 years".

Lufthansa/SAS regards a joint-venture between the two airlines. The EC authorised the agreement for a period of 10 years subject to certain conditions for the flights between Scandinavia and Germany. One such condition was that the involved airlines should give up slots at saturated airports in case there were potential entrants, to diminish the risk of foreclosure by the incumbents. The EC also decided that the parties should conclude interlining agreements with new entrants and freeze the number of flights operated to facilitate entry, and obliged them to allow entrants to participate in their frequent-flyer programmes, in case they do not have their own.[52]

Another category of behavioural remedies might consist of the so-called "vertical firewalls". When the merger creates a vertically integrated firm, say one where the upstream unit supplies not only the downstream unit but also rivals, it is possible that competitively sensitive information about downstream rivals be passed from the upstream to the downstream unit of the merged entity, thereby distorting the competitive process. It might then be required by the AA that no such information is circulated within the different units of the firm (non-disclosure provisions).[53]

5.5.2.1 Problems with Behavioural Remedies

Most of these remedies by their nature require some type of ongoing regulation or monitoring, and they are therefore likely to engage the resources of the AA long after the merger has been cleared and carried out. Some of these measures are also relatively easy to evade unless there is a careful monitoring and the regulator knows the industry very well, which is not likely to be the case for the AA.

When the AA identifies the risk of foreclosure (see Chapter 6), for instance, short of divestiture (which might be unfeasible, as the very reason behind the merger might

---

[51] This decision was not taken under the Merger Regulation but under Article 81. However, since the last revision of the Merger Regulation full-function joint-ventures are reviewed as mergers.

[52] The joint-venture effectively gave near monopoly to SAS-Lufthansa on a number of routes between Scandinavia and Germany. I doubt that the remedies imposed were enough to restore competition.

[53] US anti-trust authorities approved several vertical mergers subject to the imposition of non-disclosure and/or non-discrimination requirements upon the post-merger vertically integrated entity. For a discussion and a model of vertical firewalls, see Milliou (2001).

precisely be to integrate vertically related or complementary activities), behavioural remedies are difficult to administer and not likely to be successful unless there is monitoring. Foreclosure or discriminated access might take different forms, from obvious (say, bluntly refusing to supply an input) to more subtle ones (increasing prices, reducing quality, blaming insufficient capacity to justify missed shipments, delaying supplies, reduce accessory services and so on). Therefore, a remedy that calls for an obligation to supply is tantamount to an empty promise, but even a seemingly more sensible obligation to non-discrimination might not be easily enforceable (as just mentioned, discrimination might often occur at different levels and with different features).

These are difficult problems to cope with for a regulator, and they will *a fortiori* be for the AA, whose expertise lies elsewhere and whose knowledge of the industry is not like that of a regulator.

Behavioural remedies may also be problematic when they aim at facilitating market entry by ensuring that competitors have access to a key technology. Often, the implementation of this kind of remedy requires a (transitory) period of collaboration between the merged entity, on the one hand, and the third party to which access is going to be provided, on the other. In such cases, this third party is usually an actual or potential competitor and, therefore, it is extremely difficult to ensure that the merged entity will have the right incentives to effectively collaborate during a pre-defined transitory period to make entry by this third party successful.

In *Abbot/ALZA*, the parties proposed to sell several assets to another pharmaceutical company, but because of the risks involved in a necessary ongoing relationship between the merged entity and the potential third party, the FTC refused the commitment, leading to the parties' withdrawal of the merger proposal (Parker and Balto, 2000). In a similar case, *Astra/Zeneca*, the EC decided instead to accept the remedies proposed, which involved the merging pharmaceutical companies supporting a third party in the launch of a product which would have competed with their own.

Overall, therefore, behavioural remedies might raise several problems, not the least being that they need continuous monitoring. Given the very nature of AAs, non-discriminatory access or firewalls are best implemented when the firms involved are subject to the scrutiny of the industry regulator, which should be involved in the discussions leading to remedies in the early stages of the investigation.

5.6 MERGER POLICY IN THE EUROPEAN UNION

In the EU, mergers are regulated by the *Merger Regulation* (see Section 1.4 for a description), which establishes that only mergers which create or strengthen a dominant position will be prohibited.[54] In this section, I briefly review the current

---

[54] See Chapter 1 for a discussion of the concept of dominance. In practice, a firm will be found dominant if it has very large market power (see also Chapter 3).

EU merger policy.[55] I argue that it has two features that are at odds with economic principles. First, the dominance test does not allow the prohibition of mergers which decrease welfare without creating a dominant position. Second, so far efficiency gains have not been considered when assessing merger proposals, whereas economics strongly suggests that efficiency savings should be at the centre of the analysis of mergers (as we have seen in the previous sections).

5.6.1 Dominance Test

Economic analysis suggests that a distinction should be made between cases where the merger raises concerns of unilateral price increase and cases where the merger raises concerns of (tacit or explicit) collusive behaviour. In the latter cases, if concerns are justified the merger is said to create joint dominance. However, the former case does not correspond closely to the concept of single-firm dominance. Consider for example a merger that results in two firms with large market shares operating in the industry, but neither firm has enough market power to be considered dominant, and assume that it is very unlikely that they would collude (i.e., they would not be jointly dominant). Economics suggests that such a merger might be detrimental.[56] Yet, the European Commission could not currently prohibit it: under the Merger Regulation, the finding of a dominant position is a necessary condition for prohibiting a merger.

In what follows, I discuss the concept of joint dominance, and argue that the EC has tried to use this concept to deal with mergers that raise anti-competitive effects while not creating single-firm dominance.

5.6.1.1 Joint Dominance

The concept of joint dominance matches closely that of coordinated effects: after the merger, there is high likelihood that a collusive outcome will arise in the industry. The first merger where the EC used joint dominance was *Nestlé/Perrier* (see Section 5.7.2). At first, it was disputed whether the EC could extend the concept of dominance to deal with a situation where dominance was jointly held by two (or more) firms. However, in *France v. Commission* the European Court of Justice (ECJ) ruled that the case of joint dominance was indeed covered by the Merger Regulation.[57] The ECJ then quashed the EC decision on the substance, and seemed to set a high standard of proof for the EC to find joint dominance.[58]

---

[55] As I briefly discuss below, important changes in the EU merger policy are being considered (but have not been decided yet) as of January 2003.

[56] More precisely, welfare will decrease in the absence of efficiency gains from the merger. See Section 2.1 above.

[57] The EC decision being appealed was *Kali&Salz/MdK/Treuhand.*

[58] The judgement says that joint dominance arises when firms ". . . in particular because of correlative factors which exist between them, are able to adopt a common policy on the market and act to a

In *Gencor v. Commission,*[59] the Court of First Instance (CFI) reaffirmed that the EC can block mergers if they create joint dominance, and offered a broader interpretation of joint dominance,[60] which seemed to require a lower standard of proof.[61]

The EC took advantage of the higher degree of freedom left by the CFI judgment, and has used the joint dominance concept in a large number of cases since then. A highly publicised decision was *Airtours/First Choice,* where the EC prohibited a merger between two companies operating in the UK short-haul packaged holiday market. The industry was characterised by a large amount of product heterogeneity (specific package holidays differ in terms of destination, type of hotel and additional services: this reduces observability and makes it less likely to reach collusive prices, see Chapter 4) and by a high variability of market shares over time.[62] The extent to which internet sales of travel tickets and accommodation should have been considered in the product market definition and constrained the market power of the package holiday operators was also unclear. Further, the EC argued that collusion would take the form of capacity reduction, rather than an increase in prices.[63] This argument can be supported by economic theory,[64] but it departed from the standard joint dominance analyses.

---

considerable extent independently of their competitors, their customers, and also of consumers" (*France v. Commission*: para. 221). The reference to "correlative factors" seemed to indicate that some sort of structural links among firms must exist.

[59] Appeal from the EC's *Gencor/Lonrho decision.*

[60] The CFI argued that there is no need for oligopolists to be interrelated by some specific links in order to prove that collective dominance exists.

[61] See Caffarra and Ysewyn (1998).

[62] In 1992, Thomson had 24% of the market, Airtours 11%, First Choice 6% and Thomas Cook 4%. In 1998, Thomson had 30.7%, Airtours 19.4%, First Choice 15% and Thomas Cook 20.4% of the market, the next operator being Cosmos/Avro with 2.9% of the market.

[63] The EC was aware that full collusion in prices could not be sustained. In this industry firms' decisions are at two different levels. At a planning stage, a firm decides the overall capacity (mainly seats on charter flights and rooms in hotels) for the following 12–18 months. In the selling stage, firms compete under the constraint of the capacity previously chosen, and they have a strong incentive to fill capacity, especially if one considers that package holidays are "perishable goods" (a given package loses all its value if not sold before its departure date). For this reason, considerable price discounts with respect to catalogue prices are common when the departure dates are approaching. The temptation to deviate from a collusive price would accordingly be strong, and the threat of punishment within a selling period has little credibility due to the capacity constraint.

[64] Motta (2000) suggests to use Staiger and Wolak (1992) to rationalise the EC decision. They analyse collusion in a model, which shares many of the characteristics of the package tour industry. In the repeated game they analyse, each period is composed of three stages. First, firms choose capacity without knowing demand, then the level of demand is disclosed, and finally they choose market prices on the basis of demand and under the capacity constraints determined by the previous choice. The authors find that various price levels can be sustained at the collusive equilibrium and that collusive equilibria arise where firms collude by restricting their capacity levels but then set prices which are not the fully collusive ones. In particular, given the levels of capacity choices, "for moderately bad demand realizations, firms simply initiate a uniform price reduction below the joint monopoly price, but if demand conditions turn sufficiently sour, firms will escalate the price

Overall, the industry presented some features favourable to collusion and others less favourable to it. It was difficult to prove joint dominance here, and the EC probably wanted to rely on this concept to prohibit a merger which it could not otherwise block.[65]

However, the CFI annulled the EC decision in June 2002, arguing that it had not sufficiently proved that the merger would have led to joint dominance. This judgement is welcome in two respects. First, had its decision been upheld, the EC might have prohibited other mergers where joint dominance was far from unambiguous. Second, because it has obliged (along with two other cases, where the parties successfully challenged the EC merger prohibition decisions, see *Schneider v. Commission* and *Tetra Laval v. Commission*) the EC to fully reconsider its merger policy, in particular with respect to the issue of how to deal with unilateral effects, that is, how to prohibit mergers, which are welfare-detrimental but do not create or strengthen dominance.

In January 2003 the EC submitted a proposal for the reform of the current Merger Regulation.[66] If accepted by the Council, an amendment to Article 2 of the Merger Regulation would state that (for the purpose of that regulation) two merging firms will be deemed to be dominant "... if, with or without coordinating, they hold the economic power to influence appreciably and sustainably the parameters of competition, in particular, prices, production, quality of output, distribution or innovation, or appreciably foreclose competition". In other words, a merger which raised prices through unilateral effects could be prohibited.[67]

5.6.2 The Treatment of Efficiency Gains

As showed in this chapter, economic analysis suggests that competition agencies should carefully assess the likely efficiency gains of a merger. However difficult a task, they should try to estimate whether or not these efficiency gains are likely to offset the higher market power enjoyed by the merging firms. This is precisely the approach indicated by the US Department of Justice, which

> ... will not challenge a merger if cognizable efficiencies are of a character and magnitude such that the merger is not likely to be anticompetitive in any relevant market. To make

war and undercut one another in equilibrium". (Staiger and Wolak, 1992: 205) Note that the EC did not rely on this model in its decision.

[65] It is very possible that blocking the *Airtours/First Choice* decision might have been the correct decision (at least given the product market defined by the EC, and that no efficiency gains are mentioned in the decision) because of unilateral effects.

[66] *EC Proposal for Merger Reform.*

[67] The proposal represents a compromise between two extreme positions expressed by Member States. The first is to keep the dominance test as it is, and the second to replace it with a "substantial lessening of competition" test, under which, like in the US, a merger is blocked if it has the effect of increasing prices.

the requisite determination, the Agency considers whether cognizable efficiencies likely would be sufficient to reverse the merger's potential to harm consumers in the relevant market, e.g., by preventing price increases in that market. In conducting this analysis, the Agency will not simply compare the magnitude of the cognizable efficiencies with the magnitude of the likely harm to competition absent the efficiencies. The greater the potential adverse competitive effect of a merger . . . the greater must be cognizable efficiencies in order for the Agency to conclude that the merger will not have an anticompetitive effect in any relevant market. When the potential adverse competitive effect of a merger is likely to be particularly large, extraordinarily great cognizable efficiencies would be necessary to prevent the merger from being anti-competitive. (*US Merger Guidelines:* Section 4).

The EC has a more ambiguous approach towards efficiency gains. Looking at the wording of the Merger Regulation one cannot say that an efficiency defence is explicitly allowed, but neither that this is ruled out. Article 2.1(b) says that in its appraisal of the merger, the Commission shall take into account, among other things ". . . the interests of the intermediate and ultimate consumers, and the development of technical and economic progress provided that it is to consumers' advantage and does not form an obstacle to competition".[68]

The legislative history of the Merger Regulation has sometimes been mentioned as supporting the view that there exists no efficiency defence in EC competition law. This is because in a previous draft of the Regulation a sentence which would have allowed for some efficiency defence has been suppressed from the final text, allegedly showing explicit intention of the legislators not to allow for such a defence. However, the legislators wanted to exclude not an efficiency defence argument in general, but rather the possibility that it could be used to support industrial policy arguments. Some countries, such as France, wanted to allow mergers which could have created "national champions". This view was successfully opposed by countries such as the UK and Germany, which wanted to rule out the possibility that anti-competitive mergers could have been approved on the grounds that they could have strengthened European firms in the international marketplace.[69] Therefore, what the "travaux préparatoires" of the Merger Regulation show is that social, political and industrial policy arguments should not be used in the assessment of mergers. Since efficiency gains are a key aspect in determining the *economic welfare* impact of mergers, there is no contradiction between the spirit of the legislators and the use of an efficiency defence.

So far, the EC in its decisions has not explicitly ruled out the possibility of using an efficiency defence, but it has not showed much sympathy for this argument either. Whenever cost reductions have been claimed by the merging parties, the

---

[68] This wording is similar to Article 81 (3), which allows an efficiency defence for agreements.

[69] See Noël (1997: 503) and Goyder (1993).

EC has dismissed those claims on various grounds.[70] The most interesting decision in this respect is *Aérospatiale-Alenia/de Havilland,* where the EC argued that the cost savings would have been negligible, had not been properly quantified, were not merger-specific (they could have been attained without the need of a concentration) and would not have gone in any case to consumers' advantage.

5.6.2.1 Efficiency Offence?

At times, the EC has been accused of using an efficiency *offence* argument, that is holding cost savings against the merger, so as to protect competitors.[71] Recently, for instance, commentators made this accusation with respect to the *General Electric/ Honeywell* decision (see Chapter 6).

Similar concerns have also been expressed in other cases where the EC has proposed the so-called "portfolio theory" of merger effects.[72] This "theory" concerns mergers between firms that produce goods which do not belong to the same relevant product market but are somehow related or complementary. The merging firms could then sell them together and gain market power because buyers would prefer to be supplied by the same firm rather than by different firms.[73] In turn, the merged firms might use their market power in an anti-competitive way, and competitors would be forced to exit the industry as a result of the merger.

Behind these arguments there are in my opinion two possibly related but conceptually different issues. (1) Is it possible that merged firms become so efficient that, even if they do not behave strategically, competitors will be forced to exit the market? And if this happens, is that welfare detrimental? (2) Would two merging firms be able to exploit their (market or financial) power so as to force rivals to exit?

(1) It is theoretically possible (see technical Section 5.4.4) that two merging firms might have such important cost savings or demand efficiencies (offering a full range of products is an example) that – without engaging in any anti-competitive practice – rivals would be unable to compete on equal footing with them. Two comments should be made, though.

---

[70] See Noël (1997: 512–4). Among the cases where the defendants have raised efficiency considerations are *Aérospatiale-Alenia/de Havilland, Accor/Wagon-Lits, MSG/Media Services, Mercedes-Benz/Kässbohrer.*

[71] See Noël (1997) and Neven, Nuttall and Seabright (1993: 62), who refer to *AT&T/NCR.*

[72] See *Guinness/Grand Metropolitan, Coca-Cola/Amalgamated Beverages* and *Coca-Cola/Carlsberg* decisions.

[73] For example, in *Guinness/Grand Met,* the merger would have allowed these two firms to have a complete portfolio of alcoholic beverages (gin, vodka, whisky, rum and so on), and this would have reinforced their competitive positions due to economies of scale and of scope but also better bargaining power with buyers, who would prefer to deal with one supplier selling a whole range of products rather than many suppliers each selling a subset of products only.

First, if efficiencies are so strong, it is possible that consumer surplus is higher after the merger – even if the competitive disadvantage obliged some firms to exit – than before the merger.[74] Second, and more important, if the merger gives rise to such important cost savings, should we not expect that competitors would react to attain the same economies, rather than waiting to be forced out of the market? In the case of product portfolio, for instance, competitors will sooner rather than later realise that buyers appreciate being supplied with a full range of products, and take steps to do the same, either by merging or by starting new brands filling the gaps in their product offerings. Therefore, it would be a mistake to prohibit a merger which creates efficiencies, as competitors will react to keep their competitiveness high.[75]

(2) It is in principle also possible that the merged entity will exploit its superior market or financial position to engage in anti-competitive practices aimed at forcing rivals to exit. However, there is a good reason not to support this version of the efficiency offence argument. As I shall show in Chapter 7, predatory practices should be expected only in some particular circumstances, and are much rarer than one would expect. Rejecting a merger, which entails *certain* efficiency gains today, because of *possible* predatory behaviour in the future, does not seem a welfare-improving decision (see also the discussion of *General Electric/Honeywell* in Chapter 6). It would be better to first allow the merger and then, in case the merged entity tried to monopolise the industry, use anti-trust laws (Article 82 in the EU, Section 2 in the US) to stop anti-competitive behaviour.[76]

5.6.3 Conclusions

The EU merger policy contains several positive aspects. Among others, it gives firms a one-stop shop for mergers, thus sparing them from excessive administrative and

---

[74] Higher consumer surplus might come from demand efficiencies (such as having access to a complete portfolio of products), from lower prices due to cost savings, or from lower prices due to complementarity: a firm selling two complementary products will charge a lower price than when the same products are sold by independent firms (see Chapter 8.2, and Chapter 6 for the equivalent case of vertically related products).

[75] To formalise such arguments, one should model mergers as a dynamic process, and possibly one where firms endogenously choose which partners they want to have. For endogenous mergers, see for instance Kamien and Zang (1990), Horn and Persson (2001) and Gowrisankaran (1999). The last paper takes a dynamic setting into account, in the sense that firms also take investment decisions (but the analysis becomes extremely complex: analytical results are not obtained). See also Motta and Vasconcelos (2003) for a dynamic model dealing with the effects of efficiency gains.

[76] The reader might think that there is a similarity between the argument that calls for blocking an efficiency-enhancing merger because it might create the scope for predation and the one that calls for blocking a merger because it creates more opportunities for collusion (joint dominance). However, there is a fundamental difference. In the former case, by definition the merger creates efficiencies and therefore a prohibition decision would have a cost that would not occur in the latter case.

legal costs. It provides a reasonably quick, effective, and certain time horizon for merger decisions. The Merger Task Force of the European Commission is also doing an impressive job, given the tight deadlines and the large number of cases it has to review.

However, the EU merger policy also has two main distortions. Firstly, it prohibits only mergers which create or reinforce dominance, whereas economic analysis suggests that there exist mergers which are detrimental to welfare even though they do not bring about dominance. Hence, some mergers are allowed which should instead be prohibited. Secondly, it does not recognise the role played by cost savings, which might give rise to positive welfare effects of mergers. Accordingly, efficiency gains should explicitly be taken into account, otherwise some mergers are prohibited which should instead be allowed.[77]

However, the EC has recently formulated some proposals which might have the effect of correcting both distortions. An amendment to the current Merger Regulation – if accepted by the Council – would allow prohibition of all mergers which would have the effect of increasing prices. Further, as of January 2003 merger guidelines are being drafted, and the importance of efficiency gains in the assessment of mergers seems to be fully recognised. Hopefully, the guidelines will create also some clarity with respect of the criteria used in joint dominance cases, which has caused considerable uncertainty among the business community.[78]

5.7 CASE STUDIES

This section first summarises the main steps of a merger analysis. Then it discusses two horizontal mergers dealt with by the EC: *Nestlé/Perrier* (the first case of joint dominance) and *ABB/Daimler-Benz* (interesting for the importance given to buyer power). A third case, *General Electric/Honeywell*, which has conglomerate and vertical aspects, is discussed in Chapter 6.

---

[77] Consideration of efficiency gains would require a clarification from the relevant authority as to the relevant standard in the assessment of mergers (and more generally of competition policy). This is because different efficiency gains might be considered as acceptable according to whether a consumer surplus or a total surplus standard is adopted.

[78] In the current version of the guidelines (as of January 2003), the EC plans to use the HHI concentration index in a similar way as the US Horizontal Merger Guidelines, but not for joint dominance cases, where no quantitative threshold is offered as an indication that the merger might give rise to joint dominance or not. Instead, the EC should offer more guidance to firms, for instance committing not to review mergers in industries with a HHI lower than, say, 2000. The HHI has some foundation because – although it does not take into account the role of symmetry in helping collusion – concentration is probably a very crucial factor in affecting collusion. Further, such an index of concentration could be easily computed by all interested parties. Needless to say, many other factors should then be considered in the deeper reviews (phase II of merger investigations), but at least such a first screening device would save firms' and agencies' resources and would eliminate considerable uncertainty.

5.7.1 How to Proceed in Merger Cases

There are two main questions that competition authorities should ask themselves before allowing a merger. The first question is (1) *Will the merger create unilateral effects?*, that is: will merging firms increase prices in a considerable way? If the answer to this first question is negative, there is still a second question to be asked, that is (2) *Will the merger create pro-collusive effects?*, that is: would the merger modify the conditions of the industry so that collusion will be much more likely?[79] I briefly recall here the aspects that should be considered in each of these questions.

Unilateral Effects   The most direct way to assess the extent to which two merging firms might exercise market power is to ask whether they will be able to impose higher prices after the merger. This might be done by using the recent econometric techniques (such as those described in Chapter 3). In several cases, however, it is difficult to carry out a direct estimation, for lack of reliable data, or insufficient time to collect and elaborate them. Even when such an econometric exercise is done, its results might not give a definite answer without an additional analysis. One should then resort to a more traditional approach, by first defining the *relevant (product and geographical) market* in which the merger takes place and then assessing the degree of *market power* enjoyed by the merging companies (see both Section 5.2.2 and Chapter 3).

Whether an estimate of the market power enjoyed by the merging firms and of the likely impact on prices is carried out through econometric techniques or a more traditional approach, the following step will be to take into account likely, verifiable and merger-specific *efficiency gains*. If these gains are shown to exist, the difficult question will then be to trade-off the two effects, and predict whether efficiency gains will outweigh the negative impact of increased market power (see Section 5.2.3).

After these steps, two cases might arise: one is that the merger is likely to enable the firms to significantly raise prices beyond the current level. Hence, the merger should be prohibited, or allowed only if some *remedies* can be identified (see Section 5.5). The other case is that the unilateral effects of the merger would not jeopardise competition in the industry. However, the investigation should still deal with the possibility that collusion arises after the merger, the issue which we turn to next.

Pro-Collusive Effects   To understand whether the merger will make collusion more likely in the sector, a number of elements should be considered. Chapter 4 deals at length with the factors that facilitate collusion, and these will have

---

[79] Under the current EU Merger Regulation (as well as in all jurisdictions where a dominance test is adopted), the first step would be different: it would consist of asking whether the merger leads to single-firm dominance.

to be taken into account to establish the likelihood that the merger will have pro-collusive effects. Among other factors, recall concentration, entry barriers, structural links such as cross-ownership and joint-ventures, agreements about information exchange, multi-market contacts, regularity of market interactions, the absence of countervailing power, and the existence of clauses (such as best-price clauses and retail price maintenance) that increase observability of firms' actions.

If there exists little risk of increased collusion, the merger should be cleared. Otherwise, it might be cleared only if some remedies can be imposed that ensure that collusion will not be likely to occur in the industry after the merger.

5.7.2 *Nestlé/Perrier*

This is the first case of a merger which was challenged by the European Commission (EC) on the grounds that it would have given rise to joint dominance.

In 1991, IFINT, an Italian company belonging to the Agnelli family, launched a bid to gain control of the French company Perrier, operating in the mineral water industry. The bid was followed by a counter-offer from Nestlé, a Swiss multinational, which had previously reached an agreement with BSN, both firms being active in the mineral water industry. After a period of uncertainty the takeover battle was won by Nestlé. Under the terms of the agreement, Nestlé would have sold the Volvic source of Perrier to BSN.

After a detailed investigation, the EC decided that the operation would have resulted in joint dominance of the mineral water market in France by Nestlé/Perrier and BSN. Eventually, the merger was cleared subject to certain conditions (some of the Perrier sources would have to be transferred to an independent producer).

In what follows, I analyse the case by first looking at whether the merger might have given rise to single-firm dominance (and whether it might have lead to uni-lateral effects), and then by analysing the likelihood that it might have created joint dominance.

Product Market Definition   The first step of the investigation required the def-inition of the product and geographical market. I deal with each of these points separately.

The main problem for the definition of the product market in this case was to decide whether mineral water belongs to the same market as soft drinks and, if not, whether a distinction should be made between fizzy and still mineral water.

The EC conducted a qualitative analysis. It looked at the characteristics of the products and found differences between mineral water and soft drinks: the former has the image of a pure, natural product, it is associated with healthy living and it is thought to satisfy a basic need. The latter does not have any of these characteristics and it is consumed in a much more occasional way. It also found that both consumer surveys and interviews with retailers indicated that mineral water and soft drinks are not enough substitutes to belong to the same market.

On the production side, the EC pointed at market differences. There exist a number of regulatory constraints in the production of mineral water (especially in France), the most important being that production of mineral water needs an authorisation; bottling must be done at the source; and water must be marketed with a brand name which is associated with the source. (Spring waters, which have inferior characteristics with respect to mineral waters, have to be bottled at the source but they can be marketed with a different brand name.) None of these constraints apply to soft drink producers, whose main input is tap water and which do not have to follow particular production and marketing requirements.

As for quantitative criteria, first the EC found that there exists a considerable difference in price levels, since soft drinks are sold on average at a mill price which is two to three times higher than the price of mineral water. This would point, it argued, at a certain separation of the two markets. It also found that correlation coefficients of prices of different mineral waters range from 0.85 to 1, whereas the correlation coefficients between prices of mineral water and prices of soft drinks are either very low or negative: during the five years before 1992 mineral water prices tended to increase whereas soft drinks prices tended to decrease.[80]

As for supply substitution, it is limited. Because of the regulation on production and marketing, plants used to produce soft drinks cannot be switched to production of source water. In principle, it is possible to start production of bottled water by a process which purifies tap water (in some countries this is done). However, the EC argued that there exists no evidence that this would be accepted by consumers as a reasonably good substitute for mineral water, nor is it known whether any producer is planning to enter the market in such a way.

The EC also argued that no distinction should be made between markets for sparkling, still and flavoured waters. Despite some differences in prices, it appears that from the technical point of view it would be extremely easy for a producer to switch from sparkling to still waters and vice versa.

In the light of information published in the decision, the conclusion that the relevant product market is represented by bottled mineral water would seem difficult to object to. However, some of the arguments made by the EC are irrelevant. As discussed in Chapter 3, product market definition should be analysed by relying on the SSNIP test, and asking whether a hypothetical monopolist of mineral water would find it profitable to significantly increase prices by 5–10%. In this perspective, some of the factors analysed by the EC do not help to answer this question: differences in demand and supply characteristics between two products, as well as differences

---

[80] Cross-price elasticities and demand elasticity were not computed, but the EC argued that a small increase in the price of waters would not lead to a significant shift in demand from mineral water to soft drinks.

in price levels, do not tell us to which extent these products exercise a competitive constraint on each other (see Chapter 3 for a more detailed discussion).

Furthermore, at the stage of market definition the difference between mineral and spring waters was not analysed properly, even though the EC attached much importance to it later in the decision, when it analysed market power (see para. 55 and the tables after para. 39). In particular, the decision later argued that local spring waters are not considered a good substitute for mineral waters by most of the wholesalers and retailers (para. 84). This should have been taken into account when defining the relevant market.

Geographic Market   The EC defines the relevant market as the French market, using the following arguments: first, transport costs of mineral water are extremely high with respect to its value (between ten and twenty per cent for every 300 kilometres, depending on whether plastic or glass bottles are used). Second, there exists very little trade between EC countries, with the exception of Belgium where imports are high (but as discussed in Chapter 3, low trade flows are not necessarily an indication that two countries should be considered as separate markets: the right question, in view of the SSNIP test, is whether after a price rise imports would occur). Third, entry into the French market is also made difficult because this is a mature market with very established brand names, and a very large advertising effort would be needed to acquire considerable market shares. In the case of German producers, entry is also made more difficult by the fact that in Germany mineral water is mostly sold in glass bottles of 75 cl, while in France plastic bottles of various capacities are used.

The definition of the French market as the relevant market seems reasonable. The only possible alternative could have been to define the market as composed of both Belgium and France (a price correlation analysis could have been interesting from this point of view), but I doubt this would have affected the results of the investigation.

Single-Firm Dominance   The next step in the EC investigation (dominance being the legal test under the Merger Regulation) was to see whether the merger between Nestlé and Perrier raised fears of single-firm dominance.

Nestlé, BSN and Perrier own several sources: Nestlé owns Vittel and Hépar; Perrier owns Perrier, Contrex, Volvic, St. Yorre, Thonon and Vichy, as well as a number of local spring waters; BSN owns Evian and Badoit.[81] The three firms hold 82.3% of the market in value and 76% in volume. Individual market shares were not published in the Commission decision for business secrecy reasons. Some information about them can be found in Sutton (1991: table M.12), who estimates

---

[81] Ferrarelle and San Pellegrino, two Italian waters present in the French market, are controlled by BSN and Perrier respectively.

the BSN share at about 25%, Nestlé at 20–25%, Volvic at 7% and other sources of Perrier at about 20–25%. Since the EC found that market shares have been stable over the recent years, Sutton's estimates are useful even if they refer to 1986. Neven, Nuttall and Seabright (1993: 103) value the market share of Nestlé at 15.6% and that of Perrier at 31.9%. According to these estimates (roughly consistent with the aggregate values given in the decision), a merger of Nestlé and Perrier would result in a single firm having a market share of around 45–55%, with the largest rival having a share of about 25% of the market, enough to start an analysis of single dominance.

However, because of the transfer of the Volvic source to BSN, challenging the merger on the basis of single-firm dominance is much weaker: the largest competitor, BSN, would have more than 30% of the market. Furthermore, the analysis of capacities of the different sources reveals that Volvic had the largest capacity in the industry. For these reasons, it would seem difficult to argue that the operation involving the merger of Nestlé/Perrier and the transfer of Volvic to BSN would have created single-firm dominance: Nestlé/Perrier could not "behave independently" of BSN.

Unilateral Effects   It is interesting to wonder how different the investigation would have been if the EC had followed a different test, which requires not the finding of dominance, but rather that of a price increase: would this merger be likely to raise prices?

First, note that the market is highly concentrated (a feature which makes it more likely that prices will increase after the merger, see Section 5.2.2), with three producers (two after the merger) having more than 80% of the market. The remaining market shares are divided by a number of fragmented producers, mainly selling spring waters locally. Neven et al. (1993: 103) estimate the lower bound of the post-merger HHI at 2660 and the change in the HHI at 1000, very high values if one considers the US merger guidelines as a benchmark.

Next, we should wonder to what extent a price rise would be constrained by supply substitution or potential entry. Nestlé/Perrier and BSN do not seem to have important (actual or potential) competitors. The local producers are very fragmented. In principle, they could start to market their spring waters under a common brand name, but such waters have different features and are perceived as lower quality products relative to mineral water. None of the local producers seem to have enough financial power to start a massive advertising campaign.[82] This market is well described by a vertical product differentiation model where the product quality as perceived by the consumer depends on advertising outlays, which are a sunk cost, which would not be recovered by entrants. The endogenous sunk cost paradigm

---

[82] Promotion and advertising expenditures for the major brands have been high for years and amount to roughly 10% of the brand turnover. See para. 96.

applies neatly to this industry. One of its implications is that we should expect persistence of concentration in such a sector even when the market size increases (Sutton, 1991).

The same is true for potential entrants from other countries or other industries. Transport costs are important, entry barriers due to regulations are significant, and it is unlikely that a firm could successfully enter the market by introducing purified tap water.

Let us now consider demand variables. The EC argued that there is a low elasticity of market demand with respect to price (although no estimates are provided in the decision), which points to a certain room for raising prices. As for the power of the buyers, it turns out that the ten largest buyers of bottled mineral water account for around 70% of the total sales of Nestlé, Perrier and BSN, with the first four distribution groups (Intermarché, Leclerc, Carrefour and Promodes) representing 50% of purchases. Nevertheless, none of the buyers alone go beyond 11%. Further, the leading mineral waters are brands that most consumers are loyal customers of. Large buyers would risk losing some of their clientele (and the loss would concern all the range of goods sold, not just water) if they replaced such brands with "own labels", that is local spring waters sold under the distributors' brand name.

The majority of retailers and wholesalers interviewed by the EC indicate that the merger would further diminish their bargaining power with respect to both Nestlé and BSN. The range of mineral waters they sell would be broader and this would give them further power since discounts are usually given on the basis of the volumes purchased on the whole range of waters offered (see para. 83 and 84). This is an example of "pecuniary" economies of scope from the merger: they do not represent a gain for the economy as a whole, but just a shift in bargaining power from purchasers to suppliers.[83] In conclusion, it is unlikely that the bargaining power of the buyers could have limited the market power of the producers.

Finally, although the decision does not address this issue, we should look at possible efficiency gains. The analysis of the production process and of the industry in general suggests that the merger is unlikely to cause substantial cost savings. Regulatory constraints do not allow firms to concentrate production of different mineral waters. Hence, no scale economies could be expected from the merger. Further, since each brand should be bottled at the source and marketed under its own name, it is hard to find any economies of scope. By having a broader spectrum of brands, Nestlé and BSN might reap pecuniary scale economies at the stage of advertising and distribution, since they might be able to enjoy larger discounts from jointly advertising more brands and imposing better terms in negotiations with retailers. But these are not economies which we would classify as efficiency gains, and they might instead allow the firms to charge higher prices.

---

[83] Even Nestlé is said to acknowledge that it would be difficult for a buyer to do without the brands supplied by the leading water producers (para. 86).

Other possible synergies or economies, such as on research and development, are irrelevant given the characteristics of the industry. It is not clear at all that the merger would give rise to administrative economies or more efficient management of the firms involved. But these are hardly merger-specific economies and we know that they are extremely difficult to measure.

In conclusion, if the merger had been assessed according to a "substantial lessening of competition" test, the analysis of unilateral effects would have revealed that it was very likely to increase prices, and, most probably, it would have accordingly been prohibited.

Joint Dominance (Pro-Collusive Effects)   As seen above, the EC did not find that the merger would lead to single-firm dominance, and turned next to the issue of whether it would lead to joint dominance.

Some of the variables which might play a role in determining the ability of Nestlé/Perrier and BSN to reach a collusive outcome after the merger have already been mentioned. The industry is highly concentrated; neither existing small local producers and potential entrants nor buyers would be able to exercise a constraint on the ability of Nestlé/Perrier and BSN to jointly raise prices.

Other factors seem to facilitate a collusive outcome in this industry. First, it is characterised by short information lags and frequent transactions, which favour collusion.

Second, we know from Chapter 4 that observability of firms' market decisions is a crucial element for collusion, since it allows detection of deviations (and in turn timely punishments). Market transparency is extremely high in this industry:[84]

> The three national suppliers publish their list prices with the basic quantity rebates. Since they all supply the same customers, there is also a considerable feedback from these customers. In addition, the three suppliers provide the Chambre syndicale des eaux minérales with their monthly sales volumes and each one receives the monthly sales quantities broken down by brand of the other suppliers. In a narrow oligopoly such a practice further increases the market transparency and permits each supplier to follow the evolution of the market positions of the others. (*Nestlé/Perrier:* para. 62.)

Not surprisingly, the history of the industry does not suggest that fierce competition takes place:

> The ex-works prices (before rebates and VAT) of the five major still mineral waters of the three national suppliers have constantly increased in a parallel way since at least

---

[84] Interestingly, transportation costs are incurred directly by customers. This also increases observability, as it would be more difficult to hide a price discount behind more favourable terms of transportation. In the *Sugar Institute* case, transportation fees were a constant source of problems for the sugar retailers, and they repeatedly intervened to prevent possible price deviations through better fees offered to customers (Genesove and Mullin, 2001).

1987 . . . Whoever first increased its prices was always followed by the other two suppliers. There was no price decrease during the whole period considered. The price leader seems always to have been Perrier which has traditionally maintained the highest price level for most of its products. (*Nestlé/Perrier:* para. 59.)

There also exists a certain degree of symmetry between the firms. As for the technological point of view, Nestlé acknowledges that the main brands of the three producers have a similar cost structure (para. 63), and the merger is unlikely to create any efficiency gain that would disrupt this symmetry. Further, Compte, Jenny and Rey (2002) carefully document the symmetry existing among the firms, especially in terms of their capacities (their paper has a theoretical section, mentioned also in Chapter 4, where the symmetric distribution of capacities is a crucial element for collusion). They also show that absent the transfer of Volvic to BSN, Nestlé/Perrier would have a much larger total capacity than BSN, which could reduce the sustainability of collusion in the industry. Therefore, they identify the transfer of Volvic as an essential part of the transaction, as it ensures that the conditions for a collusive outcome are maintained.

Conclusions   The EC rightly thought that with the acquisition by Nestlé of Perrier, and the transfer of Volvic to BSN, a dominant position would be jointly held by the two firms, due to their symmetric situation in the industry and to the market environment which was favourable to collusive outcomes.[85] However, the merger with Perrier, plus the transfer of Volvic to BSN, were allowed under the condition that Nestlé would have sold to a third party the brands Vichy, Thonon, Pierval, Saint-Yorre as well as some minor local spring waters. According to the EC, these waters would represent a capacity of around 20% of Nestlé, Perrier and BSN together, even though the market shares of such brands are not very high.[86]

In my opinion, the EC should have blocked the merger *tout court.* The characteristics of the industry (high concentration, high price observability, symmetry, a history of parallel price increases) strongly suggest that the firms have been able to tacitly collude over time.

Further, the fact that Nestlé and BSN reacted immediately and of common agreement when an outsider like IFINT tried to enter the industry by taking over Perrier is a clear indicator of the coordination between them. My interpretation of the events is that the incumbent firms had managed through time to coordinate themselves in such a way to reach a collusive outcome. When a potential entrant jeopardised the stability of this outcome, they reacted together to put an end to this threat.

---

[85] The EC also argued that if Nestlé had taken over Perrier and kept the Volvic brand for itself, it would have enjoyed a single-firm dominant position.

[86] Neven, Nuttall and Seabright (1993: 103) estimate the post-merger HHI after the remedy at 2310, and the change in HHI at 640, which are still very high values of concentration.

Allowing the transfer of Volvic to BSN would only worsen matters, as it increases the degree of symmetry between Nestlé/Perrier and BSN, and facilitates a collusive outcome (see Compte et al., 2002), that the remedy accepted is unlikely to disrupt.

5.7.3 *ABB/Daimler-Benz*

This case concerns the proposed joint-venture between Asea Brown Boveri (ABB), a Swedish–Swiss company, and Daimler-Benz, a German company, to form ABB Daimler-Benz Transportation. The joint-venture would incorporate all the activities of the parent companies in the sphere of rail technology.

Product Market Definition   Defining the relevant market in this case is not easy. Rail technology can be divided into more detailed market segments. The first and most obvious division is between rolling stock (mainly rail vehicles) and stationary equipment and each of them can in turn be divided into lower segmentations. The problem is that among such market segments there exist a number of relationships of complementarity and substitutability which make the analysis more difficult. For instance, and more obviously, rolling stock and stationary equipment can be sold independently when they need to be replaced, but they are basically complementary and need to be matched. Electrical and diesel locomotives are substitutes, but locomotives and passenger coaches are complements, although taken together they are substitutable with respect to complete train sets for mainline transportation. Further, when considering rail vehicles, one should probably draw a distinction (not explicitly made in the decision) between the mechanical and the electrical elements of vehicles (the latter account for 55–60% of the value added).

Transactions in this industry do not occur frequently, and it is difficult to resort to quantitative tests such as price collinearity or cross-price elasticities.

The EC defined fifteen separate markets (see right-hand side column in Table 5.1), in the light of surveys with competitors and with customers.

Geographic Market   The relevant geographic market is defined as the German market. This is because in Europe there exist a number of particular national product specifications (e.g., different mains voltages and frequencies, track gauges and safety systems) and because public procurement policies have always favoured local suppliers, thereby separating effectively the markets into national ones. Indeed, it appears that imports into Germany have occurred very rarely.

Despite increased liberalisation in the transportation markets and a possible change in procurement policies away from the traditional national biases, this situation of market segmentation is not likely to change rapidly. Actually, it appears that the familiarity of suppliers with customers' specific requirements plays an important

Table 5.1. Product Market Definition in the Rail Technology Industry

Rolling stock		
	Mainline trains	Electrical locomotives
		Diesel locomotives
		Train sets for mainline transportation
		Passenger coaches
		Freight wagons
	Regional trains	Electrical multiple units
		Diesel multiple units
	Local trains and systems	Trams (light rail and trolleys)
		Metro vehicles
		Automated guided transportation
Stationary equipment		
	Wayside systems	Catenary systems
		Traction power supply
		Train control and protection systems
	Miscellaneous	Maintenance and refurbishment
		Information systems and ticketing

role. The existence of these "switching costs" means that customers will tend to give preference to previous suppliers. It is only when a completely new system must be put in place that potential entrants will be on an equal basis with incumbents.

The necessity of adapting to different national technical standards works as a fixed exogenous cost of entry: such an investment would be worthwhile in case of a very important contract but not of a small one. This plays an important role in the Commission's decision.

Market Shares and Concentration Table 5.2 shows market shares and concentration indices in eight selected product markets, namely those which raised substantial concerns according to the EC.[87] In the remaining product markets the joint-venture does not have enough market shares to distort competition or create a dominant position.

As Table 5.2 shows, it is unlikely that the joint-venture between ABB and Daimler-Benz could create a single-firm dominant position, since Siemens enjoys a strong market position in all the product markets considered. Nevertheless, the figures reported do show that the markets taken into account are extremely concentrated.

---

[87] The EC computed market shares by looking at the orders won in the three years before the case. I computed concentration indices by using information provided in the decision. Since information about market shares is incomplete – they do not add up to 100% – the indices reported give the lower bound of concentration.

Table 5.2. Market Shares and Concentration Indexes in the Rail Technology Industry

Product Market	Market Shares (%)						HHI	ΔHHI
	ABB	DB	Siemens	DWA	LHB	Elpro		
Electrical locom.	37	17	46	na	na	na	5032	1258
Mainline train sets	5	26	46	18	na	na	>3401	260
Reg. electr. m/units	18	26	25	17	14	na	>3046	936
Reg. diesel m/units	0	49	23	na	19	na	>3291	0
Trams	15	29	41	na	8	na	> 3681	870
Metro vehicles	42	22	19	na	11	na	>4578	1848
Catenary systems	30	31	33	na	na	6	4846	1860
Traction power supply	6	26	35	na	na	13	> 2418	312

If the merger had been proposed in a jurisdiction with a "substantial lessening of competition" test, the merger might have been blocked because of unilateral effects (but there is no information on efficiency gains in the decision).

A quick glance at the combined market shares of ABB and Daimler-Benz reveals that the merger would establish a situation of market symmetry between the merging firms on one hand and Siemens on the other. Given also the very high industrial concentration levels, the possibility that the merger might lead to joint dominance should be taken very seriously.

Joint Dominance or the Coordinated Effects of the Merger   Let us consider the different structural variables which might affect the possibility that the merger enhances the scope for collusion.

First, I look at whether existing rivals or potential entrants might limit the ability to (jointly) raise prices. The strengths of ABB/Daimler-Benz and Siemens are probably understated in Table 5.2. These firms have the technology needed to supply both the mechanical engineering and the electrical components of a rail system, whereas most of the rivals are not "full-line suppliers". Since customers tend to demand the whole product range, the ability of ABB/Daimler-Benz and Siemens to increase prices is somehow enhanced by the fact that most of the competitors would not be able to satisfy orders alone (either because they lack electrical technology, or because they do not supply the whole range of products necessary to provide the full-line product). Further, some of the existing rivals are relatively small firms which would not be able to cope with very large orders. Indeed, most of the orders won by the rivals have been obtained thanks to co-operation with either ABB or Daimler-Benz (and its subsidiary AEG) or Siemens. In particular, one of the rare orders won by a foreign firm was won by the Canadian firm Bombardier which had to rely on Kiepe, a subsidiary of Daimler-Benz/AEG, for the necessary electrical components.

A crucial point is to understand if the ability of the firms to raise prices would be limited by potential entrants. From this point of view, it should be taken into account that there exists only one firm which has the same characteristics as ABB/Daimler-Benz and Siemens, and this is the French firm GEC-Alsthom. The EC interestingly remarks that it might not be a profitable strategy for GEC-Alsthom to act aggressively in the German market, since this would probably invite a retaliatory response by ABB/Daimler-Benz and Siemens in the French market.[88] Further (see below), GEC-Alsthom has a series of co-operative arrangements with the German companies, which render less likely an aggressive entry into the German market.

There are also other foreign firms which are operating in the rail technology sectors, but so far their interest in the German market has been rather limited, or their bids have been unsuccessful. It should also be recalled that the national technical specifications do represent an obstacle for foreign firms. Finally, it should be noted that DWA – an independent firm – has been trying to create its own electrical engineering capacity through its subsidiary FAGA, but it is unclear whether these efforts are going to be successful in the future.

One point that distinguishes the different product markets considered is the bargaining *power of the buyers.* (This will lead the EC to eventually declare the merger compatible with the common market in the national and regional trains markets but not in the local trains and systems markets.)

The only client for mainline trains is the national railways company Deutsche Bahn AG. At the other extreme, there are a number of customers for local trains and systems: the EC identified 58 German municipal transport companies, which have purchased trams, buses and metro systems. Intermediate between the two cases are the regional trains.

The EC attached great importance to the fact that Deutsche Bahn is a monopsonist for the mainline transportation market, and as such in principle able to influence the structure of supply. If Deutsche Bahn decided to group orders in such a way as to invite tenders for very large single orders, it would be able to attract the interest of foreign groups such as GEC-Alsthom, for instance. Facing very large orders, foreign firms would be willing to incur the fixed costs of changing their product specifications to meet the German technical standards.

The EC maintains that a number of factors will force Deutsche Bahn to exert its bargaining power and therefore stimulate competitive behaviour. Among these factors the EC mentions the fact that it has been transformed into a private company, that there are pressures for it to behave according to commercial rules, that it faces competition from other means of transportation, and that EU public procurement directives should not allow national biases in assigning orders.

---

[88] The scope for collusion when multi-market oligopolists exist (Bernheim and Whinston, 1990) has been underlined in Chapter 4.

Surprisingly, Deutsche Bahn declared that it was not concerned by the creation of the joint-venture and maintained that there would still be enough competition in the market.

It is not clear whether Deutsche Bahn would fully exert the bargaining power it has, especially once considered that it might still be subject to pressures to buy from a national source, since train sets for mainline transportation are seen as a matter of prestige and as a key reference product (para 73).

The situation is radically different for municipal companies, not so much because their bargaining power is split (once an order is tendered, the municipal company is a monopsonist as well) but because the orders are of much smaller sizes and therefore less attractive to foreign companies, for which the fixed costs of adapting to the German specifications would be less worth incurring.[89] Indeed, it appears that such local companies are much more worried about the joint-venture than Deutsche Bahn AG is.

As for regional trains, the presence of both Deutsche Bahn and smaller regional companies implies that the bargaining power of the buyers is weaker than for mainline trains but higher than in the case of local systems. However, the Commission attaches great importance to the fact that in the future Deutsche Bahn should play a bigger role in regional trains (para. 120). This is the main argument to justify the finding that in this product market the merger does not raise concern for the creation of a dominant position.

The EC argues that there should be enough competition outside the duopoly since LHB and DWA are both in a strong position. However, it appears that their market shares have been acquired thanks to co-operation with either ABB or AEG.

Let us now turn to other possible facilitating factors. After the merger, ABB/Daimler-Benz and Siemens would be in a condition of symmetry, having similar technological capabilities and offering similar product ranges.

On the other hand, the markets under consideration do not provide the best environment for a collusive outcome. Indeed, orders are not made frequently in this industry, and when they are made they usually are of very large size. This increases the incentives for the competitors to deviate: the temptation to get a rare and important order is strong.

However, the two duopolists are likely to be the main competitors in all the procurement contracts involving rail technologies at different levels (national, regional and local). Also, there seems to be a certain transparency in the public bids which should allow the competitor to control and monitor the moves of the rivals.[90]

---

[89] See Fumagalli and Motta (2001) for a formalisation of this link between buyer power and entry.

[90] It is a pity that we do not know more about the way in which the bids are conducted. Apparently, they are extremely open since the decision mentions that suppliers obtain further information even in the course of negotiations following the submission of tenders. See Chapter 4 on collusive behaviour in bidding markets.

The rail technology industry is also characterised by a very complex network of co-operative agreements involving all the main firms, which makes it difficult to perceive this sector as one where firms compete fiercely. The EC maintains that "On the market in mainline train sets, orders for the production of high-speed trains at least have in the past been placed with domestic consortia in which it was difficult to discern any internal competitive relationship. Thus Siemens, AEG and ABB collaborated on Deutsche Bahn's ICE 1. Siemens and AEG are currently collaborating on the ICE 2" (para. 111).

Also, the main pressure towards competitive behaviour in the industry should come from outsiders, the main one being GEC-Alsthom. However, this firm has already collaborative agreements with ABB/Daimler-Benz and Siemens. In particular, Siemens and GEC-Alsthom plan to co-operate to jointly market their high-speed train technology outside Europe (para. 112). Fiat Ferroviaria, the Italian firm which has developed an innovative tilt technology is already co-operating with Siemens (and DWA).

In the market for regional trains there are also co-operative arrangements between the firms, since successful tenders have been made by Siemens with AEG, LHB with ABB, DWA with AEG, AEG with Siemens and DWA, Siemens with LHB and AEG.

In the local trains, the web of co-operative arrangements is also very well established, and each firm has been involved in co-operative arrangements with basically any other major firm (see para. 125 for a list).

Efficiency Gains   It is difficult to assess the possible efficiency gains arising from the merger, given that this issue is not covered in the decision. Probably, the most important source of gains lies in economies of scope, especially at the level of mainline trains technology. According to the EC (para. 72) Daimler-Benz/AEG does not possess the key technologies to be a full supplier of train sets for mainline transportation. Indeed, it would have obtained market shares in this product market only through co-operative agreements with Siemens, the leader in the sector. However, ABB had already the necessary technology to be a full-line supplier even before the merger (like Siemens). It is also possible that division of labour can be fostered between ABB and Daimler-Benz, resulting in economies of scale. Overall, however, it does not seem that the nature of the scale economies might possibly disrupt the scope for a collusive outcome.

Conclusions   The EC declared the concentration between ABB and Daimler-Benz incompatible with the common market in the product market of trams (including light rail vehicles and electrical equipment for trolley buses) and metro vehicles, where a jointly dominant position along with Siemens would have been created. The parties committed to divest from the AEG/Daimler-Benz's subsidiary Kiepe, which possesses the electrical engineering technology, which is a key element for supplying a complete product in the local rail technology. If this firm is kept independent, other firms which possess the mechanical engineering technology will find an available partner for competing successfully in the local trains markets.

There are no major structural differences between the mainline, regional and local product markets in rail technology. The decision taken by the EC to find only the local trains product markets incompatible with the common market is clearly driven by the different weight given to buyer bargaining power. While in the mainline and regional markets Deutsche Bahn is identified as a buyer with a very strong bargaining power, this is not the case for the municipal companies operating in the local markets.

However, it is far from clear that in the regional markets Deutsche Bahn would have the same power as in the mainline trains. More importantly, though, it is not clear that the bargaining power of the buyer would be able to limit market power in the industry, for at least two reasons. The first one is that Deutsche Bahn might not exert such power, for instance because it would be subject to political pressures to prefer national firms with respect to foreign suppliers. Secondly, even if Deutsche Bahn were willing to invite bidding from outsiders it is not clear that a more competitive outcome would arise. The main firms in the rail industry have been involved in a number of co-operative arrangements both within and outside Germany, and the overall picture is not one of a very competitive industry. Further, the fact that national markets have been so far segmented along national borders, with national firms enjoying a dominant position locally, seems hardly to be an environment where one would expect fierce competitive incursions in each other's home turf.

5.8 EXERCISES

Exercise 5.1 *(Profitability of mergers)* In the model of Salant, Switzer and Reynolds (1983), n firms produce a homogenous good and compete in quantities. The authors show that mergers are almost always unprofitable for the insiders. (a) Give the intuition for the result obtained by these authors. (b) Explain under which conditions profitability of the merger for the firms taking part in it would be restored by making reference to models proposed in the merger literature.

Exercise 5.2 *(Salant, Switzer and Reynolds, 1983)* Consider n identical firms, which produce a perfectly homogenous good at constant marginal cost c. The market demand is given by $p = a - Q$, where Q is the total output produced in the industry. The strategic variable of the firms is output (Cournot game). (i) Find the equilibrium outputs and profits at a pre-merger situation, that is when all the n firms are independent. (ii) Consider now a merger between $m + 1$ firms (note that – because the products are homogenous and there are no capacity constraints – this amounts to having m firms less in the industry), and find equilibrium output and profit for each independent firm. (iii) Show that outsiders always gain from a merger. (iv) Show that a merger to monopoly is always profitable for the merging firms. (v) Take $n = 10$ and show that a merger is profitable only if $m + 1 \geq 9$.

Exercise 5.3   *(Cournot mergers with efficiency gains)* Consider an industry with three identical firms each selling a homogenous good and producing at a cost $c > 0$. Industry demand is given by $p = 1 - Q$. Competition in the marketplace is in quantities. (i) Find the equilibrium quantities, price and profits. (ii) Consider now a merger between two of the three firms, resulting in a duopolistic structure of the market. The merger might give rise to efficiency gains, in the sense that the firm resulting from the merger produces at a cost ec, with $e \leq 1$ (whereas the outsider still has a cost c). Find the post-merger equilibrium quantities, price and profits. (iii) Under which conditions does the merger reduce prices? (iv) Under which conditions is the merger beneficial to the merging firms?

Exercise 5.4   **Consider the model as described in Section 5.2. (a) Under the assumption that all firms are single-product, find the reaction functions of a firm i and a firm k (respectively, R_i and R_k) and draw them in the plane (p_k, p_i). Show that they are positively sloped and check that stability conditions are met. (b) Now assume that two firms i and j merge and as a consequence of the merger their unit production costs are ec (with $e \leq 1$), while all the other firms have unit costs c. Derive the reaction function for product i and for product k under this assumption. Draw the reaction functions for product i and product k and compare them with the previous R_i and R_k. Do you expect the post-merger prices to be higher at the equilibrium?

Exercise 5.5   **Consider the model described in Section 5.4.2.1, where a merger would create a firm having m varieties which faces $n - m$ single-product firms. For simplicity consider the case where there are zero marginal costs, $c = 0$. (a) Find the residual demand function faced by the firm which sells m varieties. (b) Show that as the number of products m increases the elasticity of its residual demand function decreases.

Exercise 5.6   *(Mergers with quantity competition and differentiated goods)* Consumers have the following utility function for three differentiated goods:

$$U = v \sum_{i=1}^{3} q_i - \frac{3}{2(1+\gamma)} \left[\sum_{i=1}^{3} q_i^2 + \frac{\gamma}{3} \left(\sum_{i=1}^{3} q_i \right)^2 \right] + y,$$

where y is an outside good. Each of the three goods is produced at identical marginal costs $c \geq 0$. Firms choose quantities in the marketplace. (i) Derive the inverse demand functions for each good. (ii) Find the pre-merger equilibrium quantities and profits, where each good is sold by a single-product firm. (iii) Find the equilibrium quantities and profits after a merger between two firms, that is the equilibrium where products 1 and 2 are sold by the same firm I, whereas product 3 is still sold by an independent firm. (iv) Compare the profits of the merged firms with those they receive before the merger; (v) Draw the reaction functions before and after the merger and use the figure to understand the effect of the merger on profitability.

Exercise 5.7 ** (*Quantity competition*) Use the inverse demand functions given in equation (8.63) to study the model where firms compete in quantities. Keep all the other assumptions made in that section. (a) Find the quantity q_c, price p_c, and profits π_c made by the firms at the symmetric Nash equilibrium in quantities (Cournot–Nash). (b) Now consider the case of a merger between two firms (which results in the merging firm having unit costs ec, with $e \leq 1$, instead of c), and derive analytically quantity, price and profits for both insiders and outsiders. (c) (Salant, Switzer and Reynolds (1983)) Assume now $e = 1$ and $\gamma \to \infty$. Under which conditions is a merger profitable?

Exercise 5.8 ** (*Figure of mergers with strategic substitutes*) Consider the previous exercise. (a) Under the assumption that all firms are single-product derive the reaction functions of a firm i and a firm k (respectively, R_i and R_k) and draw them in the plane (q_k, q_i). Show that they are negatively sloped and check that stability conditions are met. (b) Now assume that two firms i and j merge and as a consequence of the merger their unit production costs are ec, with $e \leq 1$, while all the other firms have unit costs c. Derive the reaction function for product i and for product k under this assumption. Draw the reaction functions for product i and product k and compare them with the previous R_i and R_k. Do you expect the post-merger prices to be higher at the equilibrium?

Exercise 5.9 There are three sellers, F_1, F_2, and F_3, in an industry. They have comparable capacities, technologies and market shares. One Friday evening, firms F_1 and F_2 announce a merger. The next Monday, which is the first trading day after the announcement, the share price of firm F_3 falls by 15%. Explain: (a) Is this consistent with what economic theory would predict, and if so, under which circumstances? (b) Can information about this drop in shares prices be of any relevance at all to the competition authorities?

Exercise 5.10 In a country there are four cement producers whose names are Vodka, Tequila, Whisky and Grappa respectively. All together, they own 100% of the market. Each of these firms has tried in the past to have new production sites, but environmental regulations in the country are strictly enforced, and new permits to establish quarries (which are necessary for cement production) have not been given to cement producers for the last thirty years. The four firms jointly own (each with one-fourth of the shares) the firm Cognac, a company which coordinates the operations of transportation and distribution from the different cement plants to the consumers. Tequila has made a public offer for the purchase of the totality of Vodka's shares. The anti-trust agency of the country has refused authorisation for the takeover, on the grounds that such a merger would create a dominant position. The firm has filed an appeal with the Court of Justice, and argues that the merger would allow for considerable scale and scope economies, as well as for the rationalisation of the distribution and sales of cement. Its claim is supported by a report from a highly respected economics professor who maintains that the two firms could save up to 30% of their costs thanks to the merger and that the consumers would clearly benefit from these efficiency gains. You are the judge: what would you do?

Exercise 5.11   In a recent merger case (*Volvo/Scania*), the EC seemed to attach a lot of importance to the so-called *shrinkage test*. The EC referred to previous merger cases in the same industry where market shares of the merging firms had not considerably decreased after the merger, and used this information (no shrinkage of output) to argue that the merging firms would have a dominant position after the merger. What is, if any, the economic rationale behind such a test?

Exercise 5.12   In a small European country there are several newspapers, but only two newspapers that are specialised in international news and comments (they contain very little information about local events or national news, and even their coverage of sports and financial news is mainly international in scope). Since the country is bilingual, both newspapers are bilingual: the same articles are published in both German and French. Now the two newspapers announce that they plan to merge. The national competition authority argues that the merger is giving rise to a monopoly position in the relevant market, and proposes to block it. Under the country's competition law, though, the anti-trust authority has only an advisory role, and it is the Minister for Competition Affairs who has to decide. You are the Minister: what would you do?

Exercise 5.13   Due to high transportation costs, the relevant geographic market for cement is usually thought of as coinciding with national borders. In country 1, the main cement producer is firm A, which has almost 75% of the market, and the second producer is firm C, with roughly 20% of the market (the rest is split among minor companies). The two have always fiercely competed for the market, with recurrent price wars. In country 2, the main producer is firm B, with around 50% of the market, and the second seller is firm A, with a 30% market share (all market shares given here roughly correspond to capacity shares, and all plants are more or less equally efficient). Now firm C, which is absent from market 2, and firm B are planning to merge. Are there possible reasons why a competition authority should worry about this merger?

5.8.1 Solutions to Exercises

Exercise 5.1   (a) Salant, Switzer and Reynolds (1983) assumed (i) quantity competition and (ii) no efficiency gains from the merger, and found that a merger between two firms is always detrimental to the partners unless it gives them a monopoly. The intuition behind this result is that the merging partners internalise the negative pecuniary externality given by the too-low prices in the industry, and reduce their outputs (which would tend to increase prices). The goods being strategic substitutes (as is the case with quantity competition and linear demand functions), the outsiders to the merger will respond by increasing rather than decreasing their outputs, which allows them to gain market shares but moderates the increase in the price. As a result, insiders lose market shares and profits, as the lower quantity produced is not compensated by the price rise in the industry.

(b) This article opened a debate on the profitability of mergers, and subsequent research has showed that relaxing assumptions (i) and (ii) above, profitability of the merger would be restored. As for (i), Deneckere and Davidson (1985) showed that when goods are strategic complements, the price increase of the merging firms is followed by a price increase by the outsiders. As for point (ii), Perry and Porter (1985) showed that even under the assumption of homogenous goods and quantity competition, if there exist enough efficiency gains the merger will be profitable.

Exercise 5.2 (i) When there are n independent firms in the industry, each of them has a profit $\pi_i = (a - c - \sum_{j=1}^{n} q_j)q_i$. The FOCs are given by $a - c - 2q_i - \sum_{j \neq i} q_j = 0$. At the symmetric equilibrium, $q(n) = (a - c)/(n + 1)$ and $\pi(n) = (a - c)^2/(n + 1)^2$.

(ii) When $m + 1$ firms merge, there will be $n - m$ identical independent firms in the industry. The equilibrium quantities and profits at the post-merger equilibrium can therefore be found by replacing the number of firms $n - m$ in the equilibrium expressions above, to give $q(n - m) = (a - c)/(n - m + 1)$ and $\pi(n - m) = (a - c)^2/(n - m + 1)^2$.

(iii) A firm which is an outsider to the merger always gains from it, as $\pi(n - m) > \pi(n)$.

(iv) To see whether or not the merger benefits the insiders, one has to take into account that after the merger there is only one firm having profits $\pi(n - m)$, whereas before the merger there are $m + 1$ firms each having profits $\pi(n)$. Therefore, to see if there is a gain for the merged firms, we have to study the function $g(n, m) = \pi(n - m) - (m + 1)\pi(n)$. By substitution, $g(n, m) = (a - c)^2 \left[1/(n - m + 1)^2 - (m + 1)/(n + 1)^2 \right]$. A merger to monopoly amounts to $m + 1 = n$, hence $g(n, n - 1) = (a - c)^2 \left[1/4 - n/(n + 1)^2 \right] > 0$, which can be further simplified to $(n - 1)^2 > 0$, which is always true.

(v) If there are 10 firms in the industry, the gain function from the merger can be written as $g(10, m) = (a - c)^2 \left[1/(11 - m)^2 - (m + 1)/(11)^2 \right]$. Simple algebra shows that $g(10, m) > 0$ if $(-m^2 + 21m - 99) > 0$, which is solved by $m \gtrsim 7.15$. Hence, one needs a merger involving at least $m + 1 = 8 + 1 = 9$ out of 10 firms for the merger to be profitable.

Exercise 5.3 (i) Each firm has a profit $\pi_i = (1 - c - Q)q_i$, $i = 1, 2, 3$. The FOCs are given by $1 - c - 2q_i - q_j - q_k = 0$, with i, j, $k = 1, 2, 3$ and $i \neq j \neq k$. At the symmetric equilibrium, $q_c = (1 - c)/4$, $p_c = (1 + 3c)/4$, and $\pi_c = (1 - c)^2/16$.

(ii) After the merger, two firms are left: firm 1, with cost ce, and firm 3, with cost c. It is easy to show that deriving the FOCs and solving them gives $q_1 = (1 - c(2e - 1))/3$, and $q_3 = (1 - c(2 - e))/3$. Note that the outsider firm can sell a positive output at equilibrium only if the merger does not give rise to strong cost savings: $q_3 \geq 0$, if $e \geq (2c - 1)/c$. (If $c < 1/2$, then the outsider firm will always sell at equilibrium.) The equilibrium price is $p_m = (1 + c(1 + e))/3$, and profits are given by $\pi_1 = (1 - c(2e - 1))^2/9$, and $\pi_3 = (1 - c(2 - e))^2/9$.

(iii) Prices decrease after the merger only if there are sufficient efficiency gains: $p_m \leq p_c$ can be rewritten as $e \leq (5c - 1)/(4c)$. Note that if $c < 1/5$, prices will never fall no matter how strong efficiency gains are.

(iv) To see if the merger is profitable, we have to study the inequality $\pi_1 \geq 2\pi_c$, which after some algebra can be seen to correspond to an inequality of the second order whose relevant solution is $e \leq \left(4(1 + c) - 3\sqrt{2}(1 - c)\right)/(8c)$. In other words, the merger is profitable only if it gives rise to enough cost savings.

Exercise 5.4 (a) The reaction functions of firm i and k can be easily derived from equations (5.3) in the text as $R_i(p_k, p_j) = (3v + (3 + 2\gamma)c + \gamma p_j + \gamma p_k)/[2(3 + 2\gamma)]$ and $R_k(p_k, p_j) = (2(3 + 2\gamma)p_k - 3v - (3 + 2\gamma)c - \gamma p_j)/\gamma$. Their graphical representation in the plane (p_k, p_i) corresponds to Figure (5.2) in the text. To see that both reaction functions are positively sloped, just note that $\partial R_i(p_k, p_j)/\partial p_k = \gamma/[2(3 + 2\gamma)] > 0$, and $\partial R_k(p_k, p_j)/\partial p_k = [2(3 + 2\gamma)]/\gamma > 0$. For stability to hold, we must have $\partial R_k(p_k, p_j)/\partial p_k > \partial R_i(p_k, p_j)/\partial p_k$, which simplifies to $\gamma < 2(3 + 2\gamma)$, which holds for all $\gamma \in [0, \infty)$.

(b) Again, the reaction functions can be found in the text as $R_I^e : p_i = (3v + (3 + \gamma)ce + 2\gamma p_j + \gamma p_k)/[2(3 + 2\gamma)]$; $R_O : p_i = (-3v - (3 + 2\gamma)c - \gamma p_j + 2(3 + 2\gamma)p_k)/\gamma$. Their graphical representation in the plane (p_k, p_i) corresponds to Figure (5.4) in the text. The higher the efficiency gains from the merger (i.e., the lower e), the more likely the insiders' reaction function will shift below (rather than above) its previous position, thus giving rise to a decrease (rather than an increase) in prices at the post-merger equilibrium.

Exercise 5.5 (a) From the FOCs (5.23) of the outsiders it is possible to derive the best reply function p_o^R of each of the outsiders with respect to the price p_I set by the insiders. Given that $c = 0$, this simplifies to: $p_o^R = (\gamma m p_I + nv)/(2n + \gamma(n + m - 1))$.

The residual demand function q_I^r for a variety produced by the multi-product firm can be obtained by taking the demand (5.20) and imposing two conditions: (1) at equilibrium the prices of all symmetric varieties will be identical; (2) to see the market power enjoyed for any variety sold by the multi-product firm we shall consider a proportional increase in all the product prices set by the firm at the same time (if p_I increases, it increases simultaneously for all product varieties). We then obtain $q_I^r = \frac{1}{n}\left[v - p_I(1+\gamma) + \frac{\gamma m p_I}{n} + \frac{\gamma(n-m)p_o^R}{n}\right]$.

By substituting the value of p_o^R one finds the explicit expression of the residual demand function of the insiders.

(b) To compute the elasticity of the residual demand function $\epsilon_I^r = -\left(dq_I^r/q_I^r\right)/\left(dp_I/p_I\right)$, first find the derivative: $\frac{dq_I^r}{dp_I} = \left(-1 + \gamma\left(\frac{m}{n} - 1\right) + \frac{\gamma^2 m(n-m)}{n(2n+\gamma(n+m-1))}\right)\frac{1}{n}$.

We can now calculate the elasticity as

$$\epsilon_I^r = \frac{\left(\gamma^2(n-m)(n-1) + \gamma(3n-m-1) + 2n^2\right)p_I}{\gamma^2(n-m)(n-1)p_I + 2n^2(v-p_I) + \gamma n\left(v(2n-1)-(3n-m-1)p_I\right)}, \tag{5.57}$$

and some calculations show that

$$\frac{\partial \epsilon_I^r}{\partial m} = -\frac{\left(2n^2 + \gamma n(4n-3) + \gamma^2\left(2n^2\right) - 3n+1\right)\gamma n v p_I}{\left(\gamma^2(n-m)(n-1)p_I + 2n^2(v-p_I) + \gamma n\left(v(2n-1)-(3n-m-1)p_I\right)\right)^2} < 0. \tag{5.58}$$

The larger the number of products sold by the merging firms the lower the elasticity of the residual demand function faced by each of its product, i.e., the larger its market power. It is also possible to show that $\frac{\partial \epsilon_I^r}{\partial n} > 0$: as we would expect, for a given number of products m sold by the insiders, the larger the number of firms operating in the industry the higher the elasticity faced by the insiders (the lower the market power enjoyed by the merging firms).

Exercise 5.6 The inverse demand functions are easily found by solving the consumer's optimisation problem, that is $\max_{\{q_1,q_2,q_3,y\}} U$ subject to the income constraint $Z = \sum_{i=1}^n p_i q_i + p_y y$, after taking good y as the numéraire ($p_y = 1$). They are $p_i = v - \frac{1}{1+\gamma}\left(3q_i + \gamma \sum_{j=1}^n q_j\right)$.

(ii) Before the merger takes place, we have three identical single-product firms with a profit function $\pi_i = (p_i - c)q_i$, where p_i is given by the demand function above ($i = 1, 2, 3$).

The FOCs $\partial \pi_i/\partial q_i = 0$ are

$$q_i = \left((v-c)(1+\gamma) - \gamma q_j - \gamma q_k\right)/(2(3+\gamma)), \quad i, j, k = 1, 2, 3; i \neq j \neq k. \tag{5.59}$$

By solving the system of FOCs and imposing symmetry on quantities one obtains

$$q_c = \left((v-c)(1+\gamma)\right)/(2(3+2\gamma)). \tag{5.60}$$

Prices and profits at equilibrium are

$$p_c = \frac{v\,(3+\gamma) + 3c\,(1+\gamma)}{2(3+2\gamma)}, \qquad \pi_c = \frac{(v-c)^2\,(3+\gamma)\,(1+\gamma)}{4\,(3+2\gamma)^2}. \quad (5.61)$$

(iii) Firms 1 and 2 merge to become firm I, firm 3 continues to sell one product. They will have profits $\pi_I = \sum_{i=1}^{2}(p_i - c)q_i$ and $\pi_3 = (p_3 - c)q_3$, where prices $p_i = p_i(q_1, q_2, q_3)$ are given by the inverse demand functions found above. The FOCs $\partial \pi_I / \partial q_i = 0$ (with $i = 1, 2$), and $\partial \pi_3 / \partial q_3 = 0$ can be written as

$$q_i = \frac{(v-c)(1+\gamma) - 2\gamma q_j - \gamma q_3}{2(3+\gamma)}, \qquad q_3 = \frac{(v-c)(1+\gamma) - \gamma q_i - \gamma q_j}{2(3+\gamma)};$$

$$i,\ j = 1, 2;\ i \neq j. \quad (5.62)$$

We can then find the post-merger equilibrium quantities q_I, q_O as

$$q_I = \frac{(v-c)\,(6+\gamma)\,(1+\gamma)}{6\,(\gamma^2 + 6\gamma + 6)}; \qquad q_O = \frac{(v-c)\,(3+\gamma)\,(1+\gamma)}{3\,(\gamma^2 + 6\gamma + 6)}. \quad (5.63)$$

After substitution, one obtains the prices and per-variety profits ($\pi_{I1} = \pi_{I2} = \pi_I$) of the merged firm and the outsiders as

$$p_I = \frac{v(18 + 15\gamma + 2\gamma^2) + c\left(18 + 21\gamma + 4\gamma^2\right)}{6\,(6 + 6\gamma + \gamma^2)};$$

$$p_O = \frac{v(3+\gamma)^2 + c(9 + 12\gamma + 2\gamma^2)}{3\,(6 + 6\gamma + \gamma^2)^2}. \quad (5.64)$$

$$\pi_I = \frac{(3+2\gamma)\,(1+\gamma)(6+\gamma)^2(v-c)^2}{36\,(\gamma^2 + 6\gamma + 6)^2}, \qquad \pi_O = \frac{(1+\gamma)(3+\gamma)^3(v-c)^2}{9\,(\gamma^2 + 6\gamma + 6)^2}. \quad (5.65)$$

(iv) We can now analyse the effect of the merger on profitability for the insider firms. To do that, note that the inequality $\pi_I > \pi_c$ can be re-written as

$$-\frac{\gamma^2\,(1+\gamma)\left(\gamma^3 + 3\gamma^2 - 18\gamma - 27\right)(v-c)^2}{36\,(3+2\gamma)^2\,(\gamma^2 + 6\gamma + 6)^2} > 0, \quad (5.66)$$

which is satisfied only if $\gamma < 3.74$. In other words, the merger will be unprofitable unless the products are almost independent (recall that $\gamma \in (0, \infty)$).

(v) To understand this result, let us draw the firms' best reply functions before and after the merger. Consider for instance product 1 and product 3. In the space (q_3, q_1), and for given q_2, before the merger their best replies are obtained from

FOCs (5.59):

$$R_1 : q_1 = \frac{(v - c)(1 + \gamma) - \gamma q_2 - \gamma q_3}{2(3 + \gamma)};$$

$$R_3 : q_1 = \frac{(v - c)(1 + \gamma) - \gamma q_2 - 2(3 + \gamma)q_3}{\gamma}. \qquad (5.67)$$

After the merger, the best replies are derived from FOCs (5.62) as

$$R_1' : q_1 = \frac{(v - c)(1 + \gamma) - 2\gamma q_2 - \gamma q_3}{2(3 + \gamma)};$$

$$R_3 : q_1 = \frac{(v - c)(1 + \gamma) - \gamma q_2 - 2(3 + \gamma)q_3}{\gamma}. \qquad (5.68)$$

By drawing the reaction functions, which are negatively sloped, it is evident that the merger shifts the best reply function R_I of the insider product downwards to R_I', resulting in a new equilibrium characterised by higher production of the outsiders and lower production of the insiders. The reallocation of production explains why (unless products are extremely differentiated) the merger is unprofitable.

Exercise 5.7 (a) The Cournot–Nash equilibrium before the merger corresponds to the solution of Exercise 5.6 (ii), i.e., equations (5.60) and (5.61).

(b) The merger with efficiency gains: the merging firms' profits will be $\pi_I = \sum_{i=1}^{2}(p_i - ec)q_i$, while the outsider still has profits $\pi_3 = (p_3 - c)q_3$, where prices $p_i = p_i(q_1, q_2, q_3)$ are given by the inverse demand functions (5.19). The FOCs $\partial \pi_I / \partial q_i = 0$ (with $i = 1, 2$) and $\partial \pi_3 / \partial q_3 = 0$, can be written as

$$q_i = \frac{(v - ec)(1 + \gamma) - 2\gamma q_j - \gamma q_3}{2(3 + \gamma)}, \qquad q_3 = \frac{(v - c)(1 + \gamma) - \gamma q_i - \gamma q_j}{2(3 + \gamma)};$$

$$i, j = 1, 2; \ i \neq j. \qquad (5.69)$$

After imposing symmetry on insider quantities (i.e., $q_1 = q_2$) and solving for q_I and q_O, we obtain post-merger per-variety quantities, prices and profits:

$$q_I = \frac{(1 + \gamma)\left[(v - ec)\,2\,(3 + \gamma) - \gamma\,(v - c)\right]}{4\,(3 + 2\gamma)\,(3 + \gamma) - 2\gamma^2};$$

$$q_O = \frac{2\,(1 + \gamma)\left[(v - c)\,(3 + 2\gamma) - \gamma\,(v - ec)\right]}{4\,(3 + 2\gamma)\,(3 + \gamma) - 2\gamma^2}; \qquad (5.70)$$

$$p_I = v - \frac{(v - ec)\,2\left[(3 + 2\gamma)\,(3 + \gamma) - \gamma^2\right] + \gamma\,(v - c)\,(3 + 2\gamma)}{4\,(3 + 2\gamma)\,(3 + \gamma) - 2\gamma^2}; \qquad (5.71)$$

$$p_O = v - \frac{(v - c)\,2\left[(3 + 2\gamma)\,(3 + \gamma) - \gamma^2\right] + 2\gamma\,(v - ec)\,(3 + \gamma)}{4\,(3 + 2\gamma)\,(3 + \gamma) - 2\gamma^2}; \qquad (5.72)$$

$$\pi_I = (1+\gamma)(3+2\gamma)\left[\frac{(v-ec)\,2\,(3+\gamma)-\gamma\,(v-c)}{4\,(3+2\gamma)(3+\gamma)-2\gamma^2}\right]^2; \qquad (5.73)$$

$$\pi_O = 4\,(1+\gamma)(3+\gamma)\left[\frac{(v-c)\,(3+2\gamma)-\gamma\,(v-ec)}{4\,(3+2\gamma)(3+\gamma)-2\gamma^2}\right]^2 \qquad (5.74)$$

(c) Let $e = 1$ and $\gamma \to \infty$. For $e = 1$, the expressions obtained in Exercise 5.6 (iii) and (iv) apply. There, we saw that whenever there is an outsider left in the market, the merger will be profitable for insiders only if $\gamma < 3.74$. If $\gamma \to \infty$, the goods become more and more homogenous (and are finally perfect substitutes), so that the findings of Exercise 5.2 apply: with $n = 3$, the merger will be profitable only if it is a merger to monopoly. (To see this, just solve $g(n = 3, m) = (a-c)^2\left[\frac{1}{(n-m+1)^2} - \frac{m+1}{(n+1)^2}\right] > 0$ for m to obtain that the merger will only be profitable if $m > 1.438$, i.e., if at least $m + 1 = 3$ firms merge.)

Exercise 5.8 (a) The pre-merger reaction functions were derived in Exercise 5.6 (v) as $R_i\left(q_k, q_j\right) : q_i = \left[(v-c)(1+\gamma) - \gamma q_j - \gamma q_k\right] / [2(3+\gamma)]$; $R_k\left(q_k, q_j\right) : q_i = \left[(v-c)(1+\gamma) - \gamma q_j - 2(3+\gamma)q_k\right] / \gamma$. It is easy to see that they are negatively sloped: $\partial R_i\left(q_k, q_j\right)/\partial q_k = -\gamma / [2(3+\gamma)] < 0$, and $\partial R_k\left(q_k, q_j\right)/\partial q_k = -[2(3+\gamma)]/\gamma < 0$. For stability to hold, we must have $\partial R_k\left(p_k, p_j\right)/\partial p_k < \partial R_i\left(p_k, p_j\right)/\partial p_k$, which simplifies to $\gamma < 2(3+\gamma)$, which holds for all $\gamma \in [0, \infty)$.

(b) The post-merger reaction functions can be easily derived from the FOCs of exercise 5.7 (b), as follows: $R_i^e\left(q_k, q_j\right) : q_i = \left[(v-ec)(1+\gamma) - 2\gamma q_j - \gamma q_k\right] / [2(3+\gamma)]$; $R_k\left(q_k, q_j\right) : q_i = \left[(v-c)(1+\gamma) - \gamma q_j - 2(3+\gamma)q_k\right]/\gamma$. If $e = 1$ (i.e., there are no efficiency gains), then the insiders' reaction function will shift downward, and prices will increase. However, if efficiency gains are important enough, then the reaction function may instead shift upward, in which case prices will decrease.

6

Vertical Restraints and Vertical Mergers

6.1 WHAT ARE VERTICAL RESTRAINTS?

In most markets, producers do not sell their goods directly, but reach final customers through intermediaries, wholesalers and retailers. Further, the final good is often produced in several stages, from raw material, to intermediate good, to final product. Very often, firms at different stages of the vertical process do not simply rely on spot market transactions, but sign contracts of various types in order to reduce transaction costs, guarantee stability of supplies, and better co-ordinate actions. These agreements and contractual provisions between vertically related firms are called *vertical restraints*. This chapter analyses the welfare effects of vertical restraints as well as of vertical mergers, that is mergers between vertically related firms.[1]

To gain some initial insight on the topic, consider the classical example of the vertical relationship between a manufacturer and a retailer which distributes its products.[2] In general, both the manufacturer and the retailer decide on different actions, and what is an optimal action for one is not necessarily optimal for the other. As a result, a party can try to use contracts and clauses so as to restrain the choice of the other and induce an outcome which is more favourable to itself. (To put it another way, each party's actions create an externality on the other. Vertical contracts might be used to try to control for these externalities.)

For instance, the manufacturer would like the retailer to make a lot of effort in marketing its products (such as advertise its products, put them in evidence on shelves, employ specialised personnel who assist potential customers, offer post-sale assistance and so on), but the latter might have a lower incentive to do so, as effort and services are costly to provide. The manufacturer might then decide to use contractual

---

[1] It is worth noting that while from an economic point of view it makes sense to deal with vertical restraints and vertical mergers together (both are used to solve problems of vertical coordination), anti-trust laws resort to different provisions to deal with them. In the EU, for instance, vertical restraints might be the object of Article 81 (agreements between firms) or Article 82 (if the firm using them is dominant), whereas vertical mergers are covered by the Merger Regulation.

[2] The vertical relationship might take place between manufacturer and retailer(s), or between upstream and downstream firm(s), or between producer and distributor(s). Despite the different labels, the relationship is of the same nature.

provisions (that is, vertical restraints) in order to induce higher marketing effort from its retailer. To continue the example, it might assign an exclusive area of competence to the retailer so that it would fully appropriate the benefits of the services provided (if other retailers carry the same brand within the same region, there is a free-riding problem that further reduces the incentive to provide those services); or it might use a non-linear contract such that the retailer would have a discount if it buys a large number of units, in order to encourage its sales effort; or it might simply oblige the retailer to sell a minimum number of units of the good, which again would increase its effort; or it might convince the retailer not to carry competing brands, to stimulate its sales efforts; or it might simply take over the retailer so as to make coordination of actions easier. The objective of this chapter is to identify when these vertical restraints (and vertical mergers) should be expected to show positive or negative effects on welfare.

As the simple example above indicates, there are several types of vertical restraints.[3] Some of the most common examples are the following.

- *Non-linear pricing.* (Also called *franchise fee* (henceforth, FF) or *two-part tariff* contracts.) In the simplest possible relationship between two agents, one buys from the other on the basis of a "linear pricing" rule, that is, the total payment is proportional to the number of units involved in the transaction. Whether one buys one unit or one hundred units, the unit price would be the same.[4] A simple vertical restraint is then "non-linear pricing", a contract which specifies a fixed amount independent of the number of units bought (the "franchise fee") plus a variable component. For instance, to sell a given clothes producer's brand, a shop might have to pay 1,000 euro per year plus 10 euro for each T-shirt it buys. The effect of such a contract is that the unit cost effectively paid by the shop decreases with the number of units bought from the same producer.[5] The effect is to encourage the retailer to buy more units.

- *Quantity discounts.* Quantity discounts or *progressive rebates* have the same effect as non-linear pricing contracts, as the larger the quantity bought the cheaper the transaction on average.

- *Resale price maintenance (RPM).* The manufacturer might have different perceptions from the retailer as to which price final customers should be charged

---

[3] Tie-in sales (or tying), when they involve vertically related products, are also vertical restraints. However, they will be considered in Chapter 7 because tying might concern independent goods as well. Furthermore, some clauses that prevent a distributor from selling a product outside its home territory are also vertical restraints. But since such clauses allow a manufacturer to price discriminate (also dealt with in Chapter 7), they are not analysed here.

[4] *Royalties* are also another possible instrument used by the manufacturer, who receives a payment that is proportional to the *sales* of the downstream firm. As such, royalties are used only if downstream sales can be observed (and verified).

[5] For instance, if the shop buys one T-shirt only, its average cost is 1,010 euro, but if it buys 100 T-shirts, the average cost is only $(1{,}000 + 10 \times 100)/100 = 20$.

for the product. As a consequence, the former might want to affect the price decisions of the latter. In its most extreme form, RPM simply consists of the price at which the retailer should sell the product. But it might also be a recommended price, or it might establish either a minimum resale price (price floor) or a maximum resale price (price ceiling).

- *Quantity fixing.* The manufacturer might want to specify the number of units that the retailer should buy. Again, this might also take different forms, such as quantity forcing (the retailer cannot buy less than a certain amount) or quantity rationing (it cannot buy more than a certain amount).
- *Exclusivity clauses.* Manufacturer and retailer might also sign exclusivity agreements. For instance, an *exclusive territory* (ET) clause would imply that there is only one retailer who can sell a certain brand within a certain geographical area (or to a certain type of customers). Under *exclusive dealing* a retailer agrees to carry only the brand of a certain manufacturer. *Selective distribution* clauses allow only a certain type of retailers – usually specified in objective terms – to carry a manufacturer's brand. For instance, a luxury good producer might want to provide its product only to high-street retailers and not to supermarkets or discount stores, fearing that the latter might undermine the quality or luxury image associated with its product.

It is important to notice that in any given market – due to the nature of the transactions, or due to institutional constraints – some of these vertical restraints might be effective whereas others might not be. For instance, RPM makes sense only insofar as the effective price paid by final customers can be observed by the manufacturer. For mass products (say, the T-shirts of our example above) this might be the case; but in other circumstances there might be a bargaining process between the retailer and the final buyer whose outcome might be difficult to observe. If discounts on prices cannot be observed by the manufacturer, RPM loses its restraining power, and a manufacturer might want to rely on other restraints to achieve a certain objective. For instance, quantity fixing might be a substitute for RPM.

Arbitrage (buying where the price is cheap to resell where the price is high) might also be a force which diminishes the effectiveness of some restraints. If consumers have lower search and transport costs (with respect to the value of a good), it is unlikely that exclusive territorial clauses would be effective. If retailers could arbitrage, non-linear pricing or quantity discounts might also lose effectiveness, as one retailer could buy a large number of units and then resell some of them to retailers who plan to sell low quantities. These restraints are therefore more effective when the manufacturer can also observe retailers' sales.[6]

---

[6] Different restraints might also have a different legal status. For instance, minimum RPM is *per se* illegal in some countries and discouraged in others, obliging producers to resort to other clauses to affect the distributors of their products.

Most of the clauses above are to some extent substitutable with others. This implies that it would be largely useless, for instance, to outlaw a certain type of clause while allowing others that achieve the same objectives.

Vertical Integration (or Vertical Mergers)   In some circumstances, manufacturers might find it difficult to use clauses that induce the behaviour they want from the retailers. In such a case, they could also resort to vertical integration, that is, they could simply merge with (or take over) the retailers. They would then belong to the same firm, so that their objectives should be more easily reconciled.[7] It is important to keep in mind that vertical mergers are often an alternative to vertical restraints. It would be inconsistent to adopt a very firm stance against vertical restraints if mergers are not subject to an equally strict control.

6.1.1 Plan of the Chapter

Section 6.2 analyses the effect of vertical restraints when they affect *intra-brand* competition, that is the relationship between firms which produce and distribute the same brand, abstracting from the effect on competing brand producers or distributors. In this case, vertical restraints and vertical mergers allow firms at different stages of the vertical process to control for externalities; this is typically as beneficial for the firms as for consumers. In some circumstances, vertical restraints might improve coordination in the vertical chain but adversely affect consumer surplus and total welfare. However, I shall argue that as long as intra-brand competition is concerned, the presumption is that such restraints are welfare improving.

Section 6.3 looks at the effects of vertical restraints upon *inter-brand* competition. By affecting the actions taken by a producer and its retailer(s) (i.e., the vertical chain of a given brand), vertical restraints also generally affect the market interactions between this vertical chain and other vertical chains (i.e., producers and distributors of other brands). When the vertical restraints are adopted to solve the coordination problems within the same chain, consideration of inter-brand competition probably does not affect their evaluation. For instance, if a producer uses vertical restraints to solve the double marginalisation problem or free-riding in the provision of services, these should increase market competition, since they will tend to make the brand more competitive *vis-à-vis* rivals (through lower prices and higher sales effort). However, it is possible that vertical restraints might be adopted not so much to

---

[7] Even within the same firm there might well be problems in achieving the actions or effort levels that maximise joint profits. Indeed, the problem of giving the right incentives to employees would still be there. However, I assume for simplicity that agency problems are more easily solved within the same firm than between firms or independent agents. This leaves out – because it is beyond the scope of this work – the recent contributions in the literature on the theory of the firm, which study which transactions and tasks are better performed within a firm (hierarchical structure) than in the market.

increase efficiency of the vertical chain but to reduce competition with other vertical chains.

Section 6.4 pursues the topic further and shows that both vertical restraints and vertical mergers might have anti-competitive effects, by foreclosing competition. For instance, an incumbent firm might use exclusive contracts to pre-empt efficient entry into an industry; and a merger might allow a vertically integrated firm to foreclose an input to its downstream rivals, thereby reducing their competitiveness and possibly forcing them to exit the industry.

Section 6.5 argues that one should balance the efficiency and anti-competitive effects of vertical restraints and vertical mergers when assessing them. The same type of vertical restraint might be used with a different purpose, that is it might be used to improve coordination within the chain (which usually has a welfare improving effect) or with the aim of affecting competition with the other chains (whose effect might be to lower welfare). This has two implications. First, one cannot say that a given type of restraint is always good or always bad. For instance, RPM might improve intra-brand efficiency, but it might also affect inter-brand competition and favour collusion by increasing the observability of firms' behaviour. This means that one cannot simply outlaw certain restraints and permit others. In legal terms, this means that economic analysis suggests a *rule of reason* rather than a *per se rule* of prohibition of certain restraints. Second, in the real world both effects might co-exist to some degree, or in any case it might not be clear at first sight, which one is dominant. Often, only an elaborate analysis might shed light on whether efficiency considerations or anti-competitive ones prevail.

This would not be a satisfactory conclusion. Saying that there is no clear rule on vertical restraints, and that they should all be analysed on a case-to-case basis would amount to disaster. Given the pervasiveness of vertical agreements between firms, competition agencies would collapse because they would have to devote most of their resources to look into such cases, as happened to the EC at the beginning of its history and – to a minor degree – until the new rules on vertical agreements were adopted. Fortunately, there is a more helpful policy conclusion which can be derived from the analysis of vertical restraints. Since the only vertical restraints that raise welfare concerns are those adopted by firms which enjoy enough market power, the main policy conclusion is that only the vertical clauses adopted by firms enjoying large market power are worth investigating, and a rule of reason approach should be used on them.

Section 6.6 concludes the chapter with a discussion of two cases.

6.2 INTRA-BRAND COMPETITION

In this section, I review the main welfare effects of vertical restraints when they affect competition between retailers that sell the same product or brand. Here we consider the situation where a manufacturer (a monopolist for simplicity) sells through one or more retailers. Section 6.2.1 shows that if both a manufacturer and its retailer have market power, both charge a positive mark-up, resulting in too-high market prices for the vertical chain (the so-called *double marginalisation* problem). If vertical restraints were used, or vertical integration occurred, prices would decrease and both producer surplus and welfare would increase. Section 6.2.2 illustrates instead the free-riding problem in the provision of services by the retailers. If several retailers distributed the same brand, they might be unable to appropriate the effort made to market the brand (to the advantage of competing retailers) and, anticipating this, they would make less effort than would be optimal for the manufacturer. By using appropriate restraints, incentives for retailers to provide effort and services might be restored. Again, if consumers value such services, vertical restraints are likely to increase both producer and consumer surplus. Section 6.2.3 will study the case where several externalities co-exist. Section 6.2.4 will look at other efficiency motives for vertical restraints (in order not to fragment the analysis, I shall also consider restraints used when there is inter-brand competition). Section 6.2.5 shows that when contracts are unobservable, vertical restraints or a vertical merger might be used by a manufacturer to commit itself to sell at high prices. Otherwise, it would be tempted to renegotiate its offer to the retailers, ending up with lower prices than it would like to charge.

6.2.1 Double Marginalisation

The best known example of externalities affecting vertically separated firms is given by the *double marginalisation* problem, first identified by Spengler (1950).[8] Suppose that a manufacturer relies on a retailer for selling to final customers, and that the former sells to the latter according to a constant unit price (linear pricing). Suppose also, for simplicity, that the retailer does not have any costs other than the wholesale price.[9] Figure 6.1 illustrates the structure of the market.

Both firms want to maximise their profit and in order to do so they both choose the monopolistic mark-up (margin) over their own cost: the upstream firm chooses the wholesale price w given its cost c, and the downstream firm as a result will choose p given its own cost, namely the wholesale price w (which is higher than c because the upstream firm has a margin). The result, however, of both firms adding their margin is that they end up with consumers paying too high a price (buying too few units) with respect to what would be optimal from their joint point of view, that is from the point of view of the vertical chain (the sum of the profits made by the upstream and downstream firm).

If instead the two firms are under the same management, the final price p would be chosen so as to add only a mark-up over the cost c. Vertical integration – that is

---

[8] But Cournot (1838) had already pointed out a similar effect when firms are selling complementary products, a case which formally is similar to that of vertically related firms.
[9] The reader can easily check that the argument also holds if the retailer has an additional distribution cost.

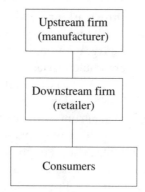

Figure 6.1. Double marginalisation.

the merger of the two firms – is efficient since it allows them to coordinate on the optimal outcome, or to "internalise" (control for) the externality that they impose on each other. The result after the correction for this externality is that not only firms but also consumers gain from the vertical merger.

If vertical integration is not possible, different types of vertical restraints might be used to control for this externality. Since the problem results in too high a market price (or too-low sales), an obvious possibility to solve the problem is resale price maintenance. The manufacturer could simply impose the resale price on the retailer, or establish a price ceiling. Of course, resale price maintenance is effective if the final price is observable.

Alternatively, quantity forcing would give the same outcome, as this would oblige the retailer to increase sales to the level, which is optimal for the integrated structure.

Yet another possibility to restore the vertically integrated outcome is for the manufacturer to use non-linear pricing (a fixed component F plus a variable component w for each unit bought) in order to make the retailer the "residual claimant" of all the profit generated in the market. By setting the variable component identical to the manufacturer's own cost, $w = c$, the retailer would effectively behave in the same way as a vertically integrated firm, and would choose the optimal final price. The retailer would then make the maximum profit. However, part of or all such profit can be appropriated by the manufacturer through the franchise fee F. In general, the distribution of the profit depends on the relative bargaining power of the two firms. If it is the manufacturer who has all the bargaining power (or if there are many possible retailers who would compete for the right to sell the manufacturer's product, and they would outbid each other until the winning bid F absorbs all the expected profit), the manufacturer can make exactly the same profit as if it owned the retailer.

However, notice that vertical restraints are not equivalent if there exists some uncertainty in the market (either on the level of final demand, or on the costs of distributing the product) and if the retailer is risk averse. In these circumstances a non-linear contract $F + cq$, by making the retailer the residual claimant of all the profit generated by the vertical chain, would ensure that the retailer reacts to demand or cost shocks in the same way as a vertically integrated firm. However, it would expose the retailer to a high risk, since his profit would not be protected against such shocks. If the retailer is risk averse, in order to insure him the manufacturer will have to guarantee him some minimum profit.

RPM gives perfect insurance under demand uncertainty, since the final price is guaranteed independently of the level of demand. However, RPM fares very badly under cost uncertainty, as a shock on the distribution cost will greatly affect the retailer's profit margin, since the price cannot be adjusted so as to cover high costs.

As a result, with a risk-averse retailer, RPM is better under demand uncertainty, non-linear pricing under cost uncertainty. (For a formal treatment, see Section 6.2.1.2.)

Conclusions   Although it is convenient to refer to the case where there exists a monopoly both upstream and downstream, the issue of double marginalisation arises whenever some market power exists at both levels. This vertical externality pushes prices *above* what would be optimal for the vertical structure.

We have seen that vertical mergers, resale price maintenance, quantity fixing and non-linear pricing are instruments which control for this externality and therefore also result in higher welfare.

An upstream firm might also resort to another means of avoiding the double marginalisation problem, namely tackling the problem at its root and eliminating market power at the downstream level. Indeed, in this particular case, the fiercer the competition among the downstream firms selling the manufacturer's brand the lower the mark-up they set on top of the upstream firm's mark-up and in turn the weaker the externality.[10] Note that by *reducing* competition downstream, for instance by assigning *exclusive territories* to retailers, which effectively give them a monopoly in a certain geographic area or for a certain type of customers, the double marginalisation problem is aggravated and welfare is reduced.

6.2.1.1 Analysis of Double Marginalisation*

Suppose there is one upstream firm U that manufactures a certain product for which it is a monopolist. Suppose also that it cannot sell the good directly, but has

---

[10] In the limit, if intra-brand competition led to final prices equal to wholesale price, $p = w$ (this would happen for instance if at least two undifferentiated retailers competed in prices), the upstream firm would be able to set the wholesale price equal to the optimal price under vertical integration, thereby restoring the efficient outcome.

to rely on a downstream firm D – the retailer – who buys the product from U and resells it to the final consumers. (Exercises 6.1 and 6.2 deal with the cases of n retailers.) Assume that the manufacturer has all the bargaining power, that is that it makes a take-it-or-leave-it offer to the retailer (although the main result would not change if we assumed a different distribution of the bargaining power).

Consumers' demand is given by $q = a - p$, where $a > 0$ is a parameter, q is quantity demanded and p is the final price charged to consumers.

The manufacturer has a unit production cost $c < a$, and the retailer's unit cost is given by the sum of the wholesale price w that it (possibly) has to pay to the manufacturer for a unit of the product and a unit cost of resale that is taken equal to zero for simplicity. I also assume that all agents have perfect information.

I analyse two different cases. First, upstream and downstream firms do not engage in any vertical contracts and the upstream firm sells to the retailer by using a simple linear price structure, that is, by fixing w. Second, upstream and downstream firms are integrated. I will show that there are several sets of vertical restraints that allow the upstream firm to reproduce the vertically integrated outcome.

Separation and Linear Pricing   The game being played is as follows. First, the upstream firm chooses the wholesale price w at which it sells to the downstream firm. Then, the downstream firm chooses the final price p at which it sells to consumers.

As usual, we first have to look for the solution of the downstream firm. Its problem is to choose p in order to maximise its profit given the wholesale price w:

$$\max_{p} \Pi_D = (p - w)(a - p). \qquad (6.1)$$

By taking the first derivative and equalling it to zero ($\partial \Pi_D / \partial p = 0$), we obtain price, quantity and profit as a function of the wholesale price: $p = (a + w)/2; q = (a - w)/2; \Pi_D = (a - w)^2/4$.

The manufacturer perfectly anticipates the decision of the retailer. In particular, it knows the quantity the retailer will order as a function of the wholesale price (for any given w, the retailer will not be willing to buy more units of the products than those that it will find optimal to sell to final consumers). Therefore, its problem is to choose w to maximise its own profit:

$$\max_{w} \Pi_U = (w - c)\frac{a - w}{2}. \qquad (6.2)$$

From the first-order condition ($\partial \Pi_U / \partial w = 0$) and after rearranging one finds the solution as $w = (a + c)/2$. Replacing the equilibrium wholesale price in the downstream solutions one finds the equilibrium final price and profits obtained by the upstream and downstream firms, as well as the sum of the profits made by the vertical chain:

$$p^{sep} = \frac{3a+c}{4}; \qquad \Pi_U^{sep} = \frac{(a-c)^2}{8}; \qquad \Pi_D^{sep} = \frac{(a-c)^2}{16}; \qquad (6.3)$$

$$PS^{sep} = \Pi_U^{sep} + \Pi_D^{sep} = \frac{3(a-c)^2}{16}. \qquad (6.4)$$

Vertical Integration (Vertical Merger) Suppose now that the upstream and downstream firms are integrated in a unique company, for instance because of a vertical merger. This implies that the manufacturer can now sell directly to consumers. Its problem will now be the standard problem of a monopolist, as follows:

$$\max_p \Pi_{vi} = (p-c)(a-p). \qquad (6.5)$$

The solution is easily obtained from the first-order condition $\partial \Pi_{vi}/\partial p = 0$:

$$p^{vi} = \frac{a+c}{2}; \qquad q^{vi} = \frac{a-c}{2}; \qquad PS^{vi} = \Pi^{vi} = \frac{(a-c)^2}{4}. \qquad (6.6)$$

Comparison The vertical merger case is unambiguously better for society.

- Prices are lower under a vertically integrated structure than under the separated one, as $p^{vi} < p^{sep}$ (recall that $a > c$, or else the market would not exist). Since vertical integration determines a price decrease (and an increase in the quantity sold to final consumers), consumer surplus improves due to the vertical merger.
- The profit created by the vertical structure is also higher under vertical integration, as $PS^{vi} > PS^{sep}$. In turn, this means that the manufacturer can always pay to the retailer at least the profit Π_D^{sep}, which the latter makes under the separated structure, to convince it to take part in the merger (otherwise, the retailer can give the manufacturer at least its outside opportunity payoff, that is the profit Π_U^{sep} it would make under vertical separation). Both firms stand to gain from merging the two vertical stages.
- Since both consumer surplus and producer surplus increase, total welfare unambiguously rises from vertical integration.

Vertical Restraints Assume now that a vertical merger – for whatever reason – is not possible. It is still possible for the upstream firm to remove the double marginalisation externality by using different vertical restraints, as follows.

- *Resale price maintenance (RPM).* Double marginalisation results in too high final prices. Imposing the retail price $p = p^{vi} = (a+c)/2$ on the downstream firm will maximise the surplus of the vertical structure. The way in which the upstream and downstream firms share the surplus will then be determined by the wholesale price w. If the upstream firm has all the bargaining power, then it will fix $w = p^{vi} = (a + c)/2$ and will get all the producer surplus. More generally, the higher w (with $w \in [c, p^{vi}]$) the higher the share of the surplus going to the upstream firm. Identical outcome would be achieved if the upstream firm sets a *price ceiling* $\overline{p} = p^{vi} = (a + c)/2$. This obliges the downstream firm to sell at a price $p \leq \overline{p}$. For any wholesale price $w \in [c, p^{vi}]$ the downstream firm would then choose precisely $p = \overline{p}$ (and again the actual w determines the division of the surplus).

- *Quantity fixing (QF)*. The mirror image of too high a price is that there is too little a quantity sold to final consumers. Therefore, the upstream firm can also restore efficiency by obliging the retailer to buy the number of units $q^{vi} = (a - c)/2$, or equivalently by imposing quantity forcing, that is establishing that the retailer should buy at least $q \geq \overline{q} = q^{vi}$. The retailer would then choose precisely the efficient output $q = q^{vi}$. As in the previous case, the level of the wholesale price determines the distribution of the producer surplus. If the upstream firm has all the bargaining power, it will choose $w = p^{vi}$ and appropriate all the profit of the vertical structure.

- *Franchise fee (FF)*. The upstream firm can make the downstream firm the residual claimant of all the profit generated in the market by setting the non-linear price scheme $F + wq$, and fixing $w = c$. The downstream firm's maximisation problem is given by

$$\max_{p} \Pi_D^{ff} = (p - c)(a - p) - F. \tag{6.7}$$

Clearly, the solution of this problem is given by the vertical integration price $p^{vi} = (a + c)/2$ and quantity $q^{vi} = (a - c)/2$, as the fixed fee does not affect the first-order condition. The distribution of the profit (equal to the vertically integrated profit) will then be determined by the amount of the fee F, as the downstream and upstream firms will respectively get $\Pi_D^{ff} = (a - c)^2/4 - F$ and $\Pi_U^{ff} = F$. If the upstream firm has all the bargaining power, then $F = (a - c)^2/4$ and it appropriates all the profit generated by the vertical structure.

6.2.1.2 Double Marginalisation with Retailers' Risk Aversion**

The following example, adapted from Rey and Tirole (1986), illustrates the different risk-insurance properties of vertical restraints when asymmetric information and risk aversion of retailers exist.[11]

Consider an extension of the double monopoly model above. A risk-neutral manufacturer has a unit cost c and its retailer is infinitely risk averse and has a unit distribution cost γ. Demand is $q = a - p$. There exist both demand uncertainty $a \in [\underline{a}, \overline{a}]$ and distribution cost uncertainty $\gamma \in [\underline{\gamma}, \overline{\gamma}]$, with $\underline{a} > c + \overline{\gamma}$, realisations of

---

[11] Rey and Tirole (1986) also analyse the case of risk neutral retailers and find that there might be a difference between private and social optimum of vertical restraints.

a and γ being independent. The game is as follows. First, when both market demand a and distribution costs γ are unknown to everybody, the manufacturer makes a take-it-or-leave-it offer to the retailer, in the form of a non-linear contract $(F + wq)$. Second, a and γ are observed by the retailer (but not by the manufacturer). Third, the retailer chooses p.

We want to (i) find the optimal contract under non-linear pricing (FF) and resale price maintenance (RPM); (ii) show that under demand uncertainty $\pi_{RPM} > \pi_{FF}$ and $W_{RPM} > W_{FF}$; (iii) show that under cost uncertainty $\pi_{FF} > \pi_{RPM}$ and $W_{FF} > W_{RPM}$.

I prove these results as follows:

(i.a) FF. The retailer maximises $\pi_r = (a - p)(p - w - \gamma)$. It is easy to check that $p = (a + w + \gamma)/2$, $\pi_r = (a - w - \gamma)^2/4$. Since the retailer is infinitely risk averse, the franchise fee F must guarantee him non-negative profits even in the worst state of nature. Therefore, it must be $F_{FF} = (\underline{a} - w - \overline{\gamma})^2/4$. The manufacturer's problem will be to choose w to maximise $E\left[(a - (a + w + \gamma)/2)(w - c)\right] + (\underline{a} - w - \overline{\gamma})^2/4$. The solutions are $w_{FF} = c + \left(a^e - \underline{a}\right) + (\overline{\gamma} - \gamma^e)$, $p_{FF} = \left[a + c + \gamma + \left(a^e - \underline{a}\right) + (\overline{\gamma} - \gamma^e)\right]/2$, $\pi_{FF} = (\underline{a} - c - \overline{\gamma})^2/4 + \left[\left(a^e - \underline{a}\right) + (\overline{\gamma} - \gamma^e)\right]^2/4$, $W_{FF} = 3(\underline{a} - c - \overline{\gamma})^2/8 + \left[\left(a^e - \underline{a}\right) + (\overline{\gamma} - \gamma^e)\right]^2/4 + \mathrm{var}(a)/8 + \mathrm{var}(\gamma)/8$.

(i.b) RPM. The retailer charges the imposed price p and has profit equal to $\pi_u = (a - p)(p - w - \gamma)$. Given infinite risk aversion, $F = (\underline{a} - p)(p - w - \overline{\gamma})$.

The manufacturer will choose p and w to maximise $(\underline{a} - p)(p - w - \overline{\gamma}) + E\left[(a - p)(w - c)\right]$, subject to $p \geq w + \overline{\gamma}$. It can be checked that π_u is increasing in w. Hence, the manufacturer will choose the maximum w compatible with the constraint $w = p - \overline{\gamma}$. The problem becomes then $\max_p E\left[(a - p)(p - \overline{\gamma} - c)\right]$, whose solution is given by $p_{RPM} = (a^e + c + \overline{\gamma})/2$. By substitution, $w_{RPM} = (a^e + c - \overline{\gamma})/2$, $F_{RPM} = 0$, $\pi_{RPM} = (a^e - c - \overline{\gamma})^2/4$, $W_{RPM} = 3(a^e - c - \overline{\gamma})^2/8 + \mathrm{var}(a)/2$.

(ii) Consider demand uncertainty only $(\overline{\gamma} = \gamma = \gamma^e)$. Then $\pi_{FF} < \pi_{RPM}$ if $(\underline{a} - c - \overline{\gamma})^2/4 + \left[\left(a^e - \underline{a}\right)\right]^2/4 < (a^e - c - \overline{\gamma})^2/4$. This inequality can be rewritten as: $(a^e - \underline{a})(c + \overline{\gamma} - \underline{a}) < 0$, which is always true since by assumption $a^e > \underline{a}$ and $\underline{a} > c + \overline{\gamma}$. It can also be checked that $W_{FF} < W_{RPM}$.

(iii) Under cost uncertainty $(E(a) = \underline{a} = \overline{a})$, $\pi_{FF} > \pi_{RPM}$ since $(\underline{a} - c - \overline{\gamma})^2/4 + \left[(\overline{\gamma} - \gamma^e)\right]^2/4 > (a^e - c - \overline{\gamma})^2/4$. One can also check that $W_{FF} > W_{RPM}$.

A variant of this example with competing retailers is considered in Exercise 6.3.

6.2.2 Horizontal Externality: Free-Riding in the Provision of Services

Besides the vertical externalities between a manufacturer and the retailers that carry its products there often exist horizontal externalities among retailers that determine an inefficient outcome from the point of view of the vertical structure as a whole. Figure 6.2 illustrates the structure of the market with more retailers.

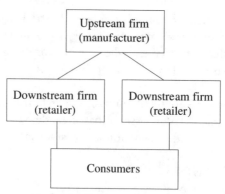

Figure 6.2. Horizontal externality.

An example of such externalities concerns the level (and quality) of services provided by retailers. If such services cannot be perfectly appropriated by one retailer (that is, if there are spillovers which benefit other retailers carrying the same brand) then services become a public good on which the retailers will free ride, thus determining an underprovision which reduces the manufacturer's profit. Again, vertical integration as well as certain vertical restraints might help the manufacturer solve this externality problem.

To capture the main reasoning behind the argument (first proposed by Telser, 1960), consider the following example. Imagine that in a city there are several shops which sell a given product, say a brand of dishwashers. (To concentrate on the issue at hand, also suppose that this is the only brand sold in this city, although it is not necessary.) There are many activities that these shops might carry out to increase consumers' appeal for the product. Think for instance of hiring shop assistants who answer potential customers' questions, illustrate the characteristics of the product to them and so on. These are all activities which might make the potential client more willing to buy the brand, but not necessarily at the shop where he gets the information. Or think of some sort of advertising that might attract customers to the brand but not to the shop that does the advertising.

Suppose also that some of the competing retailers are located very close to each other, and it is not too costly, relative to the value of the good, for the consumer to do a little search before a purchase.

In these circumstances, each shop will think twice before investing a great deal of effort to sell the brand. This is because another shop nearby would have an incentive to avoid the cost of this effort, just free ride on the provision of services and offer a better price. A consumer would first visit the shop which offers additional services, get there all of the information he needs but will then buy at the shop which offers the same product at the best price. Of course, a shop will anticipate this and will refrain from offering services that have a public good characteristic. In the limit, if services given by retailers just contribute to the brand but cannot be appropriated by the shop itself, and if the shops are close enough, no service at all will be provided. This will be sub-optimal for the producer, given that its brand will not be supported by shop services, but also for consumers, who do not receive information they highly value.

Vertical restraints might restore incentives for the retailers to invest in services. For instance, suppose that the producer divides the city in different areas, and appoints an exclusive distributor in each area (exclusive territories). This would reduce the possibility of consumers visiting several shops (it is more costly to shop around in different areas) and therefore reduces the risk that a retailer will be undercut by a free-riding competing shop. Hence, each retailer will have a higher incentive to offer brand-supporting services. Another possibility is for the producer to maintain all the shops in the city, but fix the resale price, or impose a price floor, to avoid the problem of undercutting and to allow the retailers to recoup (part of) the investment.[12]

Vertical integration would also solve the problem: if the producer owned the shops, it would take into account the externality that each of them imposes on the other, and would prevent its shop managers from undercutting each other and reducing the level of services they provide.

To sum up, vertical restraints and vertical integration avoid or reduce the free-riding problem to the benefit of both producer and consumer surplus. (For a formal treatment of this argument, see Section 6.2.2.1.)

Of course, in general there will also be many sales activities which can be appropriated by the shop, for instance credit to consumers, or post-sales service provided by the store, or physical appearance of the shop itself (some consumers do prefer to buy in shops which are located in high streets, or whose premises are nicer looking). In all these cases, the free-riding problem will not arise. In reality, services of different types will probably co-exist, and although the extreme case where no service at all is provided is unlikely to rise, the free-riding problem will probably affect to some degree the shops' investment decisions.

An Example of Welfare-Reducing Vertical Restraints (Too Much Effort)   We have just seen that vertical integration and vertical restraints might improve welfare by raising the level of effort and services provided by retailers. It is conceivable, though, that vertical restraints internalise the horizontal externality and lead to too much effort. In other words, they might increase profits, but result in lower consumer surplus and welfare. Technical Section 6.2.2.2 constructs a simple example where vertical integration (and vertical restraints) would reduce welfare: a (vertically integrated) monopolist would increase effort to attract marginal consumers to the

---

[12] Of course, if the services provided by the retailers are observable and verifiable, there is a simpler solution to the problem, which is to fix the level of services contractually. This might be the case, for instance, with advertising or certain types of after-sales services.

detriment of infra-marginal consumers who do not value extra effort.[13] Losses for the latter group might outweigh increased producer surplus.

The example illustrates that there is no reason to expect that the control of the existing externalities by means of vertical restraints or vertical mergers will always show a coincidence between the interest of the firms and the interest of consumers. However, it is worth noting that the example needs some special assumptions to show that welfare might be reduced. Furthermore, an extension of the example shows that welfare decreases only insofar as no competition exists. If infra-marginal consumers (those who do not value extra effort) have the possibility to buy from firms supplying a standard quality of the product (i.e., a product which does not incorporate extra services), vertical integration will not reduce welfare. This introduces a crucial point to which I will return later: one should worry about vertical restraints only when adopted by firms which enjoy large market power.

6.2.2.1 A Model of Underprovision of Services*

Consider a situation where there is an upstream firm U (the manufacturer) and two downstream firms D_1 and D_2 which have to decide on the level of effort (services) they want to provide to sell U's product and then compete in prices.

Assume that services increase the perceived quality of the brand but cannot be appropriated by the retailer that provides them. The perceived quality of the brand is given by $u = \bar{u} + e$, where the effort level is $e = e_1 + e_2$, that is the sum of the effort (service) provided by the two retailers. In the absence of any effort, $u = \bar{u}$ which is the basic level of quality perceived by the consumers. As for each retailer's cost, we assume that $C(q, e_i) = wq + \mu e_i^2/2$, with $\mu > 1$. Here I assume that the cost of services is fixed – it is independent of the number of units sold – rather than variable. This would correspond for instance to the case where "service" is advertising outlays.[14]

Consumers' demand is given by $q = (v + e) - p$, that is, it increases by e for any additional service above the standard quality.

The fact that downstream firms compete in prices avoids double marginalisation and will make the free-riding problem the only externality of this simple model. This is because retailers are not able to differentiate themselves (by assumption) through the use of the services they provide, and therefore retailers are perceived as perfect substitutes by consumers.

I look first at the case where there is separation between the upstream and the downstream firms and then at the case where there is vertical integration. Then,

---

[13] See Scherer and Ross (1990: 541–8) for a similar argument.
[14] Instead, services such as pre-sale assistance would probably correspond to variable costs of service provision, as each unit sold (each potential customer showing up at the shop) requires higher cost or effort. See Exercise 6.4 for the case of variable cost of effort.

I shall see which vertical restraints allow the upstream firm to restore the vertical integration solution.

Separation If the two retailers are competing in prices, the only equilibrium in the retailers' game is the one where $p_1 = p_2 = w$ and $e_1 = e_2 = 0$, for the following reason. Since there is a complete externality in the provision of services, a retailer does not manage to differentiate itself from the other no matter how much service it gives to consumers. Therefore, Bertrand competition implies that prices equal marginal cost (i.e., the wholesale price w). But since the retailers make zero profit they will never be able to cover their (fixed) cost of quality provision. No equilibrium with $e > 0$ can then be sustained.[15]

The upstream firm correctly anticipates that the final price $p = w$ and that the final demand will be $q = v - w$. Its programme is then $\max_w \Pi_u = (w - c)(v - w)$, which is solved by $w = (v + c)/2$. At the separation equilibrium, therefore, producer surplus, consumer surplus and welfare are respectively given by

$$PS_s = \Pi_u = \frac{(v-c)^2}{4}; \qquad CS_s = \frac{(v-c)^2}{8}; \qquad W_s = \frac{3(v-c)^2}{8}. \quad (6.8)$$

Vertical Integration Consider now the case where the upstream firm and the two retailers are integrated, for instance because the former takes over the retailers.[16] The programme of the vertically integrated firm is

$$\max_{p,e_1,e_2} \Pi_{vi} = (p - c)(v + e_1 + e_2 - p) - \mu \frac{e_1^2}{2} - \mu \frac{e_2^2}{2}. \quad (6.9)$$

Solving the system of the three first-order conditions, we obtain

$$\begin{cases} \dfrac{\partial \Pi_{vi}}{\partial e_i} = p - c - \mu e_i = 0, \quad (i = 1, 2) \\[2mm] \dfrac{\partial \Pi_{vi}}{\partial p} = v + e_1 + e_2 - 2p + c = 0, \end{cases} \quad (6.10)$$

one obtains the following solutions: $e_1 = e_2 = e_{vi} = (v - c)/[2(\mu - 1)]$; $p_{vi} = [\mu(v + c) - 2c]/[2(\mu - 1)]$. Each retailer will sell $q_{vi} = \mu(v - c)[4(\mu - 1)]$. By substitution, one then obtains producer surplus, consumer surplus and welfare as

---

[15] One can see the same result by contradiction. Because of fixed cost of services, $e > 0$ would require $p > w$. But then an undercutting firm would get all the demand. Hence, this cannot be an equilibrium.

[16] It turns out that it is optimal for the vertically integrated structure to have both retailers selling the good. This is because we have assumed a convex cost of services provision: to produce a given level of services, costs are lower if the provision is split among the two retailers rather than concentrated in one.

follows:

$$PS_{vi} = \Pi_{vi} = \frac{\mu(v-c)^2}{4(\mu-1)}; \quad CS_{vi} = \frac{\mu^2(v-c)^2}{8(\mu-1)^2}; \quad W_{vi} = \frac{\mu(3\mu-2)(v-c)^2}{8(\mu-1)^2}.$$

(6.11)

Vertical integration is again more efficient, as $W_{vi} > W_s$ amounts to the inequality $(4\mu - 3)(v - c)^2 / \left[8(1 - \mu)^2\right] > 0$.

In this example, vertical integration allows control for the horizontal externality which exists among retailers and which determines an underprovision of services relative to what would be optimal for the integrated structure.

Vertical Restraints   In this case the problem under a separated structure is one of free-riding among retailers, who are pushed to undercut each other thereby losing incentives to provide services. To restore incentives the manufacturer has to relax competition downstream. A non-linear contract would not solve the problem, unless it is accompanied by some measures which reduce competition.

Exclusive Territories and Franchise Fee   Suppose each retailer receives a territory or exclusive competence for a certain type of customer, plus a non-linear contract of the type $T = wq + F$, with $w = c$. For simplicity, assume that each retailer can sell to half of the total number of consumers. However, we keep the assumption that the overall perceived level of quality of the good sold by each retailer is determined by the sum of the retailers' efforts. Then each retailer will face the following problem:

$$\max_{p_i, e_i} \Pi_{et} = (p_i - c)\frac{(v + e_1 + e_2 - p_i)}{2} - \mu\frac{e_i^2}{2} - F.$$

(6.12)

The first-order conditions are

$$\begin{cases} \dfrac{\partial \Pi_{et}}{\partial e_i} = \dfrac{p_i - c}{2} - \mu e_i = 0, \\[2ex] \dfrac{\partial \Pi_{et}}{\partial p_i} = v + e_i + e_j - 2p_i + c = 0, \quad (i = 1, 2; i \neq j). \end{cases}$$

(6.13)

Note that given the level of effort the price chosen will be equivalent to the vertically integrated solution ($\partial \Pi_{et}/\partial p_i = 0$ is the same as for the vertically integrated monopolist). However, effort is not optimal since marginal profit from effort is reduced with respect to the situation where there is full internalisation of the effort externality. Each retailer knows that its effort will increase sales in a market which is half the size of the one of a vertically integrated monopolist. Therefore, exclusive territories improve the incentives to provide services and make the manufacturer closer to the optimum, but do not restore the first-best.

Giving exclusivity for the whole market to only one retailer does not restore the first-best either, since effort will be provided by only one retailer rather than two (there are diseconomies of scale from effort provision). The only retailer will choose p and e to maximise the following function:

$$\max_{p_1, e_1} \Pi_{et_1} = (p_1 - c)(v + e_1 - p_1) - \mu\frac{e_1^2}{2} - F. \tag{6.14}$$

The first order conditions will be

$$\begin{cases} \dfrac{\partial \Pi_{et_1}}{\partial e_1} = (p_1 - c) - \mu e_1 = 0, \\[2ex] \dfrac{\partial \Pi_{et_1}}{\partial p_1} = v + e_1 - 2p_1 + c = 0. \end{cases} \tag{6.15}$$

At equilibrium, the retailer will provide lower effort than at the first-best. To sum up, exclusive territories do reduce the externality problem and increase the provision of effort but do not restore the first-best.[17]

Resale Price Maintenance and Franchise Fee Another possible type of vertical restraint that can be used to give more incentives to produce services is resale price maintenance combined with a non-linear contract ($w < c; F$). If the manufacturer fixes the price $p = p_{vi}$ at which the retailers can sell, then the retailers will not price so aggressively that incentives to provide effort will be eliminated (as occurred in the Bertrand case).

Each retailer will face the following problem:

$$\max_{e_i} \Pi_{rpm} = (p_{vi} - w)\frac{(v + e_1 + e_2 - p_{vi})}{2} - \mu\frac{e_i^2}{2} - F. \tag{6.16}$$

The first-order conditions for effort is

$$\frac{\partial \Pi_{rpm}}{\partial e_i} = \frac{p_{vi} - w}{2} - \mu e_i = 0, \quad i = 1, 2; i \neq j. \tag{6.17}$$

In order for a retailer to choose the optimal level of effort, the following condition must be satisfied:

$$e_i = \frac{p_{vi} - w}{2\mu} = e_{vi} = \frac{v - c}{2(\mu - 1)}; \tag{6.18}$$

hence, the wholesale price must be $w_{rpm} = p_{vi} - \mu(v - c)/(\mu - 1)$. By replacing the expression of p_{vi} one obtains

$$w_{rpm} = \frac{3\mu c - 2c - \mu v}{2(\mu - 1)} < c. \tag{6.19}$$

Note that if $w = c$, resale price maintenance would not reproduce the vertically integrated level of effort. This is because each retailer – when choosing its effort

---

[17] If the two retailers were managed by one firm only, then giving an exclusive territory contract to this firm would restore the vertically integrated solution.

level – takes into account the marginal impact of effort only on its own profit rather than for both retailers. Since each retailer knows that it will sell to only half the market (the product is undifferentiated and the prices are fixed by the manufacturer) it will have insufficient incentives. RPM alone does not restore the first-best: the retailers must be given additional incentives to make effort, and this can be achieved by the upstream monopolist selling them the input at a wholesale price below its own marginal cost.

Note that the contract, which specifies the retail price at the level p_{vi} and the wholesale price w_{rpm}, induces the same level of price and effort as the vertically integrated structure. Therefore, the total profit generated under this contract is the same as under vertical integration. The franchise fee F can then be used to redistribute the profit from the retailers to the manufacturer. If $F = \Pi_{vi}/2 + (c-w)q_{vi}$, the manufacturer will exactly replicate the profit made under vertical integration.

Resale Price Maintenance and Quantity Forcing   Resale price maintenance can also be used in combination with another instrument, that is quantity forcing. To ensure that a retailer is selling at the optimal price, the manufacturer would set the retail price at the level $p = p_{vi}$. However, RPM alone would obviously not suffice to restore the vertically integrated solution, as we have seen above. The retailers would make insufficient effort and sell too few units of the good. As an alternative to the (w_{rpm}, F) contract specified above, the manufacturer could simply impose a minimum level of sales (quantity forcing), equal to q_{vi}. This would push the retailer to make the optimal effort level. Since price is fixed and optimal effort is determined by quantity forcing, the vertically integrated outcome would be reproduced. The manufacturer could then choose the wholesale price – which given RPM and QF does not modify the retailers' incentives – as the channel to redistribute rents away from the retailers.

More formally, the arguments just presented can be seen as follows.

Given RPM that imposes $p = p_{vi}$, and given quantity forcing, the problem of each retailer i becomes

$$\max_{e_i} \Pi = \frac{(p_{vi} - w)(v + e_i + e_j - p_{vi})}{2} - \mu \frac{e_i^2}{2}, \quad s.to: \frac{v + e_i + e_j - p_{vi}}{2} \geq q_{vi}.$$

$$(6.20)$$

We know that unconstrained maximisation would lead the retailer to insufficient effort. Therefore, its problem is solved by the minimum effort level e_i which satisfies the constraint. At the symmetric solution, effort is therefore given by $(2q_{vi} + p_{vi} - v)/2$, which is nothing else than e_{vi}. Since this contract already implements the optimal p_{vi} and e_{vi}, the wholesale price becomes incentive neutral. The manufacturer can then use it to appropriate the rents. To do so, it should choose w so as to leave retailers with zero net profit. The optimal $\widehat{w}$ solves then the following condition: $(p_{vi} - \widehat{w})(v + 2e_{vi} - p_{vi})/2 - \mu e_{vi}^2/2 = 0$, whence $\widehat{w} = (v+c)/2$.

The total profit made by the manufacturer is then given by $(\widehat{w} - c)q_{vi}$, which after substitution becomes equal to Π_{vi}.

Conclusions   In this particular example, where the overall level of services is determined by the sum of the levels provided by each retailer, and where the cost of providing services falls upon fixed costs, a vertical merger will enhance welfare with respect to a situation where competing retailers do not provide enough effort. Vertical restraints such as exclusive territories and resale price maintenance also increase welfare as they reduce competition among retailers and in doing so they restore their incentives to provide services. However, exclusive territories combined with a franchise fee are not able to reproduce the vertically integrated outcome, whereas RPM combined either with a non-linear contract $(w < c, F)$ or with quantity forcing does restore the vertically integrated outcome.[18,19]

6.2.2.2 Vertical Integration Might Reduce Welfare*: An Example

Consider a market with two types of consumers. Those with a high willingness to pay, θ_h, do not care about extra effort or services. Those with a low willingness to pay do care about extra effort or services and have therefore a valuation $\theta_l + e$ for the good, with $\theta_h > \theta_l$. Normalise the population of consumers to 1 and assume that the shares of high and low types are respectively λ and $1 - \lambda$. Assume also that price discrimination is not possible, and that two independent and undifferentiated retailers would compete in prices. As in Section 6.2.2.1 above, assume $e = e_1 + e_2$, and $C(q, e_i) = wq + \mu e_i^2/2$ (there are fixed costs of quality improvement). Assume also that $\mu > 1/(\theta_h - \theta_l)$ (which guarantees that the low types will never have the highest willingness to pay in the market).

Separation   Under separation, for the usual undercutting and free-riding arguments discussed above, no effort will be provided at equilibrium $(e = 0, p = w)$. The manufacturer will then choose the wholesale price w so as to maximise profit. If it sells to high types only, it will fix $w = \theta_h$. If it wants to sell to both types, it will choose $w = \theta_l$. Let us assume that it is convenient for the manufacturer to sell to both types. This amounts to imposing that $\lambda(\theta_h - c) \le \lambda(\theta_l - c) + (1 - \lambda)(\theta_l - c) = (\theta_l - c)$, which becomes $\lambda \le (\theta_l - c)/(\theta_h - c)$.

Under this assumption, the manufacturer extracts all the consumer surplus of the low types, while the high types have a surplus. As a result, overall consumer

---

[18]   Note, however, that the result that resale price maintenance restores the vertically integrated outcome is not necessarily robust. See also Exercise 6.4.

[19]   In this model there are two externalities. The first consists of too-strong competition, which eliminates incentives to exert effort. The second is the spillover in effort. Therefore, a necessary condition for the manufacturer to achieve the first-best is to have two instruments.

surplus is $CS_s = \lambda(\theta_h - \theta_l)$, total profit is $\pi_s = \theta_l - c$ and welfare is $W_s = \theta_l - c + \lambda(\theta_h - \theta_l)$.

Vertical Integration (with Two Retailers)   Under vertical integration (or vertical restraints which reproduce the vertically integrated outcome), the monopolist will still choose price so as to extract all the surplus of the low types, but this is now increased by the effort level. The problem of the vertically integrated monopolist will therefore be

$$\max_{e_1, e_2} \pi_{vi} = \theta_l + e_1 + e_2 - c - \mu \frac{e_1^2}{2} - \mu \frac{e_2^2}{2}, \qquad (6.21)$$

which has the solution $e_1 = e_2 = 1/\mu$. (Note that $\theta_h > \theta_l + e$ under the assumption made above on μ.) At this equilibrium, $\pi_{vi} = \theta_l + 1/\mu - c > \pi_s$ and $CS_{vi} = \lambda(\theta_h - \theta_l - 2/\mu) < CS_s$. Total welfare decreases under vertical integration if $W_{vi} = \theta_l + 1/\mu - c + \lambda(\theta_h - \theta_l - 2/\mu) < W_s$, which amounts to $\lambda > 1/2$.

In this example, effort is provided by the monopolist in order to increase the willingness to pay of the marginal consumers (whose surplus is then fully extracted by the monopolist), which increases profit but decreases the surplus of the inframarginal types. If there are many of the latter ($\lambda > 1/2 \geq (\theta_l - c)/(\theta_h - c)$), their loss outweighs the profit rise and determines a welfare loss. Note in particular that the restriction $\lambda \leq (\theta_l - c)/(\theta_h - c)$ should also be satisfied. Therefore, an interval where welfare decreases exists only if $\theta_l \geq (\theta_h + c)/2$.

Competition Reduces the Danger of Vertical Restraints   Let us slightly reinterpret the previous example in the following way. High types are willing to pay up to θ_h for a good of basic quality u but do not value any quality increase (or additional service). Low types value additional services and are willing to pay $\theta_l + e$ for a good of quality $u + e$.

There exist $n + 1$ goods. A good of basic quality u is produced by n (for simplicity vertically integrated) firms, which do not offer any additional service. Another manufacturer can instead provide a higher quality $u + e$, with $e = e_1 + e_2$, provided that its two retailers have the incentives to do so. If higher quality (or additional effort/services) is provided, it can be recognised by consumers. In other words, quality spillovers might happen between retailers of the same product but not across products (think of advertising for one particular brand).

Separation   For the usual reason, if there are two retailers competing à la Bertrand no additional effort will be provided: at equilibrium all brands will be of basic quality and $p = c$. No firm makes profit and total welfare will be $W_s = \lambda(\theta_h - c) + (1 - \lambda)(\theta_l - c)$.

Vertical Integration (with Two Retailers)   By vertically integrating, the free-riding aspect of effort provision is controlled for, and the manufacturer of the (potentially) high-quality good will indeed be able to offer a good of quality $u + e$. Low types will buy this good at a price up to $\theta_l + e$, whereas high types will continue to buy the basic quality brands at the price $p = c$. The problem faced by the vertically integrated monopolist is thus

$$\max_{e_1, e_2} \pi_{vi} = (1 - \lambda)(\theta_l + e_1 + e_2 - c) - \mu \frac{e_1^2}{2} - \mu \frac{e_2^2}{2}, \qquad (6.22)$$

whose solution is $e_1 = e_2 = (1 - \lambda)/\mu$. At the equilibrium, $\pi_{vi} = (1 - \lambda)(\theta_l + (1 - \lambda)/\mu - c)$ (all other firms still make zero profit), and $W_{vi} = \lambda(\theta_h - c) + (1 - \lambda)(\theta_l - c) + (1 - \lambda)^2/\mu > W_s$.

Therefore, vertical integration (or vertical restraints) by a monopolist hurts welfare, whereas vertical integration by a firm which faces competition does not. The presence of competing firms reduces the possibility that vertical restraints are used to the detriment of some consumers. While the example constructed here is very specific, this conclusion holds good under more general circumstances.

6.2.3 A More General Treatment*

In the previous sections, we have looked separately at the cases where there exist double marginalisation issues (Section 6.2.1) and free-riding problems in the provision of distribution services (Section 6.2.2). In general, such problems coexist. Further, there might be other possible distortions created by vertical restraints or vertical integration, such as a reduction in the number of retailers relative to the case where a manufacturer sells via linear contracts. In this section, I will sketch a more general treatment, which confirms the main insights from the two previous sections. The subject being inevitably more technical, the reader who is not particularly interested in this robustness analysis can skip this section and go directly to Section 6.2.4.

Combining Externalities   In Section 6.2.3.1 I present a model where a (monopolistic) manufacturer sells the final good through several (oligopolistic) retailers. Retailers compete against each other for the final consumers, but they also have to provide some services of which they can appropriate only a part (that is, there exists some free-riding in the provision of services). Such a situation is more general and more realistic than that developed in the previous sections. Different externalities arise there. First, there is the usual double marginalisation problem, which arises whenever firms at successive stages of the production process have some market power – not only when there are two successive monopolies. This tends to push prices above what is optimal for the chain. Second, there is the horizontal externality consisting of retailers reducing their effort because of free-riding (in a measure which is proportional to the degree to which the investment made by one spills over to the rivals). Third, there is another horizontal externality due to the fact that – other things being equal – each retailer will tend to set a lower price than would be optimal for the vertical chain because it does not internalise that a marginal reduction of its own price affects negatively the profit of the other retailers.

The model shows that the first effect prevails over the third one, and that even in this more complicated setting it is true that a vertically separated structure with linear wholesale pricing leads to higher prices and lower effort (i.e., lower services). Therefore, vertical integration and vertical restraints which restore the vertically integrated outcome will reduce prices, increase effort and ultimately increase both producer and consumer surplus. The model also emphasises that different vertical restraints (or combinations among them) can be used to alleviate the coordination problem within the chain and thus get closer to (or achieve) the same outcome as the optimal vertically integrated outcome. In other words, different types of restraints are often substitutes for each other, and a firm's preference for one over the others might be due to specific reasons (for instance, if final price is not observable, enforcement of RPM is impossible; if territorial or different customers' areas are difficult to draw, or if arbitrage among such areas is easy, ET might lose their appeal; and so on). There is *a priori* no reason to treat such restraints in a different way from the legal point of view.

Competition policy should recognise the degree of substitutability which exists among different vertical clauses in many circumstances. It would be useless to use a *per se* prohibition of, say, exclusive territorial clauses while permitting, say, resale price maintenance clauses which allow firms to reproduce a very similar outcome. (And vice versa: permitting ET but outlawing RPM.) And it would be useless to outlaw resale price maintenance practices while having lax merger control which would not stop vertical mergers: if not able to use RPM, a firm can still implement the same outcome by merging with retailers. (And, again vice versa: forbidding mergers but permitting vertical restraints.)

Vertical Integration and Variety: Endogenous Number of Retailers   So far, we have discussed only cases where one manufacturer sells through a *given* number of retailers, which in turn have to decide on price and investment levels. But the hypothesis that the number of retailers is exogenous is restrictive. While an independent retailer will open an outlet if its own profit (net of fixed cost of entry) is positive, a vertically integrated firm will introduce a new outlet only if this gives greater profit (net of fixed cost) than without it. The former condition is less strong than the latter. A vertically integrated firm would not open a new outlet if its profits came from stealing business from its other existing outlets, whereas an independent retailer would not consider externalities on competing retailers. The result is that there will be fewer outlets under vertical integration.

The existence of fewer outlets reduces consumer surplus (as long as consumers have a preference for variety, or their search cost increases with distance travelled to the closest shop) but does not necessarily decrease welfare, since more outlets also imply higher fixed costs. In many circumstances, competition generates excess of variety (or excess entry), and when this occurs vertical integration will improve welfare by reducing duplications.[20] Further, even if the impact on welfare of fewer varieties were negative, this effect should still be compared with the positive effects of vertical integration we have already discussed in the previous sections. For instance, vertical integration takes care of the double marginalisation problem, and this reduces prices to the benefit of consumers; and it increases incentives to effort, which again is efficient.

Section 6.2.3.2 illustrates the issue within a simple formal model where a vertically integrated manufacturer decides on how many outlets to have and at which price to sell in each outlet. It shows that vertical integration has the two main effects mentioned above: it decreases prices (good for welfare) but it also decreases variety (bad for welfare). It is *a priori* impossible to say which effect dominates, the answer depending mainly on the specific form that consumers' preferences take, as the following brief summary shows. However, under plausible assumptions it is likely that vertical integration increases rather than reduces welfare.

A few papers have studied the welfare impact of vertical integration when the number of retailers is endogenous. Mathewson and Winter (1983) find that vertical integration increases welfare. (The model I present in Section 6.2.3.2 shares some of the features of Mathewson and Winter, and arrives at the same result.)

Perry and Groff (1985) study a model where monopolistic competition with a CES (constant elasticity of substitution) demand function is assumed for the downstream retailers. In their model, integration does reduce final price, but this effect is outweighed by the lower variety existing under integration.

Kühn and Vives (1999) look at the impact of vertical integration of a supplier into a monopolistically competitive downstream industry for a more general family of demand functions. They confirm that the two main effects of integration are (1) eliminating the problem of double marginalisation, thus leading to lower final prices; (2) reducing variety (which might be welfare improving if there is elimination of excess variety).

They find that vertical integration is welfare improving when there is "increasing preference for variety", defined as a situation where "at low levels of total consumption a consumer cares less about variety increases (relative to total output increases) than at high consumption levels",[21] and they show that this property

---

[20] Not surprisingly, the literature shows that there is a relationship between the conditions under which vertical integration increases welfare and under which competition entails too much entry relative to the first-best. See for instance Kühn and Vives (1999).

[21] Under Perry and Groff's CES model, there is no increasing preference for variety, and welfare is decreased by vertical mergers.

is obtained under relatively mild assumptions on preferences. Their analysis suggests that under plausible assumptions on preferences vertical integration increases welfare.

6.2.3.1 Horizontal and Vertical Externalities: A Model**

In this section, I propose a simple model where externalities of different nature co-exist, and study the sets of vertical restraints that lead to an outcome equivalent to vertical integration.

This section is inspired by Mathewson and Winter (1984) who use a spatial model of product differentiation.[22] I have chosen to recast their analysis within the non-spatial model of differentiation which is already familiar to the readers of this book (see Chapter 5). Despite some differences, the main features of their analysis are preserved.

Consider an upstream manufacturer, which must sell its good through a network of n retailers that, because of location or other characteristics, sell a good, which is perceived by final consumers as differentiated, according to the following direct demand functions

$$q_i = \frac{1}{n}\left[v + e_i + \alpha \sum_{k \neq i}^{n} e_k - p_i(1+\gamma) + \frac{\gamma}{n}\sum_{j=1}^{n} p_j\right], \qquad (6.23)$$

where $\gamma \in [0, \infty)$ is the parameter of substitutability between the different products (i.e., an inverse measure of differentiation). Note that retailers' effort increases the consumers' willingness to pay, and that there exists a free-riding effect in the provision of effort, since effort made by a retailer spills over to rival retailers in a proportion which is determined by the parameter $\alpha \in [0, 1]$. When $\alpha = 0$, each retailer fully appropriates its effort; when $\alpha = 1$, its effort increases by the same amount both its demand and that of all its rivals. Note also that for $\gamma \to \infty$ and $\alpha = 1$, the model is equivalent to that analysed in Section 6.2.2.1. Similar to that model, I assume that $C_i(q_i, e_i) = wq_i + \mu e_i^2/2$, with $\mu > 1$. Each retailer's profit is given by $\pi_i = (p_i - w)q_i - \mu e_i^2/2$.

Vertical Separation and Linear Pricing Under vertical separation, retailers maximise individual profit. The first-order conditions $\partial \pi_i/\partial p_i = 0$ and $\partial \pi_i/\partial e_i = 0$ of the maximisation problem can be written, after taking derivatives and imposing

[22] In their model, an upstream manufacturer's product is sold by retailers that are located around a circle. Consumers are also located around the circle but do not know of the existence of the product unless reached by advertising messages sent by the retailers (the manufacturer cannot advertise).

symmetry, as

$$
\begin{cases}
v + e\left(1 + \alpha\left(n - 1\right)\right) - p\left(2 + \gamma - \gamma/n\right) + w\left(1 + \gamma - \gamma/n\right) = 0 \\
\dfrac{(p - w)}{n} - \mu e = 0
\end{cases}
\tag{6.24}
$$

Since we want to focus on the vertical restraints, which allow reproduction of the vertically integrated outcome and will not for the moment analyse their welfare impact, we do not need to find the closed-form solutions and we can work with the first-order conditions only.

Vertical Integration Consider now the case where the upstream monopolist owns all the retailers. In this case, each outlet will take into full account the externalities that it is imposing on the others, since effort levels and prices will be chosen to maximise $\Pi = \sum_{i=1}^{n} \pi_i$. By taking derivatives $\partial \Pi / \partial p_i = 0$ and $\partial \Pi / \partial e_i = 0$ and imposing symmetry one obtains the following FOCs:

$$
\begin{cases}
v + e\left(1 + \alpha\left(n - 1\right)\right) - 2p + c = 0 \\
\dfrac{(p - c)}{n}\left(1 + \alpha\left(n - 1\right)\right) - \mu e = 0.
\end{cases}
\tag{6.25}
$$

Note that $w = c$ since the manufacturer is now vertically integrated with all the retailers.

Externalities The comparison between (6.24) and (6.25) allows us to identify the different externalities at play, and understand why under vertical separation and linear pricing a sub-optimal outcome arises for the manufacturer. Let us start by comparing the price decisions. It is convenient to re-write these FOCs as $p^S(e) = (v + e(1 + \alpha(n - 1)) + w(1 + \gamma - \gamma/n)) / (2 + \gamma - \gamma/n)$ and $p^I(e) = (v + e(1 + \alpha(n - 1)) + c)/2$.

There are two distinct externalities at work, which push the price into opposite directions, for given effort levels. First, under separation there is the usual vertical externality: under separation, the double marginalisation problem arises, leading to $w > c$, which tends to increase the price p^S above p^I. Second, there is now a horizontal pecuniary externality, in that independent retailers would compete too much with each other, imposing a negative price externality upon each other. This can be seen by the fact that for p^S the denominator is divided by $2 + \gamma - \gamma/n$, whereas for p^I it is divided only by 2. Note that this horizontal externality increases with the degree of competition, being highest when $\gamma \to \infty$ and lowest when $\gamma = 0$. In the latter case, retailers are selling products, which are perceived as independent, and the only externality left is the vertical one. The final net effect is *a priori* ambiguous. However, it turns out that in standard models the vertical externality effect dominates the pecuniary horizontal externality effect.[23]

To analyse the incentives to make effort under the two vertical structures, write now the first derivatives with respect to effort as a function of (given) prices, as follows: $e^S(p) = (p - w)/(n\mu)$ and $e^I(p) = (p - c)(1 + \alpha(n - 1))/(n\mu)$.

Here again there are two externalities at play, but they both have a negative effect on the provision of effort under the separated vertical structure. First, the vertical externality, by increasing the marginal cost of retailers ($w > c$), reduces its marginal profit from investing in effort. Second, there is a horizontal externality, determined by the spillover, which is internalised under the vertically integrated structure and increases the effort made in that case. Therefore, $e^I > e^S$.

To sum up, in this model it is possible that vertical integration reduces welfare, but only if *all* the following conditions hold: (1) vertical integration leads to higher prices, (2) this effect outweighs the positive effect due to the rise in effort under integration, and (3) the resulting loss in consumer surplus is higher than the positive effect on producer surplus created by the internalisation of the various externalities.

Welfare Analysis   In this particular model, welfare turns out to be higher under vertical integration, because both consumer and producer surplus are higher than under separation.

To prove this, first we have to find the equilibrium price and effort under *vertical separation*. To do so, let us find the optimal wholesale price w charged by the manufacturer. By solving the system (6.24) one obtains

$$p^S = \frac{(v - w)\mu n}{2\mu n - 1 - \alpha(n - 1) + \gamma\mu(n - 1)} + w;$$

$$e^S = \frac{(v - w)}{2\mu n - 1 - \alpha(n - 1) + \gamma\mu(n - 1)}. \qquad (6.26)$$

The total output sold by the manufacturer will then be

$$Q^S = nq^S = \frac{(v - w)\mu(\gamma(n - 1) + n)}{2\mu n - 1 - \alpha(n - 1) + \gamma\mu(n - 1)}. \qquad (6.27)$$

The manufacturer's profit is given by $\pi^u = (w - c)Q^S$. By substituting and maximising with respect to w, it is immediate to see that the optimal wholesale price is given by $w^* = (v + c)/2$. We can now replace this value into p^S and e^S to find the

---

[23] See also Kühn and Vives (1999). Note that in the model I present here prices might be higher under vertical integration because of higher effort (which in turn increases the willingness to pay of consumers).

equilibrium final price and effort under vertical separation as

$$p^{S*} = \frac{1}{2}\left(v + c + \frac{(v-c)\mu n}{2\mu n - 1 - \alpha(n-1) + \gamma\mu(n-1)}\right);$$

$$e^{S*} = \frac{1}{2}\frac{(v-c)}{2\mu n - 1 - \alpha(n-1) + \gamma\mu(n-1)}. \quad (6.28)$$

Next, notice that the consumer surplus with our demand function is given by $CS = (v + e(1 + \alpha(n-1)) - p)^2/(2n)$. Therefore, we can now obtain the consumer surplus under vertical separation by substituting in this expression the equilibrium values above. We obtain

$$CS^S = \frac{(v-c)^2\mu^2(\gamma(n-1) + n)^2}{8n(2\mu n - 1 - \alpha(n-1) + \gamma\mu(n-1))^2}. \quad (6.29)$$

Now, we have to derive the equilibrium values for the case of *vertical integration*. By solving the system (6.25) one obtains

$$p^{VI*} = \frac{(v+c)\mu n - c(1+\alpha(n-1))^2}{2\mu n - (1+\alpha(n-1))^2};$$

$$e^{VI*} = \frac{(v-c)(1+\alpha(n-1))}{2\mu n - (1+\alpha(n-1))^2}; \quad (6.30)$$

Substituting these values in the expression of the consumer surplus gives

$$CS^{VI} = \frac{(v-c)^2\mu^2 n}{2(2\mu n - (1+\alpha(n-1))^2)^2}. \quad (6.31)$$

We can now compare the consumer surplus under vertical integration and separation. First of all, note that $\partial CS^S/\partial\gamma > 0$. Therefore, CS^S is bounded above by $\lim_{\gamma\to\infty} CS^S = (v-c)^2/(8n)$. Next, note that $\partial CS^{VI}/\partial\alpha > 0$ and $\partial CS^{VI}/\partial\mu < 0$. Hence, CS^{VI} is bounded *below* by $\lim_{\mu\to\infty} CS^{VI}(\alpha = 0) = (v-c)^2/(8n)$. In other words, $CS^{VI} \geq (v-c)^2/(8n) \geq CS^S$. Consumers are always better off under vertical integration. Since vertical integration allows to control for the existing externalities, it improves the profit of the vertical chain too. Hence, welfare is higher under vertical integration than under vertical separation.

Vertical Restraints That Restore the Vertically Integrated Solution Let us find the vertical restraints that allow an upstream monopolist to restore the vertically integrated outcome. As in Mathewson and Winter (1984), let us study first the case where there exist no advertising spillovers ($\alpha = 0$), which gives a useful benchmark, and then the case where advertising spillovers exist ($\alpha > 0$).[24]

---

[24] Although it is convenient to study the case $\alpha = 0$ for a fixed number of firms, the reader should note that in my model the optimal vertically integrated structure when advertising spillovers are

No advertising spillovers ($\alpha = 0$)

Exclusive territories (ET)

- $ET + FF(w = c)$. It is easy to see that exclusive territories can be used to restore the vertically integrated outcome if $\alpha = 0$. Exclusive territories imply that each of the retailers behaves as a local monopolist (as if, therefore, $\gamma = 0$). This eliminates the horizontal pecuniary externality, as the pressure to lower prices caused by competition is eliminated. Given that the advertising externality does not exist by assumption, the only other externality is given by the vertical one. But we know that the double marginalisation problem is easily solved by using a non-linear contract ($w = c, F$). Therefore, ET combined with a price scheme $F + cq$ restores the VI outcome. (Indeed, for $\alpha = 0, \gamma = 0$, and $w = c$, one can check that the FOCs under vertical separation coincide with those under vertical integration.)

- $ET + QF$. Under exclusive territories, there is an alternative way to solve the double marginalisation problem, which is to impose a minimum sale on retailers. Quantity forcing pushes the retailer to increase its output and therefore reduces price. It is enough therefore to impose $q \geq q^I$, where q^I is the optimal output under VI. The manufacturer can then use the wholesale price to redistribute profit away from the retailers.

Resale Price Maintenance (RPM)

- $RPM + FF(w = c)$. If there is no advertising spillover, the optimal price can be implemented simply by imposing it on retailers via RPM: $p = p^I$, p^I being the optimal price under VI (it is not clear *a priori* whether this should be a price floor or a price ceiling). However, to induce the optimal effort it is also necessary to guarantee the right profit margin to retailers. This is done by selling to them at a wholesale price $w = c$. A franchise fee can then be used to redistribute the profit.

- $RPM + QF$. As an alternative to the non-linear pricing scheme, RPM can be used in combination with quantity forcing. After imposing the price, if $w > c$ the retailer would not have the incentive to make the optimal effort. But the upstream monopolist can also impose a minimum quantity to the retailer. Each retailer's profit is given by $\pi = (p^I - w)q_i(p^I, e_i, e_j) - \mu e_i^2/2$, subject to $q_i(p^I, e_i, e_j) \geq q^I$. The unconstrained maximum would lead the retailer to make too low an effort: to meet the quantity forcing clause, each retailer will make enough effort to produce the vertical integration output.

---

low or nil is such that there exists only one retailer. This is because industry demand does not increase with the number of retailers and because – even under integration – the marginal profit of effort for any retailer which sells to the $(1/n)$th part of the market is reduced with respect to a unique retailer, unless spillovers are large enough. It can be shown that a necessary condition for a vertically integrated manufacturer to keep all n retailers is $\alpha > 1/(1 + n)$. If $\alpha = 1$, gross profit of the vertical structure always increases with n. (Obviously, if each retailer has to bear an entry fixed cost, then this would reduce the optimal number of outlets.)

Given that price is imposed at p^I, this will induce the optimal effort e^I. At this point, the optimal effort and price are implemented and the industry outcome reproduces the vertically integrated structure. Since the wholesale price w does not modify the retailers' choices, w can be used to redistribute rents from the retailers to the manufacturer.

Advertising Spillovers ($\alpha > 0$) When there is an advertising spillover (more generally, a horizontal externality on top of the pecuniary one), exclusive territory clauses are not able to restore the vertically integrated outcome. An exclusive territory combined with a non-linear pricing scheme solves the pecuniary externality (too much market competition relative to the optimum) and the double marginalisation problem, but downstream monopolists do not internalise the advertising spillover and would still advertise too little relative to the vertically integrated outcome. Nevertheless, resale price maintenance turns out to implement the vertically integrated outcome, if combined with other restraints, as we show next.

Resale Price Maintenance (RPM)

- $RPM + FF (w < c)$. Once the optimal price p^I is imposed upon retailers, it is easy to see from the FOCs under vertical separation that the retailers would still exert too little effort if $\alpha > 0$ and $w = c$: $e^S = (p^I - w)/(n\mu) < e^I = (p^I - c)(1 + \alpha(n-1))/(n\mu)$. To induce the optimal effort, it is therefore necessary for the manufacturer to sell the product to retailers at a wholesale price lower than its own marginal cost, $w < c$. More precisely, the wholesale price $\widehat{w}$ inducing the optimal level of effort will solve the equality $(p^I - \widehat{w}) = (p^I - c)(1 + \alpha(n-1))$. A franchise fee can then be used to redistribute the profit.

- $RPM + QF$. RPM can also be used in combination with quantity forcing, in the same way as for $\alpha = 0$. By imposing the price p^I and a minimum quantity q^I to retailers, they will be induced to make the optimal effort e^I to produce the vertical integration output. As the optimal effort and price are chosen, the industry outcome reproduces the vertically integrated structure. Since the wholesale price w is made incentive-neutral by RPM and QF, it does not modify the retailers' choices: it can then be used by the manufacturer to appropriate the retailers' rents.

6.2.3.2 Vertical Integration and Variety**

Within the same model, I now want to endogenise the number of retailers. After imposing symmetry, profit of a vertically integrated firm can be written as

$$\pi^{vi} = (p - c)(v + e(1 + \alpha(n-1)) - p) - nf, \tag{6.32}$$

whereas the profit of an independent retailer is

$$\pi^{vs} = (p - w)\frac{1}{n}(v + e(1 + \alpha(n - 1)) - p) - f. \qquad (6.33)$$

To determine endogenously the number of retailers operating at equilibrium, consider that under vertical integration entry occurs up to the point that maximises π^{vi}, whereas under vertical separation it occurs up to the point that makes $\pi^{vs} = 0$ (the standard free entry condition, under the assumption that n is continuous).

The conditions which determine the number of retailers at equilibrium are therefore

$$\frac{\partial \pi^{vi}}{\partial n} = (p - c)\alpha e - f = 0, \qquad (6.34)$$

and

$$\pi^{vs} = (p - w)\frac{1}{n}(v + e(1 + \alpha(n - 1)) - p) - f = 0. \qquad (6.35)$$

There are two different effects at work. First, a vertically integrated firm internalises the fact that the output produced by an additional variety decreases the output sold of the existing varieties. Note however that in this particular model we deal with a special case, as industry demand does not increase with the varieties available, so that there is reason to increase n only when this affects significantly the total output through the advertising spillover. In fact, if α is low enough, or if the cost of effort is very large (leading to a very low equilibrium value of e), the vertically integrated monopolist will have only one retailer. More generally, one should expect that consumers have a preference for variety and that an additional variety would increase total demand (see Exercise 6.5). However, the case analysed here provides a useful benchmark case in that a vertically integrated monopolist does not have an incentive to increase the number of outlets to attract new demand. Second, the profit margin of an additional outlet is higher under vertical integration because of the double marginalisation effect. One should expect this latter externality – which *ceteris paribus* would raise the number of varieties under vertical integration – to be outweighed by the former, so that more varieties are produced under a decentralised structure than under a centralised one.

To be able to study the welfare impact of vertical restraints in the model, abstract now for simplicity from effort considerations (i.e., from the advertising spillovers), so that the intercept is given by v alone. (Think for instance of the marginal cost of effort μ as tending to infinity, so that retailers will choose to make effort $e = 0$.)[25]

We know that *a priori* it is not clear whether the final price is higher or lower under vertical integration, since there are two distinct forces at work. First, under separation and linear pricing the horizontal pecuniary externality leads to lower

---

[25] Note that in this case the optimal number of retailers under vertical integration is one.

prices *given* the wholesale price; second, under separation and linear pricing the vertical externality leads to higher wholesale prices which in turn push prices upward. To see which force is dominant we have to find the wholesale price chosen by the upstream manufacturer. It turns out that under vertical integration prices are always smaller. Let us see why.

Under *vertical integration* the price can be easily obtained by replacing $e = 0$ in equation (6.25). One obtains $p^I = (v + c)/2$.

Under *vertical separation* and linear pricing, we have to find the optimal wholesale price w charged by the manufacturer. By replacing $e = 0$ in equation (6.24) one obtains $p^S = (v + w(1 + \gamma - \gamma/n))/(2 + \gamma - \gamma/n)$. The total output sold by the manufacturer will then be $Q^S = nq^S = (v - w)(1 + \gamma - \gamma/n)/(2 + \gamma - \gamma/n)$. The manufacturer's profit is given by $\pi^u = (w - c)Q^S$. By substituting and maximising with respect to w, one finds the optimal wholesale price as $w^* = (v + c)/2$. By replacing this value in p^S one finds the final price as $p^* = (v(3 + \gamma - \gamma/n) + c(1 + \gamma - \gamma/n))/(2(2 + \gamma - \gamma/n))$.

We can now compare the final prices under the two vertical structures. It is easy to see that $p^* \geq p^I$. Indeed, p^* decreases with the substitutability parameter γ, but $\lim_{\gamma \to \infty} p^* = (v + c)/2 = p^I$. Even when at its minimum, p^* is therefore higher than p^I.[26]

In this model, vertical integration will never reduce welfare. Independently of the number of retailers n, we have $p^* \geq p^I$: prices are always lower under vertical integration. Further, recall that in this model industry demand does not rise with the number of retailers. Therefore, $p^* \geq p^I$ implies $q^* \leq q^I$, irrespective of the number of retailers operating at equilibrium. Therefore, vertical integration leads to lower prices because it internalises the double marginalisation problem.

A second source of welfare improvement comes from the elimination of duplications. Separation results in a larger number of outlets and higher fixed costs which do not really add to consumers' utility as quantity demanded does not increase with the variety supplied. This is a very specific feature of the model. However, the reader can check in Exercise 6.5 that in a similar model, but where preferences exhibit love for variety, the impact of vertical integration on welfare is still positive. (Remember, though, that this is not always true: it is possible to devise models where the effect of reduced variety outweighs the effect of lower prices.)

6.2.4 Other Efficiency Reasons for Vertical Restraints and Vertical Mergers

We have focused so far on two efficiency motives behind vertical restraints, namely double marginalisation and externalities in the provision of retailers' services for a given brand. These are possibly among the best known (and more easily formalised

---

[26] Note that for $\gamma = 0$, $p^I < p^* = (3v + c)/4$, which is the same expression we found when discussing the double marginalisation issue.

and explained), but they are by no means the only sources of efficiency of vertical restraints and vertical mergers. Writing an exhaustive list of such efficiency reasons is beyond the scope of this work, but it is important to give an idea of how widespread they are. In what follows, I underline some of them. Note that I do not restrict the analysis to intra-brand competition, but consider also efficiency motives that exist when a manufacturer competes with rival brands.

Quality Certification   In the same spirit as the free-riding argument, Marvel and McCafferty (1984) suggest that some retailers provide customers with a quality certification service. By stocking some products, these retailers implicitly guarantee for the quality of the products in the eyes of customers. It does not really matter for this argument whether any kind of quality certification really happens or if consumers just assume that by being stocked by a certain "fancy" shop the product must be good. What matters for the argument is that such certification activity involves some costs (again, this might simply be due to the fact that a shop is located in a posh district and exhibits marble walls and smart assistants) and presents a public good characteristic: other shops might benefit from such activities and – given that they can afford a lower price because they do not engage in them – can attract consumers away from the certified product. This argument might justify restraints such as RPM (if the certifying shop cannot be undercut, there is no reason why the consumer should get the product elsewhere after having observed that the product is stocked there) and *selective distribution*. In the latter case, only a certain type of shop, showing some particular characteristics, is entitled to sell the product. For instance, a manufacturer of luxury goods might want to sell only through shops which have some characteristics, such as being located in a high street, being specialised, having dedicated personnel, having particular amenities and so on. As a consequence, it might refuse to supply the product to say discount stores or supermarkets. Although one might wonder about the use of the word "efficiency" to label such restraints, one should also recognise that not allowing a manufacturer to protect the image of its good in this way might be harmful not only to itself but also to consumers who do value the luxury features of the good. It is conceivable that – by prohibiting such marketing strategy – the luxury image would collapse and consumers would not be ready to pay for the product any longer. In turn, it might simply disappear and, strange as it may sound, the utility of all those who would have been prepared to pay for such a luxury good would diminish.[27] It should be

---

[27] Recall that the quality of a good is the quality as it is perceived by consumers, rather than the extrinsic quality of a product itself. Advertising – for instance – is another way through which a manufacturer can increase the image of its product, and most consumers are indeed happier to pay a premium for highly advertised products rather than purchasing similar products which are cheaper and not advertised. (Think of cigarettes, colas, detergents and most of mass consumer products ...) This implies that the utility of such consumers decreases if the former products disappeared from the market, or if advertising were forbidden!

noted, though, that as in the free-riding argument above, the quality certification story holds only insofar as the retailers are not able to appropriate the services they provide. For instance, a supermarket chain which invests heavily in ensuring that food products have really been produced via a fully biological process should be able to limit the spillover of its quality certification (biological labelling) investment. It is also unclear to what extent shops which provide quality certification through investing in luxury premises are not able to appropriate their investment. On the one hand, if items on sale there involve small amounts of money, it is unlikely that consumers would first go there to check what is on offer and then take the car and go and search in a discount store for its availability. On the other hand, the rumour that a certain item is sold in a certain type of shop might spread quickly, possibly ruining the luxury image, as the free-riding argument suggests. In conclusion, the free-riding and the quality certification arguments are sensible, but they do not necessarily apply to all products. Only an analysis of the industry and the market can tell to which extent they apply to a given set of products.

Free-Riding Among Producers Although restrictive by definition in that they oblige a retailer not to carry products of competing producers, exclusive contracts might be efficient. For instance, they can stimulate the investments in retailers' services made by a producer, such as technical support, promotion, training, equipment and financing. To the extent that such investments favour not a particular brand but the retail outlet in general, other producers would also benefit from them. This gives rise to a free-riding problem that may be solved by resorting to exclusive dealers (i.e., retailers cannot stock products from competing brands), as the technical treatment below formally shows. Exclusive dealing might also push a retailer to sell a brand more aggressively than if it devoted its marketing effort among different brands, thereby raising competition.[28]

Restraints which Remove Opportunistic Behaviour and Promote Specific Investments The existence of long-term contracts between a manufacturer and a retailer (or, *a fortiori*, their integration) might also have positive effects on the specific investments that both parties have to make in their relationships. There are many investments which lose most of their value outside a particular relationship, because they are tailored and dedicated to a particular partner (think for instance of a firm which devises its machinery to work with a particular intermediate good or input, or to a franchisee that devotes important investments to carry and promote a particular brand). In such cases, the danger that the relationship is broken or discontinued will generally lead to an underinvestment problem. If a distributor fears that his promotion effort to establish a brand's image might next year benefit

---

[28] However, we shall see in Sections 6.2.5 and 6.4 that such clauses are not without drawbacks and must be carefully evaluated.

another shop located in the same area and carrying the same brand, he will think twice before investing heavily in such an activity. Likewise, a producer will be deterred from investing in assets which might improve a distributor's performance if the latter is likely to switch to other brands. To avoid such opportunistic behaviour (a firm getting out of the relationship after the partner has made specific investments into it), clauses such as exclusive territories and exclusive dealing are helpful. By reducing or eliminating the underinvestment problem, they increase efficiency. Of course, the same holds for vertical mergers. In this case, the interests of the manufacturer and of the retailer are aligned, and they will coordinate so as to attain the same objective.

Exclusive Dealing Avoids Free-Riding on Manufacturers' Investment*   In this section, I formalise one of the efficiency rationales behind exclusive dealing. This is based on the idea that manufacturers often provide their retailers with services and investments which promote sales of the manufacturer's brand. In some circumstances, however, since such services and investments benefit the retailer, they might also promote sales of competing brands sold by the same retailer. This externality reduces the appropriability of the investment. Exclusive dealing (ED), obliging the retailer to carry only one brand, might then be adopted as a clause by the manufacturer, in order to avoid such an externality. ED might then increase the incentive to invest in such services, which in turn is generally welfare-improving.

The following model, a variation of Besanko and Perry (1993), formalises this idea and shows that a ban on exclusive dealing would reduce consumer surplus and welfare.

Two manufacturers produce two differentiated goods at constant unit cost (which I equal to zero for simplicity). Each manufacturer can invest in an activity which reduces the cost of the retailer carrying its brand. The level of the investment is denoted by e_i, and its cost is $(\mu/2)e_i^2$. There exists a possible spillover of such an investment, so that a retailer carrying both brands benefits from the effective investment $\widehat{e}_i = e_i + \alpha e_j$, when it sells brand i, where $\alpha \in [0, 1]$ is the externality parameter (for $\alpha = 0$, there is no spillover, whereas for $\alpha = 1$ the externality is maximal, as it equally benefits the rival manufacturer and the manufacturer who is investing). A retailer that has agreed on an exclusive dealing contract will have its cost reduced only by $\widehat{e}_i = e_i$. I assume that demand for each product is given by the (usual) following demand function:

$$q_i = \frac{1}{2}\left[v - p_i(1+\gamma) + \frac{\gamma}{2}(p_i + p_j)\right]. \tag{6.36}$$

I also assume that there are a large number of retailers in the market that compete in price and provide undifferentiated services (or, which is equivalent, that are perfectly competitive).[29] Each retailer's cost of selling brand i is given by $d + w_i - \widehat{e_i}$, where w_i is the wholesale price charged by manufacturer i, d is the distribution cost.[30]

The timing of the game is as follows. First, manufacturers make simultaneous investment and wholesale price decisions. Then, retailers choose prices. Our objective is to compare the equilibrium solutions of this game under two alternative contractual situations, one where retailers operate under ED, and one where there is no exclusive dealing (NED) – retailers can sell both brands. Besanko and Perry (1993) analyse the full game, where manufacturers decide at a pre-stage of the game whether to choose ED or NED, but this involves having at least three firms (with two firms, if one choose ED the other is *de facto* also obliged to rely on an exclusive retailer) and complicates the calculations.[31]

Solution of the Game At the last stage of the game, retailers would set prices equal to their marginal costs $p_i = d + w_i - \widehat{e_i}$. Consider first the case where there is no exclusive dealing arrangement (NED). Replacing equilibrium prices one obtains the quantities as a function of wholesale prices and investment levels. At the previous stage, manufacturers $\max_{w_i,e_i} \pi_i = w_i q_i(e_i, e_j, w_i, w_j) - (\mu/2)e_i^2$. By taking the FOCs $\partial \pi_i/\partial e_i = 0$, $\partial \pi_i/\partial w_i = 0$, imposing symmetry and solving the system, one obtains the equilibrium solutions as

$$w_i^{NED} = \frac{4\mu(v-d)}{2\mu(4+\gamma) - (1+\alpha)(2+\gamma(1-\alpha))};$$ (6.37)

$$e_i^{NED} = \frac{(2+\gamma(1-\alpha))(v-d)}{2\mu(4+\gamma) - (1+\alpha)(2+\gamma(1-\alpha))}.$$ (6.38)

---

[29] This assumption is made to avoid foreclosure issues and to bring forward in a neater way the efficiency effect of exclusive dealing. Since there are several retailers selling one same brand, strategic delegation issues (see Section 6.3.1.1) are also avoided.

[30] I also impose two conditions on parameters in order to obtain positive values at equilibrium: $\mu > (1+\alpha)(2+\gamma(1-\alpha))/2(4+\gamma)$. In addition, d has to be large enough.

[31] Please refer to their article for the full game. Notice, however, that I choose a different formalisation of the externality, and this modifies considerably the results. In particular, in my version of the model manufacturers have a collective preference for ED, whereas in Besanko and Perry it depends on the values of the externality and substitutability parameters. Their function is $\widehat{e_i} = \lambda e_i + (1 - \lambda)e_j$, and it is such that the externality not only benefits the other firms but also reduces the own marginal profit from investing. (*A priori*, I do not see any reason to prefer one formalisation over the other, and my choice was determined only by the fact that calculations turn out to be simpler.) All the results are qualitatively similar, except for the fact that in Besanko and Perry ED is not always collectively preferred by the manufacturers. In their game, a prisoner's dilemma might arise, in that ED might be chosen at equilibrium, but the manufacturers would prefer to be under NED.

By substitution, the other equilibrium values can be obtained. In particular,

$$p_i^{NED} = \frac{2d(2+\gamma)\mu + v(4\mu - (1+\alpha)(2+\gamma(1-\alpha)))}{2\mu(4+\gamma) - (1+\alpha)(2+\gamma(1-\alpha))}; \tag{6.39}$$

$$\pi_i^{NED} = \frac{\mu\left[4\gamma(2\mu - 1 + \alpha) + 16\mu - \gamma^2(1-\alpha)^2 - 4\right](v-d)^2}{[2\mu(4+\gamma) - (1+\alpha)(2+\gamma(1-\alpha))]^2}. \tag{6.40}$$

From these values, it is now easy to compute the equilibrium solutions for the case where retailers are engaged in ED agreements. Indeed, it is enough to impose $\alpha = 0$ to solve the ED case:

$$w_i^{ED} = \frac{4\mu(v-d)}{2\mu(4+\gamma) - (2+\gamma)}; \qquad e_i^{ED} = \frac{(2+\gamma)(v-d)}{2\mu(4+\gamma) - (2+\gamma)}, \tag{6.41}$$

$$p_i^{ED} = \frac{2d(2+\gamma)\mu + v(4\mu - (2+\gamma))}{2\mu(4+\gamma) - (2+\gamma)}; \tag{6.42}$$

$$\pi_i^{ED} = \frac{\mu\left[4\gamma(2\mu - 1 + 16\mu - \gamma^2 - 4\right](v-d)^2}{[2\mu(4+\gamma) - (2+\gamma)]^2}. \tag{6.43}$$

It is now easy to check that under exclusive dealing (ED): (i) investment levels are higher (this is due to the increased appropriability of the investment; in turn, this reduces the cost of distributing the brand); (ii) wholesale prices are higher (this is because lower distribution costs shift outwards the marginal revenue function of the firm, which can then increase wholesale prices); (iii) the retail price is lower (due to the dominant effect of the reduction in costs); (iv) manufacturers' profits are higher (retailers' profits are always nil due to the Bertrand competition assumption); and (v) finally, welfare is higher than under NED (since profits are higher and consumers are better off).

In this model, therefore, exclusive dealing has a welfare improving effect, and banning it would decrease both consumer surplus and manufacturers' profits.[32]

6.2.5 Vertical Restraints, Vertical Mergers, and the Commitment Problem

Vertical restraints and vertical mergers can have an adverse effect on welfare when they help a manufacturer (more generally, an upstream firm) to keep prices high, whereas without them it would not be able to commit to high prices. To understand why such a commitment problem arises, consider the following example. Suppose a manufacturer has a very successful brand of clothes which is well known everywhere,

---

[32] As indicated above, the result that profits are always higher under ED is sensitive to the specification of the externality function. However, the conclusion that ED leads to higher welfare is robust to alternative specifications. See Besanko and Perry (1993).

but that has not been sold yet in a given region. Suppose also that there is little demand uncertainty, so that total expected profit from selling these products would be π, and there is agreement on this estimate. There exist several possible franchisees ready to sell the brand. If the producer promised to give exclusivity for the region sales to one franchisee (and its promise were believed), competitive bidding would lead the winning bidder to offer π to the manufacturer. However, once it has sold the franchise, the producer has an incentive to renege on its exclusivity promise and engage in opportunistic behaviour. It could now offer a second franchise (and promise there would be no more than two) and, if its promise were believed, it would obtain up to an additional $\pi/2$ from a second franchisee (note that the first franchisee would have a loss equal to $\pi/2$). Once cashed in the second franchise, it could then renege again on the promise, and offer a third licence, etc . . .

Of course, the potential franchisees would anticipate all this, and if the manufacturer were unable to commit to give only one franchise contract, nobody would accept to buy the licence for it. Everyone knows that the manufacturer has an incentive to renege on the promise, which will entail a loss for them. In other words, the manufacturer needs to find a way to commit itself in a credible way not to add new franchises in the market. Otherwise, it would be unable to obtain the profit π that its product could fetch.

Whenever this problem arises, a firm will not be able to appropriate the market power it potentially has. In this example, for instance, the clothes producer could potentially have a monopoly profit, but the presence of a large number of potential franchisees together with the lack of commitment power might result in the buyers accepting to buy the franchise only for a very low price, and the producer earning very little profit, rather than the monopoly profit.[33]

The same commitment problem arises in more general circumstances, whenever a firm has an input (or product) and can sell it to more than one buyer (or more than one retailer): it might have an incentive to privately renegotiate the terms of the contract with some buyers after having signed with all of them. Equivalently, if the contracts were not publicly observable, it might have an incentive to agree on better terms with one or more buyers after some have already signed a contract.

To further illustrate the point, consider the following example. Suppose that there are two retailers selling the same homogenous product in the same town. If they both pay the wholesale price w, the retailers sell a quantity Q at price p and they each make profits $\pi/2$. A possible (non-linear) contract the manufacturer of the good can offer its two retailers is that they buy each at a price w if they make a fixed

---

[33] The first paper which studied the commitment problem in the context of vertical relationships is Hart and Tirole (1990). Subsequent contributions are due to O'Brien and Shaffer (1992) and McAfee and Schwartz (1994), and, more recently, Chemla (2003). Rey and Tirole (1996) analyse the incentive to foreclose access by the owner of an essential facility (or an input produced by a monopolist) and the related policy issues. It is the main reference for those who would like to understand these issues better.

payment $\pi/2$. (Each retailer would make zero profit and would accept this contract if not anticipating opportunistic behaviour by the monopolist.) After the contracts have been signed, however, the monopolist might go to one of the two retailers and offer him the product at a slightly lower unit price than w. This would allow this retailer to get a competitive advantage and increase its market share (possibly, it could get the whole market), making $\pi' > \pi/2$ under the new contract. It would therefore be willing to pay up to π' for the new terms. At the expense of the other retailer, who still has to pay $\pi/2$, the manufacturer would therefore obtain after renegotiation an additional profit $\pi' - \pi/2$. However, the temptation to renegotiate the contract will be anticipated by each retailer, who would then be unwilling to enter a contract with the manufacturer unless a very low fixed payment is set. Again, the monopolist would be unable to exploit its potential market power, being hurt by its lack of commitment, that is, by the temptation to change the terms with the retailers.

The reader will have noticed the close similarity with the problem of the durable good monopolist (see Chapter 2). There as well, it was the impossibility to commit to a certain action (the future price) which prevented the monopolist from exercising market power. Like the durable good monopolist, though, an upstream producer also has the possibility to solve the commitment problem so as to restore its market power. Vertical restraints (other than simple non-linear contracts) and vertical mergers are among such instruments, as I explain below. Before doing so, however, it is worth noting that the commitment problem arises only for an upstream firm which needs wholesalers or retailers to sell the product to final customers, not for a downstream retailer who sells directly to final customers. Suppose that the structure of the market is reversed relative to the one described above, so that there is a monopolistic downstream firm which can buy (substitutable) inputs from two or more upstream suppliers. The retailer does not have any incentive to renegotiate the supply contract with the upstream firms, since it controls the final market price itself. This means that – if it were possible to design the structure of the industry – it would be preferable to have competition at the level of the interaction with consumers.[34]

Vertical Mergers   A natural solution for the manufacturer to commit to high prices is to merge with one of the downstream firms.[35] If it did so, it would

---

[34] For instance, if there were a distributor which enjoys monopoly power, it would make sense to allow final consumers to buy directly from producers and let producers buy access from the distributor. This policy, known as "common carrier" policy, effectively turns the downstream firms upstream and vice versa. See Rey and Tirole (1996) for a discussion and some examples, mostly from the telecommunications and energy sectors. Although fascinating, I do not dwell on this topic since it is more an issue of regulation rather than competition, as it entails redesigning the structure of the industry.

[35] Obviously, complete vertical integration, that is, taking over all the downstream firms, would also solve the commitment problem. But this is not only unnecessary – as the same outcome could

internalise the profit made by its downstream affiliate, and therefore would not have any incentive to offer better terms to other downstream firms, since this would diminish the profit made by its affiliate, and therefore by itself. Foreclosure of the rival downstream firms would then be likely to arise, as the upstream unit would not have incentives to supply the input to the rival retailers. Indeed, to restore monopoly power it might be optimal to supply only the affiliate and avoid making the inputs available to rivals. It can be shown, however, that a vertical merger would not always result in complete foreclosure of rival downstream firms. If there were other substitute (but inferior) inputs, the upstream firm would prefer to supply the downstream rivals itself, rather than letting them be supplied by an upstream competitor. (See Section 6.2.5.1.)

It is interesting to note that in the absence of competing upstream suppliers a vertical merger would be maximally detrimental, because it would lead to complete foreclosure of downstream rivals and would determine a price rise up to the monopoly level. When (less efficient) upstream suppliers exist, however, a vertical merger will increase prices but not to the same extent the retailers' threat of switching to alternative suppliers limits the exercise of market power of the vertically integrated more efficient firm. Again, vertical restraints might be welfare detrimental but their adverse effect would be limited by the presence of competing suppliers of the input. This can be interpreted by saying that the larger the upstream market power the more attention should be devoted to vertical practices.

Exclusive Territories   Since the problem of the producer comes from the presence of several buyers, an obvious way to restore market power is to credibly restrict itself to supply the product (or input) to only one such buyer in each market area.[36] If a contract establishing that there is only one buyer which can sell the product within a certain specified area is legal, then the manufacturer's problem is solved. In the region protected by the exclusivity clause, competition among the potential retailers will bring them to pay up to the monopoly price to have the opportunity to be the only dealer selling the good. This will allow the manufacturer to restore all its monopoly profit. The counterpart of this is that exclusive territory harms welfare: consumers will pay the monopoly price rather than the lower price that would have arisen without the exclusivity clause. The usual allocative inefficiency occurs, as the higher producer surplus does not outweigh the lower consumer surplus.

The effect of such a contract is therefore to foreclose access to the product to all retailers apart from one. Note also that if competing upstream suppliers exist, the

---

be established with just one merger – but also very unlikely to be approved by the anti-trust authorities.

[36] Similarly to the durable good monopolist case, reputation might also help the monopolist. If a stream of inputs were brought to the market by the monopolist over time, there is a repeated game played between a manufacturer and a retailer. Even in the absence of an explicit exclusivity clause, the manufacturer might have an incentive to build for itself the reputation to deal with only one retailer at a time.

welfare impact of an exclusive dealing clause is more adverse than under a vertical merger. Indeed, if a less efficient supplier of the input existed, under a vertical merger the upstream firm of the vertically integrated firm would end up supplying the downstream rivals as well. (Since they would obtain the input anyhow, it would be better to provide them with it rather than letting them be served by the upstream rival.) But if the efficient upstream firm signs an exclusive deal, it will be prevented from serving other retailers. As a result, they will be supplied by the less efficient upstream firm, thereby adding a productive efficiency loss to the allocative inefficiency.

Resale Price Maintenance   Since the problem of the monopolist is to guarantee that there is no renegotiation which leads to higher output or lower prices, the commitment problem is solved if the monopolist commits to industry-wide prices (O'Brien and Shaffer, 1992).[37] Consider for instance RPM clauses such as those still legal in many European countries for products like books and pharmaceuticals. The producer prints the final market price on the product itself, and RPM can be enforced in the courts. Retailers cannot sell at a discount price (they can be taken to court if they did), and this clearly takes away any incentive for the producer to secretly cut wholesale prices: a price cut would not increase final sales, it would only worsen the distribution of the profit between itself and the retailer that gets a discount.[38]

Most-Favoured Nation Clause and Anti-Discrimination Laws   Suppose that the manufacturer was able to credibly commit to and enforce a clause stating that whenever it offers a price discount to one retailer, all other retailers are also entitled to it. This would remove any temptation to renege on a previously signed contract with some retailers. (Consider for instance the franchise example at the beginning of this section. If after having signed a contract with one franchisee for a price of π, the manufacturer sold a franchise to a second retailer for the price of $\pi/2$, under MFN it would have to reimburse the first retailer of $\pi/2$. Clearly, there would be no point in reneging on the promise and offering the franchise to a second retailer.)

One problem with MFN is clearly the observability of price discounts and therefore the enforceability of such a clause. (If a retailer could not observe a discount made to another, how could MFN be applied?) Since the commitment problem arises in situations where contracts are not observable, it would seem that the same

---

[37] O'Brien and Shaffer (1992), in a model with differentiated goods and price competition, also show that (bilateral) retail-level price ceilings accompanied by wholesale pricing at the same level can also restore monopoly power.

[38] In the US, industry-wide resale price floor was established thanks to state laws (so-called "non-signer" laws) according to which all retailers should abide to the RPM contract offered by the manufacturer as long as at least one retailer had signed such a contract. See O'Brien and Shaffer (1992: 306), who also offer some anecdotal evidence showing that RPM had been used in the US to solve the commitment problem.

circumstances also make it difficult to use MFN clauses. However, suppose that the producer had to pay a heavy penalty if it was caught offering better terms to some buyers than others. Then, it is likely that it would refrain from renegotiating its price offers, and this would be equivalent to enforcement of the MFN clause. This is precisely what happens under the current EU competition law. Both the Commission and the European Court of Justice consider as an abuse of a dominant position the practice of discriminating among buyers by a firm endowed with market power. As in the *Michelin* case, dominant firms would be heavily fined if they were to offer different terms of supply to different buyers,[39] and suppliers should abide to the principle of "transparent pricing": they cannot offer secret price discounts to buyers. Whatever the reason why the Commission and the ECJ introduced and enforce this rule, it is clear that it helps the provider of an input solve its commitment problem. Contrary to what they expect, the "transparency rule" will help firms endowed with market power to keep prices high, to the detriment of welfare.

Conclusions This section has shown a case where vertical restraints and vertical mergers might be welfare detrimental. If contracts between an upstream monopolist and downstream retailers are not publicly observable, the monopolist is hurt by its temptation to renegotiate supply terms (which will be anticipated by the retailers unwilling to accept high input prices). It suffers therefore from the same commitment problem as a durable good monopolist. A merger with a downstream firm, or vertical clauses such as exclusive territories and resale price maintenance, might solve the monopolist's commitment problem and help it exercise its monopoly power, to the detriment of overall welfare.

Note that the magnitude of the damage created by the vertical restraints identified above (or by a vertical merger) depends on the upstream firm being a monopolist or not. If there are competing suppliers, even if less efficient, the harm done by such practices is diminished. This suggests again that it is worth monitoring such practices only when they are undertaken by firms enjoying sufficient market power.

Another important policy conclusion, perhaps of even more practical relevance, is that laws that impose "transparency" of prices and contracts between vertically related firms, or that oblige upstream firms not to discriminate among buyers, are misguided. Rather than fostering price competition, they provide upstream firms with an efficient and credible commitment not to secretly undercut prices to buyers, thereby allowing them to enforce high prices. The EU competition rules are a case in point, and they should be revised.

---

[39] This does not mean that a firm cannot engage in any form of price discrimination. It is perfectly legitimate for a firm to offer prices based on the quantities bought by the buyers. What is not legitimate is to offer different conditions for similar contracts, or for the same number of units bought.

6.2.5.1 Vertical Restraints and the Commitment Problem**

Suppose there exists an upstream manufacturer, M, which sells a product to two retailers, R_1 and R_2. The manufacturer has a constant production cost c, and the retailers' only variable cost is given by the wholesale price they have to pay to the supplier of the input. (For simplicity, we restrict attention to contracts where they are offered the input at a unit cost c.) The two retailers produce a homogenous good and compete in quantities.[40] Final demand is given by $p = 1 - Q$, where $Q = q_1 + q_2$ is the total output. The manufacturer has all the bargaining power and makes take-it-or-leave-it offers to the retailers. The game is as follows. First, M offers each retailer a contract (F_i, q_i), where F_i is a fixed fee and q_i the number of units that the retailer wants to buy. Then, each retailer orders q_i units of the product and pays F_i. Finally, each retailer will bring q_i to the market and the market will clear.

Let me make two remarks about this game. First, note that I focus only on non-linear contracts. This is because when there is market power downstream we know that linear contracts are not optimal, in that they do not reproduce the vertically-integrated outcome.[41] Second, note that I assume that retailers pay for the input *before* they go to the final market. If they agreed on a contract but they paid for the input only *after* they go to the final market, then the upstream firm would not have an incentive to renegotiate. (See Exercise 6.7.)

Observable Contracts: A Benchmark As a benchmark case, it is easy to check that the vertically integrated outcome is given by $Q^{vi} = (1-c)/2$, $p^{vi} = (1+c)/2$, $\pi^{vi} = (1-c)^2/4$.[42] The same outcome can be obtained if contracts offered by M were observed by each retailer (and could not be renegotiated). In this case, the manufacturer would offer each of them a contract (F_i, q_i) whereby $F_i = (1-c)^2/8$ if the retailer buys $q_i = (1-c)/4$ units, and $F_i = \infty$ for any other quantity.

Unobservable Contracts The vertically integrated outcome cannot be restored under unobservability. To see why, suppose that retailer R_1 has accepted M's offer (F_i, q_i) as above. The manufacturer's profit, if it is able to appropriate R_2's profit through a fixed fee, is $\pi' = (1 - (1-c)/4 - q_2 - c)q_2 + (1-c)^2/8$. By setting $\partial \pi'/\partial q_2 = 0$, one obtains $q_2' = 3(1-c)/8 > q_1 = q^{vi}$. This is the output

---

[40] Price competition with differentiated goods gives rise to some complications, but the qualitative results are the same. See O'Brien and Shaffer (1992) and Rey and Vergé (2002b) for the analysis with price competition. See also Exercise 6.7.

[41] As emphasised by O'Brien and Shaffer (1992), this literature shows that non-linear contracts are not able either to restore the vertically integrated outcome when the upstream firm makes unobservable offers.

[42] This follows from the standard monopoly problem, which is to set Q so as to maximise $\pi = (1 - Q - c)Q$. The result is immediately obtained from $\partial \pi/\partial Q = 0$. Owning both retailers, the fully vertically integrated firm is indifferent as to how to distribute output among them, as long as $Q^{vi} = (1-c)/2$.

that M would offer to the second retailer. Since retailer 2's output is higher, the market price will fall below p^{vi}. As a result, retailer 1 will make a profit $3(1-c)^2/32 < (1-c)^2/8 = F_i$. Therefore, the contract offer (F_i, q_i) cannot be an equilibrium, since each retailer would anticipate that if it signed such a contract, the manufacturer would have an incentive to offer larger output to the rival, which in turn would create losses for it.[43]

We know then that the contract which restores the vertically integrated outcome cannot be an equilibrium. We still have to determine what the equilibrium is. To do so, given unobservability, we have to make assumptions about the beliefs that a retailer has about the offer that will be received by the other retailer. Following Hart and Tirole (1990), O'Brien and Shaffer (1992) and Rey and Tirole (1996) assume "passive beliefs" (also called market-by-market conjectures): if a retailer receives an unexpected offer from the manufacturer, it does not revise its belief about the offer received by the rival. We look for the Perfect Bayesian Equilibrium of this game, which requires each agent to choose its best action given the action of the other agents and given its beliefs.

If retailer R_1 expects that R_2 is offered to buy q_2, how much is R_1 willing to buy and at which price? Its expected market profit would be $\pi_1 = (1 - q_1 - q_2 - c)q_1$. Profit maximisation would lead it to buy $q_1 = (1 - q_2 - c)/2$ units, and pay up to $\pi_1 = (1 - q_2 - c)^2/4$. Symmetrically, the other retailer would buy $q_2 = (1 - q_1 - c)/2$ units. Note that $q_i = (1 - q_j - c)/2 = r_i(j)$, which is the usual reaction function under quantity competition. The only equilibrium occurs where both firms are on their reaction function, and it is given by the Cournot output $q^C = (1 - c)/3$ and both retailers will be ready to pay up to $(1 - c)^2/9$. Clearly, the manufacturer will make less profit than under the vertically integrated (or observable contracts) outcome, as $2(1 - c)^2/9 < (1 - c)^2/4$. It can be shown that the larger the number of retailers, the lower the profit that the manufacturer can make (the commitment problem is aggravated). See Exercise 6.6.

How to Restore Market Power

- Vertical mergers. Suppose there is a merger between M and R_1. Then, offering $q = (1 - c)/4$ to both the affiliate and the independent retailer R_2 cannot be an equilibrium, as R_2 would correctly anticipate that M has an incentive to increase the output of its affiliate. On the other hand, $q = (1 - c)/3$, that is the Cournot contract, cannot be an equilibrium because the chain $M - R_1$ can obtain higher profit simply by foreclosing access to the input to retailer R_2. Indeed, by setting $q_1 = (1 - c)/2$ and $q_2 = 0$, the vertically integrated profit can be obtained.

---

[43] Note that if M did not have all the bargaining power, the same reasoning would still hold. The sum of the profit of M and R_2 after R_1 has signed the contract (F_i, q_i) would still be $\pi' = (1 - (1 - c)/4 - q_2 - c)q_2$, leading to the same choice of output (F_i will be used to distribute profit, and it will depend on the relative bargaining power of M and R_2).

- Exclusive territories. With just one retailer downstream, market power can be exercised as the commitment problem does not arise. As long as the exclusivity clause is enforceable in courts, a retailer who is offered exclusivity and to buy $(1-c)/2$ units for a price up to $(1-c)^2/4$ will accept the contract, which then restores the vertically integrated solution.
- Industry-wide RPM (price floor). If an industry-wide price floor $p \geq p^{vi} = (1+c)/2$ is enforceable, then the commitment problem is solved. Each retailer would be offered $q = (1-c)/4$ and firm M would have no incentive to behave in an opportunistic way. Suppose R_1 has already signed the contract. If M offered a larger quantity to R_2, the total profit to be made would be $\pi^* = ((1+c)/2 - c)q_2$ for $q_2 \leq (1-c)/4$.[44] Therefore, $q_2 \geq (1-c)/4$ gives M the highest profit compatible with the price floor.
- Most-favoured nation (MFN) clause (or most-favoured customer clause). Suppose each retailer is offered a contract together with a MFN clause,[45] which states that if a price discount (or a better price) is given to one retailer, then all other retailers will also receive the same better offer. (This is also the definition of *symmetric beliefs*.) This means that whenever a retailer is offered q units of the input, it will expect its rival also to buy q. Therefore, its expected profit is $\pi = (1 - q - q - c)q$, and it will be ready to buy $q^{vi} = (1-c)/4$ units and pay up to $(1-c)^2/8$. The manufacturer is able to restore its best outcome.

Vertical Mergers and Exclusive Dealing when a Substitute Input Exists[46]   Suppose now that M is not the only supplier: there also exists a less efficient supplier of the product, S, whose cost is $s > c$, with S not being too inefficient: we assume $s \in (c, (1+c)/2]$. Look first at what happens when there is *vertical separation*. Since M will end up supplying both retailers, the solution will be the same as for the case without substitute inputs and both retailers will be offered and will order $q^C = (1-c)/3$. The market price will be $p^C = (1+2c)/3$. However, note that a retailer will not be willing to pay a fee up to the Cournot profit $(1-c)^2/9$ to the manufacturer M. By accepting that fee, it would have a zero payoff. Given that R_i accepts the contract, R_j would have an incentive to deviate and switch to the substitute good S. This deviation would give R_j a profit $\pi_j = (1 - q_j - q^C - s)q_j$. By choosing the optimising quantity $q' = (2 + c - 3s)/6$, retailer R_j would make $\pi' = (2 + c - 3s)^2/36$. Therefore, each retailer will be ready to accept the contract only if it has to pay up to π', and the manufacturer can make $2(\pi^C - \pi')$.

Suppose now that there is a vertical merger between M and, say, R_1. To understand what the equilibrium will be, consider first the case where R_2 decided to be supplied by S. This corresponds to the Cournot equilibrium with asymmetric costs c and

---

[44] The price floor is satisfied whenever $p = 1 - (1-c)/4 - q_2 \geq p^{vi}$. By substitution one obtains the condition $q_2 \leq (1-c)/4$. Higher output for R_2 would violate the RPM condition.

[45] See the discussion in the text for the conditions under which a MFN clause could be meaningful.

[46] See Hart and Tirole (1990) and Rey and Tirole (1996).

s. Quantities are $q_1^* = (1 - 2c + s)/3$, $q_2^* = (1 - 2s + c)/3$. Profits are $\pi_1^* = (1 - 2c + s)^2/9$, $\pi_2^* = (1 - 2s + c)^2/9$. Therefore, the independent retailer could always threaten to switch to S if it is not offered q_2^* units. At best, M can offer precisely the same conditions as S to the second retailer, that is q_2^* units at a unit price s. The vertical chain will then make a profit $\pi = \pi_1^* + (s - c)q_2^*$.

Note that under the vertical merger, the final price will be $p = (1 + c + s)/3$. Hence, the price increase the consumer will have to bear relative to the situation of vertical separation is $p - p^C = (s - c)/3$. In other words, the larger the efficiency gap between the upstream firms, the larger the welfare loss which will result from the vertical merger. The competition of alternative suppliers reduces the risk of vertical mergers.

One can also note that although foreclosure is not complete if an alternative supplier exists, still the independent retailer is worse off under the vertical merger, as $\pi' = (2 + c - 3s)^2/36 > (1 - 2s + c)^2/9$ for $s > c$.

6.2.6 Conclusions

This section has shown that vertical mergers and vertical restraints that affect only intra-brand competition are mostly efficiency-enhancing. They allow firms to control for externalities that affect the vertical relationship with other firms, thereby increasing profits of the vertical chain, as well as, in most cases, consumer surplus. The analysis has also unveiled some special cases (notably when they might lead to the overprovision of services – see Section 6.2.2 – and when they help a manufacturer solve a commitment problem – see Section 6.2.5) where vertical restraints and vertical mergers might reduce welfare. However, their adverse effects shrink when there is competition in the market.

The main conclusion of this section is therefore that vertical restraints which affect intra-brand competition do not raise many welfare problems; certainly, they are not worth investigating when firms that adopt them do not have high market power.

Another important implication of the analysis carried out here is that vertical restraints are often substitutable – at least to some extent – with each other. Accordingly, differential treatment of vertical restraints (for instance, allowing some and forbidding others) does not appear to be justified.

However, these conclusions are still provisional, since I have so far given little consideration to the effect of vertical restraints on inter-brand competition. It is to this topic that I turn next.

6.3 INTER-BRAND COMPETITION

In the previous section, I focused on the case where only one upstream manufacturer could use vertical contracts, so inter-brand competition was not an issue. However, by modifying the choices (investment, price and so on) made by a vertical chain (i.e., the manufacturer of a brand and its distributors), vertical restraints will generally have an impact on the competition between this vertical chain and competing ones. I now analyse the effect of vertical restraints (and mergers) when several manufacturers sell through retailers. Section 6.3.1 shows that vertical restraints can be used strategically so as to relax competition between retailers and ultimately between manufacturers; Section 6.3.2 shows that they might favour collusive agreements; and Section 6.4 shows that they might be used to deter entry. Therefore, economic analysis certainly demonstrates that vertical clauses are by no means always beneficial (contrary to what the Chicago School used to claim). Nevertheless, vertical restraints (or some of them) are not always bad. First, I point out the conditions under which such restraints are harmful. Second, I recall that one should always weigh the possible negative effects upon inter-brand competition with the likely efficiency gains of vertical restraints illustrated in the previous section. Again, the main conclusion will be that one should worry about vertical restraints only when they involve firms endowed with large market power.

6.3.1 Strategic Effects of Vertical Restraints

There is a large amount of literature that analyses the strategic rationale behind vertical restraints under imperfect competition. The main insight comes from principal-agent models, which emphasise how a principal in certain circumstances has an incentive to delegate a decision to an agent, who is more likely to perform a certain action than the principal if provided with appropriate incentives. Suppose for instance that there are two entrepreneurs in a market. Each of them would like to keep prices high, but the usual market forces would lead them to undercut each other, resulting in low prices. It would not be credible if one of them simply promised to the other that he would keep high prices and would not undercut. Each of them knows that the other will behave so as to maximise profits, and this implies that prices will be low, no matter how many promises are made. However, suppose now that one of the two entrepreneurs hired a manager, delegated to her all price and market decisions and gave her a compensation which gives her a premium if the price she charged on the market is high enough. If this contract is observable by the rival, it makes it credible that the firm's manager will keep prices high and this pushes the rival to increase prices as well. What centralisation of decisions could not do, delegation might be able to. This is a principle which is well established in game theory and which has had many applications in different fields.[47]

---

[47] See for instance Fershtman and Judd (1987) and Sklivas (1987) for an analysis of contracts in oligopoly between owners and managers. The strategic trade policy literature also starts from the same principle. The principal (a country's government) offers subsidies to (or imposes taxes on) domestic firms so as to make credible their more aggressive (or softer) behaviour in international markets. In most applications of the delegation principle, policy implications are ambiguous (as

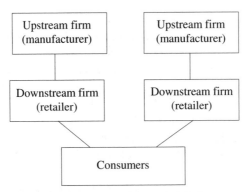

Figure 6.3. Competing vertical chains.

Gal-Or (1991), Vickers (1995), Bonanno and Vickers (1988) and Rey and Stiglitz (1988, 1995) are among the papers which have applied this principle to vertical restraints.[48] They study strategic effects of vertical restraints when there are competing vertical chains, as illustrated by Figure 6.3.

The main idea is that a manufacturer (the principal) might want to make its retailer a "softer" competitor in the final market, so as to achieve – through the strategic effect mentioned earlier – higher final prices and higher retailers' profits. The benefit from higher prices would then be recovered by the principal via a franchise fee.[49,50]

One type of vertical restraint which can be strategically used is a two-part tariff. Imagine that a manufacturer sells through an exclusive dealer. By choosing a high wholesale price, the former will make the latter raise its price in the market (since the wholesale price is the retailer's own cost, it needs to set higher prices to try and keep its mark-up), in turn making rival retailers more willing to raise prices. The effect will be higher profit for the vertical chain (the tariff can be used to appropriate the retailer's profit) but lower welfare.

Another vertical restraint that can relax inter-brand competition is exclusive territories. Consider a situation where a manufacturer sells its brands through a number of retailers (which carry only its brand). By removing intra-brand competition which would decrease the own brand prices in the market, and giving a

we shall see also below). Depending on the nature of market interactions, the principal gives very different incentives to its agent. This in turn determines different welfare effects.

[48] See Irmen (1998) for a review of this literature.

[49] In some circumstances, even without franchise fee the manufacturer will gain from vertical restraints. See for instance Rey and Stiglitz (1995).

[50] Note that the same logic applies to the case where it is the retailer – rather than the producer – that has the bargaining power. In this case, Shaffer (1991) shows that each retailer can manipulate strategically the wholesale price paid to the producer and recover the higher profit made by the vertical chain through a slotting allowance, that is a negative franchise fee that the producer pays the retailer in order to have access to the latter's shelf space. In what follows, I shall limit myself to the case where the bargaining power is on the producer.

retailer the power to behave as a brand monopolist, higher retail prices will be set. In turn, this will push rivals' prices up. Again, the brand profit will increase and welfare will be lower. Exclusive territorial clauses help also in the sense that they are visible and not easily renegotiated. (A contract has a commitment value, that is it can strategically affect the rivals' behaviour, if it can be publicly observed and cannot be easily modified.) Since they have a higher degree of commitment and visibility than non-linear contracts (the decision to delegate sales to a retailer can be easily observed, and it is likely to be irreversible in the short run, but the actual contract with the retailers will typically be private), their strategic potential is also higher.[51]

Note, however, that not all vertical restraints exercise these strategic effects. Resale price maintenance for instance cannot be used as a strategic restraint. The crucial idea is to delegate price decisions to the retailers, whereas under RPM it is still the manufacturer who decides on prices. For the same reason, a vertical merger does not raise this concern: no delegation happens there, so that exclusive territories and non-linear pricing would achieve higher profit (and cause lower welfare) than vertical integration.

However, one should note that the result that vertical restraints have strategic effects which harm welfare is not robust with respect to the nature of market competition. In some markets, like the ones I have described so far, when a firm increases its price the rival would increase its price too, thus making it profitable to have a contract pushing one's retailer to keep prices high. In other markets, however, when a firm reduces its output (that is, increases its price), the rival would increase its output (that is, would reduce its price), thus reducing the first firm's profit. When this is the case, a manufacturer will devise contracts aimed at making its retailer more, rather than less, aggressive in the market. For instance, it would decrease its wholesale price so as to stimulate retailers' sales.[52] The overall result will be larger quantities brought to the market by each brand retailer, resulting in lower equilibrium market prices. In such a case, vertical restraints will increase consumer surplus and welfare. Firms do adopt such restraints as they are privately optimal, but firms will turn out to be worse off if all of them choose this strategy. This is therefore a classical example of a prisoner's dilemma. Forbidding the restraints would favour the firms (and not the consumers).

Another important qualification to the result that vertical restraints might dampen market competition comes from the fact that the strategic effects of restraints would have sizeable effects only when the firm adopting them has some market power.

---

[51] Nevertheless, Katz (1991) shows that unobservable contracts might affect market competition under some circumstances; and Caillaud, Jullien and Picard (1995) show that under asymmetric information observable contracts carry commitment value even if they can later be renegotiated.

[52] For this reason, manufacturers will not adopt exclusive territories when retailers compete in quantities.

In conclusion, this literature establishes that vertical restraints – through strategic effects – might reduce welfare, but it does not authorise unambiguous policy implications. First, this literature suggests that only restraints set up by firms with enough market power might deserve review (if there is enough competition upstream, restraints used by one firm are unlikely to have significant effects on prices). Second, I would play down the practical utility of the strategic arguments in a concrete anti-trust case. It seems difficult to evaluate to what extent restraints are used for strategic purposes, and evaluate their quantitative impact.

6.3.1.1 Strategic Use of Vertical Restraints**

This section is structured in the following parts. First, it shows that non-linear pricing might strategically dampen competition when retailers compete in prices; second, it shows that exclusive territories might have the same effect; third, it shows that the more inter-brand competition in the industry, the weaker the negative impact of non-linear pricing; finally, it shows that under quantity competition non-linear pricing would increase rather than decrease welfare, therefore proving that the results are not robust to a change in the mode of market competition.

Two-Part Tariff with Price Competition   Consider two upstream manufacturers U_1 and U_2 which sell two differentiated products. We assume they are identical and that both production and retail costs are constant and equal to zero. The demand function for the final good i is given by

$$q_i = \frac{1}{2}\left[v - p_i\left(1 + \frac{\gamma}{2}\right) + \frac{\gamma}{2}p_j\right]. \tag{6.44}$$

This is a demand function I have repeatedly used.[53] Recall that $\gamma \in [0, \infty)$ is the degree of substitution among the products. Market decisions are on prices.

   Vertical Integration   Suppose first that the two manufacturers are both vertically integrated. All cost and demand functions are common knowledge. Then the problem is the standard one where each firm chooses price to maximise $\pi_i = p_i q_i(p_i, p_j)$. By taking $\partial \pi_i(p_i, p_j)/\partial p_i = 0$ and solving the system one obtains

$$p^{VI} = \frac{2v}{4 + \gamma}; \qquad \pi^{VI} = \frac{(2+\gamma)v^2}{(4+\gamma)^2}. \tag{6.45}$$

   Vertical Restraints: Two-Part Tariff   Suppose now that instead of selling directly, each manufacturer sells via a retailer. Call D_1 and D_2 respectively the retailer who sells good 1 and the retailer who sells good 2. There are then two competing vertical chains. Assume that the manufacturer chooses the retailer from a large number of potential retailers, and that it has all the bargaining power. In the first stage of the game, manufacturers simultaneously give non-linear pricing contracts $F_i + w_i q_i$

---

[53] For instance, disregarding effort and imposing $n = 2$, it is identical to equation (6.23).

to their retailers. These contracts are perfectly observable and not renegotiable.[54] In the second stage, the retailers simultaneously choose prices p_i, profits are realised and fees (if any) are paid to the manufacturers.

At the last stage, each retailer chooses price to maximise $\pi_i^D = (p_i - w_i)q_i(p_i, p_j)$. The first order conditions are given by

$$\partial\pi_i/\partial p_i = \frac{-2(2+\gamma)p_i + \gamma p_j + 2\nu + (2+\gamma)w_i}{4} = 0 \qquad (i, j = 1, 2; i \neq j).$$

$$(6.46)$$

By rearranging the two first-order conditions one can write the best reply functions $p_i = R_i(p_j)$ of the retailers. To draw them in the same plane (p_1, p_2), let us write R_1 and R_2 as functions of p_1. One obtains

$$R_1 : p_2 = \frac{2(2+\gamma)p_1 - 2\nu - (2+\gamma)w_1}{\gamma}; \qquad (6.47)$$

$$R_2 : p_2 = \frac{\gamma p_1 + 2\nu + (2+\gamma)w_2}{2(2+\gamma)}. \qquad (6.48)$$

Figure 6.4 shows the reaction functions in (p_1, p_2). Note that they are positively sloped, that is, goods are strategic complements (this comes from the assumption of price competition and linear demand). In other words, a retailer has an incentive to respond to a price increase of the rival by increasing the price himself. Note also that when the wholesale price w_i increases, the reaction function of retailer i shifts away from the origin: for any given price of the rival, retailer i responds with a higher price, that is he is behaving more softly.

The figure captures the intuition behind the manufacturer's incentive to increase the wholesale price. Consider first the case where both manufacturers set $w = c(= 0)$. Point E is then the market equilibrium. If instead a manufacturer charged a wholesale price $w' > c$, the reaction function of its retailer would shift outward so as to result in higher equilibrium prices, benefiting both upstream firms. If both manufacturers choose to raise wholesale prices, the final equilibrium price will correspond to the point E'. As we shall see now, this is precisely what will occur at equilibrium.

---

[54] Katz (1991) and Caillaud, Jullien and Picard (1995) – as well as Irmen's (1998) survey – have analysed whether vertical restraints affect market outcome when contracts are not observable or are renegotiable. In particular, it can be shown that a non-linear contract has no pre-commitment effect, as a producer would maximise profit by selecting $w = c$ and using F to get profit, whereas under linear pricing $w = c$ cannot be optimal because it implies that the producer gets zero profit. Therefore, at the equilibrium $w > c$ and prices are higher.

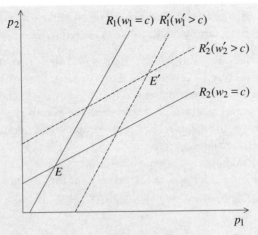

Figure 6.4. Tariffs as strategic device: Strategic complements.

By solving the system of FOCs we can now obtain the equilibrium at the price stage of the game:

$$p_i^* = \frac{2(4 + 3\gamma)v + (2 + \gamma)(2w_i(2 + \gamma) + \gamma w_j)}{16 + 16\gamma + 3\gamma^2}. \tag{6.49}$$

One can then derive $q_i^*\left(w_i, w_j\right)$ by substitution and $\pi_i^* = (p_i^* - w_i)q_i^* - F_i$. Note that the manufacturer will use the franchise fee so as to appropriate the profit of its retailer. Therefore, the manufacturer's profit will be (recall that $c = 0$) $\pi_i^U = (p_i^* - w_i)q_i^* + w_iq_i^* = p_i^*q_i^*$. In the first stage of the game the manufacturer will therefore set w_i so as to maximise

$$\pi_i^U =$$

$$\frac{(2 + \gamma)\left[2(4 + 3\gamma)v - (8 + 8\gamma + \gamma^2)w_i + 2w_i(2 + \gamma)\right]\left[2(4 + 3\gamma)v + 2(2 + \gamma)^2w_i + \gamma w_j(2 + \gamma)\right]}{4(4 + \gamma)^2(4 + 3\gamma)^2}.$$

$$\tag{6.50}$$

By solving the system $\partial \pi_i^U / \partial w_i = 0$, one obtains

$$w^{FF} = \frac{2v\gamma^2}{(2 + \gamma)(16 + 12\gamma + \gamma^2)}; \qquad p^{FF} = \frac{4(2 + \gamma)v}{(16 + 12\gamma + \gamma^2)}; \tag{6.51}$$

$$\pi^{FF} = \frac{2(2 + \gamma)(8 + 8\gamma + \gamma^2)v^2}{(16 + 12\gamma + \gamma^2)^2}. \tag{6.52}$$

Therefore, at the equilibrium both upstream manufacturers set a wholesale price $w > c = 0$ so as to relax competition among retailers (and ultimately among themselves: Rey and Stiglitz show that the vertical restraint makes manufacturers face a perceived demand elasticity which is lower than under vertical integration). As a result both prices and profits are higher than under vertical integration: $p^{FF} > p^{VI}$

and $\pi^{FF} > \pi^{VI}$ (the expressions coincide only when $\gamma \to \infty$). This increased allocative inefficiency determines a decrease in overall welfare.

Exclusive Territories   Rey and Stiglitz (1988, 1995) show that granting exclusive territories to retailers also helps manufacturers to relax competition. As a benchmark, consider the case where two manufacturers have $m \geq 2$ retailers each. Retailers who carry the same brand sell products which are perceived as homogenous by consumers. Therefore, for the usual Bertrand competition arguments, intra-brand competition leads to retailers charging $p_i = w_i$.

The upstream firm chooses its price to maximise $\pi_i^U = (w_i - c)q_i(w_i, w_j)$. Since $p_i = w_i$, this problem is identical to the problem of the vertically integrated firm we have solved above. By taking $\partial \pi_i^U(w_i, w_j)/\partial w_i = 0$ and solving the system one obtains

$$w^{VI} = p^{VI} = \frac{2v}{4 + \gamma}; \qquad \pi^{VI} = \frac{(2+\gamma)v^2}{(4+\gamma)^2}. \tag{6.53}$$

Suppose now that each retailer is given an exclusive territory by his manufacturer, and this decision is publicly observed. Exclusive territories imply that each retailer has $1/m$ share of the demand for the brand. The game is then like the one analysed in the previous sub-section: first, the manufacturer offers retailers a non-linear contract $F_i + w_iq_i$. Then, retailers simultaneously choose prices p_i, profits are realised and fees (if any) are paid to the manufacturers.

At the last stage, each retailer chooses price to maximise $\pi_i^D = \frac{1}{m}(p_i - w_i)q_i(p_i, p_j) - F_i$. Since m is only a scale factor, the first-order conditions are given by precisely the same expression as (6.46) above. All the solutions will therefore be as under the case treated above, giving rise to higher prices and profits than under intra-brand competition: $p^{FF} > p^{VI}$ and $\pi^{FF} > \pi^{VI}$.[55]

Note here that at the equilibrium $w > c$ there is double marginalisation. However, the manufacturers do not lose from this externality. By creating a monopolist (or several monopolists) downstream they strategically exploit the presence of imperfect competition as they manage to relax competition. Rey and Stiglitz (1995) show that by adding more and more layers (for instance, by creating wholesalers and other intermediaries between the production and the retail stage) manufacturers might be able to get the monopoly (i.e., the joint-profit maximising) prices.

Competition Reduces the Risk that Vertical Restraints Lower Welfare   Vertical restraints might be used so as to strategically relax competition and induce higher prices only insofar as the firm using them enjoys enough market power. To get some

---

[55] The game should be completed by endogenising the decisions to allocate exclusive territories to retailers: we have just discussed what happens when both manufacturers use ET, without proving that ET is indeed an equilibrium choice. See Rey and Stiglitz (1995) for such a proof.

intuition for this, consider the following example, where there is a manufacturer – say the firm selling product 1 – who is selling through a retailer, and offers him a contract $F + wq$, whereas all the other n manufacturers in the industry are vertically integrated. Assume the usual demand function:

$$q_i = \frac{1}{n}\left[v - p_i(1+\gamma) + \frac{\gamma}{n}\sum_{j=1}^{n} p_j\right]. \tag{6.54}$$

From the maximisation of the retailer's profit function, and after imposing symmetry on the $n-1$ vertically integrated firms, one obtains the FOCs:

$$\begin{cases} \dfrac{-\gamma(n-1)(2p_1 - p - w) + n(-2p_1 + v + w)}{n^2} = 0, \\[3mm] \dfrac{\gamma(p_1 - np) + n(-2p + v)}{n^2} = 0. \end{cases} \tag{6.55}$$

By drawing the reaction functions of the firms, one can see that they become less elastic as n increases, in the sense that their slope decrease with n. As a result, the manufacturer would need a much bigger increase in the wholesale price to obtain a given price response from the retailer: its action has lower strategic power.

From the solution of the system of FOCs one obtains

$$p_1 = \frac{n(\gamma^2(n-1)w + 2n(v+w) + \gamma v(2n-1) + \gamma w(3n-2))}{4n^2 + 2\gamma n(3n-2) + \gamma^2(2n^2 - 3n + 1)}; \tag{6.56}$$

$$p = \frac{2n^2 v + \gamma^2(n-1)w + \gamma n(w + v(2n-1))}{4n^2 + 2\gamma n(3n-2) + \gamma^2(2n^2 - 3n + 1)}. \tag{6.57}$$

By solving the manufacturer's problem, which is to choose w so as to maximise its profit $\pi^U = (p_1 - w)q_1(p_1, p)$, one obtains

$$w = \frac{\gamma^2(n-1)(2n + \gamma(2n-1))v}{2(2+\gamma)(\gamma^3(n-1)^3 + 2n^3 + \gamma n^2(5n-4) + \gamma^2 n(3 - 7n + 4n^2))}. \tag{6.58}$$

Finally, by substituting into the price expresssions, we have

$$p_1^{ff} = \frac{nv(2n + \gamma(2n-1))}{2(\gamma^2(n-1)^2 + 2n^2 + \gamma n(3n-2)}; \qquad p = \frac{v(2n + \gamma(2n-1))}{2(2+\gamma)n^2}. \tag{6.59}$$

When all firms are vertically integrated, the (Bertrand competition) equilibrium price is given by[56]

$$p_b = \frac{vn}{2n + \gamma(n-1)}. \tag{6.60}$$

---

[56] To find the equilibrium price under vertical integration, just impose $w = 0$ in the FOCs above and solve for p.

The additional mark-up that a manufacturer is able to command due to vertical restraints is therefore given by

$$p_1^{ff} - p_b = \frac{nv\gamma^2(n-1)}{2(\gamma^2(n-1)^2 + 2n^2 + \gamma n(3n-2)(2n+\gamma(n-1)))}. \tag{6.61}$$

It can be checked that $\partial(p_1^{ff} - p_b)/\partial n < 0$: the larger the number of firms, the lower the additional mark-up that strategic vertical restraints can give to the manufacturer using them.

The Results Are Not Robust: Strategic Substitutes   The previous results have been obtained by assuming that decisions in the final market were on prices. It turns out that the results obtained are very sensitive to the type of market competition. If we assume that market decisions are on quantities – rather than prices – manufacturers still want to delegate their sales to independent retailers, but first, the contracts they give their retailers make them more – rather than less – aggressive, and as a consequence final prices will be lower and welfare higher. Second, the game where manufacturers decide whether or not they want to delegate decisions is like a prisoner's dilemma: delegation is the dominant strategy, and will be chosen at equilibrium, but manufacturers would like to avoid it. In what follows, we formalise these results.

The Model   The model is the same as the one analysed above, with two manufacturers who sell differentiated goods either directly (vertical integration) or through independent retailers. To analyse what happens under quantity competition, let us use the inverse demand functions. Inverting the system (6.44), we obtain

$$p_i = v - \frac{1}{1+\gamma}(2q_i + \gamma q_i + \gamma q_j). \tag{6.62}$$

Vertical Integration   Firms choose output q_i so as to maximise $\pi_i = (p_i(q_i, q_j) - c)q_i$. By solving the system of first-order conditions $\partial\pi_i/\partial q_i = 0$ we obtain the standard Cournot equilibrium:

$$q_{vi} = \frac{(v-c)(1+\gamma)}{4+3\gamma}; \qquad \pi_{vi} = \frac{(v-c)^2(1+\gamma)(2+\gamma)}{(4+3\gamma)^2}. \tag{6.63}$$

Delegation   Suppose now that both firms have a downstream retailer, and analyse the game where first each manufacturer gives a non-linear pricing contract $F_i + w_i q_i$ to its retailer and then the retailers compete in quantities (after having observed the contract).

At the last stage of the game, retailer i chooses output q_i so as to maximise $\pi_i^r = (p_i(q_i, q_j) - w_i)q_i$. By taking the first-order conditions $\partial\pi_i^r/\partial q_i = 0$, and rearranging them one obtains the following reaction functions for each firm (to

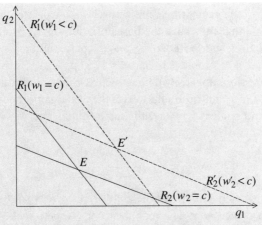

Figure 6.5. Tariffs as strategic device: Strategic substitutes.

draw them in the plane (q_1, q_2), they are written as functions of q_1):

$$R_1(q_2) \leftrightarrow q_2 = \frac{-2(2 + \gamma)q_1 + v(1 - \gamma) - w_1(1 - \gamma)}{\gamma}; \qquad (6.64)$$

$$R_2(q_1) \leftrightarrow q_2 = \frac{-\gamma q_1 + v(1 + \gamma) - w_2(1 + \gamma)}{2(2 + \gamma)}. \qquad (6.65)$$

It is easy to see that the reaction functions are now negatively sloped, that is, the goods are strategic substitutes. A firm's increased output would be followed by a rival's decrease in its own output (see Figure 6.5).

The iso-profit functions are not shown in the figure, but it would be easy to check that a shift to the right of the retailer's reaction curve (given the reaction curve of the rival) would change the equilibrium to a point where the retailer has higher profit (at the new point, the retailer would have a higher share of the market). However, Figure 6.5 also shows that if both retailers had lower marginal costs, the new equilibrium E' would result in larger quantities sold in the market than at the equilibrium E. The two firms would still have the same share of the market but since they both increase outputs, prices are lower. The figure therefore anticipates what we are now going to see more formally.

By solving the FOCs (or – equivalently – finding the intersection point of the reaction functions) one can find the retailers' equilibrium quantities and prices:

$$q_i = \frac{(1 + \gamma)\left(v(4 + \gamma) - 2(2 + \gamma)w_i + \gamma w_j\right)}{16 + 16\gamma + 3\gamma^2}; \qquad (6.66)$$

$$p_i = \frac{(8 + 6\gamma + \gamma^2)v + (8 + 8\gamma + \gamma^2)w_i + \gamma(2 + \gamma)w_j}{16 + 16\gamma + 3\gamma^2}. \qquad (6.67)$$

At the first stage of the game, the manufacturer chooses w_i to maximise profit. As before, we assume that they have the bargaining power *vis-à-vis* their retailer, so that they set the franchise fee F_i so as to appropriate all their profit: $F_i = (p_i - w_i)q_i$. Therefore, their problem is $\max_{w_i} \pi_i^u = (p_i - c)q_i$, where p_i and q_i are given by the expressions above. By taking the first-order conditions and solving the system one finds the equilibrium solutions of the whole game (because of symmetry, manufacturers and retailers will have the same equilibrium variables; we therefore drop the indices i and j):

$$w_{ff} = c - \frac{\gamma^2 v}{16 + 20\gamma + 5\gamma^2}. \tag{6.68}$$

As one can immediately see, the wholesale price is lower than the manufacturer's own production cost: $w < c$. The manufacturer wants to make the retailer more aggressive in the market and therefore it subsidises its purchase of the input so as to make it sell more in the market (of course, subsidisation does not come costly here, since the retailer's profits are appropriated by the manufacturer via the franchise fee). This is precisely the opposite result than with strategic complements (i.e., price competition), where w was optimally set higher than unit cost c.

By substituting, one can find equilibrium quantities and profits as

$$q_{ff} = \frac{2(1+\gamma)(2+\gamma)(v-c)}{16+20\gamma+5\gamma^2}; \quad \pi_{ff}^u = \frac{2(1+\gamma)(2+\gamma)(8+8\gamma+\gamma^2)(v-c)^2}{(16+20\gamma+5\gamma^2)^2}. \tag{6.69}$$

When comparing the solutions obtained at the two equilibria, it is easy to see that when firms delegate they sell a higher quantity than under vertical integration ($q_{ff} > q_{vi}$) and they obtain a lower profit ($\pi_{ff}^u < \pi_{vi}$). Here, delegation and vertical restraints increase welfare!

The result according to which at the delegation equilibrium firms earn lower profits begs the question whether choosing to delegate output decisions to an independent retailer is indeed an equilibrium (so far, we have merely assumed that both firms delegate). Exercise 6.8 proves that delegation is a dominant strategy and that the equilibrium where both producers sell through retailers is unique. This is the typical prisoner's dilemma situation, where both firms end up in an equilibrium, which is Pareto-inferior: $\pi_{ff}^u < \pi_{vi}$. The manufacturers would be better off if they were not allowed to contract with independent retailers!

6.3.2 Vertical Restraints as Collusive Devices

It has been pointed out in the literature that there are other circumstances in which vertical restraints might facilitate collusion. In this section, we consider two such arguments. The first shows that resale price maintenance might favour collusion among manufacturers. The second, that when two or more manufacturers sell through a common retailer they might be able to reach the collusive outcome.

6.3.2.1 RPM Might Facilitate Collusion (Reminder)

As seen in Section 4.2.3, resale price maintenance can facilitate collusion among manufacturers because it increases price observability. Absent RPM, when shocks in the retail markets occur, final prices will tend to change, making it more difficult for manufacturers to distinguish changes in retail prices that are caused by different retail conditions from cheating on the cartel. RPM makes collusion more likely by eliminating the retail price variation (see also Jullien and Rey, 2001).

6.3.2.2 Common Agency

If two manufacturers decide to sell their goods in the final market via a common agent (or retailer), this might have anti-competitive effects. In particular, it might give rise to the joint profit maximising prices being charged at equilibrium.[57]

There are two separate circumstances where this can happen. First, imagine that the manufacturers offer a two-part tariff contract to the common retailer and delegate the price decisions to it. In this case, it is obvious that the common agent will pick the collusive prices, given wholesale prices, since the upstream firms effectively give it the mandate to maximise joint profits. Manufacturers would still compete on wholesale prices, but have no incentive to set wholesale prices higher than their own marginal cost. As a result, the retailer behaves exactly as if the manufacturers sold directly to the final market and could maximise joint profits.

More interestingly, however, Bernheim and Whinston (1985) show that the collusive prices could be obtained even if the price choices were not delegated to the common retailer. In their setting, two manufacturers offer a franchise fee contract to a common retailer, but also impose its final price (in other words, RPM is allowed). They show that at the equilibrium both firms choose the collusive price. This is because each manufacturer makes the retailer the residual claimant and uses the franchise fee to recover its profit. At the moment of setting the final resale price, each manufacturer takes into account that the final profit of the retailer depends not only on the sales of the manufacturer's product itself, but also on the sales of the rival's product. This way, when a manufacturer chooses its price so as to maximise the retailer's profit it takes into account the externality that the price decision has on the component of the retailer's profit that comes from the sales of the rival product:

---

[57] In the literature, this is summarised by saying that common agency facilitates collusion (but interestingly, the collusive price arises even though a one-shot game is played).

this is precisely the same as when the two products were sold by the same cartel (i.e., under joint profit maximisation).[58]

Common Retailer and RPM Help Collusion**   I present here a very simplified version of Bernheim and Whinston's (1985) model, to illustrate their main result. Assume that there are two upstream producers, 1 and 2, which sell their products via a common retailer, R. To simplify the issue, assume that both products have to be sold, otherwise there is a market failure and zero profits are made by all firms.[59] Assume also that the retailer has no bargaining power, for instance because it is selected among a population of very many potential retailers who would compete fiercely to be the chosen retailer. For simplicity, the retailer has no cost other than the wholesale price and the producers have the same marginal cost c. Finally, consumer demand is given by $q_i = a - bp_i + \gamma p_j$.

Consider the following game. First, each producer $i = A, B$ simultaneously makes take-it-or-leave-it offers to R in the form of a non-linear contract $F_i + w_i q_i$. These contracts are publicly observable (they might also fix the retail price if resale price maintenance (RPM) is allowed). Second, the retailer accepts or rejects the offers. Third, if both offers have been accepted, the retailer fixes resale prices (or simply sells at the price imposed by the producer under RPM), demand and profits are realised, and franchise fees are paid. If one or both offers are rejected, no sale occurs and all firms get zero payoffs.

No RPM (Price Choices Delegated to the Common Retailer)   Let us first look at what happens if the common retailer was in charge of price decisions. At the last stage of the game, if both offers have been accepted (and therefore for a given w_i and F_i), the retailer chooses final prices p_A, p_B so as to maximise $\pi_R = (p_A - w_A)(a - bp_A + \gamma p_B) + (p_B - w_B)(a - bp_B + \gamma p_A)$. From the FOCs $\partial \pi_R / \partial p_i = 0$, one obtains $p_i = [a + w_i(b - \gamma)] / [2(b - \gamma)]$, and $q_i(w_i, w_j) = (a - bw_i + \gamma w_j)/2$.

In the first stage, the programme of a producer i will therefore be to choose its contract offer to maximise its profit given the contract of the competing producer,

---

[58]   In Rey and Vergé (2002a) there is both upstream and downstream competition, each downstream firm acting as a common retailer to both upstream firms. Under this "double common agency" structure, collusive profits arise as the unique equilibrium of a game where first upstream firms make take-it-or-leave-it offers (in the form of franchise fee contracts) to each common retailer, each retailer sets its effort level and then competes in the final product market by selling at the prices set by the manufacturers. Unfortunately, the model hinges on the ability of the manufacturers to extract all the retailer's rents, and when the retailers are endowed with some bargaining power, the model becomes too complicated.

[59]   This way, we do not have to study some deviations and the associated asymmetric cases where the retailer accepts only one manufacturer's offer. Bernheim and Whinston show that the same results are obtained relaxing this assumption.

and also taking into account the participation constraint of the retailer:

$$\max_{w_i, F_i} \pi_i = (w_i - c)q_i(w_i, w_j) + F_i,$$

$$s.to: \sum_{i=1,2; i \neq j} [(p_i(w_i) - w_i)q_i(w_i, w_j) - F_i] \geq 0. \qquad (6.70)$$

Since at equilibrium the retailer will make no profit, the retailer's constraint must be binding:

$$F_i = (p_i(w_i) - w_i)q_i(w_i, w_j) + (p_j(w_j) - w_j)q_j(w_i, w_j) - F_j. \qquad (6.71)$$

Therefore, producer i's programme can be rewritten as

$$\max_{w_i} \pi_i = (p_i(w_i) - c)q_i(w_i, w_j) + (p_j(w_j) - w_j)q_j(w_i, w_j) - F_j. \qquad (6.72)$$

By substituting the equilibrium values of the last stage of the game, this becomes

$$\max_{w_i} \pi_i = \left(\frac{a + w_i(b - \gamma)}{2(b - \gamma)} - c \right) \frac{a - bw_i + \gamma w_j}{2}$$

$$+ \left(\frac{a + w_j(b - \gamma)}{2(b - \gamma)} - w_j \right) \frac{a - bw_j + \gamma w_i}{2} - F_j. \qquad (6.73)$$

By taking $\partial \pi_i / \partial w_i = 0$ and simplifying, one can check that the symmetric equilibrium is given by $w_i = w_j = c$. In turn, this implies that the final resale price is $p_i = p_j = a/[2(b - \gamma)] + c/2$, which corresponds to the joint profit maximising price, namely, the price that the two manufacturers would set if they could sell directly and openly colluded. Indeed, by labelling π_m the joint profits, one has $\pi_m = (p_A - c)(a - bp_A + \gamma p_B) + (p_B - c)(a - bp_B + \gamma p_A)$. From $\partial \pi_m / \partial p_i = 0$, it is straightforward to check that $p_m = a/[2(b - \gamma)] + c/2$.

RPM and Common Agency If they can impose resale prices, the manufacturers have an additional strategic variable, that is p_i. Their problem is now given by

$$\max_{w_i, F_i, p_i} \pi_i = (w_i - c)q_i(p_i, p_j) + F_i,$$

$$s.to: \sum_{i=1,2; i \neq j} [(p_i - w_i)q_i(p_i, p_j) - F_i] \geq 0. \qquad (6.74)$$

At equilibrium, the retailer's constraint is binding:

$$F_i = (p_i - w_i)q_i(p_i, p_j) + (p_j - w_j)q_j(p_i, p_j) - F_j. \qquad (6.75)$$

Therefore, producer i's programme can be rewritten as

$$\max_{w_i, p_i} \pi_i = (p_i - c)q_i(p_i, p_j) + (p_j - w_j)q_j(p_i, p_j) - F_j. \qquad (6.76)$$

After substituting the specific functional form assumed for demand, this becomes

$$\max_{w_i,\,p_i} \pi_i = (p_i - c)(a - bp_i + \gamma p_j) + (p_j - w_j)(a - bp_j + \gamma p_i) - F_j. \quad (6.77)$$

By solving $\partial \pi_i / \partial p_i = 0$ one obtains the optimal price: $p_i = (a + c - \gamma w_j)/[2(b - \gamma)]$. Note that the equilibrium wholesale prices here are not determined, as π_i is not a function of w_i. However, given a pair of wholesale prices (w_i, w_j), the equilibrium (final) prices decrease with wholesale prices. More importantly, if the wholesale prices equal the manufacturers' marginal costs $(w_i = w_j = c)$, then $p_i = p_j = p_m = a/[2(b - \gamma)] + c/2$. In other words, a continuum of prices can arise as the equilibrium of the game, and the collusive price is one of these equilibria.

Note also that the collusive equilibrium would become unique under many selection criteria (for instance, Pareto dominance), as well as in a natural situation where retailers are asked to make some effort in order to sell the good. Exercise 6.9 shows that this is the case.

6.4 ANTI-COMPETITIVE EFFECTS: LEVERAGE AND FORECLOSURE

One of the most passionate and intriguing debates in the anti-trust field is whether a firm could use anti-competitive practices to protect and reinforce the market power it has in one market or to extend it to other markets. This is an issue which will be discussed at length in Chapter 7, but it is appropriate to deal with it also here, as some of the possible anti-competitive practices under consideration consist of vertical restraints.

It has been suggested, for instance, that exclusive dealing might allow a firm enjoying a dominant position to deter entry into the market, by foreclosing a crucial input (the distribution network) or by making it more difficult or expensive for the entrant to obtain such input. It has also been suggested that a vertical merger might have similar effects: if an upstream firm that has a dominant position takes over one of many downstream sellers, it might stop supplying the competitors of its downstream subsidiary, or supplying them at a higher price which puts them at a disadvantage.

We shall see in this section that – despite the appeal that such arguments might have at first sight – it is far from being the general case that a dominant firm will have the incentive to engage in such practices. In fact, it is only very recently that economic theory has managed to provide formal examples of situations where that could happen.

In what follows, I deal separately with the possible anti-competitive effects of exclusive contracts and vertical mergers. In both cases, I first recall the "Chicago School" arguments which stressed the low plausibility of foreclosure effects, then

I analyse recent ("post-Chicago") models where foreclosure effects might indeed arise. Finally, I will assess the practical value of these theories, pointing out that the anti-competitive motivations highlighted by them should be contrasted with possible efficiency effects that exclusive dealing or vertical mergers might have.

6.4.1 Anti-Competitive Effects: Exclusive Dealing

The concern that a dominant firm might use exclusive contracts to damage actual or potential competitors is an old one. However, economic theory has often reacted sceptically to the possibility that exclusive contracts might lead to foreclosure. More particularly, since the 50s the so-called Chicago School has emphasised the efficiency effects of such contracts and played down the plausibility of the foreclosure arguments. Posner (1976) and Bork (1978) summarise the "Chicago" arguments on the issue. They point out that for an exclusive contract between an incumbent seller and a buyer (or distributor) to be signed, the latter should receive a benefit from it. Instead, the argument goes, a rational buyer would not be willing to accept a contract which obliges her to buy from an inefficient incumbent if a more efficient competitor is willing to enter the industry.

Suppose for instance there is an incumbent monopolist, a potential entrant (more efficient than the incumbent) and only one buyer in a certain industry. By accepting an exclusive dealing contract, a buyer would commit to buy from a monopolist even if entry occurs. This rules out entry, and the buyer will end up paying the monopoly price for the good. By rejecting the contract offer, instead, the buyer would trigger entry and benefit from a lower price. Sure enough, the incumbent might offer a compensation to the buyer to persuade her to accept exclusivity. However, the incumbent is willing to pay a compensation no higher than its monopoly profit, whereas the buyer – by accepting the exclusive contract – would lose all the consumer surplus that arises by buying at lower prices (namely, with constant marginal cost, the profit of the incumbent plus the deadweight loss). Section 6.4.1.1 formalises this argument.

Figure 6.6 illustrates it. Suppose the incumbent has unit cost c_I and would make a profit π^m if it enjoyed a monopoly, corresponding to the area $p^m A D c_I$. The entrant has cost $c_E < c_I$: if it entered, it could set a price just slightly below c_I and get all the market for itself. Therefore, if entry occurs price would be (slightly lower than) c_I. The buyer would get a surplus CS^m, corresponding to the area $\theta A p^m$, under monopoly, and a surplus CS^e equal to the area $\theta B c_I$, if entry occurs. Therefore, to be persuaded to deal exclusively with the incumbent, the buyer should receive an offer t higher than the gain it makes if entry occurs, $CS^e - CS^m$. This is equivalent to the area $p^m A B c_I$. However, it is clear that the incumbent could never make such a high offer, since its profit would be $\pi^m < CS^e - CS^m$.

The implication of this argument is not that exclusive contracts will never be observed, but rather that, if they exist, it is because they entail some efficiency

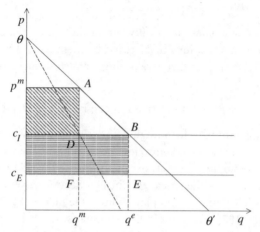

Figure 6.6. The "Chicago School" critique to foreclosure.

gains, but since these gains are beneficial both for the firm which uses such contracts and for consumers, there should be no reason why anti-trust authorities should intervene and forbid such contracts.

Post-Chicago Models   The argument above, which is still valid, emphasises that it is less likely than it might appear at first sight that a firm engages in exclusive contracts with a view to monopolising the market (and that pro-competitive effects are often behind such contracts). However, recent theoretical contributions do offer examples of circumstances under which exclusive contracts will lead to anti-competitive effects (see also Section 6.6 for a real-world case where exclusive contracts might have had entry-deterring effects).

The main insight behind the recent models of exclusion can be understood by referring to the same example used above. In that example, the incumbent is not able to make an offer large enough to persuade the buyer to accept an exclusive deal. However, there are circumstances under which this is possible, and these circumstances refer to the existence of externalities with respect to the relationship between the incumbent and the buyer who is considering the exclusive deal. For instance, imagine that by excluding the entrant the incumbent makes not only the monopoly profit in the market under consideration, but also manages to increase profit in another market (for instance because the potential entrant cannot enjoy economies of scope by producing in two markets). In this case, the incumbent, by excluding the entrant, would make π^m plus some additional profit from another market: it could now be possible to make an offer high enough to induce the buyer to accept the exclusive deal.

Most of the recent works that show that an incumbent might use exclusive deals to foreclose entry rely on different externalities that explain why foreclosure might be profitable. Such works include Aghion and Bolton (1987), Rasmusen et al. (1991), Segal and Whinston (2000a), and Bernheim and Whinston (1998).[60]

Aghion and Bolton (1987) illustrate how an incumbent and a buyer might agree on a partially exclusive contract which might prevent entry of a more efficient competitor. In their model, the buyer can be released from the exclusivity relationship by paying a penalty to the incumbent. Effectively, what happens in that setting is that incumbent and buyer agree on a contract which enables them to extract some of the rent the entrant would have in case of entry (the area $c_I B E c_E$ in Figure 6.6 above). Exclusion does not always occur, but when it does it is anti-competitive. Section 6.4.1.1 shows the argument more formally.

Rasmusen et al. (1991) and Segal and Whinston (2000a) show another circumstance where exclusive dealing might deter entry. If there are many buyers in the market that cannot coordinate their purchases, and if a potential entrant needs to secure a certain number of them to cover its fixed costs, then an incumbent might exploit the lack of coordination among buyers to deter entry. At the moment of accepting an exclusivity offer from the incumbent, each buyer does not take into account that by doing so it imposes an externality on the other buyers. In other words, if all the others accept the exclusive dealing offer from the incumbent, one of them alone has no incentive to reject the exclusivity contract from the incumbent, as a "free" buyer alone would not be able to trigger entry by addressing the entrant (as the entrant would need several buyers to cover its fixed cost of entry).

The model can be illustrated by Figure 6.6 above, but with two identical buyers rather than one. Each buyer is described by the demand function $\theta\theta'$. The incumbent makes each of them an offer in exchange for an exclusive deal, they accept or reject the offer, and then a more efficient entrant decides on entry (but it covers fixed cost only if it sells to both buyers). When the incumbent negotiates the deal with a buyer, it can offer it twice its profit, since by getting an exclusive buyer it would get monopoly profit on two markets. Provided that $2\pi^m > CS^e - CS^m$ (not a strong assumption), it can now offer a compensation t, which induces one buyer to accept

---

[60] There is also other literature that considers the anti-competitive potential of exclusive dealing through *raising rivals' costs* strategies. In Comanor and Frech (1985), exclusive dealing contracts between a dominant manufacturer (which enjoys a product differentiation advantage) and established retailers forecloses access of a rival firm to those retailers and obliges it to use a less efficient distribution channel. However, Schwartz (1987) shows that the model used by Comanor and Frech is not carefully formulated. By carrying out the correct analysis, he proves the opposite results: exclusive dealing might arise, but would lead to lower, rather than higher, prices for consumers. Mathewson and Winter (1987) also reformulate Comanor and Frech's model (by making different modelling assumptions on product differentiation) and show that exclusive dealing need not be anti-competitive even if it leads to the exclusion of rivals. These works show that first, exclusionary effects might be accounted for by theory, but tend to arise in models which require particular assumptions and settings. Second, even when exclusion does arise, it might lead to welfare improvement.

the deal, thereby blocking entry for both buyers. (In fact, there is an exclusionary equilibrium where the incumbent pays zero compensation: even if offered nothing, a buyer alone knows that it would not be enough to induce entry, and therefore accepts the deal.)

However, there is also another equilibrium where all buyers buy from the entrant.[61] If all reject the incumbent's contract, entry will occur (the entrant is more efficient), and they will all end up buying from the entrant at a lower price. This is clearly an equilibrium, as no buyer would have an incentive to unilaterally deviate and accept the incumbent's contract.

If the buyers were allowed to coordinate their purchase decisions, then they would not accept the deal and entry would occur.[62] This is not surprising, since the argument above is built upon the fact that each buyer makes its acceptance decisions separately, and does not take into account that by accepting the deal it imposes an externality upon the other buyers. If the buyers can act as if they were a single buyer, they would reject the offer from the incumbent and would buy from the entrant at a lower price. Therefore, this model speaks in favour of *central purchasing agencies*, that is agencies which coordinate (otherwise independent) buyers' decisions, thereby breaking possible inefficient mis-coordination outcomes.

Fumagalli and Motta (2002) qualify the entry deterrent power of exclusive deals. They analyse a model that incorporates the same features as Segal and Whinston (2000a), with the variant that buyers are not final consumers, but are instead competing with each other in a downstream market. They show that if buyers' competition is strong enough, a single buyer would have an incentive to break the exclusionary equilibrium, since by securing a cheaper input it would enjoy a larger share of the downstream market. Consider for instance the extreme case where downstream competition is à la Bertrand and goods are very close substitutes. In that case, any buyer would have an incentive not to accept the incumbent's offer, because in this way a buyer could address the more efficient entrant, buy from it at a lower price than all other buyers, and hence obtain most of the market for itself. (The entrant here does enter when addressed by a single deviant buyer, because the latter will buy enough units since it is able to get all the market.) An alternative way to express this result in similar terms as the Chicago argument above is that when downstream competition is strong enough, the incumbent cannot pay a large enough compensation to convince buyers to accept the exclusive contract.

Note that in the above mentioned papers (Aghion and Bolton, 1987, Rasmusen et al., 1991 and Segal and Whinston, 2000a), a key feature is that the exclusive contract between the incumbent and a buyer exercises some type or other of externality

---

[61] This is true in the simultaneous and non-discriminatory offers game. If the incumbent could discriminate, or could offer exclusive deals sequentially, the exclusionary equilibrium would be unique. See technical Section 6.4.1.1 for a discussion.

[62] More precisely, this is the only coalition-proof equilibrium of the game.

on (one or more) third parties. This principle is emphasised by Bernheim and Whinston (1998), a paper where the issue of whether exclusive dealing can give rise to foreclosure or market leverage is studied in a more general fashion.

6.4.1.1 Exclusive Dealing and Entry Deterrence*

In this section, I briefly describe the main models mentioned in the text on exclusive dealing and entry deterrence. First, I present the Chicago argument according to which exclusionary contracts would not be profitable. Then I present a simplified version of Aghion and Bolton (1987), and of the mis-coordination argument due to Rasmusen et al. (1991), as later refined by Segal and Whinston (2000a).

Exclusive Dealing: Chicago Arguments*   Consider the following model. There is an incumbent firm which produces at a cost c_I, and a potential entrant which – after paying a fixed cost of entry, f – could produce the same homogenous good at a cost c_E.[63] We assume – to make things interesting – that $c_E < c_I$ (if the incumbent was more efficient, exclusive contracts would not be relevant since entry would never occur). The game is as follows. In the first stage, the incumbent firm might offer the only buyer a compensation t in order for her to accept an exclusive contract. In the second stage, the buyer accepts or rejects the offer. If she accepted, she could buy only the incumbent's product; if she rejected, she could also buy the entrant's product. In the third stage, the potential entrant – after having observed whether a contract has been signed or not by the buyer – decides on entry (and sinks entry costs if it enters). In the last stage, firms in the market choose prices.

Demand is given by $D(p) = \theta - p$, with $\theta > 2c_I + c_E$ (this condition restricts the cases to be considered in the price game, see below).

Assume also that the entrant would find it profitable to enter in the absence of exclusive contracts: $(c_I - c_E)(\theta - c_I) > f$.

We can now solve the model backwards, to show that there are no entry-deterrent exclusive contracts which can be profitable for the incumbent and that would be accepted by the buyer.

At the last stage of the game, if no entry has occurred, the incumbent is the only seller and chooses price to maximise monopoly profit: $\max_p \pi = (\theta - p)(p - c_I)$. By taking FOCs and solving it is easy to check that under monopoly prices, profit and consumer surplus are

$$p^m = \frac{\theta + c_I}{2}; \qquad \pi^m = \frac{(\theta - c_I)^2}{4}; \qquad CS^m = \frac{(\theta - c_I)^2}{8}. \qquad (6.78)$$

---

[63] The assumption that the entrant has to pay a positive fixed cost of entry is not necessary. I just anticipate what is a crucial assumption for the entry deterrence model of Rasmusen et al. (1991) and Segal and Whinston (2000a).

If instead entry had occurred, then Bertrand competition implies that the market would be served by the more efficient entrant firm at the price which equals the marginal cost of the incumbent: $p^e = c_I$.[64] Consumer surplus is easily computed as $CS^e = (\theta - c_I)^2/2$.

At the previous stage, entry occurs if the buyer is "free", that is, she has not signed the exclusive contract. Otherwise, entry does not occur.

Next, we have to check if the buyer accepts the exclusivity offer from the incumbent. She will if the compensation offered by the incumbent will offset the loss in surplus from having to buy from a monopolist: $CS^m + t \geq CS^e$. In other words the buyer accepts if $t \geq 3(\theta - c_I)^2/8 \equiv t_{min}$.

Finally, by offering the contract the incumbent has a payoff $\pi^m - t$, whereas by not having exclusivity it will have zero payoff. After substitution, it is easy to see that the maximum compensation that the incumbent is willing to pay is $t = (\theta - c_I)^2/4 < t_{min}$. Therefore, the incumbent will not be able to induce the buyer to accept the exclusive contract, and entry will not be deterred.

Contracts as a Barrier to Entry**   Consider a homogenous good industry with an incumbent firm I having a cost $c_I = 1/2$ and a buyer with unit demand whose valuation for the good is $v = 1$. There exists a potential entrant E in this industry, whose cost c_E is uniformly distributed in $[0, 1]$. We consider an exclusive dealing contract (p, p_o) according to which – if accepted – the buyer commits to buy from the incumbent at a price p at a later stage, but it can be released from the exclusivity clause (and buy from the entrant) after the payment of a penalty (or "liquidated damages") p_o.[65]

The game is as follows. At time t_1, the incumbent I offers a contract (p, p_o) to the buyer, who can either accept it or reject it. At time t_2, the potential entrant decides on entry and sets a price p_E. (If no contract has been signed, the incumbent also chooses its price p.) At time t_3, there is product market and payoff realisation.

No Contract   First, consider the case where no exclusive dealing clause exists. Since there is price competition, firm E will enter only if its cost c_E is lower than $1/2$. In this case, it charges price $p_E = 1/2$ and gets all the market. Therefore, the probability that entry occurs is $\phi = \Pr(c_E \leq 1/2) = 1/2$ (due to the assumption of uniform distribution), and the buyer has a surplus $v - p_E = 1 - 1/2 = 1/2$. If $c_E > 1/2$, the entrant will not enter and firm I will charge $p = 1$. In this case, occurring with probability $(1 - \phi)$, the buyer has a surplus $v - p_I = 0$.

---

[64] If the entrant were much more efficient than the incumbent it could be that the entrant's monopoly price, $(\theta + c_E)/2$, is lower than c_I. The assumption made above on θ guarantees that this is not the case, and simplifies the analysis.

[65] Aghion and Bolton (1987) show that restricting attention to such a simple contract is without loss of generality.

Therefore, if no contract exists the buyer's expected surplus is $\phi(1/2) + (1 - \phi)0 = 1/4$, and the incumbent's expected payoff is $\phi(0) + (1 - \phi)(1 - 1/2) = 1/4$.

Exclusivity Contract   If the buyer has accepted the contract (p, p_o), it will buy from firm E only if the latter firm's price plus the penalty p_o due to the incumbent is lower than the incumbent's price: $p_E + p_o \leq p$. Therefore, if it enters, firm E will charge $p_E = p - p_o$. In turn, entry will occur only if the cost of the entrant is lower than the expected price. Calling ϕ' the probability of entry if a contract exists, it will be $\phi' = \Pr(c_E \leq p - p_o) = p - p_o$.[66]

Let us now look at the incumbent's problem, which is the following:

$$\max_{p, p_o} \pi = \phi' p_o + (1 - \phi')(p - 1/2) \quad s.to: 1 - p \geq 1/4. \quad (6.79)$$

In other words, the incumbent has to choose the optimal price and penalty so as to maximise its expected profit. This is given by – in expected terms – the penalty if the entrant turns out to be efficient enough so as to charge a low enough price plus the sales price if the entrant has a high enough cost. However, the contract will be accepted by the buyer only insofar as it gives the latter at least the same expected surplus $1 - p$ as without the contract (where the surplus is $1/4$): this explains the constraint in the problem above.

The problem can then be written as $\max_{p_o} \pi$ subject to: $p \leq 3/4$, whose solution is given by $(p^*, p_o^*) = (3/4, 1/2)$. This implies that firm E will enter the market with a probability $\phi' = p^* - p_o^* = 1/4$. Since efficiency would require entry whenever $c_E \leq 1/2$, whereas under the contract entry occurs only if $c_E \leq 1/4$, there is a welfare loss: for $1/4 < c_E \leq 1/2$, efficient entry does not occur due to the exclusive contract.[67]

As a last step, let us check that the incumbent is better off offering this contract than not. This is easily verified, as under the contract firm I has an expected profit which is larger than what it would get without the contract: $\pi = (1/4)(1/2) + (3/4)(1/4) = 5/16 > 1/4$.

It is worth underlining that exclusive dealing does not always deter entry. When the entrant is very efficient, the incumbent prefers to allow entry and extract some of the entrant's rent through the penalty, rather than to deter entry completely.

Naked Exclusion*   Consider an incumbent firm selling to two distinct buyers, $B1$ and $B2$, each in a separate market and with the same demand function.

Simultaneous Non-Discriminatory Offers   The incumbent simultaneously offers them a fixed compensation t (to start with, suppose it must be the same

---

[66] Provided that $p \geq p_o$ (which is the case at equilibrium). Otherwise, the probability of entry is zero.

[67] A vertical merger between the incumbent and the buyer would give exactly the same outcome. See Tirole (1988: 196).

Table 6.1. Segal–Whinston: Simultaneous Offers

B2 \ B1	Accept	Reject
Accept	$CS^m + t, CS^m + t$	$CS^m + t, CS^m$
Reject	$CS^m, CS^m + t$	CS^e, CS^e

for each buyer) in exchange for an exclusive deal. Buyers then simultaneously accept or reject the offer. Then, an entrant observes their decisions and decides about its entry. If it enters, it pays a fixed entry cost F (the same entry cost allows it to serve both buyers). Finally, price decisions are taken by operative suppliers. Assume that $\pi^m < CS^e - CS^m < 2\pi^m$ (the first inequality is a natural assumption, as seen above; the second is also satisfied under mild assumptions) and that $(c_I - c_E)q(c_I) < F < 2(c_I - c_E)q(c_I)$, which means that entry is not profitable if the entrant served only one buyer, but it would be profitable if serving both buyers (otherwise, the problem would be uninteresting).

At the last stage of the game, price decisions are straightforward. At equilibrium, if entry has occurred, the entrant charges c_I and gets every free buyer. The incumbent charges p^m to every exclusive buyer. The buyers' decisions can be illustrated by the payoff matrix in Table 6.1.

The game has two equilibria. The first equilibrium is (accept, accept), where both buyers accept the offer. When the other buyer accepts the deal, by also accepting it one buyer will obtain a payoff $CS^m + t$; by deviating and rejecting the offer it would get CS^m (recall that a buyer alone would not induce entry). Therefore, the equilibrium arises for any $t \geq 0$.

There is also a second equilibrium, (reject, reject), where no buyer accepts the deal. There is no profitable deviation from this pair: by deviating and accepting the deal when the other rejects it a buyer would have to make $CS^m + t > CS^e$. But there is no t which satisfies $t > CS^e - CS^m$, since by assumption $\pi^m < CS^e - CS^m$.

There are therefore two equilibria of the whole game. One (exclusionary equilibrium), where the incumbent offers $t = 0$ and both buyers accept the deal. The other where it offers $t = 0$ and both buyers reject it. Naked exclusion arises at equilibrium, but it is not the only outcome.

Table 6.2. Segal–Whinston: Discriminatory Offers

B2 \ B1	Accept	Reject
Accept	$CS^m + t_1, CS^m + t_2$	$CS^m + t_1, CS^m$
Reject	$CS^m, CS^m + t_2$	CS^e, CS^e

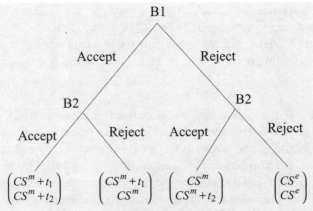

Figure 6.7. Segal–Whinston: Sequential offers.

Simultaneous Discriminatory Offers   Suppose now that the same game as above is played, but that the incumbent can differentiate the offers, so that it can offer $t_1 > t_2$. The payoff matrix of Table 6.2 illustrates the new game.

It is clear that the pair (accept, accept) is still an equilibrium of the game for any $t_i \geq 0$, since by deviating from it and rejecting the deal when the other accepts it, a buyer Bi $(i = 1, 2)$ would get $CS^m \leq t_i + CS^m$. However, the equilibrium (reject, reject) is not an equilibrium any longer. To see why, notice that when buyer $B2$ rejects the contract, buyer $B1$ would get $CS^m + t_1$ by accepting the deal and CS^e by rejecting it. However, by offering a much better deal to $B1$ than $B2$, the incumbent can make it convenient for the former to accept the deal. In other words, this equilibrium is broken if $t_1 > CS^e - CS^m$, which is possible since we assumed $CS^e - CS^m < 2\pi^m$.[68]

Sequential Offers   The neatest example of naked exclusion arises when the incumbent can make sequential offers. Figure 6.7 illustrates the game in this case.

Suppose first that the first buyer has rejected the deal in the first round, and it is up to $B2$ to decide. This buyer accepts the exclusive deal if $t_2 \geq CS^e - CS^m$, and we have just seen that the incumbent is willing to offer such high compensations. Therefore, $B2$ can always be induced to accept if $B1$ has rejected.

Suppose instead that the first buyer has accepted the deal. In this case, $B2$ accepts the deal whatever the level of the compensation, since $CS^m + t_2$ is at least as high as CS^m.

When it comes to its own decision, buyer $B1$ knows that if it accepts, the next buyer will accept too, and therefore will get $CS^m + t_1$; if it rejects, the next

---

[68] For instance, in the linear demand example above, in each market the incumbent can make $\pi^m = (\theta - c_1)^2/4$, while $CS^e - CS^m = 3(\theta - c_1)^2/8$. Since by getting an exclusive deal the incumbent would get monopoly profits in two markets, it is willing to pay up to $2\pi^m = (\theta - c_1)^2/2 > CS^e - CS^m$ to get buyer $B1$, thereby preventing entry.

buyer will always accept the deal, so that $B1$ will get CS^m. Clearly, it prefers to accept the deal for any compensation level. Therefore, at the unique equilibrium, the incumbent is able to offer zero (or slightly above zero) compensations, and have both buyers accepting the deal. Pure exclusion occurs, and it costs nothing to the incumbent.

Conclusions   Which conclusions can be drawn from this analysis? Certainly, recent models show that exclusive contracts have a strong entry-deterrent potential. However, it should not be forgotten that exclusive contracts often have efficiency reasons as well (see also Segal and Whinston, 2000b).[69] A better understanding of how to balance exclusionary and efficiency effects of exclusive contracts is needed, but it seems safe to assume that the former might dominate the latter only if the firm using exclusive contracts has a very strong market position.

6.4.2 Exclusionary Effects of Vertical Mergers

The previous sections have shown that vertical mergers have positive effects upon welfare in many circumstances, for instance, by getting rid of the double marginalisation problem or eliminating free-riding distortions. But might vertical mergers be anti-competitive? It has often been maintained that by integrating downstream, for instance, an input supplier would deny access to the input to all its downstream rivals, thereby gaining market power in the downstream market. However appealing at first sight, this argument has been debated by economists for a long time, and competition laws have also had quite different stances towards vertical mergers in different countries and at different times.

The influential Chicago School maintained that this argument was not correct, and argued that vertical mergers are efficient. This claim was based on a model where an upstream monopolist sells to perfectly competitive firms. In such circumstances (as we know already from Section 6.2.1), the upstream monopolist is able to extract all the profits from the market (since there is no problem of double marginalisation). Hence, a vertical merger would not add market power to the monopolist (hence the label *single monopoly profit* which is given to this theory): if a vertical merger takes place, it must be because some efficiencies are created. (See Section 6.4.2.1.)

In a more general framework (that is, referring to the case where there are several firms upstream and downstream), the Chicago School proponents also pointed out that even if an integrated firm reduced or ceased the supply of input to downstream

---

[69] Heide, Dutta and Bergen (1998) provide some evidence based on survey data that efficiency reasons are more likely than foreclosure reasons and entry deterrence or other anti-competitive use of exclusive dealing. However, this does not mean that their conclusion has general applicability and justifies a presumption that exclusive deals are always good. It just means that efficiency reasons behind exclusive contracts are not just a theoretical possibility but are quite common.

rivals, it is not clear that this would result in effective input foreclosure: first, other suppliers might increase their share of the input market; second, the fact that the integrated firm does not buy in the input market reduces the demand for the inputs, possibly reducing the equilibrium prices in the input markets. It might well be that wholesale prices decrease, rather than increase, after the vertical merger.

It is only recently that economists have rigorously shown that under certain circumstances vertical mergers can result in foreclosure and anti-competitive outcomes. As the reader will recall, we have already seen an instance where a vertical merger might reduce welfare. This was the case where vertical integration allowed a firm to solve a commitment problem (see Section 6.2.5) and keep its prices high.

More generally, recent game-theoretic models allow one to analyse situations where there exist several downstream and/or several upstream firms, and show that in certain cases a vertical merger *might* create foreclosure. To understand the issues at hand, consider a hypothetical situation where a vertical merger between an upstream and a downstream firm takes place. What is the effect of the merger on the input price paid by the independent downstream firms and on the price paid by consumers?

There are a number of effects that one has to take into account to answer this question. The main ones are as follows (see Section 6.6.1 for an application of the way of proceeding suggested here). First of all, one should check whether it is in the interest of the integrated firm to continue to supply the independent downstream firms, or to raise the price of the input it sells to them.[70] If the latter serve an at least partially different market than the integrated downstream firm, ceasing to supply them, or supplying them at higher prices, would entail foregoing profits. If the other upstream firms are competitive enough, raising input prices might not be a profitable strategy for the integrated firm. To understand the incentive of the integrated firm to increase price of the input sold to independent downstream firms, one has to carry out a similar analysis as in horizontal mergers to see whether the merging firms will be able to increase prices. Variables to consider will therefore be the elasticity of demand for the input; the excess capacity of the upstream rivals; the existence of potential entrants (and the ease of entry); and so on.

Second, even if the upstream integrated firm ceases to supply (or sells at higher prices to) the downstream rival firms, it does not follow that the cost of the input for the latter will increase, because (i) the other upstream firms might increase their supply of the input, and (ii) the lower demand for the input (caused by the withdrawal from the market of the downstream affiliate of the integrated firm) will tend to reduce input prices. One has therefore to check, among other things, the extent to which other upstream producers sell close enough substitute inputs and whether they are not capacity constrained.

---

[70] Ceasing to supply can be seen as the extreme case of raising input prices to downstream rivals, when the input price becomes prohibitively high so that demand would go down to zero.

Third, even if foreclosure exists (in the sense that input prices paid by independent firms will increase), this does not necessarily imply that the downstream affiliate of the integrated firm is able to raise prices. There might be enough competition in the downstream market to make it difficult for it to exercise market power (here again, supply and demand characteristics of the market will determine the extent to which the downstream firm can raise prices). Further, the final effect on consumer surplus (and welfare) might still be beneficial due to the elimination of double marginalisation within the integrated chain. The final price might decrease, rather than increase, despite the independent downstream firms paying a higher price for the input.

It is impossible to say *a priori* which effect dominates over the others, but one should none the less conclude that a number of conditions must hold for a vertical merger to give rise to anti-competitive foreclosure. Further, one should also take into account that the vertical merger might involve efficiencies (other than double marginalisation) that one should balance with the possible foreclosure effects, as I indicate in Section 6.5.

6.4.2.1 Exclusionary Effects of Vertical Mergers*

One Monopoly Profit Only*   Consider an upstream monopolist U that sells to two downstream firms, D_1 and D_2, which sell a homogenous good to final consumers (having demand $q = 1 - p$), and compete in prices.[71] Assume that for each unit of output a unit of input must be bought (fixed proportions technology). The upstream firm makes take-it-or-leave-it offers to the downstream firms; these are observable and not renegotiable. Assume also that U has a marginal cost $c < 1$ and that the downstream firms' only cost is the price of the input, w.

In this case, a vertical merger could not increase the profit of the upstream firm. Therefore, a vertical merger would take place only if it entailed some efficiency gain. To see this, compare the two alternative structures.

Vertical separation. The downstream sellers compete in prices. Denoting with w the price at which they buy the input, the market price of the final good at equilibrium will be $p_1 = p_2 = w$,[72] and the total output will be $q = 1 - w$. The upstream firm will choose w to maximise its profits $\pi^U = (w - c)(1 - w)$. Hence, $w = (1 + c)/2$ at equilibrium, resulting in market price $p = (1 + c)/2$, and total profit for U equal to $\pi^U = (1 - c)^2/4$.

Note that this is precisely the same outcome that firm U would obtain if it sold the product directly.

---

[71] The original assumption of the Chicago School theory is that downstream firms are perfectly competitive.

[72] If $w_i < w_j$ downstream firm i which pays less for the input will get all the market by selling at the price w_j. However, this will not be optimal for U, as it would leave some of its rents to downstream firm i.

Vertical merger with a downstream firm. Suppose now that the upstream firm merges with one of the retailers, say D_1. In this case, the upstream firm can either continue to set the same wholesale price as above, or sell to its affiliate D_1 only at the price $w = c$. D_1 would then choose the price $p = (1 + c)/2$ which maximises its profit $\pi = (p - c)(1 - p)$. As a result, however, the total profit of the integrated firm would still be $\pi^I = (1 - c)^2/4$ (and final prices would remain unchanged). Therefore, there is no incentive to merge in this situation: if a vertical merger arises, it is only because it would lead to efficiency gains.

Recent Theories: Is There Foreclosure from Vertical Mergers?**   The very simple model above builds on a number of assumptions that, if relaxed, would give rise to different results, although not all suggesting that vertical mergers are anti-competitive.

Unobservable Offers   First of all, consider the case where the upstream firm's offers are unobservable. In this case, we know from Section 6.2.5.1 that the upstream firm might have an incentive to merge with a downstream firm so as to solve its commitment problem. In this situation, the merger will lead to foreclosure of the downstream rival, and this will be anti-competitive, in the sense that it will lead to higher prices. However, notice that this conclusion hinges on the assumption that the upstream firm was unable to solve its commitment problem through vertical restraints.

Downstream Firms Have Market Power. Efficient Foreclosure   Second, consider the case where offers are observable but downstream firms D_1 and D_2 have some market power. In particular, assume for simplicity that they compete in quantities rather than prices (to model market power with prices we would need differentiated products). Inverse demand is given by $p = 1 - q_1 - q_2$.

Under *vertical separation,* at a symmetric equilibrium the downstream firms will pay w for the input. They choose q_i to maximise $\pi_i = (p - w)q_i$. This is the standard Cournot game, resulting in equilibrium quantities $q_1 = q_2 = (1 - w)/3$, and equilibrium price $p = (1 + 2w)/3$.

If the upstream firm is constrained to linear contracts, then it will choose w to maximise $\pi^U = 2(w - c)(1 - w)/3$. From the FOCs it follows that $w^s = (1 + c)/2$. By substitution, one obtains final prices and the upstream firm's profits as $p^s = (2 + c)/3$ and $\pi^{U,s} = (1 - c)^2/6$, whereas each downstream firm makes $\pi^{i,s} = (1 - c)^2/36$.

Consider now a vertical merger between U and D_1. The best thing that U can do is to foreclose the rival downstream firm by not providing any input to it, while providing its own affiliate at input $w = c$. In this case, D_1 will charge price $p^{vi} = (1 + c)/2$, and the vertical merger will give the integrated firm profits $\pi^{vi} = (1 - c)^2/4$. The merger is profitable, since $\pi^{vi} > \pi^{U,s} + \pi^{1,s}$.

In this simple model, therefore, there exists foreclosure and the rival downstream firm is hurt by the vertical merger. However, the merger is efficient because it removes double marginalisation. Indeed, it can be easily shown that $p^{vi} < p^s$, which implies that consumers also gain from the vertical merger. (It is easily checked that welfare increases with respect to the case of vertical separation.)

Upstream Firm Is Not a Monopolist: Possible Anti-Competitive Foreclosure
Let us analyse now an example where the upstream firm is not a monopolist any longer. To make things as simple as possible, consider a setting where the upstream firms U_1 and U_2 have respectively marginal cost $c_1 = 0$ and $c_2 \in (0, 1/2)$ and simultaneously choose the prices at which they offer the input to D_1 and D_2, which compete in quantities. Effectively, this is as if the downstream firms were making a simultaneous procurement auction. Let us consider the effect of a vertical merger between U_1 and D_1.

Consider first the case where all firms are independent. In this case, each of the two firms will receive the input from firm U_1 at a price c_2, since the upstream firms are playing a Bertrand game with asymmetric costs. The downstream firms play a standard Cournot game with cost c_2, and being otherwise symmetric the equilibrium quantities and prices are given by $q_1^{vs} = q_2^{vs} = (1 - c_2)/3$, and $p^{vs} = (1 + 2c_2)/3$. Firm U_1's profits are given by $\pi_{U1} = 2c_2(1 - c_2)/3$, whereas each downstream firm earns $\pi_i = (1 - c_2)^2/9$.

Suppose now that there is the merger between U_1 and D_1 and as a result the integrated firm decides not to provide the input to firm D_2 any longer: U_1 announces that it will not make any bid to supply D_2 (I shall discuss this assumption below). In this case, the less efficient firm U_2 will become the monopolistic supplier of firm D_2.

Since the downstream affiliate of the integrated firm will have a unit cost $c_1 = 0$, the last stage of the game is a Cournot game between firm D_1 with cost 0 and firm D_2 with cost w_2. It is easy to check that equilibrium outputs of this game will be $q_1 = (1 + w_2)/3$ and $q_2 = (1 - 2w_2)/3$.

At the first stage of the game, upstream firm U_2 chooses its wholesale price to firm D_2 to maximise $\pi^{U_2} = (w_2 - c_2)(1 - 2w_2)/3$. The optimal solution is $w_2 = (1 + 2c_2)/4$. Since $w_2 > c_2$, it is clear that downstream firm D_2 is effectively foreclosed relative to the pre-merger situation: the input has become more expensive.

By substitution, one can then show that the equilibrium quantities will be given by $q_2^f = (1 - 2c_2)/6$ and $q_1^f = (5 + 2c_2)/12$; market price by $p^f = (5 + 2c_2)/12$; and the vertically integrated firm's profits by $\pi_1^f = (5 + 2c_2)^2/144$ (the label f standing for "foreclosure").

The total profits of the merging firms are higher, since $\pi_1^f > \pi_{U1} + \pi_1$, but the merger is not necessarily efficient: $p^{vs} < p^f$ for $c_2 < 1/6$.

Therefore, if $c_2 < 1/6$, the vertical merger leads to foreclosure and it is anti-competitive (it can be checked that total surplus decreases).

Remark 1. A crucial assumption in this model is that the upstream affiliate of the integrated firm commits not to take part in the supply for the other downstream firm. But does it have an incentive to commit not to supply D_2? If it took part in the competition to supply D_2, it would win it by setting a price c_2. As a result, equilibrium quantities would be $q_2^{nf} = (1 - 2c_2)/3$ and $q_1^{nf} = (1 + c_2)/3$. The final price would be $p^{nf} = (1 + c_2)/3 < p^{vs}$ (the vertical merger would benefit consumers), and $\pi_1^{nf} = (1 + c_2)^2/9 + c_2(1 - 2c_2)/3$. It can be checked that $\pi_1^f > \pi_1^{nf}$ can be rewritten as $(28c_2^2 - 20c_2 + 3) > 0$, which corresponds to $c_2 < 3/14$.

Therefore, for $c_2 < 3/14$ it is optimal for the integrated firm to pre-commit not to supply the rival downstream firm. For $c_2 < 1/6$ the merger is anti-competitive, whereas for $c_2 \in [1/6, 1/2)$ it is not.

Remark 2. In the example I have assumed that there is only one other upstream firm apart from U_1. Assume now instead that there is at least another input supplier having the same cost c_2. In this case, after the vertical merger between D_1 and U_1 the rival downstream firm D_2 would always be supplied at the price c_2 because of the competition among the upstream firms. U_1 would find it more profitable to supply the rival downstream firm itself and the vertical merger would always be pro-competitive because it reduces double marginalisation within the vertically integrated firm.

6.5 CONCLUSIONS AND POLICY IMPLICATIONS

We have seen that vertical restraints and vertical mergers have a number of efficiency features: although in some circumstances they might have some anti-competitive effects, a *per se* prohibition rule would clearly be inappropriate, since it would forego efficiency effects which are likely to dominate in most cases. A rule of reason appears certainly more advisable.

This statement holds for all types of vertical restraints and vertical mergers: different restraints are often substitutable for each other. Furthermore, there is no unanimous ranking of vertical restraints in terms of welfare. Therefore, there is no economic justification for a policy that treats restraints in a different way, say using a *per se* rule of prohibition against retail price maintenance while always allowing all other restraints.[73] By the same token, it would be inconsistent to have, say, a tough stance against some vertical restraints, while being lenient on vertical mergers.

A rule of reason for vertical restraints and vertical mergers does not mean that all vertical agreements should be examined by the anti-trust agencies. This would simply be impossible, as they would have to use their scarce resources to monitor thousands of vertical relationships. Vertical restraints and vertical mergers are anti-competitive only if they involve firms endowed with significant market power (we have seen in several cases that the potential harm created by a vertical restraint decreases with the presence of competitors). Accordingly, there is no need to monitor

---

[73] In other words, there is no rationale for adopting block exemptions by type of vertical restraints. As discussed below, it is market power that matters, independently of the type of restraint.

restraints and mergers which involve firms with little market power. An efficient policy towards vertical restraints would grant exemption to all the vertical restraints and mergers of firms which do not have large market power. From the operational point of view, it would seem a good proxy to exempt firms with market shares below, say, 20–30% (as in the new regime created in the EU, except that practices such as RPM are black-listed: see Chapter 1).

This leaves the problem of how to deal with vertical restraints and vertical mergers which involve firms with significant market power (*a fortiori*, the same applies for dominant firms) and which have possible exclusionary effects. In these cases, a rule of reason should be adopted, and one should balance possible efficiency effects with possible anti-competitive effects.

Balancing Exclusionary and Efficiency Effects of Vertical Mergers and Vertical Restraints   The analysis of vertical mergers above emphasised that (i) input foreclosure does not necessarily follow from them; (ii) even if downstream rivals are indeed foreclosed, final prices do not necessarily increase. This suggests a two-step procedure for the cases where the vertical merger involves firms above a certain market share threshold.[74] First of all, it should be established whether the merger will likely lead to input foreclosure, that is, that input prices for independent downstream firms will increase (*competitors* will be harmed). If so, the investigation should continue to the second step. If not, the merger should be cleared. In the second step (if applicable), it should be established whether final consumer prices are likely to increase or not (*competition* will be harmed).

A similar procedure should be followed for vertical restraints that might lead to foreclosure of rivals. The anti-trust authorities should prove that exclusive dealing (or other exclusive clauses, or refusal to supply) would harm competition, in the sense of being likely to reduce consumer welfare. The defendant should then be able to produce convincing evidence that the vertical restraints adopted entail enough efficiency gains for consumers to benefit from them.

6.6 CASES

In this section, I briefly describe two EU cases. The first, *General Electric/Honeywell*, concerns a merger which has vertical aspects (as well as horizontal and conglomerate aspects, which will be dealt with here as well). The second concerns the ice-cream market in Germany, and focuses on exclusivity provisions in the contracts between ice-cream manufacturers and retailers.

---

[74] Riordan and Salop (1995) propose a four-step procedure to deal with possible exclusionary vertical mergers which blends in well with the analysis above, and which is similar to the test presented here. Their paper is devoted entirely to this issue and is richer and more complete than my analysis. It is a highly recommended reading.

6.6.1 *General Electric/Honeywell*

In February 2001, the European Commission was notified of a project according to which General Electric (GE) would have taken over Honeywell. Both firms are based in the US, but their large size implies that the merger met the thresholds for being reviewed by the EC as well. The US Department of Justice approved the deal, but in July 2001, after several negotiations and an intense debate that was abundantly reported in the media, the EC prohibited the merger (see *General Electric/Honeywell*).[75] In what follows, I describe and comment upon the case, in a necessarily brief way given its complexity.

The case touches upon issues treated in several chapters: because of horizontal overlaps, the possible effects of vertical integration, and the allegation that the merged entity could have engaged in bundling and foreclosure behaviour, references to Chapters 5, 6 and 7 naturally arise in this case.

The Product Markets Several product markets (all worldwide in geographic terms) are affected by the merger, mostly in the aerospace industry, on which I will focus.[76] Broadly speaking, there are three sectors in which the product markets at hand can be grouped: (1) jet engines, (2) aircraft systems (avionics and non-avionics) and (3) engine controls.

(1) The EC identifies four main product markets associated with jet engines.

(1a) *Jet engines for large commercial aircraft* (roughly speaking, aircraft with more than 100 seats that can travel long distances). In this market, where there are only two airframe manufacturers, Airbus and Boeing (each with roughly half of the market), there are five main active engine suppliers, GE, Rolls-Royce (RR), Pratt&Whitney (P&W), CFMI, which is a 50–50 joint-venture between GE and the French firm SNECMA, and IAE, a joint-venture between RR, P&W (each with a 32% share) and two other firms. Honeywell is not present in this market, and therefore the merger does not have a horizontal dimension.

(1b) *Engines for regional jet aircraft* (aircraft with 30 to 100 seats, manufactured by Embraer, Bombardier, Fairchild Dornier and British Aerospace), which is further divided by the EC in engines for *small* regional aircraft, where Honeywell is not present, and in engines for *large* regional aircraft, where both Honeywell and GE operate. CFMI, RR and P&W are also active if one – unlike the EC – defines the market so as to include Airbus' and Boeing's small narrow-body planes, which are also used for transport over medium distances.[77]

---

[75] The EC decision has been appealed, but as of January 2003, the CFI has not yet made a judgment.
[76] I will not deal with the concerns arising in power systems markets, since they are less important and do not raise different issues.
[77] The EC does not include them in the market definition mainly because they have a higher price and higher operating costs than other large regional jets. However, as discussed in Chapter 3, a different price of two products is not a valid criterion to establish separate product markets. Note

(1c) *Engines for corporate jet aircraft* (designed mainly for corporate activities, and therefore aimed at carrying a lower number of passengers; manufacturers are Cessna, Gulfstream, Raytheon, Bombardier and Dassault); GE, Honeywell, RR and P&W are all present in this market.

Engines for large commercial and for regional aircraft are usually sold to two distinct categories of buyers: airframe manufacturers and end-users (that is, airlines or leasing companies). Indeed, the airframe manufacturers do not necessarily choose only one type of engine for any particular aeroplane: they can certify different engines and then leave the final choice to the end-users, which might have different preferences as for the engines to be fitted in the planes they buy, for instance, due to economies from using the same make of engine (called *commonality* benefits). Engines for corporate jet aircraft are usually chosen by airframe manufacturers, not by end-users.

(1d) *Maintenance, repair and overhaul* (MRO) of engines, that is after-markets (services and spare parts).[78] These services are provided by all the original engine manufacturers (such as GE, Honeywell, RR and P&W), by airlines' maintenance departments, and by independent service shops. These are very important activities (jet engines need frequent service, maintenance and reviews), which account for a large part of the revenues of the engine manufacturers.

(2) There exist two broad categories of aircraft systems, avionics and non-avionics.

(2a) *Avionics products* include all the different equipment used for the control of the aircraft, for navigation and communication, and for the assessment of flying conditions. GE is not active in these markets, while Honeywell is active in most of them (overall it has 50–60% of total sales), with Rockwell-Collins (20–30%), Thales (10–20%) and Smiths Industries (less than 10%) being the other operators.

(2b) *Non-avionics products* include a variety of systems (such as auxiliary power units, environmental control systems, electric power, wheels, brakes, landing gear, aircraft lighting) used in operating an aircraft. Again, GE is not active, whereas Honeywell has a strong presence in most of these products; other producers are Hamilton-Sundstrand (a subsidiary of UTC, which also owns P&W), BF Goodrich and SNECMA (one of the parents in the CFMI joint-venture).

Avionics and non-avionics are just broad product categories, the relevant product markets being a number of separate systems which are not substitutable with

also that it is possible that some types of planes, such as the small narrow-bodies, might belong to both the market of large commercial aircraft and that of large regional jets: having intermediate characteristics, they might well constrain the ability of a hypothetical monopolist to raise prices in either of the two markets.

[78] Since it would probably not affect the final assessment of the merger, I will not discuss here whether after-markets should be considered in a separate product market from engines, but the reader might want to refer to Chapter 3 for some comments on market definition and market power in after-markets.

each other. The EC further divides product markets according to whether these are *buyer-furnished equipment* (BFE) or *supplier-furnished equipment* (SFE). Avionics products are generally BFE; they are purchased by the airline among the products originally certified by the airframe manufacturers (usually after consultation with advisory committees where airlines and leasing companies are represented). Non-avionics are generally SFE, that is they are purchased by the airframe manufacturers, although launch customers and other buyers (airlines and leasing companies) might influence the selection process according to the EC.

(3) *Engine controls*. These are accessories and controls that are used as inputs in the production of engines. GE is not present in these products, but Honeywell is active in some of them, and is particularly strong in the production of engine starters, where it has more than 50% of the market, its main competitor being Hamilton-Sundstrand (whose market share is put by the EC at more than 40%), which sells engine starters only to its sister company P&W.

Horizontal, Conglomerate, Vertical Aspects of the Merger   From this cursory description, it appears that the merger has several distinct aspects. First, it has a horizontal nature as far as the market for large regional jet engines is concerned, where GE and Honeywell are competing. Second, it has a conglomerate nature because in several product markets only one of the merging partners is present. Third, it has a vertical nature, because Honeywell and GE have an upstream–downstream relationship in that the former produces engine controls used by the latter in the production of engines, but also because, as I shall discuss shortly, GE is an important buyer of aeroplanes through its leasing company GECAS, and in this sense it (indirectly) purchases Honeywell products. Indeed, the EC decision argues that GECAS, after the merger, would be able to tilt the upstream avionics and non-avionics product market in favour of Honeywell.

While the horizontal aspects of this merger are relatively standard, the interesting aspects of the EC decision arise with respect to the conglomerate and vertical aspects, which usually raise few competition problems, but ultimately led the EC to prohibit this merger. To try to understand its decision, we have to turn to its analysis of GE, which according to the EC enjoys even before the merger a position of dominance in large commercial aircraft and regional aircraft engines, and can strengthen it in the markets it dominates already, or extend it to the markets where Honeywell has a leading position.

The Ingredients of GE's Dominance   Understanding whether before the merger GE has a dominant position (that is, very large market power) in jet engines markets is important. The EC believed that following the merger GE would be able to leverage its market power, through various mechanisms I describe below (GE Capital, GECAS, bundling), so as to create dominance in markets where Honeywell (but not GE) is present. Therefore, finding dominance (high-enough market power) is a necessary condition to argue that a merger between two non-competing firms (I refer here to those markets with no overlaps) could be harmful. (But recall that a finding of dominance is not sufficient to show that harm will exist.)

Market Shares   As we know from Chapter 3, the assessment of the market power of a firm entails a number of considerations, the first of which is usually market share. The EC finds that GE has a large market share, indicative of dominance, in the engines for large commercial aircraft. More particularly, the EC assigns GE a 52.5% share of the market, whereas P&W and RR have respectively 26.5% and 21% of the market.

These figures have been calculated under two assumptions contested by the parties. First, they are obtained by looking only at installed base and firm orders for aircraft that are *currently* manufactured (see *GE/Honeywell:* para. 38), and second, they consider engines produced by CFMI as if they were produced by GE alone.

Using installed base and firm orders rather than, for example, sales obtained in a given number of years (these are markets where sales occur infrequently and with large orders, so sales over say, one year, would be meaningless), is due to the value of incumbency. There are learning and switching costs associated with new engines, so an airline would prefer to continue buying the same engine when it buys a certain aircraft. The exclusion of planes whose production has been discontinued is explained by the fact that an airline can no longer order those planes.

However, this definition of sales might overlook one element that the EC stresses in other parts of the decision: the stream of revenues associated with after-markets, which appears to be crucial for the overall profitability of an engine manufacturer, and for financing research and development outlays. Since revenues from MRO and spare parts continue even for planes no longer in production (aircraft have a long life span), and given the importance attributed by the EC to these revenues, the decision to focus only on aircraft still in production might give a biased indication of GE's market power. If market shares were calculated considering aircraft in service, but no longer in production, GE would hold 41% of the market, according to Nalebuff (2002: 19), an expert who assisted GE and Honeywell.

The EC attributes all the sales made by the joint-venture between GE and SNECMA to the former company, mainly because SNECMA is not an independent engines manufacturer. Consistently, it also attributes half of the sales made by IAE to P&W and half to RR, despite the fact these firms own a lower proportion of this JV, because the remaining partners are not independent manufacturers of jet engines. This is also disputed by GE and Honeywell, which argue that – especially if financial resources matter – only half of CFMI's sales should be given to GE, since it receives only 50% of its revenues. Using this approach, GE's market share would fall to 36% (Nalebuff, 2002: 19).

To the extent that market share is looked at as an indicator of the existing market power of the firms, the EC's approach is probably correct. First, SNECMA is not a possible competitive constraint to GE, because it lacks the necessary skills to produce engines independently and it has important links with GE. Second, because it appears from the decision that GE itself in its documents, as well as independent market research publications, use the practice of attributing CFMI's sales to GE.

However, to the extent that market share is used as an indicator of the likelihood that GE/Honeywell will engage in bundling or cross-subsidisation practices among products sold in order to achieve foreclosure of Honeywell's rivals (one of the main preoccupations of the EC in this decision, see below), it might be better not to consider CFMI sales as if they were 100% GE's sales. Indeed, it is not clear that SNECMA would consent to such practices, even though GE is arguably the strongest partner in this relationship (but the president and CEO of CFMI is seconded by SNECMA).[79]

Finally, it should be noted that GE's large share depends also on the contract that makes CFMI's engines the exclusive engines for the Boeing 737, which is the most popular ever commercial plane. If one excluded those sales (to the extent that bundling or cross-subsidisation are a concern, this is a valid approach because the supply of the engines for the 737 is already secured), and even by giving it 100% of remaining CFMI's sales, GE would have 44% of the market (Kolasky, 2001: 10–11).

However large its market shares, the EC found that there exist also other reasons that justify its finding of dominance by GE in jet engines for large commercial aircraft.

GE Capital   GE Capital is the financial arm of GE, and it contributes more than 80% of GE's financial assets. This provides GE with enormous financial resources that it can use for its industrial activities. It is indisputable that, however sophisticated financial organisations might be, capital markets are imperfect, and recent research in corporate finance points at different ways in which the availability of in-house financial resources might affect product market competition.[80] According to the EC, in this particular case there are two domains where GE's financial strength gives it an advantage over its competitors.

The first is that it allows it to engage in more R&D than its competitors: "GE is able to take more risk in product development programmes than any of its competitors. This ability to absorb product failures without jeopardising its future ability to compete and develop new products in an industry characterised by long term investments is critical" (*GE/Honeywell:* para. 108).

The second is that it allows it to be more patient and not to rely on immediate profits: "GE has taken advantage of the importance of financial strength in this industry by relying heavily on discounts on the catalogue price of the engines.

---

[79] The EC's views on this point, and a mention of some of the parties' opinions, can be found in paragraphs 45–66 of the decision.

[80] See for instance Aghion, Dewatripont and Rey (1998) and Cestone and Fumagalli (2001). See also the discussion of financial models of predation, which have probably inspired the EC reasoning in this decision, in Chapter 7.

These heavy discounting practices resulted in moving the break-even point of an engine project further away from the commercial launch of a platform. Given its enormous balance sheet, GE has been in a position to increase rivals' funding costs by delaying the inception of cash flows and consequently increasing the need to resort to external financial means further raising their leverage (debt/equity ratio) and resulting borrowing costs. By doing this GE has managed to make its competitors very much vulnerable to any down cycle or strategic mistake" (*GE/Honeywell:* para. 111).

One might think that this sounds like a version of a "long purse" argument (see Chapter 7), whereby a firm (GE) makes use of its financial resources to keep its prices low and therefore hurt competitors. In fact, it is a more sophisticated argument, as the EC argues that overall prices paid by consumers have gone up, not down: "... heavily discounted original sales do not mean lower costs for the final customers. ... The total average cost of an engine has actually increased between 10% and 30% in real terms over the last 10 years. This is of course due to the offsetting effect of the significant price increases applied annually on all original spare parts manufactured by the original engine supplier" (*GE/Honeywell:* para. 113).[81]

The EC seems therefore to suggest that GE has found a way to *increase* the overall prices paid by buyers, while at the same time hurting its rivals,[82] just by modifying the stream of revenues, that is by charging low prices on the main product, engines, and increasing more than proportionately prices in the after-markets (spare parts and services). I confess I know of no rigorous economic analysis that can support such a theory.[83]

Still according to the EC, GE's vertical integration in after-markets is also important: "As the final step in the foreclosure strategy and in order to protect and grow this very lucrative part of its engine business, GE has used its financial strength to invest very large amounts of money for several years into the aftermarket through the purchase of a significant number of repair shops all over the world. This strategy applies not only to the servicing of GE's own engines but also to the engines of

---

[81] However, in the following paragraph, the EC argues that "GE can, thanks to its financial strength and incumbency advantages as an engine supplier, afford to provide significant financial support to airframe manufacturers in the form of platform programme development assistance that competitors have not been historically in a position to replicate. GE uses this direct financial support to arrange/obtain engine exclusivity on those airframes that it financially assists" (*GE/Honeywell:* para. 114). But financial support, credits, and development assistance should be equivalent to lower prices from the point of view of the customers!

[82] "Indeed, lower prices on the initial engine sales result not in net lower prices to the customer but in the weakening of engine competitors and in foreclosing them from current and future platforms and airlines competition" (para. 112).

[83] One possible explanation for it to work could be that buyers are enticed into buying GE by low engine prices and are then taken by surprise by higher prices in the after-markets, but there exist sophisticated buyers in this market: airlines must be aware that most of the expenditures related to an engine are due to servicing and maintaining it.

its competitors which as a result end up deprived of the critical aftermarket revenues needed to justify both past investments and future product developments" (*GE/Honeywell*: para. 116).

GECAS   Another factor contributing to GE's dominance, according to the EC, is its vertical integration into aircraft purchasing, financing and leasing activities through its subsidiary GE Capital Aviation Services (GECAS). GECAS is the largest single purchaser of new aircraft, accounting for around 10% of these purchases. Apart from the major airlines, another important buyer is another leasing company, ILFC, whose fleet is about half the size of GECAS' fleet.

According to the EC, GECAS – which has a policy of buying only GE engines when selecting new aircraft – has a strong influence in the market-place, mainly for two reasons. First, as the largest leasing company it has the "ability to seed smaller airlines with GE-powered aircraft, creating, maintaining and enhancing fleet commonality considerations that will influence these airlines to select similar equipment in the future, whether acquiring them from GECAS or elsewhere" (*GE/Honeywell*: para. 125). Second, it can persuade airframe manufacturers to favour GE engines through sizeable aircraft sales prospects. Also, "as a launch customer, GECAS can influence the aircraft equipment selection by the airframe manufacturers and therefore constitute, in combination with GE other features, the element that can tilt the balance in favour of GE as equipment and service supplier" (*GE/Honeywell*: para. 133).

Effectively, the EC argues here that a firm that buys 10% of aircraft is able (perhaps in conjunction with other elements, such as GE Capital's financial incentives) to manipulate aircraft manufacturers' decisions so as to persuade them to buy GE engines (thus resulting in the foreclosure of rivals). Again, the hypothesis that a firm with such small market share might have such a large market power is surprising to an economist, and it is unfortunate that most of the examples that the EC brings to support this hypothesis are omitted in the public version of the decision for confidential reasons (at the demand of the merging parties).

Is It Dominance? Other Factors to Take into Account   The EC analysis leaves us with no doubts that GE is a powerful firm, but the goal here is to understand to what extent it is able to command high prices, that is, how large its market power is. To answer this question, other elements have to be taken into account.

The markets involved in this merger are all markets where entry is difficult (both because of the sunk costs and the technological know-how required), so whatever market power exists it will not be likely to be constrained by the appearance of new firms. However, the strength of competitors and the countervailing power of buyers should also be considered.

The EC stresses the fact that neither RR nor P&W has the financial abilities of GE Capital, nor are they vertically integrated into a leasing company like GECAS. However, these firms are no minnows either: for instance, P&W is part of UTC, a large firm which is also present in non-avionics. Further, both RR and P&W operate not only in commercial aviation but also in military sectors, which have substantial technological spillovers with each other. As mentioned above, the financial resources necessary to invest might also come from engines installed in planes still operating but no longer manufactured. Therefore, if it is true that GE looks by far the leading firm in the industry, the EC might somehow underestimate the force of its rivals.[84]

The other important element to be considered is the power of the buyers. As we have seen, engines (and the same is true for the other product markets considered) are purchased by airlines (and leasing companies) and airframe manufacturers. If smaller airlines are unlikely to have large buyer power, the largest airlines and the second largest leasing company, ILFC, buy a large number of aircraft and must have some countervailing power and the possibility to influence aircraft manufacturers' decisions about engines' certification. The same must be true for aircraft manufacturers, especially in the large commercial aircraft market, where Airbus and Boeing roughly share the market. In all these cases, competition takes place through bidding, and one would expect competition among engine producers to be extremely tough. Surely, if GE tried to exercise too much market power, airlines and aircraft manufacturers might credibly threaten them to switch to RR or P&W.

The EC claims that GE Capital's financial assistance and the prospect of selling planes to GECAS play a big role in affecting buyers' decisions, but it seems doubtful that Airbus and Boeing will not be able to exercise countervailing power. The EC decision is silent as to the reaction of buyers with respect to this merger (in part, because some relevant confidential information is omitted from the decision), but knowing whether buyers would oppose this merger or not, and for which reason, would allow us to better assess its anti-competitive potential.

Conglomerate Aspects: Extending Dominance   Although in some of its parts the decision sounds as if this were a case of (past) abuse of dominance, it is time to recall that this is a merger case, and the reason why GE's strengths have been stressed is that, according to the EC, they would be used by GE to extend its dominance to product markets in which Honeywell (but not GE) operates.

There are three main arguments made by the EC to justify its finding that the merger will give dominance to GE/Honeywell in markets such as avionics and non-avionics where only Honeywell is active. Two are known from the above analysis. First, GE/Honeywell – through GE Capital – would use its financial strength to provide buyers (airlines and airframe manufacturers, depending on whether the markets are BFE or SFE) with favourable terms that rivals would not be able to

---

[84] The DOJ, which authorised the merger, had a different opinion about the competitiveness of GE's competitors, and the parties contested that GE's share was increasing over time: according to Nalebuff (2002: 20), looking at pre-orders on planes that have been launched but are not in production yet, RR would have a 40% share of engines on such planes, GE/CFMI 38%, and P&W 21%.

match.[85] Second, through GECAS, the merged entity will use its buyer power so as to persuade airframe manufacturers to buy Honeywell avionics and non-avionics products.

The third mechanism hinges on Honeywell's broad portfolio of avionics and non-avionics (as indicated above, it provides almost the complete range of products needed in aviation systems), as well as the possibility to combine together GE engines (and after-markets services) and Honeywell products, making *packaged offers* that airlines and airframe manufacturers will find very attractive: "The complementary nature of the GE and Honeywell product offerings coupled with their respective existing market positions will give the merged entity the ability and the economically rational incentive to engage in bundled offers or cross-subsidisation across product sales to both categories of customers" (*GE/Honeywell:* para. 349).

Therefore, the EC argues that after the merger the new firm will engage in *bundling* (several components will be sold only in a unique package, at a single price) or *mixed bundling* (individual components might also be available, but the whole package is sold at a price which is lower than the sum of the individual components' prices).[86]

Bundling and more generally packaged deals would have the effect of reducing prices in the market and forcing competitors to exit: "The ability of the merged entity to cross-subsidise its various complementary activities and to engage in profitable forms of packaged sales will have an adverse effect on the profitability of competing producers of avionics and non-avionics products, as a result of market share erosion. This is likely to lead to market exit of existing competitors and market foreclosure . . ." (*GE/Honeywell:* para. 398).

The EC reasoning is supported by two arguments, one theoretical and the other empirical. The theoretical is that – since work by Whinston (1990) – there exist economic models that show that a firm might use bundling so as to exclude a rival from the market (see Chapter 7).[87] The empirical is that it is plausible that the firms will engage in bundling, since bundling is already observed in this industry.

---

[85] Although the decision never makes it explicit, at times it seems as if the EC thought that the financial strength of GE Capital could provide the basis of a deep pocket predation strategy (see Chapter 7). If this argument was considered, similar considerations as in the discussion of bundling (see below) would apply. One should check whether such a predatory strategy would be profitable, whether it would lead to rivals' exit, and after how long (so as to assess the overall net effect on welfare).

[86] The EC also claims that in the medium term GE/Honeywell would also engage in *technical bundling*, that is it would make its products available only as an integrated system that is incompatible with competing individual components (para. 354).

[87] In fact, the EC did not rely on Whinston (1990). In his paper (except for particular cases that hold under more specific assumptions), a firm finds it profitable to engage in bundling only to the extent that it will lead to exit. Probably to avoid having to prove recoupment, the EC referred instead to a model (see Choi, 2001) submitted by RR, where (mixed-)bundling hurts the rivals – thus depriving them of the profits they need to be competitive or to survive – while being short-run profitable (that is, profitable without having to wait for the rival's exit). An anecdote: Choi's model was based upon work by Nalebuff, who was then retained by GE/Honeywell as an expert, and argued that this model would not apply to this particular industry (see Nalebuff, 2002).

Both arguments are disputed by the parties. The first on the grounds that finding a model where bundling hurts the rivals is not sufficient: one should also show that the model's assumptions are consistent with the basic characteristics of the industry, the latter not being the case according to the parties (Nalebuff, 2002). The second because they maintain that the EC's claim that bundling takes place in the industry is false.

This is not the appropriate place to enter a necessarily deep analysis of whether a particular economic model of anti-competitive bundling would be applicable to this industry or not, and unfortunately the examples provided by the EC to support the existence of bundling are omitted for confidentiality reasons from the decision, so it is impossible to make up one's mind on this point when reading it. Yet, I will argue below that even *assuming* that bundling is and will be done, this is not enough to prove that the merger will be anti-competitive.

Will the Merger Hurt Consumers?   Let us assume that indeed the merged entity would engage in bundling and offer packaged deals of various types. In order to win market shares and to hurt competitors, this must mean that some price reductions for buyers should follow from such practices. Another reason why we should expect prices to move downwards, although it is impossible to quantify this effect without having more detailed information, is the fact that GE and Honeywell sell products that are complementary. Like for vertically related products (where this corresponds to the elimination of double marginalisation), a firm which sells two or more complementary products will sell them at lower prices than if the same products were sold by independent firms (see Section 8.2).

But although the effect of the merger is (presumably) to reduce these prices, the EC blocked it because it expected it to result in the exit of GE's rivals, and in a subsequent price increase. Although theoretically possible, there are a number of steps that should be checked before arriving at such conclusion.

First of all, how likely is it that firms would abandon their presence in the products at issue? Some of these firms, like UTC, are large firms with a strong presence in this industry. Is it so clear that they would exit? Surely, before leaving the industry, they will also try to react in one way or other, for instance by acquiring other firms or forming alliances in order to have a broader range of products. Of course, the EC and the parties diverge on this point (see *GE/Honeywell*: paragraphs 377–86).

Although efficiency gains are never mentioned in the decision, the analysis is very similar to that conducted in Chapter 5 when discussing the possible "efficiency offence" arguments. In theory, it is possible that efficiency gains (in this case, packaged offers or bundling) might eventually lead to a welfare loss, but many circumstances must concur for this to be possible, and one of these is the lack of possible reactions from the outsiders to the merger.

Second (and this point is completely missing in the EC's analysis), let us assume that rivals will indeed exit, but how soon? The operating life of an aeroplane is very long, and since most of these products' revenues come not from initial sales but from MRO services and spare parts, presumably it will take a long time before rivals would exit. Therefore, there must be some trade-off to be considered here: the longer the phase with low prices and rivals still operating, the larger the resulting initial effect on welfare that must be outweighed by the negative impact on prices that will take place after exit.

Some final, and broader questions, arise regarding the different strategies available to the EC in dealing with the conglomerate aspects of this merger. In particular, the EC could have allowed the merger, but imposing a *behavioural remedy,* that is obliging the firm not to engage in bundling. This option was discarded because the EC did not want to have to monitor the industry on a continuous basis. This is an understandable preoccupation (see Chapter 5), but perhaps in this case the remedy was not impossible to implement, and its costs could have fallen upon the merging parties. The other possibility could have been for the EC to allow the merger but review the industry later so as to open an investigation for abuse of dominance as soon as GE/Honeywell had engaged in suspected monopolisation practices. Clearly, this option was less preferable for the EC because such an investigation would have been difficult, costly and lengthy. But the Court might say that forbidding a merger for suspected foreclosure might need a very high standard of proof, and not speculations (however well justified), thus pushing the EC to have to intervene *ex post* through Article 82, rather than *ex ante* through the Merger Regulation, to deal with such cases.

Foreclosure through Vertical Integration: Engine Starters   As said at the beginning of this section, the merger raised concerns also with respect to the vertical integration between Honeywell, a leading upstream producer of engine starters, and GE, a downstream producer of jet engines, and the EC concluded that "the merged entity would have an incentive to delay or disrupt the supply of Honeywell engine starters to competing engine manufacturers, which would result in damaging supply, distribution, profitability and competitiveness of GE's engine competitors" (*GE/Honeywell:* para. 420).

The possibility that a vertical merger leads to foreclosure has been studied in Section 6.4.2, and there are a number of conditions that should hold for foreclosure to occur.

First, one has to check whether it is profitable to stop supplying downstream competitors. In particular, RR buys engine starters in the free market, so by ceasing to supply RR, Honeywell would lose revenues. Discontinuing supplies might also be very costly in legal terms: contractual obligations prevent Honeywell from ceasing to supply non-GE engines, as the EC decision acknowledges: "Honeywell is to accept all orders placed for them. Should Honeywell fail to satisfy the order, or materially beach the agreement, it is required to grant a licence to a third party to manufacture the component and Honeywell must provide the licensee with all proprietary data necessary to enable manufacture" (*GE/Honeywell:* para. 424).

Certainly, the EC is right in saying that ceasing to supply engine starters to non-GE engines would damage the downstream competitors, but an assessment should be made as to whether this strategy is more profitable than continuing to supply RR.[88]

Second, even if Honeywell did cease supplying RR, for foreclosure to take place it must be that no other upstream manufacturer would sell enough to RR, so that the input price it pays would rise. Here again, not surprisingly, the parties and the EC disagree. The former indicate a number of firms that could have the ability to step in and replace Honeywell, but the latter argues that none of them would. According to the EC, Hamilton-Sundstrand (belonging to the same group as P&W), would have no incentive to supply RR because the profits made by foreclosing RR would be higher than the profits foregone from selling starters to RR. Another firm, Microturbo, would not have the technical ability, nor the incentive to supply RR because it is an affiliate of SNECMA (whose interests the EC regards to be aligned with GE's), and the other potential suppliers would not be a realistic alternative to Honeywell either, for various reasons.[89]

Third, imagine that foreclosure did happen, in the sense that RR would end up with higher prices paid for engine starters (the extreme case where RR would have to cease production altogether simply because engine starters are no longer available on the market at all seems very unlikely). Still, it is the final prices of the vertical chain that one should look at in order to assess the impact of vertical integration. An important consideration to be made, in this respect, is that vertical integration implies the elimination of double marginalisation (see Section 2.1): as GE becomes the owner of Honeywell, its cost for engine starters will decrease, and this will tend to decrease GE's jet engine prices.[90] This would bring us back to the points discussed above under the conglomerate aspects: even if foreclosure arises, there is still a trade-off to be assessed between lower prices and possible exit (but since P&W is also vertically integrated into starters, the arguments made here apply to the possible exit of RR alone).

Conclusions   This is a very difficult and complicated merger case, which entails several different product markets, and problems of different natures. I have discussed in particular the conglomerate aspects of the decision, where the EC makes arguments that are somehow novel, but that in my opinion are at worst incomplete or incorrect and at best not explained accurately enough (but admittedly, the

---

[88] GE and Honeywell also make the point (para. 425) that in the markets where Honeywell was manufacturing engines itself, it has continued supplying downstream rivals.

[89] Another possibility that should be checked is why RR could not start manufacturing engine starters itself. The decision does not explain if RR would not have the technical abilities required, or perhaps could not buy one of the firms active upstream and do joint development of starters.

[90] Of course, if there were any additional efficiencies from producing engine starters and engines jointly, the downward pressure on costs and prices will be higher.

published decision cannot contain all the details and explanations that one would like to have). It will be interesting to see how the European judges will deal with this case. Possibly, their decision will also bring to light details and discussions that do not appear in the published EC decision.

6.6.2 Ice-Cream

In 1991, the Mars group lodged a complaint with the European Commission, claiming that exclusive agreements linking retailers with the two leading firms, Langnese-Iglo (LI) and Schöller, hindered its sales in the German ice-cream market. In *Langnese-Iglo* and *Schöller*,[91] both dating from December 1992, the EC decided that indeed those agreements had infringed Article 81 (then art. 85) of the Treaty, and prohibited the two firms from using them. The Court of First Instance rejected the two companies' appeal in June 1995 (*Langnese-Iglo v. Commission* and *Schöller v. Commission*), and the CFI judgment was later upheld by the European Court of Justice.

The interesting aspects of this case (one of many similar cases involving Mars in different EU jurisdictions) are the definition of the relevant market, the potential for foreclosure of exclusive agreements, and the implications that exclusivity agreements might have on the incentives to invest.

A Brief Introduction to the Industry   Ice-cream can be produced either via an industrial process or by craft trade. In 1990, the former accounted for 439 million litres of sales, and the latter for 133 million litres (*Schöller*, para. 23). Industrial ice-cream can be sold in *individual portions,* which by and large corresponds to the impulse ice-cream product market as defined by the EC in its decision (131.8 million litres in 1990), *multi-packs* (26 million), *take-home packs* (212 million), and *catering packs* (69.6 million).

The main characteristic of ice-cream, as everybody knows, is that to preserve the characteristic of the product one has to guarantee that it is always kept at low temperatures. In the case of industrial ice-cream (craft trade ice-cream is almost exclusively sold directly to the final consumers), the firms need to make an important investment to make sure that the product is properly refrigerated during the various stages that bring it from the place of production to the final consumers. In particular, since retailers appear to be unwilling to spend important amounts of money to buy freezer cabinets, the main ice-cream companies have made important investments in making them available to retail outlets.

The case hinges on industrial ice-cream in Germany (the precise definition of the market will be discussed below), and in this market (which at the time of the

---

[91] Schöller is the owner of the well-known "Motta" brand that, you have already guessed it, is a high quality brand!

decision was thought of as expanding due to the recent German reunification) there are only 14 manufacturers, all of which have less than 10% market share except for LI and Schöller. The EC decision does not specify the market shares of the two companies, but says that in 1991 they held respectively 50 and 20% of *all* the ice-cream sold through the *grocery trade* (supermarkets, food shops and other stores) and respectively more than 50% and more than 25% of impulse ice-cream sales in the *traditional trade,* which consists of both specialised trade (such as kiosks, petrol stations, cake shops, cinemas, theatres) and catering trade (such as hotels, restaurants, cafés, canteens, hospitals).[92]

Ice-cream is distributed to the grocery trade either directly or through brokers (with whom there are no exclusivity agreements, and who deal with several manufacturers), and to the traditional trade either directly or through agents.

A manufacturer often uses *exclusive purchasing agreements* that require the retailer to sell in its outlet only ice-cream obtained directly from it. The manufacturer also makes available to the customer (on loan) one or more freezer cabinets, with an exclusivity clause that obliges the retailer to store only the manufacturer's products in the freezer. Although no clear distinction is made in the EC decision in this respect, it is important to note that these two exclusivity clauses are different. In principle, a manufacturer could use *freezer exclusivity* without *outlet exclusivity,* that is it might oblige a retailer not to store rivals' products in a freezer it supplies, but might allow it to carry other brands in its outlet.

The duration of these supply agreements is the object of some discussion between the parties, but they seem to last on average 2.5 years. The percentage of sales made through retailers bound by these exclusive supply agreements is also the object of a dispute, and it depends on the market definition used, as we shall see below.

The Definition of the Relevant Market   Although this is not an abuse of dominance case, the definition of the relevant market is crucial, in order to evaluate whether the firms at stake have enough market power and whether the proportion of outlets subject to exclusivity agreements is important enough.

As for the relevant product market, the EC defines as the *industrial impulse ice-cream market* ice-cream sold through all distribution channels with the exception of home delivery services. First of all, the EC decides to focus on individual portions (probably because these are mostly sold in the traditional sector, which is where the majority of exclusivity agreements is used) and mainly refers to the "impulse"

---

[92] Most of the data of this case (as well as many others) are not published because they are considered business secrets, but curiously here the EC does not even try to compute market shares for the relevant market it makes use of, which does not correspond to the markets for which shares are calculated. As for the relative importance of the various distribution channels, 55% of impulse ice-cream, as defined by the EC, is sold through the traditional trade, 35% through grocery outlets and 10% through home-delivery services.

purchase which is made by a consumer. The type of purchase they refer to is therefore the one made by somebody who is having a stroll in town and suddenly feels like having an ice-cream. Accordingly, they exclude multi-pack and take-home ice-creams, which are typically not for immediate consumption. They also exclude industrial ice-cream in individual portions but sold through home delivery, because this is not an impulse purchase.

But the definition they use is further narrowed down by the exclusion of ice-cream which is sold in bulk, but may later be sold as "scooping ice-cream", on the grounds that – even though the consumer would perceive the product as a close substitute to an individual portion – the supply technologies of the two are different: "Impulse ice-cream is purchased by the retail trade in the form in which it is resold to the consumer. It is particularly suited to consumer self-service. Catering ice-cream in tubs requires, on the other hand, a further processing operation, namely that of serving it up in individual portions" (*Schöller*, para. 85).

By using a similar argument, all craft-trade ice-cream is also excluded from the relevant market, because it does not share the same production stages as industrial impulse ice-cream: "The grocery trade and the traditional trade are distribution channels for every kind of industrial ice-cream. Craft-trade ice-cream, however, is not offered for sale to these branches of the retail trade, nor is there any demand for it" (*Schöller*, para. 83).

The CFI agrees with the EC that craft-trade ice-cream belongs to a separate market, but argues that industrial ice-cream for bulk buying customers intended for sale in individual portions should be included in the industrial impulse ice-cream (but it argues that redefining the market in this way would not alter the main assessment of the EC).

Neither the decision of the EC nor the judgement of the CFI makes use of data, but relying on the conceptual framework provided by the SSNIP test, as explained in Chapter 3, will be of help here.

Since the focus is on impulse purchase of ice-cream by an individual consumer, it is reasonable to exclude attention of multi-packs and other ice-cream which are bought for home consumption. This leaves us with the first candidate product for the relevant market, which is industrial ice-cream sold in individual portions (and not sold through door-step delivery), as proposed by the EC. Suppose that all such ice-cream is sold by a monopolist, and ask the question whether such a hypothetical monopolist would find it profitable to raise prices by 5–10%, or whether instead this price rise would not be profitable in view of possible alternatives, such as scooping ice-cream or craft-trade ice-cream.

Clearly, some estimates on cross-price elasticities, or some consumer survey data would help here, but we do not have any. Being often in Germany, having a German wife and two (half-) German children, and having German friends, I have formed a strong feeling that German consumers would regard the industrial ice-cream sold in individual portions, the scooping ice-cream sold in a café, and the craft-trade ice-cream sold in one of the many "Italian gelaterie" that one can find even in isolated German villages as close substitutes. Admittedly, however, introspection and personal experience are unlikely to give a definite answer to such questions. Fortunately, in this case, our doubts are solved by the EC decision itself, which recites (para. 80, emphasis added): "From the consumer's point of view, that part of industrial ice-cream for bulk-buying customers and of craft-trade ice-cream which is served out for consumption at or near the point of sale without the provision of any catering services, and industrial impulse ice-cream which is not sold through doorstep delivery services are *identical*."

Therefore, a hypothetical monopolist would not find it profitable to raise prices in a significant and non-transitory way unless it sold all three categories of ice-cream. The SSNIP test would unambiguously indicate that the relevant product market consists of industrial impulse ice-cream (except for that sold via home delivery services), craft-trade ice-cream and industrial scooping ice-cream. Differences in the way the ice-cream is produced or distributed are irrelevant.

From the geographical point of view, the impulse ice-cream market should be defined as quite localised, at the level of town, or of quarter within a city: clearly, the consumer who has the sudden impulse to buy an ice-cream will not be willing to travel great distances. Similarly to the way the geographic markets for food-stores are usually defined, it is likely that some substitution exists only within a certain radius from the location of the consumer. However, it seems a reasonable simplification to consider the German market as a whole rather than breaking down the market in a vast number of small geographic markets. Presumably, the pattern of competition existing at a more local level is not too different from the one existing at a national one. Also, it makes sense not to widen the market further: "Although the production of industrial ice-cream has displayed a clear trend towards internationalization, distribution is everywhere organized on a national basis. National peculiarities are reflected in different market structures, assortments and prices. Consumers prefer different brands in each country. The supply agreements at issue here and analogous distribution contracts are concluded at domestic level. The requirements governing the manufacture of ice-cream are not harmonized. The relevant market here is thus the German market" (*Schöller*, para. 95).

Market Power, and the Relative Importance of Exclusive Agreements On the basis of its definition of relevant market, the EC calculates that Schöller has something more than 20% and LI something more than 45%. The decision provides no data on this point, but certainly these market shares would be considerably lower if one took into account craft-trade ice-cream as well, which accounts for roughly the same sales as industrial impulse ice-cream (see estimates of sales in 1990 above), in which by definition industrial manufacturers have no sales. Therefore, if one could disregard scooping ice-cream (on whose sales I have seen no data in the decision),

Schöller and LI's market shares would be reduced by half. Accordingly, using a definition of the market based on the SSNIP test gives a different *prima facie* impression
of the market power of these manufacturers, and might invite more caution before intervening on the vertical contracts of these firms – particularly the weaker
of the two (Schöller). Indeed, we have seen in this chapter that it makes sense to
intervene on vertical agreements only if the firms involved have large enough market
power.

Furthermore, to assess the possible foreclosure effects of their exclusive agreements, it makes sense to look at the breadth of their coverage. By using the market
definition proposed by the EC, Schöller would sell through tied distributors something more than 10% of the total market sales, and LI more than 15% of it. By using
the broader market definition that the SSNIP test suggests, these proportions would
be considerably reduced, and the possible foreclosing effects of these contracts would
accordingly be lower.[93]

Nevertheless, suppose that the thresholds competition law provides for intervention on vertical restraints (see Chapter 1) are satisfied (if not, our analysis could
stop here, and the case be dismissed), we must then pass to the next step of the
investigation. Are these contracts more likely to have pro-competitive effects, or
foreclosing effects?

The Foreclosing Effects of the Exclusivity Clauses   According to the analysis of
the EC, entry into the industrial impulse ice-cream market is not easy,[94] because of
important fixed sunk costs necessary to establish a distribution system and to create
a brand reputation (advertising outlays are probably an important component of
success in this market). Furthermore, a large part of the existing outlets are already
tied by exclusive agreements to LI and Schöller, and a new entrant, especially if less
well known or offering a partial range of products, is unlikely to replace one of the
established firms as exclusive supplier of a retailer.

Retailers who are not tied to the leading firms should be persuaded to install
further cabinets, which – according to the EC – would be unlikely: "The possibility of installing further cabinets is limited: there may be no space available, or

---

[93] Taken together, the exclusivity agreements concern retailers that account for more than 30% of
the market as defined by the EC. The 30% share is considered as the highest acceptable threshold
by the EC. Presumably, under a broader market definition the proportion of exclusive agreements
that cumulatively tie retailers would be below that threshold. The CFI states (*Langnese-Iglo v.
Commission*, paragraphs 99–101) that, following the case law and in particular the *Delimitis* and
Brasserie de Haecht judgements, "consideration of the effects of an exclusive agreement implies
that regard must be had to the economic and legal context of the agreement, in which it might
combine with others to have a cumulative effect on competition".

[94] Of course, if the market was defined – as I propose above – also to include craft-trade ice-cream,
low-scale entry as in small ice-cream sellers with a local presence only would be easy, but let me
at this point reason according to the market definition adopted by the EC.

what space there is may be used for commercial purposes other than the sale of ice-cream. ... The existing freezer cabinets are already geared to the outlet's total requirements. Nor can it generally be expected that sales of ice-cream will increase substantially if further cabinets are installed. The effort and space devoted to a new cabinet are lost to other commercial purposes, without securing additional turnover" (Schöller, para. 137).

The extent to which a firm like Mars – an internationally renowned company with products (other than ice-cream) already established in Germany – finds considerable barriers to entry in this market is probably overstated by the EC. The existence of brokers who carry several brands might make it possible to have products reaching final outlets with a small-scale entry and some niche products only (the broker can then rely on different producers to offer a full range of products to retail outlets). Also, in many countries Mars provides retailers with small freezers that store its well-known brands. Even though it does not have the same range of products as LI and Schöller, widespread presence of its brands could be achieved by adding to the existing selection of products sold by non-exclusive dealers (and if dealers would not be willing to install a much smaller freezer or to store Mars products in their own cabinets, it means that there would be little demand for Mars brands, and its entry would hardly be beneficial).

Nevertheless, the EC worries that exclusive agreements in this industry might foreclose entry do have some foundations. Especially in the traditional trade – which accounts for some 60% of the industrial impulse ice-cream market once home-delivery services are excluded – demand is very fragmented, with a very large number of small retailers, each buying small volumes. In this context, "to run a distribution operation at reasonable cost a considerable number of customers must be secured in a geographically concentrated area which can be supplied from regional warehouses and centres" (Schöller, para. 133).

This setting should be familiar to readers from the analysis of the possible entry-deterring effects of exclusive dealing (see Section 6.4.1). When buyers are fragmented and cannot coordinate, work by Rasmusen et al. (1991) and Segal and Whinston (2000a) shows that exclusive contracts might prevent entry even of a firm more efficient than the incumbent.[95] The basic mechanism is that each outlet does not internalise the fact that when it signs an exclusive agreement with the incumbent(s) it decreases the number of outlets that the entrant can sell to, and therefore reduces the likelihood that entry will take place at all. The fact that exclusive agreements do

---

[95] In Section 4.1, I have also mentioned work by Fumagalli and Motta (2002) showing that very intense competition among buyers would eliminate the foreclosing potential of exclusive contracts. However, in this case it is unlikely that retail outlets would fiercely compete. Each outlet (café, cinema, kiosk, petrol station . . .) is likely to have its specificities that help it have some captive customers, consumers would face a limited choice of outlets within a certain range and, above all, for most outlets ice-cream is probably just a small part of total sales, which limits the incentive to look hard for the ice-cream supplier offering the best terms.

not all expire at the same time, and that discrimination in the terms made to the retailers is in principle possible (financing agreements, advance rebates, and credit terms are offered to retailers – see *Schöller*, para. 48 – and can presumably vary) make the foreclosing potential of such agreements even stronger.

Efficiency Effects of the Exclusive Agreements As argued in this chapter, exclusive agreements might also have an efficiency rationale. Before drawing a final conclusion, this aspect should be carefully assessed. Here, a distinction must also be made between two conceptually distinct aspects of the agreements, freezer exclusivity and outlet exclusivity.

The practice whereby the ice-cream manufacturers provide retail outlets with freezer outlets is – as recognised by the EC as well – largely responsible for the growth of the market for industrial ice-cream. Indeed, the manufacturer assumes the risk involved in investing in freezer cabinets and by doing so it opens up a large number of sales outlets which otherwise would not stock any ice-cream (*Schöller*, para. 55). Exclusivity of use of such freezers appears as a very important clause, necessary to protect the large investment made. If a manufacturer were obliged to allow rivals to make use of the freezers it lends to retailers, free-riding would take place which would have the inevitable effect of discouraging the installation of freezer cabinets (see also the discussion in Section 6.2.5).

It is far from clear that this type of exclusivity would have any foreclosing effect (many retail outlets would probably have room for another – possibly smaller – freezer if it supplied brands that consumers would value highly), but it is evident that freezer exclusivity has a strong efficiency rationale. Therefore, there is no reason to ask manufacturers to remove clauses requiring exclusive use of the freezers they provide.

As for outlet exclusivity, it has a much stronger foreclosing potential, since it requires that no other competing product is sold by the retail outlet, but it is less clear that an exclusive purchasing obligation would have efficiency effects. LI and Schöller claim that the exclusivity in the supply allows them to keep distribution costs as low as possible: "If every sales outlet were free to purchase at will a varying proportion of their stock from third parties, the pattern of supplies would be seriously disturbed. The efficiency of the transport system could not be assured, and its profitability could be neither planned nor maintained" (*Schöller*, para. 59).

However, it is not clear why the fact that a retailer sells competing products should create a pattern of demand which is so unstable and difficult to foresee that it might result in great difficulties in supplying the retailer. Certainly, it is true that it might not be optimal to supply some outlets whose demand falls below a certain volume, but presumably such outlets (whose *total* demand is not so small, since otherwise LI and Schöller would not have found it convenient to supply them under an exclusive contract) might be supplied instead by another company, perhaps one with a local distribution network, or by brokers who carry several brands (*Schöller*, para. 120).

One of the traditional efficiency explanations for exclusive contracts, consisting of the dealer concentrating all its efforts in selling the (exclusive) supplier's products, also seem to have little importance in this market. Retailers do not engage in any after-sales service of ice-cream, nor do they have to invest resources in advertising or to train sales-persons that would then help market the products. In most cases, all the sales effort a retail outlet makes is to make it as visible as possible a banner or a poster containing an image of the ice-cream sold and its price, and exclusivity does not seem necessary even from this point of view.

To conclude, the assessment of the possible pro- and anti-competitive effects of the exclusive agreements might justify the prohibition of clauses imposing outlet exclusivity (at least, if one adopts the market definition of the EC), but suggests that ice-cream manufacturers should be allowed to use freezer exclusivity, which has a strong efficiency rationale and a weak, if any, foreclosing effect.[96]

6.7 EXERCISES

Exercise 6.1 *Consider the same model as in Section 6.2.1.1, but with the following two differences: there exist $n > 1$ retailers downstream, who compete in quantities and have a unit distribution cost d in addition to the wholesale price w they have to pay to the manufacturer. Show that (i) the double marginalisation problem still exists, even if there are two or more retailers downstream; (ii) the double marginalisation problem disappears as $n \to \infty$.

Exercise 6.2 *Consider now the same model as in Exercise 6.1, but let the n downstream firms compete in price rather than in quantity. Show that the problem of double marginalisation disappears for $n \geq 2$. Explain.

Exercise 6.3 **Different risk-insurance properties of vertical restraints (Rey and Tirole, 1986). (Note that this is the same model as in Section 6.2.1.2 but with two retailers rather than one.) The following exercise illustrates that different vertical restraints have different properties when there exist asymmetric information and risk aversion of retailers.

Consider a risk-neutral manufacturer that has a unit cost c and sells via two identical retailers which are infinitely risk averse and have a unit distribution cost γ.

[96] The EC decision does not distinguish between these two types of exclusivity. It takes a negative approach towards freezer exclusivity, mainly on the assumption that retail outlets would be unwilling to have more than one freezer on their premises (*Schöller*, paragraphs 134–137), but the operative part of the decision is ambiguous, since it does not explicitly prohibit freezer exclusivity. This ambiguity is lamented by Korah (1994b: 175), who is "most shocked by the Commission's failure to make clearer whether it is requiring the parties to stop any outlet exclusivity or also freezer exclusivity". The ambiguity is not dispelled by the CFI judgment.

The products sold by retailers are perceived as homogenous,[97] with final demand q given by $q = d - p$. There exist both demand uncertainty $d \in [\underline{d}, \overline{d}]$ and distribution cost uncertainty $\gamma \in [\underline{\gamma}, \overline{\gamma}]$, with $\underline{d} > c + \overline{\gamma}$, and with realisations of d and γ being independent. The game is as follows. First, when both market demand d and distribution costs γ are unknown to everybody, the manufacturer makes take-it-or-leave-it offers to the retailers, in the form of a non-linear contract $(F + wq)$. Second, d and γ are observed by the retailers (but not by the manufacturer). Third, retailers take price decisions p (i.e., they compete à la Bertrand).

Assume that the refusal-to-deal and price discrimination are not possible. (i) Find the optimal contract and the equilibrium solutions for the cases of (1) Competition (C); (2) Exclusive territories (ET); (3) Resale price maintenance (RPM). (ii) Show that under demand uncertainty (fix $E(\gamma) = \overline{\gamma} = \underline{\gamma}$) the following rankings hold: $\pi_C = \pi_{RPM} > \pi_{ET}$, $W_C = W_{RPM} > W_{ET}$. (iii) Show that under cost uncertainty (fix $E(d) = \underline{d} = \overline{d}$) the following rankings hold: $\pi_C > \pi_{ET} > \pi_{RPM}$, $W_C > W_{ET} > W_{RPM}$.

Exercise 6.4 **Consider the same model as in Section 6.2.2.1, but with two differences. First, the cost of providing services now falls upon variable rather than fixed cost: $C(q_i, e_i) = wq_i + \mu \frac{e_i^2}{2} q_i$. Second, the quality of services perceived by consumers is given by the maximum quality offered in the market by any retailer: $e = \max\{e_1, e_2\}$. (This is the model briefly sketched by Tirole (1988: 182–3).) Show that (i) there is underprovision of services under a separate structure and linear pricing: each retailer offers zero services; (ii) producer surplus is higher under vertical integration with two retailers compared to vertical integration with only one retailer; (iii) vertical integration increases welfare relative to a separate structure; (iv) using exclusive territories and RPM *vis-à-vis* his two retailers allows the manufacturer to restore the outcome of vertical integration with one retailer.

Exercise 6.5 **Consider the utility function $U = v \sum_{i=1}^{n} q_i - (1/2) \left(\sum_{i=1}^{n} q_i^2 + 2g \sum_{j \neq i}^{n} q_i q_j \right) + y$ where $g \in [0, 1]$ represents the substitutability parameter. This function entails "love for variety", in the sense that demand increases as the number of retailers increases. A manufacturer has unit cost c and sells through retailers which compete in quantities and sell its product to final consumers characterised by the utility function above. (In the case of vertical separation, they buy the input at wholesale price w and the manufacturer has all the bargaining power. Retailers do not have any costs other than w.) (i) Find the equilibrium wholesale price, final price and quantity under vertical separation for any given number of retailers, n. (ii) Find the equilibrium values, again for given n, under

---

[97] To facilitate interpretation, as in Rey and Tirole (1986) think of the retailers being located away from each other but with consumers having zero cost of transportation.

the assumption of vertical integration. (iii) Endogenise now n, and show that there exist values of the fixed cost of entry, f, such that only one retailer would enter at a vertically integrated equilibrium, but two retailers would enter at a vertically separated equilibrium. (iv) Show that consumer surplus and welfare are higher under vertical integration with one retailer compared to the vertically separated structure with two retailers.

Exercise 6.6   **Consider a game where a manufacturer first offers (unobservable) contracts which specify the number of units a retailer can buy and the fixed amount for the purchase. Then, each of n retailers decides whether to accept or reject such a contract offer and orders the number of units it wants to buy accordingly. Lastly, each retailer brings quantities to the market and the market clears (compare with Section 6.2.5.1). (1) Find the Perfect Bayesian Equilibrium of this game, under the assumption that firms have passive beliefs (if a retailer receives an unexpected offer, it does not change its beliefs about the offer received by a rival retailer.) (2) Show that the larger the number of retailers the stronger the commitment problem of the manufacturer (that is, the lower the profit the manufacturer will make). (3) Find the equilibrium solution under the hypothesis that retailers have symmetric beliefs: when they receive an unexpected offer from the manufacturer, they believe that all other retailers will also receive the same unexpected offer.

Exercise 6.7   ** *(Commitment problem with linear contracts)* Assume an upstream manufacturer, M, sells a product to retailers R_1 and R_2. M has a constant production cost c, and the retailers' only variable cost is w_i, the wholesale price they pay to M (assume a one-to-one transformation technology). R_1 and R_2 produce a homogenous good and compete in prices.[98] Final demand is given by $q = 1 - \min(p_1, p_2)$, where p_i is R_i's price (retailers share the market equally if they have the same price). The manufacturer makes take-it-or-leave-it offers to the retailers. Consider two alternative games. (1) At t_0, M offers each retailer a contract (w_i, F_i), where F_i is a fixed fee. At t_1, each retailer pays F_i. At t_2, each retailer chooses p_i and consumers buy. (2) At t_0, M offers each retailer a contract (w_i). At t_1, each retailer chooses p_i and observes demand q_i. At t_2, each retailer buys q_i, pays $w_i q_i$ to the manufacturer and satisfies consumers' demand.

   (a) Find the vertically integrated solution of this game. (b) Show that in game (1) the manufacturer has an incentive to renegotiate the contract with one retailer when the contract, which would restore the vertically integrated outcome, is offered to

---

[98] Note that with homogenous products and price competition, a non-linear contract is not necessary to restore the first-best (a linear contract is optimal). However, I have chosen to deal with homogenous products for illustrative purposes. One can repeat the exercise with a demand function $q_i = (1/2)\left(v - p_i\left(1 + \gamma\right) + (\gamma/2)\left(p_i + p_j\right)\right)$ and see that the same results hold under differentiated products, as originally shown by O'Brien and Shaffer (1992).

retailers. (c) Show that in game (2) the manufacturer has no incentive to renegotiate the linear contract.

Exercise 6.8 **Consider the model in Section 6.3.1.1 and study the following game. At the first stage, each of the two producers decide on whether or not to delegate output decisions to retailers. Then, if choosing delegation, they set the (non-linear) contract to their retailer. Finally, quantities are chosen (by the manufacturer or by its retailer if delegation has been chosen). Show that (i) the equilibrium where both firms delegate is unique, (ii) this configuration makes the firms worse off than if they had both chosen not to delegate; (iii) consumers are better off at the equilibrium.

Exercise 6.9 **Consider the model of Section 6.3.2.2. Two manufacturers make take-it-or-leave-it offers to a common retailer. Each offer specifies the final resale price p_i and a franchise fee contract $F_i + w_i q_i$. The retailer can either accept or reject the offers (but the market fails unless he accepts both offers) and he then decides on the level of effort e_i to market each good i. Assume that $D(p_i, p_j, e_i) = a - bp_i + \gamma p_j + e_i$, and that the retailer's cost of effort is $C(e_i) = ke_i^2/2$. Show that at the unique equilibrium the existence of the common agent allows manufacturers to make collusive profits.

Exercise 6.10 *(A simplified version of Salinger, 1988) Consider a vertical industry where two upstream (homogenous) firms compete à la Cournot and sell to a centralised market for the input (upstream firms cannot sell directly to downstream firms, they sell to the input market auctioneer). Two downstream (homogenous) firms buy the input in the centralised input market and compete à la Cournot in the final market, where inverse demand is $p = 1 - Q$ (Q being the total output). All firms have zero costs and there is a one-to-one relationship in the production technology between input and output. (a) Find the equilibrium output and whole-sale and final prices. (b) Consider then a vertical merger between an upstream firm and a downstream firm, and assume that after the merger they withdraw from the input market (the downstream affiliate does not buy additional input from the in-put market and the upstream affiliate does not sell additional input to that market). Show that there is no foreclosure, in the sense that the wholesale price paid in the input market decreases.

Exercise 6.11 Consider an industry which produces a good X. To produce this good one needs to transform an input, call it Y, which is not substitutable with other inputs or raw materials. There is only one firm, A, which can supply input Y. Suppose now that there exists only one firm, B, which produces X. Would you allow a merger between these two firms? Justify your answer.

Exercise 6.12 Consider now the same example as before but with the following change. There are two firms, B and Q, which sell good X. Would you allow a merger between firm A and B? Explain which model supports your answer, and briefly describe it.

Exercise 6.13   An internationally successful brand which sells fashion clothes is considering to give a franchise to local agents in a country where so far it has sold only through exports (it has so far held only around 1% share of the relevant market, whereas in its home country the firm has almost 55% of the market). It plans to give the franchise only to one franchisee in each town of this foreign country. The franchisees would also have to operate under an exclusivity clause (they cannot sell competitors' products). The fashion firms operating in this market and the large distributors get to know about the franchise contracts and file a complaint with the local competition authority. You are an economic consultant hired by the authority to give advice on this case.

Exercise 6.14   In an imaginary autarkic (i.e., without foreign trade) country, film production is a quite concentrated business. Three film companies have around 30% each of the market in an average year, whereas the remaining 10% of the market is (on average) shared by 10–15 independent companies. Distribution in movie theatres is fairly concentrated as well, with 5 companies having more or less the totality of the market. The market leader has 25% of the market. One of the three big film producers has announced a takeover of the largest distribution company. What sort of economic considerations should a competition authority take into account to decide whether or not to clear the takeover proposal?

Exercise 6.15   Nimbus is the market leader of broomsticks, the key device to play the Quidditch game. Its quality is so superior to all other competing suppliers that it manages to charge a very high price premium on its products, even the low-range models. In terms of the number of units sold, it has roughly 40% of the market, but the market share rises to 80% if one looks at the total value of the broomsticks sold. Nimbus does not sell directly to the public, but through dealers specialised in magical items. The Magical Ministry for Sports has just found out that Nimbus is price discriminating among dealers. Some dealers manage to get considerable (secret) price discounts relative to others. The Ministry has fined Nimbus on the ground that it is unfairly distorting competition in the market for Quidditch broomsticks, and it has ordered the firm to be transparent on its prices, and to sell to dealers at the same price schedule (but price rebates can be justified if a larger quantity is ordered). You are sitting in Hogwarts School for Witchcraft and Wizardry and answer a question in the exam of the course for Magical Competition Policy: is the Ministry right or not? Why?

Exercise 6.16   Consider the following case. The firm "Red" is the leader in the English bicycles market, in which it has a market share of 60%. (Market definition is not an issue here, since everybody agrees that the bicycle market is the relevant market.) Two other firms, "Green" and "Yellow" have respectively 15% and 10% of the market, the rest of the sales being distributed among very small firms. "Red" produces different types of bicycles. The top of the range model is "Red Star", which incorporates all the major technological developments in the sector, and is produced by using the most sophisticated materials. This model is sold at a price which is twice as much as the average price of all the other bicycles, and can be bought only in specialised shops. The supermarket chain "Everything" has repeatedly asked "Red" about the possibility of selling the model "Red Star" in its stores, but the firm has always refused to supply it. The supermarket chain could sell all other bicycles produced by "Red", but not the top-range model. Given this continuous refusal, "Everything" has decided to denounce "Red" to the Commission. After a detailed analysis, the latter has decided that "Red" has infringed Article 82 (abuse of dominant position). The case is now on appeal at the Court of Justice, and you have to give your opinion on it.

6.7.1 Solutions to Exercises

Exercise 6.1 (i) Under vertical separation, the downstream firms solve the standard Cournot problem, $\max_{q_i} \Pi_{D_i} = (p - w - d)q_i = (a - q_i - \sum_{i \neq j}^{n} q_j - w - d)q_i$. Imposing symmetry on quantities yields $q_i^C = (a - (w + d))/(1 + n)$ and $\Pi_i^C = [(a - (w + d))/(1 + n)]^2$. The manufacturer, which perfectly anticipates this outcome on the final market, will solve $\max_w \Pi_U = (w - c)nq_i^C(w)$ which yields the optimal wholesale price $w = (1/2)(a - d + c)$ and the manufacturer's profits $\Pi_U^S = (n/(1 + n))((a - d - c)^2/4)$.

Under vertical integration, the firm chooses the standard monopoly price and output, i.e., $\max_p \Pi^{vi} = (p - c - d)(a - p)$, which yields $p^{vi} = (a + c + d)/2$, $q^{vi} = (a - c - d)/2$, and $\Pi^{vi} = ((a - c - d)/2)^2$.

We see that $\Pi_U^S < \Pi^{vi}$, i.e., the upstream firm makes less profit under vertical separation than the vertical chain makes under integration. This is due to the fact that under separation, the downstream firms still earn a positive mark-up, which leads to the problem of double marginalisation.

(ii) Note that as $n \to \infty$, $\Pi_U^S = (n/(1 + n))((a - d - c)^2/4) \to ((a - c - d)/2)^2$, i.e., the upstream firm's profits under vertical separation converge to the profits under vertical integration. As the number of downstream firms increases, their mark-ups decrease, and so double marginalisation becomes less of a problem.

Exercise 6.2 Under vertical separation, downstream (Bertrand) competition implies that all retailers charge at marginal cost, i.e., $p = w + d$, and so $Q = a - (w + d)$. Hence, the upstream firm will solve $\max_w \Pi_U = (w - c)(a - w - d)$, which yields $w = (1/2)(a - d + c)$. Now, we see that the resulting final price, quantity and upstream profits correspond exactly to the vertically integrated case, i.e. $p^S = p^{vi} = (a + c + d)/2$, $q^S = q^{vi} = (a - c - d)/2$, and $\Pi_U^S = \Pi^{vi} = ((a - c - d)/2)^2$. Since Bertrand competition implies that downstream firms' profits are driven down to zero even if there are only two of them, the problem of double marginalisation will never arise whenever $n \geq 2$.

Exercise 6.3 (i) Let us find the optimal contracts under the different cases. (1) Competition. Since retailers compete à la Bertrand, $p = w + \gamma$. They make zero profit and thus $F = 0$. The manufacturer will choose w so as to maximise its expected profit $E(\pi) = E[(d - w - \gamma)(w - c)]$. By writing $E(d) = d^e$ and $E(\gamma) = \gamma^e$, one can also find $w_C = (d^e + c - \gamma^e)/2$, $p_C = (d^e + c - \gamma^e)/2 + \gamma$, $\pi_C = (1/4)(d^e - c - \gamma^e)^2$. Total welfare can also be computed as $W_C = E((1/2)(d - p)^2) + \pi_C = (3/8)(d^e - c - \gamma^e)^2 + \text{var}(d)/2 + \text{var}(\gamma)/2$. (2) ET. Each retailer is a monopolist in its area of distribution and maximises $\pi_r = (d - p)(p - w - \gamma)/2$. Final price and retailer profit will be $p = (d + w + \gamma)/2$, $\pi_r = (1/8)(d - w - \gamma)^2$. Since the retailers are infinitely risk averse, the franchise fee F must be set in such a way as to guarantee them non-negative profits even in the worst state of nature. Therefore, it must be $F_{ET} = (1/8)(\underline{d} - w - \overline{\gamma})^2$. The manufacturer's problem will be to choose w to maximise $E[(d - (d + w + \gamma)/2)(w - c)] + (1/4)(\underline{d} - w - \overline{\gamma})^2$. The solutions are $w_{ET} = c + (d^e - \underline{d}) + (\overline{\gamma} - \gamma^e)$, $p_{ET} = [d + c + \gamma + (d^e - \underline{d}) + (\overline{\gamma} - \gamma^e)]/2$, $\pi_{ET} = (1/4)(\underline{d} - c - \overline{\gamma})^2 + (1/4)[(d^e - \underline{d}) + (\overline{\gamma} - \gamma^e)]^2$, $W_{ET} = (3/8)(\underline{d} - c - \overline{\gamma})^2 + (1/4)[(d^e - \underline{d}) + (\overline{\gamma} - \gamma^e)]^2 + (1/8)\text{var}(d) + (1/8)\text{var}(\gamma)$. (3) RPM. Retailers charge the imposed price and have profit equal to $(1/2)(d - p)(p - w - \gamma)$. Given infinite risk aversion, $F = (1/2)(\underline{d} - p)(p - w - \overline{\gamma})$. (This is the optimal fee for $p \geq w + \overline{\gamma}$. It can be shown that this is the relevant case.) The manufacturer will choose p and w so as to maximise $(\underline{d} - p)(p - w - \overline{\gamma}) + E[(d - p)(w - c)]$, subject to $p \geq w + \overline{\gamma}$. It turns out that $F_{RPM} = 0$, $w_{RPM} = (1/2)(d^e + c - \overline{\gamma})$, $p_{RPM} = (1/2)(d^e + c + \overline{\gamma})$, $\pi_{RPM} = (1/4)(d^e - c - \overline{\gamma})^2$, $W_{RPM} = (3/8)(d^e - c - \overline{\gamma})^2 + (1/2)\text{var}(d)$.

(ii) and (iii) The rankings on profits and welfare under the different restraints and under competition can be obtained directly from the equilibrium solutions identified in (i). The main point of the paper by Rey and Tirole is to show that vertical restraints are not equivalent, as the ranking shows. This is due to the two contrasting effects that the different configurations have. The first effect is on the capability of the vertical structure to exploit monopoly power. The second effect is on the risk borne by the retailers. ET, for instance, does extremely well with respect to the first problem, as the retailers are made residual claimants and will therefore respond in the same way as a vertically integrated firm when facing demand or cost shocks. However, if $w = c$ the retailers would bear too high a risk, as their profits would not be protected against such shocks. In order to insure the retailers, the manufacturer will therefore have to set $w > c$ (it can be checked that the sensitivity of the retailers' profit to variations in demand and costs decreases with

w: $\partial(|\partial \pi_R/\partial d|)/\partial w < 0$ and $\partial(|\partial \pi_R/\partial \gamma|)/\partial w < 0$), but under ET insurance is imperfect. RPM gives perfect insurance under demand uncertainty, but fares badly under cost uncertainty, as a shock to the retailer's distribution cost will greatly affect its profit margin (given that the price cannot be adjusted). As a result, RPM is better under demand uncertainty, ET under cost uncertainty. Competition scores well in terms of insurance properties (given Bertrand competition, retailers' profits will always be zero), under both demand uncertainty and cost uncertainty.

Exercise 6.4 (i) Separation. If the two retailers compete in prices, the only equilibrium in the retailers' game is the one where $p_1 = p_2 = w$ and $s_1 = s_2 = 0$. Since consumers perceive the goods sold by retailers as homogenous, Bertrand competition drives prices to equal marginal cost $w + \mu e_i^2/2$. Consider a candidate equilibrium, where $e_i = e_j > 0$, and profits are zero. Given that the quality perceived by consumers does not change if a firm i decreases its own quality to a level $e_i < e_j = e$, firm i has an incentive to decrease e_i since it will increase its unit margin and get all the demand. The usual undercutting argument leaves therefore $e_i = e_j = 0$ as the unique equilibrium, with $p_1 = p_2 = w$. The upstream firm anticipates that $p = w$ and that final demand will be $q = v - w$. It will $\max_w \Pi_u = (w - c)(v - w)$, which is solved by $w = (v + c)/2$. At the separated equilibrium, therefore, producer surplus, consumer surplus and welfare are respectively given by $PS_s = \Pi_u = ((v - c)^2)/4$; $CS_s = ((v - c)^2)/8$; $W_s = 3((v - c)^2)/8$.

(ii) Vertical integration. Assume again that if both retailers charge the same price, they will split market demand equally among each other. Then, a vertically integrated firm with **two** retailers will solve $\max_{p,e_1,e_2} \Pi_{vi} = (p - c - (1/2)\mu e_1^2/2 - (1/2)\mu e_2^2/2)(v + \max\{e_1, e_2\} - p)$. Note that it will be optimal for the manufacturer to have only one retailer provide services, while continuing to sell through both retailers (consumer valuation for retailer services is determined by the maximum of the two units).[99] Hence, set $e_2 = 0$ and derive the first-order conditions $\partial \Pi_{vi}/\partial e_1 = -\mu e_1(v + e_1 - p)/2 + p - c - (1/2)\mu e_1^2/2 = 0$ and $\partial \Pi_{vi}/\partial p = v + e_1 - 2p + c + (1/2)\mu e_1^2/2 = 0$, leading to the following solution: $e_{1,vi} = 2/\mu$; $e_{2,vi} = 0$; $p_{vi} = \frac{1}{2}(v + c + 3/\mu)$.[100] By substitution, one then obtains producer surplus, consumer surplus and welfare as follows. $PS_{vi} = \Pi_{vi} = ((\mu(v - c) + 1)^2)/(4\mu^2)$; $CS_{vi} = ((\mu(v - c) + 1)^2)/(8\mu^2)$; $W_{vi} = (3(\mu(v - c) + 1)^2)/(8\mu^2)$.

A vertically integrated firm with only **one** retailer will solve $\max_{p,e} \Pi_{vi} = (p - c - \mu e^2/2)(v + e - p)$. The only difference with respect to the two-retailers

---

[99] In fact, it can be shown that it would be optimal for the vertically integrated monopolist to have as many outlets as possible and concentrate the effort in only one of them. This will not reduce the effort but will allow to increase output where it is less costly, i.e., with all the retailers which do not have to incur the variable costs of effort.

[100] Solving the system of FOCs gives two other solution pairs. However, one is negative and the other does not correspond to a maximum since positive definiteness, i.e., $\frac{\partial^2 \pi}{(\partial p)^2} \frac{\partial^2 \pi}{(\partial e)^2} > \left(\frac{\partial^2 \pi}{\partial p \partial e}\right)^2$, is not satisfied.

case is that, now, one unit of effort will cost $\mu e^2/2$ rather than $(1/2)\mu e^2/2$. Hence, just replace μ by 2μ in the expressions obtained above to have $e'_{vi} = 1/\mu$; $p'_{vi} = (2\mu(v+c)+3)/(4\mu)$, and producer surplus, consumer surplus and welfare as follows: $PS'_{vi} = \Pi'_{vi} = ((2\mu(v-c)+1)^2)/(16\mu^2)$; $CS'_{vi} = ((2\mu(v-c)+1)^2)/(32\mu^2)$; $W'_{vi} = (3(2\mu(v-c)+1)^2)/(32\mu^2)$. We see that vertical integration with two retailers is more profitable than with only one retailer, as it allows to produce effort at half the unit cost.

(iii) It is also easy to check that vertical integration – which restores the incentives to invest in quality provision – not only increases the vertical chain profit but also enhances welfare: $PS_{vi} > PS'_{vi} > PS_s$ and $W_{vi} > W'_{vi} > W_s$.

(iv1) Exclusive territory (ET). If one retailer is given an exclusive territory, i.e., it is the only one who can sell the manufacturer's product, ET alone would not solve the problem since it would create the usual double marginalisation problem. Therefore, an ET contract should be combined with non-linear pricing of the type seen above: $(w = c; F)$. The problem of the retailer will then be $\max_{p,e} \Pi_{et} = (p - c - \mu e^2/2)(v + e - p)/2 - F$. Barring the fixed cost which does not affect the FOCs, this is precisely the same problem as a vertically integrated monopolist with **one** retailer. Therefore, the solution will be the same as in (ii), while F will be used to redistribute profits between retailer and manufacturer. If the latter has all the bargaining power, then it will appropriate all the producer surplus.

(iv2) Resale price maintenance. RPM will also have to be used in combination with a non-linear contract $(w = c; F)$. The problem of a retailer i is given by $\max_{e_i} \Pi_{rpm} = (p'_{vi} - c - \mu e_i^2/2)(v + \max\{e_i, e_j\} - p'_{vi})/2 - F$. RPM removes the price undercutting temptation. However, it leaves the incentive to free ride on services provision as $e = \max\{e_1, e_2\}$. Consider a candidate equilibrium where $e_1 = e_2 = e > 0$. This cannot be an equilibrium since a firm would prefer to deviate and provide no quality given that the other is providing a positive level of quality: $\pi_{rpm} = (p'_{vi} - c - \mu e^2/2)(v + e - p'_{vi})/2 < \pi_{dev} = (p'_{vi} - c)(v + e - p'_{vi})/2$. However, there are two asymmetric equilibria where only one firm provides effort, while the other does not, i.e. where $e_i = e'_{vi} > 0 = e_j$ for $i = 1, 2$ and $i \neq j$. First, note that the problem of the retailer who makes effort would be identical to the effort choice problem under exclusive territories, which gives $e'_{vi} = 1/\mu$ as a solution. Therefore, the profit made by the "effort" retailer is $\pi_i = \Pi'_{vi}/2 = ((2\mu(v-c)+1)^2)/(32\mu^2)$. By deviating and providing an effort $e_i = 0$, this retailer will make $\pi_d = (p'_{vi} - c)(v - p'_{vi})/2 = (2\mu(v-c)+3)(2\mu(v-c)-3)/(32\mu^2)$. As $\pi_i - \pi_d = (2\mu(v-c)+5)/(16\mu^2) > 0$, the candidate equilibrium is indeed an equilibrium. RPM therefore restores the vertically integrated solution (p'_{vi}, e'_{vi}) for the upstream manufacturer. Since it cannot enforce a contract on the basis of the effort made by the retailers, it will offer the same contract to both. Each retailer will pay the same fixed fee $F = \Pi'_{vi}/2$. Note that although the manufacturer makes the same profit, producer surplus will be higher under RPM than under the vertically integrated case with **one** retailer considered above. RPM is in some sense more efficient than ET or VI with one retailer, as it allows to exploit the beneficial effect of the effort spillovers among retailers, similar to the situation of VI with two retailers.

Exercise 6.5 (i) From the maximisation of the consumer programme one obtains the (inverse) demand function $p_i = v - q_i - g \sum_{j \neq i}^{n} q_j$. Under vertical separation, (last stage) equilibrium quantity and price for given w are given by $q^S = (v - w) / (2 + g(n - 1))$ and $p^S = (v + w(1 + g(n - 1))) / (2 + g(n - 1))$. The upstream manufacturer chooses w to maximise $\pi = (w - c)nq^S$. Hence, $w^S = (v + c)/2$. By replacing this value in q^S and p^S one finds equilibrium quantity, price and per-retailer profit: $q^* = (v - c) / (2(2 + g(n - 1)))$, $p^* = (v(3 + g(n - 1)) + c(1 + g(n - 1))) / (2(2 + g(n - 1)))$, and $\pi^* = ((v - c) / (2(2 + g(n - 1))))^2 - f$. (ii) Under vertical integration each outlet produces at marginal cost c. Equilibrium quantity, price and per-outlet profit are $q^I = (v - c) / (2(1 + g(n - 1)))$, $p^I = (v + c) /2$, and $\pi^I = ((v - c)^2) / (4(1 + g(n - 1))) - f$. (iii) Under separation, entry will occur until retailer profits are driven down to zero, i.e., $((v - c) / (2(2 + g(n - 1))))^2 - f = 0$. Under vertical integration, the firm will set n optimally, i.e., $\max_n \pi^I = ((v - c)^2) / (4(1 + g(n - 1))) - f$. Suppose that f is such that the optimal number of outlets under vertical integration is exactly 1, which implies that $f = (1/4) (v - c)^2 (1 - g)$. Then, inserting this expression for f into the zero-profit condition for retailers under separation and solving for n, we obtain $n = (1/g) (\sqrt{1/(1 - g)} - 2) + 1$. This equation will solve for $n = 2$ if $(1 - g)(2 + g)^2 = 1$, i.e., if $g \simeq 0.8793$. (iv) Given that (f, g) is such that $n_{vi}^* = 1$ but $n_S^* = 2$, i.e., $g \simeq 0.8793$ and $f = (1/4)(v - c)^2 (1 - g)$, we obtain the following expressions for welfare: under Vertical Integration, $CS_1^{VI} = ((v - c)^2) /8$; $PS_1^{VI} = ((v - c)^2) g/4$; $W_1^{VI} = (1 + 2g)((v - c)^2) /8$ under Separation, $CS_2^S = ((v - c)^2 (1 + g)) / (4(2 + g)^2)$; $PS_2^S = ((v - c)^2) / (2(2 + g))$; $W_2^S = (v - c)^2 (5 + 3g) / (2(2 + g))^2$. The inequality $C_1^{VI} > C_2^S$ implies $(1/2)(2 + g)^2 > 1 + g$, which will always hold for $g \simeq 0.8793$. Analogously, the inequality $W_1^{VI} > W_2^S$ implies $(1/2)(1 + 2g) > (5 + 3g)(1 - g)$, which holds as well for $g \simeq 0.8793$.

Exercise 6.6 (1) For passive beliefs, the solution follows from the extension of the $n = 2$ case in Section 6.2.5.1. Each retailer expects profit $\pi_i = (1 - q_i - \sum_{j \neq i} q_j - c)q_i$ and therefore will be willing to buy according to its (Cournot) reaction function. Under symmetry, the intersection of the n reaction functions gives $q = (1 - c)/(1 + n)$. Each retailer will therefore expect to make profit $(1 - c)^2/ (1 + n)^2$. (2) The manufacturer will earn $\pi^M = n(1 - c)^2/ (1 + n)^2$. Since $\partial \pi^M/\partial n < 0$, the larger the number of retailers the worse the commitment problem for the manufacturer. (3) For the case of symmetric beliefs, the reasoning is exactly the same as for the case $n = 2$ treated in Section 6.2.5.1.

Exercise 6.7 (a) The vertically integrated outcome satisfies $\max \pi = (p - c)(1 - p)$. Hence, it is given by $p^{vi} = (1 + c)/2$, $q^{vi} = (1 - c)/2$, $\pi^{vi} = (1 - c)^2/4$.

Table 6.3. A Delegation Game

	Delegation	Vert. int.
Delegation	π^u_{ff}, π^u_{ff}	$\pi_{d/i}$, $\pi_{i/d}$
Vert. int.	$\pi_{i/d}$, $\pi_{d/i}$	π_{vi}, π_{vi}

(b) The contract which would reproduce the vertically integrated outcome is one where both retailers are offered $(w_i, F_i) = (c, (1-c)^2/8)$. However, it is easy to see that the manufacturer would have an incentive to renegotiate the contract with, say, retailer R_1 given that R_2 has accepted. Indeed, if U sold the input to R_1 at a wholesale price $w_i < c$, R_1 could get the whole market by selling at a price slightly below c and earn $(1-c)^2/4$. Therefore, there is scope for an agreement between U and R_1 on renegotiating the contract. Retailer R_2 would have to pay $(1-c)^2/8$ but would have no revenue. Obviously, anticipating that renegotiation would occur, R_2 would not sign the contract in the first place. The commitment problem arises also when firms choose prices.

(c) When the contract is a pure linear pricing one, it does not commit retailers to buy a specified quantity. Under the candidate equilibrium contract, a retailer just commits to pay $w = p^{vi}$. If the manufacturer offered a lower wholesale price $w' = p^{vi} - \varepsilon$ to one retailer, the latter would get to serve the whole market, and the manufacturer would still make $\pi^{vi} = (1-c)^2/4$, but the other retailer would not be addressed by any consumer and would not buy any input. Therefore, the manufacturer would not increase its profit under renegotiation.

Exercise 6.8   At the first stage of the game, the payoff matrix is shown in Table 6.3. To check that both firms delegating and imposing a non-linear contract to retailers is an equilibrium, we should check that $\pi^u_{ff} > \pi_{i/d}$, that is, that when the rival manufacturer chooses to delegate, a manufacturer prefers to delegate as well rather than not. The symmetric payoffs in Table 6.3 have already been obtained in Section 6.3.1.1. We still have to find those corresponding to the asymmetric case where one manufacturer chooses delegation whereas the other does not. The reader can check that at the equilibrium the firm that sells through a retailer will set a wholesale price $w_{d/i} = \frac{c(64+96\gamma+44\gamma^2+5\gamma^3)-\gamma^2(4+\gamma)v}{4(2+\gamma)(8+8\gamma+\gamma^2)}$, and that the equilibrium profits are

$$\pi_{i/d} = \frac{(1+\gamma)(16+12\gamma+\gamma^2)^2(v-c)^2}{16(2+\gamma)(8+8\gamma+\gamma^2)^2}; \qquad \pi_{d/i} = \frac{(1+\gamma)(4+\gamma)^2(v-c)^2}{8(2+\gamma)(8+8\gamma+\gamma^2)}.$$

(i) It is then possible to check that a manufacturer does not have an incentive to deviate from the configuration where both manufacturers sell through retailers: $\pi^u_{ff} > \pi_{i/d}$. In other words, the configuration (delegate, delegate) is an equilibrium. One can also check that $\pi_{d/i} > \pi_{vi}$, implying that delegation is a dominant strategy and that the equilibrium where both sell through retailers is unique. (ii) This is a prisoner's dilemma game, where both firms end up in an equilibrium which yields lower payoff to them: $\pi_{ff}^u < \pi_{vi}$. The manufacturers would be better off if they were not allowed to contract with independent retailers! (iii) Section 6.3.1.1 shows that consumers are better off when there is delegation: $q_{ff} > q_{vi}$.

Exercise 6.9 If the retailer has rejected either contract he earns zero profit and the market disappears. If he has accepted both contracts, then his optimal effort level on each product is found by solving $\max_{e_i, e_j} \pi_r = \sum_{i=1}^{2} ((p_i - w_i)(a - bp_i + \gamma p_j + e_i) - ke_i^2/2 - F_i)$. From $\partial \pi_r / \partial e_i = 0$ one obtains $e_i^* = (p_i - w_i)/k$. The rest of the problem is now as in the text. In particular, complete extraction of the retailer's anticipated rents implies that each manufacturer solves $\max_{w_i, p_i} \pi_i = (p_i - c)(a - bp_i + \gamma p_j + (p_i - w_i)/k) + (p_j - w_j)(a - bp_j + \gamma p_i + (p_j - w_j)/k) - (p_i - w_i)^2/(2k) - (p_j - w_j)^2/(2k) - F_j$.

But apart from the fixed component (which does not affect equilibrium price and wholesale price), this is nothing other than the problem of a joint profit maximiser. It is easy to show in particular that $w_i = c$ at equilibrium and that the equilibrium price is the same that solves $\max_{w_i, p_i} \pi_M = \sum_{i=1}^{2}(p_i - c)(a - bp_i + \gamma p_j + e_i^*) - k(e_i^*)^2/2$, i.e. $p_i^* = p_j^* = (a + c(b - (1/k) - \gamma))/(2b - (1/k) - 2\gamma) > c$. Note that due to the effort choice made by the retailer, w_i enters retailer i's maximisation problem, and so it will be determined in equilibrium (this was not the case for the model of Section 6.3.2.2).

Exercise 6.10 (a) At the last stage of the game, both downstream firms pay the input w and have profits $\pi_i = (1 - q_i - q_j - w)q_i$. Solving $\partial \pi_i / \partial q_i = 0$ and imposing symmetry gives $q = (1 - w)/3$. Therefore, total quantity sold will be $Q = 2(1 - w)/3$. Since each unit of final output Q sold by the downstream firms corresponds to a unit of output X sold by the upstream firms, the latter will face an inverse demand function $w = 1 - 3X/2$, where $X = x_1 + x_2$. Therefore, the problem faced by the upstream firms will be $\pi_k = (1 - \frac{3}{2}(x_k + x_l))x_k$. From the FOCs $\partial \pi_k / \partial x_k = 0$ one obtains the symmetric solution $x = 2/9$. By substitution, the equilibrium wholesale price is $w = 1/3$, and the equilibrium price is $p = 5/9$.

(b) Under vertical integration, calling 1 the upstream firm and the downstream firm that merge, the downstream competition game will be between a firm with cost $w_1 = 0$ and another with cost w_2. Their profits will be respectively given by $\pi_1 = (1 - q_1 - q_2)q_1$ and $\pi_2 = (1 - q_1 - q_2 - w_2)q_2$. Solving the system of FOCs gives $q_2 = (1 - 2w_2)/3$ and $q_1 = (1 + w_2)/3$. As the integrated firm withdraws from the input market, there is now an upstream monopolist in the input market, facing inverse demand for its input $w_2 = (1 - 3x)2$, and having profits $\pi_2 = w_2 x$. From the FOC it is straightforward that $x = 1/6$ and $w_2 = 1/4$. By substitution, $q_1 = 5/12$ and $p = 5/12$. Note that the wholesale price paid by the unintegrated firm is lower than in the case of vertical separation. This might be surprising because the unintegrated upstream firm is a monopolist, but it is a monopolist which faces a reduced demand schedule. In this case, therefore, although the integrated firm does not supply the input any longer, the input is cheaper: there is no foreclosure. Further, note that the final price paid by consumers is lower and total industry output increases under the vertical merger.

7

Predation, Monopolisation, and Other Abusive Practices

7.1 INTRODUCTION

This chapter deals mainly with exclusionary practices, that is, practices carried out by an incumbent with the aim of deterring entry or forcing the exit of rivals. By and large, such practices correspond to the legal concepts of monopolisation in the US and abuse of dominance in the EU (see Chapter 1).[1]

The identification of exclusionary behaviour is one of the most difficult topics in competition policy, as often exclusionary practices cannot be easily distinguished from competitive actions that benefit consumers. For instance, suppose that following entry into an industry a dominant firm reduces its prices considerably: should this be considered an anti-competitive strategy aimed at forcing the new entrant out of the industry (after which prices will be raised again, damaging consumers in the long-run), or is it instead just a competitive response that will be beneficial to consumers? Most of this chapter will be devoted to understanding how to answer this question.

Exclusionary practices by incumbents are certainly not a new phenomenon, but there are at least two reasons why such practices should receive fresh attention. The first is that in many countries there have been processes of liberalisation, privatisation, and deregulation that have resulted in several sectors having an incumbent facing potential entrants. This asymmetric structure creates strong incentives for potential exclusionary behaviour. The second is that a growing share of today's advanced economies is composed of sectors (for example computer software, Internet and telecommunications) that exhibit network and lock-in effects. In such environments, entrants might find it very difficult to compete with incumbents, and particular attention should be paid to possible exclusionary practices.

Section 7.2 focuses on pricing strategies, and Section 7.3 on non-pricing strategies, such as over-investment, tying and bundling, and incompatibility choices. (Other non-price exclusionary practices focusing on vertical restraints, such as exclusive dealing and refusal to supply, have already been analysed in Chapter 6.)

---

[1] Exploitative practices – consisting mainly of excessive prices – are covered by Article 82 of the Treaty in the EU, but not by Section 2 of the Sherman Act in the US. I argued in Chapter 2 that excessive pricing should not be dealt with by competition policy.

Section 7.4 deals with price discrimination in general, although only some forms of price discrimination can be thought of as exclusionary.

Section 7.5 ends the chapter with a description of an important recent case, US v. Microsoft.

7.2 PREDATORY PRICING

Throughout this book we have seen that low prices are generally associated with higher consumer and social welfare. It might therefore seem surprising at first sight that competition authorities could be concerned with situations where a firm charges "too low" prices. Yet, although rare, there are circumstances where a dominant firm might set low prices with an anti-competitive goal: forcing a rival out of the industry or pre-empting a potential entrant. In these cases, low prices improve welfare only in the short-run, for the time predation lasts; once the prey has succumbed, the predator will increase its price. The final effect of this predatory behaviour (if successful) will be to worsen welfare in the long-run, because it eliminates competition in the industry.

Predatory pricing therefore occurs when a firm sets prices at a level that implies the sacrifice of profits in the short-run in order to eliminate competition and get higher profits in the long-run. This definition, for the moment still vague, contains the two main elements for the identification of predatory behaviour in practice: first, the existence of a short-term loss; second, the existence of enough market power by the predator so that it can reasonably expect to be able to raise prices so as to increase profits in the long-run once a rival (or more rivals) has been driven out of the market.

The very nature of predatory pricing, which involves low prices for a period, makes it difficult to analyse. To distinguish low prices due to a genuine and lawful competitive response to rivals from low prices due to a predatory and unlawful behaviour is far from an easy task in practice. Furthermore, a very cautious approach by anti-trust agencies and courts is needed to avoid the risk that firms endowed with market power keep prices high to avoid being charged with predatory behaviour. Suppose for instance that in a certain jurisdiction a low standard of proof is accepted for a finding of predatory pricing. Anticipating possible anti-trust problems, a firm will have a lower incentive to cut prices, even though this would be due to normal competitive behaviour. As a result, prices will be higher than they might otherwise be, causing an allocative efficiency loss, and inefficient competitors might feel encouraged to enter the market, adding a productive inefficiency to the welfare loss.

This does not mean, of course, that predatory pricing should be eliminated from the possible set of anti-competitive actions, but it does suggest that it should be dealt with cautiously. In the rest of this section I will try to give some indications on how to build a cautious but rigorous policy towards it.

7.2.1 Predation: Search for a Theory

Allegations of predatory pricing are certainly not a new phenomenon. Indeed, as seen in Chapter 1, one of the reasons behind the Sherman Act was the small entrepreneurs' complaint that large firms acted predatorily, setting low prices to drive them out of the market.[2] Of course, some allegations were (as they are today) unfounded: a large firm often charges lower prices than rivals simply because it enjoys stronger scale and scope economies and it is therefore more efficient. But the point is that predatory pricing cases, although relatively rare, are as old as anti-trust laws themselves.[3]

Although findings of predatory pricing have not been uncommon in the US and, later, in the EU, a convincing economic theory of predation has not appeared until recently. The main explanation for predation was probably the "deep pocket" (also called "long purse") story. A large firm might drive a small competitor out of the market by waging a price war that gives losses to both. But the small competitor has limited resources (a "small pocket") and will therefore be unable to survive such losses for a long time. Sooner or later, it will have to give up and leave the industry, allowing the large firm to increase prices and recoup losses. Unfortunately, however, a solid theory to support this story has appeared only very recently (see below), and sceptics have pointed out the weak points of predation arguments.

McGee (1958), in a very influential article, criticised the idea that a firm could drive out competitors by using predatory pricing on four main grounds, which I loosely summarise as follows. First, due to its larger market share, a large firm will usually have to suffer greater losses than a small firm: other things being equal, the same unit loss will be multiplied by a larger number of units (McGee, 1958: 140). Second, predation makes sense only if the large firm will increase prices when the prey leaves. But, McGee (1958: 140–1) argues, the assets and plants of the small firm will not disappear, and as soon as prices rise the small firm can re-enter, or its assets might be bought and used by somebody else, reducing the profits the predator can expect to make. Third, the predation theory assumes that the predator has a deep pocket and the victim a small one, while this should rather be explained than assumed (McGee, 1958: 139). In this perspective, one should understand why a small firm,

[2] Section 2 of the Sherman Act, prohibiting monopolisation or attempts to monopolise an industry, and later the Clayton Act are the legal instruments to protect the interest of firms that consider themselves victims of predatory pricing. In Europe, it is Article 82 of the Treaty.

[3] Or even older: see the *Mogul Steamship Co. v. McGregor, Gow and Co. et al.,* a classical case of predation, which started in 1885. It concerned a conference of shipowners that excluded competition from non-members in the China–England trade (see Yamey, 1972) by a variety of practices among which the use of "fighting ships" which had the task of undercutting freight rates of competing vessels whenever they tried to get business on the China–England route.

Two famous early cases, which have kept researchers busy even in recent years, are *Standard Oil* and *American Tobacco*, with Supreme Court decisions taken as early as 1910 and 1911 (see also below).

even if financially constrained, could not explain the situation (including the fact that the predator is suffering more losses than it does, and cannot sustain them forever) to its creditors, thereby obtaining funds until predation will end. Fourth, for predation to be rational, it must be not only feasible but also more profitable than alternative instruments. If a large firm would like to get rid of a competitor, this criticism goes, predation is an inefficient tool because it destroys industry profits for the time it lasts. Merging with the rival would be a more profitable strategy, as it would allow the preservation of high profits in the industry.

The first two arguments above can be taken care of relatively easily. Indeed, the first point does not hold if the large firm could price discriminate and decrease prices selectively only in those markets or for those clients where the small firm is competing. This allows the predator to preserve high margins on most of the units it sells, therefore reducing the cost of the predation strategy.[4]

As for the second point, it relies on the idea that entering and re-entering the industry does not entail sunk costs. But as we have seen throughout the book, fixed sunk costs are pervasive. A firm that leaves a sector will probably not be able to recover more than a small fraction of the fixed costs it has incurred to start production and sales, and a firm cannot close down its plants, fire its workers, cease to supply its product one day and return costlessly the day after.

Furthermore, the very fact that the incumbent has successfully preyed once will probably have an influence over other firms that are considering entry into the same market. A potential entrant will not rush into the industry after seeing the end of its predecessor. This is one of the important counter-objections made by Yamey (1972), who pointed out that predation will discourage further entry into the industry. If an incumbent develops a reputation for reacting toughly and aggressively towards entry, potential competitors might be discouraged from entering the industry at all. Although it has taken game theorists quite a long time to prove this reputation argument formally, it is now rigorously established, as we shall see in Section 7.2.2 and in technical Section 7.2.3.2 below.

Perhaps the most challenging point made by McGee is the third. Suppose that the incumbent is indeed endowed with extensive financial resources and a small rival is not, although they are equally efficient. Why should the small firm not be able to get further financing from banks or other lending institutions? After all, they should understand that predation could not be successful if they gave unlimited funding to the prey, and anticipating that, predation would not take place at all. Again, it is only recently, with developments in corporate finance, that a convincing story has emerged of why predation might make the financial constraints of firms tighter, as I shall discuss in Section 7.2.2 and, more technically, in Section 7.2.3.6 below.

Finally, note that the fourth point made by McGee stresses an important general issue, namely that predation must not only be feasible but it must also be more

---

[4] However, in his detailed analysis of *Standard Oil*, McGee argues that there is no evidence that supports the claim that local price cutting was used as a discriminatory predatory pricing strategy.

profitable than alternative options available to the incumbent. On the particular point that a merger would be more profitable than predatory prices, three counter-objections can be made. First, buying out a competitor might encourage new ones to enter the industry with the aim of selling out to the incumbent at a profit: if it gains the reputation that new competitors will be bought out, a merger might not be a cheap option. Second, under some anti-trust laws, taking over rivals might not be allowed for dominant firms. Third, as both Telser (1966) and Yamey (1972) argued, predation and mergers are not necessarily mutually exclusive options: aggressive price behaviour might well result in the prey being ready to sell out at a lower price. The merger strategy is therefore not necessarily in contradiction with a predation strategy.

Indeed, Burns (1986) looks at the expenditures made by American Tobacco to take over forty-three competing firms between 1891 and 1906, and finds economet-ric evidence that predation substantially decreased the acquisition prices. Aggressive price behaviour helped both directly (by reducing the price of acquiring a victim) and indirectly (by establishing a reputation for being a predator, that persuaded other rivals to sell out before any predatory episode would start).[5]

This discussion of McGee's (1958) arguments and their possible counter-objections has brought up the main issues related to predatory pricing. In what follows, I briefly summarise how economic theory has addressed such issues, pro-viding convincing stories of why predation might indeed take place.

7.2.2 Recent Theories of Predatory Pricing

There is a common thread behind all the recent models of predatory pricing: pre-dation is a phenomenon that can be fully explained only in a context of *imperfect information*, that is a situation where players have some uncertainty.[6] In all cases, the predator will try to use the entrant's imperfect knowledge (or that of the outside investors that finance it), and behave so as to make it believe that the entrant would not make high profits in the industry. As a result, the entrant will exit, or its lenders will not be willing to provide it with more funding.

This manipulation of beliefs can exist only if there is some uncertainty. In a world where all the firms (and other active agents in the economy, such as outside investors) knew perfectly what the technologies and financial resources available

---

[5] The fact that predation might depress profit expectations of competitors, persuading them to sell out at lower prices, has been modeled by Saloner (1987) and is discussed in technical Section 7.2.3.4.

[6] More precisely, in game theory a player has *imperfect information* when it does not know the moves that its opponents have taken beforehand; it has *incomplete information* when it does not know the payoff or the set of actions available to its opponents. However, it has been shown that a game of incomplete information can be re-written as one of imperfect information, which is therefore a more general concept (the equilibrium concepts of Perfect Bayesian Equilibrium and Sequential Equilibrium apply to both types of game).

to each are, their preferences and those of consumers, and their ability to behave rationally, predation would never be observed: either it is clear that a dominant firm will have an incentive to fight entry, and in this case the entrant would not dare enter in the first place (or the small firm would exit immediately); or the dominant firm knows that predation will not be successful, and therefore would not prey at all. Either way, predatory pricing would not be observed.

Within this set of recent (game theoretic) predation models of imperfect information, there are three main types that can be identified: (i) reputation models, (ii) signalling models, (iii) financial market models of "deep pocket" predation.[7]

7.2.2.1 Reputation Models

The discussion of McGee's critique pointed out that the behaviour of an incumbent firm towards a current competitor is likely to have an impact on future (potential) competitors as well. A price war today might therefore find its rationale in the attempt to create a reputation of being a strong and aggressive incumbent to discourage entry (in other markets by the same competitor, or in the same market by others) tomorrow. To understand how economic theory explains this reputation-based model of predation, consider the following example.

Suppose that there is an incumbent monopolist that is active in a number of identical markets, where it has the same technology and products (e.g., a "chain-store"). In each of these markets, it faces a potential entrant. Entrants can enter one at a time. The game is as follows. In the first market, first the potential entrant decides whether to enter or not, and if entry occurs the incumbent decides whether to fight or accommodate it. Then this same game is repeated, one by one, for all the markets.

Call now a "weak" incumbent one that has costs as high as the entrants and, if the game was played only once, would not fight entry, because it would be unprofitable: fighting amounts to setting a low price that causes losses to both the entrant and the weak incumbent. Selten's (1975) insight is to show that the same result – the entrant enters and is accommodated – applies also when the game is played for (finitely) many times, as long as it is *certain* that the incumbent is weak. Consider for instance the case where there are two entrants. Whatever might have happened in the first market, it is clear that the second and last entrant will be accommodated, since the incumbent would incur losses from fighting and would have no reason to build a reputation to be strong if the game ends. But then, since the only reason to fight entry could be to deter future entrants, in the first period there is no incentive to fight either: both the incumbent and the first market entrant correctly anticipate

---

[7] The distinction between reputation and signalling models is done mainly for exposition purposes, and it is to some extent arbitrary. Both types of models are incomplete information games that use sequential equilibrium or perfect Bayesian equilibrium as a solution method.

that the following period the incumbent will not fight, and entry will occur. In other words, fighting the first entrant would not deter second-period entry. Hence, the incumbent has no incentive to fight and the first entrant knows it and will enter.[8]

Selten himself was puzzled by the result (that he thought "paradoxical") that predation would never be observed. He was convinced that in reality there would be a strong reason for the incumbent to prey on entrants to build up a reputation to deter further entry.

The main reason behind this result comes from the fact that the entrants know with certainty (i.e., have perfect information) that the incumbent has an incentive to accommodate if the game was played just once. Kreps and Wilson (1982) show that if some uncertainty is introduced, predation will occur.[9] Suppose that when the game starts entrants believe that with some (possibly very small) probability the incumbent might not be as weak as described above, but rather "strong". In other words, it might be a very efficient firm whose costs are so low that it could make profits (rather than losses) if it charged a price below the costs of the entrant.

Clearly, a strong incumbent will always fight entry, but this will not be predation: simply, it is so efficient that it can set prices below the costs of the entrant. The interesting issue is another, that is that a weak incumbent might exploit the entrants' uncertainty and fight entry to make them believe it is strong instead.[10] Indeed, Kreps and Wilson (1982) prove that a weak incumbent would fight entry at the beginning of the game, to establish a reputation for being strong and thus discourage further entry. It would be only towards the last periods of the game that the weak incumbent will accommodate entry, as the closer to the end of the game the lower the expected gain from pretending to be strong. In general, in any period, the weak incumbent's decision to fight reinforces its reputation of being efficient, but involves the sacrifice of current profits in order to deter entry and earn higher future profits. At the beginning of the game, the future is remote enough and the trade-off is in favour of fighting, whereas at the end of the game there is less to be gained from deterring

---

[8] With more than two periods, the same logic is applied repeatedly: see Section 7.2.3.1.

[9] Kreps and Wilson's *incomplete information* model is presented technically – albeit in a much simpler two-periods version – in Section 7.2.3.2. Predation by an incumbent facing successive entry can also be explained in an *infinite horizon* model with perfect information, as shown in Exercise 7.1. Both models are a reaction to Selten's chain-store paradox model, which is based on perfect information and assumes a *finite* stream of successive entrants.

[10] Note that uncertainty precludes the same reasoning as in Selten's perfect information game. Consider for instance the last entrant's problem. Under perfect information, it is sure that entry will be accommodated, and it will accordingly enter, no matter how many times before the incumbent has fought entry. But under incomplete information, things change. Suppose for instance that entry has always been fought so far: the last entrant will have revised its beliefs about the incumbent, and start to think that the probability it is strong is much higher than it thought at the beginning of the game! Accordingly, it will not necessarily enter.

further entry (at the limit, in the last period there is no future gain at all), and the trade-off is in favour of accommodating.

7.2.2.2 Signalling Models

Signalling models of predation are based, like reputation models, on imperfect information. Again, the potential entrant does not know whether the incumbent has low costs (strong) or high costs (weak), and the incumbent will try to exploit this uncertainty to deter entry. The first signalling model is due to Milgrom and Roberts (1982b) and it can be roughly summarised as follows (see Section 7.2.3.3 for a formal presentation).

Before taking its entry decisions, a potential entrant observes the price set by the incumbent when it is still a monopolist. If it is certain that the incumbent is weak, entry would be profitable. If it is certain that the incumbent is strong, entry would entail a loss. But the entrant cannot tell them apart. It thinks it will face a strong incumbent with some probability, but it can revise this probability only by observing the monopoly price of the incumbent (if it enters, instead, it will immediately learn if the incumbent is weak or strong). In this context, it is clear that a weak incumbent might want to mimic a strong one, to try and deter entry. However, a strong one would not like to be mistaken for a weak one, because that would attract entry, which lowers its profits.

There are two possible equilibria in the game. In the first (called "separating equilibrium"), the efficient incumbent will set a price lower than its normal monopoly price in the first period (when it is the only active firm) that is so low that no weak incumbent would like to set it, because it would involve too high losses. Since there is no scope for mimicking the efficient incumbent, the inefficient one will instead choose its normal monopoly price. The entrant will immediately learn which incumbent it faces: if the price is low, it can only be the efficient one, and it will stay out. If it is high, it will face the inefficient incumbent, and will enter.

Note that in this equilibrium one could say that there is predation, in that the low-cost incumbent is acting "strategically" and sacrifices current profits to deter entry and gain more in the future. But, interestingly, its behaviour does not hurt welfare. To see why, note that in a perfect information world the entrant facing the low-cost incumbent would never enter (by assumption of the model), and consumers would have to pay the normal monopoly prices in both periods. In this equilibrium, instead, the low-cost incumbent charges a much lower price than it would otherwise do to signal its efficiency. Therefore, while in the second period the sales price is the same, consumers will be better off in the first period. In a sense, by signalling its true nature through low prices the low-cost incumbent is providing a service that enhances social efficiency.

In the second equilibrium (called "pooling equilibrium"), instead, there is no price at which the low-cost incumbent can profitably sell and be distinguished from the high-cost one. As a result, it will simply set its normal monopoly price and the high-cost incumbent will imitate it in order to deter entry.[11]

In this case, we observe predation from the inefficient incumbent, who sets a lower price than it would otherwise set in the first period (even though, it is important to notice, that price might be above or below the incumbent's costs), but it can act as a monopolist in the second: it sacrifices current profits to increase the future ones. The impact on welfare is more likely to be negative in this case.[12]

Milgrom and Roberts' signalling model is reminiscent of the old concept of "limit pricing" proposed by Bain (1949) and Sylos-Labini (1979), which is very popular in pre-game theory industrial organisation. Limit pricing refers to the possibility that an incumbent monopolist sets a low price to deter entry, the rationale of this practice being that observing a low price a potential entrant would also expect lower margins in the industry, and therefore lower profits. If we read those early works today we would not find them very convincing, since they rely on some strong assumptions (one of them being that a firm commits to a certain price for a time, while we know that prices can be easily changed in the short-run), but Milgrom and Roberts (1982b) have cast the theory of limit pricing in rigorous terms, with a low price being a signal that expected profits from entry might be low.

However, signalling models of predation are not inherently associated with the incumbent setting a low price. In the cost-signalling model described above, the costs of the entrant are not correlated with those of the incumbent, so the low costs of the incumbent are bad news for the entrant, and it makes sense for the incumbent to pretend to be low cost by setting a low price. However, consider a situation where the entrant – new to the industry – does not really know what costs it will have itself, and expects them to be identical (or highly correlated) to those of the incumbent. Further, note that in most cases where two firms with identical costs compete, each firm's duopoly profits decrease with costs.[13] In this situation, the incumbent might deter entry by setting a *high* price, because this would signal the existence of high costs in the industry for both (see Harrington, 1986).

---

[11] The entrant does not learn anything from the observation of the first period prices, and decides on whether to enter or not on the basis of its *ex ante* probability of facing a weak incumbent. For the pooling equilibrium to exist, this probability must be low enough: the entrant will stay out only if it expects a high likelihood to face an efficient incumbent. If it expected with a high probability to meet a weak incumbent, it would enter. But then, it could not be an equilibrium as the high-cost incumbent would have no reason to sacrifice current profits if it knows it will not deter entry.

[12] To be precise, the net effect is ambiguous *a priori*, since it involves a gain in the first period and a loss in the second. In Section 7.2.3.3, I show for a specific example that the net effect on consumer surplus is negative, but this need not always be the case. Incidentally, one should recall that entry might in some circumstances involve a productive inefficiency. If this was the case, there would be an additional reason for entry deterrence not to be detrimental.

[13] The reader can immediately check that this holds, for instance, in a duopoly with homogenous goods, linear demand $p = 1 - Q$, and Cournot competition. With a marginal cost c, a firm's profit is $\pi = (1 - c)^2/9$, and therefore is the higher, the lower the cost c.

Predation for Mergers   An extension of the signalling model above allows us to explain why predation might be used to lower the price of taking over rivals, a strategy that has been discussed in Section 7.2.1 above. Saloner (1987) changes Milgrom and Roberts' model slightly, to allow for the possibility that firms merge after the first period (also, in his model, entering when facing a low-cost incumbent would not give rise to losses, but just lower profits). In this case, setting a lower price than would otherwise be optimal signals to the entrant whether it should expect to make high or low profits after entry, and therefore whether it should be willing to sell out to (to merge with) the incumbent at a high or at a low price.

Again, predation takes the form of setting lower prices than a short-run calculation would imply, but this time its objective is not to deter entry but rather to improve the terms at which the rival will accept to be taken over.[14]

Other Signalling Models   There are several other models where the incumbent might want to act strategically so as to make the entrant (or an existing competitor) expect lower profitability if it entered (or if it stayed in) the industry. Scharfstein (1984), for instance, analyses a model of "test-market predation", where the entrant has a new product and is uncertain about the demand for it. Given this uncertainty, it introduces the product in a test-market first to see how it would be received. The incumbent might engage in various predatory practices (for instance secret price discounts to consumers) to make the entrant believe demand for its product will be low, thus leading it to abandon the market or reduce its scale of activity.

Fudenberg and Tirole (1986) suggest that the incumbent might also engage in "signal-jamming predation", which inhibits the entrant from improving its information. In a test-market model, for instance, the purpose of the entrant is to gather information about demand, and the predator defeats this purpose by openly cutting prices. The entrant knows that its demand is artificially low due to the incumbent's cut-throat prices, but it cannot have any information about what demand would be in normal competitive circumstances. In the absence of information, it will prefer to exit. A similar "signal-jamming" mechanism might also be used in other circumstances where there is imperfect information (for instance, in imperfect capital markets, see below).

7.2.2.3 Predation in Imperfect Financial Markets

As we have seen above, a weak point of the deep-pocket theory of predation is that it does not explain why the prey has limited access to funding. If capital markets were perfect, a profitable project would always find a financial sponsor.

Modern corporate finance theory, focusing on the imperfections existing in capital markets, provides an answer to these questions, leading to a deep-pocket theory

---

[14] See Section 7.2.3.4 for a technical presentation.

of predation where the prey's limited access to funding is endogenous, since predation affects the perceived risk of lending money, thereby reducing financial sources
available to the prey.

The key point of this theory is the existence of imperfect information on the
side of the lenders (be they banks, equity holders, or other financial institutions).
Lenders do not have their hands on the industry and cannot have precise knowledge
about it (or cannot observe some of the actions taken by firms). This characterises
the relationship between the lender and the borrower. (In these principal-agent
models, the bank is the "principal" and the borrower the "agent".) The bank cannot
be sure that the money lent is used in an efficient and competent way rather than
being used by the entrepreneur for its private benefit, or in an exceedingly risky way
(there is a so-called "moral hazard" problem), and will accordingly have to devise a
contract that protects its interests. For instance, it will give credit to a borrower only
if it has a certain amount of internal assets (such as retained earnings). Because of
credit constraints, therefore, a profitable project might not be financed.

Consider now the competition between an incumbent and a new firm. The
incumbent is a well-established firm that has accumulated enough resources in the
past, whereas the new firm does not have enough own resources and needs to borrow
heavily to compete on a par with the incumbent. In such a situation, predation by
the incumbent will reduce the possibility for the new firm to get funding, since it
reduces its profits, its retained earnings and thus the own assets that are needed to
obtain further funding. It is therefore the aggressive behaviour by the incumbent
that endogenously reduces the funds available to the rival (see Section 7.2.3.6 for a
formalisation).

A possible objection to this predatory argument is that the lender, understanding
that predation might occur, thus destroying its opportunity to make profits out of the
loan, might have an interest in preventing it by announcing that it will finance the
prey no matter what its performance in the market will be. However, it might not
be optimal for the bank to do so because it would create the scope for further
agency problems. If the firms' managers knew that whatever they do their firm will
be refinanced, they would have an incentive to use the money lent by the bank to
increase their salaries, embellish the firm's premises and so on, rather than making
all the necessary effort to ensure that the venture will be competitive. The bank,
anticipating this moral hazard problem, will therefore not be ready to commit to
renew the loan independently of the repayment ability of the firm.[15]

To summarise, these models provide a convincing story of why predation takes
place. Once again, aggressive market behaviour is used by the incumbent to modify
the expectations of the profitability of the prey. In this particular case, predation

---

[15] I shall discuss this argument more formally in Section 7.2.3.6. There, I also show that a critical
assumption for the unlimited lending contract to deter predation is that such a contract should
involve a fully credible commitment and cannot be re-negotiated.

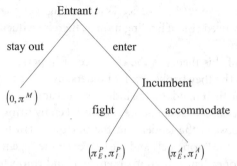

Figure 7.1. Stage game at time t, chain-store paradox game.

affects the lender's evaluation that the firm they finance will be successful. As a result, the prey will have a lower ability to borrow and will be obliged to exit the industry or to reduce the scale of its operations.

7.2.3 Models of Predatory Pricing*

In this technical section, I review the main models of price predation.

7.2.3.1 Selten's Chain-Store Paradox*

Selten (1978) considers an incumbent firm which owns a chain of stores, one in each of T different cities (with T being a finite number). In each market in succession, the incumbent faces a local entrant, say firm 1 can enter market 1 in period 1, firm 2 can enter market 2 in period 2, and so on.

In each period t, the stage game between the incumbent and potential entrant firm t is the same, and it is illustrated in Figure 7.1. First, firm t has to decide whether to enter or not; then, the incumbent has to decide whether it wants to fight entry (that is, choose an aggressive market action), or to accommodate it. If the entrant stays out, then the payoffs for the incumbent and the entrant are respectively π^M and 0. If there is entry, and the incumbent chooses to accommodate it, then their respective payoffs are π_I^A and π_E^A. If entry is followed by an aggressive reaction (or predation, or fight), payoffs are π_I^P and π_E^P. Assume that the fight is costly for both players, in the sense that $\pi_I^A > \pi_I^P$ and $\pi_E^A > 0 > \pi_E^P$. Assume also that the incumbent gets the highest profits under monopoly: $\pi^M > \pi_I^A$.

If the game was played just once ($T = 1$), it is clear that the threat of a fight in case of entry is not credible, and that entry would take place and be accommodated at the sub-game perfect equilibrium. Indeed, if entry occurs, the incumbent will prefer to accommodate than to fight it, as $\pi_I^A > \pi_I^P$. The entrant correctly anticipates the incumbent's choice, and in the first period it knows that if it enters a soft market reaction will occur, so that it will get a payoff π_E^A, whereas if it does not enter its payoff is $0 < \pi_E^A$. Therefore, it prefers to enter.

Selten's insight is to show that nothing changes in this result if the same stage game is repeated a number of times, as long as this number is finite. To look for the sub-game perfect equilibrium when the incumbent faces T entrants, we have to work by backward induction.

Consider what happens when the incumbent and the potential entrant play the game in the last market T. Whatever has happened before (if entry occurred or not, if it has been accommodated or not), the decisions to be taken in this market will not have any effect other than on the current payoffs, since it is the last play. Therefore, the firms will behave as if they were playing the game for the first and only time. The only equilibrium is therefore the one found above in the case where $T = 1$: the entrant anticipates that entry would be accommodated, and therefore entry occurs (and it is indeed accommodated: why should the incumbent prefer to have a payoff $\pi_I^P < \pi_I^A$?).

Consider now what happens at period $T - 1$, where the incumbent and firm $T - 1$ play the game on market $T - 1$. Again, firms know that independently of what has happened in any period before and what they do today, in the next period T entry will occur. Therefore, the play at period $T - 1$ again does not have any bearing on future play, and the incumbent will play as if this was the only (or the last) period of the game. Firm $T - 1$ knows that the incumbent does not have any reason to fight entry, and will accordingly enter; and, of course, entry will be accommodated.

The same reasoning will occur for the $T - 2$ period and any other previous period, so that the only sub-game perfect Nash equilibrium of the game is one where each entrant will enter its respective market, and each entry will be accommodated.

Contrary to what one might expect, there is no effect of reputation building in this game, and predation will not occur.

7.2.3.2 A Reputation Model of Predation**

In this section, I present a simplified two-period version of Kreps and Wilson's (1982) incomplete information model of predation (see also Ordover and Saloner, 1989). Consider the same model as the chain-store paradox for $T = 2$, but with a variant. Entrants do not know with certainty the per-period payoff of the incumbent. In particular, there is a small (prior) probability x that firm I is a *tough* ($\Pr(t) = x$), or low cost, incumbent, with profits $\pi_I^P > \pi_I^A$, whereas with probability $1 - x$ it is a *weak* (or high cost) incumbent ($\Pr(w) = 1 - x$), whose profits are $\pi_I^P < \pi_I^A$ as in the chain store game above. In other words, an entrant might face a tough opponent, that prefers fighting (predating) over accommodating even in a one-period game.[16]

---

[16] The predatory strategy might be thought of as a low price, and the accommodating strategy as a high price. A tough incumbent is one that has such low costs that it would be optimal for it to set the low price regardless of strategic considerations.

This is a multi-stage game with incomplete information, and I look for the Perfect Bayesian Equilibrium (PBE) of the game. In this case, given the strategies of the players and the beliefs of the entrants, at the PBE each player chooses the optimal strategy given the strategy of the rival and the entrant's beliefs, and the beliefs are consistent (that is, they are derived using Bayes' rule). Note that the strategies might be stochastic rather than deterministic functions; there might be mixed strategy equilibria.

A game of this type admits three types of equilibria, two in pure strategies (*separating* and *pooling* equilibria) and one in mixed strategies (*hybrid* or *semi-separating* equilibrium). We briefly indicate the conditions for each type of equilibrium, but then focus on the last one, which in this case is the most interesting.

Separating Equilibrium   At a separating equilibrium a tough incumbent fights entry and a weak one accommodates it. The second period entrant has complete information after observing the behaviour of the incumbent in the first period: $\Pr(w \mid a) = 1, \Pr(t \mid f) = 1$, where w, t stand for "weak" and "tough" respectively, and a, f stand for "accommodate" and "fight". (So, $\Pr(w \mid a)$ is the probability that the incumbent is weak given that accommodation is observed in the first period, and $\Pr(t \mid f)$ is the probability that it is tough given that fight is observed in the first period.) Accordingly, it will enter only if it observes that entry has been accommodated in the first period. At such an equilibrium there would be no predation: the tough incumbent is not behaving strategically, it just maximises its static payoff, and the weak incumbent is unable to deter entry.

A necessary condition for such an equilibrium to hold is that the weak incumbent prefers to accommodate rather than mimic the tough one, that is predate and deter entry:

$$\pi_I^A + \delta\pi_I^A \geq \pi_I^P + \delta\pi^M. \tag{7.1}$$

Pooling Equilibrium   At a pooling equilibrium, both the tough and the weak incumbent fight entry. The entrant correctly understands it, and does not revise its beliefs when observing aggressive behaviour in the first period. The posterior belief coincides with the prior: $\Pr(t \mid f) = x$. For this to be an equilibrium, it must be that the entrant will not enter after observing a fighting episode:

$$x\pi_E^P + (1 - x)\pi_E^A \leq 0. \tag{7.2}$$

To see that a pooling equilibrium cannot exist if condition (7.2) is violated, reason *a contrario*. If $x\pi_E^P + (1 - x)\pi_E^A > 0$, the second entrant would enter after observing predation. But then it cannot be optimal for the weak incumbent to fight in the first period, since sacrificing profits would make sense only in order to deter entry. However, a pooling equilibrium of this type is not very interesting, since condition (7.2) means that the entrant would not enter the market in a static game.

Semi-Separating Equilibrium Let us focus therefore on a situation where both conditions (7.1) and (7.2) are violated, and assume that $(1')$ $\pi_I^A + \delta\pi_I^A < \pi_I^P + \delta\pi^M$, and that $(2')$ $x\pi_E^P + (1-x)\pi_E^A > 0$. I now show that there is a semi-separating equilibrium (i.e., an equilibrium in mixed strategies, since assumptions $(1')$ and $(2')$ rule out pure strategy equilibria) as follows.[17]

Description of the equilibrium

(i.) The first potential entrant enters.

(ii.a) The second potential entrant enters if the first was accommodated.

(ii.b) The second potential entrant enters with probability $1 - (\pi_I^A - \pi_I^P)/[\delta(\pi^M - \pi_I^A)]$ if the first entrant was fought.

(iii.) The tough incumbent fights in both periods.

(iv.) The weak incumbent fights in the first period with probability $-x\pi_E^P/[(1-x)\pi_E^A]$.

(v.) The weak incumbent accommodates entry in the second period, if it occurs.

Proof First of all, note that actions (ii.a), (iii.) and (v.) are trivially optimal: if entry is ever accommodated, it is clear that the incumbent is weak (ii.a); a tough incumbent is by definition one whose payoff is higher from fighting even in a static game (iii.); in the last period of the game, a weak incumbent does not have any reason to fight entry (v.).

I now prove the optimality of the remaining actions as follows.

(iv) If entry has been fought in the first period, the second entrant will use Bayes' rule to revise its prior belief when facing a tough incumbent. The revised probability that the incumbent is tough given a fight is observed is

$$\Pr(t \mid f) = \frac{\Pr(f \mid t)\Pr(t)}{\Pr(f \mid t)\Pr(t) + \Pr(f \mid w)\Pr(w)} = \frac{x}{x + \Pr(f \mid w)(1-x)}. \quad (7.3)$$

For a mixed strategy to be optimal, the second entrant must be indifferent between entering or staying out (that gives a zero payoff), that is,

$$\Pr(t \mid f)\pi_E^P + (1 - \Pr(t \mid f))\pi_E^A = 0, \quad (7.4)$$

which after substituting and re-arranging can be rewritten:

$$\Pr(f \mid w) = -\frac{x\pi_E^P}{(1-x)\pi_E^A}. \quad (7.5)$$

Note that $\pi_E^P < 0$, so this probability is positive, and by $(2')$, $\Pr(f \mid w) < 1$.

(ii.b) For the weak incumbent to randomise in the first period, it must be indifferent between fighting (which would be followed by entry with some probability

---

[17] In this characterisation, I follow closely Ordover and Saloner (1989).

$\Pr(Entry \mid f))$ or not:

$$\pi_I^P + \delta \left[\Pr(Entry \mid f)\pi_I^A + \left(1 - \Pr(Entry \mid f)\right)\pi^M \right] = \pi_I^A(1+\delta). \qquad (7.6)$$

By rearranging, we find the indifference condition as

$$\Pr(Entry \mid f) = 1 - \frac{\pi_I^A - \pi_I^P}{\delta(\pi^M - \pi_I^A)}, \qquad (7.7)$$

which is lower than one by assumption $(1')$.

(i.) The first potential entrant enters if its expected payoff is higher than staying out:

$$x\pi_E^P + (1 - x)\left[\Pr(f \mid w)\pi_E^P + (1 - \Pr(f \mid w))\pi_E^A\right] > 0. \qquad (7.8)$$

After substitution, this amounts to

$$x\pi_E^P + (1 - x)\pi_E^A - x\pi_E^P \left(\frac{\pi_E^P}{\pi_E^A} - 1 \right) > 0. \qquad (7.9)$$

Therefore, some restrictions on the payoff must be imposed for the previous condition to hold. As long as (7.9) holds, the semi-separating equilibrium we have described exists. ∎

Comment The general case $T > 2$ is much more complex but also much richer. The main result is that if T is large enough, in the earlier periods of the game even a weak incumbent fights with certainty, and anticipating this early entrants stay out. As the game proceeds, the optimal strategies become mixed, as in the $T = 2$ case.

The main insight of this model is that even a small departure from the perfect information setting might give rise to predation, if the horizon is finite but long enough: a weak incumbent will play at the beginning of the game as if it were a strong one, and this gives it the reputation of a fighter, which will convince entrants to stay out in early periods. Towards the end of the game, however, a weak incumbent will not find it convenient to fight, and anticipating it some entrants will try their luck (recall, there is always the possibility that the incumbent is a tough one).

Finally, note that Milgrom and Roberts (1982a) examine an extension where there is two-sided uncertainty (the incumbent does not know the payoff of the entrant), and confirm that predation might arise also in this more complex incomplete information game.

7.2.3.3 Milgrom and Roberts' Limit Pricing Model**

Here I present a simplified version of Milgrom and Roberts (1982b). Consider an industry with an incumbent (firm 1) and a potential entrant (firm 2), and demand for the homogenous good is given by $p = 1 - Q$.[18] The potential entrant has a marginal cost c and, if it enters, a fixed sunk cost F. Its costs are common knowledge. The incumbent's marginal cost, instead, might be low ($c_l = 0$) or high ($c_h = c < 1/2$). This cost is private information: the incumbent knows it, but the entrant believes that it is low with a probability $\Pr(c_1 = 0) = x < 1$, and high with a probability $\Pr(c_1 = c) = 1 - x$.[19] I also assume for simplicity that if the entrant actually enters the industry, it will immediately learn the true cost of the incumbent.

The game is as follows. In the first period, firm 1 chooses its output. In this period, it is a monopolist. In the second period, firm 2 decides whether to enter or not; if it does, it sinks its cost F; if it does not, it gets a zero payoff. Active firms choose outputs. For simplicity, I assume no discounting across periods: firm 1 just maximises the sum of its payoff.

I look for the Perfect Bayesian Equilibria of the game. In this case, given the strategies (s_1, s_2) of the players and the beliefs p of the entrant, the PBE consists of a triple (s_1^*, s_2^*, p) such that each player chooses the optimal strategy given the strategy of the rival and the entrant's beliefs, and the beliefs are correct.

In such a game, there are two possible types of equilibrium in pure strategies. In a *separating equilibrium*, the low-cost incumbent chooses a large-enough output, and the entrant correctly infers the incumbent's type by observing its first-period output. In a *pooling equilibrium*, both the low- and the high-cost incumbent choose the same output. If the entrant has a high enough *ex ante* probability to meet a low-cost incumbent, it will not enter. It knows that the output observed in the first period does not carry any additional information about the incumbent's type, and its posterior beliefs are accordingly the same as in the first period.

(The fact that the low-cost incumbent in a separating equilibrium and a high-cost incumbent in a pooling equilibrium set a low enough price to make the entrant stay out makes the model resemble the so-called *limit pricing* arguments of entry deterrence.)

Before characterising these equilibria, let me briefly summarise the first- and second-period outputs under the different possibilities. Firm 1's optimal quantities if there were no potential entrant would be

$$q_{1h}^m = \frac{1-c}{2}; \qquad q_{1l}^m = \frac{1}{2}, \qquad (7.10)$$

where labels h and l stand for high- and low-cost incumbent respectively, and m stands for monopoly. Under duopoly, equilibrium quantities in the Cournot game

[18] I will focus for simplicity on the case of Cournot competition in the second stage, but this is just to have simpler payoff functions. The type of competition in the second stage does not play any role in the analysis.

[19] In this specific example, where demand is linear and there are constant marginal costs, the model could be re-interpreted as one where uncertainty is on the demand intercept, rather than on the incumbent's costs.

are

$$q_{1h}^d = q_{2h}^d = \frac{1-c}{3}; \qquad q_{1l}^d = \frac{1+c}{3}, \qquad q_{2l}^d = \frac{1-2c}{3}, \qquad (7.11)$$

where d stands for duopoly (the first pair refers to the case of a high-cost incumbent, the second of a low-cost incumbent). All equilibrium profits are given by $\pi_{ij}^k = (q_{ij}^k)^2$. To make the analysis interesting, I assume that in a full information context the entrant would never enter if it faced a low-cost incumbent ($\pi_{2l}^d - F < 0$), but would always enter if it faced a high-cost one ($0 < \pi_{2h}^d - F$), or

$$\frac{(1-c)^2}{9} > F > \frac{(1-2c)^2}{9}. \qquad (7.12)$$

Finally, denote by $\pi_{1j}^m(q_{1l})$ the profit obtained by an incumbent of type $j = h, l$ when selling an output q_{1l} (not necessarily coinciding with the monopoly output of type j).

Separating Equilibrium   I shall now show that the following is an equilibrium:

$$\begin{cases} q_{1l}^* = q_{1l} > q_{1l}^m \\ q_{1h}^* = q_{1h}^m \\ s_2^* = Enter, \text{ if } q_1^m < q_{1l}; \text{ } Not\ Enter, \text{ if } q_1^m \geq q_{1l}, \\ x' = 0, \text{ if } q_1^m < q_{1l}; \text{ } x' = 1, \text{ if } q_1^m \geq q_{1l}, \end{cases} \qquad (7.13)$$

where $x' = \Pr(c_1 = 0 \mid q_1^m)$ is the entrant's belief of facing a low-cost incumbent given the observed first-period output q_1^m.

At this equilibrium, the low-cost incumbent sets a higher output than its monopoly output (that is, the output set if it were in a monopoly unthreatened by entry) in the first period, and the high-cost incumbent sets its own monopoly output, thereby revealing its type. The entrant correctly infers the incumbent's type and behaves accordingly, entering only when if faces a high-cost firm 1.

For this to be an equilibrium, no firm should have an incentive to deviate. Given its beliefs and firm 1's strategies above, it is clear that the entrant cannot do better than that: entering with a low-cost firm would entail losses, and not entering with a high-cost one would imply foregoing positive profits.

Let us now check that the high-cost incumbent has no incentive to deviate. If it plays the candidate equilibrium strategy it will get its monopoly profit in the first period but would attract entry: $\pi_{1h}^m + \pi_{1h}^d$. Alternatively, it could set q_{1l} thus mimicking the low-cost incumbent and deterring entry: under this deviation, it would get $\pi_{1h}^m(q_{1l}) + \pi_{1h}^m$. Its incentive constraint (IC) therefore amounts to

$$\pi_{1h}^m + \pi_{1h}^d \geq \pi_{1h}^m(q_{1l}) + \pi_{1h}^m, \qquad \text{or} \qquad \frac{(1-c)^2}{9} \geq (1 - q_{1l} - c)q_{1l}. \qquad (7.14)$$

As for the low-cost incumbent, by playing the (candidate) equilibrium strategy it would get a lower profit than by setting its monopoly output in the first period, but it deters entry: $\pi_{1l}^m(q_{1l}) + \pi_{1l}^m$. This strategy involves a sacrifice in the profits earned in the first period; the alternative could be to set the monopoly output in the first period (since any output lower than q_{1l} would attract entry, choosing q_{1l}^m is clearly the best deviation output) but this would not deter entry, and would therefore give duopoly profits in the second period. This deviation gives the payoff $\pi_{1l}^m + \pi_{1l}^d$, giving rise to the following incentive constraint:

$$\pi_{1l}^m(q_{1l}) + \pi_{1l}^m \geq \pi_{1l}^m + \pi_{1l}^d, \quad \text{or} \quad (1 - q_{1l})q_{1l} \geq \frac{(1+c)^2}{9}. \quad (7.15)$$

It is easy to check that the high-cost IC (7.14) is satisfied for $q_{1l} \geq 1/2 + \sqrt{5}(1-c)/6$ and that this is bigger than $1/2$ for $c < (3\sqrt{5} - 5)/4 \simeq .4271$ (for values of c higher than this threshold, separating equilibria would exist where the low-cost incumbent simply sets its monopoly output and is not mimicked by the high-cost incumbent).

The low-cost IC (7.15) is satisfied for $q_{1l} \leq 1/2 + \sqrt{5 - 8c - 4c^2}/6$.[20] Therefore, there exists an interval of values which satisfies both ICs as long as $1/2 + \sqrt{5}(1 - c)/6 \leq 1/2 + \sqrt{5 - 8c - 4c^2}/6$, or $c \leq 2\sqrt{5}/3 - 1 \simeq .49$.

Note also that the best possible equilibrium for the incumbent corresponds to the output that makes the high-cost IC's bind: $q_{1l} = 1/2 + \sqrt{5}(1-c)/6$ (any output larger than this would decrease the first-period profit without changing the second-period profit).[21]

Pooling Equilibrium   I shall now check if the following is an equilibrium:

$$\begin{cases} q_{1l}^* = q_{1h}^* = q_{1l}^m \\ s_2^* = Enter, \text{ if } q_1^m < q_{1l}^m; \ Not \ Enter, \text{ if } q_1^m \geq q_{1l}^m, \\ x' = 0, \text{ if } q_1^m < q_{1l}^m; \ x' = x, \text{ if } q_1^m \geq q_{1l}^m, \end{cases}$$

At this equilibrium, the high-cost incumbent imitates the low-cost incumbent. Since the potential entrant understands that it cannot infer the incumbent's type from the first-period play, it decides on the basis of its *ex ante* beliefs, which say that the incumbent is a low-cost one with a probability x. Accordingly, the pooling equilibrium can exist only if the entrant's expected payoff (which is the same before and after observing firm 1's first-period choice) is negative:

$$x(\pi_{2l}^d - F) + (1 - x)(\pi_{2h}^d - F) < 0 \quad \text{or} \quad x > \frac{(1-c)^2 - F}{2 - 3c}. \quad (7.16)$$

---

[20] The lower root of the second-order equation is discarded because it is lower than $1/2$.

[21] Since the high-cost incumbent would have the same payoff anyway, this equilibrium would be selected if the criterion of Pareto dominance (for the active players, that is the firms) is used.

In other words, the *ex ante* probability that the entrant will meet a low-cost incumbent must be high enough if the pooling equilibrium is to exist.[22] Otherwise, since at a pooling equilibrium first-period play does not lead to a revision of beliefs, the entrant would always enter. In turn, the fact that entry will not be deterred implies that the high-cost incumbent had better play its monopoly output rather than bluffing.

As for the incentive constraints of firm 1, the high-cost incumbent must prefer to imitate the low-cost firm and deter entry rather than reduce its output and attracting entry:[23]

$$\pi_{1h}^m + \pi_{1h}^d \leq \pi_{1h}^m(q_{1l}^m) + \pi_{1h}^m, \qquad \text{or:} \qquad \frac{(1-c)^2}{9} \leq (1 - 1/2 - c)/2, \quad (7.17)$$

which holds for $c < (3\sqrt{5} - 5)/4 \simeq .4271$.

As for the low-cost incumbent, it is clear that it prefers to play the candidate equilibrium output, where it deters entry by choosing its monopoly profit: any other output would lower first-period profit and possibly (if setting an output lower than $1/2$) also trigger entry.

Conclusion   The analysis shows that by setting a low enough price (a large enough output) and pretending to be an efficient producer, an incumbent would be able to deter entry. In the example above, this is possible whenever the high-cost incumbent is not too inefficient ($c < (3\sqrt{5} - 5)/4$) and the *ex ante* probability that the entrant attaches to the incumbent being low cost is high enough.

Note, however, that the policy implications of the model are far from straightforward. First of all, predation here occurs without the high-cost incumbent selling below its cost: in the pooling equilibrium, entry is deterred by setting $q = 1/2$, that corresponds to a price $p = 1/2$ higher than the cost of the inefficient incumbent. Second, suppose, for the sake of the argument only (as such a policy would be based on unobservables), that a competition authority imposed a rule which prevents a firm from "acting strategically" and selling at a price lower than the one it would set if there was no threat of entry. Such a rule would eliminate entry deterrence by the high-cost firm, and might therefore increase welfare.[24] However, it would also reduce welfare if the incumbent was low-cost and a separating equilibrium arose. Indeed, in such

---

[22] Note that, other things being equal, as c increases condition 7.16 is less likely to hold. In other words, the more inefficient the high-cost incumbent the less likely it can deter entry by mimicking the low-cost incumbent.

[23] Since, given the entrant's belief, any output below q_{1l}^m would trigger entry, the high-cost optimal deviation would entail setting its monopoly output. Note also that the IC for the high cost is basically the opposite condition as (7.14).

[24] Under a pooling equilibrium, consumers would buy a total of $1/2 + (1 - c)/2$ units in the two periods. If strategic behaviour was prevented, they would buy $(1 - c)/2 + 2(1 - c)/3$ units. The deadweight loss would therefore be reduced, but only for $c < 1/4$.

a case, by acting strategically the efficient incumbent would decrease price below the myopic monopoly level in the first period, and consumers would be better off.[25]

7.2.3.4 Predation to Merge**

The Chicago School's critique to predation maintained that mergers would be a more profitable strategy than predation. The argument was criticised by Yamey (1972) who pointed out that even with a view to take over a rival, predation might be profitable because it would have the effect of decreasing the price at which the rival is bought. Saloner (1987) gives formal support to this argument. In what follows, I present a very streamlined version of his model.[26]

Consider the same incomplete information model as in the previous Section 7.2.3.3, but with some differences. First, assume that $F = 0$, so that the entrant always finds it profitable to enter (to focus on predation and merge at more convenient terms). Second, modify the game so as to introduce a stage where firms can merge, as follows. In the first period, the incumbent (that, as above, might be a low-cost or a high-cost firm) is alone in the market and chooses its output, that is observed by the potential entrant. In the second period (the novelty with respect to Milgrom and Roberts' analysis) there is bargaining over the merger terms. For simplicity, assume that all the bargaining power is on the incumbent, that makes a take-it-or-leave-it merger offer to the potential entrant. In the third period, active firms set outputs.[27]

Note that third-period equilibrium quantities and profits are already known from Section 7.2.3.3 above. In case a merger has taken place in the second period, the incumbent simply becomes a monopolist in the third.[28]

As for the merger process at period two, the price Q at which firm 2 is willing to be bought will depend on whether it expects to face a high- or a low-cost incumbent. In the former case, it expects to make a profit π_{2h}^d and in the latter a lower profit π_{2l}^d. Therefore the takeover will take place for $Q \geq \pi_{2h}^d$ and $Q \geq \pi_{2l}^d$ respectively. One

---

[25] Under a rule that excludes strategic behaviour the entrant would observe that the low cost sets $q = 1/2$ and correctly infer that it is efficient, and therefore would not enter. In both periods, there would be a monopoly with $1/2$ units sold. Under the separating equilibrium, instead, the output would be $1/2$ in the second period, but higher than $1/2$ in the first one.

[26] A similar presentation can be found in Tirole (1988: 374–6).

[27] In Saloner (1987) there is product market competition in the first period as well, so predation to make rival firm 2 exit, rather than to deter entry, takes place. He also considers an extension where a third firm (more efficient than firm 2 but not efficient enough to compete with a low-cost incumbent) could enter the market. Therefore, the extended model is one where both predation for mergers and entry deterrence can occur. Indeed, there exist separating equilibria where a low enough ("limit") price is chosen by the low cost firm 1 so as to take over firm 2 more cheaply, and deter entry of firm 3. There also exist pooling equilibria where a high-cost incumbent imitates the low-cost one, thus both predating for merger and for entry deterrence.

[28] Goods being homogenous, this can only be a very stylised model of a merger, where assets of the taken-over firm simply disappear. See Chapter 5 for a proper analysis of mergers with asset-based models.

can see immediately that the incumbent has an interest in being believed to be low-cost. Since the bargaining power is all on the incumbent side, firm 2 will sell out at a price equal to its reservation price. If firm 2 believes it faces an efficient incumbent, the merger occurs at a price $Q_l = \pi_{2l}^d$. If it believes it faces an inefficient incumbent, the price will be $Q_h = \pi_{2h}^d > Q_l$.

I can now turn to the characterisation of the separating equilibria, whereas pooling equilibria are studied in Exercise 7.2.

Separating Equilibrium   Let me focus on the following equilibrium, where the low-cost incumbent sets an output larger than its monopoly output in the first period to signal it is efficient and buy firm 2 at a lower price, whereas the high-cost incumbent simply sets its monopoly output and it is recognised as inefficient (and therefore has to pay a higher price for the takeover):

$$\begin{cases} q_{1l}^* = q_{1l} > q_{1l}^m; & Q^* = Q_l = \pi_{2l}^d \\ q_{1h}^* = q_{1h}^m; & Q^* = Q_h = \pi_{2h}^d \\ s_2^* = \begin{cases} \text{if } q_1^m < q_{1l}: & \text{Sell, if } Q \geq Q_h; & \text{Reject, if } Q < Q_h \\ \text{if } q_1^m \geq q_{1l}: & \text{Sell, if } Q \geq Q_l; & \text{Reject, if } Q < Q_l \end{cases} \\ x' = 0, \text{ if } q_1^m < q_{1l}; & x' = 1, \text{ if } q_1^m \geq q_{1l}. \end{cases}$$

Given its beliefs, it is clear that the entrant cannot do better than selling out at the high price Q_h if $q_1^m < q_{1l}$ and at the low price Q_l otherwise.

As for the high-cost firm 1, playing according to the candidate equilibrium strategy is optimal if it is better to have the monopoly profit in the first period but having to pay a high price for the merger, rather than pretending to be a low-cost incumbent, which entails a lower initial payoff but a higher later gain due to saving on the takeover price:

$$\pi_{1h}^m - \pi_{2h}^d + \pi_{1h}^m \geq \pi_{1h}^m(q_{1l}) - \pi_{2l}^d + \pi_{1h}^m. \tag{7.18}$$

This can be re-written after substitution as $\pi_{1h}^m - \pi_{1h}^m(q_{1l}) \geq \pi_{2h}^d - \pi_{2l}^d$, or

$$\frac{(1-c)^2}{4} - (1 - q_{1l} - c)q_{1l} \geq \frac{(1-c)^2}{9} - \frac{(1-2c)^2}{9}, \tag{7.19}$$

which simplifies to $q_{1l} \geq (1-c)/2 + \sqrt{(2-3c)c}/3$,[29] with $q_{1l} = (1-c)/2 + \sqrt{(2-3c)c}/3$ being the natural equilibrium among all the possible ones.

The low-cost firm 1 will find the candidate equilibrium strategy optimal if it is better to sacrifice first-period monopoly profit to pay a lower price for the merger, rather than getting its monopoly profit in the first period but having less convenient

---

[29] Note that $(1-c)/2 + \sqrt{(2-3c)c}/3$ is bigger than $1/2$ for $c < 8/21$. Therefore, for $c \geq 8/21$, the low-cost incumbent does not need to set a lower price (a higher output) than its monopoly price (output) to separate from the high-cost incumbent.

terms for the takeover (as the entrant would mistake it for a high-cost firm):

$$\pi_{1l}^m(q_{1l}) - \pi_{2l}^d + \pi_{1l}^m \geq \pi_{1l}^m - \pi_{2h}^d + \pi_{1l}^m. \tag{7.20}$$

This can be re-written after substitution as $\pi_{1l}^m - \pi_{1l}^m(q_{1l}) \leq \pi_{2h}^d - \pi_{2l}^d$, or

$$\frac{1}{4} - (1 - q_{1l})q_{1l} \leq \frac{(1-c)^2}{9} - \frac{(1-2c)^2}{9}, \tag{7.21}$$

which simplifies to $q_{1l} \leq 1/2 + \sqrt{(2-3c)c}/3$, always satisfied for $q_{1l} = (1-c)/2 + \sqrt{(2-3c)c}/3$.

7.2.3.5 Deep-Pocket Predation*

For a very simple model of deep-pocket predation, due to Benoit (1984), consider the following *perfect information* game that lasts for $T + K$ periods with $K \geq 1$. In the first period, an entrant firm E decides whether to enter or not a given sector, and the incumbent firm I decides whether to prey (fight) or accommodate entry. In each of the following periods, firm E decides whether to stay or exit, and firm I whether to prey or accommodate. (As an alternative, firm E is already in the market, and decides whether to continue or not from the first period.) If it preys, both firms have a per-period payoff $\pi^P < 0$, if it does not prey, they have $\pi^A > 0$.

The two firms are perfectly symmetric in their technologies and products, but differ in their assets. The entrant has lower assets than the incumbent, and can survive a maximum of T periods: $A_E = -T\pi^P < A_I$.[30] In other words, the incumbent can survive longer in the event of a price war, that is it has a deeper pocket.

Under this set of assumptions, at the only sub-game perfect equilibrium the entrant will not enter (or will immediately exit). It is easy to see this result by backward induction. Figure 7.2 illustrates the game in the simple case where $T = 1$ and $K = 1$, that is, the entrant has resources only for one period fight, and the firms meet in the marketplace only twice. I first solve the model for this two-period case, and then for the general case.[31]

Solution for the Two-Period Case: $T = K = 1$ The game is solved by moving backwards. Let us start by the second period. If the entrant has entered and has been fought, in the second period it has to exit. If entry has been accommodated, it will decide to stay. This is because the entrant anticipates that – if it stays – the incumbent prefers to accommodate and get π^A rather than fight and make a loss π^P. Therefore, in the second period, it prefers to stay and get π^A rather than exiting and getting 0.

---

[30] For simplicity, disregard here the possibility that firms borrow funds. As an alternative think of assets as the maximum financing they can obtain. This raises of course the crucial question of why one firm can raise more funds than another, a point that is dealt with in Section 7.2.3.6.

[31] See also the slightly more difficult Exercise 7.3 for a two-period game of predation.

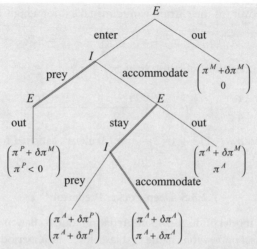

Figure 7.2. Deep-pocket predation, with $T = K = 1$.

In the first period, if the entrant has entered, the incumbent knows that by fighting it will induce exit (and get monopoly profits π^M), whereas by accommodating it will not (we have just seen that if it is not fought, the entrant will stay). The former strategy is preferred if

$$\pi^P + \delta\pi^M > \pi^A(1 + \delta). \tag{7.22}$$

Let us now move to the very first decision. If the above condition holds, the entrant knows that its entry will be followed by a fight and it will lose all its assets: it will thus prefer to stay out. If the condition is violated, the entrant will enter since it anticipates that the threat of predation is not credible.

Solution of the General Case   At period $T + 1$, if firm E has always been fought, it will go bankrupt and will have to exit, and firm I will get monopoly profits forever, $\pi^M + \sum_{j=1}^{K-1} \delta^j \pi^M$. Else, predation in this period by the incumbent would not be credible: by accommodating it would get $\pi^A + \sum_{j=1}^{K-1} \delta^j \pi^A > \pi^P + \sum_{j=1}^{K-1} \delta^j \pi^A$.[32] Anticipating it, firm E would stay, and they would both earn π^A forever.

At period T, if the entrant is still in the industry and it has always been fought, the incumbent knows that by fighting the entrant one more time it would make it exit. Therefore, it would prefer to fight as long as

$$\pi^P + \sum_{j=1}^{K} \delta^j \pi^M > \pi^A + \sum_{j=1}^{K} \delta^j \pi^A. \tag{7.23}$$

---

[32] Since there is discounting, if the incumbent wants to fight entry for T periods, it would fight the first T periods. In other words, it would not make sense for it to restart predation after a period of accommodation.

If this condition is satisfied, the entrant anticipates that it will be preyed upon once more and would prefer to exit immediately, in order to save π^P.

At period $T-1$, if the incumbent fights one more period it knows that it will induce exit in the next period, giving a payoff $\sum_{j=1}^{K+1} \delta^j \pi^M + \pi^P$. By accommodating, it will get $\sum_{j=1}^{K+1} \delta^j \pi^A + \pi^A$. Clearly, fighting is more profitable as long as condition (7.23) holds. Anticipating this, the entrant will prefer to exit immediately to avoid the losses caused by a period of fighting.

The argument then continues backwards in the same way until the first period, where the entrant prefers to exit immediately (or not enter at all) rather than incurring any losses.

Comments This simple model illustrates why the deep-pocket arguments of predation might work. In a situation where a firm is financially stronger than another, the former can use its deeper pockets to force the latter out of the industry. Note also that there need not be any relationship between financial strength and efficiency: a more efficient firm might have – for several reasons, some to be seen in the following Section 7.2.3.6 – cash constraints and be forced out of the market by a richer but less efficient rival (see Exercise 7.3). If this is the case, predation is twice harmful for welfare: first, because it eliminates one firm where instead two could co-exist; second, because it eliminates the most efficient firm, adding a productive inefficiency to the allocative inefficiency.

None the less, the model has some limits. First, note that the information requirements for predation to work are quite strong, with the incumbent that should know not only the costs of the entrants but also the precise amount of funds available to it, and the entrant who should know that the incumbent does not have any cash (or credit) constraint (and there must be common knowledge of these elements). Second, the model is somewhat unsatisfactory in the sense that along the equilibrium path predation would never be observed: given perfect information and common knowledge, the entrant will never enter the industry (or, if already in, would leave it immediately), without any price war being observed. However, Benoit (1984) shows that predation would still occur under incomplete information (where some uncertainty exists about how deep a firm's pocket is), and that – similarly to the reputation model of Section 7.2.3.2 – a price war might well be observed along the equilibrium path.[33] The third and most important limit of this simple model is that it exogenously assumes that a firm is not able to raise outside funds. This leads us to the models that endogenously explain why predation might reduce the ability of an entrant firm to borrow, which is the object of the next section.

---

[33] Note that the same remark applies also to the financial models of predation seen below. There as well the introduction of incomplete information would allow for predation to be observed at equilibrium.

7.2.3.6 Deep-Pocket Predation with Imperfect Financial Markets**

To understand why predation might occur when an incumbent has financial strength, one has to understand why an entrant or a smaller firm is vulnerable when it does not have enough financial means. The key issue is to recognise that if capital markets are imperfect, then the assets (such as cash and retained earnings) owned by a firm matter and determine its ability to raise external funds. Once this point is established, it will be easy to understand why predation might occur: by behaving aggressively in the marketplace, the incumbent will reduce the assets available to the smaller firm, reducing its ability to raise capital, and therefore obliging it either to exit or to reduce its ambitions in the industry.

This section, based on Holmström and Tirole (1997) and Cestone (2001), formalises this point.[34]

Financing Investments in an Imperfect Capital Market   Consider first the financing problem of a risk-neutral entrepreneur, abstracting from product market competition. The firm needs to invest a given amount to enter a certain sector, or to continue operations in that sector, and that entails the payment of a fixed cost F. The firm has own assets for a total of A, so it needs to borrow from a risk-neutral bank the amount $D = F - A > 0$ to finance the investment.

If the investment is financed, the entrepreneur decides whether to work diligently on the project or shirk. If he works diligently, the business project will succeed with probability p and will give a revenue R, and it will fail with a probability $1 - p$, giving a revenue 0. If he shirks, the project will fail with certainty, but he will get a private benefit $B < F$. The private benefit can also be interpreted as the disutility of effort saved when shirking, conditional on the project being financed; for instance, as the time the entrepreneur can spend reading newspapers or calling his family and friends rather than working on the project.

Effort is not observable (or, if observable, it is not verifiable), so it is not possible to write a financing contract that directly fixes its level. This creates an information asymmetry (with moral hazard) between the outside investors and the entrepreneur, that is the reason for capital market imperfection in this example.

Assume that if the entrepreneur had enough assets to finance the project itself, or if there was no information asymmetry (that is, if effort was objectively verifiable and it was possible to write a contract contingent on it), the investment would always be made:

$$pR > F. \tag{7.24}$$

But the outside investor will finance the investment only if it is sure that it is going

---

[34] Cestone (2001) provides a nice survey of the literature on the interaction between capital and product markets.

to elicit diligent work from the entrepreneur. Otherwise, it will lose D. (Assume that there is limited liability: the investor (or bank) cannot recover the amount it lent by seizing the personal assets of the entrepreneur.)

Consider now the following contract between the bank and the firm. The bank lends D to the firm, and if the project is successful, the former receives a payment $R - S$, where S is kept by the firm. The entrepreneur's net expected utility is given by $U = pS$ in case of high effort, and $U = B$ in case of low effort. Therefore, S must be chosen to satisfy the following incentive constraint:

$$pS \geq B. \tag{7.25}$$

So, if the contract is to elicit high effort, the entrepreneur must receive at least $S = B/p$ or, which is the same, the firm could not promise to repay more than $R - B/p$ to the bank ($R - B/p$ is called *pledgeable income*).

The bank will finance the project if and only if its expected value (subject to the entrepreneur making high effort, that is subject to condition (7.25) being satisfied) is higher than its cost (that is, the funds lent):

$$p(R - S) \geq F - A, \tag{7.26}$$

that is, if the expected pledgeable income is higher than the cost of the investment:

$$p\left(R - \frac{B}{p}\right) \geq F - A. \tag{7.27}$$

This clearly shows that the firm's financial position, summarised by the assets A it owns, plays a key role in the bank's lending decision: the larger A the more likely that the firm's project will be financed.[35] Indeed, (7.27) can be re-written as

$$A \geq B - (pR - F) \equiv \overline{A}, \tag{7.28}$$

which makes it clear that a project with positive net present value will not be financed (the firm is credit constrained) if the firm has assets below a certain threshold $\overline{A}$.

If involved in a price war that reduces its assets, a firm's likelihood to get further financing from banks will be jeopardised. This is the key insight from recent deep-pocket models of predation, as I now show.

A Deep-Pocket Model of Predation Let us now introduce product market competition in the financing model seen above. There are two firms: firm I is the incumbent, and firm E is a recent entrant into the industry (or the predator and the prey). The firms are perfectly identical in their technologies and products, but

---

[35] There are different alternative models that lead to similar results. For instance, Fudenberg and Tirole (1985) look at a contract where either the firm repays its debt augmented by an interest rate ($D + rD$), or it goes bankrupt (such a contract is showed to be optimal by Gale and Hellwig (1986)). Again, the final result is that the higher the assets owned by the firm the more likely the project is financed.

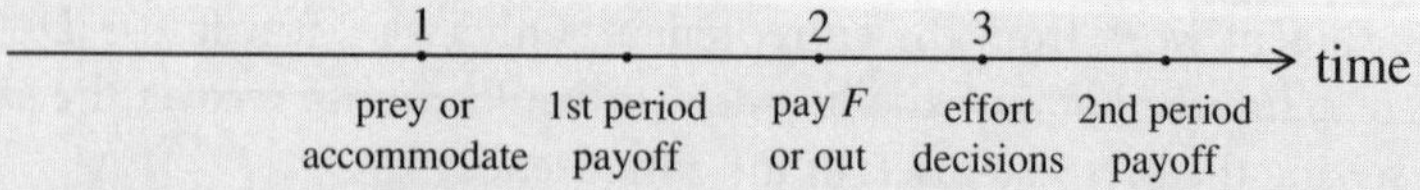

Figure 7.3. Time line: A (financial) long-purse model of predation.

they differ in that I has a deep pocket whereas E has limited assets, in a sense to be specified below.

Assume that both firms have already incurred their fixed recurrent cost F for period 1, but still have to pay it to continue production in period 2.[36] The game is as follows (see Figure 7.3 for an illustration).

At stage 1, firm I decides on whether it preys or accommodates entry. If it preys, both firms get (first-period) profits π^P; if it does not, they get profits $\pi^A > \pi^P > 0$. At stage 2, each firm either pays F or goes out of business; a firm that does not own enough assets has to find a bank to finance the investment. At stage 3, each entrepreneur has to make effort decisions, and then second (and last) profit re-alisation occurs. Conditional on making high effort, if both firms have invested they will earn π^A with the same probability p,[37] whereas if only one firm has invested it will earn monopoly profits $\pi^M > 2\pi^A$ with probability p.

Assume that $p\pi^A > F$: this implies that the investment would always be financed if capital markets were perfect. Assume also that firm I has own assets $A_I > F$, so that it will always be able to finance the investment, whereas firm E's assets in the first period are $A_E = 0$; therefore, its second period assets coincide with its first period retained earnings (I abstract from discounting). Assume that

$$F - \pi^A < p\left(\pi^A - \frac{B}{p}\right) < F - \pi^P. \tag{7.29}$$

It is now easy to look for the sub-game perfect Nash equilibrium of this game. Note that from stage 2 onwards, the game is exactly the same as the basic model studied in the previous subsection, where π^A replaces R and where assets A are equal to either π^A in case of accommodation or π^P in case of predation. Therefore, condition (7.29) tells us that firm E's investment would be financed only if firm I does not prey.

So far, this shows that predation would indeed make firm E exit the industry. However, I also have to establish that firm I will have an incentive to predate. This is the case if and only if

$$p\pi^M + \pi^P > p\pi^A + \pi^A. \tag{7.30}$$

---

[36] Alternatively, one can think that entering the industry does not involve any cost, but then a new superior technology which requires paying a cost F becomes available. This is a drastic innovation: A firm that does not adopt it will be excluded from the market.

[37] I assume that the probability of success of the two firms is the same. This will happen, for instance, if p is the probability that market demand exists for the good.

Therefore, predation will occur if the future prospect of higher profits, $p(\pi^M - \pi^A)$, outweighs the current losses from predation, $\pi^A - \pi^P$.

Some Comments   First, note that I have assumed the entrant to have less financial means than the incumbent, but this might not always be the case. An interesting implication of this model is that large or financially strong entrants should be welcome. In an industry where a strong incumbent is present, a small firm might never be able to survive, whereas a large multinational company or a dominant firm in another sector that wishes to diversify into a new sector will not run the risk of being preyed upon by the incumbent. At present, I have the impression that whenever a large firm, possibly dominant in some market, plans to enter a new market, this is regarded with suspicion by anti-trust authorities. Such a suspicion might be warranted in many cases, but not always, as the deep-pocket model teaches us.

Second, note that a strong market position is a necessary condition for predation. Predation involves monetary losses that a firm can hope to recoup in the future only if it enjoys enough market power.

Third, it should be noticed that exit of the rival is not strictly necessary for predation to be profitable, as shown in Exercise 7.4: predation might not force a smaller firm to exit, but might prevent it from adopting innovations or from growing.

Extensions: Renegotiation and Bolton and Scharfstein's Model   A critique of this model is that predation could be avoided by the bank's agreement to finance the entrant independently of first-period payoff realisation. In other words, if the bank and firm E signed a long-term contract whereby the bank *commits* to finance firm E whether or not there is predation, in exchange of a repayment $\pi^A - B/p$, then there would be no scope for predation. Two important points should be stressed in this contract: first, it should be observable to the incumbent; second, it must be non-renegotiable, that is, the bank cannot withdraw from its commitment to finance firm E.

If both conditions are satisfied, then it is easy to see that predation will not occur. This is because firm I knows that no matter what it does in the first period, that is no matter what assets are available to firm E at the moment of investing, the bank will finance the investment. Hence, it would be pointless to engage in predation which involves foregoing profits that cannot be recovered later.

First, note that this reasoning hinges on firm I's observing the contract between the bank and its rival, not necessarily a weak assumption (consider also that firm E has all interest in having firm I believe that it enjoys an unconditional line of credit).

Second, it also hinges on the credibility of the commitment of this long-term contract. If it were impossible for the bank to commit to such a contract, that is if the bank could renegotiate it at a zero or small cost, predation would not be avoided.

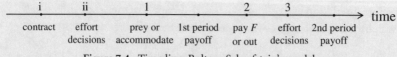

Figure 7.4. Time line: Bolton–Scharfstein's model.

Indeed, consider what happens if the contract is renegotiable after observing the first-period payoff realisation. Suppose predation has occurred. Then firm E has insufficient assets for the bank to be willing to finance its second-period investment (since $p\pi^A - B < F - \pi^P$), and will not be able to borrow. Anticipating this, the incumbent will prey in the first period.

The Trade-Off between Moral Hazard and Deterring Predation   Considering all the possible uncertainties of the market, it seems unlikely that a bank wants to commit to continuing to finance operations of a firm no matter how its business is developing. Bolton and Scharfstein (1990) add the following argument to explain why it might not be wise for the bank to give such a long-term contract to the firm. If an entrepreneur knew that its firm will be financed in the future independently of its results, it would not have the right incentives to make an effort. To see why such an agency problem might arise following a long-term contract with the bank, consider an extension of the model where after the contract is signed but before first-period market realisation firm E's entrepreneur should decide whether to make a high or low effort.

To repeat, the model illustrated in Figure 7.4 is as follows (to stress the agency problem, disregard renegotiation issues and assume that the bank fully commits to the long-term contract). At stage i, the bank and firm E sign a long-term contract, whose details we shall see below. At stage ii, each entrepreneur takes effort decisions, which leads to success with a probability q (success rates are the same for both firms).[38] First-period shirking gives private benefit b (with $b < qB$). At stage 1, firm I decides on whether to prey or accommodate, (first-period) profits being respectively π^P and $\pi^A > \pi^P$ in case of effort and success for both firms. If an entrepreneur shirks or if he makes effort but the project fails, the firm's first period profits are zero. At stage 2, each firm either pays F or exits. At stage 3, each entrepreneur has again to make effort decisions (success rate, again perfectly identical, is p), after which, second (and last) profit realisation occurs, with payoffs π^A if both firms invest, and $\pi^M > 2\pi^A$ if only one does.

We know from the sub-section above that firm E will be able to borrow if its assets at the beginning of the second period are $A_E = \pi^A$ (recall that we assume $F - \pi^A < p\pi^A - B < F - \pi^P$). But the long-term contract also establishes that the bank will finance the fixed investment F with a probability $x < 1$ in case firm E's second period assets are lower than π^A, in exchange of a repayment $\pi^A - B/p$.

---

[38] I introduce an effort decision for firm I as well to preserve symmetry, but this is of course not necessary.

The optimal contract corresponds to the value of x that maximises the value of firm E subject to two incentive constraints to be satisfied: first, the incumbent does not prey ($IC_{I,NP}$); second, firm E's entrepreneur makes high effort in the first period ($IC_{E,1}$). In other words, the programme is

$$\max_x V = q\pi^A + [q + (1-q)x](p\pi^A - F), \qquad \text{subject to:} \qquad (7.31)$$

$$IC_{I,NP}: q\pi^A + [q + (1-q)x]\, p\pi^A + (1-q)(1-x)\, p\pi^M$$

$$\geq q\pi^P + xp\pi^A + (1-x)\, p\pi^M, \qquad (7.32)$$

$$IC_{E,1}: [q + (1-q)x]\, p(B/p) \geq xp(B/p) + b. \qquad (7.33)$$

$IC_{I,NP}$ says that the incumbent prefers to accommodate entry than to prey. By accommodating, it earns π^A in the first period, and in the second period π^A if the rival has been successful or has been refinanced, and π^M if it has not been successful and not refinanced (which happens with probability $1-x$), of course weighted by own probability of success. By preying, it gets π^P in the first period, and in the second period π^A if firm E receives funding (which occurs with probability x) and π^M otherwise (again, all payoffs are expressed in expected terms).

$IC_{E,1}$ says that the entrepreneur prefers to exert high effort than shirking in the first period (the IC in the second period is already taken care of under the stipulated contract that guarantees firm E a payoff B/p in case of success). The first-period effort does not give an immediate payoff to the entrepreneur, but increases the likelihood of financing in the second period. Financing occurs with probability $[q + (1-q)x]$ under high effort, and with probability x under low effort.

After re-arranging, the two ICs can be re-written as

$$x \geq \frac{p\pi^M + \pi^P - \pi^A(1+p)}{p\pi^M} \equiv x_{I,NP}, \qquad (7.34)$$

where the numerator is positive because of condition (7.30), and

$$x \leq 1 - \frac{b}{qB} \equiv x_{E,0}. \qquad (7.35)$$

These two conditions show that predation might be deterred at the cost of reducing the entrepreneur's incentive to exert effort. For instance, in the extreme case where $x = 1$, that is firm E is financed no matter what firm I does, the entrepreneur's incentive constraint is always violated. More generally, the two ICs can be simultaneously satisfied only if $x_{I,NP} \leq x_{E,0}$, that is if

$$\frac{b}{qB} \geq \frac{\pi^A(1+p) - \pi^P}{p\pi^M}. \qquad (7.36)$$

In such a case, the optimal probability of refinancing will be $x^* = x_{E,0}$ (the higher x the larger the present value of the firm). But if condition (7.36) is violated, then predation can be deterred only at the cost of having low effort in the first period.

7.2.4 Practice: How to Deal with Predatory Pricing Allegations

One clear lesson from Section 7.2.2 is that incumbent firms might well use aggressive pricing strategies in order to deter entrants and/or to force competitors out of their industry, by relying on different mechanisms: they can build a reputation for being tough, so as to scare potential entrants out of the business; they might want to set low prices to signal entrants or smaller competitors not to expect high profits; or they might want to erode a rival's resources to make it more difficult for it to get funding. No doubt, anti-trust agencies should watch out and expect some incumbents to use such predatory practices to create or strengthen a dominant position.

However, we should also try to get something more from economic theory, not just the result that predatory pricing might occur. In what follows, I give my interpretation of the policy implications from the theory.

In all theories of predatory pricing there is a common mechanism: the predator sets low prices for a period, thereby sacrificing short-run profits, in order to make a rival (or its lenders) believe that it should not expect high profitability. When the rival revises its plans (or its lenders stop financing it) and exits, or abandons the project of entering, or reduces the scale of its operations, the incumbent will increase its prices and reap high profits, which in the long-run outweigh early losses.

Two elements should be stressed from this mechanism: (a) the sacrifice of short-run profits; and (b) the ability to increase profits in the long-run by exercising market power once predation has been successful. It is on these two elements that the legal treatment of predatory pricing should be built. Accordingly, it makes sense to have a two-tier test of predation, as follows:[39]

1. Analysis of the industry to determine the degree of market power of the allegedly dominant firm. If the firm is not dominant, dismiss the case; if the firm is dominant, proceed with:
2. Analysis of the relationship between price and costs:[40]
   - A price above average total costs should definitely be considered lawful, without exceptions.
   - A price below average total costs but above average variable costs should be presumed lawful, with the burden of proving the opposite on the plaintiff.
   - A price below average variable costs should be presumed unlawful, with the burden of proving the opposite on the defendant.

Note that the test reverses the logical order of (a) and (b). This is because the analysis of the industry might in many cases turn out to be simpler to carry out than the price-above-cost test, and would allow to screen out some cases (those where

---

[39] Joskow and Klevoric (1979) were probably the first to suggest a two-tier test for predatory pricing. Relative to their test, the one I propose is probably more stringent in the first part (I would require dominance) and less stringent in the second part (I would presume prices below average total costs as lawful – provided they are above average variable costs).

[40] See below for the definition of average variable costs and average total costs.

the alleged predator is clearly not dominant) saving time and resources. In what follows, I discuss the proposed test.

7.2.4.1 Ability to Increase Prices (Is There Dominance?)

A necessary element for predation is the ability to more than compensate after the exclusion of the competitor for the minor profits made during the predation episode. Clearly, this requires the existence of market power on the side of the firm, and the stronger its market power the more likely for it to gain in the long-run from the exit (or down-sizing) of the prey. Since market power is a matter of degree, the issue is where to set the line above which a firm might be accused of predatory behaviour: can an oligopolistic firm, among many in its sector that can exercise some market power, be accused of predation?

In EU law, this is not an issue, since predation would fall under the category of abuse of dominant position. Accordingly, an oligopolistic firm that does not have a dominant position would not be found guilty of predatory behaviour. In current practice, this means that a firm with a market share below 40% would probably not be accused of predation (see Chapter 3 on dominance).

In the US, the issue is much less clear, and courts have found firms guilty of predation even when they held relatively small market shares. A case in point is *Brooke Group*, although the final Supreme Court decision eventually dismissed the predation allegations, after an initial guilty verdict. In that case, a small cigarette producer, Liggett & Myers (later part of the Brooke Group) had filed a suit against Brown & Williamson – which held 12% of the cigarette market – accusing the latter of having entered the generic and private label segment of the market and of selling below cost to drive Liggett – the main firm in that segment – out of the market.[41]

A high market power standard is needed to avoid the risk of jeopardising competition in oligopolistic markets. It would be paradoxical if anti-trust authorities put hurdles to practices used by non-dominant firms to increase their market power. Suppose for instance that a firm with a sizeable market share (say, 20%) in an oligopolistic industry where there is a much stronger firm (say, one with 60% of the market) tries to increase its custom by decreasing its price. Suppose also that the lower price allows it to steal customers from both the market leader and a smaller competitor, one that, say, has 5% of the market. The latter might then accuse the price-cutting firm of predatory pricing, and – if the price is found to be below some specific measure of cost (see following sub-section), the court would indeed find predation. Yet, rather than behaving predatorily, the alleged non-dominant predator is just trying to increase its market share through an aggressive but lawful behaviour.

There are many reasons why a non-dominant firm might price below costs as part of a normal competitive process. Consider for instance an industry characterised

[41] For discussions of this case, see Burnett (1999), Bolton et al. (2000) and Elzinga and Mills (2001).

by *switching costs* (see also Chapter 2): most consumers would be locked-in with the dominant firm, and only a significant price cut might convince many of them to address another seller instead. The same argument holds for markets with *network externalities* (see also Chapter 2): if they are important enough, a substantial price cut might be necessary for a firm to win enough customers and reach a critical mass. Or think of industries characterised by steep *learning curves* or important economies of scale: rather than being confined to be a niche player, a firm might want to sharply decrease prices and increase its output so as to go down the cost curve and increase its efficiency.[42] Finally, a firm might charge a price below cost if there is some *product complementarity* with another market.[43] If the latter is more important for the firm, it is short-run profitable (and good for consumers as well) that it decreases prices in the market at stake to increase demand in the complementary market.

Note also that the same arguments (with the exception of the complementarity defence) would *not* apply to a firm which is dominant in the industry where the alleged predation takes place. A dominant firm cannot claim that it needs promotional pricing to increase its sales, since it is already well established in the market: its consumers are already locked-in by switching costs and network effects, and presumably it has already reached the minimum efficient scale of production and benefited from learning effects.

Therefore, the market power test should catch only dominant firms, and not just any oligopolistic firm that has some market power. Admittedly, in exceptional circumstances there might be a non-dominant predator, and such a test would leave it unpunished. Yet, this would be a small price to pay compared to a test that sets a lower barrier. The latter would create higher legal uncertainty, as most oligopolists might be the target of a predatory action. As a result, the normal competitive process would be damaged, since firms might fear predatory actions if setting too-low prices. Further, it would invite many more predatory litigations, which would absorb the energy and resources of the anti-trust authorities and would distort the attention of both plaintiffs and (above all) defendants away from productive activities and into legal ones.

Finally, note that the existence of dominance should refer to the period when the first allegedly predatory episode starts, not at some later dates. Otherwise, one might find predation where instead two or more firms are fiercely competing in a

---

[42] In this last example, the firm might defend itself by showing that its price is below current costs, but not below expected future costs. For this reason, whatever measure of costs is adopted, it is important that "reasonably anticipated" costs are considered, as discussed by Areeda and Turner (1974). See also below.

[43] In Chapter 8, I show that a multi-product monopolist charges lower prices when it produces complementary goods than two independent firms that monopolise those same markets, a result due to Cournot (1838), and already seen in Chapter 6 as well. This result carries over to oligopolistic firms. It might also involve below-cost pricing on one good.

market characterised by switching costs, network effects or scale economies, and are initially competing on equal terms but only one is successful *ex post*. (See also Section 7.2.4.3 below.)

7.2.4.2 Sacrifice of Short-Run Profits

In the predatory price models analysed above, sacrifice of short-run profits means that the incumbent-predator is not choosing the price, say p^*, that it would optimally choose were it taking as given the presence of the rival–prey, but rather a lower price, say p', at which it will make lower current profits.[44] However, there is no necessary relationship between the price p' chosen to exclude the rival and any measure of costs of the incumbent (for instance, p' could be above or below the incumbent's marginal costs). In other words, theory just says that the incumbent chooses a price at which it makes less profit than it could otherwise make in the short-run, but it does not say whether such profit is negative or not.

If one wanted to apply the theory literally, one should be ready to enter into very troubled waters, where one of the necessary steps of the predation investigation would be the calculation of the optimal price p^*, and a proof that the actual short-run price p' is lower than that. Clearly, this would not be feasible in practice. However sophisticated the managers of a firm might be, it is unlikely that they could have a notion of what *the* optimal price is: *a fortiori*, anti-trust agencies and courts would find it impossible to establish that profits have been sacrificed in the sense that the price actually set by the incumbent is below the one it would have set had it not tried to force a rival out of the industry.

However, there is an alternative route to establish the sacrifice of current profits. This is to re-interpret the concept and define it not as making lower profits than otherwise possible, but making *negative* profits. In other words, the sacrifice of short-run profits is established if the alleged predation price p' is lower than (some appropriate measure of) costs.

This approach introduces a clearer benchmark: during the alleged predation episode, the predator's profits should be lower than zero, or its price below costs. Unfortunately, however, this rule is still far from being easily implementable in practice. But before discussing the practical implementation of the rule, let me make some additional remarks.

This rule is nothing else than what most courts have done and anti-trust commentators have suggested, for a long time: a necessary (although not sufficient) condition for proving an allegation of predatory monopolisation (or abuse of dominance) is

---

[44] To be sure, Harrington (1986) has shown that in some circumstances the incumbent might manage to exclude by using a higher price than would be optimal in the short-run, but I will focus on the more likely case where predation involves low prices. The considerations that follow will lead me to propose a rule whereby a necessary element of predation is pricing below (some measure of) cost. Hence, any predation through *high* prices would be undetected.

that the predator makes losses during the predation period. This rule makes a lot of sense. A firm that makes profits should be excluded from predatory charges because nobody could prove that it could have made even more profits had it acted differently. A firm that makes negative profits, instead, *might* be a predator, although there are other reasons why a firm might want to charge below costs, such as selling perishable products that would otherwise be unsold (thus causing even greater losses), making promotional offers, stimulating sales of complementary products, and so on (see more below).

This rule, however, admittedly leaves some possible predation cases uncovered, as we have seen that – in theory – a firm might choose prices strategically to exclude rivals even without going as far as selling below costs.[45] Given the difficulty of proving that price has been lower than some optimal price, there could still be yet another possibility, which is to find documents at the alleged predator's premises that show that the managers have indeed been willing to sacrifice profits in the short-run in order to exclude rivals.

However, such evidence should not replace an objective proof. Statements like "let us decrease prices so as to signal to them that we are efficient", or "... so as to make them exit", or even the existence of a business plan aimed at reducing prices to make life difficult for competitors, can be complementary evidence, but they should not be taken as an independent and objective proof of sacrifice of short-run profits, if at those prices the incumbent is making profits. After all, if an inefficient rival enters the industry, an efficient incumbent might well be entitled to reduce its prices in response to entry, and it might well know that this is going to determine the rival's exit. Yet, this is simply part of the competitive process that anti-trust agencies should stimulate: exit of an inefficient firm does not harm welfare.

In a similar vein, if an incumbent causes a rival to exit by reducing prices but at a level at which it still makes profits, this means that the rival is likely to be much less efficient than the incumbent. Hence, it is unlikely that there is a great welfare loss from its exit.

To summarise, a "price below cost" test might not allow us to catch all the possible instances of predation. Yet, the cases not covered by this test would probably be few and very special. The cost of making such an error seems small.

Compare it instead to the error that we would make if we allowed a finding of predation with prices above costs. The absence of an objective rule based on observables ("optimal" prices are not observable) would introduce an element of legal uncertainty and arbitrariness. This might not only have an effect on the particular cases at hand (firms might be found guilty of monopolisation while they are not) but would have serious consequences across the economy, as firms endowed with market power would hesitate to decrease their prices lest they are accused of forcing smaller competitors out of the industry or pre-empting the entry of new rivals. Since

---

[45] In other words, this approach reduces type-I errors but not type-II errors.

low prices improve consumer surplus and welfare, and it should be an objective of any competition policy to create circumstances favourable to low prices, the risk of deterring firms from setting low prices is simply too great.

Which Definition of Cost in a "Price below Cost" Test?   Determining whether at a certain price a firm is making positive profits or not (i.e., is selling above or below cost) is a very hard task. First of all, one should decide which measure of cost to use in this assessment exercise.

Areeda and Turner (1974), in an article that has influenced anti-trust practice worldwide, argue that the best measure from a conceptual point of view would be that of *marginal cost*,[46] since a firm that sets price below marginal cost would clearly not maximise short-run profits. However, they suggest using in practice *average variable cost* – defined as the sum of all variable costs divided by output – as a surrogate for marginal cost, given "the difficulty of ascertaining a firm's marginal cost. The incremental cost of making and selling the last unit cannot readily be inferred from conventional business accounts, which typically go no further than showing observed average variable cost. Consequently, it may well be necessary to use the latter as an indicator of marginal cost".[47]

Hence, Areeda and Turner (1974: 733) suggest that:

(a) A price at or above reasonably anticipated average variable cost should be conclusively presumed lawful.
(b) A price below reasonably anticipated average variable cost should be conclusively presumed unlawful.

There are probably not enough cases on predatory pricing to say what courts in different jurisdictions would currently deem a predatory price. However, according to Bolton, Brodley and Riordan (2000),

> Under current US law, a price above average total cost (ATC) is conclusively lawful, while a price below average variable cost (AVC) is at least suspect. A price between AVC and ATC is sometimes held unlawful, depending on other factors.

---

[46] Marginal cost is "the increment to total cost that results from producing an additional increment of output. It is a function solely of variable costs, since fixed costs, by definition, are costs unaffected by changes in output". "[Variable costs] typically include such items as materials, fuel, labor directly used to produce the product, indirect labor such as foremen, clerks and custodial help, utilities, repair and maintenance and per unit royalties and license fees". Of course, such a concept leaves out fixed costs, that do not vary with output, which ". . . typically include most management expenses, interest on bonded debt, depreciation (to the extent that equipment is not consumed by using it), property taxes, and other irreducible overhead". (Areeda and Turner, 1974: 700).

[47] Areeda and Turner (1974: 716). Using average variable cost instead of marginal cost is clearly an imperfect proxy (as Areeda and Turner themselves recognise) and has been criticised in the literature, giving rise to alternative measures of costs to be used in predatory tests. Some will be mentioned below. For a review of predation tests, see Ordover and Saloner (1989).

But judicial decisions are not consistent and courts have increasingly relied on the AVC benchmark as the main criterion for illegality.[48]

Not only courts, but also some scholars would rule out predatory pricing only if price is above average *total* cost (that is, if the firm is able to recover its fixed costs as well), rather than above average *variable* cost. Joskow and Klevoric (1979) suggest that it would be more appropriate to deem any price below ATC as predatory (provided that the structural part of their test is met, that is if the alleged predator does enjoy enough market power), since a situation where a firm has losses cannot be an equilibrium. However, a problem with using ATC is that it would require a firm to cover all the fixed sunk costs, which is a very stringent standard. Suppose for instance that an incumbent firm makes some fixed expenditure that it expects to recover through monopoly profits. Soon afterwards, a new firm unexpectedly enters the market, with normal competition leading the incumbent to decrease its price to a level where the fixed sunk investment cannot be recovered. In this case, a price below ATC rule would find predation even if there is none. This drawback is avoided by the concept of *average incremental costs* (AIC), defined by Bolton et al. (2000) as

> the per unit cost of producing the added output to serve the predatory sales. AIC differs from average variable cost in at least two ways. First, it is not measured over the firm's whole output, but only over that increment of output used to supply the additional predatory sales. Second, incremental cost includes not only variable cost, but any fixed costs incurred in expanding to serve the new sales. Incremental cost is a better standard than either average variable cost or full costs because it most accurately reflects the costs of making the predatory sales.[49]

Accordingly, these authors would presume illegal a price below AIC and lawful one above ATC with a grey area in between.

To sum up, a number of different cost standards have been proposed in the literature. In particular, both average variable cost and average incremental cost are reasonable standards. Perhaps AIC better matches the concept of predation, but it might not be always easy in practice to identify precisely the costs that are sustained for a given output, and/or isolate the predatory output from total output.

However, I would be cautious in finding predatory behaviour in cases where the price is above average variable cost (or average incremental cost): the possibility that a firm is charged with predatory pricing if it sets a price that allows it to recover variable cost but not total fixed costs (that is, a price above average variable cost but below average total cost) seems too strict and might encourage firms to keep prices higher than they otherwise would.

---

[48] Average total costs are all costs (including fixed costs) divided by output.
[49] AIC is a concept that is very close to the measure of *average avoidable cost* suggested by Baumol (1996).

Accordingly,

1. A price above average total costs should definitely be considered lawful, without exceptions.
2. A price below average total costs but above average variable costs should be presumed lawful, with the burden of proving the opposite on the plaintiff or the anti-trust authority.
3. A price below average variable costs should be presumed unlawful, with the burden of proving the opposite on the defendant.

For the cases where average incremental costs can be calculated, they might be used instead of average variable cost.

It would obviously be very important, to safeguard legal certainty, that anti-trust agencies express the criterion they want to follow in clear guidelines.

7.2.4.3 Testing Predatory Pricing: Further Discussion

This section comments upon further elements that might be raised during a predatory pricing case: intent, proof of recoupment, proof of anti-competitive effects and matching competitors' prices as a defence. It also deals with predatory pricing allegations in high-technology markets, an issue that has recently been debated. Finally, it criticises recent laws and regulations adopted in some EU countries, which forbid firms to sell below costs.

Intent (Existence of a Predatory Scheme) In many predation cases, there is evidence from internal documents that the alleged predator's managers intended to exclude a new entrant, or force a competitor out of the industry. How should one treat these documents?

On the one hand, e-mail, minutes and other internal papers where one or more managers adopt a very strong language against competitors and state they want to eliminate them, "kill" them or the like, should not be given much importance, as they are probably to be found in any company's headquarters and – right or not – are part of usual business language. (I would be much more suspicious of managers who say they want to be nice to their competitors, and would suggest immediately opening a collusion investigation!)

On the other hand, it would be hard to dismiss evidence that there is an articulated plan to try to exclude smaller rivals, at the cost of temporarily sacrificing profits. If there is proof that a coherent business strategy has been put in place with exclusionary purposes, and especially if those documents reveal the intention to produce at a loss to achieve that aim, then the burden of proving that there was no predation after all should be on the shoulders of the alleged predator.

No Need to Prove Recoupment or Success of Predation *Ex Post* The proposed test suggests looking at the existing market power of the alleged predator to see if there is the ability to recoup losses in the long-run. Note that this is very different from assessing whether there has actually been recoupment of losses, or whether this is under way. This assessment should be in any case done from an *ex ante*, rather than *ex post*, vantage point, and the firm could not defend itself showing that after all it did not manage to recoup losses. In other words, the predator should not benefit from the fact that it has miscalculated the opportunity to recover losses, or that the prey has turned out to be a "tougher cookie" than initially thought, or that prompt anti-trust action has led to conclusion of the predatory episode before it could achieve its aim.

Likewise, if the market power and price above cost tiers of the test are both satisfied, one should not admit as a defence the fact that predation has not been effective and exclusion has not happened.

No Need to Prove *Ex Post* Damage to Consumers   Anti-trust policy aims at protecting competition, not competitors. So, it might appear strange that there is no explicit requirement of harm to consumers in a predation test. However, predatory pricing as established by the proposed test will result in lower consumer surplus in the vast majority of cases. Sure enough, it is possible to conceive models where predation occurs without consumer surplus being harmed (this might happen, for instance, in signalling models). However, the fact that the predator expects to recover losses from raising prices after exclusion points to a horizon long enough for (future) high prices to have a higher weight than (current) low prices. Consequently, one should expect a negative effect on net consumer surplus, leading to a presumption of anti-competitive effects.[50]

In particular, it should not be accepted as a defence that consumers have *ex post* turned out to benefit from the alleged predatory episode, for the reasons expressed in the previous sub-section: the fact that low prices have not been followed by high-enough prices might be due to the predator's miscalculations, anti-trust action, or stronger than expected resistance from the prey.

Conversely, the alleged predator might conceivably have an efficiency defence for its below-cost prices (for instance, when it is active in complementary markets). If it has a convincing case in this respect, and the burden of proving this should be on it if prices are found to be below average variable costs, then this would exclude anti-competitive harm.

Meeting Prices of a Competitor as a Defence   It is part of the normal competitive process that entry by a competitor would trigger a response by the incumbent firms, leading them to decrease their prices.[51] Therefore, observing that a dominant firm's

---

[50] Note that this presumption applies only to predatory pricing. I will argue in Section 7.3.1 below that quite a different approach should be taken for allegations of predatory investments.

[51] The reader can check that this would happen in most, if not all, oligopolistic models.

price decreases following entry is *per se* no proof of strategic behaviour. Clearly, a rule which dictates otherwise, and obliges a dominant firm not to react to entry would harm the competitive process and lead to market distortions (any inefficient firm would be invited to enter).

However, matching a rival's price should not be accepted if it leads the incumbent to price below average variable costs.[52] As we have seen above, there exist many reasons why an entrant, or a less established firm, might want to set prices below costs for a period in order to gain new customers and overcome the competitive disadvantage created, for instance, by switching costs, network effects, and scale economies. In such situations, as we have seen in Chapter 2, a very aggressive price might be the only instrument available for a new firm to win customers away from the incumbent. While some initial losses for a new firm are perfectly justified and are part of the normal competitive process, the same is not true for an incumbent which enjoys a dominant position. Accordingly, matching a competitor's price should not be an accepted defence if it implies prices below average variable costs for the incumbent. Conversely, a price above average total costs is lawful even if it implies undercutting a smaller competitor or a new firm.

Predatory Prices in High-Technology Markets   In recent years, there have been a stream of high-profile cases involving high-technology firms, such as IBM, Intel, and Microsoft. Microsoft in particular has been the object of several investigations in both the US and the EU. These cases are very complex and involve several allegations of anti-competitive behaviour, including the possibility that Microsoft aimed at excluding a competitor, Netscape, from the browser market as a way to avoid being challenged in the OS (Operating System) market (see Section 7.5).

Without discussing the merit of these allegations here, some commentators have argued that traditional anti-trust analysis is not well suited to high-technology markets such as the computer software markets.[53] Such markets are characterised by extremely high fixed costs and very low – if not nil – marginal costs (as well as average variable costs). Think for instance of software, where R&D is the main expenditure firms incur to develop a new software package, and where the cost of producing and selling an additional unit of it, whether in the form of CDs or downloads, is next to zero. They are also characterised by very important network externalities, either direct (the more other people use my same software the happier I will be because the more likely I can exchange files with them) or indirect (the more people use my same OS the happier I will be because the more likely that software developers will write applications that will run on my OS).[54] This means

---

[52] See also Areeda and Turner (1974: 715).

[53] See Ahlborn et al. (2001) and Schmalensee (2002).

[54] Computer OS, like many other markets characterised by network externalities, are *two-sided* markets, that is markets where the success of a product depends on it being accepted by two different groups of consumers. Another examples of two-sided market is the market for credit

that we should expect very intense competition in the early stages of the market, until the market tips in favour of one firm, which will then become dominant and use its market power to recover the losses incurred in the initial periods, until a new technology will appear that replaces the old one, bringing to an end the previous leadership.[55]

While I agree that caution should be used in dealing with predatory charges, (1) these markets do not present unique features unknown to industries in the pre–information technology age, and (2) nor is a new anti-trust policy necessary to deal with them. As for the first point, examples of industries with very strong fixed sunk costs and relatively low variable costs can be found everywhere: think for instance of consumer products characterised by heavy advertising outlays and industries such as chemicals, pharmaceuticals, and engineering characterised by heavy R&D outlays.[56] Nor are new information technology industries the only ones where network effects are at play. Network effects can be seen in such traditional industries as toys, shoes, and design for instance, that is whenever fashion and fads play a role (whereas some people are happier to buy unique pieces, the vast majority seems to want what other people have), and of course network externalities play a role in electricity appliances, fixed telephones, railways, records, and so on.

As for the second point, note that the proposed test for predatory pricing above (which is a variant on a long tradition dating from Areeda and Turner, 1974) allows coping with many of the fears expressed by, for instance, Ahlborn et al. (2001). A firm that is charging below average total costs (which can easily be the case when fixed costs are important) is not necessarily found guilty even if it has a dominant position. And, most certainly, if two or more firms are competing for the market in a particular sector and none of them has a dominant position at the outset, the fact that they charge below costs to win the market (and that they do have intent to exclude, since each of them is struggling to become the firm which wins the race and becomes the monopolist) should not lead to any charge since the first tier of the test (no dominance) is not satisfied. In other words, if there is no *ex ante* dominance, the case for predation should be dismissed.

The existence of network effects and important R&D outlays should be no excuse for a dominant firm that tries to keep its market power through anti-competitive means. The rules should apply to high-technology markets as well as traditional ones, and if a dominant firm tries to preserve its position by predatory pricing, it should be punished for it.

---

cards (shop-keepers and consumers). For an analysis of pricing strategies and competition effects in such markets, see Rochet and Tirole (1999, 2001), Schmalensee (2002) and Evans (2002).

[55] See Shapiro and Varian (1999) for an interesting and accessible analysis of information technology markets, and Shy (2001) for a simple analysis of network industries. Breshanan (1998) presents a theory of successive monopolies in a dynamic context.

[56] Sutton (1991, 1998) provides a detailed analysis – rich also in case studies – of industries with high fixed sunk costs and low variable costs.

Another interesting case is the one where a firm dominant in one product tries to enter a new market for a complementary or independent product, which is often the case in high-technology markets (think for instance of Microsoft, which has moved progressively into Internet browsers, audio and video software, instant messaging services, software for hand-held devices, and so on). How should it be treated? There is no *a priori* answer to this question, but a couple of observations seem worth making. First, if the products are complementary, recall that a firm will have an (honest) interest in charging lower prices than two separate firms would, in order to stimulate demand, and that this is to the advantage of consumers as well. As we have seen repeatedly (see also Chapter 6), being served two products by the same monopolist is usually better than being served those same products by two different monopolists!

Second, people are generally concerned about large and well-endowed firms extending their power from one market to the other. However, if markets are complementary we have seen that this is more likely than not to be beneficial for consumers. If markets are independent, this is not necessarily bad news either. In markets characterised by important network effects and other attritions, it might be very difficult to leapfrog the current leader, and a firm that can rely on important R&D, marketing and financial assets might manage to achieve what a small firm might not have.[57]

Therefore, it might not necessarily be always bad news when a large firm tries to enter a new product market.

Price below Average Variable Cost: Not a General Rule   In most EU countries, there exist laws and regulations that apply to specific sectors or are economy-wide, and that forbid below-cost pricing, promotional sales, free gifts, "two-for-one" offers, and retail discounts above a certain threshold. Retailers are not entitled to sell goods at a loss in France, Spain, Italy, Ireland, Luxembourg, Belgium, Portugal and Greece (*Financial Times*, 22 August 2002: 1, 3). In general, these laws are the result of lobbying from shop-keepers and small businesses that regard aggressive price cuts by national supermarket chains or large firms as predatory and unfair. However, the resulting obligation to charge above costs applies to any firm, regardless of the market power it holds and the reasons why the price cut is made.

There is no justification for such a regulatory approach, which protects competitors (for political or social reasons) rather than promoting competition. To repeat, there are many reasons (switching costs, network externalities, price promotions, complementary products) why firms might want to sell at a loss temporarily, and

---

[57] Cestone and Fumagalli (2001) show that the allocation of financial resources within a business group (even when it is not observable to outsiders) affects the business units' product market behaviour. Being affiliated to a well-endowed business group might facilitate entry in a market relative to a stand-alone firm; however, an incumbent firm, which is part of a large business group, might also deter entry more easily.

they are part of a normal competitive process. Forbidding them *a priori* and on a generalised basis has the effect of hampering competition and decreasing consumer welfare.[58] If there are reasons to believe that, say, a supermarket chain is selling at a loss to force small shop-keepers out of business, a specific anti-trust action should be started. If instead the concern is the survival of small shops and small firms in general, then, as I have argued also in Chapter 1, this might well be the objective of a public policy, but should be addressed with different means (for instance, income tax rebates) that are less distortive of competition.

7.3 NON-PRICE MONOPOLISATION PRACTICES

There are a number of instruments other than price that a dominant firm might use to try to force the exit of smaller rivals or to deter entry into the industry. They include strategic investments (Section 7.3.1), tying (Section 7.3.2), and incompatibility decisions (Section 7.2.1); other instruments, such as exclusive dealing and refusal to supply, have already been analysed in Chapter 6.

7.3.1 Strategic Investments

We have seen that when a dominant firm reduces prices, first it is very difficult to understand whether this is due to genuine, lawful competition or to anti-competitive behaviour; second, since low prices are something that consumers like, one has to be extra careful not to discourage firms from decreasing prices. This basic problem re-appears when one looks at investments in capacity, R&D, advertising, product quality, new brands, and so on. Theory shows that – as for price decisions – a dominant firm might use its investment decisions in a strategic way, in order to drive competitors out of the industry, or to persuade them not to enter at all.[59] However, first it is difficult to recognise in practice whether a certain investment level is the fruit of the "honest" attempt of a firm to be more competitive and more appealing to consumers, or whether instead it is driven only by the desire of attaining or reinforcing a monopolistic position. Second, since most investments have a positive effect upon welfare, a very cautious approach has to be taken not to discourage firms from undertaking projects that should be welcome. I will argue that because of these difficulties, only in truly exceptional cases might it make sense to accuse a firm of over-investment; further, the burden of proof should be on the plaintiff or the competition agency, not on the defendant.

---

[58] Compare with the following statement by the European Parliament's internal market committee: "the prohibition of loss-making sales . . . is a useful instrument that not only serves consumer interests but also helps to prevent unfair trade practices" (*Financial Times*, 22 August 2002: 1).

[59] See for instance the classic papers by Spence and Dixit on investments in capacity; and the more recent papers by Choi (1996) and Farrell and Katz (2000) on R&D investments in complementary markets.

The basic mechanism behind anti-competitive choice of investments is similar to predatory pricing: an action is taken that involves the sacrifice of current profits, to be outweighed by future profits. In other words, for a period, a firm invests more than is profitable in the short-run, with the expectation of increasing profits in the long-run, when the rival has left (or a potential competitor abandons plans of entering the market).

Consider a situation (analysed formally in Section 7.3.1.1) where an incumbent monopolist has to decide how much to invest in process R&D, knowing that a firm is considering entry into the industry. Suppose for simplicity that the R&D outcome is not stochastic, for instance because there are technologies already available elsewhere and the incumbent has to decide which ones to adopt. Facing competition, it makes sense that the incumbent wants to improve its technology and abate its production costs. Indeed, we would all say that such an investment in R&D is one of the welcome effects of increased competition. Let me call x^i, where i stands for innocent, the optimal investment level chosen by the incumbent firm when it takes for given that the new competitor will be in the market in the following period.

However, the incumbent might also act strategically, and try to discourage the new firm from entering at all. For instance, it might choose to invest in a particularly costly and efficient technology, so costly and efficient that the new entrant would not expect to be sufficiently profitable when the incumbent adopts it. In other words, investing in the more efficient technology represents a credible commitment to be a fierce competitor in case of entry. Call x^p, where p stands for predatory, the investment level (higher than x^i) that would make the entrant re-consider its entry decisions.[60] When the rival observes that the incumbent has invested (or committed to invest) x^p, it will withdraw.

Clearly, x^p is higher than short-run profitability would require, since it is the lower investment level x^i that the incumbent would choose if it did not try to affect the entry decisions of the potential rival. Nonetheless, the expectation of continuing monopolistic profits (due to entry deterrence) might make the more costly investment profitable.

Some remarks are needed here. First, it is not said that the entry deterrence level of investment would always be chosen. Even if it was *feasible* to deter entry (for instance, because it is known that the rival would drop its entry plans after observing x^p), it is not necessarily *profitable*. For instance, the sunk cost required by technology x^p might be so high that it is more convenient to co-exist with the competitor.

Second, authorities should protect competition, not competitors. In other words, even in the unrealistic case where we could establish that x^p has been decided only to pre-empt entry, from the above example we could not necessarily conclude

---

[60] For the sake of simplicity, I am assuming that the entrant cannot use the same technology, for instance because the size of the market is not large enough for two firms to recover such important (endogenous) sunk costs. See also Chapter 2 on endogenous sunk costs.

that the over-investment is anti-competitive for two reasons:[61] The first reason is that the lower its costs the lower the price a monopolist charges, so it is conceivable that consumers might gain from the more efficient technology (in the period prior to the planned entry date of the other firm, prices would be lower; prices might also be lower under an efficient monopolist than under a less efficient duopoly).

The second and most important reason is that it would be very difficult to identify predation for strategic motives such as the one described above in practice, as there are no observable variables and no evident benchmark levels that one could use to decide whether there has been strategic over-investment or not. Imagine a court having to evaluate a complaint by a competitor that there has been strategic over-investment by the incumbent in order to deter entry. The only observable variable here is the actual investment level made by the incumbent, x^p. How can it be proved that had it not wanted to deter entry, the incumbent would have chosen another, and lower investment level? The incumbent will say that it has chosen an investment that makes it competitive *vis-à-vis* an entrant, and in any case in the real world it could never be sure whether after observing x^p the rival would call off its entry plans or not.

The very notion that a court or an anti-trust authority could find a firm guilty of anti-competitive behaviour because it has "invested too much" would create a dangerous precedent: firms might refrain from investing fearing that they could be investigated for abuse of dominance or monopolisation.

Similar considerations also applied to predatory pricing, but with two differences. Firstly, for allegedly predatory prices a possible benchmark exists: if a firm sets a price below average variable costs, a presumption that the firm is taking an anti-competitive action exists. But no such benchmark exists when it comes to investments.

Secondly, low prices are reversible, whereas most investments are not. And indeed, a full commitment is crucial for the strategic entry deterrence argument (if the investment decision was reversible, the entrant would enter). As a result, consumers will benefit from the investment even after "predation" ends, whenever the incumbent's action involves the installation of new capacity, investments in R&D (think for instance of the creation of a new laboratory and the hiring of related personnel and scientists), the introduction of a new brand if supported by specific advertising and marketing expenses (provided they are specific to the new brand), and so on.[62] Other things being equal, this argument indicates that the loss from anti-competitive investment would be lower than under predatory pricing.

---

[61] An additional argument, that I will not consider here, is that entry might not always be welfare enhancing, because of duplications of fixed costs. Accordingly, it is in principle possible that welfare is higher when the incumbent acts strategically than otherwise.

[62] Judd (1985) analyses a model where an incumbent might use product positioning to deter entry, and he finds that if the incumbent could later withdraw the brand at a low cost, it might want to do so. Accordingly, the commitment of the investment is reduced and the entrant will not be deterred.

Overall, therefore, while it is theoretically possible that an incumbent over invests in advertising, R&D, or capacity, or that it introduces new brands, or engages in product proliferation for the purpose of strategically deterring entry or forcing exits of smaller rivals, it would seem difficult to suggest any rule that allows identifying such behaviour in practice.

7.3.1.1 Strategic Investments to Deter Entry*

There are a number of variables that could fit the analysis carried out in Section 7.3.1, and indeed many works have shown that a firm might pre-empt entry by investing strategically. Spence (1977) and Dixit (1980) are the classical references in this respect: they show that a monopolist can strategically accumulate capacity so as to deter a potential entrant. Here I present a slightly different (and perhaps simpler) model that gives similar insights.[63]

There is an incumbent, firm 1, that faces a potential entrant, firm 2, in the market for a homogenous good whose demand is $p = 1 - q$. The game they play is as follows. In the first stage, firm 1 decides how much it wants to invest in a cost-reducing technology. Absent any investment, the incumbent produces at a marginal cost c; by investing x_1 it can become more efficient, with total cost of production given by $C(x_1, q_1) = (c - x_1)q_1$. Assume a quadratic cost for the investment, $F(x_1) = x_1^2$. For simplicity, assume that firm 2 cannot invest in R&D prior to entry and that if it enters, it will have a constant marginal cost c. (Exercise 7.5 studies the case where firm 2 can also invest in R&D, and shows that the main results obtained here carry over to that case.) In the second stage, firm 2 decides whether to enter or not, after observing the investment of firm 1. If it does, it has to pay a fixed sunk cost F. In the last stage, active firms choose outputs.

To look for the sub-game perfect Nash equilibrium of the game, start by the Cournot game at the last stage.

If there is a duopoly, firm $i = 1, 2$ will choose the output q_i so as to maximise $\Pi_i = (1 - q_i - q_j - c_i)q_i$, where $c_1 = c - x_1$ and $c_2 = c$. Rearranging the FOCs $\partial \Pi_i / \partial q_i = 0$, one obtains the reaction functions:

$$R_1 : q_2 = 1 - 2q_1 - c + x_1; \qquad R_2 : q_2 = \frac{1 - q_1 - c}{2}. \qquad (7.37)$$

Their intersection gives the usual Cournot outputs, prices and profits:

$$q_i^c = \frac{1 - 2c_i + c_j}{3}, \qquad p^c = \frac{1 + c_i + c_j}{3}, \qquad \Pi_i^c = \frac{\left(1 - 2c_i + c_j\right)^2}{9}. \qquad (7.38)$$

If there is a monopoly, firm 1's optimal values are $q_1^m = (1 - c_1)/2$, $p^m = (1 + c_1)/2$, $\Pi_1^m = (1 - c_1)^2/4$.

---

[63] For a textbook presentation of entry deterrence models of capacity see for instance Tirole (1988).

458 Predation, Monopolisation, and Other Abusive Practices

Going backwards, we find two different cases, according as to whether firm 1 behaves innocently or strategically.

Innocent Behaviour   The first case is the one where firm 1 takes as given firm 2's entry. Its programme will be

$$\max_{x_1} \pi_1 = \frac{(1 - c + 2x_1)^2}{9} - x_1^2.$$ (7.39)

From $\partial \pi_1 / \partial x_1 = 0$, and further substitutions, we obtain

$$x_1^{inn} = \frac{2(1-c)}{5}; \qquad q_1^{inn} = \frac{3(1-c)}{5}; \qquad q_2^{inn} = \frac{(1-c)}{5}; \qquad p^{inn} = \frac{1+4c}{5};$$ (7.40)

corresponding profits for firms 1 and 2 respectively are

$$\pi_1^{inn} = \frac{(1-c)^2}{5}; \qquad \pi_2^{inn} = \frac{(1-c)^2}{25} - F.$$ (7.41)

Therefore, firm 2 would enter the market as long as $F \leq (1 - c)^2 / 25$. In the words of Bain (1956), if $F > (1 - c)^2 / 25$, entry would be blockaded: there would be no need for firm 1 to behave strategically in its technology choice: firm 2 would not enter.

Strategic Behaviour   Observing firm 2's profits one can notice that they decrease with the investment of firm 1: $\Pi_2^c(x_1) = (1 - c - x_1)^2 / 9 - F$. Call x_1^P the level of investment such that $\Pi_2^c(x_1^P) = 0$. It is easy to see that

$$x_1^P = 1 - c - 3\sqrt{F}.$$ (7.42)

For a level of investment slightly above x_1^P, firm 2 will prefer to stay out of the market, as it would not be able to recover its fixed costs if it entered.

To see the intuition behind the existence of such a level of investment at which entry is deterred, consider Figure 7.5. The solid lines represent the reaction functions of the two firms absent investments by firm 1. Expressions (7.37) reveal that they are negatively sloped and that an increase in x_1 shifts firm 1's reaction function to the right. The figure also draws the iso-profits of firm 2: the closer to the vertical axis (where $q_1 = 0$) the higher firm 2's profits. By appropriately selecting its investment levels, firm 1 can therefore move the equilibrium to the right, up to the point where firm 2's profit is just a shade short of covering its fixed cost F. In other words, if firm 1 chooses the investment level x_1^P, it will move its reaction function from R_1 to $R_1(x_1^P)$ and firm 2 will prefer not to enter.

So far, I have proved only that entry deterrence is *feasible*: by choosing a level slightly above x_1^P, firm 2 would be deterred from entering. But is such a strategy

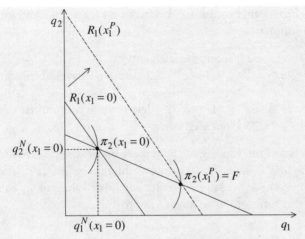

Figure 7.5. Entry-deterring R&D investment.

profitable? To see if this is so, note first that by investing x_1^P firm 1 would be a monopolist. Therefore

$$q_1^P = 1 - c - \frac{3\sqrt{F}}{2}; \qquad p^P = c + \frac{3\sqrt{F}}{2}; \qquad \pi_1^P = \frac{12(1-c)\sqrt{F} - 25F}{4}.$$
(7.43)

The question is then whether by behaving strategically (that is, preying) firm 1 will obtain higher profits than by accommodating firm 2. This happens if $\pi_1^P > \pi_1^{inn}$. By rearranging, one has that

$$\pi_1^P - \pi_1^{inn} > 0 \Leftrightarrow 125F - 60(1-c)\sqrt{F} + 4(1-c)^2 < 0. \qquad (7.44)$$

By setting $\sqrt{F} = \phi$, one has a standard second-order equation which is solved for $2(1-c)/25 < \phi < 2(1-c)/5$, or $4(1-c)^2/625 < F < 4(1-c)^2/25$. Note that the second root is beyond the interval we are considering. Therefore, we can conclude the analysis by saying that

- $F \leq 4(1-c)^2/625$, there is accommodated entry.
- $4(1-c)^2/625 < F \leq (1-c)^2/25$, there is deterred entry.
- $F > 4(1-c)^2/25$, there is blockaded entry.

Is Entry Deterrence Anti-Competitive? There is still an important point to be clarified. Suppose that $4(1-c)^2/625 < F \leq (1-c)^2/25$, so that incumbent firm 1 does engage in entry-deterrence behaviour by strategically over-investing in process innovation. Does such behaviour harm consumers? Is the price under entry deterrence higher than under accommodated entry? This is not the case if $p^P \leq p^{inn}$, or $F \leq 4(1-c)^2/225$. For low-enough values of the fixed cost F, entry deterrence is possible and profitable, but firm 1 has to invest so much to pre-empt entry that it becomes so efficient that consumers are better off than if the entrant was accommodated. To summarise:

- $F \leq 4(1-c)^2/625$: accommodated entry.
- $4(1-c)^2/625 < F \leq 4(1-c)^2/225$: deterred entry; but consumer surplus is higher.
- $4(1-c)^2/225 < F \leq (1-c)^2/25$: deterred entry; consumer surplus is lower.
- $F > 4(1-c)^2/25$: blockaded entry.

Note that here I am looking at the impact on prices (i.e., consumer surplus) rather than on total welfare. This is just to avoid unnecessary calculations: Looking at total welfare would give similar results: for some values of F, entry would be deterred but this turns out to be welfare-improving.

7.3.2 Bundling and Tying

In many situations, a product is offered by a seller under the condition that another product is also bought, a phenomenon which is called *tie-in sales*. For instance, your favourite newspaper might come with a "trends and fashion" supplement on Sundays, and you will be forced to pay a higher price for your newspaper that day (compared to the regular weekdays when the newspaper does not have a supplement) even though you might not be interested in trends and fashion. However, there are also less obvious examples of tying which show how widespread the phenomenon is: a travel agent might sell a plane ticket only together with the purchase of a hotel accommodation; a car manufacturer sells a car as a whole, and does not sell separately tyres, air-conditioning, engine, seats and car body; shoes are sold with laces, computers might include both OS and application software, and so on. All these are instances of *bundling* (or *package tie-in*): different goods are sold together in *fixed proportions*.[64]

A different class of examples pertains to so-called *requirements tying*, that occurs when a seller requires the buyer to purchase not only a certain good, but also all the units that the latter wishes to buy of another good: here the two goods are sold together in *variable proportions*. For instance, a mobile phone company might want to sell you the mobile telephone set only under the condition that you make all the phone calls from that same company and not from those of other operators, or a photocopier company might sell a copy machine only if one agrees to buy toner only from it.

This section analyses why firms might want to use tie-in sales (I use indifferently the terms tying and tie-in sales), and what are the likely effects of such business

---

[64] To be more precise, these are instances of pure bundling. *Mixed bundling* occurs when a firm offers consumers the choice between a bundle and separate products or components. For instance, a restaurant might offer both a fixed menu and the possibility to order *à la carte*.

strategies. Section 7.3.2.1 shows that tying often has a very natural efficiency ratio-nale (and therefore has pro-competitive effects). But there are two possible reasons why tying might decrease welfare. The first (Section 7.3.2.2) is that it allows firms to price discriminate across consumers with different preferences (this is true for both bundling and requirements tying). Unfortunately, as for price discrimination in general (see Section 7.4), the welfare effects of tie-in practices are ambiguous. The second (Section 7.3.2.3) deals with the old contention that by tying sales of two products, a monopolist in one product might be able to extend its monopoly onto a second product market. Chicago School thinking maintained that this would be unprofitable, but recent models of tying indicate strategic reasons why tying might allow monopolisation in a second market. Section 7.3.2.4 presents the main policy conclusions from the analysis.

7.3.2.1 Efficiency Reasons for Tying

In some cases, selling components together has obvious efficiency justifications. For instance, assembling all the different parts that compose a computer is much more costly for a typical consumer than for a computer maker that can rely on specialised personnel and appropriate machines; it would be time-consuming to buy separately shoes and laces, or the different parts of a car, and having to assemble them. Therefore, in many cases the principles of *division of labour* and *scale economies* imply that it is more efficient that certain components are marketed together rather than separately.

In other cases, tying different components or products together might also be an efficient response to *asymmetric information*. Imagine for instance that a computer would work at its best only with certain components, or that driving a car with another type of tyres than the ones recommended by the producer might become dangerous, or a copy machine would give poor copies without a specific type of toner. Then firms might wish to incorporate the right components or parts into the final product, to overcome possible reputation problems that would arise if the consumers did not combine them properly. Such a practice would be profitable for the firm but would also be efficient: consumers enjoy the highest possible quality of the products they buy.

Of course, when assessing efficiency gains, one should take into account that tying might not always be the only available way to overcome information problems. For instance, a car manufacturer could specify which types of tyres should be installed on its cars, the computer maker could point out which components should or should not be installed on its computer, and the copy producer could indicate which toner can be used in its photocopy machine. Sometimes this would solve the problem, in others they would not, it depends on the specific case.

In a widely cited US case on tying in the old-generation computer sector, *International Business Machines Corporation v. US*, IBM claimed that its requirement

Table 7.1. Consumers' Valuations of Goods

	1's willingness to pay	2's willingness to pay
Good A	7	4
Good B	5	8
Goods A and B	12	12

that customers should use only IBM punch-cards for IBM computers was justified on quality grounds: poor cards might have led to malfunctioning and jamming of its computers, with a loss in its reputation. However, the Supreme Court found that IBM could have solved the possible quality problem by either properly publicising the higher quality of its cards, or making leases conditional on a minimum standard requirement for cards to be used with IBM machines.[65]

7.3.2.2 Tying as a Price Discrimination Device

Even if none of the previous technological or informational justifications exist, firms might still have other reasons to use tie-in sales. In particular, both bundling and requirements tying allow firms to increase profits by working as a price discrimination device, as explained in what follows.

Bundling   Consider a very simple example where a monopolist sells two goods, call them A and B, to two consumers, 1 and 2. Consumer 1 has a maximum willingness to pay 7 for good A and 5 for good B. Consumer 2 has a maximum willingness to pay 4 for good A and 8 for good B (see illustration in Table 7.1). Assume also that the monopolist knows their willingness to pay but cannot charge different prices to them (for instance, because it is illegal), that consumers buy at most one unit of each good, and that for simplicity's sake the monopolist's production cost is zero.

If the monopolist sells the two products separately, it will choose the price of A to equal 4 and sell to both consumers, making a profit of 8 on good A (if it sold at 7, it would sell only one unit and have a profit of 7); and it would sell B at 5, making a profit of 10 on B (by selling at 8, it would sell only one unit and make lower profits). In total, it would gain 18.

If instead the monopolist sold the two products as a bundle, it could charge a bundle price of 12, and since both consumers would buy, its total profits would be 24. Clearly, bundling allows it to extract more surplus from consumers and increase profits.

[65] For more on this case and other examples of tie-in sales, see Scherer and Ross (1990: 562–9).

There have been several contributions in the economic literature trying to understand under which conditions firms have an incentive to bundle. More interestingly for our purpose, however, is to notice that the welfare implications from such a bundling practice are ambiguous:[66] one can devise examples where bundling increases welfare and others where it decreases it.[67]

Requirements Tying as a Metering Device   Sometimes consumers use a certain product in a more or less intensive way. For instance, some might use a copy machine very often, while others use it only occasionally, which would reflect itself in a different willingness to pay for the photocopier.[68] When this happens, a firm might want to have a metering device, which is a way to sort consumers according to their intensity of use (and therefore willingness to pay), and make them pay accordingly so as to extract as much surplus as possible from them. Ideally, the firm would like to measure intensity of use directly. However, if the copy machine producer requires consumers to buy toner only from it, this would effectively work as a measure of intensity of demand, since the more often one makes copies the more frequently one needs to replace the toner cartridges. The firm can then keep the price of the copy machine low (so as to attract people with lower intensity of demand to buy it) and charge a higher price on each unit of the complementary good (the toner cartridges) so as to extract surplus according to the willingness to pay of consumers.[69]

While it is clear that tie-in sales benefit the firm, the welfare effects are ambiguous. It can be shown that if all consumers buy both when there is tying and when it is banned, then welfare will be lower under tying. However, the tying strategy might allow sales to some consumers who would otherwise not buy the good (that is, it might increase demand), and cause a net positive effect on welfare. (See technical Section 7.3.2.5 for a formal analysis.)

So far, in view of the facts that tying might well have important efficiency effects, and that even in the absence of an efficiency rationale its impact on welfare is *a priori* ambiguous,[70] there would be little economic basis for a harsh treatment of

---

[66] Bundling here works very much like price discrimination (see Section 7.4), whose welfare impact is also *a priori* unclear.

[67] See Adams and Yellen (1976). One reason why more insightful conclusions on the welfare effects of bundling are not available is that it is difficult to analyse bundling with general hypotheses on consumers' preferences.

[68] Scherer and Ross (1990, Chapter 15) use the same example.

[69] This is a very similar price discrimination mechanism as that used by a seller which offers two-part tariffs (in turn equivalent to quantity discounts): by using a fixed fee and a variable component in its price, it manages to extract surplus from consumers with different intensities of demand. See Section 7.4.1.

[70] Note that, so far, tying works in a very similar way as price discrimination (see Section 7.4 below). However, an efficiency defence might possibly exist for tying, but is less likely for price discrimination (quantity discounts might be associated with savings in transaction costs and scale economies).

tying. Before drawing any conclusion, however, we should look into the possible exclusionary effects of tying.

7.3.2.3 Exclusionary Tying in Recent Models

The first author to offer a convincing explanation about why exclusionary tying might be profitable is Whinston (1990) (see Section 7.3.2.6 for a formal analysis). He shows that an incumbent monopolist in a market for product A that commits to bundling it with an independent product B can exclude a competitor from the latter market. This is because the commitment to sell the two products together effectively acts as a commitment to be more aggressive in market B: the incumbent knows that every consumer who prefers to buy the rival's version of product B is also a consumer who will not buy its product A (on which there are high margins since it is a monopolist).[71] In turn, fiercer competition in the market will decrease the rival's profits with respect to the case where the incumbent does not bundle its sales, and might force it to leave the industry if the reduced profits are not large enough to cover fixed costs. (Note also that more aggressive competition would decrease the incumbent firm's profits as well, if the rival continued to be active: I shall come back to the implication of this point.)

Note, however, that the exclusion of the rival is not necessarily profitable for firm 1: if it has committed to selling the products as a bundle, it might well be that some consumers who would have bought A only in combination with the rival's variety of B would not buy the bundle at all; this might happen, for instance, if they do not value A very highly, and if they much prefer the rival's version of product B. In other words, if the incumbent is selling a poor quality version of product B, it seems unlikely that – even if it can exclude the superior quality rival's product – the incumbent would find it profitable.

It is important to stress that the exclusionary effects of this mechanism take place as long as the bundle has commitment value, that is if the incumbent can irreversibly commit to selling the two products together, for instance by product design or in the technological process. Otherwise, exclusion would not occur: the rival knows that, if it entered or it stayed in the market, the incumbent would reverse its bundling decision, as it also earns lower profits when both firms are active (remember, bundling implies more aggressive competition, and this destroys profits if both firms are in the market).

Note also that in this model tying does not have by assumption any efficiency role (this is done to stress the possibility of anti-competitive effects). When assessing welfare in practice, however, one should keep in mind that tying might have efficiency

---

[71] Although under bundling the incumbent just sets a single price for the two products sold together, everything works as if it sold product B independently but it had a lower cost, that is the true unit cost of producing B minus the unit margin on product A sales. And a lower cost implies a more aggressive market behaviour.

effects that enhance consumer utility directly, and that might outweigh its exclusionary effect. In other words, an efficiency defence should be allowed to the incumbent monopolist that allegedly used tying to exclude competitors.[72]

Whinston also shows that when goods are complements, exclusion is in general not profitable. Continue the example above, but suppose now that products A and B are complements in fixed proportions: good A is a necessary product, and no consumer would buy good B alone. In this context, a commitment to bundling would trivially exclude the rival: if A is sold only in combination with the incumbent's variety of product B, nobody would buy rival's product B.

However, by not bundling the incumbent can only do better. Call $\widetilde{p}$ the optimal price of the bundle under monopoly. Suppose that when it does not bundle the incumbent chooses for market B a price p_B equal to c_B, its marginal cost of producing B, and for market A a price p_A equal to $\widetilde{p} - c_B$. Given this pricing policy, two cases might happen. Consider first the case where the rival is not active in the market. In this case, the only thing that matters for consumers is the sum of the prices of the two goods, and the incumbent will do just as well as with the bundle, since $p_A + p_B$ equals $\widetilde{p}$ (both price and demand are the same as under bundling).

Consider next the case where the rival is active when the incumbent does not bundle and uses the above pricing policy. In general, there will be two effects from the presence of the rival. (a) Some consumers who were buying from the incumbent will switch to the rival (others stay with the incumbent). But this does not reduce the incumbent's profits: it will still sell product A to all consumers (those who buy B from it and those who buy B from the rival), and make on them the same margin as $(\widetilde{p} - c_B) - c_A$ as when it sells under bundling. Lost demand on B's products does not amount to lost profits, though: B is sold at unit cost under the pricing scheme above, so profits on B are zero anyway. (b) Some consumers who were not buying from the incumbent under bundling will instead start to buy when an alternative choice of B exists. Clearly, this effect increases the incumbent's profits, since it attracts to product A additional demand (on which the incumbent makes positive profits).

Whinston (1990) finds two specific examples where an incumbent profitably uses tying to exclude competitors in a complementary market: one where product A is not essential, the other where an inferior alternative to product A exists. Overall, however, complementarity makes it less likely (albeit not impossible) that an incumbent will use tying for exclusionary purposes.

Choi and Stefanadis (2001) also consider complementary products (see technical Section 7.3.2.7). In their paper, an incumbent firm is monopolising both

---

[72] Whinston (1990: 845) also points out that, even when it does exclude and it is profitable, tying is not necessarily welfare detrimental: consumers will lose from it (monopoly prices under bundling will probably be higher, and less variety of product B is on offer), but in principle this adverse effect on welfare might be outweighed by the saved fixed costs of the rival. This presumes, however, that there might be excess of entry in the market from a social welfare point of view: an occurrence that is theoretically possible but it has no clear application, as it is impossible to verify empirically.

components, and faces an entrant in each market. Each potential entrant can enter the market for one component if it has a successful innovation. However, innovating involves an initial fixed investment, and it is therefore risky. In this context, if the incumbent commits to bundling, entry in one component market is possible only if both innovations are simultaneously successful (when the incumbent is bundling, if only one entrant obtains the innovation it will have no demand since the goods are complements). Therefore, bundling reduces the incentives to invest and consequently it will be less likely that innovations will appear, and that entrants will oust the incumbent.[73]

Even in this model, however, it is not always clear that the incumbent will find it profitable to tie sales of the two goods. On the one hand, tying would avoid being forced out if both rivals were simultaneously successful; on the other hand, it would decrease the profit the incumbent makes were only one rival successful. In the latter case, indeed, it would gain from the rival's investment, since it will use the monopoly power it has on the other component to extract some of the rent created by the rival's innovation.

Carlton and Waldman (2002) present a similar mechanism whereby tying would allow an incumbent to deter entry in a complementary market B in order to protect its monopoly in market A.[74] Initially, the incumbent faces a potential entrant in market B; only subsequently can another firm decide on entering market A. By tying A and B, the incumbent could deter the first entrant in the B market (this happens as long as it is sufficiently uncertain that there will be future entry in market A), which in turn makes it less likely that the second entrant wishes to enter the A market (because the incumbent would be the only producer of the complementary product).

Both in Carlton and Waldman (2002) and in Choi and Stefanadis (2001) the basic mechanism of exclusion is the same, in that entry in one market is made dependent on the success of entry in a complementary market. This mechanism reminds us of the papers where exclusive dealing deters entry exploiting externalities among buyers (see Chapter 6). Here there are also externalities among the potential entrants, which begs the question of what happens when the entrants can coordinate. (In Choi and Stefanadis the entrants can belong to the same firm, but probabilities of success in the two markets are still independent, a hard assumption to make. It would seem

---

[73] Exclusionary tying in the presence of R&D investments is also considered in Choi (1996). Farrell and Katz (2000) look at incentives to invest, and resulting welfare effects, when a monopolist in a component is also present in a competitive complementary market (their analysis does not necessarily refer to tying).

[74] The model therefore tells a story which is reminiscent of US v. Microsoft (see Section 7.5), where Microsoft was alleged to tie Internet Explorer, its internet browser, with its operating system (OS), Windows, to force exit of Netscape Navigator and preserve Microsoft's monopoly in the OS market.

reasonable to expect that there exists correlation among the probabilities of success when the same firm contests entry in both markets.)[75]

In all these models, tying can have its strategic (exclusionary) effects only to the extent that it really involves a credible commitment, as for instance bundling directly in the product design or in the way production is carried out. If bundling is obtained through marketing or packaging decisions that can be easily reversed, then the commitment effect is absent (and no strategic effect exists). For instance, these models could not have been invoked in two often-mentioned US cases: *Times-Picayune v. US*, and *United Shoe v. US*. In the first case, a New Orleans publisher that had the only morning newspaper was tying sales of advertising space in that newspaper with advertising in its evening newspaper (where it faced other competitors). In the second case, United Shoe tied repair services with the leasing of its machinery. In both cases, it would be difficult to argue that there was a technological commitment to bundling (see also Whinston, 1990: 839).

In a more recent EC merger decision, *Boeing/Hughes,* the merging entity would have produced two complementary products, geo-stationary satellite operations and services to launch satellites to their orbit. The Commission considered whether the new entity might have had an interest in engaging in exclusionary tying. It concluded that this was unlikely, among other things because a commitment to offer the two services only in a bundle was unlikely: customers seemed to have a strong preference for flexibility in the choice of launchers, and would not have liked incompatibility of their satellites with all launchers but Boeing's.

7.3.2.4 Practice: Assessment of Tying Practices

As the previous discussion has hinted, the welfare implications of tie-in sales are far from unambiguous, and to deal with them in practice is extremely complex. In most cases, tying will have efficiency effects that will benefit consumers; in a few (probably rare) cases, it might have harmful exclusionary effects that should be balanced with any possible efficiency effects. In some other cases, tie-in sales might be made to price discriminate; in this case the immediate impact on consumer and total surplus is ambiguous even in the absence of any efficiency effect; therefore, it is even less likely to be detrimental when efficiency considerations are present.

Traditionally, tying has been looked upon very suspiciously by anti-trust authorities and courts, and for a long time in the US it had a status very close to *per se* prohibition (see Chapter 1). This harsh approach is not justified.

To start with, it would make sense to investigate tying practices only when they are carried out by firms endowed with considerable market power. Since it is the exclusionary effect of tying that one should fear the most, firms that do not have a

---

[75] See also Rey, Seabright and Tirole (2001) for specific criticisms to Carlton and Waldman's model.

dominant position should be free to use tie-in sales as they like. Accordingly, a safe harbour might be prescribed such that firms with market shares of less than, say, 40% in each product market involved will not be investigated.

This approach might seem generous at first sight, but it is justified by the number of possible efficiency effects that derive from tying: consumers gain in many cases where they do not have to bother assembling products themselves, or look for different suppliers to collect the different components they want, and so on. Tying might therefore allow a non-dominant firm to become more competitive, resulting in a positive welfare effect.

Particularly instructive in this respect is the *Ilford* case, where UK authorities stopped Ilford from bundling sales of photographic films with their development, speeding up its downfall with respect to Kodak. In the mid-60s, the colour film market was dominated by Kodak worldwide. In the UK, Kodak had around 80% of sales, with Ilford holding less than 15% market share. One of the reasons why Ilford found it difficult to catch up with Kodak was due to (indirect) network effects: Ilford used a processing system that differed from the dominant Kodak's, and this represented an obstacle to its diffusion with independent processors. Ilford's response to this problem was to sell film with processing included. A customer would buy the film and after taking pictures would send back the exposed film to Ilford, which would process it in its laboratories and then send it back to the customer. Following a complaint by independent processors that this practice would have reduced the demand for their services, the Monopolies and Mergers Commission found the tying of film and processing to be anti-competitive in 1966. As Sutton (1998: 126) puts it, "this finding greatly increased Ilford's problems. The independents could not easily process the company's film, and this appears to have been the last straw for Ilford's retail business. . . . Ilford withdrew its brand from the color film market in 1968".

When a firm does not pass the first screening test and it has market shares above that certain threshold, a full investigation should weigh possible anti-competitive effects against possible efficiency reasons behind the practice. Note that theory tells us that the higher the complementarity between the products the less likely it is that tying will be used for exclusionary purposes, so allegations of monopolisation when a firm bundles two fully complementary products should be received with more scepticism. Theory also says that exclusionary effects are more likely when there is a credible commitment to bundling, such as when two previously separate components are combined in a new product design. Therefore, it is less likely to have exclusionary effects when, for instance, two products are sold together but this marketing decision is reversible. However, when such a commitment exists, it is far from automatic that it will have detrimental effects. Furthermore, extreme care should be taken in this case because stopping a tying practice amounts to intervening and modifying the product design of a good.

7.3.2.5 Models of Tying, I: Requirements Tying as a Metering Device*

In this section, I show that a monopolist of an essential good A has an incentive to tie the use of a complementary good B, whose demand intensity differs across consumers.[76] The welfare consequences of tying will be ambiguous.[77]

A consumer of type $i = l, h$ who buys one unit of product A and q units of product B has the following utility function:

$$U_i = q - \frac{q^2}{2v_i}. \tag{7.45}$$

Consuming the goods separately gives zero utility, and buying more than one unit of good A does not add to utility. Type-l consumers have lower intensity of demand ($v_l < v_h$) and are a share λ of the population (of size 1 for simplicity), $1 - \lambda$ being the share of type-h consumers.

Good A is monopolised by firm 1, whereas several firms having identical technology – including firm 1 – are involved in the production of good B. The cost of producing one unit of the products are respectively c_A and $c_B < 1$. There are no fixed costs.

To look at the effects (requirements) of tying first consider the case where firm 1 sells separately goods A and B. Assume that there is price competition in the B market.

No Tying (If All Consumers Buy)   Suppose first all consumers buy. Demand of type-i consumers is obtained as $\max_q U_i - p_A - p_B q$. By setting $\partial U_i / \partial q = 0$, one has

$$q_i = v_i(1 - p_B). \tag{7.46}$$

A type-i consumer will then buy good A if its surplus $CS_i = U_i - p_A - p_B q_i$ is non-negative or, after substitution, if $CS_i = v_i(1 - p_B)^2/2 - p_A \geq 0$.

Price competition on the good B market implies that $p_B = c_B$. Therefore, in the case where firm 1 chooses prices so that all consumers buy, it must be

$$p_A^{NT} = \frac{v_l(1 - c_B)^2}{2}. \tag{7.47}$$

In this case, type-l consumers will have zero surplus, whereas type-h consumers will have a surplus $CS_h^{NT} = (v_h - v_l)(1 - c_B)^2/2$.

---

[76] Note that complements here are not used in fixed proportions, unlike the case I analyse below in Section 7.3.2.6.

[77] I follow here Tirole (1988: 142–8) quite closely, with a different utility function that gives rise to slightly simpler calculations.

Producer surplus equals firm 1's profits from good A: $\pi^{NT} = v_l(1 - c_B)^2/2 - c_A$. Welfare will therefore be equal to

$$W^{NT} = \frac{((1 - \lambda)\,v_h + \lambda v_l)(1 - c_B)^2}{2} - c_A. \tag{7.48}$$

No Tying (Only High Types Buy)   Firm 1 might prefer to serve only high-type consumers, though, fixing a price that allows to extract all surplus from them and leaves consumers with lower intensity of demand unserved:

$$p_A^{NTh} = \frac{v_h(1 - c_B)^2}{2}. \tag{7.49}$$

In this case, both types will have zero surplus: $CS^{NTh} = 0$, and producer surplus is $\pi^{NTh} = (1 - \lambda)\left[v_h(1 - c_B)^2/2 - c_A\right] = W^{NTh}$.

Selling only to high types is profitable as long as $\pi^{NTh} > \pi^{NT}$, which is the more likely the smaller the proportion of low-type consumers and the higher the difference in demand intensities. Formally, this strategy is profitable if

$$\lambda < \frac{(v_h - v_l)(1 - c_B)^2}{v_h(1 - c_B)^2 - 2c_A}. \tag{7.50}$$

Tying   Consider now the case where firm 1 requires consumers who want to buy good A also to buy good B from it. Assume also, and it is a strong assumption, that it is endowed with some technology that allows it to monitor consumers' purchases of good B, and to prevent them from addressing competitors to buy good B after having bought one unit of good A with a symbolic quantity of B.

Recalling that demand of product B is given by equation (7.46), firm 1's profits are

$$\pi = (p_B - c_B)\left[\lambda v_l(1 - p_B) + (1 - \lambda)\,v_h(1 - p_B)\right] + p_A - c_A. \tag{7.51}$$

From $\partial\pi/\partial p_B = 0$, one obtains

$$p_B^T = \frac{(1 - \lambda)(v_h - v_l) + c_B\left[\lambda v_l + (1 - \lambda)\,v_h\right]}{2v_h - v_l - 2\lambda(v_h - v_l)}, \tag{7.52}$$

where it is easy to check that $p_B^T > c_B$. (Therefore, it is crucial that firm 1 is able to prevent consumers from buying good B from competitors.) As for the price of good A, note that profits increase with it, but consumers will buy as long as $CS_i = v_i(1 - p_B^T)^2/2 - p_A \geq 0$. After replacement, one obtains the optimal price for good A:

$$p_A^T = \frac{(1 - c_B)^2 v_l\left[\lambda v_l + (1 - \lambda)\,v_h\right]^2}{2\left[2v_h - v_l - 2\lambda(v_h - v_l)\right]^2}, \tag{7.53}$$

which can be either bigger or smaller than c_A. Note that here tying works in a very similar way as a two-part tariff scheme $T + pq$ that segments consumers according to their intensity of demand.[78] Here, the fixed fee part of the tariff, T, corresponds to p_A^T, that is the price of one unit of the (essential) good A, whereas the variable part of the tariff corresponds to the price p_B^T of one unit of good B. The lower the intensity of demand of a consumer the lower the number of units of good B he will buy from the monopolist, as $q_i = v_i(1 - p_B^T)$, and therefore the lower the total amount paid to it.

Firm 1's profits under tying are

$$\pi^T = \frac{(1 - c_B)^2 \left[\lambda v_l + (1 - \lambda) v_h\right]^2}{2 \left[2v_h - v_l - 2\lambda(v_h - v_l)\right]} - c_A. \tag{7.54}$$

Type-l consumers have zero surplus, whereas type-h consumer surplus is

$$CS_h^T = \frac{(1 - c_B)^2(v_h - v_l) \left[\lambda v_l + (1 - \lambda) v_h\right]^2}{2 \left[2v_h - v_l - 2\lambda(v_h - v_l)\right]^2}. \tag{7.55}$$

Welfare can be computed as

$$W^T = \frac{(1 - c_B)^2 \left[\lambda v_l + (1 - \lambda) v_h\right]^2 \left[1 + (1 - \lambda)(v_h - v_l)\right]^2}{2 \left[2v_h - v_l - 2\lambda(v_h - v_l)\right]^2}. \tag{7.56}$$

Comparisons of Equilibria (a) Let us first consider the case where both types are served anyhow. One can check that tying is profitable:

$$\pi^T - \pi^{NT} = \frac{(1 - c_B)^2(1 - \lambda)^2(v_h - v_l)^2}{2 \left[2v_h - v_l - 2\lambda(v_h - v_l)\right]} > 0. \tag{7.57}$$

This is not surprising, as it allows the monopolist to impose higher payments from consumers who have a higher intensity of demand, namely, to price discriminate among the two types of consumers. It is also possible to check that tying is detrimental to welfare, as

$$W^{NT} - W^T = \frac{(1 - c_B)^2 (1 - \lambda)(v_h - v_l)^2 \left[\left(1 + \lambda - 2\lambda^2\right) v_h + 2\lambda^2 v_l\right]}{2 \left[2v_h - v_l - 2\lambda(v_h - v_l)\right]^2} > 0. \tag{7.58}$$

Even without doing tedious calculations, one can notice that welfare should be lower under tying. Indeed, if there is no tying, consumers buy at marginal cost, and welfare is therefore the highest possible, whereas tying introduces a source of allocative inefficiency as good B is sold above marginal cost. We have therefore the usual case where a higher price decreases consumer surplus (of high types, since low types have zero surplus in either regime) more than it increases producer surplus.

(b) The above comparisons have been made for the case where both types of consumers buy in the regime where there is no tying. If only high types buy, however,

---

[78] For two-part tariffs as a price discrimination device, see Section 7.4.2.2.

it turns out that tying *increases* welfare. To see that, notice that consumer surplus is positive under tying whereas it is zero when there is no tying and low types do not buy. Therefore, whenever tying is more profitable for firm 1 it will also be welfare improving.

To check that tying might indeed be profitable, and to save on tedious calculations, just consider a simple example where $c_A = c_B = 0$, $v_h = 2$, and $v_l = 1$. For these values, under no tying firm 1 would serve only high types for $\lambda < 1/2$. It is straightforward to check that $\pi^T - \pi^{NTh} > 0$ for $\lambda > 1 - \sqrt{3}/3 = .423$; above this threshold, tying is profitable, and it is welfare improving.

7.3.2.6 Models of Tying, II: Tying, Foreclosure, and Exclusion in Whinston (1990)*

Consider two markets for *independent products* (see below for the complementary products case), A and B, and two firms, 1 and 2. Firm 1 is a monopolist in market A, where it is not challenged, and produces at constant marginal cost c_A. Both firms 1 and 2 are potential entrants in market B. To enter, they have to incur a fixed cost F_1 and F_2, and they can then operate at constant marginal costs respectively equal to c_{B1} and c_{B2}.

The game is composed of three stages. In the first stage, firm 1 decides whether it wants to bundle good A and B1 together, or not.[79] If they are bundled, assume that this decision is irreversible (that is, it has full commitment value). In the second stage, each firm simultaneously decides whether to enter or not market B, and accordingly pays (or not) the fixed cost F. In the third stage, active firms simultaneously set prices: firm 1 either sets a single price $\tilde{p}$ if it has committed to a bundle, or two independent prices p_A and p_{B1};[80] firm 2, if active, sets the price p_{B2}.

A Simple Example of Exclusion with Homogenous Goods* Assume first that consumers have mass one and have valuations (that is, a maximum willingness to pay) $v > c_A$ for product A, and $w > c_{B1} > c_{B2}$ (firm 2 is more efficient than firm 1 in market B) for products $B1$ and $B2$ that in this first example are assumed homogenous. Consumers buy one unit of each good A and B as long as prices are lower than their valuations; otherwise, they do not buy the good. Also assume that firm 1 has already sunk its fixed cost in market B (this is therefore a slight variation

---

[79] Assume also that firm 1 cannot use a *requirements contract*, that is it cannot sell good A only under the condition that a consumer will not buy $B2$ (for instance because firm 1 is unable to observe what consumers buy).

[80] I exclude for simplicity the case where firm 1 does mixed bundling, that is it allows consumers to choose between the bundle or separate prices. However, this is never optimal in this model. The only reason to choose a bundle is for its strategic value: either the firm commits to technologically bundle the products (in which case they cannot be sold separately any longer), or it does not, in which case selling them together is dominated by selling them separately.

of the above-described game, since firm 1 is already active in both markets), whereas firm 2 has not, and that $c_{B1} - c_{B2} > F_2$.

To look for the sub-game perfect Nash equilibrium we move backwards. Two cases should be studied, according to whether in the first stage firm 1 has bundled the goods or not.

Independent Pricing (No Tying)   Since market B products are perfectly homogenous, and firm 2 is more efficient, it will set a price equal to (a shade less than) the marginal cost of firm 1 and get all the market. It will make a profit $c_{B1} - c_{B2}$. Since this is higher than its fixed cost, it will enter the market. Market A is independent, and firm 1 will set $p_A = v$. It will therefore make a total profit $\pi_1 = v - c_A$.

Tying   Suppose now that firm 1 has bundled the two goods A and B1 and sells them at a price $\widetilde{p}$. One can think of this price as $\widetilde{p} = v + \widetilde{p}_{B1}$, where $\widetilde{p}_{B1} = \widetilde{p} - v$ is the *fictitious* price set by firm 1 under bundling (since it would not make sense to charge consumers in market A less than their valuation for it). Since there is Bertrand competition, consumers will buy the bundle from firm 1 if $\widetilde{p}_{B1}$ is a shade less than the marginal cost of firm 2: $\widetilde{p}_{B1} = \widetilde{p} - v = c_{B2} - \varepsilon$. Therefore, with $\widetilde{p} = c_{B2} + v$, no consumer would buy from firm 2.

Since firm 2 observes that firm 1 has bundled the two products (and since this is irreversible), it knows that if it entered it would not be able to recoup its fixed costs (since it would not sell anything). Hence, it stays out.[81]

Finally, note that under bundling and when firm 2 decides not to enter, at the last stage of the game firm 1 will set the bundle price at $\widetilde{p} = v + w$, therefore extracting all the surplus from the consumers, and making a profit $\widetilde{\pi}_1 = v + w - c_A - c_{B1}$.

First Stage   It is now easy to look at the decision between bundling or not at the first stage of the game. Firm 1 will prefer to commit to bundling and tying sales of the two goods if $\widetilde{\pi}_1 > \pi_1$, which is always satisfied since by assumption $w - c_{B1} > 0$. This shows that tying might allow to exclude entry in a profitable way.[82]

Let us now look at a slightly more general case.

The Model with Differentiated Goods in Market B[**]   Assume consumers are located on the $[0, 1]$ line, where they are uniformly distributed with unit density. They can consume at most one unit of good A, for which they have a valuation $v > c_A$, and one unit of good B. The net utility they derive from buying variety $i = 1, 2$ of good B is given by $U_{Bi} = w - t_i \mid x - x_{Bi} \mid - p_{Bi}$, where $w > \max(c_{B1}, c_{B2})$ is the maximum valuation for good B, t_i measures the disutility parameter of buying

---

[81] Note that this equilibrium occurs only if the bundle profit under duopoly is positive: $v + c_{B2} - c_A - c_{B1} > 0$, otherwise firm 1 would be better off not selling at all in case firm 2 entered.

[82] This example is not suitable to study welfare effects of tying, since it involves the special case of perfectly inelastic demands. Exclusion just shifts the surplus between firms and between firms and consumers. Further, it has the beneficial effect of saving the fixed cost of entry of firm 2 (goods are perfectly homogeneous, so consumers do not value variety here), so its overall impact is positive.

a variety located in x_{Bi} for a consumer located in x.[83] I assume that $x_{B1} = 0$ and $x_{B2} = 1$. This is a simple Hotelling model (see Chapter 8) where location should not necessarily be intended in physical terms.[84]

The game is the one described at the beginning of the section, and its solution is found by backward induction.

Independent Pricing (No Tying)   To find the solution of the price game, in the case where firm 2 has entered, one first has to derive the demand functions for goods B1 and B2 (in this case, A is sold independently, so it does not affect the game in market B). A consumer located at x will prefer to buy product B1 if $U_{B1} \geq U_{B2}$, or: $w - t_1 x - p_{B1} \geq w - t_2(1 - x) - p_{B2}$. Define x_{12} as the location of the consumer indifferent between buying from B1 or B2, such that

$$x_{12}(p_{B1}, p_{B2}) \equiv \frac{t_2 + p_{B2} - p_{B1}}{t_2 + t_1}. \tag{7.59}$$

All consumers located between 0 and x_{12} will prefer variety B1. Those located between x_{12} and 1 will prefer B2. Therefore, demand functions will be $q_{B1} = x_{12}(p_{B1}, p_{B2})$ and $q_{B2} = 1 - x_{12}(p_{B1}, p_{B2})$. Profit functions are

$$\pi_{B1} = (p_{B1} - c_{B1})\frac{t_2 + p_{B2} - p_{B1}}{t_2 + t_1}; \qquad \pi_{B2} = (p_{B2} - c_{B2})\left(\frac{t_1 + p_{B1} - p_{B2}}{t_2 + t_1}\right). \tag{7.60}$$

Set the first derivatives equal to zero ($\partial \pi_{Bi}/\partial p_{Bi} = 0$) and write the reaction functions of the two firms in the plane (p_{B2}, p_{B1}):

$$R_{B1}: p_{B1} = \frac{t_2 + c_{B1} + p_{B2}}{2}; \qquad R_{B2}: p_{B1} = 2p_{B2} - c_{B2} - t_1. \tag{7.61}$$

From the intersection of the two reaction functions we find the equilibrium prices and (after substitution) profits in the no-tying price game:

$$p_{Bi}^* = \frac{t_i + 2t_j + c_{Bj} + 2c_{Bi}}{3}; \qquad \pi_{Bi}^* = \frac{(t_i + 2t_j + c_{Bj} + 2c_{Bi})^2}{9(t_i + t_j)}$$

$$\text{(for } i, j = 1, 2, i \neq j). \tag{7.62}$$

As for market A, it is clear that firm 1 will set its price as to extract all the surplus from consumers in that market: $p_A = v$. The total profits under the independent pricing (no tying) game for firm 1 will then be $\pi_1^* = (v - c_A) + \pi_{Bi}^*$.

Tying   When firm 1 has irreversibly bundled the two goods A and B1, market A is clearly not independent from B any longer, as the firm chooses a unique price $\tilde{p}$ for the whole bundle, rather than two separate prices. A consumer x now has the

---

[83] For $t_1 = t_2 = t$, we have the standard Hotelling game.
[84] This model differs from the examples chosen by Whinston in his paper, but it reproduces his main results and shares a similarity with his examples.

choice between buying either the bundle A/B1, or variety B2 alone. (Note that if a consumer buys variety B2, this implies one lost sale of good A for firm 1.) She will prefer the bundle A/B1 if $\widetilde{U} \geq U_{B2}$, or: $v + w - t_1 x - \widetilde{p} \geq w - t_2(1-x) - p_{B2}$. In order to have both firms selling at a bundling equilibrium assume:

(A1) $0 < v - c_A < t_2 + 2t_1 + c_{B1} - c_{B2}$, and
(A2) $v - c_A > -2t_2 - t_1 + c_{B1} - c_{B2}$.

The consumer indifferent between A/B1 and B2 is at

$$\widetilde{x}_{12}(\widetilde{p}, p_{B2}) \equiv \frac{t_2 + p_{B2} + v - \widetilde{p}}{t_2 + t_1}. \tag{7.63}$$

Therefore, demand functions will be $\widetilde{q} = \widetilde{x}_{12}(\widetilde{p}, p_{B2})$ and $q_{B2} = 1 - \widetilde{x}_{12}(\widetilde{p}, p_{B2})$. Profit functions are

$$\widetilde{\pi} = (\widetilde{p} - c_A - c_{B1})\frac{v + t_2 + p_{B2} - \widetilde{p}}{t_2 + t_1};$$

$$\pi_{B2} = (p_{B2} - c_{B2})\left(\frac{v + t_1 + \widetilde{p} - p_{B2}}{t_2 + t_1}\right). \tag{7.64}$$

From $\partial \pi_{Bi}/\partial p_{Bi} = 0$, the reaction functions are

$$R_1 : \widetilde{p} = \frac{v + c_A + t_2 + c_{B1} + p_{B2}}{2}; \qquad R_2 : \widetilde{p} = 2p_{B2} - c_{B2} + v - t_1. \tag{7.65}$$

Solving the system we find the equilibrium prices under tying:

$$\widetilde{p}^* = \frac{t_1 + 2t_2 + c_{B2} + 2c_{B1} + v + 2c_A}{3};$$

$$\widetilde{p}_{B2}^* = \frac{t_2 + 2t_1 + c_{B1} + 2c_{B2} - v + c_A}{3}, \tag{7.66}$$

and by replacement the equilibrium profits:

$$\widetilde{\pi}_1^* = \frac{(t_1 + 2t_2 + c_{B2} - c_{B1} + v - c_A)^2}{9(t_1 + t_2)};$$

$$\widetilde{\pi}_{B2}^* = \frac{(t_2 + 2t_1 + c_{B1} - c_{B2} - v + c_A)^2}{9(t_1 + t_2)}. \tag{7.67}$$

Profit Comparisons and Interpretation of the Results   First of all, it is straightforward to see that bundling by firm 1 hurts rival firm 2: $\pi_{B2}^* > \widetilde{\pi}_{B2}^*$, as $v > c_A$. However, note that bundling also hurts firm 1 if firm 2 enters the market. To see this, first check that

$$\widetilde{\pi}_1^* < \pi_1^* \text{ iff } v - c_A < 5t_2 + 7t_1 + 2c_{B1} - 2c_{B2}. \tag{7.68}$$

Then, note that for inequality (7.68) to be compatible with assumption (A2), it must be $7t_2 + 8t_1 + c_{B1} - c_{B2} > 0$, which is always satisfied by assumption (A1).

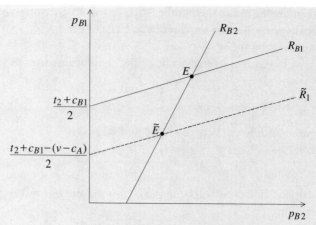

Figure 7.6. Strategic effect of bundling.

To sum up, conditional on firm 2 being active, both firms would be worse off by bundling. Therefore, for bundling to be chosen by firm 1, it must be that it deters entry of firm 2. Before showing the conditions under which this occurs, let us interpret the results obtained: Why does bundling depress profits of both competitors?

To see this, it is useful to think of $\tilde{p}$ as composed of two fictional prices: the price on market A (that can only be equal to v, since firm 1 is monopolist on that market) and the price in market B:

$$\tilde{p} = v + \tilde{p}_{B1}. \tag{7.69}$$

By replacing this expression in the reaction functions (7.65), we can write them in the plane $(\tilde{p}_{B1}, p_{B2})$, as

$$\tilde{R}_1 : \tilde{p}_{B1} = \frac{t_2 + c_{B1} + p_{B2} - (v - c_A)}{2}; \qquad R_2 : \tilde{p}_{B1} = 2p_{B2} - c_{B2} - t_1. \tag{7.70}$$

As Figure 7.6 shows, and as easily checked from comparing expressions (7.61) and (7.70), bundling shifts downwards, from R_{B1} to $\tilde{R}_1$, the reaction function of firm 1 when it competes in market B. In other words, bundling represents a credible commitment for firm 1 to be more aggressive when it competes in that market, because it knows that any lost sale in market B is lost profit $(v - c_A)$ in market A. As a result, equilibrium prices and profits will be lower for both firms under tying.

Entry Decisions   Firm 2 will enter market B if and only if its profits offset its fixed costs. It is then straightforward to see that there are parameter values where it would enter if firm 1 did not use tying, but it would not enter if it committed to tying. This occurs if $\pi_{B2}^* \geq F > \tilde{\pi}_{B2}^*$. This is also the case where firm 1 might find it profitable to bundle, as we show next.

Bundling Decisions   At the first stage of the game, firm 1 decides on bundling. The previous comparison between profits shows that if firm 2 is expected to enter, bundling is unprofitable. Therefore, when $F \leq \tilde{\pi}_{B2}^*$, the equilibrium is such that firm 1 does not bundle, and firm 2 enters.

However, it does not follow *a priori* that firm 1 necessarily wants to bundle when it expects firm 2 not to enter. Bundling is optimal only if the monopoly profit under bundling, π_m, (remember, the firm commits to bundling, so it cannot reverse the decision when firm 2 decides not to sink its entry costs) is higher than the duopoly profit when there is no bundling, π_1^*. To find the former profit, note that a consumer located in x will decide to buy the bundle rather than not buying at all, if $U_m = v + w - t_1 x - \tilde{p}_m \geq 0$. Therefore, the indifferent consumer will be at $x_m = (v + w - \tilde{p}_m)/t_1$. There are two cases according to whether $x_m < 1$ (the market is not covered) or $x_m \geq 1$ (the market is covered: all consumers buy the bundle):

$$q_m = \begin{cases} 1, & \text{if } \tilde{p}_m \leq v + w - t_1 \\ \dfrac{v + w - \tilde{p}_m}{t_1}, & \text{if } \tilde{p}_m > v + w - t_1 \end{cases} \tag{7.71}$$

$$\pi_m = \begin{cases} \tilde{p}_m - c_A - c_{B1}, & \text{if } \tilde{p}_m \leq v + w - t_1 \\ (\tilde{p}_m - c_A - c_{B1})\dfrac{v + w - \tilde{p}_m}{t_1}, & \text{if } \tilde{p}_m > v + w - t_1. \end{cases} \tag{7.72}$$

One can then find the optimal price at the internal solution as $\tilde{p}_m = (v + w + c_A + c_{B1})/2$, and check that it can apply only if $v + w < c_A + c_{B1} + 2t_1$ (otherwise $\tilde{p}_m \leq v + w - t_1$ and the corner solution holds). Therefore, the equilibrium profits will be

$$\pi_m^* = \begin{cases} v + w - t_1 - c_A - c_{B1}, & \text{if } v + w \geq c_A + c_{B1} + 2t_1 \\ \dfrac{(v + w - c_A - c_{B1})^2}{4t_1}, & \text{if } v + w < c_A + c_{B1} + 2t_1. \end{cases} \tag{7.73}$$

The conditions obtained make sense: the higher the consumers' willingness to pay for the goods, the more likely they will all end up buying. The higher the disutility from purchasing a variety B1 distant from the most preferred one (that is, from the consumer's location), the less likely they will all buy.

We can now proceed to compare monopoly profits under the bundling strategy with duopoly profits when products are sold separately. Rather than carrying out tedious calculations, let me focus on two very special cases, just to show that different outcomes can arise.

Suppose first that $c_A = c_{B1} = c_{B2} = t_2 = 0$, and that $v + w < 2t_1$: the market is not covered under monopoly. Then

$$\pi_m^* - \pi_1^* = \frac{(v + w)^2}{4t_1} - \frac{t_1}{9} - v. \tag{7.74}$$

Clearly, this expression decreases with t_1, which means that there exist parameter values such that the above expression is negative, that is, bundling would not be chosen even if it leads to the exit of firm 2.[85]

Suppose now that $c_A = c_{B1} = c_{B2} = t_2 = 0$, but that $v + w \geq 2t_1$: the market is covered under monopoly. Then

$$\pi_m^* - \pi_1^* = -t_1 - \frac{t_1}{9} + w. \qquad (7.75)$$

Here, it is easy to see that it would be enough to choose a high enough w or a low enough t_1 for the monopoly with exclusion to be profitable.

To conclude, bundling in this model might lead to exclusion. However, this does not necessarily mean that it will be profitable for the incumbent to choose this option, as obliging consumers to buy the bundle or abstain may imply fewer sales on market A, and decrease the profitability of the monopoly solution.

Welfare Analysis   One last item remains to be checked, and this is the effect of exclusionary bundling upon welfare. To keep things short, let me skip derivations and just recall Whinston's conclusions. He shows that the effects of bundling, even when it profitably excludes an entrant, are ambiguous. Under monopoly, consumers tend to suffer from lower variety (those located to the right of the interval, for instance, have to content themselves with a more distant specification than their ideal one, or give up buying the bundle altogether) and prices tend to increase; but a duplication of fixed costs can be avoided when firm 2 stays out. Overall, however, it seems sensible to expect that consumer welfare will decrease from exclusionary bundling (when it is profitable), and if one disregards the argument that there might be excess of variety under free entry, total welfare will decrease too.

When Goods are Complementary*   I have so far looked at the case where products A and B are independent. Suppose now that they are complementary. More particularly, assume a one-to-one relationship between them, so good A is essential. Therefore, consumers derive zero utility from buying B alone. We shall see that bundling is not a profitable strategy for firm 1.

Assume that, like above, consumers are distributed uniformly on $[0, 1]$, and that their utility is given by $U_{A/Bi} = \theta - t_i \mid x - x_{Bi} \mid - p_{Bi} - p_A$, and keep the same assumptions as before.[86]

Tying (and Exclusion)   If firm 1 commits to bundling, the very fact that A can be sold only in a bundle with B1 automatically implies that firm 2 is excluded from the market. Note first that we have already seen the case where firm 1 is a

---

[85] The most restrictive among the assumptions we have made above is (A1), which becomes in this case $v < 2t_1$. Therefore, t_1 can be made large at will.

[86] One can think of θ as $v + w$. Note that here it does not make sense to give separate valuations to good A and B. Assume also for simplicity (but the results would not change otherwise) that θ is high enough for all consumers to buy when both firms are active.

monopolist selling a bundle. The market is covered ($q_m = 1$) if $\widetilde{p}_m \leq \theta - t_1$, and is not otherwise ($q_m = (\theta - \widetilde{p}_m)/t_1$ for $\widetilde{p}_m > \theta - t_1$). From the analysis above it follows that equilibrium prices and profits will be

$$\widetilde{p}_m^* = \begin{cases} \theta - t_1, & \text{if } \theta \geq c_A + c_{B1} + 2t_1 \\ \dfrac{(\theta - c_A - c_{B1})^2}{4t_1}, & \text{if } \theta < c_A + c_{B1} + 2t_1 \end{cases} \tag{7.76}$$

$$\widetilde{\pi}_m^* = \begin{cases} \theta - t_1 - c_A - c_{B1}, & \text{if } \theta \geq c_A + c_{B1} + 2t_1 \\ \dfrac{(\theta - c_A - c_{B1})^2}{4t_1}, & \text{if } \theta < c_A + c_{B1} + 2t_1. \end{cases} \tag{7.77}$$

No Tying Suppose now that firm 1 decides instead to sell the goods separately. Regardless of whether firm 2 is active or not, suppose it sells at prices $\widehat{p}_{B1} = c_{B1} - \varepsilon$, and $\widehat{p}_A = \widetilde{p}_m^* - \widehat{p}_{B1}$. There are two possible cases.

(a) If firm 2 is not active, then this pricing policy will give exactly the same profits as bundling. Indeed, consumers will buy the system A/B1 if $U_{A/Bi} = \theta - t_1 x - \widehat{p}_{B1} - \widehat{p}_A \geq 0$. But then demand and profits will just depend on the sum of the prices, $\widehat{p}_A + \widehat{p}_{B1} = \widetilde{p}_m^*$, and therefore the total profits will be the same as under bundling.

(b) If firm 2 is active and sells at a price p_{B2}, consumers will choose B1 if $U_{A/B1} > U_{A/B2}$, or $\theta - t_1 x - \widehat{p}_{B1} - \widehat{p}_A \geq \theta - t_2(1 - x) - p_{B2} - \widehat{p}_A$. The indifferent consumer is $x_{12} = (t_2 + p_{B2} - \widehat{p}_{B1})/(t_2 + t_1)$. The demand for B1 is given by $q_{B1} = x_{12}$, whereas demand for good A is given by all consumers. Firm 1's profits are then

$$\pi_1 = (\widehat{p}_A - c_A + \widehat{p}_{B1} - c_{B1})x_{12} + (\widehat{p}_A - c_A)(1 - x_{12}) \tag{7.78}$$

$$= (\widetilde{p}_m^* - c_A - c_{B1}), \tag{7.79}$$

which cannot be lower than under the monopoly with bundling: in both cases, the firm has the same unit profit ($\widetilde{p}_m^* - c_A - c_{B1}$), but under independent pricing total demand cannot be lower, since everybody buys.

In other words, what happens here is the following. If under monopoly with bundling all consumers were buying, then firm 1's profits cannot decrease when there is no bundling: some consumers might replace B1 with B2, but since under the chosen pricing scheme B1 is sold at (slightly below) marginal costs c_{B1}, and everybody continues to buy A, profits are not lower (they increase by ε).

If the market was not covered under monopoly, then the presence of firm 2 would allow to increase sales of A. Some consumers might switch from B1 to B2, but we have seen that this does not harm firm 1's profits, but some others will buy the system A/B2, thus increasing sales of A, and overall profits.

7.3.2.7 Models of Tying, III: Tying to Deter Entry in Complementary Markets*

This subsection provides a variant of Choi and Stefanadis (2001). Consider two complementary products, A and B, which are combined in fixed proportions on a one-to-one basis and have value only if consumed together. Firm 1 is an incumbent in both products. It produces them (call them A1 and B1) at unit cost c_h each. In each of the two markets there is a potential entrant that can sell products which are perfect substitutes of A1 and B1: call them A2 and B2 respectively. By making an investment in R&D, I_{i2}, which costs $C(I_{i2}) = \gamma(I_{i2})^2/2$, with $\gamma > (c_h - c_l)$,[87] each potential entrant affects the probability $p(I_{i2}) = \varepsilon + I_{i2}$ (with $i = A, B$) that it will obtain a successful innovation, defined as an innovation that gives it a unit cost $c_l < c_h$. With probability $1 - p(I_{i2})$, the entrant's unit cost will be prohibitively high.

Consumers' utility is given by $U_{Aj/Bj} = \theta - p_{Bj} - p_{Aj}$, with $j = 1, 2$, and I normalise consumer size to one, without loss of generality.

Consider the following game. In the first period, firm 1 decides whether to commit to selling A1 and B1 as a bundle, or not. In the second period, firms A2 and B2 simultaneously take investment decisions. In the third period, active firms name prices (Bertrand competition). Let us solve the game backwards.

Price Sub-Game   Consider the case of *no tying* first. If only the incumbent is active, it will extract all the surplus from the consumers by setting prices for its components such that their sum equals θ, and earns $\theta - 2c_h$. If both entrants are active (i.e., their innovations have been successful), each will charge a price that equals c_h, and get the whole market for its product, making gross profits $c_h - c_l$. Less straightforward is the case where only one entrant, say A2, is active, as it gives rise to a continuum of equilibria. The two extreme ones are as follows: (a) both the entrant and the incumbent set price c_h in product A, with the entrant getting all demand and extracting the rent from the innovation, $c_h - c_l$,[88] and the incumbent sets price $\theta - c_h$ on product B. (b) Both the entrant and the incumbent set price c_l in market A, with the entrant still getting all demand but zero profits, and the incumbent setting $\theta - c_l$ in market B, thereby extracting all the rents from the innovation itself through a price squeeze. All intermediate cases are also equilibria of the price game.

Following Choi and Stefanadis, assume that when only one entrant enters, the incumbent obtains a share λ of the innovation rent, $c_h - c_l$, with the remaining

---

[87] One can check that this ensures at the same time that the equilibrium probability is lower than 1, and that the stability conditions are met.

[88] As usual in all Bertrand games with cost asymmetries, there are two ways to present equilibrium outcomes. One is to say that both firms set the price that equals the highest marginal cost, and consumers are assumed to choose the low cost firm. The other is to say that the low cost firm sets a price that is a shade (that is, an ε, with ε arbitrarily small) lower than the highest cost.

part $1 - \lambda$ obtained by the entrant, with $\lambda \in [0, 1]$ being the measure of the price squeeze that the incumbent can exercise due to its monopoly position on market for the complementary product. Therefore, the incumbent's profits are $\theta - 2c_h + \lambda(c_h - c_l)$.

Next, consider the case of *tying*. If only the incumbent is active, it will extract all the consumer surplus and earn $\theta - 2c_h$. If both entrants are active, at the symmetric equilibrium each entrant sets a price equal to c_h, and gets the whole market for its product, making gross profits $c_h - c_l$. If only one entrant has been successful, it will not be able to market its product, since the other complementary product is sold by the incumbent as a bundle (tying trivially excludes a rival active in only one market when two products must be combined in fixed proportions).

Investment Sub-Game   Under *no tying*, the profits obtained by an entrant are

$$\pi_{i2} = p(I_{i2})[1 - p(I_{k2})](1 - \lambda)(c_h - c_l) + p(I_{i2})p(I_{k2})(c_h - c_l) - C(I_{i2}),$$

$$\text{with} \quad i, k = A, B, i \neq k \tag{7.80}$$

where the first term indicates firm $i2$'s profits when it innovates whereas the other entrant does not, and the second term profits when both entrants innovate. By substituting the specific functions chosen for $p(I_{i2})$ and $C(I_{i2})$, one obtains FOCs as

$$\frac{\partial \pi_{i2}}{\partial I_{i2}} = [1 - (\varepsilon + I_{k2})](1 - \lambda)(c_h - c_l) + (\varepsilon + I_{k2})(c_h - c_l) - \gamma I_{i2} = 0,$$

$$\text{with} \quad i, k = A, B, i \neq k. \tag{7.81}$$

At the symmetric equilibrium $I_{A2}^* = I_{B2}^* = I_2^*$ the optimal investment is therefore given by

$$I_2^*(\lambda) = \frac{(1 - \lambda(1 - \varepsilon))(c_h - c_l))}{\gamma - \lambda(c_h - c_l)}. \tag{7.82}$$

Note that, not surprisingly, equilibrium investments fall with the degree of price squeeze (if the incumbent appropriates most of the surplus created by the innovation, the returns from innovating decrease): $\partial I_2^*/\partial \lambda < 0$.

Under *tying*, entrant $i2$'s profits are

$$\tilde{\pi}_{i2} = p(I_{i2})p(I_{k2})(c_h - c_l) - C(I_{i2}), \quad \text{with} \quad i, k = A, B, i \neq k, \tag{7.83}$$

since only when both entrants innovate will they be able to sell their product. FOCs are

$$\frac{\partial \tilde{\pi}_{i2}}{\partial I_{i2}} = (\varepsilon + I_{k2})(c_h - c_l) - \gamma I_{i2} = 0, \quad \text{with} \quad i, k = A, B, i \neq k. \tag{7.84}$$

At the symmetric equilibrium the optimal investment is

$$\widetilde{I}_2^* = \frac{\varepsilon(c_h - c_l)}{\gamma - (c_h - c_l)}. \tag{7.85}$$

A simple inspection of (7.82) and (7.85) reveals that tying lowers the investments made by the potential entrants, and thus reduces the probability that there will be entry at equilibrium. (Only if $\lambda = 1$, the two investment levels coincide: $\widetilde{I}_2^* = I_2^*(1)$: when entrants anticipate a perfect price squeeze, the returns from being the only innovator are nil, as in the case of tying.) In this sense, tying has exclusionary effects. However, we still have to check if this practice is profitable. For this, consider the first stage of the game.

Tying Decisions   If there is *no tying*, firm 1's expected profits are

$$\pi_1^*(\lambda) = [1 - (\varepsilon + I_2^*(\lambda))^2](\theta - 2c_h)$$
$$+ 2(\varepsilon + I_2^*(\lambda))[1 - (\varepsilon + I_2^*(\lambda))]\lambda(c_h - c_l). \tag{7.86}$$

Note that for $\lambda = 0$, the second term is zero, as the incumbent does not extract any rent from the innovation.

If there is *tying*, firm 1's expected profits are

$$\widetilde{\pi}_1^*(\lambda) = [1 - (\varepsilon + \widetilde{I}_2^*)^2](\theta - 2c_h), \tag{7.87}$$

since when only one entrant is successful, there will be no entry, and the incumbent cannot extract any rent from the innovation.

It can be shown that there exists a value $\widetilde{\lambda} \in (0, 1)$ such that $\widetilde{\pi}_1^*(\lambda) \geq \pi_1^*(\lambda)$ for $\lambda \leq \widetilde{\lambda}$. Rather than doing tedious calculations to find the precise expression for $\widetilde{\lambda}$, note that there is a trade-off for the incumbent in tying the goods. On the one hand, tying decreases the risk of entry, which increases its profits (exclusion effect); on the other hand, tying decreases the profit that the incumbent makes when only one entrant makes it (price squeeze effect). But the latter effect on profits is absent when $\lambda = 0$, since the incumbent is not able to extract profits (hence, tying is more profitable in this case), whereas it is very strong when $\lambda = 1$, as the incumbent appropriates all the surplus created by the innovation.

Indeed, when $\lambda = 0$, bundling is preferred as

$$\pi_1^*(\lambda) = [1 - (\varepsilon + I_2^*(0))^2](\theta - 2c_h) < \widetilde{\pi}_1^*(0) = [1 - (\varepsilon + \widetilde{I}_2^*)^2](\theta - 2c_h), \tag{7.88}$$

which always holds since $I_2^*(0) > \widetilde{I}_2^*$.

When $\lambda = 1$, bundling is unprofitable, since $I_2^*(1) = \widetilde{I}_2^*$, which implies that

$$\pi_1^*(1) = [1 - (\varepsilon + \widetilde{I}_2^*)^2](\theta - 2c_h) + 2(\varepsilon + \widetilde{I}_2^*)[1 - (\varepsilon + \widetilde{I}_2^*)]\lambda(c_h - c_l) >$$
$$\widetilde{\pi}_1^*(1) = [1 - (\varepsilon + \widetilde{I}_2^*)^2](\theta - 2c_h). \tag{7.89}$$

To sum up, tying can indeed lead to exclusion, but it might still be more profitable for the incumbent not to resort to such strategy.

7.3.3 Incompatibility and Other Strategic Behaviour in Network Industries

This section first deals with *compatibility* (or *inter-operability*) issues when an incumbent sells two complementary products and faces competition in one of them. Then it discusses compatibility issues when said incumbent sells a product that is characterised by network effects and faces a rival that offers a substitutable product (i.e., a competing network, if the products are not compatible). Finally, it offers some remarks about strategic behaviour – other than incompatibility choices – that could be used by incumbents in network industries.

Complementary Products   Suppose that an incumbent monopolist sells both a product A and a complementary product B – the latter is also sold by competing firms – to final consumers. By denying compatibility between A and competing versions of B, the incumbent could leverage its monopoly position into market B, in very much the same way as we have seen in tying models (see Section 7.3.2):[89] to tie the sales of A and their own version of B amounts to making rivals' B product incompatible with A. However, we have seen when discussing tying that A's producer would generally have little interest in excluding rivals from the complementary product market. Therefore, despite the easy way available to foreclose rivals, it is far from obvious *a priori* that a monopolist will want to use incompatibility as a way to leverage power into another market, although in some particular circumstances exclusion might indeed be profitable,[90] leaving us with no clear policy for compatibility.

The same sort of arguments also applies where A is not sold directly to consumers, but is instead just used as an input in the production of product B. We know, from the discussion of vertical mergers (Chapter 6.4), that it is possible, but not very likely, that the upstream monopolist will want to foreclose rival versions of the final product B.

Competing Networks   The issue of whether competition policy should promote (or impose) compatibility is particularly crucial in network industries,[91] where entry by a new firm is made very difficult when it has no access to the customer base of an incumbent network (note that here I refer to competing versions of substitute – networks think for instance of two cellular phone networks). Indeed, in network

---

[89] A difference between incompatibility and tying decisions is that the former is more likely to be built in product design and is therefore unlikely to have the commitment problems.

[90] Again, this conclusion comes from a straightforward application of the results of the literature on tying. See the discussions of Whinston (1990), as well as the short descriptions of the models of Choi and Stefanadis (2001) and Carlton and Waldmann (2002) in Section 7.3.2.

[91] See also the discussions in Chapter 2 (on the main features of network effects) and in Chapter 4 (on co-operative standard setting, an issue very close to the one touched upon here).

markets, a firm endowed with a large installed base often has no incentive to offer inter-operability to a smaller rival. This topic is analysed in technical Section 7.3.3.1, which shows that granting compatibility (or inter-operability, or connectivity) to a smaller network is optimal for a large firm only if it expects that access to two fully compatible networks will exhibit such strong network externalities that it will attract a large number of new consumers. The large firm then prefers to share a larger market with the small rival over dominating a smaller market.

It would be very tempting to argue that in a network industry dominated by an incumbent one should force compatibility to allow for otherwise very difficult entry. However, this *ex post* intervention would not take into account what has happened in the industry beforehand. Very often, when products are incompatible, network industries are characterised by a very intense period of early competition until one firm establishes itself as the market leader, and strong market power is the reward for a tough battle between competing networks (a process often described as "competition *in* the market being replaced by competition *for* the market"). If this is the case, forcing compatibility onto the incumbent would imply depriving it of the returns it expected which after all motivated the initial strong competition.[92] This would also send the wrong signals to firms in other industries, leading them to revise their expectations of profits if they are successful in a network war, and therefore reducing their incentives to compete.

Nevertheless, there might exist situations where a more interventionist public policy in this sphere might make some sense. Consider for instance an industry where the incumbent derives its strong customer base from a legal monopoly (think of the national telecommunications operators in pre-deregulation Europe): In such a case, obliging the incumbent to open up its network to rivals looks like an appealing policy.[93]

In general, one is left with the impression that network markets under incompatibility are prone to problems, especially because the role of entry in moderating the market power of the incumbent is strongly reduced, but it is hard to come up with solid and clear policy implications that have general validity.[94]

---

[92] Another way to explain the same concept is that the apparently high prices set by the incumbent are the other side of the coin of the low prices set by the rivals at the early periods of the market. Concluding that the industry is not competitive just looking at the *ex post* situation overlooks what has happened beforehand.

[93] Further, Farrell and Katz (1998: 649) find that in some cases incumbent networks enjoy a monopoly for reasons that have little to do with R&D or investment strategies, and an exceptional relaxation of intellectual property rights might be justified. Think for instance of number portability. An incumbent telephone operator might argue that the phone number it has assigned to a customer is protected by copyright laws. However, it would be difficult to argue that this is an innovation which deserves protection, and allowing the customer to keep its number if it moves to a new provider would strongly increase competition.

[94] Under network effects, policy assessments become more complex because a number of externalities come into play. For instance, persistence of a monopolist might even have some positive

Product Pre-Announcements in Network Industries The importance of consumers' expectations in network markets (prophecies tend to be self-fulfilling: if consumers expect an entrant not to win much custom, this prediction will turn out to be correct, and the entrant will fail even if it has a superior product) opens the way for further manipulation by the incumbent. *Product pre-announcement,* for instance, is a strategy whereby the incumbent declares it will release a new version of its product soon, so as to possibly persuade consumers to wait rather than buying the currently superior product made by a rival company that enjoys a smaller network base.[95] How to deal with such a strategy is not straightforward. Probably the only feasible way is to judge it anti-competitive only to the extent that such announcements are not truthful and are made in bad faith.

7.3.3.1 Inter-operability Choices in Asymmetric Networks*

This section, which is based on Crémer, Rey and Tirole (2000), analyses the different incentives of providing inter-operability of two firms that have asymmetric networks.[96]

There exists a market for a network product and two firms. Firm 1 is the incumbent, and has already an installed base of β_1 consumers, and firm 2 is a new firm, with an installed base of $\beta_2 = 0$ consumers. There exists a mass 1 of new consumers uniformly distributed along the segment $[0, 1]$. The consumer located in $T \in [0, 1]$ attaches an intrinsic value T to the network. Thus, for a consumer the net benefit from network product i is

$$S_i = T + s_i - p_i, \tag{7.90}$$

where p_i is network i's price, and s_i represents the network externality, given by

$$s_i = v \left[\beta_i + q_i + \theta \left(\beta_j + q_j \right) \right], \tag{7.91}$$

where q_i and q_j represent the number of new consumers buying respectively from firm i and j, $v < 1/2$ is a parameter (common to all consumers) that indicates the importance of the network externalities,[97] and $\theta \in [0, 1]$ is a parameter that indicates the quality of the inter-operability between the two networks: if $\theta = 0$,

---

effects in that it allows network effects to be larger and avoids consumers being *stranded* when a new incompatible product becomes the new standard. Fudenberg and Tirole (2000) analyse an overlapping generation model where an incumbent engages in limit-pricing to increase its customer base and deter entry in a network industry. But the welfare effects of entry-deterrence are ambiguous, due to the presence of stranded users and other externalities that might lead to excess entry.

[95] See Dranove and Gandal (2000) and the discussion in Chapter 2.

[96] Crémer et al. (2000) is based itself on Katz and Shapiro (1985). See also Malueg and Schwartz (2001) for an extension and a discussion of Crémer et al. (2000).

[97] I show below that $v < 1/2$ guarantees stability of the interior equilibrium of the Cournot game. See Chapter 8 for an explanation of the stability concept.

there is no compatibility between the networks, whereas if $\theta = 1$, they are perfectly compatible. (Intermediate cases of imperfect inter-operability can describe cases where a consumer who has joined a network might use the other network, but in an imperfect way, for instance because there is a lower performance, or because it takes more time to get the same service, or because some services are unavailable.)

If each firm is to attract some of the new consumers, it must be that the net benefit is the same: $S_1 = S_2$, which can be re-written as

$$p_1 - s_1 = p_2 - s_2 = \widehat{p}. \tag{7.92}$$

The new consumer who is indifferent between joining either network or not buying the network product at all is the one such that $S_i = T + s_i - p_i = T - \widehat{p} = 0$. Therefore, all consumers with $T \in [\widehat{p}, 1]$ will buy either product, whereas those with $T \in [0, \widehat{p})$ will not be in the market. It must then be

$$q_1 + q_2 = 1 - \widehat{p}. \tag{7.93}$$

From expression (7.92) it follows that $p_i = \widehat{p} + s_i$, which after using expression (7.93) becomes $p_i = 1 - q_i - q_j + s_i$, and finally by (7.91), one can write firm i's demand function as

$$p_i = 1 + v(\beta_i + \theta\beta_j) - (1 - v)q_i - (1 - v\theta)q_j, \qquad i, j = 1, 2, i \neq j. \tag{7.94}$$

Competition in the Product Market   Given the inter-operability parameter θ, each firm chooses output so as to maximise its profits $\pi_i = \left(p_i \left(q_i, q_j \right) \right) - c)q_i$. It turns out that there exist two types of equilibrium in this game. The first is an interior solution, the second a corner solution.

To find the *interior solution*, compute $\partial\pi_i/\partial q_i = 0$ and obtain the best-reply functions in the plane (q_2, q_1) as follows:[98]

$$R_1 : q_1 = \frac{1 - c + v\beta_1 - (1 - v\theta)q_2}{2(1 - v)}; \qquad R_2 : q_1 = \frac{1 - c + v\theta\beta_1 - 2(1 - v)q_2}{1 - v\theta}.$$

$$\tag{7.95}$$

The intersection of the best-reply functions gives the interior equilibrium of the

---

[98] Stability requires R_2 to be steeper than R_1, that is $2(1 - v)/(1 - v\theta) > (1 - v\theta)/(2(1 - v))$, or equivalently $v < 1/(2 - \theta)$. Assuming that $v < 1/2$ is therefore sufficient to guarantee stability for all values of $\theta \in [0, 1]$.

game:[99]

$$q_i^* = \frac{1}{2}\left(\frac{2(1-c) + v(1+\theta)(\beta_i + \beta_j)}{2(1-v) + (1-v\theta)} + \frac{(1-\theta)v(\beta_i - \beta_j)}{2(1-v) - (1-v\theta)}\right). \quad (7.96)$$

Note that, to be precise, in this game we are using a concept that extends the usual concept of Nash equilibrium in quantities, since we have to consider consumers' expectations. Katz and Shapiro (1985) call this concept "Fulfilled Expectations Cournot Equilibrium"; and it is an equilibrium where not only the firms' output decisions form a Nash equilibrium, but also consumers' expectations are fulfilled: they make their purchase decisions expecting the sizes of the networks to be (q_1^*, q_2^*) and such expectations are fulfilled.

Note also that

$$q_1^* - q_2^* = \frac{(1-\theta)v\beta_1}{2(1-v) - (1-v\theta)} > 0, \quad (7.97)$$

which implies that more consumers will join the incumbent's network than the rival network's, except for the case $\theta = 1$ (perfect inter-operability), where the networks are perceived identical by consumers. Note also that the lower θ the higher $q_1^* - q_2^*$: the lower inter-operability the stronger the competitive advantage enjoyed by the incumbent because of its installed base.

Let us now look for the *corner solutions*, or "tipping equilibria" as Malueg and Schwartz (2001) call them (because the market "tips" in favour of one or the other firm).

We have seen in Chapter 2 that models with network externalities can be characterised by multiple equilibria, caused by the fact that each consumer's choice depends on all other consumers' choices. Here, expectations may support tipping equilibria where only one firm gets new consumers.

Tipping to the Firm with the Large Installed Base   Check first that there exists an equilibrium where all consumers expect that no consumer will patronise firm 2, that is, expect $q_2 = 0$. Under these expectations, firm 1 will behave as a monopolist, and maximise $\pi_1^m = (1 + v\beta_1 - (1-v)q_1 - c)q_1$. From $\partial \pi_1^m / \partial q_1 = 0$, one obtains the monopoly output:

$$q_1^m = \frac{1 - c + v\beta_1}{2(1-v)}. \quad (7.98)$$

For $(q_1^m, 0)$ to be an equilibrium, it must be that firm 2 has no incentive to deviate. This will be the case if, given the quantity q_1^m produced by firm 1, firm 2 would

---

[99] For the model to hold, the market must be uncovered, i.e., some consumers should not buy. (Otherwise, inverse demand functions cannot be obtained.) This requires $q_1^* + q_2^* < 1$, which amounts to $v < (1 + 2c)/[2 + \theta + \beta_1(1+\theta)]$.

experience losses if it sold a positive quantity. Or, equivalently, if given the output sold by firm 1 it would not be able to impose a price above cost even when producing an arbitrarily small output: $p_2(q_1^m, 0) \leq c$. By recalling the inverse demand function (7.94), this condition becomes

$$1 + v\theta\beta_1 - (1 - \theta v)\frac{1 - c + v\beta_1}{2(1 - v)} - c \leq 0. \qquad (7.99)$$

Note that the lower θ the more likely this condition will be satisfied. For the case where the networks are fully incompatible ($\theta = 0$), tipping to firm 1 will occur if

$$v \geq \frac{1 - c}{2(1 - c) + \beta_1}, \qquad (7.100)$$

and this condition is compatible with $v < 1/2$.

Tipping to the Entrant   Let us now check if an equilibrium exists where all consumers expect that $q_1 = 0$. Under these expectations, firm 2 will behave as a monopolist, and maximise $\pi_2^m = (1 + v\theta\beta_1 - (1 - v)q_2 - c) q_2$. From $\partial\pi_1^m/\partial q_1 = 0$ one obtains the monopoly output:

$$q_2^m = \frac{1 - c + v\theta\beta_1}{2(1 - v)}. \qquad (7.101)$$

For $(0, q_2^m)$ to be an equilibrium, firm 2 must have no incentive to deviate. This will be the case if $p_1(0, q_2^m) \leq c$. By recalling the inverse demand function (7.94), this condition becomes

$$1 + v\beta_1 - (1 - v\theta)\frac{1 - c + v\theta\beta_1}{2(1 - v)} - c \leq 0. \qquad (7.102)$$

The lower θ the more likely this condition will be satisfied. For $\theta = 0$, tipping to firm 2 would occur if

$$c \geq 1 + \frac{2\beta_1 v (1 - v)}{1 - 2v}$$

but this condition never holds, as it must be $c < 1$ in order for $q_2^m > 0$. Tipping towards the incumbent might occur, but tipping towards the entrant in this example does not.[100]

The Choice of Inter-operability   So far we have regarded the parameter θ as exogenous. However, it is likely that it is a strategic variable of the firms, which can decide the degree of inter-operability they want among networks. Sometimes, to increase inter-operability might be costly, but assume for simplicity that it is not. Assume also that $\theta = \min(\theta_1^*, \theta_2^*)$, where θ_i^* is firm i's optimal degree of inter-operability.

---

[100] Malueg and Schwartz (2001) show that, within the same model but with more than two firms, tipping away from the incumbent might occur.

We want to study the firms' preferences for inter-operability.

To start with, note that we have to separate the analysis according to the type of solutions arising in the Cournot game. For tipping equilibria, the incumbent's preference for a low inter-operability was already seen above: if $\theta = 0$, we have seen that the condition for a tipping equilibrium towards firm 1 is maximal, whereas the market cannot tip towards firm 2.

For interior solutions, the results are less straightforward. Firstly, note that $\pi_i^* = (1 - v)(q_i^*)^2$. This means that the higher the output the higher the profits of the firms. Therefore, firm i's desired degree of inter-operability is the one that maximises output q_i^*.

Crémer et al. (2000) show that the new firm would always choose the maximum degree of inter-operability, whereas the incumbent's preferred choice is either $\theta = 0$ or $\theta = 1$, the latter when the installed base is small relative to the new consumers. To gain some insight while keeping to a simple example, consider the case where $c = 0$,[101] and suppose that firms can choose only between $\theta = 0$ and $\theta = 1$ (given Crémer et al.'s result, this is without loss of generality).

Firm 1 will prefer full inter-operability if

$$q_1^*(\theta = 1) - q_1^*(\theta = 0) = \frac{v\left(1 - 2v - \beta_1\left(3 - 4v + 2v^2\right)\right)}{3(1 - v)(3 - 8v + 4v^2)} > 0, \quad (7.103)$$

which is true for $\beta_1 < (1 - 2v) / \left(3 - 4v + 2v^2\right) \equiv \bar{\beta}_1$. Hence, if the installed base is small enough relative to the new consumers, the incumbent will want to guarantee full inter-operability. If the installed base is large enough, the incumbent will prefer incompatible networks. (Note that $\bar{\beta}_1$ decreases with v, so the more important the network externalities the more likely that firm 1 prefers low inter-operability.)

Firm 2 always prefers full inter-operability because

$$q_2^*(\theta = 1) - q_2^*(\theta = 0) = \frac{v\left(1 - 2v + \beta_1\left(6 - 11v + 4v^2\right)\right)}{3(1 - v)(3 - 2v)(1 - 2v)} > 0. \quad (7.104)$$

To sum up, this model, however simple, shows that in network markets an incumbent (more generally, a firm with a large installed base) might have an incentive to lower the degree of inter-operability (or compatibility, or connectivity) with new entrants (more generally, firms with a smaller customer base). However, this is not always the case: The incumbent might actually gain from full inter-operability. This is because full inter-operability eliminates the incumbent's competitive advantage due to its larger customer base, but it increases the demand of new consumers in the market.[102]

---

[101] From the previous conditions imposed on the model, it follows that $c = 0$ excludes tipping equilibria, but it does not matter here as I am considering interior solutions.

[102] New demand is given by $q_1^* + q_2^* = [2(1 - c) + v(1 + \theta)\beta_1] / [2(1 - v) + (1 - v\theta)]$, which increases with the degree of inter-operability θ.

If the installed base is small relative to the new demand, the market expansion effect dominates (recall that the smaller the installed base the lower the competitive advantage of the incumbent, as measured by $q_1^* - q_2^*$): the incumbent prefers to share equally a bigger cake than to get a larger slice of a small cake.

7.3.4 Refusal to Supply and Exclusive Contracts (Reminder)

Some anti-competitive practices have already been analysed elsewhere in the book. Refusal to supply a key input, resulting in foreclosure of rivals, has been analysed in Chapter 2 with reference to the *essential facilities* doctrine. I have argued there that obliging a firm to give access of a key asset to a rival might have the effect of discouraging investments. Accordingly, such policy should be used only in very specific circumstances (see also Chapter 6, where some situations where a firm has an incentive to foreclose, resulting in lower welfare, have also been identified).

Chapter 6 has also shown that exclusive contracts might have exclusionary effects, but that these should be balanced against possible efficiency reasons before concluding that they are anti-competitive.

7.3.5 Raising Rivals' Costs

Krattenmaker and Salop (1986) claim that among the monopolisation tools available to firms there are also so-called *raising rivals' costs* practices.[103] These practices all aim at increasing the costs of one or more rivals, thus leaving room for the firm that engages in these practices to increase prices without losing market share. These practices would be particularly appealing for a firm that has anti-competitive aims because they do not require it to run losses in the short-run, as in predatory pricing. If the impact on rivals' costs is immediate, there will also be an immediate positive impact on profits.

A number of practices have been interpreted as belonging to the category of raising rivals' costs strategies. Some of them are probably of little relevance, such as those that increase rivals' costs directly, either through sabotage (if one destroys the rivals' plants it also increases its costs, but there is no need for anti-trust laws to take care of such behaviour); or through lobbying and regulation (think for instance of domestic firms that convince the government to introduce tariffs or other taxes on imported products).[104] More interestingly, a number of practices

---

[103] See also Salop and Scheffman (1987).

[104] An interesting US case is *Pennington,* where a large mine operator and the miners' trade unions lobbied for a minimum wage. The resulting increase in production costs would have hurt smaller competitors more than the large firm.

that we have already analysed might be seen as raising rivals' costs. Exclusive dealing might make it more difficult or more costly for a rival to find distributors that can sell its products. A vertically integrated firm might refuse to supply a key input to a downstream rival (or to engage in a price squeeze, that is sell the input to the rival but at a prohibitively high price), increasing the production costs of the latter. Furthermore, denying inter-operability to a rival network might also be seen as a strategy which increases the rival's cost of doing business.

Not all actions that increase rivals' costs are necessarily anti-competitive. For instance, one might argue that a firm that carries out significant R&D activities to increase its product quality is also raising the cost of its rivals: if they want to be competitive and keep their appeal, they also have to sustain higher R&D expenses. Yet, this is not a practice that harms competition: R&D will benefit consumers.[105] Therefore, a crucial step in the theory is to distinguish between practices that only harm competitors from those that also reduce welfare.

To sum up, raising rivals' costs theories provide a concept that encompasses many very different practices. Due to the specificities of such practices, I have preferred to deal with them separately.

7.4 PRICE DISCRIMINATION

Price discrimination is a pervasive phenomenon, of which examples from our daily life abound.[106] Books are sold at different prices according to whether they are hardback or paperback (but the cost of the hardback binding alone does not explain the price difference); journals charge a higher price for libraries and institutions than for private citizens (and sometimes make further discounts to students); if we buy pencils and paper in a shop for our private use we certainly pay more per item than our university or firm that buys a large amount of them; airlines apply very different tariffs not only for business versus economy trips, but often charge very different prices for the same type of seat and trip according to whether the passenger is a student, a senior citizen, has booked early or at the last minute, and so on. Some of the strategies firms use to discriminate across consumers (and as we shall see, price

---

[105] The same considerations hold for advertising outlays, as they increase the perceived quality of products.

[106] I do not give a precise economic definition of price discrimination, which can easily become a thorny issue. Varian (1989: 598) follows Stigler's definition: There exists price discrimination when two or similar goods are sold at prices that are in different ratios to marginal costs. (Note that if a firm charges the same price to two different consumers, but it has to pay a higher cost to ship the good to one than to the other, this will effectively be price discrimination.) Tirole (1988: 134) warns that "a general equilibrium theorist might rightly point out that goods delivered at different locations, in different states of nature, or of different quality are distinct economic goods and thus that the scope of 'pure' discrimination is very limited".

discrimination increases their profits) are fascinating and extremely sophisticated, but the main purpose of this chapter is not to study firms' discriminating practices but rather to identify the likely effects of price discrimination.

The Two Main Ingredients of Price Discrimination   There are two principal conditions for price discrimination.[107] The first one is that a firm must have a way to sort consumers so as to charge them different prices. Different situations can arise, which broadly correspond to different types of price discrimination identified by economic theory.[108]

Under *first-degree* price discrimination, for instance, a monopolist would know each consumer's precise willingness to pay for its good, charge each of them exactly the maximum they would pay and therefore capture all the consumer surplus. Under *second-degree* discrimination, a firm offers different deals to everybody and lets different consumers "self-select", that is choose one particular deal. Quantity discounts are a natural example: a cinema, for instance, might offer to all customers the option to pay a lower unit price for a film if they buy a ten-film card, but some customers will prefer just to buy one film ticket at a time. *Third-degree* discrimination refers to the possibility that a firm charges different prices to consumers having different (observable) characteristics. For instance, a student might be able to fly cheaper; a citizen over 65 years old might receive discounts on train tickets; the same good might be sold at a lower price in Portugal than in Germany.

The second crucial feature for price discrimination is that *arbitrage* should be absent. In other words, a firm would not manage to price discriminate successfully if consumers could re-sell the goods among each other. Under first-degree discrimination, a monopolist would not be able to appropriate the consumer surplus if Mr. A – who has a lower valuation for the good than Ms. B – could buy the good not only for himself but could also buy it to re-sell it to Ms. B. Under second-degree discrimination, arbitrage opportunities arise if I can buy a ten-film card at a $5 unit price and then offer its use to ten spectators who would be charged $10 each by the cinema. Under third-degree discrimination, the firm would not be able to segment national markets if a Portuguese consumer could buy the good at the lower Portuguese market price and then ship it to Germany where it commands a higher price. (This practice of arbitraging across countries is called *parallel imports,* and it attracts a lot of attention in EU law, as we shall see below).

Arbitrage is of course not always feasible, either because of natural obstacles or because of obstacles created by the firms themselves. For instance, transportation

---

[107] Varian (1989) suggests that another ingredient is that firms should have market power. As I have repeatedly said in this book, it is unlikely that real-world firms (as opposed to firms in perfect competition models) lack all market power: therefore, we should expect all firms to have an incentive to discriminate, although I will show below that firms with very little market power have also very limited ability to have an impact on market prices through discriminatory practices.

[108] This, now standard, classification is due to Pigou (1920).

costs, tariffs, transaction costs and red-tape might prevent parallel imports from one country to another; firms might require proof that the purchaser is a student (or a senior citizen); a ten-film card might be nominative and an ID required at the cinema; a firm might require an exclusive distributor not to sell the product beyond a particular territory and to unauthorised dealers; a car manufacturer might require its dealers in a country not to sell their car to citizens resident in other countries (a practice systematically outlawed and heavily fined in the EU), and so on.

Therefore, *if* competition authorities think that price discrimination should be forbidden, they will try to intervene in the practices on which firms rely to prevent arbitrage. For instance, they could require a firm not to include any clause limiting the ability of dealers to re-sell the product in other territories; or they could prevent an airline clerk or a train conductor from asking passengers for their ID cards, and so on. (I am just following a hypothetical reasoning, and not suggesting what should be done: This will have to wait until an analysis of welfare effects is complete.)

7.4.1 Welfare Effects of Price Discrimination

7.4.1.1 First-Degree (Perfect) Price Discrimination

To understand that it is not self-evident that price discrimination hurts welfare, it is enough to look at first-degree price discrimination. Suppose a monopolist (whose marginal cost is equal to c) faces a demand function as in Figure 7.7: this demand can be interpreted as the aggregation of unit demands of very many consumers, each with a different willingness to pay for a certain good. If it were able to set a different price for each different consumer (and of course knew their valuations), the monopolist would be able to extract all the consumer surplus: it would make each consumer pay exactly their maximum willingness to pay, and get a profit equal to the whole area of the triangle Op_cS. Since welfare is the sum of profits and consumer surplus, welfare will also be equal to the area of Op_cS. Perfect price discrimination would then lead to the highest possible welfare.[109]

To see this, just note that allocative efficiency under uniform pricing would require the monopolist to sell to all consumers at a price equal to marginal cost, leading to welfare being equal again to the area of the same triangle Op_cS. By contrast, if the monopolist were forced not to discriminate, it would sell at a price p^m and welfare would equal the area of the trapezoid $ORTp_c$, which is lower.[110]

This example should not be over-emphasised because perfect price discrimination is unrealistic, as it would require firms to have perfect knowledge of consumers

---

[109] The reader can check that the same welfare level would be attained under Bertrand (or perfect) competition: See Chapter 2.

[110] More generally, any (uniform) price above marginal cost would create a deadweight loss. For the price p^m the deadweight loss equals the area of the triangle RST. See also Chapter 2.

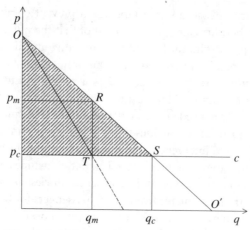

Figure 7.7. Welfare under perfect price competition.

and their preferences. However, it serves my purpose, which is to make the reader aware that price discrimination should not necessarily be thought of as a practice detrimental to welfare.[111]

7.4.1.2 Quantity Discounts

Another form of price discrimination (second-degree) occurs when a firm offers consumers different price–quantity packages – which give discounts to those buying a larger number of units of the product – or it imposes a two-part tariff, which requires the consumer to pay a flat fee T independent of the quantity bought plus a variable component pq which does depend on the quantity bought.[112] For instance, in many countries the price of gas, electricity, phone services is composed of a fixed fee plus a variable one. Note that two-part tariffs and quantity discounts are equivalent: for a consumer buying q units of a good or service, and subject to a

---

[111] Of course, a reader who thinks that the appropriate objective of competition policy is maximisation of consumer surplus and not of total welfare, would not accept the case of perfect price discrimination as an example showing that price discrimination is not necessarily "bad". I have explained in Chapter 1 why most economists prefer a total welfare standard.

[112] Quantity discounts are not the only instance of second-degree price discrimination, which refers to all situations in which firms provide different packages to consumers, who then self-select among the available packages. For instance, airline companies offer business and (much cheaper) economy fares, the latter requiring a Saturday night stay, and are therefore less interesting for those travelling for business purposes (whose willingness to pay is higher since the ticket is on a company's budget). Note also that the airline's cost of providing a seat does not vary (or varies only marginally) with the type of fare offered, whose rationale lies only in separating consumers with different willingness to pay. See Tirole (1988: ch. 3) for modelling issues.

two-part tariff, the average price is given by $p + T/q$, and therefore decreases with the number of units bought.

This type of price discrimination also tends to be welfare improving. The firm will use the flat fee to extract surplus from consumers with a lower intensity of demand (those who buy fewer units of the good at any given price) but will use a lower marginal price than the price it would set if it was obliged to use only a variable component. The result is similar (although less extreme) to that under perfect price discrimination: the lower marginal price reduces the allocative ineffi- ciency, and therefore increases welfare (the firm compensates for the lower marginal price by using the flat fee). To better see the similarity with the case of perfect price discrimination, note that in that case a monopolist might appropriate all the con- sumer surplus by using a marginal price equal to c (its marginal cost) and then charge each consumer a fixed fee that equals her surplus. A two-part tariff (where only one fixed fee is used) therefore aims at (imperfectly) replicating this outcome.

In most jurisdictions, such as for instance the EU and the US, quantity discounts are not prohibited by competition law. Economic analysis, as we have just seen, suggests that this is a sensible approach.[113]

7.4.1.3 Price Discrimination between Countries

As seen in Chapter 1, EU law takes a negative view of price discrimination between member countries: some practices used by firms to prevent parallel imports (that is, arbitrage) are basically under a status of *per se* prohibition and are considered, along with cartels, the gravest competition offence under EU law.

It is therefore very important to see what economic analysis has to say on this issue, not only with respect to the usual standard of total welfare, but also to the objective of "economic integration" that the Commission and the Community Courts seem to pursue when dealing with inter-country price discrimination.

Suppose that a monopolist (but the same arguments can be made to any firm enjoying some market power) sells the same product in two different markets, say Germany and Portugal; assume also that transportation costs are nil, for simplicity. In Germany there exists a higher intensity of demand for the good than in Portugal, which can be thought of as reflecting the higher German incomes.[114] If the mo- nopolist is allowed to price discriminate, it will set a higher price in Germany, say p^D, than in Portugal, say p^P. (Of course, it will be able to enforce this price differ- ence only if it can prevent consumers and intermediaries from exploiting arbitrage opportunities. For instance, if it forbids Portuguese buyers to re-sell outside their home country.)

---

[113] See Section 7.4.2.2 for a technical treatment.
[114] See Tirole (1988: 143–4) for why different incomes generate different tastes.

Suppose instead that price discrimination is prohibited by law. One would then expect the new uniform price, p^u, to be located somewhere in between p^D and p^P, if the firm wants to serve both markets. What is the effect on welfare of imposing the same price across countries? *A priori*, it is ambiguous: profits decrease (as the firm is not able to exploit the different intensities in demand), Germans would gain (since they buy at a price p^u lower than p^D) and Portuguese would lose (the new price p^u is higher than p^P).[115]

Nevertheless, technical Section 7.4.2.1 shows that aggregating losses and gains, overall welfare increases when banning price discrimination *if* both markets are served under both regimes.

This result would seem to support the claims of critics of price discrimination. However, there is a strong assumption behind the result above, which is that the firm has always an interest in serving both markets. This is not necessarily the case: if the Portuguese market is very small compared to the German one, and/or if Portuguese demand is much smaller than the German one, the firm that cannot price discriminate will prefer to set the price p^D in both markets even if it implies losing all sales in Portugal. In this case, banning price discrimination is clearly welfare detrimental: it reduces the profits of the firm, reduces Portuguese consumer surplus and leaves German consumer surplus unchanged.

More generally, price discrimination would allow firms to reduce prices to categories of consumers who would not buy otherwise, thus increasing the total quantity sold. Economic theory shows that price discrimination unambiguously reduces welfare only when it does not raise total output, whereas the sign of welfare change is ambiguous in all other cases.

If a clear assessment of price discrimination cannot be reached when using the welfare criterion that economists prefer, note that banning price discrimination need not fare better under the criterion of "achieving market integration": its effect might well be that a product will completely disappear from one market (in the example above, no unit of the good will be sold in Portugal).[116]

7.4.1.4 Dynamic Effects of Price Discrimination: Incentives to Invest

Price discrimination might affect welfare in a long-run perspective too, by modifying firms' incentives to innovate. A simple argument that does not require any technical treatment is as follows. Suppose that a firm has to decide whether to introduce a new product in the EU or not, and that the cost of developing and launching the product is

---

[115] For those who think that equity is an issue, note that higher income consumers are better off and lower income consumers are worse off from the prohibition of price discrimination.

[116] This seems to have been the final effect in the *UK Distillers* case, where following the judgement of the ECJ, a whisky brand (previously sold in Continental Europe at a lower price than in the UK) was not sold outside the UK.

independent of output, as is reasonable to assume. Since price discrimination allows the firm to have higher profits, if the fixed cost falls between the price discrimination and the uniform pricing profits, then the product will be introduced if the firm expects to be able to prevent parallel imports, but will not be introduced if price discrimination practices were outlawed. More generally, price discrimination can affect the marginal profits from investing or innovating, creating more incentives to engage in such activities (See technical Section 7.4.2.3).

This is an important issue in some recent EU cases, where pharmaceutical companies have been fined by the European Commission for having forbidden intermediaries in one country from selling the product in countries where the sales price was higher. In 1996, Bayer was fined by the EC because it reduced supplies of the cardiovascular drug Adalat to French and Spanish wholesalers that have been re-exporting to the UK, where the price for the drug was higher.[117] In *Glaxo/Wellcome* (2001), the EC prohibited the dual pricing system introduced by Glaxo/Wellcome for all its pharmaceutical products in Spain. According to this system, Spanish wholesalers were charged a higher price for supplies which were to be re-sold abroad than those aimed at the local market, a practice that effectively impeded parallel exports.

The pharmaceutical market is unusual since prices are often regulated by national governments (or set after negotiations between the government and the companies), and because patent protection might differ across countries. Therefore, it is not surprising that firms want to avoid low prices in one country (due to regulations and/or less intellectual property protection that raises competition) from preventing them from commanding higher prices in another countries. Although the effect is probably not easily quantifiable, reduced profits are likely to reduce the R&D investments that pharmaceutical companies make, thus harming both consumer surplus and total welfare.

7.4.1.5 Does Market Power Matter?

As I have hinted above, any firm that has some degree of market power will have an incentive to price discriminate. Indeed, small and large firms, operating in very different sectors of activity, try to price discriminate to increase their profits. In the EU, all firms are currently prevented from prohibiting parallel imports. For instance, in 2000, the European Commission has – after investigations and even surprise inspections – prohibited Triumph, a small manufacturer of motorcycles of large engine capacity (750 cc and over) from banning exports of motorcycles from Belgium and the Netherlands to the UK (where its products commanded

---

[117] The *Adalat* decision by the EC was later annulled by the Court of First Instance (mostly for formal reasons, although the Advocate General's opinion seemed for the first time to accept that forbidding parallel trade should not necessarily be a *per se* anti-competitive practice). The case is under appeal at the European Court of Justice as of January 2003.

a higher price). Triumph's market share for this kind of motorcycles in any individual EU country is below 5% except in the UK where it oscillates around 10%.[118] The question is: does it make sense to extend the prohibition of preventing parallel imports to firms with little market power, as is currently the case in the EU?

First, it should be noted that – whatever its effect on welfare – one should expect price discrimination by firms with little market power to have a small effect in magnitude on welfare. Second, we have seen above that price discrimination might also – by increasing profits – boost investments. As such, price discrimination by firms having small market power should be welcomed rather than prohibited, as it may allow them to become more competitive.[119] It is therefore difficult to justify, *on welfare grounds*, why the EC does not introduce a safe harbour according to which firms with a market share below a certain threshold will not be investigated for practices hampering parallel trade. The objective of such a tough stance against price discrimination seems to be dictated only by political reasons (giving citizens of different countries access to the same deal), but the EC should be aware that this comes at a cost in terms of efficiency, and might also backfire in some cases (when a firm sets a price that effectively implies ceasing supplying a country altogether).

7.4.1.6 Price Discrimination as a Monopolisation Device

So far, I have dealt only with the effects of price discrimination on consumer surplus and welfare *given the structure of the market* in which the discriminating firm operates. A different question is whether price discrimination can be used to change such a market structure, for instance by pre-empting entry, or forcing exit, of competitors.

To discuss whether discrimination might be used in an anti-competitive way, imagine that an incumbent-monopolist that produces a good with relevant transportation costs is located in the centre of a country whose population is concentrated around two cities, one in the north and the other in the south. Suppose also that a new competitor sets up a plant in a neighbouring country which lies north. It is then clear that the monopolist has an incentive to price discriminate, charging a higher price in the southern city than in the northern one. Is this anti-competitive behaviour or not?

As seen in Section 7.2.4, there is little doubt that this behaviour should be seen as predatory if the price is below average variable cost. But one might wonder if price discrimination is sufficient to evaluate this as monopolisation or abuse of dominance independently of whether prices are above or below any cost benchmark.

Banning price discrimination in such a circumstance has similar ambiguous effects as the ones seen for price discrimination in general. If uniform pricing leads

---

[118] See *Triumph*.

[119] Both effects can be seen formally in technical Section 7.4.2.4.

the incumbent to serve both cities at an intermediate price, one would expect a positive welfare impact. But it might also happen, if the northern city is less important in income or population, that the incumbent prefers to comply with the uniform pricing requirement by keeping the same high price as in the south. If this happens, welfare will likely decrease (see also technical Section 7.4.2.5). Note also that in this case some productive inefficiency might also arise *if* the incumbent is more efficient than the entrant, as a more efficient producer is replaced by a less efficient one. Further, there is the risk that a rule preventing a monopolist from discriminating gives an incentive to inefficient producers to enter the market: knowing that the incumbent cannot cut prices unless it cuts them in all its markets, they will expect a weak reaction to their entry and get higher profits than otherwise.

Selective Discounts and Fidelity Rebates   Apart from setting different prices to final consumers, a firm might also discriminate among its retailers and distributors. Examples of such practices are not only quantity discounts (which are usually considered lawful) but also discounts and rebates that firms give to push their buyers to purchase more from them. *Fidelity rebates,* for instance, are discounts that a producer gives to a customer to reward the latter for purchasing most or all of its requirements of a given product from the former.[120] *Aggregate rebates* are discounts given to a customer that buys most or all of its products from that same producer.

In the EU, the European Commission and the European Court of Justice have always taken a tough stance on discriminatory prices adopted by dominant firms and which are not justified by cost savings.[121,122]

First of all, it should be recalled that not only cost but also demand and market conditions might explain why firms would want to engage in discriminatory pricing (and that price discrimination is not always a welfare reducing business practice). Therefore, automatically outlawing selective discounts, even when used by a dominant firm, does not appear a robust policy recommendation: as seen above, it is part of a normal competitive process that a firm charges lower prices when its rivals are stronger (but of course, prices below average variable costs should be deemed predatory).

That said, some types of rebates made by dominant firms should be carefully monitored because of their exclusionary potential. The effect of fidelity rebates, for instance, is to try and induce the retailer not to buy from rivals, and it is therefore

---

[120] For example, a firm A might give a fidelity rebate that consists of a 10% discount if the customer buys more than 50% of its requirements from A, a 15% discount if it buys more than 70%, and a 20% discount if it buys more than 90% of its requirements from A.

[121] Examples of discounts justified by cost savings might be discounts based on the quantity bought (that leads to economies of scale), for immediate payments, or that reflect lower transportation costs, or that reward retailers that engage in promotional activities.

[122] The classic cases are *United Brands, Hoffman-La Roche* and *Michelin;* a more recent case is *Virgin/British Airways,* regarding British Airways' discounts to travel agents.

similar to exclusive dealing; and aggregate rebates are similar in their effects to tying or full-line forcing (when the supplier imposes a purchaser to buy all of its range of products). Accordingly, these types of discounts achieve a similar purpose to exclusive dealing and tying, whose possible anti-competitive effects have been discussed at length above.

Price Transparency   In Chapter 6, we have seen that a monopolist might be unable to fully exploit its market power due to a commitment problem. This is because given the input price contract signed with a buyer, it might have an incentive to offer a better deal to another buyer. Anticipating this, a buyer will be unwilling to accept a high price contract in the first place.

The EC has repeatedly stated that a dominant firm should give the maximum transparency to its buyers, that it should be guaranteed that they will all receive an equal deal from the monopolist when they buy similar quantities.[123] This effectively removes any temptation from the monopolist to offer a price discount to a buyer after having signed with another (since a discount should be offered to all buyers), and therefore provides it with a commitment mechanism that allows it to command high prices. Perhaps paradoxically, therefore, the effect of requiring transparency is to restore all the market power of the monopolist.

7.4.1.7 Anti-Dumping

Anti-dumping laws have been adopted by many countries (USA, Australia, Canada and the EU are the main users of such laws, whereas less developed countries are usually defendants) and are often enforced vigorously.[124] They are generally seen as an instrument of trade policy rather than one of competition law (for instance, in the EU it is not DG Competition that deals with anti-dumping). My objective here is to underline the competition implications of anti-dumping.

The World Trade Organisation (the organisation that presides over multi-lateral trade agreements) recognises the right of its members to take unilateral actions to protect themselves when their domestic industry is injured by unfair trade practices, such as foreign firms "dumping" their products (i.e., selling at an exceedingly low price). More precisely, anti-dumping actions are legitimate when two conditions are verified. These are, first, when export prices are *below their normal value*; and second, when exports cause or threaten *material injury* to the domestic industry of the importing country.

The ambiguity of the WTO provisions leaves room for quite different notions of dumping. For instance, there exists a substantial margin of discretion and

---

[123] See for instance the *Michelin* case.
[124] See Trebilcock and Howse (1995) for a discussion of anti-dumping law and practice.

arbitrariness in the calculation of the "normal price".[125] As for the determination of the injury created by dumping (however one would measure the latter), some commentators have suggested that it is too open to political influences (Tharakan and Waelbroeck, 1994).

From the way in which anti-dumping regulations are implemented in both the EU and in other countries, more than an instrument to avoid unfair practices, they appear as an instrument of trade protection in disguise. As such, it should not come as a surprise that its relevance has increased over the years, seemingly caused by the lower availability of more traditional instruments of protection (such as tariffs, reduced over time by successive multi-lateral negotiations).

Independent of the specific ways in which dumping is calculated by the different national laws and regulations, it should be emphasised that there is little economic rationale for considering the difference between the home price and the export price as an "unfair practice". As we have seen in this chapter, price discrimination between different markets is compatible with the simple objective of profit maximisation and neither necessarily entails the intention of forcing rivals out of the market, nor is necessarily welfare detrimental.

In international trade, price discrimination naturally takes the form of different prices in different markets. Normally, since firms tend to have a larger market share and more faithful demand in their domestic market, this implies that domestic price is higher at home than abroad.[126]

The welfare effect of anti-dumping measures, which is so loosely defined as to comprehend most situations where foreign producers are more competitive than domestic ones, is clearly negative, as not only consumers but also firms which use the good as an input might be penalised by the anti-dumping actions. This implies that a measure which is supposed to help the national industry might actually be detrimental to it. Furthermore, anti-dumping laws might remove threats to domestic

---

[125] One way to compute the normal price is to look at the price in the exporters' home market. By using this method, however, the EC excludes from such a calculation all the sales which occur at "less than fully allocated cost", as well as those which do no not occur "under the ordinary course of business". In most cases, however, the normal value is found by using the "constructed cost method", which consists of adding up all the average costs of production, average fixed costs, general expenses, and a "reasonable" profit margin (which can vary across industries and which is not specified once-and-for-all). The exclusion of transactions in which price is lower than costs because "not in the ordinary course of trade" clearly inflates the normal value, by rendering the finding of dumping more likely. In the same way, the inclusion of all sorts of fixed costs and of a profit margin in the calculation of the normal price also tends to find dumping more frequently than it should be. The EC has been in particular criticised for the procedure used, which biases the results of the investigation towards the outcome of dumping.

[126] A well-known model where each firm sets a lower (f.o.b.) price abroad than in the domestic market is given by Brander (1981) where reciprocal dumping occurs in a Cournot setting.

firms which are not competitive enough. This has productive efficiency implications (as domestic firms devote their energy more to lobbying for state intervention than in improving their processes and products) and might allow them to preserve market power positions.[127]

One case which illustrates the conflict that anti-dumping laws have with economic efficiency is that of the soda-ash industry, whose two main European producers (Solvay had 70% of the market share in Continental Europe in 1990, while ICI had a quasi-monopoly in the UK market) received heavy fines for collusive agreements and for abuse of dominant position. It is then surprising to discover that the industry has been repeatedly protected from foreign competition by anti-dumping actions.[128]

Of course, the European anti-dumping laws are not the only ones which can be criticised. The US anti-dumping measures, for instance, have also attracted a number of criticisms. Empirical analyses have shown the anti-competitive effect of anti-dumping policies. Further, they have confirmed the theoretical suspicion that anti-dumping laws have a negative effect even when they do not result in final duties. The mere threat of anti-dumping sanctions can be enough to induce foreign competitors to be less aggressive, and very often investigations end up with a suspension decision, in exchange for the promise of the foreign firms to stop "dumping" their goods.[129]

Anti-dumping duties should be justified only when predatory pricing is involved. Accordingly, dumping should not be considered as belonging to the domain of trade policy, but rather to that of competition policy. And to justify anti-dumping actions, the standards set up in Section 7.2 should be used.

7.4.2 Price Discrimination*

I offer here a technical presentation of the arguments made in the previous section. Section 7.4.2.1 deals with the case of price discrimination across national markets, Section 7.4.2.2 with quantity discounts,[130] Section 7.4.2.3 with price discrimination and incentives to invest, Section 7.4.2.4 with the role of market power, and Section 7.4.2.5 with the effects of discrimination when a monopolist faces an entrant.

---

[127] Messerlin (1990), for instance, finds that anti-dumping actions have been crucial for the survival of collusive agreements among European firms in two sectors.

[128] Less surprisingly, the EC found that "one of the major preoccupations of Solvay's commercial policy in the soda sector is to ensure the maintenance of the anti-dumping measures in place against the United States producers of heavy ash as well as the East European producers of light ash" (*Soda-ash, Solvay*: 23, my translation).

[129] See Staiger and Wolak (1994).

[130] For presentation reasons, it is more convenient to invert the order followed in the previous section, and deal with second-degree price discrimination after third-degree discrimination.

7.4.2.1 Third-Degree Price Discrimination*

A monopolist serves two markets, l and h, which one can think of as two regions that are part of the same country (or two countries that are part of a union). The weight of the two regions in the country is respectively λ and $1 - \lambda$, with $0 < \lambda < 1$. Market $i = l, h$ demand is given by $q = v_i - p$, with $v_h > v_l$. This can be rationalised by assuming that a type-i consumer has a utility function $U_i = v_i q - q^2/2$.[131]

The monopolist serves both countries from the same plant, and has a unit cost $c < v_l$ (we disregard transport costs for simplicity). We want to compare the case where the monopolist can discriminate to the one where it cannot.

Price Discrimination The monopolist can choose two different prices and its profits in each market are given by $\pi_i = (p_i - c)(v_i - p_i)$. From $\partial \pi_i/\partial p_i = 0$ the equilibrium solutions are easily found (total profits should be weighted by population shares):

$$p_i^d = \frac{v_i + c}{2}; \qquad \pi^d = \lambda\frac{(v_l - c)^2}{4} + (1 - \lambda)\frac{(v_h - c)^2}{4}. \qquad (7.105)$$

The consumer surplus in each market can easily be found as the area of triangle between the demand function and the market price; aggregate consumer surplus and welfare are obtained by weighting each market:

$$CS^d = \frac{\lambda(v_l - c)^2}{8} + \frac{(1 - \lambda)(v_h - c)^2}{8};$$

$$W^d = \frac{3}{8}\left(\frac{\lambda(v_l - c)^2}{4} + \frac{(1 - \lambda)(v_h - c)^2}{4}\right). \qquad (7.106)$$

Uniform Pricing (Both Markets Served) Suppose now that there is a ban on price discrimination. The monopolist is then obliged to set the same uniform price p for both markets and its programme is $\max_p(p - c)[\lambda(v_l - p) + (1 - \lambda)(v_h - p)]$. Suppose for the moment that both markets are served. From $\partial \pi/\partial p = 0$, the equilibrium solutions are

$$p^u = \frac{\lambda v_l + (1 - \lambda)v_h + c}{2}; \qquad \pi^u = \frac{(\lambda v_l + (1 - \lambda)v_h - c)^2}{4}. \qquad (7.107)$$

One can easily check that the uniform price is in between the prices the monopolist would charge if it were allowed to price discriminate: $p_h^d > p^u > p_l^d$. Consumer

---

[131] From the maximisation of its utility subject to the budget constraint, it follows that $v_i - q = p$.

surplus and welfare under uniform pricing are

$$CS^u = \frac{(\lambda v_l + (1 - \lambda)v_h - c)^2}{8} + \frac{\lambda(1 - \lambda)(v_h - v_l)^2}{2};$$

$$W^u = \frac{3(\lambda v_l + (1 - \lambda)v_h - c)^2}{8} + \frac{\lambda(1 - \lambda)(v_h - v_l)^2}{2}. \qquad (7.108)$$

We can now compare the two equilibria. It is easily checked that the firm prefers to be free to discriminate ($\pi^u < \pi^d$), which should not come as a surprise since under discrimination it has two instruments to maximise its objective function, whereas under uniform pricing it has only one. A few steps of algebra also show that

$$W^u - W^d = \frac{\lambda(1 - \lambda)(v_h - v_l)^2}{8} > 0, \qquad (7.109)$$

which implies that welfare is higher under uniform pricing. Indeed, it is a general result that price discrimination decreases welfare if it does not increase total output,[132] and one can check that here total output sold is the same under the two regimes, making it an application of the general result:

$$Q^d = \lambda q_l^d + (1 - \lambda)q_l^d = \frac{\lambda v_l + (1 - \lambda)v_h - c}{2} = Q^u = \lambda q_l^u + (1 - \lambda)q_l^u.$$
$$(7.110)$$

Uniform Prices (One Market Not Served)   There is a strong assumption behind the analysis just carried out: viz., the monopolist serves both markets. However, uniform pricing to serve both markets entails reducing prices (and profits) in the high-demand market. The monopolist might prefer instead just to set the price $p_h = (v_h + c)/2$ that maximises its profits in the high-demand market, even if this implies losing all sales in the low-demand market. For instance, assume that $v_h + c > 2v_l$. In this case, demand in the low-demand market is zero, and the monopolist will earn

$$\pi_h^u = (1 - \lambda)\frac{(v_h - c)^2}{4}. \qquad (7.111)$$

Standard calculations show that

$$\pi_h^u > \pi^u \text{ if } \lambda < \frac{(v_h - c)(v_h - 2v_l + c)}{(v_h - v_l)^2}, \qquad (7.112)$$

that is, the lower the share of the low-demand market in total demand the more likely it will not be served if price discrimination was banned. It can also be checked that the RHS of expression (7.112) increases with v_h and decreases with v_l: the higher the gap between the demands, the more likely one market only will be served.

---

[132] For a proof, see Varian (1989), for Tirole (1988: 137–8).

Finally, it is straightforward to check that if only one market is served (that is, if (7.112) holds) welfare is higher under price discrimination, since the high-demand market has the same consumption and profits under both regimes, but the low-demand market contributes zero to both under uniform pricing.

7.4.2.2 Quantity Discounts: Two-Part Tariffs as Price Discrimination*

I consider here the case where the monopolist uses a two-part tariff $T + pq$: a consumer buying q units of the good will have to pay a fixed fee T plus a variable component p. Note that this amounts to a quantity discount, as the average cost of the purchase, $p + T/q$, decreases with the number of units bought.

Let me continue with the example of the previous Section 7.4.2.1: there are two different types of consumers, low-types having demand $q = v_l - p$ (they are a share λ of the population) and high-types having demand $q = v_h - p$ (a share $1 - \lambda$ of the population).

Assume that $v_l > (c + v_h)/2$, which ensures that everybody buys under both uniform pricing and two-part tariffs.[133]

Non-Discrimination This case has been already analysed in the previous section.

Quantity Discounts (Two-Part Tariff) Since low-types have lower intensity of demand, the fixed fee will be chosen so as to make them willing to pay. Given that their consumer surplus is given by $CS_l = (v_l - p)^2/2 - T$, it follows that the monopolist will set $T = (v_l - p)^2/2$. As for the variable component of the tariff, it is found as the one which solves the problem:

$$\max_p \pi = (p - c)[\lambda (v_l - p) + (1 - \lambda)(v_h - p)] + (v_l - p)^2/2. \quad (7.113)$$

From $\partial \pi / \partial p = 0$, it follows that

$$p^{qd} = c + (1 - \lambda)(v_h - v_l). \quad (7.114)$$

Note that the quantity bought by the low-types is $q = v_l - p^{qd}$, so that $q > 0$ amounts to $v_l > [c + (1 - \lambda) v_h]/(2 - \lambda)$, which is satisfied by the assumption $v_l > (c + v_h)/2$. At this price, the surplus of high-types is

$$CS_h^{qd} = (v_h - v_l)[v_l(2 - \lambda) - c - (1 - \lambda) v_h] > 0 = CS_l^{qd}, \quad (7.115)$$

and the monopolist's profits are

$$\pi^{qd} = \frac{1}{2}\left[(v_l - c)^2 + (1 - \lambda)^2 (v_h - v_l)^2\right], \quad (7.116)$$

and welfare can be found by substitution as $W^{qd} = \pi^{qd} + (1 - \lambda) CS_h^{qd}$.

---

[133] For future reference, note that $(c + v_h)/2 > (c + (1 - \lambda) v_h)/(2 - \lambda)$.

Quantity Discounts and Uniform Pricing: A Comparison   The reader can check that the monopolist will be better off by using this form of price discrimination: $\pi^{qd} > \pi^{u}$. But even without doing any calculations, this is straightforward, since two-part tariffs provide the monopolist with two instruments, T and p, rather than only one as under uniform pricing (the monopolist could always replicate the result under uniform pricing simply by setting $T = 0$ and choosing the same unit price).

As for marginal prices, it is easy to check that $p^{qd} < p^{u}$ for $v_l > [c + (1 - \lambda) v_h] / (2 - \lambda)$, which is true: when two-part tariffs are used, the variable component consumers will pay is lower (but the monopolist will gain from the marginal price decrease because it can use the fixed fee).

Therefore, welfare will also be higher under quantity discounts than under uniform pricing, as the lower marginal price entails a smaller distortion.[134]

7.4.2.3 Price Discrimination and Investments*

In this section, I analyse a simple model of a monopolist that invests in the quality of its good. I show that under price discrimination the equilibrium quality offered will be higher.

Consider a monopolist that sells a good of quality u to two different markets, each of size one. Consumers in both markets have preferences $CS = \theta u - p$ if they buy one unit of the good, and 0 otherwise. In market h, consumers' taste for quality, θ, is uniformly distributed on $0 \leq \theta \leq \theta_h$. In market l, the taste parameter is uniformly distributed on $0 \leq \theta \leq \theta_l$ with $\theta_l < \theta_h$.

The monopolist has to decide first on the quality u it wants to supply, and it has a fixed cost of quality improvement $C(u) = ku^2/2$ (assume for simplicity that there is zero variable cost of production); then, it has to decide on the price at which it wants to sell the good. Consider two variants of the game: in the first, it has to choose the same price for both markets; in the second, it can price discriminate.[135]

Uniform Pricing   First of all, note that the demand faced by the monopolist is determined by finding the consumer who is indifferent between buying or not. Given a price p and a quality u, the indifferent consumer θ_0 is given by solution of $CS = \theta u - p = 0$. Therefore, $\theta_0 = p/u$. Therefore, demand is given by all consumers in both markets such that $\theta \geq \theta_0$. Profits in the second stage are

$$\Pi = p \left[\left(\theta_h - \frac{p}{u} \right) + \left(\theta_l - \frac{p}{u} \right) \right]. \tag{7.117}$$

---

[134] The reader can check that $W^{qd} > W^{u}$, for $v_l > [c + (1 - \lambda) v_h] / (2 - \lambda)$.

[135] In international trade theory, the case of price discrimination across markets is called "segmented markets", whereas choosing one price for both markets is called "integrated markets".

From the FOC $\partial \pi / \partial p = 0$, it follows that equilibrium prices and profits are

$$p^u = \frac{u(\theta_h + \theta_l)}{4}; \qquad \Pi^u = \frac{u(\theta_h + \theta_l)^2}{8}. \tag{7.118}$$

The total quantity sold by the monopolist is $q^u = \theta_h - (\theta_h + \theta_l)/4 + \theta_l - (\theta_h + \theta_l)/4 = (\theta_h + \theta_l)/2$. The optimal quality choice can be found as the solution of the programme $\max_u \pi = \Pi^u - ku^2/2$; from $\partial \pi / \partial u = 0$, it follows that

$$u^u = \frac{u(\theta_h + \theta_l)^2}{8k}. \tag{7.119}$$

Price Discrimination Under price discrimination, the monopolist can charge a different price in the two markets. The indifferent consumer θ_0^i in market i is given by solution of $CS = \theta u - p_i = 0$. Whence $\theta_0^i = p_i/u$. Profits in the second stage are

$$\Pi = p_h \left(\theta_h - \frac{p_h}{u} \right) + p_l \left(\theta_l - \frac{p_l}{u} \right). \tag{7.120}$$

From the FOC $\partial \Pi / \partial p_i = 0$, it follows that equilibrium prices and profits are

$$p_i^d = \frac{u\theta_i}{2}; \qquad \Pi^d = \frac{u(\theta_h^2 + \theta_l^2)}{4}. \tag{7.121}$$

Note also that the total quantity sold by the monopolist is $q^d = \theta_h - \theta_h/2 + \theta_l - \theta_l/2 = (\theta_h + \theta_h)/2$, which is the same as under uniform pricing. The optimal quality choice can be found as the solution of the programme $\max_u \pi = \Pi^d - ku^2/2$; from $\partial \pi / \partial u = 0$, it follows that

$$u^d = \frac{u(\theta_h^2 + \theta_l^2)}{4k}. \tag{7.122}$$

It is then straightforward to check that $u^d > u^u$.

7.4.2.4 Price Discrimination and Market Power*

Consider a vertical product differentiation model where firm 1 sells a product of quality u_1 and firm 2 a product of quality u_2, with $u_1 > u_2$. Both firms sell in two different markets, each of size one. (A firm does not differentiate quality across markets.) Consumers in both markets have preferences $CS_j = \theta u_j - p_j$ if they buy one unit of the good of quality $j = 1, 2$, and 0 otherwise. In market h, consumers' taste for quality, θ, is uniformly distributed on $0 \leq \theta \leq \theta_h$. In market l, it is uniformly distributed on $0 \leq \theta \leq \theta_l$, where $\theta_l < \theta_h$.

I show here that both firms have an incentive to price discriminate, but that there is little reason to care about price discrimination practices of a firm with little market power.

Uniform Pricing To find demand functions of the firms, we first need to identify two indifferent consumers: the consumer indifferent between buying from the low-quality good and not buying, θ_0, and the consumer indifferent between buying the low-or the top-quality good, θ_{12}.

From $CS_2 = 0$ it follows that $\theta_0 = p_2/u_2$. From $CS_2 = CS_1$ it follows that $\theta_{12} = (p_1 - p_2)/(u_1 - u_2)$. Therefore, demand functions are $q_1^i = \theta_i - \theta_{12}$ and $q_2 = \theta_{12} - \theta_0$, with $i = l, h$. Firms' profits are

$$\Pi_1 = p_1\left[\theta_h + \theta_l - 2\frac{p_1 - p_2}{u_1 - u_2}\right]; \qquad \Pi_2 = 2p_2\left(\frac{p_1 - p_2}{u_1 - u_2} - \frac{p_2}{u_2}\right). \quad (7.123)$$

Equilibrium prices in the price sub-game are found from $\partial\Pi_j/\partial p_j = 0$ as

$$p_1^u = \frac{u_1(u_1 - u_2)(\theta_h + \theta_l)}{(4u_1 - u_2)}; \qquad p_2^u = \frac{u_2(u_1 - u_2)(\theta_h + \theta_l)}{2(4u_1 - u_2)}. \quad (7.124)$$

Given u_1, a low u_2 implies that firm 2 can command a low price. For u_2 which tends to zero, for instance, firm 2's price would also tend to zero, that is, the low-quality firm would have very little market power (which is the ability of raising prices above marginal costs, here zero).[136]

By substitution, one can find equilibrium profits as

$$\Pi_1^u = \frac{2u_1^2(u_1 - u_2)(\theta_h + \theta_l)^2}{(4u_1 - u_2)^2}; \qquad \Pi_2^u = \frac{u_1 u_2(u_1 - u_2)(\theta_h + \theta_l)^2}{2(4u_1 - u_2)^2}. \quad (7.125)$$

Price Discrimination Under price discrimination, both firms can charge a different price in the two markets. Firms' profits are

$$\Pi_1 = \sum_{i=h,l} p_{1i}\left[\theta_i - \frac{p_{1i} - p_{2i}}{u_1 - u_2}\right]; \qquad \Pi_2 = \sum_{i=h,l} p_{2i}\left(\frac{p_{1i} - p_{2i}}{u_1 - u_2} - \frac{p_{2i}}{u_2}\right).$$

$$(7.126)$$

Equilibrium prices in the price sub-game are found from $\partial\Pi_{ji}/\partial p_{ji} = 0$ as

$$p_{1i}^d = \frac{2u_1(u_1 - u_2)\theta_i}{(4u_1 - u_2)}; \qquad p_{2i}^d = \frac{u_2(u_1 - u_2)\theta_i}{(4u_1 - u_2)}. \quad (7.127)$$

Therefore, it is clear that both firms discriminate across markets at equilibrium (in other words, not only monopolists want to segment markets!) By substitution, equilibrium profits are

$$\Pi_1^d = \frac{4u_1^2(u_1 - u_2)(\theta_h^2 + \theta_l^2)}{(4u_1 - u_2)^2}; \qquad \Pi_2^d = \frac{u_1 u_2(u_1 - u_2)(\theta_h^2 + \theta_l^2)}{(4u_1 - u_2)^2}. \quad (7.128)$$

---

[136] Note that there is no monotonic relationship here between u_2 and its equilibrium price (market power). This is because when u_2 becomes close enough to u_1, the products become closer substitutes and equilibrium prices decrease.

Market Power and Price Discrimination In this simple model, the distortion created by price discrimination in each market differs across firms:[137]

$$p_{1i}^d - p_1^u = \left| \frac{u_1(u_1 - u_2)(\theta_h - \theta_l)}{(4u_1 - u_2)} \right|; \qquad p_{2i}^d - p_2^u = \left| \frac{u_2(u_1 - u_2)(\theta_h - \theta_l)}{2(4u_1 - u_2)} \right|. \tag{7.129}$$

Clearly, the distortion becomes irrelevant when a firm does not have much market power. For small values of u_2 (that is, when firm 2 has little market power), the price difference becomes very small. More formally,

$$\frac{\partial(p_{2i}^d - p_2^u)}{\partial u_2} = \frac{(4u_1^2 - 8u_1 u_2 + u_2^2)(\theta_h - \theta_l)}{2(4u_1 - u_2)^2}. \tag{7.130}$$

From studying the second-order inequality $4u_1^2 - 8u_1 u_2 + u_2^2 > 0$ one obtains that the equilibrium price difference between the two pricing regimes increases with u_2 for $u_2 < .53u_1$ and decreases for higher values. In other words, when the quality gap is the highest (market power of firm 2 is the lowest), an increase in u_2 (an increase in firm 2's market power) raises the price differential up to a point where the qualities are similar enough.

This strongly suggests that when a firm has little market power (as is the case with firm 2 here for low enough values of u_2), the impact that its pricing policy might have is unlikely to be significant.

The Effect on Investments Suppose now that, for some reason, firm 1's quality was fixed but firm 2 (the firm in a disadvantaged position) could invest to improve its quality level at a convex cost $C(u_2)$. It is easy to see that price discrimination would allow the firm to have a higher incentive to invest in quality, thereby helping it to fill the gap more than in the case of uniform pricing.

Firm 2's problem is then to choose its quality endogenously so as to maximise its net profits: $\max_{u_2} \Pi_2(u_2) - C(u_2)$. The gross profits and the first-order condition of this problem are different according to the price regime. Under uniform pricing, it is given by

$$\frac{\partial \Pi_2^u(u_2)}{\partial u_2} = \frac{u_1^2(4u_1 - 7u_2)(\theta_h + \theta_l)^2}{2(4u_1 - u_2)^2} = \frac{\partial C(u_2)}{\partial u_2}, \tag{7.131}$$

[137] Obviously, for both firms the price is higher (respectively lower) under price discrimination in the market with higher (resp. lower) intensity of demand, v_h (resp. v_l). Although the sign of the price difference is opposed, the absolute magnitude of the difference is the same for each firm.

whereas under price discrimination it is given by

$$\frac{\partial \Pi_2^d(u_2)}{\partial u_2} = \frac{u_1^2(4u_1 - 7u_2)(\theta_h^2 + \theta_l^2)}{(4u_1 - u_2)^2} = \frac{\partial C(u_2)}{\partial u_2}. \tag{7.132}$$

It is easy to check that $\partial \Pi_2^d(u_2)/\partial u_2 > \partial \Pi_2^u(u_2)/\partial u_2$ as $(\theta_h - \theta_l)^2 > 0$, which entails that the equilibrium quality chosen by firm 2 will be higher under price discrimination (marginal revenue from the investment is higher, whereas the marginal cost is the same). Therefore, by forbidding a firm with low quality to price discriminate, its chance to reduce the gap that separates it from the high-quality firm is reduced.

7.4.2.5 Price Discrimination under Entry*

Two cities are located along the horizontal line $[0, 2t]$ that delimits a country. The first, city A, is at 0, and the second at $2t$. Firm 1, the incumbent monopolist, is located between the two cities, at t. Demand in each city is given by $q = 1 - p$; there is no demand elsewhere. Suppose now that firm 1's monopoly is challenged by imports from a foreign firm that is located at $2t + T$. Assume that both firms have zero production costs, but have to incur a unit transportation cost which is proportional to distance: for instance, it costs T (resp. $T + 2t$) for firm 2 to bring each unit to city B (resp. A). Assume that $(1 + t)/2 \geq T \geq (1 - 3t)/2$: firm 2 is close enough to challenge firm 1 in city B, but not enough to endanger its monopoly in city A.

Firms Compete in Prices   I want to compare the regime where firm 1 is allowed to price discriminate between cities with the one where it is not. (Note that the assumption of identical demands ensures that competition is the only reason for price discrimination.)

Price Discrimination   Under the assumptions above, firm 1 is undisturbed in city A, where it will set the monopoly price, $p_A^d = (1 + t)/2$. (This comes from $\max_p \pi = (p - t)(1 - p)$, and setting $\partial \pi / \partial p = 0$.) Bertrand competition in city B implies instead that it will get all demand, but at the price $p_B^d = T$. Its total profits are $\pi^d = (1 - t)^2/4 + (T - t)(1 - T)$.

Uniform Pricing   If price discrimination was banned, and the incumbent wanted to serve both markets, it would have to set $p_A^u = p_B^u = T$, and would make profits $\pi^u = 2(T - t)(1 - T)$.

However, the incumbent might decide instead to serve only its captive market A, and sets prices in both markets equal to $p^m = (1 + t)/2$. It would then make monopoly profits $\pi^m = (1 - t)^2/4$ in market A but it would not get any demand in market B, where firm 2 would obtain all demand by just slightly undercutting p^m.[138]

---

[138] Note that the monopoly price of firm 1 is higher than the export monopoly price of firm 2, $(1 + T)/2$.

One can check that serving only market A is more profitable if $T < (1 + t)/2 - \sqrt{2}(1 - t)/4$.[139] This is because when firm 2 is close enough, serving city B would involve a big drop in prices and profits in city A as well, so it is more convenient not to serve the border city.

Therefore, a ban on price discrimination by the monopolist threatened by entry on one side of its market has an ambiguous welfare impact. If the monopolist serves both markets under uniform pricing, prices drop in both markets, the deadweight loss in each market decreases, and the total welfare goes up. However, imposing uniform pricing on the incumbent would be detrimental, if it would consequently not serve the border city. In this market, a monopoly by the incumbent would simply be replaced by a monopoly of the entrant, and consumer surplus and overall welfare would decrease.[140] More generally, the ban on price discrimination would increase the market power enjoyed by the entrant. Exercise 7.7 shows that if the monopolist is challenged by firms that cannot have market power, then the ban on price discrimination will not hurt consumers (but may still decrease welfare).

7.5 *US V. MICROSOFT*

This is certainly one of the most publicised cases in the history of anti-trust policies, and it involves a number of interesting aspects for competition policy.[141]

7.5.1 A Short Description of the Case

In May 1998, the US Department of Justice and a group of states filed separate complaints (which were later consolidated) asserting anti-trust violations by Microsoft. The company's alleged anti-competitive practices dealt with business practices related to its internet browser, Internet Explorer (IE), which competed with Netscape Navigator, initially the leading browser.

---

[139] $\pi^m > \pi^u$ if $8T^2 - 8T(1 + t) + 1 + t^2 + 6t > 0$. This standard second-order inequality is solved for external roots, but the highest is outside the interval of values assumed for T.

[140] This is straightforward if one assumes that profits earned by the foreign firm are not computed in national welfare. But the result is unchanged if one includes any share of the foreign firms' profits earned in the domestic market in the welfare function. It just requires to check one more inequality and few steps of algebra.

[141] I refer here only to the US case. In the EU, there is another case – still open as of January 2003 – regarding Microsoft, whose defence team I have collaborated with. Even though the two cases are very different, initially I had planned not to discuss even the US case because I felt that, inevitably, I would lack impartiality. Eventually, I have been convinced that there has been so much interest in this case that one cannot write a book on competition policy today without commenting upon, or at least describing, *US v. Microsoft*. Nevertheless, due to my "conflict of interest", I prefer to abstain from giving my own comments on the case, and I will limit myself to summarising the case by following very closely the judgement of the Court of Appeal. Further, I am not using any other source of information than its judgement, which is publicly available.

In October 1998, the trial started. After the District Court for the District of Columbia (Judge Thomas Penfield Jackson) issued its *Findings of Facts,* an attempt to reach a settlement, with Judge Richard Posner serving as mediator, failed.

In April 2000, the District Court issued its *Conclusions of Law.* Microsoft was found liable for three separate violations of anti-trust laws: (I) maintenance of monopolisation in the market of Intel-compatible operating systems (OS) for personal computers (PC) – Windows OSs belong to this category – (an infringement of Section 2 of the Sherman Act); (II) attempted monopolisation of the internet browser market (again, a violation of Section 2); (III) tying its Windows OS with IE (in violation of Section 1).[142]

In June 2000, the District Court issued its *Final Judgment,* imposing on Microsoft behavioural remedies and structural remedies: the latter would have split Microsoft into two separate companies, one devoted to operating systems and the other to applications.

Microsoft filed an appeal, and the Court of Appeals (CA) issued its decision in June 2001. It ruled that (I) Microsoft was guilty of maintenance of monopolisation for some of the business practices it had adopted (but on others the CA reversed the District Court), but (II) it was not guilty of attempted monopolisation, and (III) found that the tying allegations should be analysed under a rule of reason, rather than under a *per se* rule as Judge Jackson had done, and therefore remanded the case to the District Court for an assessment on tying.

The CA also disqualified Judge Jackson from the case for improper behaviour (he had given interviews about the case while it was open, which is contrary to the judges' code of conduct, and made public comments about Microsoft which put his impartiality in doubt). Hence, another judge of the District Court was put in charge of the case. However, the CA deferred to Judge Jackson's factual findings, implying that it was Microsoft which had the burden of challenging those factual findings, or arguing that they did not support the District Court's conclusions.

Finally, it also remanded the case to the District Court for an assessment of the appropriate remedies (both because of procedural violations by the District Court and because the remedies should be commensurate to the infringement of the anti-trust laws, and the latter was found in appeal more limited than in the lower court).

Following remand, the parties entered into settlement negotiations, and a resolution was reached between Microsoft and the DOJ. Several states joined the settlement, but other states did not, and proposed different remedies. In November 2002, the District Court issued its ruling (*State of New York et al. v. Microsoft Corp.,* No. 98-1233) and decided on the remedies to be adopted, which are behavioural remedies aiming at preventing Microsoft from using exclusionary practices against firms that challenge its monopoly position in the OS market. Two states have decided to appeal this decision.

---

[142] The Court also found insufficient evidence for a Section 1 exclusive dealing violation.

Before describing the case, it is useful to look at the concept of "middleware", which is central to this case.

Middleware   One of the tasks of OSs is to function as "platforms for software applications. They do so by 'exposing' – i.e., making available to software developers – routines or protocols that perform certain widely-used functions. These are known as Application Programming Interfaces, or 'APIs'. . . . For example, Windows contains an API that enables users to draw a box on the screen. . . . Software developers wishing to include that function in an application need not duplicate it in their own code. Instead, they can call – i.e., use – the Windows API" (*US v. Microsoft*: 17).

Each OS has different APIs, and thousands of them. "Accordingly, a developer who writes an application for one operating system and wishes to sell the application to users of another must modify, or 'port', the application to the second operating system. This process is both time-consuming and expensive" (*US v. Microsoft*: 17–18).

Middleware products expose their own APIs. Middleware products written for Windows can take over some or all of Windows' platform functions, so software developers can rely upon APIs exposed by the middleware instead of relying upon the APIs included in Windows. Middleware written for multiple OSs reduces the cost of porting applications to other OSs. This is because a software developer could rely on APIs exposed by middleware to run on all OSs on which the middleware is present.

Netscape Navigator and *Java,* both at the centre of this case, are middleware products written for multiple OSs, and the accusation against Microsoft is that it perceived them as a threat to Windows. By allowing developers to write software applications which would run on different OSs, these products would endanger Windows' monopoly, because a consumer who wanted to use a given application would not need to use Windows but could rely instead on other OSs.

7.5.2 Monopolisation

In the US, to find that a firm is guilty of monopolisation requires first proof that there is monopoly power in the relevant market and second that this monopoly power has been acquired or (as in this case) maintained through anti-competitive means.[143] Therefore, the CA looks at each point in turn.

7.5.2.1 Monopoly Power

The first step in the assessment of monopoly power is to define the *relevant market.* The District Court defined the market as that of all *Intel-compatible PC OS worldwide*, whereas Microsoft claims that the product market definition should be wider,

---

[143] This is not dissimilar from the EU, where one has to first prove that there is dominance, and then that there has been an abuse of dominance.

and should also include 1. non-Intel compatible OS (mainly, Mac OS), 2. OS for non-PC devices (hand-held computers and portal Web sites), and 3. "middleware" products which are not OS.

The CA accepts the definition of the District Court, that excluded these types of products for the following reasons:

1. If there was a substantial price increase of Windows, consumers would not switch to Mac OS, because of the costs of acquiring new hardware (Mac OS does not run on Intel-compatible PCs) and compatible software applications, and because of the effort needed to learn the new system and to transfer files to its format. Additionally, Mac OS supports fewer software applications, which makes it less interesting to consumers.[144]

2. Hand-held devices do not perform all the functions of a PC, and are perceived by customers as a supplement rather than a substitute for their PC; portal Web sites that host server-based applications do not host enough applications to induce the consumers to switch to them. Neither product would therefore constrain the profitability of a price increase in Intel-compatible PC OS.

3. Although potentially middleware could take over the OS' platform function, this is a lengthy process. Navigator, Java and other middleware would take a long time to expose enough APIs to serve as a platform for popular applications. As a result, middleware would not constrain the ability to increase prices in Intel-compatible PC OS for a long time.

After defining the market, the following step is the assessment of *market power*. The CA confirms the District Court's finding that Microsoft enjoys monopoly power in the market, based on two elements: first, Microsoft enjoys extremely high market shares, which are suggestive of dominance; and second, there exist significant barriers to entry.

As for market shares, Windows was found to have more than 95% of the market (more than 80% if the market included Mac OS). The CA acknowledges that market shares, however high, do not always correspond to monopoly power, but argues that in this case there is a strong barrier to entry that protects Microsoft position: "That barrier – the 'applications barrier to entry' – stems from two characteristics of the software market: (1) most consumers prefer operating systems for which a large number of applications have already been written; and (2) most developers prefer to write for operating systems that already have a substantial consumer base. . . . This 'chicken-and-egg' situation ensures that applications will continue to be written for the already dominant Windows, which in turn ensures that consumers will continue to prefer it over other operating systems" (*US v. Microsoft*: 20).

---

[144] This is a market characterised by strong physical and indirect network effects (see Chapters 2 and 7), and the relationship between OS and applications is an example of the latter: The more people buy a certain OS the more applications will be written for it, which increases the utility from buying that OS.

Microsoft disputes the Court's arguments, mainly arguing that middleware would erode the applications barrier to entry (but, as seen above, the CA believes that this would not happen in the foreseeable future), and that if such an applications barrier to entry exists, it is because of the large investments Microsoft made in the past to convince software developers to write programmes for Windows. This argument is not accepted by the CA because "when Microsoft entered the operating system market with MS-DOS and the first version of Windows, it did not confront a dominant rival operating system with as massive an installed base and as vast an existing array of applications as the Windows operating system have since enjoyed" (*US v. Microsoft:* 23).

As a result, Microsoft is found to have monopoly power in the relevant market.

7.5.2.2 Anti-Competitive Conduct

For a firm to be found guilty of monopolisation, there must not only exist monopoly power, but also the acquisition or maintenance of monopoly power through anti-competitive conduct rather than "as a consequence of a superior product, business acumen, or historic accident".

There are a number of deleterious business practices of which Microsoft is accused, and the CA makes it clear that they should be evaluated according to the following principle. "First, to be condemned as exclusionary, a monopolist's act must have an 'anticompetitive effect.' That is, it must harm the competitive *process* and thereby harm consumers. In contrast, harm to one or more *competitors* will not suffice.... Second, the plaintiff, on whom the burden of proof of course rests.... must demonstrate that the monopolist's conduct indeed has the requisite anticompetitive effect.... Third... if the monopolist asserts a procompetitive justification... then the burden shifts back to the plaintiff to rebut that claim.... Fourth, if the monopolist's procompetitive justification stands unrebutted, then the plaintiff must demonstrate that the anticompetitive harm of the conduct outweighs the procompetitive benefit.... Finally,... our focus is upon the effect of that conduct, not upon the intent behind it. Evidence of the intent behind the conduct of a monopolist is relevant only to the extent it helps us understand the likely effect of the monopolist's conduct" (*US v. Microsoft:* 26–8).

The business practices under consideration are now described.

Licenses Issued to OEMs Microsoft is accused of having used a number of provisions in its agreements licensing Windows to original equipment manufacturers (OEMs) aimed at reducing *usage share* of Netscape Navigator, and thus at protecting Windows' monopoly.

Usage share is important because only if enough consumers use a browser will software developers write applications which rely on the APIs it exposes. In turn, these applications will run on any computer using that browser independently of the underlying OS, and consumers could have access to applications simply by installing the browser rather than by using Windows. In this perspective, gaining market share in the browser market would help Microsoft since it would prevent other browsers from gaining the critical mass of users necessary to make software developers interested in writing applications for them.

There are three restrictions in the contracts with the OEMs that are considered. For each, it must be decided whether they have anti-competitive effects; if so, whether they might be motivated by efficiency gains, and again if so, whether the latter outweighs the former.

The first clause prohibits the OEMs from *removing desktop icons, folders and Start menu entries* related to IE. This implies that Windows users will always be able to use IE even if another browser is installed on their PC. This provision is said to be anti-competitive because for a OEM it would be very costly to have more than one browser pre-installed in its computers. The cost would not come from pre-installation, but from having to answer calls from consumers who do not know which browser to use. Accordingly, in order to minimise costs for support calls from "confused end-users", OEMs would simply not pre-install another browser.

The CA finds that this story is convincing (*US v. Microsoft:* 30–1) and judges these provisions anti-competitive. It also finds that Microsoft does not provide any valid efficiency justification for them, thereby concluding that they violated Section 2 of the Sherman Act.

The second clause prohibits OEMs from *modifying the initial boot sequence.* Absent this clause, OEMs could introduce sign-up procedures which appear the first time users turn on the computer, and which encourage them to choose Internet Access Providers (IAPs) using Navigator as their browser.

This provision is also found to be anti-competitive, because it prevents OEMs from promoting browsers competing with IE. However, the CA agrees with Microsoft that "a shell that automatically prevents the Windows desktop from ever being seen by the user is a drastic alteration of Microsoft's copyrighted work, and outweighs the marginal anticompetitive effect of prohibiting the OEMs from substituting a different interface automatically upon completion of the initial boot process" (*US v. Microsoft:* 34). Accordingly, this is not a practice that violates Section 2 of the Sherman Act.

The third clause prohibits OEMs from *changing the appearance of the desktop.* This clause is also considered anti-competitive because it prevents OEMs from promoting IE's rival browsers and IAPs which do not rely on IE. Microsoft argued that there is an efficiency rationale for such a provision, because altering the appearance of the desktop (as well as changing the initial boot sequence) could undermine "the principal value of Windows as a stable and consistent platform that supports a broad range of applications and that is familiar to users" (*US v. Microsoft:* 34–5). However, the CA finds that Microsoft did not substantiate this claim, and concludes that these contract restrictions are in violation of Section 2 of the Sherman Act.

Integration of IE and Windows   Microsoft is also accused of technologically binding IE to Windows, that is integrating them so tightly that IE cannot be removed from Windows. This would prevent OEMs from pre-installing other browsers, which in turn makes it more difficult for consumers to use them. OEMs would not pre-install a second browser for two reasons: because it would increase its training and testing costs (a OEM has to train its support staff to answer calls related to each product pre-installed on its computers); and because to install two software items, which belong to the same category, would not be efficient use of the scarce space on a PC's hard drive.

Three specific actions increasing the integration of IE and Windows are considered. As above, first there must be an assessment of their anti-competitive effects and then of their possible efficiency justifications.

The first action is the *exclusion of IE from the "Add/Remove Programs"* utility in Windows 98. The second action is the design of Windows so that in certain circumstances it could *override the users' choice* of a browser other than IE. The third action is *commingling code related to browsing and other code* in the same files, having the effect that deleting IE files could cripple the OS. (On this technical point, there is contradictory testimony in the record, some experts denying that there was commingling of the two codes, while others arguing there was, and the CA cannot conclude that the District Court had erred in its factual findings: see *US v. Microsoft*: 38–9.)

All three actions are found to have anti-competitive effects, in that they make it difficult for rival browsers to gain usage share. Turning to the possible efficiency justifications, Microsoft argued that integration of IE with Windows was beneficial to both consumers and developers, but the CA finds that this claim was not specified and substantiated enough. However, the CA does accept that there are valid technical reasons for Windows to be designed so as to override the user's preferences in some very special circumstances. Since the plaintiffs did not offer any rebuttal of this efficiency claim, the CA does not hold Microsoft liable for this aspect of its product design, while finding that the other two actions are in violation of Section 2 of the Sherman Act.

Agreements with IAPs   Internet access providers (IAPs) include both internet service providers, which give internet access to consumers, and online services, such as America Online (AOL), which offer proprietary content in addition to internet access.

The actions attributed to Microsoft regarding its dealing with IAPs are of two types.

First, actions that result in IE being offered to IAPs at very favourable terms or in giving them strong incentives to use IE. These include offering IE free of charge; offering a bounty to each customer the IAP signs up for service using IE; having developed an IE Access Kit (IAEK), which allows easy customisation of IE; and offering the IAEK free of charge.

The District Court had condemned all these actions, but the CA reverses its decision. It argues that offering a product at an attractive (or even negative) price or developing a new product are the hallmark of competition, and that, even if taken by a monopolist, they do not usually violate the laws. The exception is when prices are predatory, but the CA finds that it had not even been argued – by the plaintiffs or the District Court – that there had been below-cost pricing, that these would have led to exit, and that the losses so incurred would have been recouped by higher future prices after rivals' exit (see Section 7.2 above for a discussion of predatory pricing). Therefore, the CA finds that these practices do not violate the Sherman Act.

The second type of action considered here are the deals offered by Microsoft to IAPs concerning desktop placement. The most important is the agreement with AOL, the leading IAP, that accounts for a substantial portion of all existing internet access subscriptions and of new subscribers. Under the agreement, Microsoft puts the AOL icon on the Windows desktop and AOL does not promote IE's rival browsers, nor provides these browsers except at the customer's request, and in this case AOL cannot supply those browsers to more than 15% of its subscribers.

The CA underlines that exclusivity provisions in contracts may serve many useful purposes (see Chapter 6), and that "because an exclusive deal affecting a small fraction of a market clearly cannot have the requisite harmful effect upon competition, the requirement of a significant degree of foreclosure serves a useful screening function" (*US v. Microsoft*: 44).

In this case, the CA finds that the exclusive deal at hand does have a substantial foreclosing effect, since together with diffusion through OEM's pre-installation, IAPs provide the other main efficient way by which Netscape Navigator could reach customers, and this deal excludes it from this efficient distribution channel.

Turning to the possible efficiency effect of these exclusive agreements, Microsoft argues that they aimed at keeping developers focused on its APIs, an argument that is not accepted by the CA as a pro-competitive justification. Accordingly, the CA finds these exclusive contracts with IAPs in violation of Section 2 of the Sherman Act.[145]

Java   Java is a set of technologies developed by Sun Microsystems. Like Netscape Navigator, it is middleware that might pose a threat to Windows as a platform for software development. Java technologies include a set of programmes, the "Java class libraries", which expose APIs and are written in a specific programming language; and a Java Virtual Machine (JVM) that allows passing from the code written by a developer to instructions to the OS. Programmes calling upon Java APIs run on any machine with a "Java runtime environment", that is with Java class libraries and a JVM.

Following an agreement with Netscape, Navigator became the main channel by which the Java runtime environment entered the PC of Windows users. Microsoft

---

[145] Deals with internet content providers (ICPs), independent software vendors (ISVs), and Apple had also been considered as exclusionary. The CA finds that the first ones are not in violation of the Sherman Act, while the other two are (*US v. Microsoft*: 47–51).

is accused of four actions aimed at preventing Java from becoming a viable cross-platform threat. The CA's finding with respect to these actions are discussed in what follows.

(a) *The incompatible JVM.* As stated in the District Court's *Findings of Fact*, Microsoft developed a JVM which allows Java applications to run faster on Windows than with Sun's Java, but it is incompatible with the latter. Based on these findings, the CA concludes that Microsoft's development and promotion of its JVM does not have an anti-competitive effect, because it improves the Java runtime environment. In other words, developing a product which is incompatible with the rivals' products is not by itself anti-competitive, and in this case there is a pro-competitive justification (speed of processing) that outweighs the incompatibility features.

(b) *The first-wave agreements.* Microsoft had a number of agreements with important ISVs whereby it offered advantages in exchange of using Microsoft and not Sun's JVM. Since these agreements have the same effects as exclusive deals, they should be assessed in the same way (see the discussion on agreements with IAPs). The CA finds that these agreements substantially foreclose distribution channels for JVM, and they are anti-competitive because they protect Microsoft's monopoly from a middleware threat. Given the absence of pro-competitive justifications, the CA concludes that these clauses are in violation of Section 2 of the Sherman Act.

(c) *Deception of Java developers.* Microsoft is also accused of deceiving developers regarding the Windows-specific nature of software-development tools it created to assist ISVs in the design of Java applications. Microsoft denied the accusations, but the CA finds that "... Microsoft documents confirm that Microsoft intended to deceive Java developers, and predicted that the effect of its actions would be to generate Windows-dependent Java applications that their developers believed would be cross-platform; these documents also indicate that Microsoft's ultimate objective was to thwart Java's threat to Microsoft's monopoly in the market for operating systems". (*US v. Microsoft*: 56)

Given the anti-competitive nature of these actions and their lack of efficiency justifications, these practices are held by the CA to violate the Sherman Act.

(d) *The threat to Intel.* In 1995, Intel was developing a high-performance JVM compatible with Windows. Microsoft is accused of threatening Intel with retaliatory actions if the latter did not abandon this project, that would have created a fast, cross-platform JVN that could jeopardise Windows' monopoly. Based on the evidence gathered and absent pro-competitive justifications, the CA finds this conduct exclusionary and in violation of Section 2 of the Sherman Act.

7.5.2.3 Causation

Microsoft asked the CA to reverse the monopolisation findings because the causal link between Microsoft's conduct and the maintenance of Windows' monopoly had not been established (that is, there is no evidence that Netscape and Java would have developed into viable platform substitutes). However, the CA rejects this argument for two reasons: first, and second, because it would imply putting onto the plaintiff the burden of proving that an infant firm would grow into a strong competitor; and second, because according to the factual findings of the District Court both Navigator and Java had shown potential as middleware platform threats.

This concludes the first part of the judgement concerning the monopolisation charge. In sum, the CA finds that some of the business practices previously condemned by the District Court are indeed in violation of Section 2 of the Sherman Act for maintenance of monopolisation, whereas others are not.

7.5.3 Attempted Monopolisation

The District Court found that Microsoft was guilty of *attempted monopolisation* of the browser market. In order to establish a violation for attempted monopolisation, the CA argues that the following test must be satisfied: first, the defendant is shown to have engaged in anti-competitive conduct; second, it had a specific intent to monopolise; and third, "a dangerous probability of achieving monopoly power" must have existed (*US v. Microsoft:* 62).

The CA finds that the District Court and the plaintiffs had not even tried to prove attempted monopolisation: "simply put, plaintiffs have made the same argument under two different headings – monopoly maintenance and attempted monopolisation" (*US v. Microsoft:* 63). In particular, to establish a "dangerous probability" of success, one should show that the browser market can be monopolised, which in turn requires defining the relevant market and then demonstrating that because of substantial barriers to entry a hypothetical monopolist would enjoy market power in that market.

The CA finds that this analysis had not been carried out either by the plaintiffs or by the District Court. First, the "browser market" is never properly defined, so it is not clear which types of products it would include. Second, the District Court mentioned network effects as possible barriers to entry, but failed to explain to what extent a high market share in the browser market (however defined) would lead to a substantial entry barrier due to network effects.

Accordingly, the CA reverses the District Court's finding of a Section 2 violation for attempted monopolisation.

7.5.4 Tying

The District Court found that Microsoft's contractual and technological bundling of the IE Web browser with Windows OS was a tying arrangement *per se* unlawful (in violation of Section 1 of the Sherman Act).[146] The CA argues instead that this

---

[146] *Technological bundling* of IE and Windows has already been discussed above under the possible monopolisation effects of integration of these two software products. *Contractual tying* had been identified by the District Court in the form of Microsoft requiring licensees of Windows 95 and 98 (the "tying" products) also to license IE (the "tied" products) as a bundle at a single price.

case should be dealt with under a rule of reason, because the integration of added functionality into the OS represents an innovation and its pro-competitive effects might outweigh the possible anti-competitive potential of tying. As a consequence, it remands the case to the District Court.

Following *Kodak* and *Jefferson Parish Hospital*, the CA argues that "There are four elements to a *per se* tying violation: (1) the tying and tied goods are two separate products; (2) the defendant has market power in the tying product market; (3) the defendant affords consumers no choice but to purchase the tied product from it; and (4) the tying arrangement forecloses a substantial volume of commerce" (*US v. Microsoft*: 70).

The CA then discusses the four-pronged test above, and in particular it deals with point (1). It argues that the requirement of separate products serves as a proxy for net efficiencies, which are otherwise not included in the test. An assessment of the CA's legal arguments on this point (*US v. Microsoft*: 70–85) is beyond my abilities, but its conclusion is that the existing four-pronged test above for the application of the *per se* rule is inadequate in this case, because it fails to consider the innovative component of the tying of IE with Windows, and the possible welfare advantages deriving from a close integration of these two products.

The CA argues that the application of the *per se* rule above might prevent valuable innovation. Indeed, under this rule a firm which is the first to integrate two previously separate products risks being condemned of tying. Conversely, a rule of reason analysis would allow the firm to demonstrate that efficiency gains from tying offset any distortion in consumer choice.

The CA is particularly concerned with the absence of an efficiency defence in platform software markets, where integration is common and widespread, since all firms, even those which do not have market power, integrate software products: "firms without market power have no incentive to package different pieces of software together unless there are efficiency gains from doing so. The ubiquity of bundling in competitive platform software markets should give courts reasons to pause before condemning such behavior in less competitive markets" (*US v. Microsoft*: 83).

Further, "... because of the pervasively innovative character of platform software markets, tying in such markets may produce efficiencies that courts have not previously encountered and thus the Supreme Court had not factored into the *per se* rule as originally conceived. For example, the bundling of a browser with OSs enables an independent software developer to count on the presence of the browser's APIs, if any, on consumers' machines and thus to omit them from its own package" (*US v. Microsoft*: 83).

After mentioning other examples of efficiencies in software markets that a *per se* rule would not take into account, the CA concludes that a more accurate analysis of the effects of Microsoft's tying arrangements should be made. As a consequence, it remands the case for the evaluation of tying under the rule of reason. It also instructs the District Court on how to assess the case with a test similar to the one adopted above for exclusionary practices: if Microsoft offers pro-competitive justification, it is the plaintiffs' burden to show that the anti-competitive effect of tying outweighs its benefit.

7.5.5 Remedies

The CA vacates the District Court's remedies decree (and therefore annuls the order that Microsoft should be split into two separate companies) for three reasons: first, because Microsoft was not granted the opportunity to present its views on the remedies; second, because the District Court did not provide adequate reasons for the remedies it wanted to impose; and third, because the CA has revised the scope of Microsoft's liability and cannot determine how this should affect the remedies provisions.

With respect to the first point, the CA argues that Microsoft had presented a number of facts suggesting that the remedy was not appropriate, and that therefore an evidentiary hearing on remedies should have been held.

In particular, the CA stresses that ". . . in two separate offers of proof, Microsoft identifies 23 witnesses who, had they been permitted to testify, would have challenged a wide range of plaintiffs' factual representations, including the feasibility of dividing Microsoft,[147] the likely impact on consumers,[148] and the effect of divestiture on shareholders" (*US v. Microsoft:* 97).

Finally, the CA says that it does not intend to dictate to the District Court which precise form relief should take, but it notes that "it should be tailored to fit the wrong creating the occasion for the remedy" (*US v. Microsoft:* 106).

7.5.6 Conclusions

Independent of its final outcome (that is based on the factual findings of the District Court), the CA's line of reasoning is very clear and its judgement is instructive for the way in which the test for the assessment of anti-competitive practices is formulated and the decision is made. In particular, and again independently of the particular case to which it is applied and its result, the multi-tier test adopted by the CA to

---

[147] Microsoft argued that it is organised as a unified company and there are no natural lines along which it could be broken without causing serious problems. This is an important issue, as we know from the discussion of merger remedies in Chapter 5 that certain criteria for divestitures must be verified in order to ensure the viability of a company created from divested assets. As emphasised by the CA, the risk is that dismembering a unitary company would cause a marked loss of efficiency (*US v. Microsoft:* 103–5).

[148] Microsoft argued that the division into two companies would have an adverse effect on consumers, by increasing prices, reducing efficiency and discouraging innovation. When two firms produce complements or vertically related goods, integration enables to coordinate better and improve product design and innovations; further, it avoids double-marginalisation (see Chapter 6) and "Cournot effects" (see Section 8.2), determining lower final prices.

assess potentially anti-competitive business practices is sound and consistent with economic theory and its implications (as discussed in Chapter 6 and in this chapter). It is very important to stress that an alleged abusive practice infringes competition laws if (1) it is found to harm the competitive process substantially *and* (2) if it does not have efficiency justifications, or if these efficiency justifications do not outweigh the anti-competitive effect of the practice.

7.5.7 The District Court Judgement on Remedies

Following the settlement between the DOJ and some of the states, the District Court had to endorse the remedies envisaged in the proposed consent decree and decide on the alternative remedies proposed by the remaining states.

The Court (*State of New York et al. v. Microsoft Corp.*) adopts a number of behavioural remedies that aim at prying open competition in the Intel-compatible OS market. It does not simply limit itself to prohibit provisions that had been found in violation of the Sherman Act, but also extends its attention to new middleware and related products that could challenge Windows' monopoly.

The main remedies will (1) provide OEMs with the flexibility of deciding their configuration of Windows OS, for instance by lifting illegal license restrictions related to non-Microsoft middleware or services provided by IAPs; (2) require Microsoft to alter its Windows technology to ensure that OEMs and end-users may disable various functions of Windows; (3) protect OEMs from possible retaliation, among other things by introducing some uniformity in the licenses for Windows (so as to provide OEMs with security), and obliging Microsoft not to terminate licenses without due notice; and (4) include various provisions avoiding that Microsoft could restrict diffusion of middleware through IAPs and ISVs.

Furthermore, the Court also adopts "explicitly forward-looking remedies" that will (1) require Microsoft to disclose those APIs and related technical information that Microsoft middleware uses to interoperate with the Windows platform; (2) mandate disclosure and licensing of protocols used by clients running on Windows to inter-operate with Microsoft servers, the rationale of this measure being that server OSs could develop into a platform threat to Windows; and (3) require limited disclosures of APIs, communication protocols, and related technical information in order to facilitate inter-operability.

Finally, the Court adopts some compliance and enforcement provisions to ensure that the remedies will be properly implemented. Among other things, it charges plaintiffs (who have the incentive to vigilate on the compliance with the remedies) with the obligation of monitoring Microsoft's compliance, and it introduces the figure of a compliance officer who will serve as a high-level Microsoft employee, but will retain significant autonomy and independence from the company.

These remedies have a validity of five years, but could be extended for up to two years if Microsoft engaged in systemic violation of the decree.

7.6 EXERCISES

Exercise 7.1   *(The chain-store model with infinite horizon)* Consider the model described in Section 7.2.3.1, but with the variant that the stage game of Figure 7.1 is repeated for an infinite number of times. (a) Show that predation exists under the following strategies and for a large enough discount factor δ. The incumbent's strategy is "fight entry, if entry occurs and it has never been accommodated before; accommodate entry, if entry has been accommodated before". The entrant's strategy is "enter, if entry has ever been accommodated before; stay out, otherwise". (b) Discuss the model: do you think it offers a valid formalisation of predatory behaviour?

Exercise 7.2   ** *(Pooling equilibria in the predation for merger model, Section 7.2.3.4.)* Consider the version of Saloner's (1987) model presented in Section 7.2.3.4, and check under which conditions there exists a pooling equilibrium where both the low-cost and the high-cost firm set the low-cost firm 1 monopoly output ($q_{1l}^* = q_{1h}^* = q_{1l}^m$), and offer $Q^* = x\pi_{2l}^d + (1-x)\pi_{2h}^d$ to buy the entrant; if firm 2 observes $q_1^m \geq q_{1l}^m$, it accepts any offer $Q \geq Q^*$ and rejects it otherwise; if firm 2 observes $q_1^m < q_{1l}^m$, it accepts any offer $Q \geq \pi_{2h}^d$ and rejects it otherwise; and firm 2 has beliefs $x' = 0$, if $q_1^m < q_{1l}^m$; $x' = x$, if $q_1^m \geq q_{1l}^m$.

Exercise 7.3   *(Deep pocket predation under perfect information: quantity competition.)* Consider a variant of the model analysed in Section 7.2.3.5. Market demand for a homogenous good is $p = \max(0, 1 - Q)$, where Q is total output. Firm 1 and firm 2 have respectively costs $c_1 < 1$ and c_2, and have to incur a fixed recurrent cost F before production if they are to operate in the industry (if one does not pay this cost once, one has to exit the industry forever). Also assume that it is impossible for a firm to get credit. Firm 2 is more efficient ($c_2 < c_1$) but is cash constrained: its total assets are $A_2 = 2F - \varepsilon$ (whereas firm 1 has deep pockets: $A_1 > 2F + 1$). Consider a two-period game (assume no discounting: $\delta = 1$), where in each period (i) each firm decides whether to pay F and stay in the industry or leave forever; (ii) active firms choose outputs. Find (a) what is the optimal quantity produced by firm 1 if it wants to prey; (b) under what conditions will predation occur as a sub-game perfect Nash equilibrium.

Exercise 7.4   ** *(Deep pocket predation without exit)* Consider a variant of the model seen in Section 7.2.3.6, where firm 1 has no cash constraint and firm 2 has zero resources. Firms produce a homogenous good whose demand is $p = 1 - Q$ and compete in quantities. Both firms are in the market when the game starts, and produce at a technology that involves marginal costs c. The game is as follows. In the first period, firm 1 decides whether to set the Cournot output, $q(c, c) = (1 - c)/3$ (accommodate) or set an aggressive output, $q_1^P(c, c) = 1 - c$ (prey). In the former case both firms earn $\pi(c, c) = (1 - c)^2/9$, in the latter case they each get $\pi^P(c, c) = 0$. (Check that firm 2's best response when firm 1 sells $1 - c$ units is not to sell anything, and that firm 1 sells at marginal cost.) In the second period, each firm has to decide whether to invest an amount I in a new technology that abates the marginal cost to $c' = 0$, or not. If a firm decides not to invest, it will have marginal cost c in the second period as well, and make profits $\pi(c, \cdot)$.

Unlike firm 1 that has enough own assets, firm 2 needs to borrow from banks to pay I. If it obtains financing, the manager of each firm has to decide whether it wants to exert high effort or zero effort (a binary decision for simplicity). If the manager implements the innovation properly ("high effort"), the innovation will succeed with probability $p = 1$, allowing the firm to produce at marginal cost $c' = 0$; if the manager shirks ("low effort"), he obtains private benefits B (which he does not get if he makes "high" effort or does not innovate at all), but the innovation will fail with probability 1, i.e., the firm will produce at marginal cost c in the second period as well. Finally, second period profits are realised.

Assume that with perfect capital markets the innovation would always be financed: (A1) $\pi(0, 0) - I > \pi(c, c)$, and that a firm which finances the innovation itself would never shirk; (A2) $B + \pi(c, c) < I$; if there is accommodation, firm 2's manager will be able to raise funds; (A3) $\pi(0, 0) - B > I - \pi(c, c)$, but in case of predation in the first period the innovation will not be financed; and (A4) $\pi(0, 0) - B < I$. Will predation occur?

Exercise 7.5 *(Over-investment in R&D)* This is a slightly richer version of the model seen in Section 7.3.1.1, since the entrant firm is also allowed to invest in R&D. The incumbent, firm 1, faces a potential entrant, firm 2, in the market for a homogenous good with demand $p = 1 - q$. Consider two games. (a) Find the solution of the following simultaneous decisions game. In the first stage, firm 1 and 2 simultaneously decide investment x_i in a cost-reducing technology, with total cost of production given by $C(x_i, q_i) = (c - x_i)q_i$. Assume a quadratic cost for the investment, $F(x_i) = x_i^2$. At this stage, firm 2 also decides on entry, and pays a fixed sunk cost F. In the last stage, active firms observe each other's investment decision and choose outputs. (b) Find the solution of the sequential investment game, which is like the previous one, with the only variant that firm 1 invests in the first stage; in the second stage, after observing firm 1's investment decision, firm 2 decides on investment and on entry; in the last stage, active firms choose outputs.

Show that there is a range of values of the fixed sunk cost F where entry deterrence is profitable, in the sense that firm 1 prefers to invest more in the new technology than it would if it took firm 2's entry for granted.

Exercise 7.6 *(Credibility of product pre-emption, inspired by Judd (1985) and Tirole's (1988) comments.)* When the game starts, firm 1 is already established in market A, where demand for its product is $Q = 1 - p$, whereas in market B, no firm is active and there is no demand for the good. At time T, firm 1 can decide whether it wants to set a plant in market B, at a fixed sunk cost F. It then sets prices in the market where it is active. At time $T+1$, a potential entrant, firm 2, decides whether to set a plant in market B at the fixed sunk cost $F < 1/4$. After the entry decision is taken, active firms set prices. Firms 1 and 2 sell the same homogenous good in both markets. However, transporting the good from one market to the other entails a transportation cost $t < 1/2$. Assume also that at time T demand for the good in market B is zero, whereas at time $T+1$, demand is given by $Q = 1 - p$. Firms serving both markets from the same plant have to choose the same mill price across markets (i.e., prices can differ only by the transportation cost), they have the same discount factor $\delta = 1$ and the same marginal costs $c = 0$. (i) Assume that firm 1 cannot withdraw from market B if it enters there, and show it will enter at time T to pre-empt entry by firm 2. (ii) Assume that, after observing firm 2's entry decision at time $T+1$, firm 1 can withdraw from market B at no cost if it wishes so. Show that market pre-emption will not occur at the (sub-game perfect) equilibrium.

Exercise 7.7 *Assume the same setting as in Section 7.4.2.5. City A is located at 0, and city B at $2t$ along the horizontal axis. Firm 1 is located at t. Demand in each city is given by $q = 1 - p$. There are two foreign firms located at $2t + T$. Assume that all firms have zero production costs, but incur a unit transportation cost equal to distance. Assume that $(1 + t)/2 \geq T \geq (1 - 3t)/2$. Firms compete in prices. Find the equilibrium solutions for the cases where (a) price discrimination is allowed; (b) price discrimination is banned. Then show that (c) a ban on price discrimination reduces welfare.

Exercise 7.8 *(Quantity discounts and incentives to invest)* Consider the model described in Sections 7.4.2.1 and 7.4.2.2. The monopolist faces λ (resp. $1 - \lambda$) consumers with demand $p = v_l - q$ (respectively $p = v_h - q$). It has an initial marginal cost $A < v_l$ of providing the good. Consider the two following games:

Game 1: Uniform pricing. First, the monopolist decides on the investment x to reduce its marginal cost. By investing a given level x, its new marginal cost will be $c = A - x$. The cost of the investment is $C(x) = \mu x^2/2$ (assume that $\mu > 1$ for the second-order condition to be satisfied in both Game 1 and 2.) Second, it chooses the uniform price p at which both markets are served (assume that it is not convenient to supply one market only: $v_l > [A + (1 - \lambda) v_h] / (2 - \lambda)$).

Game 2: Quantity discounts. Same game as game 1, but in the second stage the monopolist can use a two-part tariff $T + pq$.

Show that the monopolist invests more in Game 2.

Exercise 7.9 Suppose you hear the CEO of a small firm complaining about the difficulties he faced as he tried to enter a market that has a strong incumbent firm: "as soon as we started to market our product, our rival would basically give away his stuff for free! He did everything to try and drive us out of the market. It was so unfair! We never had a real chance to make it . . . A firm should not be allowed to do a thing like that. I think the government should pass a law that prohibits to price below cost . . . " Discuss this proposal. Do you agree?

Exercise 7.10 *(Exercise 7.9 continued)* To get a clear picture of the situation, you decide to confront the incumbent's CEO with the smaller firm's allegations and ask for their point of view. Here is what they tell you: "come on, this is ridiculous! These guys were just not competitive enough . . . Their product was junk, and their pricing was beyond the beyonds! Do you want to blame us for having the better product and better prices? Let's face it: The marketplace is like the Olympics – it's always the best guy who will win!" Discuss this statement.

Exercise 7.11 Fernando, who lives in Vienna, recently bought himself a car and went on a long vacation with it. When he arrived in Florence, he happened to stop at a local car dealer's premises, where he discovered that "his" car – the exact same make and model – was sold there for two-thirds of the price he had paid in Vienna. Fernando frets and fumes: he somehow feels like he had been ripped off mightily, and he thinks that firms should not be allowed to do that – as a matter of fairness, the same car should be sold at the same price everywhere in the world! Discuss.

Exercise 7.12 In a recent case, the European Commission has fined the pharmaceutical company British Chemicals for abuse of dominant position. The firm has been found guilty of artificially segmenting the markets of member countries because it had forbidden its Spanish subsidiary to export to other EU countries a well-known medicine used for heart disease. In Spain the price of this medicine (as well as of many others) is lower than in other EU countries because Spanish law does not protect patents to the same extent as in the other EU countries. As a result, there are many more firms which can produce and sell this product, which brings prices down. Would you agree with the Commission's decision?

Exercise 7.13 Until the end of 1995, the airline "Golden Wings" was the only one authorised to operate in the passenger air transport business in the country "Eagleland". To operate flights to or from this country, other airlines had to strike co-operative agreements with Golden Wings, which could impose its conditions without any restriction from the domestic government. Due to the existing situation, Golden Wings had 80% of the national market, and basically all the Eaglelandish population had been participating in the frequent-flyer programme of the company (out of four trips, one is free), which had been set up in 1994. Since 1996, the market has been deregulated, and other airlines are now free to sell their services in the country. Immediately after deregulation, the large multinational company "Albion

Airways" bought landing slots in the major airports of the country and started to sell aeroplane tickets to and from the country at a price which is roughly half that set by Golden Wings. The latter firm lost 30% of the market in a few months. It filed a complaint to the national competition authority accusing Albion of predatory pricing. According to the complaint, Albion was using its strength on the world market (it has 40% of it) to evict Golden Wings from the Eaglelandish market. The national authority decided that Albion Airways had used a predatory practice, and the company received a fine. In particular, the authority attached much weight to the fact that Albion's prices to and from Eagleland were on average 20% lower than flights operated by Albion on other routes, and 10% lower than Golden Wings average costs. Albion has appealed to the Court of Justice, and you have to give your opinion as the Advocate General.

7.6.1 Solutions to Exercises

Exercise 7.1   (a) The incentive constraint for the incumbent is as follows. If it sticks to the strategy when entry occurs, it earns the low payoff π_I^P today but entry will not occur forever afterwards. By deviating and accommodating entry, it would get the higher current payoff π_I^A but then all potential entrants will enter (and will be accommodated). This trade-off is summarised by the condition $\pi_I^P + \delta \pi^M/(1-\delta) \geq \pi_I^A/(1-\delta)$, which simplifies to $\delta \geq (\pi_I^A - \pi_I^P)/(\pi^M - \pi_I^P)$.

Note that from $\pi^M > \pi_I^A$ it follows that the RHS is smaller than one, so that there always exists a discount factor large enough for this incentive constraint to hold.

As for the entrants, if the incumbent's IC is satisfied, they prefer to follow the candidate equilibrium strategy, and earn 0, rather than entering and get $\pi_E^P < 0$. As a result, entry will never occur at equilibrium.

(b) There are at least two features of the infinite horizon version of the chain-store game that make it unsatisfactory. First, as all super games, this model is characterised by multiplicity of equilibria. In particular, the game has an equilibrium where entry takes place and is accommodated forever. Just consider the following strategies. The entrant enters at the beginning of the game, and always enters as long as entry is accommodated; if entry is ever fought, no entrant will enter. The incumbent accommodates whenever entry takes place. These strategies are nothing other than the equilibrium strategies in the one-shot game, and it is easy to see that they represent an equilibrium. (We have already seen in Chapter 4 that the one-shot equilibrium repeated forever is an equilibrium of the supergame.)

Second, in this model even when "predation" is an equilibrium it is never observed along the equilibrium path: entrants simply anticipate that entry would be fought, and abstain from entering the market. According to this story, one should never see any episode of predatory pricing in the real markets. Hence, this does not represent a convincing model of predation.

Exercise 7.2   At the pooling equilibrium, the high-cost incumbent imitates the low-cost incumbent, and the potential entrant (firm 2) decides on the basis of its *ex ante* beliefs, according to which the incumbent (firm 1) is a low-cost one with probability x. Let us now check if the strategy profile and system of beliefs given above will indeed constitute a Perfect Bayesian Equilibrium.

We start with the entrant's strategy with respect to Q, taking firm 1's strategies and firm 2's beliefs as given. At the pooling equilibrium, the entrant will accept the incumbent's offer only if the entrant's expected payoff from entering is lower than the offer Q received. If firm 2 observes a quantity choice $q_1^m \geq q_{1l}^m$ by firm 1, firm 2 will not revise its beliefs about firm 1 being low-cost, and will accept the takeover if $x(\pi_{2l}^d) + (1 - x)(\pi_{2h}^d) \leq Q$. If, however, firm 2 observes $q_1^m < q_{1l}^m$, it will revise its beliefs and attach probability 1 to facing a high-cost incumbent, and will accept only offers $Q \geq \pi_{2h}^d$ (recall that $\pi_{2h}^d > \pi_{2l}^d$).

Let us now turn to the incumbent's strategies, taking firm 2's strategies and beliefs as given. Suppose first that firm 1 is high-cost. Then, firm 1 has no incentive to make any offer $Q \neq Q^*$. Any offer $Q < Q^*$ would be rejected by firm 2, leading to lower second-period profits for firm 1 (π_{1h}^d instead of $\pi_{1h}^m - Q^*$). Moreover, firm 1 will find it optimal to imitate the low-cost type with respect to first-period output ($q_1^m = q_{1l}^m$) if doing so yields higher profits than setting the high-cost monopoly quantity in the first period, thus revealing its true type and having to make a higher takeover offer, $Q = \pi_{2h}^d > Q^*$. We obtain **condition 1**: $\pi_{1h}^m(q_{1l}^m) - \left[x(\pi_{2l}^d) + (1 - x)(\pi_{2h}^d) \right] \geq \pi_{1h}^m - \pi_{2h}^d$.

If firm 1 is instead low-cost, it obviously has no incentive to produce any $q_1^m \neq q_{1l}^m$. Moreover, given firm 2's beliefs, it will be optimal for firm 1 to offer Q^* if taking over the rival at this cost is more profitable than offering zero and accommodating entry, which yields **condition 2**: $\pi_{1l}^m - \left[x(\pi_{2l}^d) + (1 - x)(\pi_{2h}^d) \right] \geq \pi_{1l}^d$.

What remains to be checked is if firm 2's beliefs are consistent with the equilibrium strategy profile. Note that if conditions 1 and 2 above hold, the only first-period output observed along the equilibrium path will be q_{1l}^m, and the only takeover offer made will be Q^*. Since both high-cost and low-cost incumbents behave the same way, first-period actions do not convey any information about the incumbent's type, so following Bayes' Rule the posterior beliefs will indeed coincide with the prior ones. Off the equilibrium path, any assignment of beliefs is admissible, in particular the one chosen here (i.e., if $q_1^m < q_{1l}^m$, $x' = 0$; if $q_1^m \geq q_{1l}^m$, $x' = x$).

Exercise 7.3   (a) Note that firm 2 has resources just below $2F$. Hence, if firm 1 is to make it exit the market, firm 1 just needs to inflict a loss equal to F upon firm 2. Firm 2 will be left with resources slightly lower than F and will have to exit since it cannot pay up-front the recurrent fixed cost. Firm 2's per-period profits are $\Pi_2 = (1 - q_2 - q_1 - c_2)q_2 - F$, and its best reply function will be given by $q_2 = (1 - q_1 - c_2)/2$. Therefore, by selling $q_1 = 1 - c_2$, firm 1 would induce firm 2 to produce zero output and incur a loss equal to $-F$.

(b) Of course, the issue is whether this is profitable for firm 1 to do. By selling $q_1 = 1 - c_2$ units at a price $p = c_2 < c_1$, firm 1 will suffer a loss $\pi_1^P = -(c_1 - c_2)(1 - c_2) - F$ but it will induce exit of the rival, and operate as a monopolist in the following period (note that firm 1's loss is never higher than $F + 1$). Therefore, it will get a payoff from predation $-(c_1 - c_2)(1 - c_2) - F + (1 - c_1)^2/4 - F$. If it accommodates entry, both firms will get duopoly profits and firm 1's total payoff will be $2[(1 - 2c_1 + c_2)^2/9 - F]$. By comparing these two payoffs and rearranging one obtains a second-order equation which is solved for $c_1 < (1 + 22c_2)/23$ (the other root is irrelevant since it is lower than c_2). This is therefore the condition for predation to prevail.

Exercise 7.4 Note first that $\pi(0, c) > \pi(0, 0) > \pi(c, c) > \pi(c, 0)$. (A1) and (A2) imply that firm 1 will always want to invest and never shirk. By applying the model seen in Section 7.2.3.6 (there is only a slight variation, in that a firm is not forced to exit the market even if it decides not to invest), one can see that firm 2 is unable to raise funding if predation occurs in the first period. However, the question is whether predation is profitable for firm 1 or not. For it to be profitable, it must be that $0 + \pi(0, c) > \pi(c, c) + \pi(0, 0)$ (P1), or $\pi(0, 0) < \pi(0, c) - \pi(c, c)$. (Recall that predation gives zero first-period profit to both the predator and the prey.)

Using (A1) and (A2), we have $(1 - c)^2/9 + B < I < 1/9 - (1 - c)^2/9$. For this interval to be non-empty, we must have $c > 1 - \sqrt{1/2} \simeq 0.29$. Using this lower bound on c in (A3), we can re-write (A3) and (A4) as $I + B \in (1/9, 1/9 + 1/18)$. Note that (P1) implies $c > 1/4$, which will always be satisfied if (A1) and (A2) hold. Hence, predation will always occur in this model.

Exercise 7.5 (a) In the last stage, given investment decisions from the previous period, firms will play a Cournot game with (potentially) unequal marginal costs. Output, price and profits are given by $q_i^C = (1 - 2c_i + c_j)/3$, $p^C = (1 + c_i + c_j)/3$, $\Pi_i^C = (1 - 2c_i + c_j)^2/9$.

In the first stage, each firm chooses its optimal level of investment, taking the other firm's investment as given. The firm's programme, $\max_{x_i} \pi_i^C = (1/9)(1 - 2(c - x_i) + (c - x_j))^2 - x_i^2$, gives rise to the following reaction function: $x_i(x_j) = (2/5)(1 - c - x_j)$. The equilibrium level of investment will be $x_i^* = x_j^* = (6/21)(1 - c)$. Firm 2 will enter if net profits cover fixed cost, i.e., $\pi_2^C(x_i^*) = \Pi_2^C(x_i^*) - (x_i^*)^2 > F$, or $(5/49)(1 - c)^2 > F$. Note that under simultaneous investment decisions, there is no room for entry-deterring use of investment by the incumbent.

(b) In the last stage, given investment decisions from previous periods, firms will play the same Cournot game as in (a). Now, however, firm 2 will make its investment decision only after observing firm 1's preceding decision. Firm 2 will invest optimally when $x_2(x_1) = (2/5)(1 - c - x_1)$.

Firm 1 has now two options: it can behave "innocently", i.e., optimise its investment taking firm 2's entry as given, or it can use a "predatory" strategy, i.e., invest so much that firm 2 is discouraged from entry. Under the "innocent strategy", the incumbent's problem is $\max_{x_1} \pi_1^C = (1/9)(1 - 2(c - x_1) + (c - x_2(x_1)))^2 - x_1^2$, which yields equilibrium solutions $x_{1inn}^* = (4/9)(1 - c)$ and $x_2(x_{1inn}^*) = (2/9)(1 - c)$. Notice the asymmetry in the investment levels, which derives from firm 1's first-mover advantage. Firm 2 will enter if $\pi_2^C(x_{1inn}^*) - F = (5/81)(1 - c)^2 - F > 0$, otherwise, entry will be blockaded, and so there is no need for firm 1 to even consider entry deterrence.

Suppose now that entry is not blockaded. Then, under the "predatory" strategy, firm 1's problem is to set x_1 such that firm 2's profits are driven down to zero, i.e., x_{1pred}^* solves $\pi_2^C(x_1) - F = 0$. We obtain $x_{1pred}^* = 1 - c - \sqrt{5F}$. Of course, firm 1 will want to predate only if this yields higher overall profits than accommodating firm 2's entry, i.e., if $\pi_1^m(x_{1pred}^*) = (1/4)\left(1 - \left(c - x_{1pred}^*\right)\right)^2 - \left(x_{1pred}^*\right)^2 > \pi_1^C(x_{1inn}^*)$. Solving for F, we obtain a similar ranking as in Section 7.3.1.1: if $F \leq (1/5)(2/3)^2\left(1 - \sqrt{2/3}\right)^2(1 - c)^2$, entry will be accommodated; if $(1/5)(2/3)^2\left(1 - \sqrt{2/3}\right)^2(1 - c)^2 < F \leq (5/81)(1 - c)^2$, entry will be deterred; and if $F > (5/81)(1 - c)^2$, entry will be blockaded. Note that the first-mover advantage is crucial for firm 1: as we saw in (a), no predatory behaviour can emerge if investment decisions are taken simultaneously.

Exercise 7.6 (i) At time $T + 1$, suppose firm 1 has entered market B in the previous period. By entering as well, firm 2 would suffer losses: price competition with homogenous goods implies zero gross profit, which would not allow it to recoup the fixed cost F. Therefore, firm 2 would not enter. Firm 1 will make monopoly profits in each market, $\pi = 1/4$ (the monopoly price is found as the price that maximises the profit in each market, $\pi = p(1 - p)$: from $\partial \pi / \partial p = 0$, it follows that $p = 1/2$ and $\pi = 1/4$). Therefore, total profits will be $\pi = 1/2$.

If firm 1 has not entered market B, and firm 2 entered, it will make monopoly profit $\pi = 1/4 - F$ in that market. This is because firm 1 will set the monopoly price in its own market (since it cannot price discriminate and it has to incur an additional cost to serve market B, it does not have any incentive to set a price lower than the monopoly price in market A). Therefore, firm 1 will have profits $\pi = 1/4$.

At period T, firm 1 will enter since it anticipates that its own entry deters by firm 2, thus giving it higher profits. By entering, it will gain $\pi = 1/2 - F$. By not entering, it will make $\pi = 1/4 < 1/2 - F$ (recall that $F < 1/4$).

(ii) In the previous point (i), firm 1's investment deters entry by firm 2. The issue here is what happens if firm 2 decided to enter the market nevertheless. Price competition would lead to an equilibrium price $p = 0$ in market B. But this implies that firm 1 will not be able to sustain the monopoly price in market A: consumers there can import the good by paying $t < 1/2$. Therefore, firm 1 will set its price in market A so as to be slightly lower than t and make profits $t(1 - t)$.

If it closed down its plant in market B, it would relax competition in market B (where firm 2 would become a monopolist) and be able to set the monopoly profits in market A, thus earning $1/4$. It is easy to see that $1/4 > t(1 - t)$ can be re-written as $(1 - 2t)^2 > 0$, which holds true.

Firm 2 anticipates that if it enters market B, firm 1 would prefer to withdraw from it if it had invested there, and so firm 2 will always enter. In turn, firm 1 will anticipate this and not enter market B in period T, thus saving its fixed costs.

Exercise 7.7 (a) As in the text, under price discrimination, firm 1 sets $p_A^d = (1 + t)/2$ and $p_B^d = T$. Its total profits are $\pi^d = (1 - t)^2/4 + (T - t)(1 - T)$.

(b) Under uniform pricing, as in the text, if the incumbent serves both markets, $p_A^u = p_B^u = T$, and it makes profits $\pi^u = 2(T - t)(1 - T)$. If it serves only market A, it sets prices in both markets equal to $p^m = (1 + t)/2$. It would then make total profits $\pi^m = (1 - t)^2/4$. The difference with respect to the case treated in Section 7.4.2.5 is that Bertrand competition among foreign firms ensures that the price in market B will not rise above T.

(c) We know that if both cities are served, welfare is higher if there is a ban on price discrimination. However, if only one city is served when a ban on discrimination exists, the two regimes are equivalent for consumer surplus, since they lead to the same prices $(1 + t)/2$ in market A and T in market B. However, firm 1 makes positive profits in market B under discrimination, and no profits under a ban.

Exercise 7.8 Game 1. As usual, we have to move backwards. The solution of the second stage is given in Section 7.4.2.1. In the first stage, the monopolist chooses x to maximise the net profits under uniform pricing, $\pi^u = (\lambda v_l + (1 - \lambda)v_h - c)^2/4 - \mu x^2/2$, with $c = A - x$. Maximisation requires $\partial \pi^u/\partial x = (\lambda v_l + (1 - \lambda)v_h - A + x)/2 - \mu x = 0$.

Game 2. The solution of the second-stage is given by Section 7.4.2.2. In the first stage, the monopolist's programme is $\max_x \pi^{qd} = (1/2) \left[(v_l - A + x)^2 + (1 - \lambda)^2 (v_h - v_l)^2\right]$. The first-order condition is $\partial \pi^{qd}/\partial x = (v_l - A + x) - \mu x = 0$.

Comparison of the equilibrium investment levels does not require finding the explicit solution. Just note that the marginal cost of the investment, μx, is the same in both games, but that the marginal revenue is higher under game 2: $(v_l - A + x) > (\lambda v_l + (1 - \lambda)v_h - A + x)/2$, since $v_l > [A + (1 - \lambda) v_h]/(2 - \lambda)$. Therefore, x will be higher under quantity discounts (that is, two-part tariffs).

8

A Toolkit: Game Theory and Imperfect Competition Models

8.1 INTRODUCTION

This chapter introduces the reader to imperfect competition models that are used in the technical sections of the book (specifically, the intermediate technical sections, labelled*; the advanced technical sections, labelled**, will likely need a stronger background than the one which is offered in this chapter).

Of course, this is no replacement for more proper training in basic industrial organisation models, but the chapter should help some students who have already some background in economics and in simple mathematical analysis (I use little more than derivatives of real functions in the book and in this chapter), or those who want to refresh a knowledge acquired some time ago, to follow the formal arguments made in the book.

The choice of the topics analysed here is functional, with the objective of helping the reader follow the book. The chapter starts with a short treatment of monopoly (Section 8.2), then introduces the reader to elementary game theory (Section 8.2.2.3), which is indispensable for understanding modern oligopoly theory, which for convenience I divide into static models (Section 8.3) and dynamic models (Section 8.4).

8.2 MONOPOLY

This section offers an introductory treatment of monopoly pricing. First the case of a single-product monopoly and then that of a multi-product monopoly are analysed.

8.2.1 Single-Product Monopoly

The easiest possible model of imperfect competition is one where there is a monopolist that sells only one good. I will first solve the monopolist's problem with general cost and demand functions, and then offer some specific examples.

Denote demand for this good as $q = D(p)$, where p is the price and q output, and assume that demand is negatively sloped: $\partial D/\partial p < 0$.

For later use, define the *elasticity of demand* ε as the percentage change in the quantity demanded by consumers that follows a one percent change in price:

$\varepsilon = -(\partial D/D)/(\partial p/p) = -p(\partial D/\partial p)/D > 0$. (Note that the elasticity is defined as a positive number).

Production costs are given by the function $C(q)$, with non-negative marginal costs: $\partial C/\partial q \geq 0$. For the second-order conditions to be satisfied (that is for the profit function to be concave), assume also that $\partial^2 D/(\partial p)^2 \leq 0$ and $\partial^2 C/(\partial q)^2 \geq 0$.[1]

Let us now find the optimal price and quantity set by the monopolist in this market. Its objective is to choose the price that maximises its profits, that is $\max_p \pi = pq - C(q)$, or

$$\max_p \pi = pD(p) - C(D(p)). \tag{8.1}$$

The first-order condition (FOC) of this problem is

$$\frac{\partial \pi}{\partial p} = p\frac{\partial D(p)}{\partial p} + D(p) - \frac{\partial C(q)}{\partial q}\frac{\partial D(p)}{\partial p} = 0, \tag{8.2}$$

that can be re-written as

$$p - \frac{\partial C(q)}{\partial q} = -\frac{D(p)}{\partial D(p)/\partial p}. \tag{8.3}$$

By using the definition of demand elasticity and substituting, one obtains

$$\frac{p - \partial C(q)/\partial q}{p} = \frac{1}{\varepsilon}. \tag{8.4}$$

The left-hand side (LHS) of condition (8.4) is the so-called Lerner index, a measure of market power, that is the ability of a firm to set prices above marginal costs.[2] This condition therefore tells us that the higher the elasticity of demand the lower the monopolist's market power (that is, the lower the relative mark-up it earns). Consider for instance the two extreme cases: if market demand were so inelastic that consumers would be willing to buy the good at whatever price ($\varepsilon = 0$), then the monopolist's mark-up would tend to infinity. If instead demand was extremely elastic, so that consumers would switch to some other goods whenever the monopolist tries to marginally increase the price of its product ($\varepsilon \to \infty$), then its market power would be nil, and the monopolist's price would be equal to its marginal cost (since $p - \partial C(q)/\partial q$ must equal zero).

A Specific Functions Example Let me now use explicit demand and cost functions to analyse the monopolist's problem. Consider for the sake of simplicity the

---

[1] These assumptions are satisfied when adopting a linear demand function and constant marginal costs, which is the case I most often use in this chapter and throughout the book.

[2] See Chapter 2 for a discussion of market power (of which a monopoly is an extreme expression) and its relationship with welfare. See Chapter 3 for a discussion of how to measure market power.

case of linear demand $q = 1 - p$ and of constant marginal cost $C(q) = cq$, with $c < 1$ to guarantee viability of the market (otherwise, nobody would buy the product even if the monopolist offered it at marginal cost).

The monopolist's problem is $\max_p \pi = (p - c)(1 - p)$. The FOC is given by

$$\frac{\partial \pi}{\partial p} = 1 - 2p + c = 0, \tag{8.5}$$

whence

$$p^M = \frac{1 + c}{2}. \tag{8.6}$$

It is worth noting that the higher the marginal cost the higher the price the monopolist will set at equilibrium, $dp^M/dc > 0$: for consumers, better to face an efficient monopolist than an inefficient one![3]

By substitution, one can also find optimal quantities and profits: $q^M = (1 - c)/2$, and $\pi^M = (1 - c)^2/4$.

Note also that whether the monopolist chooses price or quantity the market outcome will be the same (a property that does not hold in oligopoly markets, as we shall see below). To see this, write the inverse demand function as $p = 1 - q$. The monopolist's problem is then $\max_q \pi = (1 - q - c)q$. The FOC is $\partial \pi/\partial q = 1 - 2q - c = 0$, which becomes $q^M = (1 - c)/2$ (and by substitution $p^M = (1 + c)/2$).

8.2.2 Multi-Product Monopoly

In the real world, firms often produce and sell more than one product. It is natural, therefore, to ask how a multi-product monopolist prices its different products. I start with the simplest case, where demand and cost of one product do not affect demand and cost for other products, and move later to the cases of interdependent demands and, in turn, interdependent costs. For simplicity, and without losing insights, I restrict attention to the case of two products.

8.2.2.1 Independent Demand and Cost Functions

Suppose the monopolist sells two products, 1 and 2, that affect neither each other's demands nor costs. The monopolist's total profit is given by $\pi = \pi_1 + \pi_2 = p_1 D_1(p_1) - C_1(D_1(p_1)) + p_2 D_2(p_2) - C_2(D_2(p_2))$. The monopolist's problem is given by $\max_{p_1, p_2} \pi$, but this decomposes to two completely separate problems: $\max_{p_1} \pi_1$ and $\max_{p_2} \pi_2$. Each of these problems reduces to the problem studied

---

[3] See Tirole (1988: 66–7) for a general proof of this result.

above for the single-product monopolist, giving as a result condition (8.4):

$$\frac{p_i - \partial C_i(q_i)/\partial q_i}{p_i} = \frac{1}{\varepsilon_i}, \qquad \text{with} \qquad i = 1, 2. \qquad (8.7)$$

This condition tells us that the monopolist sets the price in each market i according to its demand elasticity ε_i: in a market characterised by higher demand elasticity, consumers will pay less than in the other. This is a simple application of a principle of price discrimination that is analysed more at length in Chapter 7.

Of course, the assumptions that the price for one good does not affect demand for the other good, and that production costs are independent, make this case very special. Let us now turn to the cases where interdependence exists, first on the demand side, then on the cost side.

8.2.2.2 Interdependent Demands

Very often, a firm sells a range of products that are to some extent substitutable with each other. Think for instance of a car manufacturer that offers cars with different engine powers, colours and versions (station-wagon, sedan, cabriolet), or a food producer that offers different types of pasta. For substitute products, an increase in the price of one product will increase the demand for the others, which become relatively more convenient: $\partial q_i/\partial p_j > 0$.

At times, firms might sell instead (or in addition) products that are complements to each other: a telecom operator might sell both a cellular phone and a subscription to its services, and a food producer might sell both pasta and prepared sauces. For complementary goods, an increase in the price of one product will decrease the demand for the others (by decreasing the demand for the first product, demand for complements is also discouraged): $\partial q_i/\partial p_j < 0$.

To see how a monopolist sets prices for two products whose demands are interdependent, assume products have the following demand functions:

$$q_i = a - bp_i + gp_j \qquad \text{with} \qquad i, j = 1, 2, i \neq j. \qquad (8.8)$$

If the parameter $g > 0$, then the two products are substitutes; if $g < 0$, they are complements; if $g = 0$, their demands are independent of each other (a case that we shall use as a useful benchmark). Assume also that $|g| < b$, to guarantee that the own-price effect on demand of a product is stronger than the cross-price effect, a natural assumption, and that $a > c(b - g)$, to ensure that output is positive at equilibrium.

Assume also that the costs of producing one good are not affected by how much is produced of the other, to focus on the interdependence of demands. More particularly, assume that $C(q_1, q_2) = cq_1 + cq_2$.

The monopolist's total profits are given by

$$\pi = (a - bp_1 + gp_2)(p_1 - c) + (a - bp_2 + gp_1)(p_2 - c); \qquad (8.9)$$

its problem being $\max_{p_1, p_2} \pi$, the FOCs are

$$\frac{\partial \pi}{\partial p_i} = a - 2bp_i + 2gp_j + c(b - g) = 0, \qquad \text{with} \qquad i, j = 1, 2; \; i \neq j. \qquad (8.10)$$

At the symmetric solution, $p_1 = p_2 = p_m$, we have

$$p_m = \frac{a + c(b - g)}{2(b - g)}, \qquad (8.11)$$

where $p_m > c$. Since we are interested in the effect of demand relationship on equilibrium price, note that

$$\frac{\partial p_m}{\partial g} = \frac{a}{2(b - g)^2} > 0. \qquad (8.12)$$

As g increases in the interval $(-b, b)$, the price charged by the monopolist on both products also increases.[4]

Relative to the benchmark case where the two products are independent ($g = 0$), this implies that the monopolist reduces the price of its products when they are complements ($g < 0$) and it increases them when they are substitutes ($g > 0$). The intuition for this result is straightforward. When the products are complements, they exercise a positive externality on each other and the monopolist internalises it by decreasing its prices (a lower price of good 1 stimulates sales of good 2 and vice versa). In other words, if products 1 and 2 were sold by two distinct monopolists, consumers would pay more for them than when they are sold by the same firm, a result that dates back to Cournot (1838), and that is also discussed both in Chapters 6 (a vertically integrated firm being a particular case of a firm that sells complements) and 7 (when studying tie-in sales).

When instead the products are substitutes, the externality they exercise on each other is negative, and the monopolist controls for it by raising prices (a lower price of good 1 crowds out sales of good 2 and vice versa). If products 1 and 2 were sold by two distinct firms, consumers would pay less than when they are sold by the same firm.

To complete the analysis, use the equilibrium price (8.11) and substitute into output and profit function to obtain

$$q_m = \frac{a - c(b - g)}{2}; \qquad \pi_m = \frac{[a - c(b - g)]^2}{2(b - g)}, \qquad (8.13)$$

q_m being the output per product and π_m being the total profits.

---

[4] It is easy to check that p_m is concave, with its lowest possible value (equaling $(a + 2bc)/(4b)$) obtained as g tends to $-b$ and an asymptote as g tends to b.

A Dynamic Interpretation of Demand Interdependence   So far, I have treated the two products as two distinct products sold simultaneously by a monopolist. However, the insights obtained above carry over to the case where the monopolist sells the same product in sequential markets simply by re-interpreting the demand relationship as one of inter-temporal substitutability or complementarity.

Continue to consider the case where each good is produced at constant marginal cost c, but assume that demand in the first period is given by $q_1 = a - bp_1$ and demand in the second period by $q_2 = a - bp_2 + \lambda q_1$. If $\lambda > 0$, then higher sales in the first period stimulate demand in the second; if $\lambda < 0$, the opposite holds. The monopolist's total profits (assuming for simplicity a zero interest rate, that is the future gains count as the current ones) are

$$\pi = (a - bp_1)(p_1 - c) + (a - bp_2 + \lambda(a - bp_1))(p_2 - c). \qquad (8.14)$$

The monopolist chooses p_1 and p_2 so as to maximise π, therefore the two FOCs are given by $\partial \pi / \partial p_i = 0$. Solving the resulting system gives

$$p_1 = \frac{a(1 - \lambda) + cb}{b(2 - \lambda)}, \qquad p_2 = \frac{a + cb(1 - \lambda)}{b(2 - \lambda)}. \qquad (8.15)$$

It is easy to see that as λ rises the first-period price goes down and the second-period price goes up:

$$\frac{\partial p_1}{\partial \lambda} = -\frac{a - cb}{b(2 - \lambda)^2} < 0, \qquad \frac{\partial p_2}{\partial \lambda} = \frac{a - cb}{b(2 - \lambda)^2} > 0. \qquad (8.16)$$

The effect of the inter-temporal externality over prices is different. The second-period price varies with λ only because it shifts up (or down, if $\lambda < 0$) its demand intercept from a to $a + \lambda q_1$. More interesting is the reason why the first period price varies.

Intertemporal Complementarity: Introductory Price Offers   When $\lambda > 0$, the monopolist realises that there is a positive intertemporal demand externality, and it internalises it by decreasing the price relative to the price it would set if there was no future market. In other words, it anticipates that by lowering the first-period price it would increase first-period demand, which in turn will stimulate demand in the second period. This is an example of a well-known business strategy, that consists of *promotional pricing*, or introductory pricing: in the early stages of the life of a product, the firm sets initially a low price that is progressively increased as consumers get to know and appreciate the product (goodwill effect) or as more consumers have already bought the product (network effects, see Chapter 2 for a discussion).[5,6]

Intertemporal Substitutability: Durable Goods In the case where $\lambda < 0$, higher sales in the first period decrease the demand in the second period. As a result, the monopolist keeps the first-period price higher than in the hypothetical case where the product is sold only once, to internalise the negative demand externality arising across periods. This situation can be seen as a reduced form of the case of a durable good monopolist: the more consumers buy in the first period, the fewer will buy in the second. Note that it can be shown that in a durable good monopoly equilibrium prices tend to decrease over time, as is the case in this example.[7]

8.2.2.3 Interdependent Costs: Economies (or Diseconomies) of Scope

Let us now turn to the impact that cost externalities have over pricing of a multi-product monopolist. Assume that the overall cost function of the monopolist is given by $C(q_1, q_2) = cq_1 + cq_2 + \mu q_1 q_2$.[8] When $\mu > 0$, there exist diseconomies of scope between the two products, as the higher the output of one product, the higher the marginal cost of the other product ($\partial^2 C / \partial q_i \partial q_j = \mu > 0$). This is the case, for instance, where both products make use of limited natural resources or inputs: increase in output of one product exerts pressure on the common input by driving up its cost.

When $\mu < 0$, there exist instead economies of scope (or of joint production) between the two products: the higher the output of one product the lower the marginal cost of the other ($\partial^2 C / \partial q_i \partial q_j = \mu < 0$). There are many instances in the real world where producing two goods jointly gives rise to cost savings relative to the case where each product is produced separately.

For simplicity, assume that product demands are independent, so that $q_i = a - bp_i$.

---

[5] Another reason why a firm might offer introductory prices is the existence of switching costs (see Chapter 2). While the simple model used here can be seen as a reduced form of a more sophisticated model containing some goodwill effects or network effects, it cannot be easily interpreted as the result of switching costs.

[6] In the particular example chosen here, the first-period price does not go below marginal costs. However, one could find examples where the firm charges below marginal cost in the first period.

[7] See Chapter 2 for a brief discussion of the durable good monopoly, and Chapter 6 for an application that shares many features with the durable good monopoly case (the firm is hurt by its inability to commit to a certain price).

[8] Assume also that $\mu > -2c/a$. This guarantees that marginal costs are positive when μ is negative.

The monopolist's total profits are

$$\pi = (a - bp_1)p_1 + (a - bp_2)p_2 - cq_1 - cq_2 - \mu q_1 q_2. \tag{8.17}$$

Its problem amounts to $\max_{p_1, p_2} \pi$, so the FOCs are

$$\frac{\partial \pi}{\partial p_i} = a(1 + b\mu) - 2bp_i - b^2 \mu p_j + cb = 0, \qquad \text{with} \qquad i, j = 1, 2; \ i \neq j. \tag{8.18}$$

Under symmetry, $p_1 = p_2 = p_m$, and the solution becomes

$$p_m = \frac{a(1 + b\mu) + cb}{b(2 + b\mu)}. \tag{8.19}$$

To see the effect of the cost externality on the equilibrium price, write

$$\frac{\partial p_m}{\partial \mu} = \frac{a - bc}{(2 + b\mu)^2} > 0. \tag{8.20}$$

The stronger the cost externality between the two products, the higher the equilibrium price set by the monopolist. In particular, note that the function $p_m(\mu)$ is increasing over all its domain. This implies that when there exist economies of scope ($\mu < 0$), prices are lower than in the benchmark case where the production costs are independent. The firm anticipates that there exists a positive externality between the two products, and reduces the price of each good in order to stimulate its output, and in turn the output of the other product, through the cost reduction. In this case, a multi-product monopolist charges lower prices than two distinct monopolists, each producing one product, would charge.

When instead there exist diseconomies of scope ($\mu > 0$), prices are higher than in the case where production costs are independent. Here there exists a negative externality between the two products, and the monopolist increases the price of each good to internalise it (by reducing the output of one product the marginal cost of the other is lowered). In this case, a multi-product monopolist charges higher prices than two distinct monopolists would charge.

An Intertemporal Example: Learning-by-Doing   The cost of production of many goods and services decreases with the experience accumulated in producing those goods and services. This is a phenomenon known as "learning-by-doing" (see Arrow, 1961), and that provides an example of inter-temporal externalities on the cost side. As one can see from the following simple example, a monopolist that expects a learning effect will want to decrease prices (relative to a situation where such learning effects are absent) in the early stages of life of a product, in order to increase output and "go down the learning curve", which in turn will make it more efficient in later periods.

Suppose that in each of the two periods of life of its product a monopolist faces demand $p_t = 1 - q_t$, with $t = 1, 2$. Because of learning effects, marginal costs decrease with past production: they are $C'_1 = c$ in the first period and $C'_2(q_1) = c - lq_1$ in the second.[9]

Total profits of the monopolist (assuming there is no discounting for simplicity) are

$$\pi = (p_1 - c)q_1 + (p_2 - c + lq_1)q_2. \tag{8.21}$$

Since it has to choose q_1, q_2 so as to maximise π, the FOCs are given by $\partial \pi / \partial q_1 = 0$ and $\partial \pi / \partial q_2 = 0$, which can be re-written as

$$q_1 = \frac{1 - C'_1 + lq_2}{2}; \qquad q_2 = \frac{1 - C'_2}{2}. \tag{8.22}$$

The previous expressions tell us that while in the second period (the last one in this simple example) the monopolist will behave as usual, that is by simply equating marginal revenue to marginal cost, in the first period it will produce more than it would in a static setting, since it internalises the positive externality that this will have on its second-period costs (and the higher l the higher the first-period quantity).

By solving the system of FOCs (8.22) one obtains equilibrium values as

$$q_1^* = q_2^* = \frac{1 - c}{2 - l}; \qquad p_1^* = p_2^* = \frac{1 + c - l}{2 - l}. \tag{8.23}$$

Note that in this simple example it turns out that the quantity and price set by the monopolist at the equilibrium are the same over time. However, they are so for quite different reasons. In the first period, the monopolist increases quantities because it internalises the learning effect; in the second period, this externality is absent (it is the last period), but the equilibrium quantity increases because marginal costs have decreased.[10]

However, there is a sense in which learning makes the monopolist behave more competitively in the earlier periods. If one computes the market power (as proxied by the Lerner index: $L_t = (p_t^* - C'_t)/p_t^*$) exercised by the monopolist one finds that market power is lower in the first period than in the second:

$$L_1 = \frac{(1 - c)(1 - l)}{1 + c - l} < L_2 = \frac{(1 - c)}{1 + c - l}. \tag{8.24}$$

[9] Assume also that l is positive but small enough, to guarantee that costs are positive in the second period.

[10] These two effects exactly compensate each other in this model. See Tirole (1988: 72) for a learning model where output might even increase over time.

8.3 AN INTRODUCTION TO ELEMENTARY GAME THEORY

In this section, I give a simple and short introduction to the most elementary concepts of game theory, which are also the ones that I use in most of the technical sections of the book.[11]

Perhaps the simplest way to introduce the reader who is not familiar with game theory is to start with a simple example of a game, that I keep as abstract as possible so as not to distract attention with real world stories (I turn later to some more realistic applications).

Consider a game played between two *players,* call them player A and player B. Player A has to decide between two possible *actions:* a_1 or a_2; simultaneously, player B chooses among three possible actions b_1, b_2, or b_3. Each pair of actions will be associated with a certain *payoff* for each player, that is what a player receives after each of them has chosen an action. The payoffs can be summarised in a payoff matrix such as in Table 8.1. For instance, if player A chooses action a_1 and player B action b_2, that is, for the pair (a_1, b_2), the players' payoff is (2, 5): A receives 2 and B receives 5. Assume also this is a game with *perfect information,* that is players have perfect knowledge of the actions available to each and of the payoffs associated with them; they know what the table looks like (this assumption is kept throughout unless otherwise indicated).

Moreover, assume that both players are perfectly *rational,* i.e., each player chooses his/her actions so as to maximise his/her payoff from the game, and also assume that players' rationality is *common knowledge,* i.e., A knows that B knows that A knows that B knows . . . that the other player is rational.

When one looks at a game, one would like to be able to predict its outcome. In this particular game, for instance, one would like to answer the question "if A and B were called to play this game, which actions will they choose?" or, which is equivalent, "what will be the final result of the game?"

It is clear that we can have reasonable expectations as to how the game is played. For instance, the pair (a_2, b_1) is unlikely to occur. To see why, put yourself into player B's shoes first. Player B looks at the payoff table and realises that, whatever player A does, the best thing for B to do is to play b_2 (if A chooses a_1, then playing b_2 will give B a payoff of 5, while b_1 only yields 0 and b_3 only yields 1; a similar reasoning applies if A chooses a_2 instead: b_2 yields 3, while b_1 and b_3 only yield 2). In technical terms, we say that actions b_1 and b_3 are *strictly dominated* by action b_2. Since we have assumed that player B is rational, we can conclude that he will never choose any other action that b_2.

Next, put yourself into player A's shoes: recall that we have assumed that player A is perfectly aware of B's rationality, and that A is rational as well. Hence, A

---

[11] Some sections marked with ** use concepts, such as Bayesian Nash equilibrium and sequential equilibrium, that are not explained here but are briefly introduced directly in those sections.

Table 8.1. A Simple Game

A \ B	b_1	b_2	b_3
a_1	2, 0	2, 5	1, 1
a_2	0, 2	0, 3	2, 2

anticipates that B will never choose b_1 (or b_3), but always play b_2. Now, player A has to figure out what is the best thing for her to do given that she rationally expects B to choose b_2. Looking at the payoff table, we see that the obvious choice is a_1 (which yields payoff 2), while a_2 would never be chosen by A (as it only yields payoff 0).

In technical terms, we say that player A *responds* to B's choice of b_2 by choosing either action a_1 or a_2, and that a_1 is A's *best response* to B's playing b_2. Note that the term *best response* is used no matter if the two players make their choices at the same time (like in our example here) or one after the other (in which case the term *response* may be more intuitive). The term *response* refers to the (hypothetical) rounds of reasoning that precede the final actions rather than to those actions themselves.

Hence, we expect from two rational players that the final outcome of the game they play is a pair (a, b) such that a is the best response to b and vice versa. For instance, in the game above, (a_1, b_2) is such a pair (as a_1 is A's best response to b_2, and b_2 is B's best response to any of A's actions, hence also to a_1), while the pair (a_2, b_1) is no such pair of best responses.

8.3.1 Nash Equilibrium

The concept of *Nash equilibrium* is based on such an idea: it predicts that the outcome of the game (the "equilibrium") is given by the set of actions such that, for each player, each action is the best response to the actions of all other players. Equivalently, a set of actions represents a Nash equilibrium if none of the players has an incentive to deviate from its action given the actions of all other players.[12]

More formally, in a game with n players, denoting with A_i the set of actions available to player i (with $i = 1, \ldots, n$), and with player i's payoff $\pi_i(\alpha_1, \alpha_2, \ldots, \alpha_i, \ldots, \alpha_n)$, the n-tuple $(\alpha_1^*, \alpha_2^*, \ldots, \alpha_i^*, \ldots, \alpha_n^*)$ is a Nash equilibrium

---

[12] To keep things as simple as possible, the Nash equilibrium is defined here in terms of *actions*. It could also be defined in terms of strategies. A *strategy s* is a "rule", which tells a player which action to choose at any given time t of the game, for any given history of the game prior to t. Denoting with S_i the set of strategies available to player i (with $i = 1, \ldots, n$), and with $\pi_i(s_1, s_2, \ldots, s_i, \ldots, s_n)$ player i's payoff, the n-tuple $(s_1^*, s_2^*, \ldots, s_i^*, \ldots, s_n^*)$ is a Nash equilibrium if $\pi_i(s_1^*, s_2^*, \ldots, s_i^*, \ldots, s_n^*) \geq \pi_i(s_1^*, s_2^*, \ldots, s_i', \ldots, s_n^*)$, for all $i = 1, 2, \ldots, n$, and all $s_i \in S_i$. In one-shot simultaneous games, the concepts of strategy and action coincide.

Table 8.2. The Prisoners' Dilemma Game

A \ B	*High*	*Low*
High	10, 10	5, 15
Low	15, 5	6, 6

if

$$\pi_i(\alpha_1^*, \alpha_2^*, \ldots, \alpha_i^*, \ldots, \alpha_n^*) \geq \pi_i'(\alpha_1^*, \alpha_2^*, \ldots, \alpha_i', \ldots, \alpha_n^*),$$

$$\text{for all} \quad i = 1, 2, \ldots, n, \quad \text{and all} \quad \alpha_i \in A_i. \quad (8.25)$$

In other words, $(\alpha_1^*, \alpha_2^*, \ldots, \alpha_i^*, \ldots, \alpha_n^*)$ is a Nash equilibrium if, for each player i, playing α_i^* is the best possible response given that all the other players play $(\alpha_1^*, \alpha_2^*, \ldots, \alpha_{i-1}^*, \alpha_{i+1}^*, \ldots, \alpha_n^*)$.

We can now return to the game described in Table 8.1, and look for the Nash equilibrium (or equilibria) of that game. To do so, let us write down the best responses for each player: the equilibrium, if it exists, will be given by the pair of actions that are mutually best responses.

Player A's best responses (indicated in bold) to each of B's actions are $(\mathbf{a}_1, b_1)$, $(\mathbf{a}_1, b_2)$, $(\mathbf{a}_2, b_3)$.

Player B's best responses (indicated in bold) to each of A's actions are $(a_1, \mathbf{b}_2)$, $(a_2, \mathbf{b}_2)$.

It is straightforward to see that (a_1, b_2) is the unique Nash equilibrium of this game, as it is the only pair of actions that is the best response to each other. Equivalently, it is the only pair of actions such that no player has an incentive to deviate from given the action of the rival.

8.3.1.1 The Prisoners' Dilemma

Perhaps the most famous game, since it has applications in several fields, from economics to politics, is the so-called prisoners' dilemma,[13] illustrated by the payoff matrix of Table 8.2.

This is a perfectly symmetric game that has only one Nash equilibrium (*low, low*). (The reader can easily check by drawing the best responses for each player, as indicated above; or by verifying that no player would play *high* given that the other plays *low*, whereas any other pair of actions cannot be an equilibrium since a player would have an incentive to deviate from it.)

First, note that the game is very particular because each player has a *dominant strategy*: whether its rival plays *high* or *low*, a player always prefers to play *low*.

---

[13] So-called, because the original story behind this game is one where the players are two prisoners accused of a crime, and kept in separate cells, each of them having to decide whether to confess or deny the crime.

Table 8.3. The Battle of the Sexes Game

A \ B	Indian	Thai
Indian	3, 2	0, −1
Thai	−1, 0	2, 3

Second, the outcome of the game is *Pareto inferior:* both players would be better off if they played (*high, high*).

8.3.1.2 Coordination Games and Equilibrium Selection

In the previous two games there was a unique Nash equilibrium. It is possible, though, that several equilibria co-exist, as in the game (a version of the so-called *battle of the sexes*) described in Table 8.3.

Anna and Bruno have decided to go to a restaurant together, but have not discussed which one, and cannot communicate with each other before dinner time. There are two good restaurants in town; one offers Indian and the other Thai food. Anna would prefer Indian and Bruno Thai, but for both the most important thing would be to end up in the same place. It is easy to check that this game has two Nash equilibria: (*Indian, Indian*) and (*Thai, Thai*).

It is far from uncommon to find games with multiple equilibria, and the problem in such cases is how to choose among them. In many economic applications, for instance, we are faced with such a situation, and unless we could refine our analysis the game would have scarce predictive power. This issue is addressed by *refinements* to the Nash equilibrium concept that try to select between different equilibria.

Pareto Dominance as an Equilibrium Selection Device   Sometimes, as in the battle of the sexes game above, which is perfectly symmetric, even these refinements would not help much, but in others there might be one equilibrium that, for one reason or the other, might be more appealing and more likely for players to coordinate upon.[14]

[14] History or other circumstances might in some particular cases suggest that one equilibrium is more likely to be played than another. In the words of Schelling (1960), there might be *focal* points. For instance, if Anna and Bruno have so far always met at the Indian restaurant and never had dinner at the Thai restaurant, the former equilibrium is more likely than the latter. Some discussions on how certain prices might be focal can be found in Chapter 4, where models having several more or less collusive equilibria are analysed. There, I also discuss other elements that might resolve the uncertainty about the equilibrium, such as communication or first-mover advantages (Anna might move first, make a reservation at the Indian, and then make it known to Bruno). But of course all these are different games than the one-shot simultaneous moves game I am discussing here.

Table 8.4. A Pure Coordination Game

A \ B	Indian	Italian
Indian	2, 2	0, 0
Italian	0, 0	1, 1

Consider for instance a slightly different version of the battle of the sexes, as in Table 8.4.

Here there are again two equilibria: (*Indian, Indian*), and (*Italian, Italian*). However, ending up in the Italian restaurant would be Pareto-inferior for the players: that is, in plain words, both Anna and Bruno would have higher payoffs if they had dinner in the Indian restaurant. Therefore, using Pareto-dominance as a criterion for selection among different equilibria, we would predict that Anna and Bruno will go to the Indian restaurant, a somehow reasonable prediction, and one which enjoys support from experimental evidence.[15,16]

Another criterion for equilibrium selection is the elimination of weakly-dominated strategies.

Elimination of Weakly Dominated Strategies   Consider two players A and B whose set of possible strategies is S_i (with $i = A, B$). We say that for player i a strategy s_i is weakly dominated if there exists a strategy s_i' such that $\pi_i(s_i', s_j) \geq \pi_i(s_i, s_j)$ for all s_j (with $i \neq j$), and there exists at least one strategy s_j for which this inequality holds with a strict sign.

Consider for instance the game illustrated in Table 8.5.

It is easy to check that this game has two equilibria: (p_L, p_L) and (p_H, p_H). The criterion of the elimination of weakly dominated strategies uniquely selects the equilibrium (p_H, p_H). Indeed, for player A we have $\pi_A(p_L, p_L) = \pi_A(p_L, p_H) = 0$ and $\pi_A(p_H, p_L) = 0 < \pi_A(p_H, p_H) = 2$, which implies that for A strategy p_L is weakly dominated by strategy p_H. Further, for player B we have $\pi_B(p_L, p_L) = \pi_B(p_L, p_H) = 0$ and $\pi_B(p_H, p_L) = -2 < \pi_B(p_H, p_H) = 0$, that is, for B strategy p_L is weakly dominated by strategy p_H.[17]

---

[15] Some experimental evidence is mentioned in Chapter 4, that analyses repeated games that are very similar to the one described in this simple game, as they present a multitude of equilibria that can be Pareto-ranked.

[16] It is important to stress that here I am using Pareto-dominance to select between two Nash equilibria, whereas in the prisoners' dilemma game the pair giving the Pareto-superior outcome was not an equilibrium of the game, and therefore very unlikely to be the outcome of the game.

[17] Note that in this example Pareto dominance would also select the same (p_H, p_H) equilibrium pair.

Table 8.5. An Asymmetric Game

A \ B	p_L	p_H
p_L	0, 0	0, 0
p_H	0, −2	2, 0

8.3.1.3 Mixed Strategies

So far, I have restricted attention to so-called *pure strategies*: players decide whether to play a certain action or not but cannot randomise between them, that is they have to choose one action with probability one. Some games have no equilibrium in pure strategies, and it is easy to check that one such game is that described in Table 8.6 (a version of the *matching pennies* game).

Mixed Strategies   However, one might want to consider the possibility that players use *mixed strategies*, that is, that they have a probability distribution over their pure strategies (in other words, players randomise among pure strategies).[18] For instance, in the matching pennies game of Table 8.6, player A might play *heads* with a certain probability p, *tails* with probability $1 - p$; and player B might play *heads* with a probability q, *tails* with probability $1 - q$. The concept of Nash equilibrium and of best responses must then be re-cast in terms of mixed strategies. Note that for a mixed strategy to make sense, it must be that a player is indifferent between two (or possibly more) pure strategies, that is, they should give her the same payoff given the (mixed) strategy of the other player(s).

In the game of Table 8.6, for instance, the equilibrium in mixed strategies is the one where $p = q = 1/2$. To see why, look first at the payoff player A makes given the mixed strategy of player B. If A chooses *heads*, she gets $\pi_A(heads) = -1(q) + 1(1 - q) = 1 - 2q$. If she chooses *tails*, she gets $\pi_A(tails) = 1(q) - 1(1 - q) = -1 + 2q$. To be willing to randomise between *heads* and *tails*, player A must be indifferent between the two, that is it must be $\pi_A(tails) = \pi_A(heads)$. It is easy to check that this is true for $q = 1/2$.

A similar easy calculation (here everything is symmetric) shows that player B is indifferent between *heads* and *tails* (that is, he is willing to randomise between the

---

[18] If it sounds strange that a player "throws dice" to decide which action to take, a more appealing interpretation of mixed strategies exists: "the crucial feature of a mixed-strategy Nash equilibrium is not that player j chooses a strategy randomly, but rather that player i is uncertain about player j's choice; this uncertainty can arise either because of randomization or (more plausibly) because of a little incomplete information". Gibbons (1997: 140). Gibbons (1997: 138–40) shows how to interpret mixed strategies using games with *incomplete information,* that is where at least one player is not sure about the other player's payoff.

Table 8.6. The Matching Pennies Game

A \ B	Heads	Tails
Heads	−1, 1	1, −1
Tails	1, −1	−1, 1

two) if player A chooses *heads* with probability $p = 1/2$ and *tails* with probability $1 − p = 1/2$.

Nash (1950) has shown that any game with a finite number of players, where each player has a finite number of pure strategies, has a Nash equilibrium (in mixed strategies if no equilibrium in pure strategies exists).

Note also that equilibria in mixed strategies can co-exist in the same game with equilibria in pure strategies. For instance, the reader can check that the battle of the sexes game of Table 8.3 admits one Nash equilibrium in mixed strategies where B chooses (*Indian*) with probability 1/3 and A chooses (*Thai*) with probability 1/2.

8.3.2 Dynamic Games and Sub-Game Perfect Nash Equilibrium

So far we have just looked at static games, where players choose their actions simultaneously. Dynamic games are games where players move sequentially or they move more than once. Such a game might be as follows. First, player 1 chooses an action a_1 from the set of her feasible actions; second, player 2 chooses an action a_2 from the set of his feasible actions; after both have played, players 1 and 2 receive the payoffs associated with the pair (a_1, a_2).

An example will help illustrate why the concept of Nash equilibrium needs to be refined to deal with dynamic games. Consider two players: firm I is an incumbent firm, firm E is a potential entrant in the industry. First, firm E decides whether to enter or not in the market; second, firm I decides whether to *accommodate* entry (for instance, setting a high price) or to *fight* entry (setting a low price). Table 8.7 represents this game in the so-called *normal form*, that is with the usual payoff matrix.[19]

This game has two Nash equilibria: (*enter, accommodate*) and (*stay out, fight*). However, the second equilibrium, (*stay out, fight*), is an unlikely outcome of this game. At this equilibrium, firm E chooses to stay out because firm I would fight

---

[19] Note that at first sight, the second line of this payoff matrix may seem confusing. It is *not* meant to read: "If E stays out, then I can fight or accommodate, where either action will yield the same payoffs of 10 (for I) and 0 (for E)". Instead, if E stays out, there is of course nothing left to be done for I (he remains the uncontended incumbent in this market), and the game is over for both of them. Yet, to reflect this fact in the payoff matrix, the conventions require to treat this case as shown in Table 8.7.

Table 8.7. The Entry Deterrence Game

E \ I	Accommodate	Fight
Enter	4, 5	−1, 0
Stay out	0, 10	0, 10

entry, thereby making entry unprofitable to E. However, the threat of fighting entry by firm I if entry occurs is not credible. Indeed, if entry did take place, firm I would rather accommodate it, since it would get a higher payoff than if it fought it, and E knows this.

We therefore need a refinement of the Nash equilibrium concept that allows ruling out equilibria – such as the one described above – that are based on non-credible threats. In other words, we need to ensure that each player always plays optimally in each situation, even in those that are not along the equilibrium path. (In the game above, an equilibrium is given by (*stay out, fight*) but *fight* is not optimal if the game reached a point where *entry* occurs.)

The concept of *sub-game perfect Nash equilibrium* (SPNE) corresponds to this requirement. It is the set of strategies for each player such that the strategies form a Nash equilibrium in any sub-game of the game (and not only along the equilibrium path), that is any subset of the game that starts from any point at which the complete history of the game prior to that point is common knowledge for all the players (each player knows it, and knows that the other knows it . . .).

To see how to look for the SPNE of a game, it is useful to describe a game in its *extensive form* (or game tree). For the game above, this is done in Figure 8.1.

The game tree of Figure 8.1 contains two sub-games: the whole game; and the subset of the game which starts when player I is about to move after player E has played *enter*. What the SPNE equilibrium concept requires is then that all players play optimally at each sub-game.

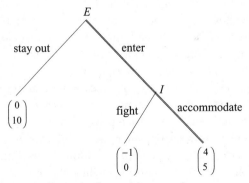

Figure 8.1. Extensive form of the entry deterrence game.

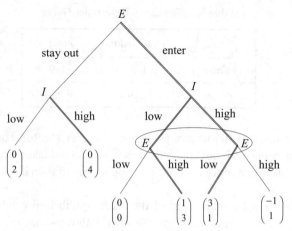

Figure 8.2. Extensive form of a quality game.

8.3.2.1 Backward Induction

To find the (pure strategy) SPNE equilibrium, we have to start from the last branches of the tree and move backwards. At the sub-game starting after player E has chosen *enter*, player I will choose *accommodate* (it gets 5 rather than 0). We can now move backwards to the first sub-game, which is the initial node of the game. Player E knows that if it chooses to stay out it will get 0 whatever I does, and anticipates correctly that if it enters player I will accommodate and it will make a profit of 4. Therefore, it will enter: (*enter, accommodate*) is the only SPNE of this game.

Note that SPNE is used also in games of "almost perfect information", where more than one player moves in the same sub-game. Consider for instance the game depicted in Figure 8.2. This is a game where player E decides first whether to *stay out or enter*; after observing E's decision, active firms decide (simultaneously, if E has entered) whether to sell *low* or *high* quality.

Figure 8.2 represents the game in its extensive form. The "oval" around E's nodes is called an *information set*: it is a convention to represent the idea that when E decides it does not know at which node it is, that is whether I has chosen *low* or *high* quality (this can be either because I and E take decisions on quality simultaneously, as I have said above, or because I takes its choice before but E does not observe I's choice before its own choice: the two are equivalent).

Note that this game has three sub-games: the whole game; the subset of the game, which starts when player I is about to move after player E has played *stay out*; and the subset of the game which starts when player I is about to move after player E has played *enter*. (The nodes starting after I has played are not sub-games because the complete history of the game prior to that point is not common knowledge for all the players: at the moment of choosing quality, player E does not know what I has played.)

By using backward induction, it is easy to find that there are two pure strategy SPNE of this game: (*enter, low, high*) and (*enter, high, low*).[20]

Another type of game that belongs to the category of games of "almost perfect information", which can be solved by backward induction, is that in which the same game is repeated finitely many times. For instance, the prisoners' dilemma game repeated over and over, but for a finite number of times, is one such game (see also Section 8.4.3.1). However, backward induction cannot be used for *infinite horizon* games: backward induction requires starting from the final node of the game and moving backwards, whereas no such final node can be found if the game lasts forever.

The concept of SPNE, and the method of backward induction to look for it, can be found everywhere in this book since it is used to solve dynamic games that are widely used in industrial organisation theory (see also below in this section). Examples of a game being played for infinite number of times are at the core of Chapter 4 on collusion (see also Section 8.4.3.2 below).

8.4 OLIGOPOLY I: MARKET COMPETITION IN STATIC GAMES

This section introduces the reader to simple models of product market competition in static games, and under exogenously given investment choices of firms (Section 8.5 will consider games where firms decide their investments in capacities, R&D, advertising, quality or product positioning). Section 8.4.1 also assumes that the firms produce a perfectly homogenous good, and examines the different benchmark cases of product market competition: price competition (the *Bertrand* model), quantity competition (the *Cournot* model) and joint-profit maximisation. Section 8.4.2 assumes that the firms sell differentiated products, and again derives the equilibrium outcomes for the three benchmark cases of price competition, quantity competition and joint-profit maximisation. Throughout these two sections, we shall use the Nash equilibrium concept introduced in the previous section: for given characteristics of the goods (that is, whether they are homogenous or differentiated), the firms play a one-shot game where their actions might consist of prices or quantities, and the Nash equilibrium is the appropriate concept to study the outcome of the game.

Section 8.4.2.1 will consider a repeated game of product market interaction: again, firms have exogenously given product characteristics, but they meet period after period in the marketplace. For those games, the relevant equilibrium concept is the one of sub-game perfect Nash equilibrium.

8.4.1 Product Market Competition with Homogenous Goods

In this section I assume that the firms' products are homogenous, that is are seen as perfect substitutes by consumers. I will analyse in turn the three benchmark cases

---

[20] If *E* enters, the last stage of the game has two equilibria: (*low, high*) and (*high, low*). Find first the equilibrium of the whole game if (*low, high*) is played; then, if (*high, low*) is played.

where firms compete in prices, in quantities, and where they choose their actions so as to maximise joint profits.

8.4.1.1 Price Competition (Bertrand Model)

Consider two firms (but the extension to n firms would be straightforward and offer the same results) that:

A1) sell *homogenous* goods;
A2) play a *one-shot game;*
A3) independently and simultaneously choose the *price* at which they want to sell their product;
A4) have *no capacity constraints,* that is, they are able to serve all demand that is addressed to them;
A5) have the same *identical marginal cost, c,* and no fixed costs.

Consumers address the firms according to the following demand function:

$$D_i(p_i, p_j) = \begin{cases} D(p_i), & \text{if } p_i < p_j \\ D(p_i)/2, & \text{if } p_i = p_j \\ 0, & \text{if } p_i > p_j \end{cases} \qquad (8.26)$$

that is, if a firm sets a price lower than its rival, then all consumers will address it (and vice versa: nobody addresses the firm setting the higher price); if both firms set the same price, consumers are indifferent between one or the other, and it is assumed that they equally split their demand between the two firms.

This being a one-shot game, the appropriate solution concept is the Nash equilibrium. In this model, a Nash equilibrium in prices, or Bertrand equilibrium, is a pair of prices (p_i^*, p_j^*) such that $\pi_i(p_i^*, p_j^*) \geq \pi_i'(p_i, p_j^*)$, for any i, $j = 1, 2$, with $i \neq j$ and any p_i in the real numbers. I am going to show the following result:

Result   (*Bertrand equilibrium*) *The unique price equilibrium of this game is given by* $p_i^* = p_j^* = c$, *with* $\pi_i(p_i^*, p_j^*) = \pi_j(p_i^*, p_j^*) = 0$.

Proof   To prove this result, we need to prove first that the proposed one is a Nash equilibrium of the game, and then that it is the only one.

Step 1. To see that $p_1^* = p_2^* = c$ is a Nash equilibrium is straightforward. To be in a Nash equilibrium, no firm must have incentives to deviate from it given that the other plays according to the equilibrium strategy. Suppose then that $p_1^* = c$, does firm 2 have an incentive to deviate and sell at a different price than $p_2^* = c$? By selling at marginal cost, firm 2 serves half of the market but makes zero profit. If it deviates and sets a *lower* price than c, it will serve all the market, but make losses; if it deviates and sets a *higher* price, no consumers will address it, and therefore it will make zero profits, thus not improving its situation relative to playing the candidate equilibrium. Therefore, firm 2 will have no incentive to deviate. Likewise, given the perfect symmetry between the two firms, firm 1 has no incentives to deviate.

Step 2. Let us reason by contradiction. Suppose that there is a different candidate equilibrium, and show there is at least one deviation that would make better off a firm, thereby breaking the candidate equilibrium.

- $p_i^* = p_j^* = p^* > c$: at this candidate equilibrium, firms share the market equally and make positive profits $\pi(p^*, p^*) = (p^* - c)D(p^*)/2$. However, given the price p^* of firm i, its rival firm j can set a price p_j' which is a shade less than p^* (that is, $p_j' = p^* - \varepsilon$) and get the whole market. It would therefore make a profit $\pi_j'(p_i^*, p_j') = (p^* - c - \varepsilon)D(p^* - \varepsilon)$ that, for ε small enough, is clearly higher than $\pi(p^*, p^*)$ (since a marginal reduction in the price results in a disproportionate increase in demand, which doubles). Therefore, this cannot be a Nash equilibrium of the game.

- $p_i^* = p_j^* = p^* < c$: at the candidate equilibrium, both firms take losses. Trivially, this cannot be an equilibrium since a firm would have an incentive to deviate and set a price at or above marginal cost: it would not sell anything and therefore make zero profits (better than negative profits).

- $p_i^* > p_j^* \geq c$: if $p_j^* = c$, firm j makes zero profits, but given that firm i sets a price above cost, it can improve its position by charging any price between c and firm i's price, since it would still get the whole demand but would command a positive margin. In particular, the optimal deviation would be to set the price $p_i^* - \varepsilon$ and get profits $(p_i^* - c - \varepsilon)D(p_i^* - \varepsilon) > 0$. Therefore, this candidate equilibrium, and by similar reasoning all pairs with asymmetric prices, cannot be a Nash equilibrium of the game. If $p_j^* > c$, firm i would also have an incentive to deviate, and charge a price just below p_j^*. ∎

The Bertrand result is a striking one. Despite the fact that there are only two firms in the industry, they will end up selling at marginal cost, and get zero profits. As we shall see below, this is not a robust result, as it crucially depends on a series of strong assumptions: by relaxing in turn each of assumptions A1)–A5), one obtains equilibria where prices are above marginal cost and firms make positive profits. Nevertheless, this case provides a useful benchmark, corresponding to the lower bound that equilibrium prices can take. In other words, the Bertrand equilibrium corresponds to the toughest possible degree of product market competition.

Before introducing the other main benchmark case, that of Cournot competition, let me briefly describe the Bertrand game in two interesting cases: (1) under asymmetric firms; and (2) under capacity constraints.

Bertrand under Cost Asymmetric Firms   Consider exactly the same game as above, but relax assumption A5) and assume that the two firms have asymmetric costs. Firm 1 and 2 have respectively marginal cost c_1 and c_2 with $c_1 < c_2$. There are two possible solutions to this game. In the first case, firm 1 is so much more efficient than firm 2 (firm 1's costs are much lower) that it can behave as if it was a monopolist: firm 2's cost is so high that firm 1's monopoly price p_1^m is below c_2. In the second case, if the firms' costs are close enough to each other (how close is to be specified below), then firm 1 will set a price slightly below firm 2's marginal cost and get the whole market.

To keep the analysis simple, I develop these two cases under the assumption that firm i's demand function is given by $D_i = 1 - p_i$ if $p_i < p_j$, $D_i = 0$ if $p_i > p_j$, and $D_i = (1 - p_i)/2$ if $p_i = p_j$.

Large Asymmetries Consider the case where firm 2's costs are large enough relative to firm 1's (more precisely, $c_2 \geq (1 + c_1)/2$, as will be seen below). If firm 1 were alone in the market, it would choose its price so as to maximise $\pi = (1 - p)(p - c_1)$. We have seen that the monopolist's problem is easily solved by taking $\partial \pi / \partial p = 0$ and rearranging, which gives the result

$$p_1^m = \frac{1 + c_1}{2}. \tag{8.27}$$

As long as p_1^m is below the marginal cost of firm 2, firm 1 can charge the monopoly price and get the whole market undisturbed, as firm 2 would have no incentive to undercut it: if it did set a price below p_1^m, all consumers would address it and it would accumulate losses. Better then to charge a price higher than p_1^m and get zero profits.

Therefore, if $c_2 \geq (1 + c_1)/2$, at equilibrium firm 1 will set $p_1^m = (1 + c_1)/2$, firm 2 a price $p > p_1^m$. Firm 1 will get monopoly profits $(1 - c_1)^2/4$, and firm 2 zero profit.

In the study of innovations, this case corresponds to the case where a firm gets a *drastic innovation*, that is an innovation that makes it so much more competitive than its rival that it can behave as a monopolist (see Chapter 2 for some applications of this case).

Small Asymmetries Consider now the case where the firms' costs are close enough: $c_1 < c_2 < (1 + c_1)/2$. In this case, firm 1 setting its monopoly price cannot be the equilibrium of the game: if firm 1 sets $p_1^m = (1 + c_1)/2$, firm 2 will charge a price $p = (1 + c_1)/2 - \varepsilon$, get all the market, and make a positive profit (on each unit sold, it will make a gain equal to $(1 + c_1)/2 - \varepsilon - c_2$).

The following is instead a Nash equilibrium of the game: $(p_1^*, p_2^*) = (c_2 - \varepsilon, c_2)$, that is, firm 2 charges a price equal to marginal cost and firm 1 a price which is a shade below that. It is easy to check that firm 2 has no incentive to deviate from this pair, as undercutting $p_1^* = c_2 - \varepsilon$ would leave it with losses rather than zero profits, whereas increasing the price above c_2 leaves it again with zero profits. Firm 1 has no incentive to deviate either: by setting a higher price, say $p_1 = c_2$ it would have to share the market with the rival (or lose it completely to firm 2 if the price was above c_2),[21] whereas by setting a lower price it would continue

---

[21] There is a very minor technical detail here, which is that firm 1 wants to choose ε as close as possible to zero, but of course for any given small number ε it is always possible to find another number smaller than it. To resolve this technical problem, an *escamotage* is sometimes used, by assuming that for identical prices all the demand goes to the firm that has lower costs. The equilibrium of the game then becomes $(p_1^*, p_2^*) = (c_2, c_2)$, with all demand going to firm 1.

to get all the market but it would sell at a lower margin, and thus making lower profits.

At this equilibrium, firm 1 makes profits $(c_2 - c_1)(1 - c_2)$, and firm 2 gains zero.

In principle, there exist other equilibria of this game, but they are less "reasonable". Consider for instance a price $p \in (c_1, c_2)$. It is easy to see that the pair $(p_1^{**}, p_2^{**}) = (p - \varepsilon, p)$ represents an equilibrium of the game.

However, such an equilibrium looks less appealing than the equilibrium (p_1^*, p_2^*) identified above, and indeed the main criteria of equilibrium selection would select the latter over the former. Under Pareto-dominance, for instance, (p_1^*, p_2^*) would be chosen because it gives higher profits for firm 1 while keeping the same profits (zero) for firm 2. Elimination of weakly dominated strategies also selects (p_1^*, p_2^*) as the only equilibrium of the game. To see this, note that when player 2 chooses action $p_2^* = c_2$ it gets $\pi_2(c_2 - \varepsilon, c_2) = 0$ and $\pi_2(p - \varepsilon, c_2) = 0$, where $p \in (c_1, c_2)$; when it chooses action $p_2^{**} = p$, it gets $\pi_2(p - \varepsilon, p) = 0$, if player 1 chooses $p - \varepsilon$, but it gets $\pi_2(p + \varepsilon, p) < 0$, if player 1 chooses $p + \varepsilon$. The equilibrium (p_1^{**}, p_2^{**}) contains a strategy that is weakly dominated for player 2.

Bertrand under Capacity Constraints   Let us now go back to the symmetric case treated initially, but relax now assumption A4), and assume instead that each firm holds a capacity $k_i < D(p_i = c)$: When charging at marginal cost, a firm would have to supply a larger number of units than its capacity would allow it to do. It is then easy to see that under this new assumption $p_i^* = p_j^* = c$ is not a Nash equilibrium of the game any longer:

Remark 8.1   *If $k_i < D(p_i = c)$, $(p_i^*, p_j^*) = (c, c)$ is not a Nash equilibrium of the game.*

Proof   To prove this result, we just need to find a deviation that leaves one of the firms better off. Now, at the candidate equilibrium $p_i^* = p_j^* = c$, firm i makes zero profits. But if it deviates and sells at a price $p_1' > p_j^* = c$, some consumers will address it (at least as long as p_1' is not too high) and it will make positive profits. This is because all consumers would like to buy from firm j, which sells at a lower price, but j cannot serve them all (as its capacity $k_j < D(c)$). Some consumers are rationed, and will have to buy instead from firm 1, which will therefore make positive profits (it will sell a positive number of units at a positive margin). ∎

I limit myself here to this proof that under capacity constraints the Bertrand result does not hold. To find the equilibrium of the price competition game under capacity constraints requires specifying a *rationing rule*, that is a rule that allocates consumers between the firms (some cannot buy from the low price firm). It also turns out that an equilibrium in pure strategies does not exist if firms have large enough capacities. Since throughout the book I never deal with capacity constrained models, it would be an unnecessary complication to carry out the complete analysis of the capacity-constrained price competition game. I refer the interested reader to

Kreps and Scheinkman (1983): in a two-stage game where firms (simultaneously) first choose capacities and then prices, the final equilibrium outcome is the same as in a one-shot game where firms choose quantities. In other words, the Cournot equilibrium could be interpreted not only literally, that is as the outcome of a game where firms choose the output they bring to the market, but also as the outcome of a game where firms choose their capacities and then their prices.[22]

8.4.1.2 Quantity Competition (Cournot Model)

Consider now the same one-shot game analysed in Section 8.4.1.1, but relax assumption A3) and assume instead that firms choose *quantities* they want to bring to the market, rather than prices. For simplicity, let us look first at the symmetric case, where both firms have the same marginal cost $c < 1$, and they face a linear demand function $p = 1 - Q$, with $Q = q_1 + q_2$ being total industry output.[23]

Firm i's profit is given by $\pi_i = p(q_i, q_j)q_i - cq_i$. The first step to identify the Nash equilibrium of this game is to look for the best reply function of a firm for any given quantity chosen by its rival. Taking q_j as given, firm i solves therefore the following problem (for $i, j = 1, 2$, and $i \neq j$):

$$\max_{q_i} \pi_i(q_i, q_j) = (1 - q_i - q_j - c)q_i, \text{ given } q_j. \tag{8.28}$$

This problem is solved by taking $\partial \pi_i(q_i, q_j)/\partial q_i = 0$, that is,

$$1 - 2q_i - q_j - c = 0. \tag{8.29}$$

The previous expressions ($1 - 2q_1 - q_2 - c = 0$ for firm 1, and $1 - 2q_2 - q_1 - c = 0$ for firm 2) implicitly represent the *reaction functions* (or *best-reply*, or *best-response functions*) of each firm, whose meaning we have already discussed in Section 8.2.2.3. It is convenient to represent the reaction functions in the same plane (q_1, q_2). To this end, let us write them as

$$R_1 : q_2 = 1 - 2q_1 - c; \qquad R_2 : q_2 = \frac{1 - q_1 - c}{2}. \tag{8.30}$$

Figure 8.3 illustrates the two reaction functions. Note that they are negatively sloped: the higher firm j's output q_j the lower firm i's best-reply output. The slope of the reaction functions carries important effects when analysing dynamic models, as we shall see in Section 8.5.1 below. The figure also illustrates the iso-profit functions of

[22] See also Maggi (1996), where constraints are "soft", as a firm can increase its output beyond capacity by incurring an additional variable cost. Maggi's formulation is simpler as it allows us to find an equilibrium in pure strategies of the price game independently of the capacity levels. Note, however, that the Kreps–Scheinkman result applies only when using the efficient-rationing allocation rule, as shown by Davidson and Deneckere (1986).

[23] The assumption $c < 1$ serves to guarantee the viability of the market. Otherwise, there is no price at which firms would be willing to supply demand as they would get negative profits.

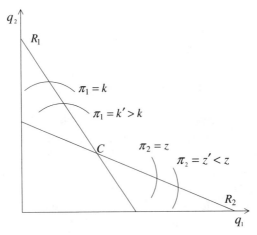

Figure 8.3. Reaction functions in the Cournot model.

each firm, that is the locus of the points such that different values of q_1, q_2 give the same value of profit to a firm, $\pi_i(q_i, q_j) = k$. Note that lower iso-profit curves for firm 1, and iso-profit curves more to the left for firm 2, are associated with higher profits (given the same q_i, a lower q_j would increase prices and profits of firm i).[24]

As we know from the discussion of the game theory section, the Nash equilibrium of the game will be determined by the intersection of the two reaction functions, which elementary algebra shows to be

$$q_1^C = q_2^C = \frac{1-c}{3}, \qquad (8.31)$$

the label "C" standing for Cournot.[25] After substituting, one obtains also prices and

---

[24] Note also that an iso-profit function of firm 1 must be tangent to the horizontal line when it crosses firm 1's best reply function, and an iso-profit function of firm 2 must be tangent to the vertical line when it crosses 2's best reply function. To see this, write a generic iso-profit function of firm 1 as $\pi_1(q_1, q_2) = (1 - q_1 - q_2 - c)q_1 = k$. To find its slope, write the total differential as $d\pi_1 = (1 - 2q_1 - q_2 - c)dq_1 - q_1 dq_2 = 0$. Therefore, its slope must be $dq_2/dq_1 = (1 - 2q_1 - q_2 - c)/q_1$, whose numerator is nil when the FOC is satisfied (that is, along the reaction function). Similarly, write a generic iso-profit function of firm 2 as $\pi_2(q_1, q_2) = (1 - q_1 - q_2 - c)q_2 = z$. The total differential is $d\pi_2 = (1 - q_1 - 2q_2 - c)dq_2 - q_2 dq_1 = 0$. Its slope must be $dq_2/dq_1 = q_1/(1 - q_1 - 2q_2 - c)$, whose denominator is zero when the FOC is satisfied: Therefore, along the reaction function, the slope is infinity.

[25] I focus here on the symmetric equilibrium of the game. There also exist two possible asymmetric Nash equilibria, where a firm, say 1, produces zero output and the other firm produces such a large output that if firm 1 brought even a very small quantity to the market the price would fall below marginal costs (thus giving it no incentive to deviate from zero output). This case is considered in detail in Chapter 7.3.3.1 (on inter-operability) and omitted here to save space.

profits as

$$p^C = \frac{1+2c}{3}, \qquad \pi_1^C = \pi_2^C = \frac{(1-c)^2}{9}. \tag{8.32}$$

Note that at the Cournot equilibrium the market price is above marginal costs (recall that $c < 1$, so $(1+2c)/3 > c$) and firms make positive profits. The fact that at an equilibrium under quantity competition firms set a higher price than under a price competition equilibrium descends from the very concept of Nash equilibrium. In a Bertrand game, a firm has to choose its optimal price by taking as given the price of the rival. By undercutting the latter, it will get all the demand, which gives a very strong incentive to decrease one's price. In a Cournot game, instead, a firm chooses its quantity given the quantity of the rival. Therefore, an expansion of one's output might allow one to capture a higher market share but does not allow one to capture all demand precisely because the rival's output is taken as given. The incentives to compete aggressively are accordingly weaker than in the price competition game. In other words, price competition is tougher than quantity competition and other things being equal, firms' prices and profits are lower. This result will be confirmed also when looking at the differentiated products case.

Cournot with Cost Asymmetries   Consider the same Cournot game as before, but assume that firms differ in their marginal costs, with $c_1 < c_2$. Each firm i's problem is $\max_{q_i} \pi_i(q_i, q_j) = (1 - q_i - q_j - c_i)q_i$, given q_j. The reader can check that the reaction functions are given by $q_i = (1 - q_j - c_i)/2$, and that the Cournot equilibrium quantities and profits (determined by the intersection of the reaction functions and substitution) are given by

$$q_i^* = \frac{1 - 2c_i + c_j}{3}; \qquad \pi_i^* = \frac{(1 - 2c_i + c_j)^2}{9}. \tag{8.33}$$

However, note that this solution holds only if costs are close enough to each other. Indeed, the equilibrium output is meaningful only if $q_2^* \geq 0$, or $c_2 \leq (1 + c_1)/2$. Otherwise, similarly to the case of Bertrand competition, firm 2 is so much less efficient than firm 1 that the latter can set, undisturbed, its monopoly output and make monopoly profits.

Cournot with n Firms   Consider now again the case of symmetric cost firms, but extend the base model to n firms. For the ith firm, the problem is

$$\max_{q_i} \pi_i(q_1, \ldots, q_i, \ldots, q_n) = \left(1 - q_i - \sum_{j \neq i} q_j - c\right) q_i, \text{ given } q_j. \tag{8.34}$$

The FOC is given by $\partial \pi_i(q_1, \ldots, q_i, \ldots, q_n)/\partial q_i = 0$, that is

$$1 - 2q_i - \sum_{j \neq i} q_j - c = 0. \tag{8.35}$$

At the symmetric equilibrium, $q_i = q_j$, and the FOC simplifies to $1 - 2q_i - (n-1)q_i - c = 0$. One can immediately derive the equilibrium outputs, and by substitution the equilibrium price and profits, as

$$q^* = \frac{1-c}{1+n}; \qquad p^* = c + \frac{1-c}{1+n}; \qquad \pi^* = \left(\frac{1-c}{1+n}\right)^2. \tag{8.36}$$

One can check that for $n = 2$ the equilibrium values in (8.36) correspond to the ones found above in expressions (8.31) and (8.32). These results are interesting because they allow us to study how the Cournot equilibrium outcome changes with n. In particular, it is easy to see that the larger the number of firms in the industry the closer one gets to the Bertrand outcome: $\lim_{n \to \infty} p^* = c$.

The Cournot model allows us therefore to capture the intuitive result that the more firms that co-exist in the industry, the stronger the competition will be in it, ranging from the monopoly outcome corresponding to $n = 1$ to the Bertrand outcome ($p = c$) when n tends to infinity. Such a result did not arise in the Bertrand model, where already with $n = 2$ one obtains that firms charge at marginal cost, a result which holds independently of the number $n \geq 2$ of firms in the industry.

8.4.1.3 Joint-Profit Maximisation

The final benchmark case of product market competition corresponds to the case where the oligopolists maximise joint profits, that is they behave as if they were a single firm. This case therefore corresponds to that analysed in Section 8.2.2. As an illustration, consider n perfectly symmetric firms. Joint-profit maximisation implies that

$$\max_{q_1, \ldots, q_i, \ldots, q_n} \Pi = \sum_{i=1}^{n} \pi_i(q_1, \ldots, q_i, \ldots, q_n) = \sum_{i=1}^{n} \left(1 - q_i - \sum_{j \neq i} q_j - c\right) q_i. \tag{8.37}$$

In this particular case where firms are perfectly symmetric, this problem amounts to $\max_Q (1 - Q - c)Q$. The FOC is given by $\partial \Pi/\partial Q = 0$, that is $1 - 2Q - c = 0$, which results in the following equilibrium levels:

$$Q^M = \frac{1-c}{2}; \qquad p^M = \frac{1+c}{2}; \qquad \Pi^M = \frac{(1-c)^2}{4}. \tag{8.38}$$

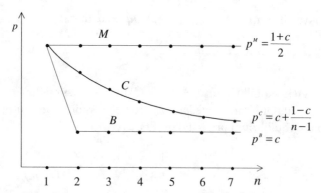

Figure 8.4. Toughness of product market competition: Bertrand (B), Cournot (C) and joint-profits maximisation (M).

Obviously, per-firm outputs and profits can be obtained by dividing by n:

$$q^M = \frac{1-c}{2n}; \qquad \pi^M = \frac{(1-c)^2}{4n}. \tag{8.39}$$

The symmetric case is extremely simple because it is natural to assume that outputs and profits are shared equally, but the treatment of joint-profit maximisation becomes more complex when asymmetries among the firms exist.[26]

Note also that the joint-profit maximisation case should be seen as a benchmark case, that is as the limit of a situation where competition among the firms in the product market is very weak. For a treatment of collusion, that is how and whether firms are able to sustain a joint-profit maximisation outcome, see Section 8.4.2.1 and, above all, Chapter 4.

8.4.1.4 Benchmark Models of Product Competition: A Comparison

As a summary of the different cases analysed here as benchmarks of product market competition, it might be helpful to illustrate the equilibrium price as a function of the number n of firms in the industry, under the hypotheses that firms compete in prices and quantities and that they behave as if they were a monopolist. Figure 8.4 does this, and shows for any given number of firms how the toughness of product market competition – or *toughness of price competition,* as Sutton (1991) calls it – varies across these cases, being highest under Bertrand (equilibrium prices are the lowest) and lowest under joint-profit maximisation (equilibrium prices are the highest).

[26] I do not deal with this issue because it does not arise anywhere in the book.

The three cases analysed are useful benchmarks when discussing oligopoly issues. It would be difficult to say when in the real world one should expect product market competition to take one form or another. Joint-profit maximisation might perhaps correspond to a (nowadays very rare) situation where anti-trust enforcement is so weak that a cartel can be easily sustained. Cournot competition might be associated with industries where firms cannot easily adjust their capacities (that is, when they choose prices after they have committed to a certain capacity or output), and Bertrand competition with industries where firms are instead not much constrained by capacities; that is, where they can easily adjust output in response to the demand they receive.[27]

8.4.2 Product Market Competition with (Exogenously) Differentiated Goods

This section studies (one-shot) product market competition within two (non-spatial) differentiated good models. This amounts to relaxing assumption A1) of Section 8.4.1.1, and again this will result in an equilibrium price above marginal cost (except in limiting cases). Throughout this section firms' products choices are taken as given.

8.4.2.1 A Linear Demand Model of Differentiated Goods

Following Singh and Vives (1984), consider two firms, 1 and 2, that sell two products. Denote q_1 and q_2 the quantities of each good. There exists a continuum of consumers of the same type in the economy, each having the following utility function:

$$V = y + U(q_1, q_2),\qquad (8.40)$$

where the linearity in the composite good y avoids income effects and provides a rationale for a partial equilibrium analysis of the differentiated sector. Indeed, the consumer's problem is $\max_{q_1, q_2, y} V$ subject to the budget constraint $p_1 q_1 + p_2 q_2 + p_y y = R$. To solve this problem, write the Lagrangian:

$$L = y + U(q_1, q_2) + \lambda(R - p_1 q_1 - p_2 q_2 - p_y y).\qquad (8.41)$$

---

[27] Most manufacturing industries will probably be closer to Cournot than Bertrand. Industries where procurement is important might be an example of Bertrand competition: first a firm selects price and gets a contract, and then it has to fulfil the order within a certain time. Sectors where it is costless and immediate to ship a good would also resemble Bertrand competition (think for instance of the music industry, where once the original track is recorded, making an additional CD is easy and cheap).

The FOCs are given by

$$
\begin{cases}
\dfrac{\partial L}{\partial q_i} = \dfrac{\partial U(q_i, q_j)}{\partial q_i} - \lambda p_i = 0, & i = 1, 2; i \neq j, \\[2mm]
\dfrac{\partial L}{\partial y} = 1 - \lambda p_y = 0, \\[2mm]
\dfrac{\partial L}{\partial \lambda} = R - p_1 q_1 - p_2 q_2 - p_y y = 0.
\end{cases}
\tag{8.42}
$$

By taking the composite good as the numéraire, $p_y = 1$, one obtains $\lambda = 1$. Therefore, the FOCs relative to the differentiated good market become $\partial U(q_i, q_j)/\partial q_i -$
$p_i = 0$, and can be analysed independently of the market for the composite good.

Having established that the quasi-linearity in the utility function V justifies a
partial equilibrium analysis of the differentiated good market, let us use a specific
functional form for the utility function. In particular, assume

$$
U(q_1, q_2) = \alpha q_1 + \alpha q_2 - \frac{1}{2}\left(\beta q_1^2 + \beta q_2^2 + 2\gamma q_1 q_2\right),
\tag{8.43}
$$

with the parameters used in the utility function satisfying the following assumptions
(for $i = 1, 2, i \neq j$): (i) $\alpha > 0$, (ii) $\beta > 0$, (iii) $\beta > |\gamma|$. Assumption (iii) guarantees
that the demand functions can be inverted, are of the right sign, and that there is a
positive intercept in direct demands (see below).

Parameter γ indicates whether goods 1 and 2 are substitutes, independent or
complements (and to what degree). As one can see from the utility function, if
$\gamma > 0$ consuming the two goods together diminishes the consumer's utility (that
is, they are substitutes); if $\gamma < 0$ consuming the two goods together increases the
consumer's utility (that is, they are complements); if $\gamma = 0$ consuming the two
goods together does not affect the consumer's utility (that is, they are independent).

The FOCs of the consumer problem are given by $\partial U(q_i, q_j)/\partial q_i - p_i = 0$, which
become

$$
p_i = \alpha - \beta q_i - \gamma q_j, \qquad i = 1, 2, i \neq j.
\tag{8.44}
$$

This is the system of inverse demands that can be used to study quantity competition. An inspection of these demand functions immediately suggests further
interpretation of the parameters. The closer γ to β the better substitutes the two
goods will be, with the case of perfect substitutes arising as the limiting case $\gamma \to \beta$.
For $\gamma > 0$, one could therefore define an inverse measure of product differentiation
as γ/β. This index takes values in $[0, 1)$, and attains its minimum value when the
goods are independent (for $\gamma = 0$, that is when they are maximally differentiated),
and its highest value when they tend to be perfect substitutes (for $\gamma \to \beta$).

By inverting the two expressions in (8.44) one obtains the system of direct demand functions as

$$q_i = a - bp_i + gp_j, \qquad i = 1, 2, i \neq j, \tag{8.45}$$

where a, b, g satisfy

$$a = \frac{\alpha(\beta - \gamma)}{\beta^2 - \gamma^2}; \qquad b = \frac{\beta}{\beta^2 - \gamma^2}; \qquad g = \frac{\gamma}{\beta^2 - \gamma^2}. \tag{8.46}$$

Note, therefore, that this is the linear demand function already used in Section 8.2.2. Armed with the inverse and direct demand functions, we can now derive the equilibrium solutions under the usual benchmark cases of product market competition. For simplicity, assume that the two firms have the same constant marginal cost c and assume that $c = 0$ without loss of generality.

Quantity Competition Consider first the case where firms compete in quantities. Each firm $i = 1, 2$ chooses q_i so as to maximise its profits $\pi_i = p_i(q_i, q_j)q_i$ for any given q_j, where $p_i(q_i, q_j) = \alpha - \beta q_i - \gamma q_j$. The FOCs are

$$\frac{\partial \pi_i}{\partial q_i} = \alpha - 2\beta q_i - \gamma q_j = 0. \tag{8.47}$$

Note that each FOC defines implicitly a best-reply function, and that such a function is negatively sloped, as was the case under Cournot competition with homogenous goods.

At the symmetric equilibrium, $q_i = q_j = q$, and by rearranging the FOCs the equilibrium output is obtained:

$$q^C = \frac{\alpha}{2\beta + \gamma}. \tag{8.48}$$

By substitution one can then find the equilibrium output and profits as

$$p^C = \frac{\alpha\beta}{2\beta + \gamma}; \qquad \pi^C = \beta \left(\frac{\alpha}{2\beta + \gamma} \right)^2. \tag{8.49}$$

Price Competition If firms compete in prices, each firm $i = 1, 2$ chooses p_i so as to maximise its profits $\pi_i = q_i(p_i, p_j)p_i$ taking p_j as given, where $q_i(p_i, p_j) = a - bp_i + gp_j$. The FOCs are

$$\frac{\partial \pi_i}{\partial p_i} = \alpha - 2bp_i + gp_j = 0. \tag{8.50}$$

The FOCs define the following two best-reply functions in the plane (p_1, p_2):

$$R_1: p_2 = \frac{a - 2bp_1}{g}; \qquad R_2: p_2 = \frac{a + gp_1}{2b}. \tag{8.51}$$

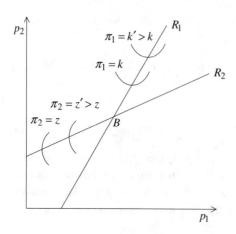

Figure 8.5. Reaction functions under price competition.

Figure 8.5 illustrates the reaction functions and shows that they are positively sloped.[28] (Hence, the higher p_j the higher the price p_i which is the best reply to it.) It also illustrates the iso-profit curves of the two firms, that is the locus of the points such that a firm earns a given profit. For both firms, the further an iso-profit curve from the origin the higher the associated profits.[29]

At the symmetric equilibrium, $p_i = p_j = p$, and by rearranging the FOCs the equilibrium price is obtained:

$$p^B = \frac{a}{2b - g} = \frac{\alpha(\beta - \gamma)}{2\beta - \gamma}. \tag{8.52}$$

By substitution one can then find the equilibrium output and profits as

$$q^B = \frac{ab}{2b - g} = \frac{\alpha\beta(\beta - \gamma)}{2\beta - \gamma}; \qquad \pi^B = \frac{a^2 b}{(2b - g)^2} = \frac{\alpha^2\beta(\beta - \gamma)}{(\beta + \gamma)(2\beta - \gamma)^2}. \tag{8.53}$$

It is worth noting that – although it was a good exercise to derive the equilibrium solutions – I could have found the solution of the price game just by noting the duality of the quantity and price problems, and substituting in the Cournot solutions already found above. Indeed, under quantity competition for firm i the problem

---

[28] Stability requires R_1 to be steeper than R_2, that is $2b/g > g/(2b)$, or $4b^2 > g^2$, always satisfied since $b > g$ by assumption.

[29] The iso-profit curves of firm 1 are described by the function $\pi_1 = (a - bp_1 + gp_2)p_1 = k$. By totally differentiating, we obtain the slope of one such curve. First, take $d\pi_1 = (a - 2bp_1 + gp_2)dp_1 + gp_1 dp_2 = 0$, from which $dp_2/dp_1 = -(a - 2bp_1 + gp_2)/(gp_1)$, the iso-profit slope. (Note that along R_1 the numerator is zero, so crossing the reaction function the iso-profit must be flat.) Firm 2's iso-profits are given by $\pi_2 = (a - bp_2 + gp_1)p_2 = z$. Total differentiation gives $d\pi_2 = (a - 2bp_2 + gp_1)dp_2 + gp_2 dp_1 = 0$. Hence, one has $dp_2/dp_1 = -gp_2/(a - 2bp_2 + gp_1)$, the slope of firm 2's iso-profit. (Note that along the reaction function, R_2, the denominator is zero, so when crossing R_2 the iso-profit must be vertical.)

is $\max_{q_i} \pi_i = (\alpha - \beta q_i - \gamma q_j) q_i$ given q_j, whereas under price competition the problem is $\max_{p_i} \pi_i = (a - bp_i + gp_j) p_i$, given p_j. These expressions are the dual of each other, as one can obtain the latter from the former by replacing q_i by p_i; α by a; β by b; γ by $-g$.[30]

Equilibrium Comparison It is now possible to compare the results obtained under price and quantity competition. To do so, write the difference in the equilibrium prices as

$$p^C - p^B = \frac{\alpha \gamma^2}{4\beta^2 - \gamma^2} > 0. \tag{8.54}$$

First, note that the difference is always positive: prices are always higher (and accordingly quantities are always lower) under quantity competition than under price competition, regardless of whether the goods are substitutes, independent, or complements.[31]

Second, $p^C - p^B$ increases with γ for given β: when $\gamma = 0$, the prices coincide (the markets being independent, it is irrelevant whether firms compete in quantities or in prices); when $\gamma \to \beta$, the difference is highest, with $p^C - p^B \to \alpha/3$ (the reader will have already recognised that this is the case corresponding to homogenous goods).

Strategic Substitutes v. Strategic Complements We have seen above that under quantity competition the firms' reaction functions are negatively sloped, whereas under price competition they are positively sloped.[32] In what follows, I briefly relate the slope of firms' reaction functions to a property of the profit function, and introduce the concepts of strategic substitutes and strategic complements due to Bulow et al. (1985).[33]

Consider a simultaneous move game where each firm $i = 1, 2$ can choose actions a_i. Define $\pi_i(a_i, a_j)$ firm i's profit function, and assume that it is twice differentiable in both a_i and a_j, with $\partial^2 \pi_i / (\partial a_i)^2 < 0$ on its domain to ensure a maximum exists.

---

[30] This also implies that Cournot competition with substitute (respectively complement) products is the dual of Bertrand competition with complement (respectively substitute) products: $\gamma > 0$ corresponds to $g < 0$, and vice versa.

[31] One might also check another of the results obtained by Singh and Vives: consumer surplus and total surplus are (weakly) larger under price competition than under quantity competition. Profits are higher, equal or lower under quantity than under price competition, according to whether goods are substitutes, independent or complements.

[32] Note, however, that this holds for linear demand, but need not always be the case for more general demand functions.

[33] This section follows closely Tirole (1988: 207–8).

As we know already, firm i's *reaction function* is given by the function $R_i(a_j)$ that identifies the best possible response a_i to any given action a_j of the rival:[34]

$$\frac{\partial \pi_i(R_i(a_j), a_j)}{\partial a_i} = 0. \tag{8.55}$$

Differentiation of (8.55) with respect to a_j gives

$$\frac{\partial (\partial \pi_i/\partial R_i)}{\partial a_i} \frac{\partial R_i}{\partial a_j} da_j + \frac{\partial (\partial \pi_i/\partial a_i)}{\partial a_j} da_j = 0, \tag{8.56}$$

which can be re-written as

$$\frac{\partial^2 \pi_i}{\partial a_i^2} \frac{\partial R_i}{\partial a_j} + \frac{\partial^2 \pi_i}{\partial a_i \partial a_j} = 0. \tag{8.57}$$

Denote $\partial R_i/\partial a_j \equiv R_i'$ as the slope of firm i's reaction function, and rearrange it to give

$$R_i' = -\frac{\partial^2 \pi_i/(\partial a_i \partial a_j)}{\partial^2 \pi_i/\partial a_i^2} = 0. \tag{8.58}$$

Therefore, the sign of the slope of the reaction function is given by the sign of $\partial^2 \pi_i/(\partial a_i \partial a_j)$. (Recall that $\partial^2 \pi_i/\partial a_i^2 < 0$.)

Bulow et al. (1985) introduce the following definition:

- *Actions are strategic substitutes if* $\dfrac{\partial^2 \pi_i}{\partial a_i \partial a_j} < 0.$

- *Actions are strategic complements if* $\dfrac{\partial^2 \pi_i}{\partial a_i \partial a_j} > 0.$

Actions are strategic substitutes (respectively, strategic complements) when an increase in a_j reduces (resp. raises) firm i's marginal profitability ($\partial \pi_i/\partial a_i$), thus leading firm i to choose a lower (resp. higher) a_i. This explains why the best-reply functions are negatively (resp. positively) sloped.

As we shall see in Section 8.5.1 below, the implications for an oligopoly model might turn out to be dramatically different according to whether the firms' actions are strategic complements or substitutes.

Stability of the Equilibrium   A property that is sometimes required of Nash equilibria in oligopoly models is that of *stability*. Stability of the equilibrium refers to the following question: would the equilibrium be reached through a sequence of movements along the reaction functions starting from any arbitrary point? Figure 8.6

---

[34] This best response is unique, due to the assumption that the profit function is strictly concave.

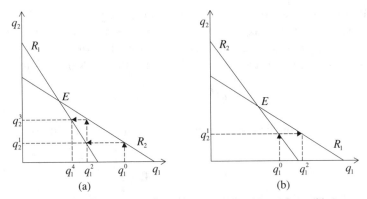

Figure 8.6. (a) Stable Nash equilibrium; (b) Unstable Nash equilibrium.

illustrates the adjustment process involved by this thought experiment, under two different possibilities.

Figure 8.6(a) illustrates a case of stable equilibrium (such as in the Cournot model analysed in this section). Suppose for instance that firm 1 produces a quantity q_1^0; firm 2's best reply would be to produce the quantity q_2^1; in turn, the best reply for firm 1 to the quantity q_2^1 would be to produce q_1^2; and so on, until the firms end up producing the quantities corresponding to the equilibrium pair at point E.

In Figure 8.6(b), instead, the equilibrium would not be stable, as movements along the reaction functions would push the firms further and further away from the equilibrium point E. Firm 2's best response to firm 1 producing quantity q_1^0 would be quantity q_2^1; in turn, the best reply for firm 1 to the quantity q_2^1 would be to produce q_1^2; however, firm 2's best reply would at this point be to produce nothing. The equilibrium point E cannot be reached through this adjustment process and is therefore said to be unstable.

As one can see from these two examples, the stability property is related to the slope of the reaction functions. In a game where firms 1 and 2 choose actions (a_1, a_2) and where reaction functions are drawn in the plane (a_1, a_2), for instance, it must be that R_1 is steeper than R_2. By recalling the expression of the slope of the reaction function, this condition can be written as $(\partial^2 \pi_1/\partial a_1^2)(\partial^2 \pi_2/\partial a_2^2) > (\partial^2 \pi_1/\partial a_1 \partial a_2)(\partial^2 \pi_2/\partial a_2 \partial a_1)$.

It is important to stress that the type of adjustment process that the stability concept supposes is very particular. The sequence of moves described above makes sense only if players are completely *myopic*, as each firm ignores the impact that its choice has on the rival's next move.[35]

---

[35] Alternatively, one can think that each player does look ahead but attaches no importance to the future, that is it has a zero discount factor.

Joint-Profit Maximisation   If firms maximise joint profits and choose quantities, their problem is $\max_{q_1, q_2} \Pi$, where $\Pi = \pi_1 + \pi_2 = (\alpha - \beta q_1 - \gamma q_2)q_1 + (\alpha - \beta q_2 - \gamma q_1)q_2$. From the FOCs $\partial \Pi / \partial q_i = 0$, it follows $\alpha - 2\beta q_i - 2\gamma q_j = 0$. At the symmetric equilibrium, $q_1 = q_2$. Therefore, the FOCs simplify to

$$q^M = \frac{\alpha}{2(\beta + \gamma)}. \tag{8.59}$$

By substitution one obtains equilibrium prices and per-firm profits as

$$p^M = \frac{\alpha}{2}; \qquad \pi^M = \frac{\alpha^2}{4(\beta + \gamma)}. \tag{8.60}$$

It can be checked that under price competition one gets exactly the same results:

$$p^M = \frac{a}{2(b - g)} = \frac{\alpha}{2}; \qquad q^M = \frac{a}{2} = \frac{\alpha}{2(\beta + \gamma)}. \tag{8.61}$$

8.4.2.2 A Differentiated Goods Model with Some Nice Properties

The differentiated goods model used in the previous section has the advantage of being very easy to deal with. However, its extension from 2 to n firms (which I omit here for simplicity) is not completely satisfactory because aggregate demand increases with the number of firms (as well as with the degree of substitutability among products), at given prices. For this reason, I usually prefer to use another simple model due to Shubik and Levitan (1980), where market size does not vary either with the degree of substitutability or the number of products. This is based on the following utility function for the differentiated products:[36]

$$U(q_1, \ldots, q_i, \ldots q_n) = v \sum_{i=1}^{n} q_i - \frac{n}{2(1 + \mu)} \left[\sum_{i=1}^{n} q_i^2 + \frac{\mu}{n} \left(\sum_{i=1}^{n} q_i \right)^2 \right], \tag{8.62}$$

where q_i is the quantity of the ith product, v is a positive parameter, n is the number of products in the industry, and $\mu \in [0, \infty)$ represents the degree of substitutability between the n products.[37]

From the maximisation of the utility function subject to the income constraint, one can write $\partial U(\cdot)/\partial q_i - p_i = 0$, resulting in the inverse demand functions

$$p_i = v - \frac{1}{1 + \mu} \left(nq_i + \mu \sum_{j=1}^{n} q_j \right). \tag{8.63}$$

---

[36] Of course, as above, consumers preferences can be expressed as $V = U(q_1, \ldots, q_i, \ldots, q_n) + y$, so that a partial equilibrium analysis is fully justified.

[37] A drawback of this utility function is instead that it does not allow to deal with both complements and substitutes.

By inverting this system (see Appendix for details) we can find the following direct demand functions:

$$q_i = \frac{1}{n}\left[v - p_i(1+\mu) + \frac{\mu}{n}\sum_{j=1}^{n} p_j\right]. \tag{8.64}$$

Two nice properties of this demand function are: (1) aggregate demand $Q = \sum_{i=1}^{n} q_i$ does not depend on the degree of substitution among the products, as $Q = \sum_{i=1}^{n} q_i = v - \frac{1}{n}\sum_{i=1}^{n} p_i$; (2) in the case of symmetry $p_i = p_j = p$ aggregate demand does not change with the number of products n in the industry, as $Q = \sum_{i=1}^{n} q_i = v - p$.

Price Competition   Assume that all the firms have identical cost functions $C(q_i) = cq_i$, with $c < v$. Firm i's profits are given by $\pi_i = (p_i - c)q_i$ $(p_1, \ldots, p_i, \ldots, p_n)$, where $q_i(\cdot)$ is given by (8.64). By writing the FOCs $\partial\pi_i/\partial p_i = 0$ and imposing symmetry $(p_i = p_j = p$ for all $j \neq i)$ one obtains the "Bertrand" equilibrium prices as

$$p_b = \frac{(nv + c(n + n\mu - \mu))}{2n + n\mu - \mu}. \tag{8.65}$$

The quantity sold and the profits earned by each firm at equilibrium are found by substitution as[38]

$$q_b = \frac{(v-c)(n+n\mu-\mu)}{n(2n+n\mu-\mu)}; \qquad \pi_b = \frac{(v-c)^2(n+n\mu-\mu)}{(2n+n\mu-\mu)^2}. \tag{8.66}$$

Quantity Competition   To study the case of quantity competition, write firm i's profits as $\pi_i = [p_i(q_1, \ldots, q_i, \ldots, q_n) - c]q_i$, where $p_i(\cdot)$ is given by (8.63). From the FOCs $\partial\pi_i/\partial q_i = 0$ and imposing symmetry $(q_i = q_j = q$ for all $j \neq i)$ one obtains the "Cournot" equilibrium prices as

$$q_c = \frac{(v-c)(1+\mu)}{2n+n\mu+\mu}. \tag{8.67}$$

Prices and profits at the Cournot equilibrium are

$$p_c = \frac{v(n+\mu) + cn(1+\mu)}{2n+n\mu+\mu}; \qquad \pi_c = \frac{(v-c)^2(1+\mu)(n+\mu)}{(2n+n\mu+\mu)^2}. \tag{8.68}$$

---

[38] Note that $\lim_{\mu\to\infty} p_b = c$ and $\lim_{\mu\to\infty}\pi_b = 0$: When goods become perfect substitutes, the equilibrium tends to the usual Bertrand case with homogenous goods.

The reader can check that – as in the previous model – quantity competition results in higher equilibrium prices and profits than price competition:

$$p_c - p_b = \frac{(v - c)(n - 1)\mu^2}{(2n + n\mu + \mu)(2n + n\mu - \mu)} \geq 0;$$

$$\pi_c - \pi_b = \frac{(v - c)^2 (n - 1)^2 \mu^3 (2 + \mu)}{(2n + n\mu + \mu)^2 (2n + n\mu - \mu)^2} \geq 0, \qquad (8.69)$$

the two equilibria coinciding when $\mu = 0$.

Joint-Profit Maximisation   If firms maximise joint profits and choose prices, their problem is $\max_{p_1, \ldots, p_i, \ldots, p_n} \Pi = \sum \pi_i(p_1, \ldots, p_i, \ldots, p_n)$. From the FOCs $\partial \Pi / \partial p_i = 0$ and imposing symmetry one has

$$p^M = \frac{v + c}{2}. \qquad (8.70)$$

By substitution one obtains equilibrium prices and per-firm profits as

$$q^M = \frac{v - c}{2}; \qquad \pi^M = \frac{(v - c)^2}{4n}. \qquad (8.71)$$

8.4.3 Repeated Product Market Interaction

So far, we have analysed only one-shot games. This section looks at the case where firms still have only one strategic variable (be it price or quantity) but they repeatedly interact in the product market. In other words, I relax assumption A2) of the Bertrand game. It turns out that the result of the modified game is very different according to whether the game is repeated for a finite or infinite number of times.

8.4.3.1 Finite Horizon

Consider the Bertrand game described in Section 8.4.1.1, but with firms playing that basic game for $T + 1$ periods, that is from period $t = 0$ to period $t = T$, with T being a *finite* number.

Each firm $i = 1, 2$ wants to maximise the present discounted value of its profits, $\sum_{t=0}^{T} \delta^t \pi_{i,t}$, with δ being the discount factor[39] and $\pi_{i,t}$ the profit earned in period t. I am going to show the following result:

---

[39] The discount factor measures the importance that a player attaches to the future: if $\delta = 0$, then only current profits matter; if $\delta = 1$, profits earned at any time in the future (however distant) hold the same importance as current profits. Since $\delta = 1/(1 + r)$, where r is the interest rate, $\delta = 0$ corresponds to the case where $r \to \infty$, and $\delta = 1$ to the case $r = 0$.

Result *(Repeated Bertrand game, with finite horizon). If T is finite, the only sub-game perfect Nash equilibrium of the game is the Bertrand equilibrium repeated T times.*

Proof   This is a game of "almost perfect information" that can be solved by backward induction (see Section 8.3.2.1). At the last period of the game, $t = T$, whatever happened in the previous periods, everything is as if the two firms were playing the one-shot Bertrand game. Therefore, the only equilibrium of the game will be the one-shot Bertrand price $p_{1,T} = p_{2,T} = c$.

In period $t = T - 1$, players know that their current choices will not affect the equilibrium solution in the following period T. Therefore, whatever happened in periods $0, 1, \ldots, T - 2$, the game they are playing at $T - 1$ is effectively the same as if they were playing for the last time, and again the only equilibrium is the Bertrand equilibrium $p_{1,T-1} = p_{2,T-1} = c$.

The same reasoning can be applied to all previous periods, leading firms to choose $p_{1,t} = p_{2,t} = c$ at any period t. ∎

This shows that when the Bertrand game is repeated a finite number of times, its outcome is exactly the same as the one-shot game, with firms setting prices at marginal cost and making no profits in any period. This result, however, holds only insofar as firms play a complete information game. If firms had *incomplete information* about their opponents (that is, if they were uncertain about their pay-offs), then the equilibrium outcome would not be the Bertrand equilibrium repeated T times. Although I am not going to analyse the Bertrand game under incomplete information, the interested reader can look at the incomplete information version of the chain-store paradox game in Chapter 7, which shares similar features.[40]

A very different result arises also when firms repeatedly play the Bertrand game over an infinite horizon, as I show next.

8.4.3.2 Infinite Horizon

Take now the number of times for which the price competition game is being played to be infinite.[41] Consider the following *trigger strategies*. Each firm sets the price p in the initial period $t = 0$. It sets price p at time t if both firms have set p in every period before t. Otherwise, each firm sets $p = c$ forever. In other words, each firm behaves in a "collusive" fashion as long as the rival does, but if one of them deviates

[40] Kreps et al. (1982) have first formalised the repeated prisoner's dilemma game (that is very similar to the Bertrand game) under incomplete information. See also Tirole (1988: 258–9).

[41] Equivalently, suppose that the game has an uncertain final date, with the probability that the market exists in the following period being $\phi \in (0, 1)$. Call the firms' discount factor under this alternative interpretation d. One can then set $\delta = d\phi$, and carry out the analysis as in the text.

from the "collusive" price, then the punishment is triggered and they both revert to the one-shot Bertrand equilibrium for the rest of the game.

These trigger strategies form an equilibrium if each firm's incentive compatibility constraint holds:[42]

$$\frac{\pi(p)}{2}(1 + \delta + \delta^2 + \delta^3 + \cdots) \geq \pi(p). \tag{8.72}$$

The LHS gives the present discounted value of the profits a firm receives if it colludes (i.e., if it follows the trigger strategy when the other firm does). In each period, the firm receives half of the aggregate monopoly profit. The RHS gives the present discounted value of the profits if the firm (optimally) deviates from the trigger strategy. By setting $p - \varepsilon$, all consumers will buy from the deviating firm, that will thus earn a profit $\pi(p - \varepsilon)$. For $\varepsilon \to 0$, this will therefore ensure profits very close to $\pi(p)$ in the period the deviation takes place. In the following period, however, the punishment occurs as both firms revert to the Nash equilibrium forever. Therefore, the deviating firm (as well as the rival) will make zero profit in all following periods of the game.

Note that $\sum_{t=0}^{\infty} \delta^t = 1/(1 - \delta)$. Hence, after simple algebra, the incentive constraint above becomes

$$\delta \geq \frac{1}{2}, \tag{8.73}$$

that is, the price $p \in [c, p_m]$ can be sustained at the equilibrium provided that the discount factor is high enough.

There is little point in elaborating further here, since this is discussed at length in Chapter 4. The main purpose of this section is just to show that prices above marginal costs might be sustained as the equilibrium of a game with infinite horizon (or uncertain final date). Note, however, that an important issue is that of the multiplicity of equilibria arising in this game. Any price $p \in [c, p_m]$ that is between marginal cost and monopoly price might be the equilibrium of the game (for a high enough discount factor). This leads to important policy implications that are discussed in Chapter 4.

8.5 OLIGOPOLY II: DYNAMIC GAMES

So far, I have assumed that the only strategic variables available to firms were either prices or quantities, and that all their other characteristics were exogenously given. Clearly, this is not the case in reality, where firms also make a number of decisions that affect their costs and their products, and even the very choice of being in the market in the first place. When studying models where firms have several strategic variables, it is important to recognise that some are typically more

---

[42] The constraint is the same for both firms, due to their symmetry. See Chapter 4 for collusion under asymmetries.

"long-run" variables than others. Suppose for instance that we want to study a game where firms make entry, R&D investment and price decisions. It is reasonable to expect that price decisions are "short-run" decisions that can be revised relatively often, R&D investment decisions are more costly to revise, and entry decisions are "long-run" decisions that are taken only once and are taken as given forever afterwards. Accordingly, it would make sense to formalise the game played by the firms as a dynamic (or multi-stage) game where in the first stage firms choose whether to enter or not; in the second stage they decide how much R&D they want to carry out; and in the third stage at what price they want to sell their products.

Dynamic games have been described in general terms in Section 8.3.2, and many such games are analysed throughout the book. For instance, Chapter 2 analyses games where entry decisions are taken before (cost-reducing R&D or quality) investments and product market competition. Chapter 4 looks again at R&D-then-product market decisions when there are R&D spillovers. Chapter 5 analyses games where firms first decide whether to merge or not and then compete in the marketplace. In Chapter 6, retailers make effort decisions or manufacturers take investment decisions before competition takes place; and in exclusive dealing models decisions are taken sequentially by an incumbent monopolist, buyers and a potential entrant. In Chapter 7, again incumbents take some actions before potential entrants decide on entry, or new firms decide whether to continue operations or not.

In what follows, rather than offering yet other examples of dynamic games, I focus on the strategic effects that actions taken in the early stages of a game can have on oligopolistic interaction in the marketplace.

8.5.1 Strategic Investments

In oligopoly models where firms take decisions sequentially, firms can act strategically, that is they can take actions in the early stages of the game that modify to their advantage some of the variables which are taken as given in the following stages. To understand how such strategic effects take place, consider the following game.[43]

In stage one of the game, Nature moves and picks the magnitude and sign of a "shock" parameter, $s \in \mathbb{R}$, that affects the marginal cost of firm 1, that equals $k - s$, in stage two.[44]

In stage two, firms 1 and 2 make product market decisions in a differentiated good market where consumers have utility function (8.43). Except for the shock that affects firm 1, firms would have the same marginal cost, k. However, to study possible entry-deterrence effects, assume that firm 2 also incurs a fixed cost f.

I consider two variants of the game: (i) firms choose quantities (in this case, decisions will be strategic substitutes) and (ii) firms choose prices (decisions will be

---

[43] This is a very simplified, one-market-only version of Bulow et al. (1985). The other important reference for this section is Fudenberg and Tirole (1984).

[44] We shall see below that one could extend and re-interpret the model so that s is chosen by a firm, or by a third party such as a government.

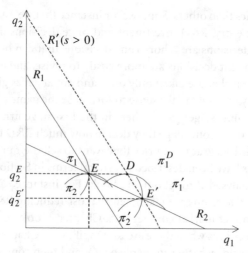

Figure 8.7. Effects of a shock ($s > 0$) that reduces firm 1's marginal cost: Strategic substitutes.

strategic complements). I am interested in studying the impact of the shock s on the product market equilibrium (in particular, firms' profits) at stage two.

8.5.1.1 Quantity Competition (Strategic Substitutes)

To analyse quantity competition, consider the inverse demands given by (8.44). Given the shock, the firms' problem is given by $\max_{q_1} \pi_1 = (\alpha - \beta q_1 - \gamma q_2 - k + s)q_1$ and $\max_{q_2} \pi_2 = (\alpha - \beta q_2 - \gamma q_1 - k)q_2 - f$. By taking the first derivatives, equalling them to zero and rearranging, we can write the reaction functions in the plane (q_1, q_2) as follows:

$$R_1 : q_2 = \frac{\alpha - (k - s) - 2\beta q_1}{\gamma}; \qquad R_2 : q_2 = \frac{\alpha - k - \gamma q_1}{2\beta}. \qquad (8.74)$$

Figure 8.7 illustrates the firms' reaction functions. First, note that the reaction functions are negatively sloped: hence, in this model decisions are *strategic substitutes*. Then, note that the position of firm 1's reaction function is shifted by the shock s. In particular, if $s > 0$ as in the figure, R_1 shifts to the right to R_1'. To evaluate the strategic effect of the shock, it is convenient to distinguish between two cases. In the first, entry by firm 2 is not an issue (for instance, because $f = 0$ and the shock is such that at the intersection between R_1' and R_2 firm 2 sells a positive output). Call this the *accommodation* case.[45] In the second case, firm 2's entry is an issue (for instance, because at the equilibrium absent the shock, firm 2 has positive *net* profits and a movement to a new equilibrium might put it on an iso-profit curve associated with negative profits, thus making entry unprofitable). Call this the *entry deterrence* case. I analyse each case in turn.

---

[45] The term is drawn from Fudenberg and Tirole (1984), where the shock is endogenous. It refers then to an investment that will bring about a new equilibrium at which firm 2 has positive profits: In this sense, the investment accommodates entry.

Accommodation Assume that entry will be accommodated. A difficulty in assessing the impact of the shock which moves the equilibrium from E to E' is that it has two effects on firm 1's profits. First, the shock has a *direct effect* on firm 1's profits in that it decreases the costs of production of firm 1 at any pair of actions (q_1, q_2). Second, it has a *strategic effect* in that, since the shock is observed by its rival, it modifies the latter's choice. It is the second effect that we are interested in, as the first effect is independent of firm 2's response, and would take place even if firm 2 could not see the shock affecting firm 1.

To disentangle these two effects, reason in the following way. Once the shock occurs, it modifies firm 1's reaction function, shifting it to the right. The direct effect of the shock on firm 1's profits could therefore be seen as a movement which takes place absent any response on the side of firm 2. In other words, suppose that firm 2 does not change its action and still produces the quantity q_2^E. Then, firm 1 would end up in point D, that is on its new reaction function corresponding to the lower marginal costs, but where the quantity produced by firm 2 is unchanged. Firm 1's iso-profit passing by point D is associated with a profit level π_1^D.

However, firm 2 does observe the shock, and it knows that firm 1's reaction function is now R_1' and it will therefore revise its output accordingly, producing $q_2^{E'}$: Firms end up in equilibrium E'. The strategic effect of the shock on firm 1's profits can therefore be seen as the move from D to E'. In words, the shock raises the output q_1 produced by firm 1. This decreases the marginal profitability of firm 2 (decisions being strategic substitutes), which will then lower its output q_2. In turn, lower q_2 increases firm 1's profits.

Since profits are higher (at E' firm 1 is on a lower iso-profit curve than at D), we can conclude that the strategic effect has a positive impact on π_1.

As for the strategic effect on firm 2's profitability, it is clearly negative. We have assumed no direct impact on firm 2's profits, and as the equilibrium shifts from E to E', firm 2 moves to an iso-profit function with lower profits.

Entry Deterrence At the new equilibrium E', firm 2 is on an iso-profit function π_2' which corresponds to lower profits than the function π_2. Suppose that firm 2's *net* profits after the shock are $\pi_2' < 0$ (whereas they would be positive absent the shock: $\pi_2 > 0$). In this case, firm 1 will certainly be better off under the shock, since it would shift the duopoly equilibrium to a point where firm 2 would prefer to stay out. Hence, the shock would deter entry, and firm 1 would gain both because the shock has a positive direct effect on its profits (its costs are lower) and because it has the (positive) strategic effect to deter entry, and make it a monopolist.[46]

To sum up the quantity competition (strategic substitutes) case, the strategic effect of a cost-reducing shock on firm 1 is positive whether entry will be accommodated or deterred.

---

[46] We know from the accommodation case that firm 1 would be better off even if firm 2 stayed in the market. *A fortiori,* the shock will increase its profits when it makes firm 1 the only seller.

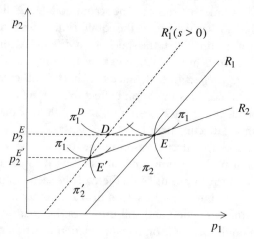

Figure 8.8. Effects of a shock ($s > 0$) that reduces firm 1's marginal cost: Strategic complements.

8.5.1.2 Price Competition (Strategic Complements)

To analyse price competition, consider the system of direct demands given by (8.45). Firms' problems are $\max_{p_1} \pi_1 = (p_1 - k + s)(a - bp_1 + cp_2)$ and $\max_{p_2} \pi_2 = (p_2 - k)(a - bp_2 + cp_1) - f$. By taking the FOCs and rearranging, we obtain the reaction functions in (p_1, p_2):

$$R_1 : p_2 = \frac{-a - b(k - s) + 2bp_1}{c}; \qquad R_2 : p_2 = \frac{a + bk + cp_1}{2b}. \qquad (8.75)$$

Figure 8.8 illustrates the firms' reaction functions. As we have already seen in Section 8.4.2.1 above, the reaction functions are positively sloped: decisions are *strategic complements*. If $s > 0$ as in the figure, R_1 shifts to the left to R_1' following the cost-reducing shock.

Accommodation   If entry is accommodated, the strategic effect associated with the shock might hurt firm 1. To see this, let me use the same trick as above to decompose direct and strategic effects on firm 1's profits. Absent any response to the shock from firm 2, that is if it set the same action p_2^E as in the case $s = 0$, firm 1 would be in point D. At such point, its profits would be π_1^D. But firm 2 modifies its price, determining a new equilibrium in E', where firm 1 has profits π_1'. The strategic effect is given by the move from D to E', and it is therefore negative for firm 1: $\pi_1' < \pi_1^D$ (any downward movement along the reaction function is associated with lower profits). What happens here is that the shock reduces firm 1's marginal cost and its price. Since price decisions are strategic complements in this model, the lower p_1 reduces firm 2's marginal profitability and accordingly its price p_2. In turn, the more aggressive pricing behaviour of firm 2 will reduce firm 1's profits.

Table 8.8. Strategic Effect of a Shock that Reduces Firm 1's Costs

Strategic Substitutes	Strategic Complements
Accommodation: $\pi_1 \uparrow; \pi_2 \downarrow$	Accommodation: $\pi_1 \downarrow; \pi_2 \downarrow$
Entry deterrence: $\pi_2 \downarrow (\Rightarrow \pi_1 \uparrow)$	Entry deterrence: $\pi_2 \downarrow (\Rightarrow \pi_1 \uparrow)$

The shock has also a negative effect on firm 2's profits, which are lower at E' than at E.

Entry Deterrence Suppose that firm 2's *net* profits after the shock (that is, at E') are not only lower but also negative: $\pi_2' < 0$ (whereas they would be positive absent the shock: $\pi_2 > 0$). In this case, the shock will make firm 1 better off. This is because the shock would deter entry, and firm 1 would gain both because the shock has a positive direct effect on its profits (its costs are lower) and because it has the (positive) strategic effect to deter entry, and make it a monopolist.

To sum up the price competition (strategic complements) case, the strategic effect of a cost-reducing shock on firm 1 is negative when entry will be accommodated, but positive when it will be deterred.

Table 8.8 summarises the analysis.[47]

Discussion and Interpretation So far I have treated the shock as an exogenous variable, decided by nature or fate. However, the analysis above can be endogenised in a straightforward manner. Suppose for instance that s is determined by an investment decision of firm 1. For instance, consider a decision on R&D investment that reduces firm 1's costs and that is observable to firm 2, that is, a credible commitment to shift firm 1's reaction function.

The above analysis sheds light on whether oligopolistic interaction would push firm 1 to over- or under-invest, relative to a situation where the strategic effects were not taken into account and therefore would not affect the behaviour of firm 1's rival. Consider for instance the case where decisions are strategic substitutes: a reduction in its costs will have a positive strategic effect on firm 1, which will therefore be led to over-invest in cost-reducing activities (in this case, independently of whether entry of firm 2 is at stake or not).

Table 8.9, derived from the previous one, summarises the effects.

Examples of Strategic Investments The strategic effects that I have illustrated above play an important role in a number of economic contexts analysed in this book.[48] For instance, manufacturers might use exclusive territorial clauses to induce retailers to choose higher prices, and in turn relax competition in the market-place

---

[47] Clearly, exactly the opposite results hold if the shock affected firm 1 adversely, that is if $s < 0$.

[48] See Bulow et al. (1985) and Tirole (1988: 328–36) for a number of other interesting applications.

Table 8.9. Strategic Investments to Reduce Firm 1's Costs

Strategic Substitutes	Strategic Complements
Accommodation: *over-invest*	Accommodation: *under-invest*
Entry deterrence: *over-invest*	Entry deterrence: *over-invest*

among both retailers and manufacturers when decisions are strategic complements (see Chapter 6.3); an incumbent firm might over-invest in capacity, R&D and advertising to pre-empt entry by a new firm (see Chapter 7.3); tie-in sales effectively make an incumbent more aggressive in the market where there exist competing sellers and can exclude the latter (Chapter 7.3).

8.6 APPENDIX

I show here how to obtain the system of direct demands (8.64) from inverse demands (8.63).[49] The system of inverse demand functions can be written in matrix form as $p - v = -\frac{1}{1+\gamma} Aq$, where p, q are respectively the price and quantity $(n, 1)$ vectors, v is an $(n, 1)$ vector having the scalar v in each entry, γ is a scalar, and A is an (n, n) matrix having elements $n + \gamma$ on the diagonal and elements γ everywhere off the diagonal. It is evident that the direct demand functions can be re-written in matrix form:

$$q = -(1+\gamma)A^{-1}(p - v). \tag{8.76}$$

Our problem is therefore to find A^{-1}, that is the inverse of matrix A.

Define $d = \frac{\gamma}{n}$. It is easy to show that $A = n(I + dO)$, where I is the identity matrix having 1's on the diagonal and 0's off the diagonal, and where O is the matrix with 1 in all its entries. Therefore, it must be $A^{-1} = \frac{1}{n}(I + dO)^{-1}$.

It turns out that $(I + dO)^{-1} = I - \left(\frac{d}{1+dn}\right) O$. We can check this by recalling that the product of a matrix by its inverse must be I. This requires a few steps, as follows. $(I + dO)\left(I - \left(\frac{d}{1+dn}\right) O\right) = I + dO - \left(\frac{d}{1+dn}\right) O - \left(\frac{d^2}{1+dn}\right) O^2$.

One can immediately check that $O^2 = nO$. The previous expression can therefore be rewritten:

$$I + dO - \left(\frac{d}{1+dn}\right) O - \left(\frac{nd^2}{1+dn}\right) O = I + \left[d - \frac{d}{1+dn} - \frac{nd^2}{1+dn}\right] O$$

$$= I + \left[\frac{d + d^2 n}{1+dn} - \frac{d}{1+dn} - \frac{nd^2}{1+dn}\right] O = I + 0O = I.$$

[49] I am grateful to Felipe Cucker, great mathematician and gastronomer, who showed me a long time ago how to invert similar matrices.

We can then conclude that the inverse of matrix A is given by

$$A^{-1} = \frac{1}{n}\left[I - \left(\frac{\gamma}{n + n\gamma}\right)O\right]. \qquad (8.77)$$

With few steps of algebra one can then simplify the expression $q = -(1 + \gamma)A^{-1}(p - v)$ and check that it corresponds to the system of direct demand functions in the text.

Bibliography

Abreu, D. 1986. "Extremal Equilibria of Oligopolistic Supergames." *Journal of Economic Theory*. 39: 191–225.

Abreu, D. 1988. "On the Theory of Infinitely Repeated Games with Discounting." *Econometrica*. 56: 383–96.

Abreu, D., D.P. Pearce and E. Stacchetti. 1986. "Optimal Cartel Equilibria with Monitoring." *Journal of Economic Theory*. 39: 251–69.

Adams, W.J. and J.L. Yellen. 1976. "Commodity Bundling and the Burden of Monopoly." *Quarterly Journal of Economics*. 90: 475–98.

Aghion, P., N. Bloom, R. Blundell, R. Griffith and P. Howitt. 2002. "Competition and Innovation: An Inverted U Relationship." Cambridge, MA: National Bureau of Economic Research Working Paper 9269.

Aghion, P. and P. Bolton. 1987. "Contracts as a Barrier to Entry." *American Economic Review*. 77: 388–401.

Aghion, P., M. Dewatripont and P. Rey. 1998. "Agency Costs, Firm Behavior and the Nature of Competition." Université de Toulouse: IDEI. Unpublished manuscript.

Aghion, P., M. Dewatripont and P. Rey. 1999. "Competition, Financial Discipline and Growth." *Review of Economic Studies*. 66: 825–52.

Ahlborn, C., D.S. Evans and A.J. Padilla. 2001. "Competition Policy on Internet Time: Is European Competition Law Up to the Challenge?" *European Competition Law Review*. 22: 156–67.

Amato, G. 1997. *Antitrust and the Bounds of Power: The Dilemma of Liberal Democracy in the History of the Market*. Oxford: Hart.

Anderson, S.P., A. de Palma and J.-F. Thisse. 1992. *Discrete Choice Theory of Product Differentiation*. Cambridge, MA: MIT Press.

Areeda, P.E. and D.F. Turner. 1974. "Predatory Pricing and Related Practices under Section 2 of the Sherman Act." *Harvard Law Review*. 88: 697–733.

Arrow, K. 1961. "Economic Welfare and the Allocation of Research for Invention." In R. Nelson, ed. *The Rate and Direction of Inventive Activity: Economic and Social Factors*. Princeton University Press.

d'Aspremont, C. and A. Jacquemin. 1988. "Cooperative and Noncooperative R&D in Duopoly with Spillovers." *American Economic Review*. 78: 1133–7.

d'Aspremont, C. and M. Motta. 2000. "Tougher Competition or Lower Concentration: A Trade-Off for Antitrust Authorities?" In G. Norman and J. F. Thisse, eds. *Market Structure and Competition Policy: Game-Theoretic Approaches*. Cambridge, UK: Cambridge University Press.

Athey, S. and K. Bagwell. 2001. "Optimal Collusion with Private Information." *Rand Journal of Economics*. 32: 428–65.

Baily, M.N., C. Hulten and D. Campbell. 1992. "Productivity Dynamics in Manufacturing Plants." *Brookings Papers on Economic Activity. Microeconomics*. 187–267.

Baily, M.N. and H. Gersbach. 1995. "Efficiency in Manufacturing and the Need for Global Competition." *Brookings Papers on Economic Activity. Microeconomics.* 307–47.

Bain, J. 1949. "A Note on Pricing in Monopoly and Oligopoly." *American Economic Review.* 39: 448–64.

Bain, J. 1956. *Barriers to New Competition.* Cambridge, MA: Harvard University Press.

Baker, J.B. and T.F. Bresnahan. 1985. "The Gains from Merger or Collusion in Product Differentiated Industries." *Journal of Industrial Economics.* 33: 427–44.

Baker, J.B. and T.F. Bresnahan. 1988. "Estimating the Residual Demand Curve Facing a Single Firm." *International Journal of Industrial Organization.* 6: 283–300.

Barla, P. 2000. "Firm Size Inequality and Market Power." *International Journal of Industrial Organization.* 18: 693–722.

Barnes, M. and J. Haskel. 2000. "Productivity in the 1990s: Evidence from British Plants." Queen Mary and Westfield College. Unpublished manuscript.

Barros, P.P. 2001. "Looking Behind the Curtain. Effects from Modernization of European Competition Policy." Universidade Nova de Lisboa. Unpublished manuscript.

Baumol, W. 1996. "Predation and the Logic of the Average Variable Cost Test." *Journal of Law and Economics.* 39: 49–72.

Baumol, W., J. Panzar and R. Willig. 1982. *Contestable Markets and the Theory of Industrial Structure.* New York: Harcourt, Brace, Jovanovich.

Beggs, A. and P. Klemperer. 1992. "Multi–Period Competition with Switching Costs." *Econometrica.* 60: 651–67.

Bellamy, C. and G. Child. 2001. *European Community Law of Competition.* London: Sweet & Maxwell.

Benoit, J.P. 1984. "Financially Constrained Entry in a Game with Incomplete Information." *Rand Journal of Economics.* 15: 490–9.

Benoit, J.-P. and V. Krishna. 1987. "Dynamic Duopoly: Prices and Quantities." *Review of Economic Studies.* 54: 23–35.

Bergès, F., F. Loss, E. Malavolti and T. Vergé. 2002. "Competition Policy and Agreements Between Firms." Université de Toulouse: IDEI. Unpublished manuscript.

Berhneim, B.D. and M.D. Whinston. 1985. "Common Marketing Agency as a Device for Facilitating Collusion." *Rand Journal of Economics.* 16: 269–81.

Bernheim, B.D. and M.D. Whinston. 1990. "Multimarket Contact and Collusive Behavior." *Rand Journal of Economics.* 21: 1–26.

Bernheim, B.D. and M.D. Whinston. 1998. "Exclusive Dealing." *Journal of Political Economy.* 106: 64–103.

Berry, S.T. 1994. "Estimating Discrete Choice Models of Product Differentiation." *Rand Journal of Economics.* 25: 242–62.

Berry, S.T., J. Levinsohn and A. Pakes. 1995. "Automobile Prices in Market Equilibrium." *Econometrica.* 63: 841–90.

Besanko, D. and M.K. Perry. 1991. "Resale Price Maintenance and Manufacturer Competition for Exclusive Dealerships." *Journal of Industrial Economics.* 39: 517–44.

Besanko, D. and M.K. Perry. 1993. "Equilibrium Incentives for Exclusive Dealing in a Differentiated Products Oligopoly." *Rand Journal of Economics.* 24: 646–67.

Besanko, D. and D.F. Spulber. 1989. "Antitrust Enforcement under Asymmetric Information." *Economic Journal.* 99: 408–25.

Besanko, D. and D.F. Spulber. 1993. "Contested Mergers and Equilibrium Antitrust Policy." *Journal of Law, Economics, and Organization.* 9: 1–29.

Besen, S.M. and J. Farrell. 1994. "Choosing How to Compete: Strategies and Tactics in Standardization." *Journal of Economic Perspectives.* 8: 117–31.

Bishop, S.B. 1999. "Power and Responsibility: The ECJ's Kali–Salz Judgment." *European Competition Law Review.* 1: 38–9.

Bittlingmayer, G. 1985. "Did Antitrust Policy Cause the Great Merger Wave?" *Journal of Law and Economics.* 28: 77–118.

Bolton, G. and D. Scharfstein. 1990. "A Theory of Predation Based on Agency Problems in Financial Contracting." *American Economic Review.* 80: 93–106.

Bolton, P., J. Brodley and M. Riordan. 2000. "Predatory Pricing: Strategic Theory and Legal Policy." *Georgetown Law Journal.* 88: 2239–330.

Bonanno, G. and J. Vickers. 1988. "Vertical Separation." *Journal of Industrial Economics.* 36: 257–65.

Boone, J. 2000. "Competitive Pressure: The Effects on Investments in Product and Process Innovation." *Rand Journal of Economics.* 31: 549–69.

Borenstein, S. 1999. "Rapid Price Communication and Coordination: The Airline Tariff Publishing Case (1994)." In J.E. Kwoka and L.J. White, eds. *The Antitrust Revolution.* (3rd ed.). Oxford: Oxford University Press.

Bork, R. 1978. *The Antitrust Paradox.* New York: Basic Books.

Brander, J.A. 1981. "Intra-Industry Trade in Identical Commodities." *Journal of International Economics.* 11: 1–14.

Bresnahan, T.F. 1989. "Empirical Studies of Industries with Market Power." In R. Schmalensee and R.D. Willig, eds. *Handbook of Industrial Organization.* New York: Elsevier Science.

Bresnahan, T.F. 1998. "New Modes of Competition. Implications for the Future Structure of the Computer Industry." In J.A. Eisenach and T.M. Lenard, eds. *Competition, Innovation and the Microsoft Monopoly: Antitrust in the Digital Marketplace.* Boston: The Progress & Freedom Foundation.

Bresnahan, T.F. and P.C. Reiss. 1991. "Entry and Competition in Concentrated Markets." *Journal of Political Economy.* 99: 977–1009.

Brock, W.A. and J. Scheinkman. 1985. "Price Setting Supergames with Capacity Constraints." *Review of Economic Studies.* 52: 371–82.

Bulow, J., J. Geanakoplos and P. Klemperer. 1985. "Multimarket Oligopoly: Strategic Substitutes and Complements." *Journal of Political Economy.* 93: 488–511.

Burnett, W.B. 1999. "Predation by a Nondominant Firm: The Liggett Case." in J.E. Kwoka and L.J. White, eds. *The Antitrust Revolution.* (3rd ed.). Oxford: Oxford University Press.

Burns, M.R. 1986. "Predatory Pricing and the Acquisition Costs of Competitors." *Journal of Political Economy.* 94: 266–96.

Cabral, L. 2003. "Horizontal Mergers with Free-Entry: Why Cost Efficiencies may be a Weak Defense and Asset Sales a Poor Remedy." *International Journal of Industrial Organization.* 5: 607–23.

Caffarra, C. and J. Ysewyn. 1998. "Two's Company, Three's a Crowd: The Future of Collective Dominance after the Kali & Salz Judgment." *European Competition Law Review.* 7: 470.

Caillaud, B., B. Jullien and P. Picard. 1995. "Competing Vertical Structures: Precommitment and Renegotiation." *Econometrica.* 63: 621–46.

Camesasca, P. 1999. "The Explicit Efficiency Defence in Merger Control: Does It Make the Difference?" *European Competition Law Review.* 1: 25–7.

Carlton, D.W. and M. Waldman. 2002. "The Strategic Use of Tying to Preserve and Create Market Power in Evolving Industries." *Rand Journal of Economics.* 33: 194–220.

Caves, R.E. 1989. "Mergers, Takeovers and Economic Efficiency. Foresight vs. Hindsight." *International Journal of Industrial Organization*. 7: 151–74.

Caves, R.E. and Barton, D.R. 1990. *Efficiency in U.S. Manufacturing Industries*. Cambridge, MA and London: MIT Press.

Cestone, G. 2001. "Corporate Financing and Product Market Competition: An Overview." *Giornale degli Economisti*. 58: 269–300.

Cestone, G. and C. Fumagalli. 2001. "Internal Capital Markets, Cross-Subsidization, and Product Market Competition." London: CEPR Discussion Paper 2935.

Chandler, A.D. 1990. *Scale and Scope: The Dynamics of Industrial Capitalism*. Cambridge, MA: Harvard University Press.

Chemla, G. 2003. "Downstream Competition, Foreclosure and Vertical Integration." *Journal of Economics and Management Strategy*. 12: 261–89.

Choi, J.P. 1996. "Preemptive R&D, Rent Dissipation and the 'Leverage Theory'." *Quarterly Journal of Economics*. 110: 1153–81.

Choi, J.P. 2001. "A Theory of Mixed Bundling Applied to the GE/Honeywell Merger." *Antitrust*. 16: 32–3.

Choi, J.P. and C. Stefanadis. 2001. "Tying, Investment, and the Dynamic Leverage Theory." *Rand Journal of Economics*. 32: 52–71.

Coase, R. 1972. "Durability and Monopoly." *Journal of Law and Economics*. 15: 143–9.

Comanor, W.S. 1990. "United States Antitrust Policy: Issues and Institutions." In W. S. Comanor et al., eds. *Competition Policy in Europe and North America: Economic Issues and Institutions*. New York: Harwood Academic. 43–72.

Comanor, W.S. and H.E. Frech. 1985. "The Competitive Effects of Vertical Agreements?" *American Economic Review*. 75: 539–46.

Compte, O. 1998. "Communication in Repeated Games with Imperfect Private Monitoring." *Econometrica*. 66: 597–626.

Compte, O., F. Jenny and P. Rey. 2002. "Capacity Constraints, Mergers and Collusion." *European Economic Review*. 46: 1–29.

Connor, J.M., R.T. Rogers and V. Bhagavan. 1996. "Concentration Change and Countervailing Power in the U.S. Food Manufacturing Industries." *Review of Industrial Organization*. 11: 473–92.

Cooper, R., D.V. DeJong, R. Forsythe and T.W. Ross. 1992. "Communication in Coordination Games." *Quarterly Journal of Economics*. 107: 739–71.

Cooper, T.E. 1986. "Most-Favored-Customer Pricing and Tacit Collusion." *Rand Journal of Economics*. 17: 377–88.

Correia, E. 1998. "Joint Ventures: Issues in Enforcement Policy." *Antitrust Law Journal*. 66: 737–71.

Cournot, A.A. 1838. *Recherches sur les Principes Mathématiques de la Théorie des Richesses*. Paris: L. Hachette.

Cramton, P. and J.A. Schwartz. 2001. "Collusive Bidding: Lessons from the FCC Spectrum Auctions." *Journal of Regulatory Economics*. 17: 229–52.

Crémer, J., P. Rey and J. Tirole. 2000. "Connectivity in the Commercial Internet." *Journal of Industrial Economics*. 48: 433–72.

Crocker, K.J. and T.P. Lyon. 1994. "What Do Facilitating Practices Facilitate? An Empirical Investigation on Most-Favored Nation Clauses in Natural Gas Contracts." *Journal of Law and Economics*. 37: 297–322.

Dansby, E. and R. Willig. 1979. "Industry Performance Gradient Indexes." *American Economic Review*. 69: 249–60.

Davidson, C. and R.J. Deneckere. 1986. "Long-Term Competition in Capacity, Short-Run Competition in Price, and the Cournot Model." *Rand Journal of Economics.* 17: 404–15.

Davidson, C. and R.J. Deneckere. 1990. "Excess Capacity and Collusion." *International Economic Review.* 31: 521–41.

Deneckere, R.J. and C. Davidson. 1985. "Incentives to Form Coalitions with Bertrand Competition." *Rand Journal of Economics.* 16: 473–86.

Dierickx, I., C. Matutes and D.J. Neven. 1991. "Cost Differences and Survival in Declining Industries: A Case for 'Picking Winners'?" *European Economic Review.* 35: 1507–28.

Disney, R., J. Haskel and Y. Heden. 2000. "Restructuring and Productivity Growth in UK Manufacturing." Queen Mary and Westfield College. Unpublished manuscript.

Dixit, A. 1980. "The Role of Investment in Entry Deterrence." *Economic Journal.* 90: 95–106.

Dobson, P.W. and M. Waterson. 1997. "Countervailing Power and Consumer Prices." *Economic Journal.* 107: 418–30.

Dranove, D. and N. Gandal. 2000. "The DVD vs. DIVX Standard War: Network Effects and Empirical Evidence of Preannouncement Effects." Northwestern University. Unpublished manuscript.

Eckbo, B.E. 1983. "Horizontal Mergers, Collusion, and Stockholder Wealth." *Journal of Financial Economics.* 11: 241–73.

Ellison, G. 1994. "Theories of Cartel Stability and the Joint Executive Cartel." *Rand Journal of Economics.* 25: 37–57.

Elzinga, K.G. and T.F. Hogarty. 1973. "The Problem of Geographic Market Definition in Antimerger Suits." *Antitrust Bulletin.* 18: 45–81.

Elzinga, K.G. and D.E. Mills. 2001. "Predatory Pricing and Strategic Theory." *Georgetown Law Journal.* 89: 2475–94.

Encaoua, D. and A. Jacquemin. 1980. "Degree of Monopoly, Indices of Concentration and Threat of Entry." *International Economic Review.* 21: 87–105.

Eswaran, M. 1994. "Cross-Licensing of Competing Patents as a Facilitating Device." *Canadian Journal of Economics.* 27: 689–708.

European Commission. 1996. *XXV Competition Policy Report, 1995.* Brussels: Commission of the European Communities.

European Commission. 2000. *XXIX Report on Competition Policy, 1999.* Brussels: Commission of the European Communities.

European Commission. 2001. *XXX Report on Competition Policy, 2000.* Brussels: Commission of the European Communities.

Evans, D.S. 2002. "The Antitrust Economics of Two-Sided Markets." Unpublished manuscript.

Evans, W.N. and I.N. Kessides. 1994. "Living by the 'Golden Rule': Multimarket Contact in the U.S. Airline Industry." *Quarterly Journal of Economics.* 109: 341–66.

Fabra, N. 2001a. "Tacit Collusion in Electricity Markets: Uniform-Price versus Discriminatory Auctions." *Journal of Industrial Economics.* Forthcoming.

Fabra, N. 2001b. "Collusive Behavior with Capacity Constraints over the Business Cycle." Florence: European University Institute. Unpublished manuscript.

Farrell, J. 1987. "Cheap Talk, Coordination and Entry." *Rand Journal of Economics.* 18: 34–9.

Farrell, J. and M.L. Katz. 1998. "The Effects of Antitrust and Intellectual Property Law on Compatibility and Innovation." *Antitrust Bulletin.* Fall/Winter. 609–50.

Farrell, J. and M. Katz. 2000. "Innovation, Rent Extraction, and Integration in Systems Markets." *Journal of Industrial Economics.* 48: 413–32.

Farrell, J. and P. Klemperer. 2001. "Coordination and Lock-In: Competition with Switching Costs and Network Effects." University of California, Berkeley. Unpublished manuscript.

Farrell, J. and M. Rabin. 1996. "Cheap Talk." *Journal of Economic Perspectives.* 10: 103–18.

Farrell, J. and G. Saloner. 1985. "Standardization, Compatibility and Innovation." *Rand Journal of Economics.* 16: 70–83.

Farrell, J. and C. Shapiro. 1990. "Horizontal Mergers: An Equilibrium Analysis." *American Economic Review.* 80: 107–25.

Farrell, J. and C. Shapiro. 2001. "Scale Economies and Synergies in Horizontal Merger Analysis." *Antitrust Law Journal.* 68: 685–710.

Faulí-Oller, R. and M. Motta. 1996. "Managerial Incentives for Takeovers." *Journal of Economics and Management Strategy.* 5: 497–514.

Federal Trade Commission. 1999. *A Study of the Commission's Divestiture Procedure.* Washington, D.C.: Federal Trade Commission.

Fershtman, C. and Judd, K.L. 1987. "Equilibrium Incentives in Oligopoly." *American Economic Review.* 77: 927–40.

Fingleton, J., E. Fox, D. Neven and P. Seabright. 1996. *Competition Policy and the Transformation of Central Europe.* London: CEPR.

Fisher, F. 1985. "The Social Costs of Monopoly and Regulation: Posner Reconsidered." *Journal of Political Economy.* 93: 410–16.

Foster, L., J. Haltiwanger and C. J. Krizan. 1998. "Aggregate Productivity Growth: Lessons from Microeconomic Evidence." NBER Working Paper 6803.

Fox, E. 2002. "What is Harm to Competition? Exclusionary Practises and Anticompetitive Effect." *Antitrust Law Journal.* 70: 371–412.

Frank, J., R.S. Harris and S. Titman. 1991. "The Postmerger Share–Price Performance of Acquiring Firms." *Journal of Financial Economics.* 29: 81–96.

Fridolfsson, S.-O. and J. Stennek. 2002. "Why Mergers Reduce Profits and Raise Share Prices: A Theory of Preemptive Mergers." Stockholm: IUI. Unpublished manuscript.

Friedman, J. 1971. "A Noncooperative Equilibrium for Supergames." *Review of Economic Studies.* 28: 1–12.

Froeb, L.M. and G.J. Werden. 1991. "Residual Demand Estimation for Market Delineation: Complications and Limitations." *Review of Industrial Organization.* 6: 33–48.

Fudenberg, D. and J. Tirole. 1984. "The Fat Cat Effect, the Puppy Dog Ploy and the Lean and Hungry Look." *American Economic Review, Papers and Proceedings.* 74: 361–8.

Fudenberg, D. and J. Tirole. 1985. "Preemption and Rent Equilization in the Adoption of New Technology." *Review of Economic Studies.* 52: 383–401.

Fudenberg, D. and J. Tirole. 1986a. "A Signal-Jamming Theory of Predation." *Rand Journal of Economics.* 17: 173–90.

Fudenberg, D. and J. Tirole. 1986b. "A Theory of Exit in Duopoly." *Econometrica.* 54: 943–60.

Fudenberg, D. and J. Tirole. 2000. "Pricing a Network Good to Deter Entry." *Journal of Industrial Economics.* 48: 373–90.

Fumagalli, C., L. Karlinger and M. Motta. 2003. "A Model of Physical Networks." Florence: European University Institute. Unpublished manuscript.

Fumagalli, C. and M. Motta. 2000. "Buyers' Coordination and Entry." London: CEPR Discussion Paper 2908.

Fumagalli, C. and M. Motta. 2001. "Advertising Restrictions in Professional Services." In G. Amato and L. Laudati, eds. *The Anticompetitive Impact of Regulation.* Edward Elgar Publishers.

Fumagalli, C. and M. Motta. 2002. "Exclusive Dealing and Entry, When Buyers Compete." London: CEPR Discussion Paper 3493.

Galbraith, J.K. 1952. "American Capitalism: The Concept of Countervailing Power." Reprint edition. *Classics in Economics Series.* New Brunswick, NJ and London: Transaction. 1993.

Gale, D. and M. Hellwig. 1986. "Incentive Compatible Debt Contracts: The One-Period Problem." *Review of Economic Studies.* 52: 647–64.

Gal-Or, E. 1991. "Duopolistic Vertical Restraints." *European Economic Review.* 35: 1237–53.

Genesove, D. and W.P. Mullin. 2001. "Rules, Communication, and Collusion: Narrative Evidence from the Sugar Institute Case." *American Economic Review.* 91: 379–98.

George, K.D. and A. Jacquemin. 1990. "Competition Policy in the European Community." In W.S. Comanor et al., eds. *Competition Policy in Europe and North America.* New York: Harwood Academic. 206–45.

Gibbons, R. 1997. "An Introduction to Applicable Game Theory." *Journal of Economic Perspectives.* 11: 127–49.

Gilbert, R. and X. Vives. 1986. "Entry Deterrence and the Free Rider Problem." *Review of Economic Studies.* 53: 71–83.

Gowrisankaran, G. 1999. "A Dynamic Model of Endogenous Horizontal Mergers." *Rand Journal of Economics.* 30: 56–83.

Goyder, D.G. 1993. *EC Competition Law.* 2nd ed. Clarendon: Oxford University Press.

Goyder, D.G. 1998. *EC Competition Law.* 3rd ed. Clarendon: Oxford University Press.

Green, E.J. and R.H. Porter. 1984. "Noncooperative Collusion Under Imperfect Competition." *Econometrica.* 52: 87–100.

Green, A. and D. Mayes. 1991. "Technical Inefficiency in Manufacturing Industries." *Economic Journal.* 101: 523–38.

Grossman, G.M. and C. Shapiro. 1986. "Research Joint Ventures: An Antitrust Analysis." *Journal of Law, Economics and Organization.* 2: 315–37.

Gual, J. 1995. "The Three Common Policies: An Economic Analysis." In Pierre Buigues, Alexis Jacquemin and Andre Sapir, eds. *European Policies on Competition, Trade and Industry: Conflict and Complementarities.* Aldershot: Elgar. 3–48.

Haltiwanger, J. and J.E. Harrington, Jr. 1991. "The Impact of Cyclical Demand Movements on Collusive Behavior." *Rand Journal of Economics.* 22: 89–106.

Harberger, A.C. 1954. "Monopoly and Resource Allocation." *American Economic Review.* 44: 77–87.

Harrington, J.E., Jr. 1986. "Limit Pricing When the Potential Entrant Is Uncertain of Its Cost Function." *Econometrica.* 54: 429–37.

Harrington, J.E., Jr. 1989a. "Collusion among Asymmetric Firms: The Case of Different Discount Factors." *International Journal of Industrial Organization.* 7: 289–307.

Harrington, J.E., Jr. 1989b. "Collusion and Predation under (Almost) Free Entry." *International Journal of Industrial Organization.* 7: 381–401.

Hart, O. 1983. "The Market Mechanism as an Incentive Scheme." *Bell Journal of Economics.* 14: 366–82.

Hart, O. and J. Tirole. 1990. "Vertical Integration and Market Foreclosure." *Brookings Papers on Economic Activity.* Special Issue 0: 205–76.

Hausman, J., G. Leonard and J.D. Zona. 1994. "Competitive Analysis with Differentiated Products." *Annales d'Economie et Statistique.* 34: 159–80.

Hay, D.A. and G.S. Liu. 1997. "The Efficiency of Firms: What Difference Does Competition Make?" *Economic Journal.* 107: 597–617.

Hay, G.A. 1999. "Facilitating Practices: The Ethyl Case (1984)." In J.E. Kwoka, Jr. and L.J. White, eds. *The Antitrust Revolution.* (3rd ed.). Oxford University Press.

Heide, J.B., S. Dutta and M. Bergen. 1998. "Exclusive Dealing and Business Efficiency: Evidence from Industry Practice." *Journal of Law and Economics.* 41: 387–407.

Hermalin, B.E. 1992. "The Effects of Competition on Executive Behavior." *Rand Journal of Economics.* 23: 350–65.

Holmström, B. and J. Tirole. 1997. "Financial Intermediation, Loanable Funds and the Real Sector." *Quarterly Journal of Economics.* 62: 663–91.

Holt, C.A. and D.T. Scheffman. 1987. "Facilitating Practices: The Effects of Advance Notice and Best-Price Clauses." *Rand Journal of Economics.* 18: 187–97.

Horn, H., H. Lang and S. Lundgren. 1994. "Competition, Long–Run Contracts and Internal Inefficiencies in Firms." *European Economic Review.* 38: 213–33.

Horn, H. and L. Persson. 2001. "Endogenous Mergers in Concentrated Markets." *International Journal of Industrial Organization.* 19: 1213–44.

Inman, R.P. and D.L. Rubinfeld. 1997. "Making Sense of the Antitrust State–Action Doctrine: Balancing Political Participation and Economic Efficiency in Regulatory Federalism." *Texas Law Review.* 75: 1203–99.

Irmen, A. 1998. "Precommitment in Competing Vertical Chains." *Journal of Economic Surveys.* 12: 333–59.

Jacquemin, A. 1990. "Mergers and European Policy." In P.H. Admiraal, ed. *Merger and Competition Policy in the European Community.* Oxford: Basil Blackwell.

Jacquemin, A. and M. Slade. 1989. "Cartels, Collusion, and Horizontal Merger." In R. Schmalensee and R.D. Willig, eds. *Handbook of Industrial Organization.* New York: Elsevier Science.

Joskow, P.L. and A.K. Klevorick. 1979. "A Framework for Analyzing Predatory Pricing Policy." *Yale Law Journal.* 89: 213–70.

Jovanovic, B. 1982. "Selection and the Evolution of Industry." *Econometrica.* 50: 649–70.

Judd, K.L. 1985. "Credible Spatial Preemption." *Rand Journal of Economics.* 16: 153–66.

Jullien, B. and P. Rey. 2001. "Resale Price Maintenance and Collusion." Université de Toulouse: IDEI. Unpublished manuscript.

Kamecke, U. 1998. "Vertical Restraints in German Antitrust Law." In S. Martin, ed. *Competition Policies in Europe.* Amsterdam: Elsevier.

Kamien, M.I. and I. Zang. 1990. "The Limits of Monopolization through Acquisition." *Quarterly Journal of Economics.* 105: 465–99.

Kamien, M.I. and I. Zang. 1991. "Competitively Cost Advantageous Mergers and Monopolization." *Games and Economic Behavior.* 3: 323–38.

Kandori, M. 1992. "The Use of Information in Repeated Games with Imperfect Monitoring." *Review of Economic Studies.* 59: 581–93.

Kandori, M. and H. Matsushima. 1998. "Private Observation, Communication and Collusion." *Econometrica,* 66: 627–52.

Katz, D. 1991. "Game-Playing Agents: Unobservable Contracts as Precommitments." *Rand Journal of Economics.* 22: 307–28.

Katz, M.L. and C. Shapiro. 1985. "Network Externalities, Competition and Compatibility." *American Economic Review.* 75: 424–40.

Katz, M.L. and C. Shapiro. 1994. "Systems Competition and Network Effects." *Journal of Economic Perspectives.* 8: 93–115.

Kim, H. and V. Singal. 1993. "Mergers and Market Power: Evidence from the Airline Industry." *American Economic Review.* 83: 549–69.

Klemperer, P. 1987a. "Markets with Consumer Switching Costs." *Quarterly Journal of Economics.* 102: 357–94.

Klemperer, P. 1987b. "The Competitiveness of Markets with Switching Costs." *Rand Journal of Economics*. 18: 138–51.

Klemperer, P. 1987c. "Entry Deterrence in Markets with Switching Costs." *Economic Journal. Conference Supplement*. 1–17.

Klemperer, P.D. 1988. "Welfare Effects of Entry into Markets with Switching Costs." *Journal of Industrial Economics*. 37: 159–65.

Klemperer, P. 1995. "Competition when Consumers Have Switching Costs: An Overview." *Review of Economic Studies*. 62: 515–39.

Klemperer, P. 2002. "What Really Matters in Auction Design." *Journal of Economic Perspectives*. 16: 169–89.

Kolasky, W.J. 2001. "Conglomerate Mergers and Range Effects: It's a Long Way from Chicago to Brussels." Washington, D.C. Unpublished manuscript.

Korah, V. 1994a. *An Introductory Guide to EC Competition Law and Practice*. London: Sweet and Maxwell.

Korah, V. 1994b. "Exclusive Purchasing Obligations: *Mars v. Langnese and Schöller*." *European Competition Law Review*. 15: 171–75.

Korah, V. 1999. "*Gencor v. Commission*: Collective Dominance." *European Competition Law Review*. 6: 337.

Kovacic, W.E. and C. Shapiro. 2000. "Antitrust Policy: A Century of Economic and Legal Thinking." *Journal of Economic Perspectives*. 14: 43–60.

Krattenmaker, T.G. and S.C. Salop. 1986. "Anticompetitive Exclusion: Raising Rival's Costs To Achieve Power Over Price." *Yale Law Journal*. 96: 209–93.

Kreps, D., P. Milgrom, J. Roberts and R. Wilson. 1982. "Rational Cooperation in the Finitely Repeated Prisoner's Dilemma." *Journal of Economic Theory*. 27: 245–52.

Kreps, D. and J. Scheinkman. 1983. "Quantity Precommitment and Bertrand Competition Yield Cournot Outcomes." *Bell Journal of Economics*. 14: 326–37.

Kreps, D. and R. Wilson. 1982. "Reputation and Imperfect Information." *Journal of Economic Theory*. 27: 253–79.

Krueger, A. 1974. "The Political Economy of the Rent–Seeking Society." *American Economic Review*. 64: 291–303.

Kühn, K.-U. 1997. "Germany." In E.M. Graham and J. Richardson, eds. *Global Competition Policy*. Washington, D.C.: Institute for International Economics.

Kühn, K.-U. 2001. "Fighting Collusion by Regulating Communication between Firms." *Economic Policy*. 16: 167–204.

Kühn, K.-U. and M. Motta. 1999. "The Economics of Joint Dominance." Florence: European University Institute. Unpublished manuscript.

Kühn, K.-U. and X. Vives. 1995. "Information Exchange Among Firms and their Impact on Competition." European Commission Document.

Kühn, K.-U. and X. Vives. 1999. "Excess Entry, Vertical Integration, and Welfare." *Rand Journal of Economics*. 30: 575–603.

LaCasse, C. 1995. "Bid Rigging and the Threat of Government Prosecution." *Rand Journal of Economics*. 26: 398–417.

Laffont, J.-J. and J. Tirole. 1994. *A Theory of Incentives in Procurement and Regulation*. Boston: MIT Press.

Landes, W.M. and R.A. Posner. 1981. "Market Power in Antitrust Cases." *Harvard Law Review*. 94: 937–96.

Leahy, D. and J.P. Neary. 1997. "Public Policy Towards R&D in Oligopolistic Industries." *American Economic Review*. 87: 642–62.

Leibenstein, H. 1966. "Allocative Efficiency vs. X-Efficiency." *American Economic Review*. 56: 392–415.

Levin, R.C., W. Cohen and D.C. Mowery. 1985. "R&D Appropriability, Opportunity, and Market Structure: New Evidence on Some Schumptereian Hypothesis." *American Economic Review. Papers and Proceedings*. 75: 20–4.

Levy, D.T. and J.D. Reitzes. 1992. "Anticompetitive Effects of Mergers in Markets with Localized Competition." *Journal of Law, Economics and Organization*. 8: 427–40.

Lin, P., B. Raj, M. Sandfort and D. Slottje. 2000. "The US Antitrust System and Recent Trends in Antitrust Enforcement." *Journal of Economic Surveys*. 14: 255–306.

Lustgarten, S.H. 1975. "The Impact of Buyer Concentration in Manufacturing Industries." *Review of Economics and Statistics*. 57: 125–32.

Lyons, B.R. 2002. "Could Politicians Be More Right than Economists? A Theory of Merger Standards." Norwich: UEA. Unpublished manuscript.

McAfee, R.P. and Schwartz, M. 1994. "Opportunism in Multilateral Vertical Contracting: Nondiscrimination, Exclusivity, and Uniformity." *American Economic Review*. 84: 210–30.

McAfee, P. and M.A. Williams. 1992. "Horizontal Mergers and Antitrust Policy." *Journal Industrial Economics*. 40: 181–87.

McCutcheon, B. 1997. "Do Meetings in Smoke-Filled Rooms Facilitate Collusion?" *Journal of Political Economy*. 105: 330–50.

McFadden, D. 1973. "Conditional Logit Analysis of Qualitative Choice Behavior." In P. Zarembka, ed. *Frontiers in Econometrics*. New York: Academic Press.

McGee, J. 1958. "Predatory Price Cutting: The Standard Oil (NJ) Case." *Journal of Law and Economics*. 1: 137–69.

McGuckin, R. and S. Nguyen. 1995. "On the Productivity and Plant Ownership Change: New Evidence from the Longitudinal Research Database." *Rand Journal of Economics*. 26: 257–76.

Maggi, G. 1996. "Strategic Trade Policies with Endogenous Mode of Competition." *American Economic Review*. 86: 237–58.

Malueg, D.A. and M. Schwartz. 2001. "Interconnection Incentives of a Large Network Facing Multiple Rivals." Washington, D.C.: Georgetown University. Unpublished manuscript.

Martin, S. 1993. "Endogenous Firm Efficiency in a Cournot Principal-Agent Model." *Journal of Economic Theory*. 59: 445–50.

Martin, S. 1995. "R&D Joint Ventures and Tacit Product Market Collusion." *European Journal of Political Economy*. 11: 733–41.

Martinez Lopez, M. 2000a. "Commission Approves an Agreement to Improve Efficiency of Washing Machines." *Competition Policy Newsletter*. 1: 13–14.

Martinez Lopez, M. 2000b. "Horizontal Agreements on Energy Efficiency of Appliances: A Comparison of CECED and CEMEP." *Competition Policy Newsletter*. 2: 24–5.

Marvel, H.P. and S. McCafferty. 1984. "Resale Price Maintenance and Quality Certification." *Rand Journal of Economics*. 15: 346–59.

Maskin, E. and J. Tirole. 1988. "A Theory of Dynamic Oligopoly, II: Price Competition, Kinked Demand Curves, and Edgeworth Cycles." *Econometrica*. 56: 571–99.

Mathewson, G.F. and R.A. Winter. 1983. "Vertical Integration by Contractual Restraints in Spatial Markets." *Journal of Business*. 56: 497–517.

Mathewson, G.F. and R.A. Winter. 1984. "An Economic Theory of Vertical Restraints." *Rand Journal of Economics*. 15: 27–38.

Mathewson, G.F. and R.A. Winter. 1987. "The Competitive Effects of Vertical Agreements: Comment." *American Economic Review*. 77: 1057–62.

Mathewson, G.F. and R.A. Winter. 1998. "The Law and Economics of Resale Price Maintenance." *Review of Industrial Organization.* 13: 57–84.

Matsusaka, J.G. 1993. "Takeover Motives during Conglomerate Merger Wave." *Rand Journal of Economics.* 24: 357–79.

Merges, R.P. 2001. "Institutions for Intellectual Property Transactions: The Case of Patent Pools." In R. Dreyfuss, D.L. Zimmerman and H. First, eds. *Expanding the Boundaries of Intellectual Property.* Oxford University Press.

Messerlin, P.A. 1990. "Anti-Dumping Regulation or Pro-Cartel Law? The EC Chemical Cases." *World Economy.* 645–92.

Milgrom, P. and J. Roberts. 1982a. "Limit Pricing and Entry under Incomplete Information: An Equilibrium Analysis." *Econometrica.* 50: 443–59.

Milgrom, P. and J. Roberts. 1982b. "Predation, Reputation and Entry Deterrence." *Journal of Economic Theory.* 27: 280–312.

Milliou, C. 2001. "Vertical Integration and R&D Spillovers: Is There a Need for 'Firewalls'?" International Journal of Industrial Organization. Forthcoming.

Morck, R., A. Schleifer and R. Vishny. 1990. "Do Managerial Incentives Drive Bad Acquisitions?" *Journal of Finance.* 45: 31–48.

Motta, M. 1992. "Cooperative R&D and Vertical Product Differentiation." *International Journal of Industrial Organization.* 10: 643–61.

Motta, M. 1996. "Research Joint Ventures in an International Economy." *Ricerche Economiche.* 50: 293–315.

Motta, M. 2000. "EC Merger Policy and the Airtours Case." *European Competition Law Review.* 21: 199–207.

Motta, M. and F. Onida. 1997. "Trade Policy and Competition Policy." *Giornale degli Economisti e Annali di Economia.* 56: 67–97.

Motta, M. and M. Polo. 1999. "Leniency Programs and Cartel Prosecution." Florence: European University Institute. Unpublished manuscript.

Motta, M. and M. Polo. 2003. "Leniency Programs and Cartel Prosecution." *International Journal of Industrial Organization.* 21: 347–79.

Motta, M., M. Polo and H. Vasconcelos. 2002. "Merger Remedies in the European Union: An Overview." Antitrust Bulletin. Forthcoming.

Motta, M. and T. Rønde. 2002. "Trade Secret Laws, Trade Mobility, and Innovations." London: CEPR Discussion Paper 3615.

Motta, M., J.-F. Thisse and A. Cabrales. 1997. "On the Persistence of Leadership or Leapfrogging in International Trade." *International Economic Review.* 38: 809–24.

Motta, M. and H. Vasconcelos. 2003. "Efficiency Gains and Myopic Antitrust Authority in a Dynamic Merger Game." Florence: European University Institute. Unpublished manuscript.

Mueller, D.C. 1985. *Profits in the Long-Run.* Cambridge University Press.

Mueller, D.C. 1996. "Lessons from the United States's Antitrust History." *International Journal of Industrial Organization.* 14: 415–45.

Nalebuff, B.J. 2002. "Bundling and the GE-Honeywell Merger." Yale School of Management Working Paper 22.

Nash, J.F. 1950. "Equilibrium Points in *N*-person Games." *Proceedings of the National Academy of Sciences.* 18: 155–62.

Neven, D.J., R. Nuttall and P. Seabright. 1993. *Merger in Daylight: The Economics and Politics of European Merger Control.* London: CEPR.

Neven, D.J., P. Papandropoulos and P. Seabright. 1998. *Trawling for Minnows. European Competition Policy and Agreements between Firms.* London: CEPR.

Neven, D.J. and L.-H. Röller. 1996. "Rent Sharing in the European Airline Industry." *European Economic Review*. 40: 933–40.

Neven, D.J. and L.-H. Röller. 2000. "Consumer Surplus versus Welfare Standard in a Political Economy Model of Merger Control." WZB Working Paper FS IV 00-15.

Neven, D.J. and L.-H. Röller. 2002. "Discrepancies between Markets and Regulators: An Analysis of the First Ten Years of EU Merger Control." Unpublished manuscript.

Nevo, A. 2000. "A Practitioner's Guide to Estimation of Random-Coefficients Logit Models of Demand." *Journal of Economics and Management Strategy*. 9: 513–48.

Nevo, A. 2001. "Measuring Market Power in the Ready-to-Eat Cereal Industry." *Econometrica*. 69: 307–42.

Nickell, S. 1996. "Competition and Corporate Performance." *Journal of Political Economy*. 104: 724–46.

Nickell, S., D. Nicolitsas and N. Dryden. 1997. "What Makes Firms Perform Well?" *European Economic Review*. 41: 783–96.

Nöel, P.-E. 1997. "Efficiency Considerations in the Assessment of Mergers." *European Competition Law Review*. 8: 498–519.

O'Brien, D.P. and G. Shaffer. 1992. "Vertical Control with Bilateral Contracts." *Rand Journal of Economics*. 23: 299–308.

Olley, G.S. and A. Pakes. 1996. "The Dynamics of Productivity in the Telecommunications Equipment Industry." *Econometrica*. 64: 1263–97.

Ordover, J.A. 1990. "Economic Foundations of Competition Policy." In W.S. Comanor, K. George and A. Jacquemin, eds. *Competition Policy in Europe and North America: Economic Issues and Institutions*. Chur: Harwood Academic.

Ordover, J. and G. Saloner. 1989. "Predation, Monopolization, and Antitrust." In R. Schmalensee and R. Willig, eds. *Handbook of Industrial Organization*. Amsterdam: North-Holland.

Ordover, J.A. and R.D. Willig. 1993. "Economics and the 1992 Merger Guidelines: A Brief Survey." *Review of Industrial Organization*. 8: 139–50.

Padilla, A.J. 1991. "Consumer Switching Costs: A Survey." *Investigaciones Economicas*. 15: 485–504.

Padilla, A.J. and M. Pagano. 1997. "Endogenous Communication among Lenders and Entrepreneurial Incentives." *Review of Financial Studies*. 10: 205–36.

Parker, R. and D. Balto. 2000. "The Evolving Approach to Merger Remedies." *Antitrust Report*. 2: 2–28.

Parker, P.M. and L.-H. Röller. 1997. "Collusive Conduct in Duopolies: Multimarket Contact and Cross-Ownership in the Mobile Telephone Industry." *Rand Journal of Economics*. 28: 304–22.

Peritz, R.J.R. 1999. "Il prodotto di marca e il suo prodotto derivato. Analisi economica e inquadramento giuridico." *Mercato Concorrenza Regole*. 2: 195–221.

Perry, M.K. and R.H. Groff. 1985. "Resale Price Maintenance and Forward Integration into a Monopolistically Competitive Industry." *Quarterly Journal of Economics*. 100:1293–311.

Perry, M.K. and R. Porter. 1985. "Oligopoly and the Incentive for Horizontal Merger." *American Economic Review*. 75: 219–27.

Pesendorfer, M. 2000. "A Study of Collusion in First-Price Auctions." *Review of Economic Studies*. 67: 381–411.

Pigou, A.C. 1920. *The Economics of Welfare*. London: McMillan.

Porter, R.H. 1983a. "Optimal Cartel Trigger Strategies." *Journal of Economic Theory*. 29: 313–38.

Porter, R.H. 1983b. "A Study of Cartel Stability: The Joint Executive Committee, 1880–1886." *Bell Journal of Economics*. 14: 301–14.

Porter, R.H. 1985. "On the Incidence and Duration of Price Wars." *Journal of Industrial Economics.* 33: 415–26.

Posner, R.A. 1975. "The Social Cost of Monopoly and Regulation." *Journal of Political Economy.* 83: 807–27.

Posner, R.A. 1976. *Antitrust Law: An Economic Perspective.* Chicago: University of Chicago Press.

Posner, R.A. 2001. *Antitrust Law.* Chicago: *University of Chicago Press.*

Raith, M. 1996a. "Product Differentiation, Uncertainty and the Stability of Collusion." London School of Economics–STICERD. Discussion Paper Series EI/16:49.

Raith, M. 1996b. "A General Model of Information Sharing in Oligopoly." *Journal of Economic Theory.* 71: 260–88.

Rasmusen, E.B., J.M. Ramseyer and J.S. Wiley, Jr. 1991. "Naked Exclusion." *American Economic Review.* 81: 1137–45.

Ravenscraft, D.J. and F.M. Scherer. 1987. *Mergers, Sell-Offs, and Economic Efficiency.* Washington, D.C.: Brookings Institution.

Rey, P. 2000. "Towards a Theory of Competition Policy." Université de Toulouse: IDEI. Unpublished manuscript.

Rey, P. 2002. "Collective Dominance in the Telecommunications Industry." Université de Toulouse: IDEI. Unpublished manuscript.

Rey, P., P. Seabright and J. Tirole. 2001. "The Activities of a Monopoly Firm in Adjacent Competitive Markets: Economic Consequences and Implications for Competition Policy." Université de Toulouse: IDEI. Unpublished manuscript.

Rey, P. and J. Stiglitz. 1988. "Vertical Restraints and Producers' Competition." *European Economic Review.* 32: 561–68.

Rey, P. and J. Stiglitz. 1995. "The Role of Exclusive Territories in Producers' Competition." *Rand Journal of Economics.* 26: 431–51.

Rey, P. and J. Tirole. 1986. "The Logic of Vertical Restraints." *American Economic Review.* 76: 921–39.

Rey, P. and J. Tirole. 1996. "A Primer on Foreclosure." Université de Toulouse: IDEI. Unpublished manuscript.

Rey, P. and T. Vergé. 2002a. "Resale Price Maintenance and Horizontal Cartel." Université de Toulouse: IDEI. Unpublished manuscript.

Rey, P. and T. Vergé. 2002b. "Bilateral Control with Vertical Contracts." Université de Toulouse: IDEI. Unpublished manuscript.

Riordan, M.H. and S.C. Salop. 1995. "Evaluating Vertical Mergers: A Post-Chicago Approach." *Antitrust Law Journal.* 63: 513–68.

Ritter, L., W.D. Braun and F. Rawlinson. 2000. *European Competition Law: A Practitioner's Guide.* 2nd ed. The Hague: Kluwer.

Rochet, J.-C. and J. Tirole. 1999. "Cooperation Among Competitors: The Economics of Credit Card Associations." London: CEPR Discussion Paper 2101.

Rochet, J.-C. and J. Tirole. 2001. "Platform Competition in Two-Sided Markets." Université de Toulouse: IDEI. Unpublished manuscript.

Roll, R. 1986. "The Hubris Hypothesis of Corporate Takeovers." *Journal of Business.* 59: 197–216.

Ross, T.W. 1992. "Cartel Stability and Product Differentiation." *International Journal of Industrial Organization.* 10: 1–13.

Rotemberg, J.J. and G. Saloner. 1986. "A Supergame-Theoretic Model of Price Wars During Booms." *American Economic Review.* 76: 390–407.

Rubinfeld, D.L. 1998. "Antitrust Enforcement in Dynamic Network Industries." *Antitrust Bulletin.* 43: 859–82.

Salant, S., S. Switzer and R. Reynolds. 1983. "Losses from Horizontal Mergers: The Effects of an Exogenous Change in Industry Structure on Cournot–Nash Equilibrium." *Quarterly Journal of Economics.* 98: 185–99.

Salinger, M.A. 1988. "Vertical Mergers and Market Foreclosure." *Quarterly Journal of Economics.* 103: 345–56.

Saloner, G. 1987. "Predation, Mergers, and Incomplete Information." *Rand Journal of Economics.* 18: 156–86.

Salop, S.C. 1986. "Practices that (Credibly) Facilitate Oligopoly Co-ordination." In J. Stiglitz and G. Mathewson, eds. *New Developments in the Analysis of Market Structure,* Basingstoke: MacMillan.

Salop, S.C. and D.T. Scheffman. 1987. "Cost-Raising Strategies." *Journal of Industrial Economics.* 36: 19–34.

Scharfstein, D.S. 1984. "A Policy to Prevent Rational Test-Marketing Predation." *Rand Journal of Economics.* 2: 229–43.

Scharfstein, D.S. 1988. Product-Market Competition and Managerial Slack." *Rand Journal of Economics.* 19: 147–55.

Scheffman, D.T. and P.T. Spiller. 1987. "Geographic Market Definition under the U.S. Department of Justice Merger Guidelines." *Journal of Law and Economics.* 30: 123–47.

Schelling, T.C. 1960. *The Strategy of Conflict.* Cambridge, MA: Harvard University Press.

Scherer, F.M. 1980. *Industrial Market Structure and Economic Performance.* 2nd ed. Boston: Houghton Mifflin.

Scherer, F.M. 1994. *Competition Policies for an Integrated Economy.* Washington, D.C.: Brookings Institution.

Scherer, F.M. and D. Ross. 1990. *Industrial Market Structure and Economic Performance.* 3rd ed. Boston: Houghton Mifflin.

Schmalensee, R. 1979. "On the Use of Economic Models in Antitrust: The Realemon Case." *University of Pennsylvania Law Review.* 127: 994–1050.

Schmalensee, R. 1982. "Another Look at Market Power." *Harvard Law Review.* 95: 1789–816.

Schmalensee, R. 2002. "Payment Systems and Interchange Fees." *Journal of Industrial Economics.* 50: 103–22.

Schmidt, K.M. 1997. "Managerial Incentives and Product Market Competition." *Review of Economic Studies.* 64: 191–213.

Schnitzer, M. 1994. "Dynamic Duopoly with Best-Price Clauses." *Rand Journal of Economics.* 25: 186–96.

Schumacher, U. 1991. "Buyer Structure and Seller Performance in U.S. Manufacturing Industries." *Review of Economics and Statistics.* 73: 277–84.

Schumpeter, J. 1912. *Theorie der Wirtschaftlichen, Entwicklung.* Leipzig: Duncker & Humblot.

Schwartz, M. 1987. "The Competitive Effects of Vertical Agreements: Comment." *American Economic Review.* 77: 1063–68.

Scott Morton, F. 1997. "Entry and Predation: British Shipping Cartels 1879–1929." *Journal of Economics and Management Strategy.* 6: 679–724.

Segal, I.R. and M.D. Whinston. 1996. "Naked Exclusion and Buyer Coordination." Harvard Institute of Economic Research. Unpublished manuscript.

Segal, I.R. and M.D. Whinston. 2000a. "Naked Exclusion: Comment." *American Economic Review.* 90: 296–309.

Segal, I.R. and M.D. Whinston. 2000b. "Exclusive Contracts and Protection of Investment." *Rand Journal of Economics.* 31: 603–33.

Selten, R. 1975. "Reexamination of the Perfectness Concept for Equilibrium Points in Extensive Games." *International Journal of Game Theory.* 4: 25–55.

Selten, R. 1978. "The Chain-Store Paradox." *Theory and Decision.* 9: 127–59.

Shaffer, G. 1991. "Slotting Allowances and Resale Price Maintenance: A Comparison of Facilitating Practices." *Rand Journal of Economics.* 22: 120–36.

Shaked, A. and J. Sutton. 1982. "Relaxing Price Competition through Product Differentiation." *Review of Economic Studies.* 49: 3–13.

Shaked, A. and J. Sutton. 1983. "Natural Oligopolies." *Econometrica.* 51: 1469–84.

Shaked, A. and J. Sutton. 1987. "Product Differentiation and Industrial Structure." *Journal of Industrial Economics.* 36: 131–46.

Shapiro, C. 1989. "Theories of Oligopoly Behavior." In R. Schmalensee and R.D. Willig, eds. *Handbook of Industrial Organization.* New York: Elsevier Science.

Shapiro, C. 2000. "Navigating the Patent Thicket: Cross Licenses, Patent Pools, and Standard Setting." University of California, Berkeley. Unpublished manuscript.

Shapiro, C. 2001. "Setting Compatibility Standards: Cooperation or Collusion?" In R.C. Dreyfuss, D.L. Zimmerman and H. First, eds. *Expanding the Boundaries of Intellectual Property: Innovation Policy for the Knowledge Society.* New York: Oxford University Press.

Shapiro, C. and H.R. Varian. 1999. Information Rules: A Strategic Guide to the Network Economy. Boston: Harvard Business School Press.

Shelling, T. 1960. *The Strategy of Conflict.* Cambridge, MA: Harvard University Press.

Sherwin, R.A. 1993. "Comments on Werden and Froeb: Correlation, Causality, and All that Jazz." *Review of Industrial Organization.* 8: 355–58.

Shubik, M. and R. Levitan. 1980. *Market Structure and Behavior.* Cambridge, MA: Harvard University Press.

Shy, O. 2001. *The Economics of Network Industries.* Cambridge: Cambridge University Press.

Singh, N. and X. Vives. 1984. "Price and Quantity Competition in a Differentiated Duopoly." *Rand Journal of Economics.* 15: 546–54.

Sklivas, S. 1987. "The Strategic Choice of Managerial Incentives." *Rand Journal of Economics.* 18: 452–58.

Slade, M.E. 1986. "Exogeneity Tests of Market Boundaries Applied to Petroleum Products." *Journal of Industrial Economics.* 34: 291–303.

Snyder, C.M. 1996. "A Dynamic Theory of Countervailing Power." *Rand Journal of Economics.* 27: 747–69.

Spagnolo, G. 1999. "On Interdependent Supergames: Multimarket Contact, Concavity, and Collusion." *Journal of Economic Theory.* 89: 127–39.

Spagnolo, G. 2000. "Optimal Leniency Programs." Milano: Fondazione Eni Enrico Mattei Note di Lavoro 42/2000.

Spence, A.M. 1977. "Entry, Capacity, Investment and Oligopolistic Pricing." *Bell Journal of Economics.* 8: 534–44.

Spengler, J.J. 1950. "Vertical Integration and Anti-Trust Policy." *Journal of Political Economy.* 58: 347–52.

Spratling, G.R. 1999. "Making Companies an Offer They Shouldn't Refuse." Speech of the Deputy Assistant Attorney General presented at the Bar Association of the District of Columbia. 16 February 1999.

Staiger, R.W. and F.A. Wolak. 1992. "Collusive Pricing with Capacity Constraints in the Presence of Demand Uncertainty." *Rand Journal of Economics.* 23: 203–19.

Staiger R.W. and F.A. Wolak. 1994. "Measuring Industry-Specific Protection: Anti-Dumping in the United States." *Brookings Papers on Economic Activity.* Microeconomics. 51–118.

Stigler, G.J. 1964. "A Theory of Oligopoly." *Journal of Political Economy*. 72: 44–61.

Stigler G.J. and R.A. Sherwin. 1985. "The Extent of the Market." *Journal of Law and Economics*. 28: 555–85.

Sutton, J. 1991. *Sunk Costs and Market Structure*. Cambridge, MA: MIT Press.

Sutton, J. 1998. *Technology and Market Structure*. Cambridge, MA: MIT Press.

Sylos Labini, P. 1979. *Oligopolio e Progresso Tecnico*. Torino: Einaudi.

Symeonidis, G. 1998. "The Evolution of UK Cartel Policy." In S. Martin, ed. *Competition Policies in Europe*. Amsterdam: Elsevier.

Telser, L.G. 1960. "Why Should Manufacturers Want Fair Trade?" *Journal of Law and Economics*. 3: 86–105.

Telser, L.G. 1966. "Cutthroat Competition and the Long Purse." *Journal of Law and Economics*. 9: 259–77.

Tharakan, P.K.M. and J. Waelbroeck. 1994. "Antidumping and Countervailing Duty Decisions in the E.C. and in the U.S." *European Economic Review*, 38: 171–93.

Thisse, J.-F. and X. Vives. 1992. "Basing Point Pricing: Competition Versus Collusion." *Journal of Industrial Economics*. 40: 249–60.

Tirole, J. 1988. *The Theory of Industrial Organization*. Boston: MIT Press.

Trebilcock, M.J. and R. Howse. 1995. *The Regulation of International Trade*. London: Routledge.

Tybout, J.R. 2000. "Manufacturing Firms in Developing Countries: How Well Do They Do, and Why?" *Journal of Economic Literature*. 38: 11–44.

UNCTAD. 2000. *World Investment Report 2000*. Geneva: UNCTAD.

von Ungern–Sternberg, T. 1996. "Countervailing Power Revisited." *International Journal of Industrial Organization*. 14: 507–19.

US Department of Justice and Federal Trade Commission. 1992. "Horizontal Merger Guidelines."

Utton, M. 2000. "Fifty Years of UK Competition Policy." *Review of Industrial Organization*. 16:267–85.

Varian, H.R. 1989. "Price Discrimination." In R. Schmalensee and R.D. Willig, eds. *Handbook of Industrial Organization*. Amsterdam: North-Holland. 597–654.

Vasconcelos, H. 2001a. "Entry Effects on Cartel Stability and the Joint Executive Committee." Florence: European University Institute. Unpublished manuscript.

Vasconcelos, H. 2001b. "Tacit Collusion, Cost Asymmetries and Mergers." Florence: European University Institute. Unpublished manuscript.

Vickers, J. 1995. "Entry and Competitive Selection." Oxford University. Unpublished manuscript.

Viscusi, W.K., J.M. Vernon and J.E. Harrington, Jr. 1995. *Economics and Regulation and Antitrust*. Cambridge, MA: MIT Press.

Werden, G.J. 1998. "Antitrust Analysis of Joint Ventures: An Overview." *Antitrust Law Journal*. 66: 701–35.

Werden, G.J. and L.M. Froeb. 1993. "Correlation, Causality, and All that Jazz: The Inherent Shortcomings of Price Tests for Antitrust Market Delineation." *Review of Industrial Organization*. 8: 329–53.

Werden, G.J. and L.M. Froeb. 1994. "The Effects of Mergers in Differentiated Products Industries: Logit Demand and Merger Policy." *Journal of Law, Economics and Organization*. 10: 407–26.

Werden, G.J. and L.M. Froeb. 1998. "The Entry-Inducing Effects of Horizontal Mergers: An Exploratory Analysis." *Journal of Industrial Economics*. 46: 525–43.

Werden, G.J., L.M. Froeb and T.J. Tardiff. 1996. "The Use of the Logit Model in Applied Industrial Organization." *International Journal of the Economics of Business*. 3: 83–105.

West Group. 1988. *West's Law and Commercial Dictionary.* St. Paul, MN.: West Information Pub. Group.

Whinston, M.D. 1990. "Tying, Foreclosure, and Exclusion." *American Economic Review,* 80: 837–859.

Whish, R. 2001. *Competition Law.* 3rd ed. London: Butterworths.

Williamson, O.E. 1968. "Economies as an Antitrust Defense: The Welfare Trade-offs." *American Economic Review.* 59: 954–59.

Willig, R.D. 1991. "Merger Analysis, Industrial Organization Theory, and Merger Guidelines." *Brookings Papers on Economic Activity. Microeconomics.* 281–312.

Yamey, B. 1972. "Predatory Price Cutting: Notes and Comments." *Journal of Law and Economics.* 15: 129–42.

References to Cases and Legislation

European Cases: Decisions of the Commission of the European Communities

- *ABB/Daimler-Benz*, (M.580), OJ 1997 L11/1, *120n32, 122, 237, 277, 286–92*
- *Accor/Wagon-Lits*, (M.126), OJ 1992 L204/1, *275n70*
- *Adalat*, OJ 1996 L201/1, *497, 497n117*
- *Aérospatiale-Alenia/de Havilland*, (M.53), OJ 1991 L334/42, *109, 115n20, 120n32, 275*
- *Airtours/First Choice*, (M.1524), OJ 2000 L93/1 ("*Airtours*"), *120n33, 272–3*
- *Astra/Zeneca*, (M.1403), OJ 1999 C335/3, *269–70*
- *AT&T/NCR*, (M.50), OJ 1991 C16/1, *275n71*
- *B&I Line/Sealink Harbours*, [1992] 5 CMLR 255 ("*B&I Line/Sealink*"), *67n53*
- *Boeing/Hughes*, (M.1879), dated 27 September 2000, *467*
- *Boeing/McDonnell Douglas*, (M.877), OJ 1997 L336/16, *115n20, 119n30, 120n32*
- *CECED*, OJ 2000 L187/47, *27–8*
- *CEWAL*, OJ 1993 L34/20, *144n13*
- *CLT/Disney/SuperRTL*, (M.566), OJ 1995 C144/23, *115n21*
- *Coca-Cola/Amalgamated Beverages GB*, (M.794), OJ 1997 L218/15, *275n72*
- *Coca-Cola/Carlsberg*, (M.833), OJ 1998 L145/41, *275n72*
- *Du Pont/ICI*, (M.214), OJ 1993 L7/13, *109*
- *Dyestuffs*, OJ 1969 L195/11, *188, 219*
- *Enso/Stora*, (M.1225), OJ 1999 L254/9, *122*
- *Ford/Volkswagen*, OJ 1993 L20/14, *15–6*
- *Gencor/Lonrho*, (M.619), OJ 1997 L11/30, *37n95, 119n29*
- *General Electric/Honeywell*, (M.2220), dated 3 July 2001, *37n95, 115n20, 120n32, 275, 277, 378–91*
- *Glaxo Wellcome and Others*, OJ 2001 L302/1 ("*Glaxo Wellcome*"), *497*
- *Guinness/Grand Metropolitan*, (M.938), OJ 1998 L288/24, *275n72–3*
- *Irish Continental Group/CCI Morlaix*, (1995) 5 CMLR 177, *67n53*
- *Kali & Salz/MdK/Treuhand*, (M.308), OJ 1994 L186/30, *238n21, 271*
- *Kirch/Richemont/Telepiù*, (M.410), OJ 1994 C225/3, *115n21*
- *Langnese-Iglo*, OJ 1993 L183/19, *391–8*
- *Lufthansa/SAS*, OJ 1996 L54/28, *81n67, 104n5, 269*

European Cases: Decisions of the Court of First Instance and the European Court of Justice

European Treaties

European Legislation and Guidelines

- Commission Notice, *on the definition of the relevant market for the purposes of Community competition law*, OJ 1997 C372/5 (the "*Market Definition Guidelines*"), *102n3*
- Commission Notice, *on the non-imposition or reduction of fines in cartel cases*, OJ 1996 C207/4 (the "*Commission Notice on the non-imposition or reduction of fines in cartel cases*"), *194n107*
- Commission Press Release, *Commission adopts new leniency policy for companies which give information on cartels*, IP/02/247 of 13/02/2002, *194n108*
- Commission Recommendation, *concerning the definition of small and medium-sized enterprises*, OJ 1996 L107/4, *16n46*
- Commission Regulation 2659/2000, *on the application of Article 81(3) of the Treaty to categories of research and development agreements*, OJ 2000 L304/7 (the "*R&D Block Exemption*"), *205*
- Commission Regulation 2790/99, *on the application of Article 81(3) of the Treaty to categories of vertical agreements and concerted practices*, OJ 1999 L336/21 (the "*Vertical Block Exemption*"), *32–3*
- Council Regulation 17, OJ 1959–1962 ("*Regulation 17*"), *33*
- Council Regulation 4064/89, *on the control of concentrations between undertakings*, OJ 1990 L257/13, as corrected and amended (the "*Merger Regulation*"), *14, 16, 19, 29, 36–8, 118–9, 231–3, 270–7*
- Council Regulation, *on the implementation of the rules on competition laid down in Articles 81 and 82 of the Treaty and amending Regulations 19/65/EEC, (EEC) No. 1017/68, (EEC) No. 2821/71, (EEC) No. 2988/74, (EEC) No. 4056/86, (EEC) No. 3975/87, (EEC) No. 3976/87, (EEC) No. 1534/91 and (EEC) No. 479/92), not yet published in the OJ, (the "Regulation implementing Articles 81 and 82 of the Treaty*"), *33–4*
- Proposal for a Council Regulation on the control of concentrations between undertakings, OJ C20, dated 28 January 2003, (*EC Proposal for Merger Reform*), *273*

UK Cases and MMC Reports

- Colour film: a report on the supply and processing of colour film, 1966–7 HC 1 (MMC Report) ("*Ilford*"), *468*
- *Mogul Steamship Co., Ltd. v. McGregor, Gow & Co. et al.* (1891–4) All E.R. Rep 263, *413n3*

UK Legislation and Guidelines

- Competition Act 1998, *11–3*
- Monopolies and Mergers Act 1965, *11*
- Monopolies and Restrictive Practices (Inquiry and Control) Act 1948, *11*
- Office of Fair Trading, UK Competition Act Guideline on "Market Definition," 1999 ("*Market Definition Guidelines*"), *102n3, 110n14*
- Office of Fair Trading, UK Competition Act Guideline on "Assessement of Market Power," 1999 ("Assessement of *Market Power Guidelines*"), *118*
- Profiteering Act 1919, *11*

- Resale Prices Act 1964, *11*
- Restrictive Trade Practices Act 1956 (the *"RTPA"*), *11–12*

US Cases

- *US v. Addyston Pipe and Steel Co.*, 85 Fed. 271 [6th Cir. 1898] (*"Addyston Pipe and Steel"*), *4, 5*
- *Airline Tariff Publishers Co. v. US*, 1994 WL 454730 [DDC 1994] (*"Airline Tariff Publishers"* or *"ATP"*), *154, 155n46, 189*
- *US v. Aluminum Co. of America*, 148 F.2d 416 [2nd Cir. 1945] (*"Alcoa"*), *7–8, 119*
- *US v. American Tobacco Co.*, 221 US 106 [1911] (*"American Tobacco, 1911"*), *4–5, 413n3, 415*
- *American Tobacco Co. v. US*, 328 US 781 [1946] (*"American Tobacco, 1946"*), *7n20*
- *Appalachian Coals v. US*, 288 US 344 [1933], *6–7*
- *Board of Trade of the City of Chicago v. US*, 246 US 231 [1918] (*"Board of Trade of Chicago"*), *6n18*
- *Brooke Group Ltd. v. Brown and Williamson Tobacco Corp.*, 509 US 209 [1993] (*"Brooke Group"*), *443*
- *Brown Shoe Co. v. US*, 370 US 294 [1962] (*"Brown Shoe"*), *8*
- *Dr. Miles Medical Co. v. John D. Park & Sons Co.*, 220 US 373 [1911], *4*
- *US v. E.I. Du Pont de Nemours & Co.*, 351 US 377 [1956] (*"du Pont"*), *105*
- *In the matter of Ethyl Corp. et al.*, 101 FTC 425 [1983] (*"Ethyl"*), *154n41, 156, 188n97*
- *Continental TV Inc. v. GTE-Sylvania Inc.*, 433 US 36 [1977] (*"GTE-Sylvania"*), *8*
- *International Business Machines Corporation v. US*, 298 US 131 [1936], *461–2*
- *International Salt Co. v. US*, 332 US 392 [1947] (*"International Salt"*), *7*
- *Interstate Circuit, Inc. v. US*, 306 US 208 [1939] (*"Interstate Circuit"*), *7n20*
- *Jefferson Parish Hospital Dist. No. 2 v. Hyde*, 466 US 2 [1984] (*"Jefferson Parish Hospital"*), *8n26, 119, 521*
- *Eastman Kodak Co. v. Image Technical Services, Inc.*, 504 U.S. 451 (1992) (*"Kodak"*), *112, 521*
- *Northern Securities Co. v. US*, 193 US 197 [1904], *5n15*
- *United Mine Workers v. Pennington*, 381 US 657 [1965] (*"Pennington"*), *490n104*
- *US v. Philadelphia National Bank*, 374 US 321 [1963] (*"Philadelphia National Bank"*), *8*
- *FTC v. Procter & Gamble Co.*, 386 US 568 [1967] (*"Procter & Gamble"*), *8*
- *US v. Arnold, Schwinn & Co.*, 388 US 365 [1967] (*"Schwinn"*), *7*
- *US v. Socony-Vacuum Oil Co.*, 310 US 150 [1940] (*"Socony-Vacuum Oil"*), *7*
- *Standard Oil Co. of New Jersey v. US*, 221 US 1 [1911] (*"Standard Oil"*), *4, 413n3, 414n4*
- *State Oil Co. v. Kahn*, 522 US 1 [1911], *4n11*
- *Sugar Institute Inc. v. US*, 297 US 553 [1936] (*"Sugar Institute"*), *175, 189n99, 214n137, 284n84*

US Legislation and Guidelines

Index